# Aruba Certified Switching Professional

OFFICIAL CERTIFICATION STUDY GUIDE
(EXAM HPE6-A45)

## First Edition

Miriam Allred

HPE Press
660 4th Street, #802
San Francisco, CA 94107

**Aruba Certified Switching Professional**
**Official Certification Study Guide (Exam HPE6-A45)**
Miriam Allred



Published by:

Hewlett Packard Enterprise Press
660 4th Street, #802
San Francisco, CA 94107



ISBN: **978-1-942741-81-7**

Printed in Mexico

## WARNING AND DISCLAIMER

This book provides information about the topics covered in the Implementing Aruba Campus Switching Solutions (HPE6-A45) certification exam. Every effort has been made to make this book as complete and as accurate as possible, but no warranty or fitness is implied.

The information is provided on an "as is" basis. The author, and Hewlett Packard Enterprise Press, shall have neither liability nor responsibility to any person or entity with respect to any loss or damages arising from the information contained in this book or from the use of the discs or programs that may accompany it.

The opinions expressed in this book belong to the author and are not necessarily those of Hewlett Packard Enterprise Press.

**Note:** Books and courses developed prior to the Hewlett-Packard Company separation contain branding, logos, web page links, and other elements/information that has not been updated for each HP Inc. and Hewlett Packard Enterprise. The general knowledge and skills are still considered of value to HP Inc. and Hewlett Packard Enterprise employees (partners/customers) respectively, so these legacy materials are being made available here. Plans are in place for updating the most highly-used content for each HP Inc. and Hewlett Packard Enterprise.

## TRADEMARK ACKNOWLEDGEMENTS

All third-party trademarks contained herein are the property of their respective owner(s).

## GOVERNMENT AND EDUCATION SALES

This publisher offers discounts on this book when ordered in quantity for bulk purchases, which may include electronic versions. For more information, please contact U.S. Government and Education Sales 1-855-447-2665 or email sales@hpepressbooks.com.

## Feedback Information

At HPE Press, our goal is to create in-depth reference books of the best quality and value. Each book is crafted with care and precision, undergoing rigorous development that involves the expertise of members from the professional technical community.

Readers' feedback is a continuation of the process. If you have any comments regarding how we could improve the quality of this book, or otherwise alter it to better suit your needs, you can contact us through email at hpepress@epac.com. Please make sure to include the book title and ISBN in your message.

We appreciate your feedback.

**Publisher**: Hewlett Packard Enterprise Press

**HPE Contributors**: Don McCracken, Gerhard Roets, Wim Groeneveld and Craig Maxwell

**HPE Press Program Manager**: Michael Bishop

## About the Author

Miriam Allred has spent the last 12 years configuring, testing, and troubleshooting HP and HPE Aruba wired and wireless networks. Miriam combines this wide range of technical expertise with pedagogy and instructional design training, allowing her to create technical training courses for both advanced and entry-level networking professionals. Miriam Allred has a Masters degree from Cleveland State University and a Bachelors degree from Brigham Young University.

## Introduction

This study guide is based on the Aruba course titled *Implementing Aruba Campus Switching Solutions.* It is designed to help you study for the Implementing Aruba Campus Switching Solutions certification exam (HPE6-A45) and delta exam (HPE6-A46) to achieve the Aruba Certified Switching Professional (ACSP) certification. The ACSP certification validates that you have the networking skills and expertise to design, implement and manage the modern network, based on Aruba wired and wireless solutions for campus networks.

Beyond certification, this guide will serve as a useful on-the-job reference for designing and configuring Aruba networking solutions. Learn how to implement layer 2 technologies and layer 3 routing protocols to ensure a loop-free topology and resilient network. Study the essential mechanisms for securing the network such as access control lists (ACLs), 802.1X with Aruba ClearPass, MAC authentication, and SNMPv3 as well as methods for controlling wireless access for guest users on campus. You will also learn how to configure Quality of Service (QoS) on AOS-Switches and understand how to implement features such as backplane stacking, Virtual Switching Framework (VSF), tunneled-node, and more.

## Certification and Learning

Hewlett Packard Enterprise Partner Ready Certification and Learning provides end-to-end continuous learning programs and professional certifications that can help you open doors and succeed in the idea economy. We provide continuous learning activities and job-role based learning plans to help you keep pace with the demands of the dynamic, fast paced IT industry; professional sales and technical training and certifications to give you the critical skills needed to design, manage and implement the most sought-after IT disciplines; and training to help you navigate and seize opportunities within the top IT transformation areas that enable business advantage today.

As a Partner Ready Certification and Learning certified member, your skills, knowledge, and real-world experience are recognized and valued in the marketplace. To continue your professional and career growth, you have access to our large HPE community of world-class IT professionals, trend-makers and decision-makers. Share ideas, best practices, business insights, and challenges as you gain professional connections globally.

To learn more about HPE Partner Ready Certification and Learning certifications and continuous learning programs, please visit http://certification-learning.hpe.com

## Audience

This book is designed for networking IT professionals involved in implementing Aruba networking solutions. Implementation tasks include interpreting network architectures and customer requirements to install, configure, and manage Aruba networking solutions.

## Assumed Knowledge

Typical candidates for this certification are networking IT professionals who have advanced-level implementation experience with Aruba wired switching solutions. It is assumed you have a minimum of 4 to 5 years of general networking experience and 2 years of experience focused on interpreting network architectures and customer requirements to install and configure Aruba solutions.

## Minimum Qualifications

The pre-requisite qualification for the Aruba ACSP certification is the Aruba Certified Switching Associate (ACSA) V1.

## Relevant Certifications

After you pass these exams, your achievement may be applicable toward more than one certification. To determine which certifications can be credited with this achievement, log in to The Learning Center and view the certifications listed on the exam's More Details tab. You might be on your way to achieving additional certifications.

## Preparing for Exam HPE6-A45

This self-study guide does not guarantee that you will have all the knowledge you need to pass the exam. It is expected that you will also draw on real-world experience and would benefit from completing the hands-on lab activities provided in the instructor-led training.

## Recommended HPE Training

Recommended training to prepare for each exam is accessible from the exam's page in The Learning Center. See the exam attachment, "Supporting courses," to view and register for the courses.

## Obtain Hands-on Experience

You are not required to take the recommended, supported courses, and completion of training does not guarantee that you will pass the exams. Hewlett Packard Enterprise strongly recommends a combination of training, thorough review of courseware and additional study references, and sufficient on-the-job experience prior to taking an exam.

## Exam Registration

To register for an exam, go to http://certification-learning.hpe.com/tr/certification/learn_more_about_exams.html

# CONTENTS

1 Introduction to Aruba Solutions ........ 1
Assumed knowledge ........ 1
Introduction ........ 1
Digital workplace ........ 1
Digital workplaces require a Mobile First Network ........ 2
Aruba Switch solutions ........ 3
Aruba 5400R zl2 Switch Series ........ 4
Aruba 3810 Switch Series ........ 5
Aruba 2930F Switch Series ........ 5
Unified wired and wireless management ........ 5
Unified, policy-based access management: Aruba ClearPass ........ 6
Campus architectures ........ 7
Review basic networking concepts ........ 8
Summary ........ 9
Learning check ........ 9
Answers ........ 10
Review: Basic technologies for a campus network ........ 10
Learning check ........ 11

2 Data Link Layer Redundancy Technologies ........ 13
Assumed knowledge ........ 13
Introduction ........ 13
Rapid Per-VLAN Spanning Tree Plus (RPVST+) ........ 14
Why RPVST+ ........ 14
Comparison: RPVST+, RSTP, and MSTP ........ 15
Rapid Spanning Tree Protocol Plus BPDUs ........ 16
Path cost differences ........ 18
RPVST+ setup ........ 19
MSTP versus RPVST+ ........ 19
Vulnerability: Rogue device becomes root bridge ........ 20
BPDU protection ........ 21
PVST protection ........ 23
BPDU protection versus BPDU filtering ........ 23
Root guard ........ 24
BPDU throttling ........ 25
STP loop guard ........ 26

Loop protection ........ 28
- Vulnerability: Edge loops in a network without spanning tree ........ 28
- Vulnerability: Loops undetectable by spanning tree ........ 29
- Loop protection overview ........ 30

Unidirectional Link Detection (UDLD) ........ 33
- UDLD frames ........ 35
- Guidelines for configuring UDLD ........ 36
- Tagged or untagged UDLD frames ........ 37
- View information about UDLD-enabled ports ........ 38

Summary ........ 38

Learning check ........ 39

Answers ........ 40
- MSTP versus RPVST+ ........ 40
- Learning check ........ 41

**3 Virtual Router Redundancy Protocol (VRRP) ........ 45**

Assumed knowledge ........ 45

VRRP use case ........ 45

VRRP overview ........ 47

Controlling VRRP states ........ 48
- Controlling the states with a VRRP owner (legacy) ........ 48
- Controlling the roles without a VRRP owner ........ 49

Configure VRRP ........ 49

VRRP basic operation ........ 51
- Choosing the virtual router settings ........ 52

VRRP failover ........ 52
- Supplemental information on controlling the failover time ........ 54
- Supplemental information on electing the new master ........ 54

Ping response behavior ........ 55

VRRP preemptive and nonpreemptive modes ........ 56

Considerations for setting up VRRP ........ 57

Load sharing routing within a subnet ........ 58

Load sharing routing across different subnets ........ 59

Combining VRRP and MSTP ........ 59
- Configure MSTP ........ 61
- Configure VRRP ........ 61

Summary ........ 62

Learning check ........ 62

Answers ........ 66
- Considerations for setting up VRRP ........ 66
- Learning check ........ 66

4 Aruba Backplane Stacking and Virtual Switching Framework (VSF) ....71
Assumed knowledge....71
Introduction ....72
Backplane stacking....72
Backplane stacking topologies ....73
Roles in the backplane stack ....74
Configuring a backplane stack....76
Election of the commander and standby member....78
Stack operations ....79
Stack fragments ....80
Virtual Switching Framework (VSF)....81
Plug-and-play VSF configuration ....82
VSF provisioning use cases....84
Manual VSF configuration ....86
Viewing the VSF fabric....88
Implementing VSF on Aruba 2930F Series switches....88
Configuring VSF on Aruba 2930F Series switches ....91
Compare unicasts on backplane stacking and VSF forwarding ....92
Compare flooding on backplane stacking and VSF forwarding ....93
Protection against split brain with MAD ....94
OOBM MAD....94
LLDP MAD setup ....95
LLDP MAD behavior ....96
VLAN MAD....97
VSF Fast Software Updates (FSU) ....99
Summary....99
Learning check....100
Answers ....101
Virtual Switching Framework (VSF) ....101
Learning check ....102

5 Advanced Open Shortest Path First (OSPF) ....105
Assumed knowledge....105
Introduction ....105
OSPF overview ....106
Basic OSPF setup ....106
Background information on OSPF ....107
Configure OSPF for a one area topology....116
Review basic OSPF concepts....125

OSPF multi-area overview ....................................................................126

ABRs....................................................................................128

Need for route aggregation between areas......................................130

Aggregating summaries ..................................................................131

Filtering inter-area routes..............................................................133

Review multi-area OSPF concepts....................................................134

OSPF external routes..........................................................................136

Need for redistributing external routes into OSPF ..............................137

External routes and ASBRs..............................................................138

Summary ASBR advertisements.......................................................140

Need for eliminating excessive external routes ..................................143

Using stub areas to eliminate external routes.....................................144

Need for eliminating all inter-area and external routes .......................146

Using totally stub areas ..................................................................147

Need for advertising local external routes in a stub area....................148

Using NSSAs...................................................................................148

Review external route advertisement...............................................149

Best route selection in redundant OSPF network......................................151

Setting interface cost .......................................................................151

Best practices for networks with redundant ABRs ..............................152

Choosing best inter-area routes.......................................................154

Options for external route metrics ...................................................156

Choosing between external routes to the same network: Type 2 metric..........................................................................................156

Learning check ..............................................................................158

Choosing between external routes to the same network: Type 1 metric..........................................................................................160

Learning check ..............................................................................161

Review factors that affect OSPF route selection .................................163

OSPF failover and convergence..............................................................165

Detecting failed neighbor relationships .............................................166

Using BFD to speed OSPF failed neighbor detection ..........................168

BFD control messages and asynchronous mode.................................170

BFD echo mode .............................................................................171

The need for graceful restart ...........................................................172

OSPF graceful restart process .........................................................174

Implementing OSPF graceful restart.................................................176

Implementing OSPF and VRRP .......................................................177

Virtual links .........................................................................................179

Example situations that require virtual links .....................................179

Virtual link ........ 179
Virtual link configuration process ........ 180
OSPF authentication ........ 181
Simple authentication configuration ........ 183
MD5 authentication configuration ........ 184
Summary ........ 184
Learning check ........ 185
Answers ........ 185
Review basic OSPF concepts ........ 185
Review multi-area OSPF concepts ........ 188
Review external route advertisement ........ 190
Learning check for "Choosing between external routes to the same network: Type 2 metric" ........ 191
Learning check for "Choosing between external routes to the same network: Type 1 metric" ........ 192
Learning check ........ 193

6 Internet Group Management Protocol (IGMP) ........ 195
Assumed knowledge ........ 195
Introduction ........ 195
Multicast overview ........ 196
Multicast uses ........ 198
Multicast flooding within VLANs ........ 198
IGMP use cases ........ 200
IGMP queriers ........ 202
Enabling IGMP ........ 202
Multiple IGMP queriers and elections ........ 203
Behavior without PIM enabled ........ 204
Behavior with PIM enabled ........ 204
Building membership tables with IGMP reports ........ 205
Supplemental information on how AOS-Switches handle reports ........ 206
Filtering traffic based on membership tables ........ 207
IGMP snooping ........ 207
Configuring IGMP snooping ........ 209
How AOS-Switches handle unknown multicasts ........ 209
Data-driven mode and fast leave ........ 210
Nondata-driven mode (legacy) ........ 211
Summary ........ 211
Learning check ........ 212
Answers ........ 213
Learning check ........ 213

7 Protocol Independent Multicast (PIM) ........................................ 215
Assumed knowledge ........................................ 215
Introduction ........................................ 215
Multicast routing use cases ........................................ 216
Multicast routes ........................................ 216
Discovering multicast routes ........................................ 217
PIM-DM versus PIM-SM ........................................ 219
PIM-DM ........................................ 220
PIM-DM operation: flooding and pruning ........................................ 221
PIM-DM operation: grafts ........................................ 222
Interpreting PIM-DIM (*, G) entries ........................................ 223
Interpreting PIM-DM (S, G) entries ........................................ 224
Using state refreshes to minimize flooding ........................................ 227
Understanding the relationship between the PIM-DM tree and the unicast routing table ........................................ 229
Understanding how a multicast forwarder is elected ........................................ 231
PIM-SM ........................................ 232
RPT ........................................ 233
Behavior as source begins forwarding ........................................ 234
Switching to SPT ........................................ 235
Specifying the RP ........................................ 237
Bootstrap mechanism ........................................ 238
Selecting an RP from the RP set ........................................ 240
Summary ........................................ 243
Learning check ........................................ 244
Answers ........................................ 247
Learning check ........................................ 247

8 Border Gateway Protocol (BGP) ........................................ 251
Assumed knowledge ........................................ 251
Introduction ........................................ 251
BGP use case: Multihomed ISP connections ........................................ 252
Other BGP use cases ........................................ 253
BGP AS ........................................ 253
BGP TCP sessions ........................................ 255
BGP neighbor addresses ........................................ 255
eBGP neighbors ........................................ 256
iBGP neighbors ........................................ 257
MD5 authentication ........................................ 257
Enable BGP ........................................ 258

BGP connection states ... 258
View information about the BGP session ... 260
Receiving routes from BGP neighbors ... 260
First criteria in best BGP route selection ... 261
More criteria in BGP best route selection ... 263
Advertising routes in BGP ... 265
Inject routes into the BGP routing table ... 266
Advertise external routes in OSPF ... 267
Avoid becoming a transit AS ... 268
Review activity ... 269
Summary ... 269
Learning check ... 270
Answers ... 273
Review activity ... 273
Learning check ... 273

9 Access Control Lists ... 277
Assumed knowledge ... 277
Introduction ... 277
What is an ACL? ... 278
Reasons to implement ACLs ... 278
ACL IDs and types ... 279
ACL types ... 279
ACL IDs ... 280
ACL rule components ... 281
Sequence ID ... 281
Action ... 281
Matching criteria ... 282
Example IP ACL rules ... 282
IPv4 standard ACLs ... 282
IPv4 extended ACLs ... 283
Example MAC ACL rules ... 287
Standard MAC ACLs ... 287
Extended MAC ACLs ... 288
Determine use cases for ACL types ... 289
Processing order and implicit deny ... 290
Implicit action ... 290
Applying ACLs to interfaces ... 291
Tips ... 293

Example ACL ... 294
Activity: Plan ACLs ... 294
- Scenario 1: Protect the mobility infrastructure ... 295
- Scenario 2: Control access for less trusted users ... 295
- Configuring the ACL for Scenario 1 ... 296
- Configuring the ACL for Scenario 2 ... 297

Detailed look at source and destination IP addresses in ACLs ... 300
Specifying IP address ranges with prefix length ... 300
- Subnet masks ... 301
- Prefix lengths ... 301
- Rules of thumb for specifying ranges with prefix lengths ... 301

Using and interpreting wildcard bits ... 302
- Wildcard bits ... 302
- Examples ... 303
- Add a rule using the correct wildcard bits ... 305

Specifying MAC addresses ranges ... 306
Managing ACL rule sequence ... 306
- Automatic numbering ... 307
- Manual numbering ... 307
- Sequence renumbering ... 307

Logging ACL matches ... 308
Activity: Analyzing an ACL ... 309
Inbound RACLs ... 310
Outbound RACLs ... 311
- Supplemental information: Inbound and outbound RACLs on multinetted VLANs ... 312

Inbound VACLs ... 312
Outbound VACLs ... 314
VACLs at the edge ... 315
Port-based ACLs (PACLs) ... 318
ACL grouping ... 319
Activity: Predict filtering behavior ... 321
Summary ... 322
Learning check ... 323
Answers ... 324
- Determine use cases for ACL types ... 324
- Activity: Plan ACLs ... 325
- Activity: Analyzing an ACL ... 327
- Activity: Predict filtering behavior ... 328
- Learning check ... 328

10 802.1X Authentication.............331
Assumed knowledge.............331
Introduction.............331
Port-based authentication use models.............331
802.1X overview.............332
802.1X logical ports.............332
802.1X roles.............333
802.1X requirements.............335
EAP framework.............336
EAP and RADIUS together.............337
EAP methods.............338
EAP-Transport Layer Security.............339
PEAP and EAP-Tunneled TLS.............341
Choosing an EAP method.............343
802.1X configuration.............344
Specifying the RADIUS server.............344
Managing multiple RADIUS servers and RADIUS groups.............345
Ensuring compatibility with ClearPass.............348
Viewing the RADIUS settings on AOS-Switches.............349
Enabling 802.1X.............350
Customizing authenticated users' access.............352
How the RADIUS server sends dynamic settings.............353
How dynamic port ACLs are applied.............357
Applying dynamic settings with Aruba ClearPass.............358
Viewing dynamic settings.............359
Port-based mode.............361
Additional examples of how port-based mode operates.............361
User-based mode.............362
Additional examples of how user-based mode operates.............363
User role-based authorization.............366
Summary.............368
Learning check.............368
Answers.............369
Learning check.............369

11 MAC Authentication.............373
Assumed knowledge.............373
Introduction.............373
MAC-Auth use cases.............373
RADIUS-based MAC-Auth.............374
RADIUS-based MAC-Auth options.............375

MAC-Auth and provisioning with ClearPass ..... 377
RADIUS-based MAC-Auth configuration process ..... 378
Local MAC-Auth ..... 379
MAC groups ..... 380
Profiles ..... 382
LMA Unauthorized-client VLAN ..... 384
Implementing MAC-Auth on ports connected to multiple clients ..... 385
Combining MAC-Auth and 802.1X ..... 386
Combining MAC-Auth and 802.1X in multiple client scenarios ..... 388
Using Authorized-client VLANs ..... 389
Summary ..... 389
Learning check ..... 390
Answers ..... 390
Learning check ..... 390

12 Captive Portal and Other Guest Options ..... 393
Assumed knowledge ..... 393
Introduction ..... 393
Guest access ..... 394
Web-based authentication ..... 394
Advantages of Web-Auth ..... 394
Disadvantages of Web-Auth ..... 395
Types of Web-based authentication ..... 395
Additional capabilities of a solution such as Aruba ClearPass ..... 395
AOS-Switches' support for Web-based authentication ..... 396
Captive portal authentication ..... 397
Authentication enforced on the AOS-Switch ..... 398
High-level authentication process ..... 399
More detailed look at the redirection to the captive portal ..... 400
More detailed look at the login process ..... 402
Optional VLAN for unregistered devices ..... 405
Configuring an AOS-Switch to integrate with the Aruba ClearPass captive portal ..... 406
Web-Auth and EWA ..... 409
Local Web-Auth to a RADIUS server ..... 410
Basic Web-Auth setup ..... 411
EWA ..... 413
Limited access with no authentication ..... 415
802.1X Unauthorized-client VLAN ..... 415
Guidelines for using the 802.1X Unauthorized-client VLAN ..... 416

Supporting multiple employees and guests with the Unauthorized-client VLAN ........ 417
Summary ........ 418
Learning check ........ 419
Answers ........ 420
Learning check ........ 420

13 Integrating with an Aruba Mobility Solution ........ 423
Assumed knowledge ........ 423
Introduction ........ 423
Use cases ........ 423
Tunneling traffic to an MC ........ 425
Using PAPI enhanced security ........ 426
Modes ........ 427
Port-based tunneled-node ........ 429
Enabling tunneled-node on ports ........ 429
How the MC handles tunneled-node traffic ........ 430
Role-based tunneled node ........ 432
User role-based authorization ........ 432
Roles for role-based tunnel-node ........ 432
How the MC handles role-based tunneled-node traffic ........ 435
High availability ........ 435
Supporting high availability with VRRP ........ 436
Supporting high availability with clustering ........ 437
Supporting high availability with a backup controller ........ 438
Controlling failure behavior ........ 440
Implementation restrictions ........ 441
Guidelines for the path between tunneled-node switch and MCs ........ 444
MC licensing and capacity considerations ........ 445
Summary ........ 446
Learning check ........ 446
Answers ........ 448
Learning check ........ 448

14 Secure Device Management ........ 451
Assumed knowledge ........ 451
Introduction ........ 451
Management user authentication options ........ 451
Access types ........ 452
Access level ........ 452
Review of default authentication methods ........ 453

RADIUS servers for authenticating management users....................454
RADIUS authorization of operator or manager access....................455
RADIUS-based command authorization....................457
VSAs for defining command authorization....................458
Secondary authentication method....................460
SNMP....................461
SNMP review....................462
SNMP objects, OIDs, and MIBs....................463
SNMPv3 benefits....................463
SNMPv3 users....................464
SNMPv3 groups....................465
SNMPv3 predefined groups and associated rights....................466
SNMPv1/2c versus SNMPv3 operation....................467
Ensure SNMPv3 settings match on AOS-Switches and AirWave....................469
SNMPv3 notifications....................475
Defining traps....................476
SNMPv3 notification targets....................479
Configuration auditing....................482
Monitoring network traffic and events....................483
RMON—collect information on a port....................484
RMON—generate alarms....................486
Other monitoring features....................488
sFlow....................488
Local traffic mirroring....................491
Remote traffic mirroring....................493
Summary....................495
Learning check....................496
Answers....................497
RADIUS servers for authenticating management users....................497
SNMP review....................497
Learning check....................499

15 Quality of Service....................503
Assumed knowledge....................503
Introduction....................503
Dealing with congestion....................504
TCP and UDP response to congestion....................505
Impact of congestion on real-time traffic....................505
The challenges in providing QoS....................507
QoS use case....................508

Queuing and scheduling .......... 508
SP scheduling .......... 509
GMB .......... 510
Viewing how traffic is forwarded in egress queues .......... 513
Controlling the number of queues .......... 514
Introduction to QoS marks .......... 515
Layer 2: 802.1p .......... 516
Layer 3 protocols .......... 516
Methods for prioritizing and queuing traffic .......... 518
Honoring QoS marks .......... 518
Classifying traffic .......... 518
Mix of strategies .......... 519
Honoring QoS marks .......... 519
Honoring 802.1p .......... 519
Honoring DSCP .......... 522
Controlling trusted value at a port level .......... 525
Classifying traffic for QoS .......... 528
Classifying at Layer 2 versus Layer 3 .......... 528
Classifying based on interface .......... 529
Classifying with global QoS policies .......... 531
Interaction of QoS classifications and incoming values .......... 532
Classifying traffic with classifier-based QoS policies .......... 533
Summary of how traffic is marked and prioritized .......... 540
Rate limiting .......... 544
Port-based rate limiting .......... 545
Rate limit all traffic .......... 546
Rate limit ICMP traffic .......... 546
Rate limit broadcast and multicast traffic .......... 547
Combining rate limits .......... 547
Egress per-queue rate limiting .......... 548
Class-based rate limiting .......... 549
User-based rate limits .......... 553
LLDP-MED .......... 554
Review interoperation with authentication .......... 554
Enabling LLDP-MED .......... 555
Configuring information advertised in the LLDP-MED TLVs .......... 556
Summary .......... 558
Learning check .......... 558
Answers .......... 561
Review .......... 561
Learning check .......... 562

16 Additional Security Features ....................565
Assumed knowledge....................565
Introduction ....................566
DHCP attacks....................566
Using DHCP snooping to protect against DHCP attacks ....................567
How DHCP snooping works ....................568
Configuration ....................569
Authorized servers....................570
Inserting option 82 with DHCP snooping....................571
Filtering option 82 from connected devices ....................573
ARP snooping and poisoning ....................574
ARP protection....................575
Additional checks ....................577
DHCP snooping and ARP protection ....................577
Guidelines for using dynamic ARP protection ....................579
The dangers of eavesdropping and unauthorized access....................580
Port security....................581
Port security learn modes....................582
The address limit parameter....................583
Port security actions ....................583
Use case 1: Limit devices on an edge port....................583
Use case 2: Preventing changes to the devices connected to ports .....585
Use case 3: Exactly controlling devices that can connect to a port .....587
Use case 4: Combining port security with 802.1X port-based authentication....................588
Eavesdropping protection ....................590
MAC lockdown....................591
Considering redundant links ....................593
MAC lockdown versus port security....................593
Connection rate filtering ....................594
Operation ....................594
Action....................595
Unblocking a blocked host....................596
Sensitivity ....................597
Implementation recommendations ....................598
Excluding hosts from filtering ....................599
Summary....................600
Learning check....................601
Answers ....................601
Learning check ....................601

17 Practice Exam ........................................................ 603
Introduction ........................................................ 603
Minimum qualifications........................................................ 603
HPE6-A45 exam details........................................................ 603
HPE6-A45 testing objectives........................................................ 604
Test preparation questions and answers ........................................................ 605
Questions........................................................ 605
Answers........................................................ 632

Index........................................................ 643

# 1 Introduction to Aruba Solutions

EXAM OBJECTIVES

✓ Describe market trends that are leading companies to implement a digital workplace

✓ Describe how the Mobile First Network from Aruba, a Hewlett Packard Enterprise company, delivers the digital workplace

## Assumed knowledge

Before reading this chapter, you should have a basic understanding of:

- IP addressing
- Open Systems Interconnection (OSI) model
- Wired networking protocols and technologies such as Spanning Tree Protocol (STP), link aggregation, Virtual LANs (VLANs), switching, and routing
- Aruba Virtual Switching Framework (VSF)

## Introduction

You will begin this chapter by examining the trends that are driving companies to move to a digital workplace and how Aruba's Mobile First Network delivers the digital workplace. You will also briefly explore the solutions that are highlighted in this study guide.

Finally, you will review several technologies that you should understand before moving on to other chapters.

## Digital workplace

HPE helps companies enable workplace productivity by helping them create a digital workplace.

As you know only too well, the nature of work is changing. The new generation of collaborative digital workplaces, an increase in Internet of Things (IoT) devices, and the increased speed of doing business on mobile are just part of this change that leads IT to ask the question—Is the network infrastructure ready?

In addition to the nature of work, the workforce itself is changing. According to *Time* magazine, millennials will make up three-fourths of the global workforce by 2025. ("Millennials vs. Baby Boomers: Who Would You Rather Hire?" Time.com, Mar. 2012.) These GenMobile workers are tech savvy and like to do their work using a variety of devices. They thrive when they can collaborate with new tools in an open environment. To be productive and experience job satisfaction, these new workers need a network that provides access for any device, anywhere they want to work.

Employers that want to attract and retain the best of this new workforce must pay attention to employees' need to work where and how they want. A study by Cornell University reports 33% less attrition rate within companies that allow their workforce to work wherever they roam.

Creating and delivering new business models, solutions, and experiences require harnessing new types of applications, data, and risks. It also requires implementing new ways to build, operate, and consume technology.

## Digital workplaces require a Mobile First Network

The Aruba Mobile First Network helps adapt to the challenges that attend mobile and Internet of Things (IoT), Bring Your Own Device (BYOD), and Unified Communications (UC). At the heart of the Mobile First network is the Aruba Mobile First platform, the intelligent software layer between the Aruba technology ecosystem and the Aruba Mobile First infrastructure (see Figure 1-1).

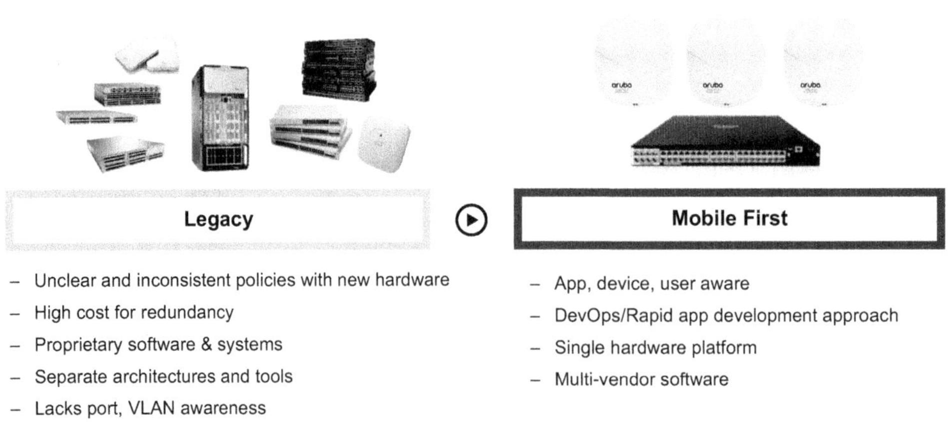


Figure 1-1 Digital workplaces require a Mobile First Network

The infrastructure must become application aware to adapt and respond in real time to meet these requirements.

The Mobile First platform makes the underlying Aruba Mobile First infrastructure smarter, enabling it to adapt to idea-economy innovations in real time. And because all products within the Mobile First infrastructure share a single architecture, you can deploy a single set of hardware components across the entire company and manage them all from anywhere with the Mobile First platform.

Designed to enrich the mobile experience and secure IoT for operational technologies, the Mobile First platform acts as a rich source of insights for business and IT. The platform's focus on mobile and IoT clearly differentiates Aruba and helps companies accelerate innovation within the Aruba technology ecosystem, which speaks to Aruba's commitment to open standards.

Consisting of third-party IT services as well as business and end-user facing applications, the Aruba technology ecosystem allows developers to freely innovate and customize networking functions dynamically in real time by using the rich contextual data that mobile and IoT devices collect.

## Aruba Switch solutions

Although Aruba is known for its industry-leading wireless solutions with technologies such as ClientMatch, AppRF, and 802.11ac Wave 2, as an HPE company, it has also gained strength as a wired solution provider. The sample architecture shown in Figure 1-2 illustrates the power of a unified wired and wireless architecture. The wired network consists of Aruba 3810 or 5400R switches at the core and Aruba 3810 or 2930F switches at the access layer. Aruba AP 330s, controlled by centralized Aruba Mobility Controller 7240s, provide wireless services, while Aruba AirWave delivers on-premises network management and Aruba ClearPass Policy Manager, user and access management.

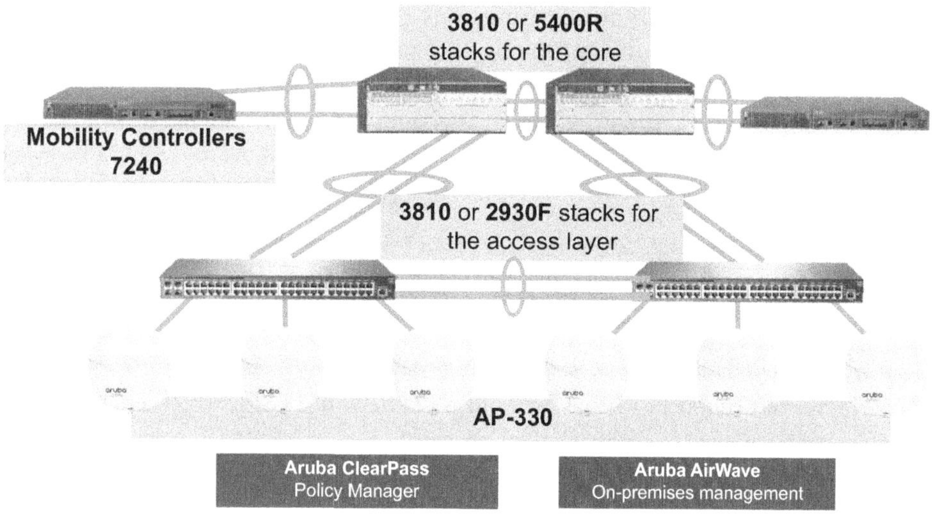


Figure 1-2 Aruba Switch solutions

This study guide focuses on Aruba's wired solutions—with emphasis on the Aruba 5400R zl2, 3810, and 2930F Series switches (see Figure 1-3). You will learn how to manage these switches in AirWave and how to integrate them with ClearPass as part of a security solution. You should visit the Aruba website (www.arubanetworks.com) to see the full range of Aruba solutions and to obtain detailed information about each one.

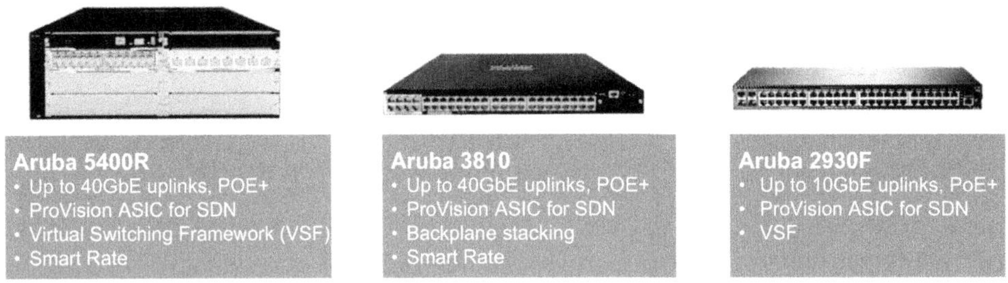


Figure 1-3 Aruba Switch solutions

## Aruba 5400R zl2 Switch Series

The Aruba 5400R zl2 Switch Series can be deployed at the access or core of a campus network and consists of advanced intelligent switches available in either a 6-slot or 12-slot chassis. (If you are familiar with the HPE switch portfolio, this switch was formerly called the HPE 5400R zl2 Switch Series.) The foundation for the switch series is a purpose-built, programmable ProVision ASIC that allows the most demanding networking features (such as Quality of Service, or QoS, and security) to be implemented in a scalable yet granular fashion.

Aruba 5400R zl2 Switch Series supports redundant management modules as well as redundant power supplies, providing high availability for environments that cannot tolerate down time. The switch series supports many combination of 10/100 Gigabit Ethernet, 10 Gigabit Ethernet, and 40 Gigabit Ethernet interfaces and full Power over Ethernet Plus (PoE+) on all ports simultaneously (with the appropriate power supply unit). The switch series also supports Smart Rate ports, which deliver both high speed and power for 802.11ac Wave 2 devices, using existing CAT5e and CAT6 twisted pair wiring.

In addition, the 5400R zl2 Switch Series provides Layer 3 features such as Open Shortest Path First (OSPF), Border Gateway Protocol (BGP), Virtual Router Redundancy (VRRP), and Protocol Independent Multicast (PIM), and it provides support for emerging technologies such as Software Defined Networking (SDN).

Finally, the switch series supports Virtual Switching Framework (VSF), which enables you to combine two switches into one virtual switch called a fabric.

## Aruba 3810 Switch Series

The Aruba 3810 Switch Series is a family of fully managed Gigabit Ethernet switches available in 24-port and 48-port models, with or without PoE+ and with either SFP+, 10 GbE, or 40 GbE uplinks. One model in the series also supports Smart Rate ports. Like the 5400R zl2 Switch Series, the 3810 Switch Series is built on the latest ProVision ASIC technology and advances in hardware engineering to deliver one of the most resilient and energy-efficient switches in the industry.

If you want to take advantage of Smart Rate technology, 3810 stacks can form an agile, flexible, and intelligent access layer. You can also use backplane stacking to deploy stacks of 3810 switches and form a powerful, intelligent, and highly available core. Similar to VSF, backplane stacking technology is implemented in the 3810 Switch Series to deliver chassis-like resiliency in a flexible, stackable form factor.

## Aruba 2930F Switch Series

The Aruba 2930F Switch Series is a family of basic Layer 3 Gigabit Ethernet switches that are ideal for the enterprise edge, small and midsize businesses (SMBs), and branch offices. This powerful access layer switch supports 1 GbE or 10 GbE uplinks and up to 370 W PoE+. VSF stacking provides simplification, cost savings, and redundancy.

The Aruba 2930F Switch Series provides basic Layer 3 features, such as static and RIP routing, access control lists (ACLs), and Access (single area) OSPF, with no software licensing required. Designed with a powerful, programmable ProVision ASIC, the Aruba 2930F enables the mobile campus with low latency, increased packet buffering, and adaptive power consumption, and with support for OpenFlow, this switch is ready to take advantage of SDN applications.

Finally, the 2930F switches support VSF so that you can deploy them in flexible, easily managed stacks.

# Unified wired and wireless management

Aruba AirWave is a multivendor wired and wireless network management solution that gives organizations deep visibility into the access network (see Figure 1-4). Available as software or as a combined hardware and software appliance, AirWave reduces cost and complexity, improves service quality, and enables IT administrators to make intelligent, well-informed decisions about network design and usage.

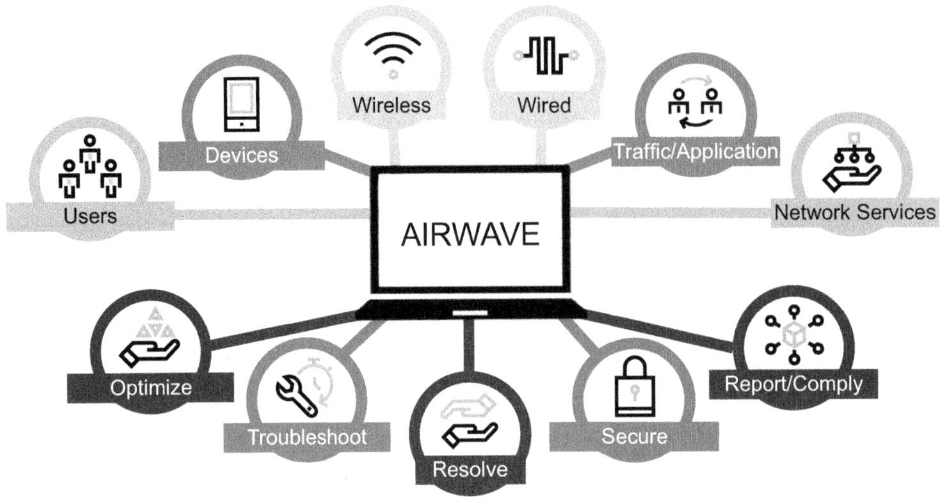


Figure 1-4 Unified wired and wireless management

With a single interface, IT administrators can view the entire network with real-time performance monitoring of every device, every user, and every application running on the wired and wireless network, as well as other network services impacting the user experience (Figure 1-4).

Granularity, end-to-end visibility, and predictive insight make AirWave unique in the industry and perfect for mobile-first access networks.

Aruba AirWave is ideal for mid-size to large enterprise networks. The management solution supports all Aruba controller-managed and controller-based APs as well as Mobility and Cloud Controllers. AirWave even supports Aruba campus switches. More importantly, AirWave supports third-party wired and wireless networks from vendors such as Cisco, Brocade, Alcatel-Lucent, Meru, and Motorola.

## Unified, policy-based access management: Aruba ClearPass

Aruba ClearPass is an enterprise-ready, scalable policy management solution that secures network access for a mobile world. As Figure 1-5 shows, the comprehensive Policy Manager includes ClearPass Onboard to manage device and employee access, ClearPass OnGuard to manage device health, and ClearPass Guest to manage guest access with a customizable portal. ClearPass Policy Manager can control who can access the network and on what devices. It can then customize users' access to control devices, data, infrastructure, and applications.

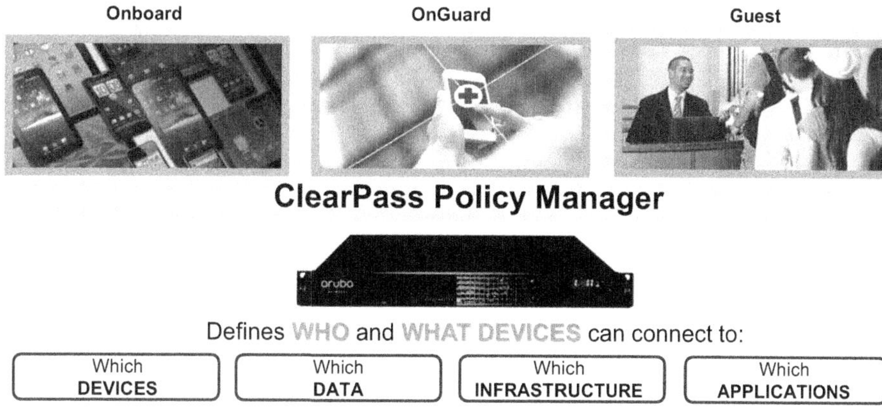


Figure 1-5 Unified, policy-based access management: Aruba ClearPass

In the world of virtual workplaces, mobile devices, and wireless connectivity, ClearPass provides secure, high-performance connectivity. This policy engine for mobility is the perfect foundation for network security in any organization, with unprecedented scale and integration for multivendor architectures.

Aruba ClearPass comes as a hardware appliance combined with a virtual machine (or VM) or as a VM that can be deployed on the customer's hardware. Three different-sized appliances are available, and each can be purchased for use in remote locations.

In this study guide, you will focus on integrating AOS-switches into ClearPass employee and guest authentication and access control solutions. You will not learn how to set up Aruba ClearPass itself, but you will examine policies already configured on ClearPass and learn how to deploy your switches to work with ClearPass to enforce the solution.

## Campus architectures

You will begin by examining the architecture for the wired network. You can classify the architecture based on the number of tiers or the layers. In Figure 1-6, the topology, the two-tier topology, includes an access layer, to which endpoints connect, and a core, which interconnects the access layer switches. The core might also connect the access layer to external resources such as the Internet, and it might provide connections for centralized servers. (Companies with more servers might place those servers in a dedicated data center, which would have a two- or three-tier topology of its own.)

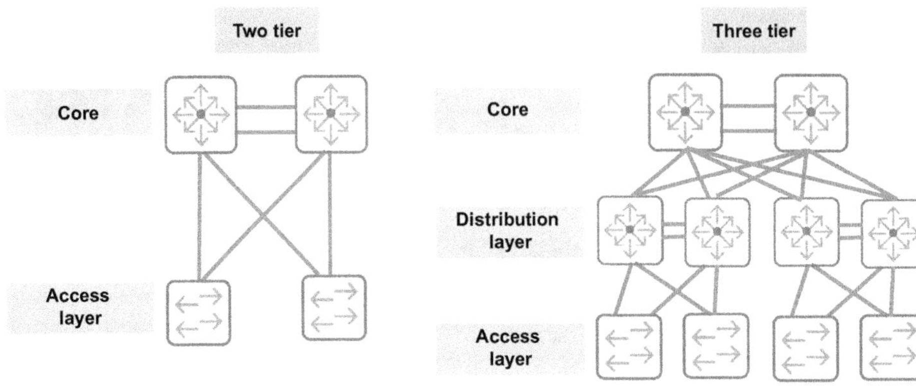


Figure 1-6 Campus architectures

Aruba recommends the two-tier topology whenever the environment supports it.

Sometimes, however, legacy solutions or cabling restraints force you to use a three-tier topology, and Aruba offers optimized solutions for these cases as well. Figure 1-7 shows a recommended three-tier topology. The added distribution layer consists of several pairs of stacked 3810 switches or 5400R VSF fabrics.

Figure 1-6 shows the physical connections between switches in a redundant design.

## Review basic networking concepts

Take a minute to answer the following questions. This will help you review technologies within a simple campus network such as the one shown in Figure 1-7.

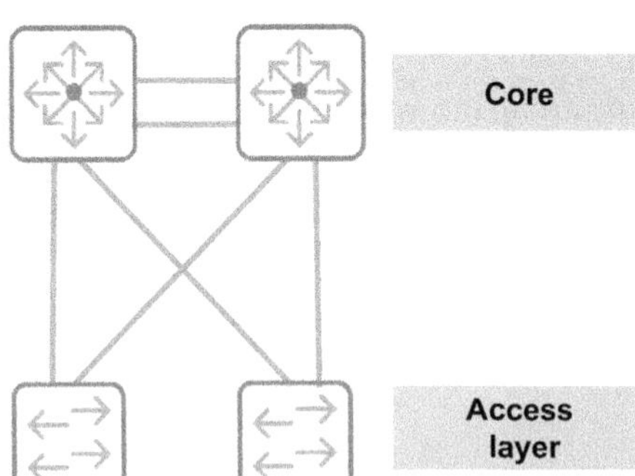


Figure 1-7 Simple campus network

1. Which technology or technologies should you implement on the redundant links between Access-1 and the two core switches in Figure 1-7 to prevent network loops? Your choice should allow the switches to use as much of the bandwidth on those links as possible.
2. Which technology allows two core Aruba 5400R zl2 Series switches to act as single logical switch? The same technology can stack up to four Aruba 2930F Series switches at the access layer, allowing you to treat each stack as a single logical switch.
3. In Figure 1-7 the core is routing traffic, and the access layer is switching traffic. What functions can VLANs fulfill in a topology such as this? How do you configure VLANs on edge ports as opposed to switch-to-switch links? What is required for traffic to flow between VLANs?
4. You want to be able to access the CLI of your switches remotely and securely using Secure Shell (SSH).
   - What should you configure on the switches to set up this form of access?
   - What feature of the switches can you use if you want to completely separate management traffic from production traffic?
5. You are managing a 5400R switch remotely. You think that this switch connects to a specific other switch on interface A23, but you are not sure. What command can you use to verify? What technology needs to be running on the switches?

## Summary

In this chapter, you reviewed the demands that employees are placing on IT as they look for a digital workplace, which allows them to use any device anywhere to access their data. You also learned how the Aruba Mobile First Network delivers this digital workplace, providing the WLAN, switch, and management solutions that companies need.

## Learning check

1. Which Aruba switch series supports backplane stacking?
   a. 5400R zl2
   b. 3810
   c. 2930F
   d. 2530
2. Which Aruba solution provides policy-based access management?
   a. Aruba AirWave
   b. Aruba Meridian
   c. Aruba Central
   d. Aruba ClearPass

# Answers

## Review: Basic technologies for a campus network

1. Which technology or technologies should you implement on the redundant links between Access-1 and the two core switches in Figure 1-7 to prevent network loops? Your choice should allow the switches to use as much of the bandwidth on those links as possible.

   You should place all of these links in a single link aggregation (or trunk). You should generally use Link Aggregation Control Protocol (LACP) on the link aggregation to decrease the chance of misconfigurations causing loops.

2. Which technology allows two core 5400R switches to act as single logical switch? The same technology can stack multiple 2930F switches at the access layer, allowing you to treat each stack as a single logical switch.

   VSF

3. In Figure 1-7 the core is routing traffic, and the access layer is switching traffic. What functions can VLANs fulfill in a topology such as this? How do you configure VLANs on edge ports as opposed to switch-to-switch links? What is required for traffic to flow between VLANs?

   VLANs allow you to separate endpoints according to flexible criteria such as user types or device types. For example, you could place employee endpoints in one VLAN, guest endpoints in a different VLAN, and servers in a third VLAN.

   Edge ports typically supported untagged traffic. To place a device in a VLAN, you must configure the edge port connected to it as an untagged member of the VLAN. In order to extend the VLANs across the topology and connect the devices in those VLANs to their default router (the core VSF fabric), you must tag those VLANs on the links between the access layer and the core. VLAN tagging allows a link, or a link aggregation, to carry traffic in more than one VLAN.

   IP routing, implemented in this example at the core, allows traffic to flow between VLANs. The core routing switch—in this case the core VSF fabric—can act as the default router for all of the VLANs. It should have an IP address in each VLAN, the same IP address that the endpoints have configured as their default gateway address. The core VSF fabric should have IP routing enabled on it. When the server providing DHCP services is in a different VLAN from DHCP clients, the core VSF fabric should also implement DHCP relay (an IP helper address) in the clients' VLANs. The access switches do not require IP addresses on the user VLANs because they are acting at Layer 2.

4. You want to be able to access the CLI of your switches remotely and securely using SSH.

   – What should you configure on the switches to set up this form of access?

   – What feature of the switches can you use if you want to completely separate management traffic from production traffic?

To enable SSH access to the switches, you must make sure that every switch has an IP address. SSH is enabled by default and uses a default private/public keypair. You should typically generate a new key. You should also set a manager password, operator password, or both to secure access to the switch.

You can use the switches' out-of-band management (OOBM) ports to completely separate management traffic from production traffic. You would connect these ports and your management stations in a network separate from the network used by users and servers. You would then configure the IP addresses at which you manage your switches on the OOBM ports.

If you are not using OOBM ports, you should generally create a different VLAN for the switches' management IP addresses.

5. You are managing a 5400R switch remotely. You think that this switch connects to a specific other switch on interface A23, but you are not sure. What command can you use to verify? What technology needs to be running on the switches?

   You can use the **show lldp info remote-device** or **show lldp info remote-device <interface ID>** command. LLDP must be running on the switches (it is by default).

## Learning check

1. Which Aruba switch series supports backplane stacking?
   a. 5400R zl2
   **b. 3810**
   c. 2930F
   d. 2530
2. Which Aruba solution provides policy-based access management?
   a. Aruba AirWave
   b. Aruba Meridian
   c. Aruba Central
   **d. Aruba ClearPass**

# 2 Data Link Layer Redundancy Technologies

EXAM OBJECTIVES

- ✓ Compare Rapid Per-VLAN Spanning Tree Plus (RPVST+) with Rapid Spanning Tree Protocol (RSTP) and Multiple Spanning Tree Protocol (MSTP)
- ✓ Implement spanning tree protocol and loop protections
- ✓ Describe how Unidirectional Link Detection (UDLD) detects and handles unidirectional links

## Assumed knowledge

Before reading this chapter, you should have a basic understanding of:

- IP addressing
- Open Systems Interconnection (OSI) model
- Spanning Tree Protocol (STP)
- Multiple Spanning Tree Protocol (MSTP)
- Rapid Per-VLAN Spanning Tree Plus (RSTP+)
- Link aggregation
- Virtual LANs (VLANs)
- Switching
- Static and dynamic routing

## Introduction

In this chapter, you will explore technologies beyond spanning tree alone for establishing a network infrastructure that is both redundant and loop free.

If a network does not provide redundancy, a link failure could prevent users from accessing essential network services. However, to function properly, an Ethernet network must have only one active pathway between two devices. Adding redundant links can create loops, which result in broadcast storms that make the network inaccessible.

Aruba Switching Fundamentals for Mobility introduced you to the role of various spanning tree protocols in creating a redundant and loop-free network environment, including Spanning Tree Protocol (STP), Rapid Spanning Tree Protocol (RSTP), and Multiple Spanning Tree Protocol (MSTP). This chapter introduces a proprietary Cisco protocol that provides similar capabilities: Rapid Per-VLAN Spanning Tree Plus (RPVST+). It explains how to configure RPVST+ on AOS-Switches to provide interoperability between switches and routers in heterogeneous networks.

This chapter also introduces loop protection, which helps prevent loops at edge ports, and protections that help prevent STP-based network attacks.

To remain resilient, networks need a way to detect problems that can occur on links. This chapter also includes Unidirectional Link Detection (UDLD), which helps to detect and mitigate issues that can occur on fiber links. It explains how to configure this technology on your AOS-Switches.

## Rapid Per-VLAN Spanning Tree Plus (RPVST+)

Not all Cisco switches and IOS versions support MSTP. Many companies with Cisco networks use the default mode on Cisco switches, Rapid Per VLAN Spanning Tree Plus (RPVST+). Many vendors' devices also support RPVST+. Therefore, when administering a heterogeneous network, network administrators who are very familiar with RPVST+ may not want to change to MSTP, even if the latter is an option.

### Why RPVST+

You can implement RPVST+ on AOS-Switches so that you can deploy them in heterogeneous environments that use the RPVST+ protocol.

---

**Note**

RPVST+ was preceded by PVST+, a similar Cisco standard that was based on STP. Most modern networks use RPVST+, and this is the version of the protocol supported on AOS-Switches when you enable PVST+ mode. However, if the AOS-switch does connect to a switch that uses only basic PVST+, the AOS-switch interoperates in much the same way that an RSTP switch interoperates with an STP switch.

---

## Comparison: RPVST+, RSTP, and MSTP

RPVST+ is essentially RSTP that is operating on a per-VLAN basis in a single Layer 2 domain. As with MSTP, RPVST+ allows each RSTP spanning tree to have a different root switch. A redundant link might be active for one topology but blocked for another, enabling per-VLAN load sharing of traffic across redundant links.

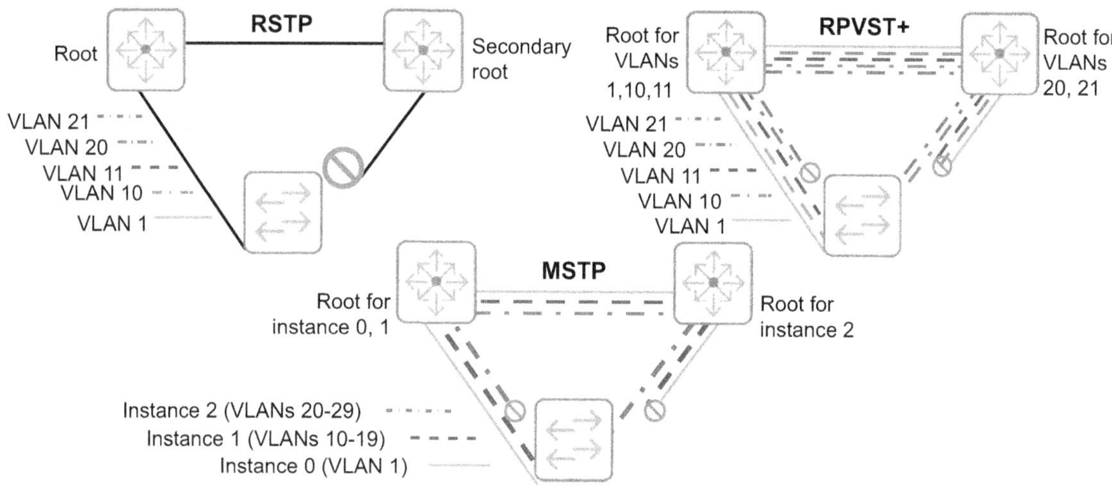


Figure 2-1 Comparing RPVST+, RSTP, and MSTP

In the simple network shown in Figure 2-1, for example, the link between Switch B and Switch C is blocked for VLAN 10, but in a forwarding state for VLAN 20. Likewise, the link between Switch A and Switch C is blocked for VLAN 20, but active for VLAN 10.

RPVST+ creates a unique spanning tree for each VLAN, while MSTP creates just one spanning tree per instance and maps multiple VLANs to each instance.

This difference has several implications.

Because RPVST+ creates a separate spanning tree for each VLAN, topology changes affecting a particular VLAN are propagated only inside that VLAN. RPVST+ is also VLAN-aware. The spanning tree only extends on links that actually support the VLAN, helping to prevent misconfigurations and accidentally blocked links. However, in a network with a large number of per-VLAN spanning tree instances, RPVST+ can increase the load on the switch's CPU. It must always create one spanning tree for each VLAN, even if many VLANs use the same paths, as is often the case. Therefore, the load balancing comes with some tradeoffs; the switches need to process more Bridge Protocol Data Units (BPDUs) and maintain more spanning trees, creating a higher CPU usage that can cause issues.

This means that you might need to follow different guidelines in networks that use RPVST+ from networks that use MSTP. For example, you should generally propagate VLANs only where they need to go rather than on all switch-to-switch links as you do with MSTP. In addition, in networks with 100 or more VLANs, you might consider migrating to MSTP, if possible.

With MSTP, on the other hand, a single untagged BPDU carries information for every instance. This enables load sharing across the network while keeping the switch's CPU load at a moderate level. You should be aware that, although each instance specifies its associated VLANs, the instance spanning tree is built without regard to the VLANs that are actually carried on the ports. To ensure a true loop-free topology, every switch must agree on the tree that carries traffic for a specific VLAN. Therefore, MSTP only operates within an MSTP region in which every switch uses the same region name, configuration revision number, and VLAN-to-instance mappings. In addition, it is best practice to support all VLANs used in the network on every switch-to-switch link. This prevents MSTP from choosing a path for an instance that does not actually carry the VLANs mapped to that instance.

**Note**

If you are familiar with Cisco switches, you might be familiar with UplinkFast and BackboneFast technologies. Cisco developed these technologies for PVST+ to speed convergence times. RSTP has similar mechanisms to speed convergence built into it. Because each RPVST+ per-VLAN spanning tree uses RSTP (just as each MSTP spanning tree uses RSTP), RPVST+ does not need to use UplinkFast and BackboneFast. Similarly, the AOS-Switches do not support, nor need to support, these technologies. They provide the same fast convergence using RPVST+.

## Rapid Spanning Tree Protocol Plus BPDUs

As a proprietary protocol, RPVST+ uses different BPDUs from the standard BPDUs. First, a port on a switch that implements RPVST+ sends and receives multiple BPDUs—one for each VLAN and spanning tree.

The RPVST+ BPDUs use a Cisco destination MAC address, multicast address 01:00:0c:cc:cc:cd, and their version indicates Rapid Spanning Tree Protocol. The BPDU is tagged or untagged based on the configuration of the port. Because a port supports at most one untagged VLAN, most BPDUs are tagged. Often the untagged VLAN is VLAN 1, so the RPVST+ port sends the VLAN 1 BPDU as untagged. However, this is not required.

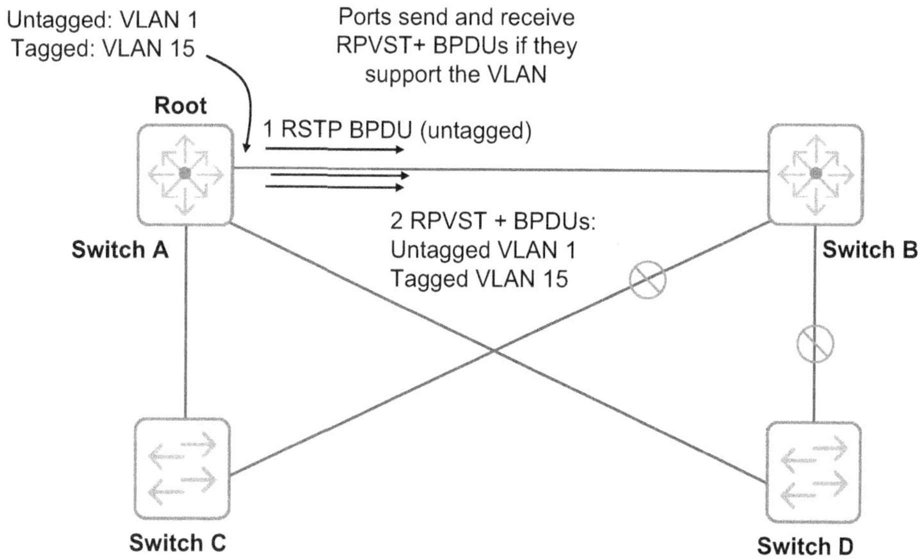


Figure 2-2 RPVST+ BPDUs

To provide compatibility with RSTP, RPVST+ switches also send RSTP BPDUs. To send these BPDUs, an AOS-switch port must support VLAN 1. VLAN 1 can be either tagged or untagged on the port, but the switches always send the RSTP BPDUs as untagged frames.

Consider the example port on the root bridge for the RPVST+ network in Figure 2-2. This port is configured to support untagged traffic for VLAN 1 and tagged traffic for VLAN 15. The port sends the following BPDUs:

- RSTP BPDUs, which are untagged frames in VLAN 1 (of course, untagged frames do not include VLAN information but the BPDUs use VLAN 1's costs and priorities)
- RPVST+ BPDUs, which are untagged frames in VLAN 1
- RPVST+ BPDUs, which are tagged frames in VLAN 15

If the port supports tagged traffic for VLAN 1 and untagged traffic for VLAN 15, on the other hand, it would send the following BPDUs:

- RSTP BPDUs, which are untagged frames in VLAN 1
- RPVST+ BPDUs, which are untagged frames in VLAN 15
- RPVST+ BPDUs, which are tagged frames in VLAN 1

It is important for you to understand that:

- RPVST+ uses different BPDUs to construct the spanning tree for each VLAN.
- The BPDUs carried on each port depend on the VLANs supported on those ports.

This is why the topologies constructed by RPVST+ are VLAN aware. In other words, the spanning tree for a particular VLAN only extends as far as that VLAN extends. This provision can make it easier for you to design the network.

**Important**

Because RPVST+ BPDUs are sent in each VLAN, they create overhead. It is often recommended that you reduce the number of VLANs on the switch to reduce overhead. The forwarding and reception of RPVST+ BPDUs depends on whether a VLAN exists on a particular link.

## Path cost differences

You should also be aware of the port cost differences for the STP protocols. Take a minute to study the costs outlined in Table 2-1.

Table 2-1 Path cost differences for the Spanning Tree protocols

| Path cost | STP/RPVST+ Cisco short path cost 802.1D-1998 | RSTP/MSTP 802.1t-2001 |
|---|---|---|
| Fast Ethernet (100 Mbps) | 19 | 200,000 |
| Gigabit | 4 | 20,000 |
| 10 Gigabit | 2 | 2000 |

AOS-Switches that run RPVST+ use the 802.1t-2001 standard (200,000/20,000/2000) by default. You can also set AOS-Switches to use the 802.1D costs, although the newer costs are recommended. However, if other switches in the network are using the default RPVST+ switches, you should configure the AOS-Switches to use these costs as well.

## RPVST+ setup

The basic steps for configuring RPVST+ are provided for your reference below:

1. Set spanning tree to RPVST+ mode.

   ```
   Switch(config)# spanning-tree mode rapid-pvst
   ```

2. By default, RPVST+ runs on every VLAN configured on the switch. You can disable or re-enable RPVST+ on a VLAN with this command:

   ```
   Switch(config)# spanning-tree vlan <ID><disable | enable>
   ```

3. If you want the switch to act as the root or secondary root for any VLANs, configure the appropriate priority settings on each VLAN (typically 0 for root and 1 for secondary root). In this example, you configure priority 0 on VLAN 10 and priority 1 on VLAN 20. Another switch will have priority 1 on VLAN 10 and priority 0 on VLAN 20.

   ```
   Switch(config)# spanning-tree vlan 10 priority 0
   Switch(config)# spanning-tree vlan 20 priority 1
   ```

4. Enable spanning tree.

   ```
   Switch(config)# spanning-tree
   ```

5. You can configure other settings such as per-VLAN port priority. Refer to your switches' *Advanced Traffic Management* guide for more details.

## MSTP versus RPVST+

You now have a basic understanding of the differences between how MSTP and RPVST+. What are the advantages and disadvantages of RPVST+ as opposed to MSTP?

Use Figure 2-3 as a reference to compare RPVST+ and MSTP in terms of:

- Number of trees
- Number of BPDUs
- Traffic flow

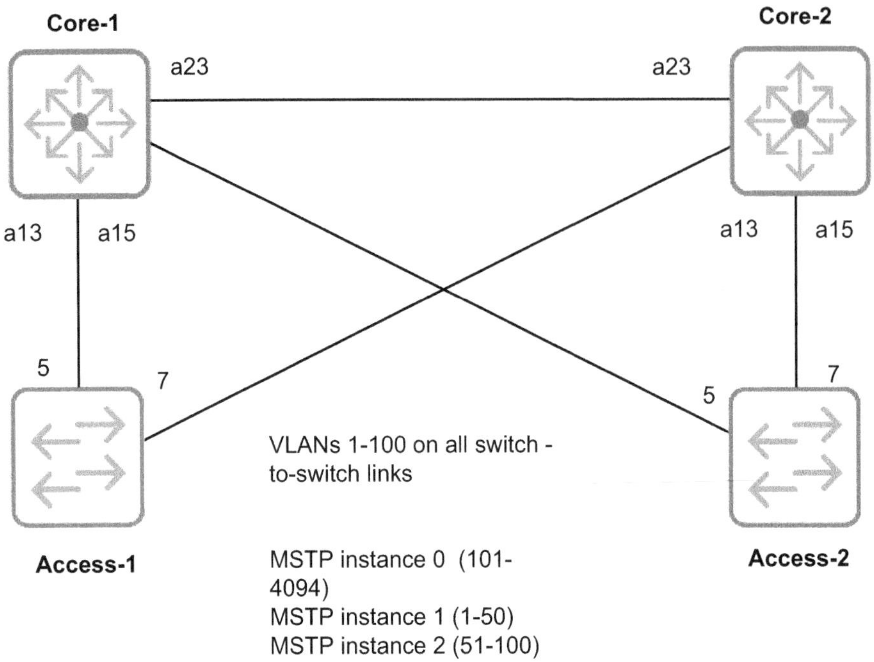


Figure 2-3 MSTP versus RPVST+

Now consider the following:

- What would happen if you removed some VLANs from Access-1? How would MSTP and RPVST+ handle this differently?
- What could happen if the link between Core-1 and Core-2 fails? How would MSTP and RPVST+ handle this differently?

You will find the answers to these questions at the end of this chapter.

## Vulnerability: Rogue device becomes root bridge

Sometimes issues can occur that cause your spanning tree protocol—whether RSTP, MSTP, or RPVST+—to choose an unfavorable link or to fail to block the appropriate link. You will now learn several ways that you can increase the security of your spanning tree network.

AOS-Switches protect against attacks that target spanning tree protocol's inherent vulnerability to BPDU spoofing attacks and unauthorized switches.

By design, STP allows any network device to join the spanning tree. While this design's openness ensures that all loops are eliminated, it leaves choices about disabling links vulnerable to manipulation from unauthorized devices. Because BPDUs have no authentication, it's easy for rogue devices to send legitimate BPDUs and join the spanning tree. Whether the rogue device is a malicious attacker or simply an unauthorized device such as an unmanaged switch added by users, it can negatively affect the network in a significant number of ways. For example, it can affect path selection, inactivate correct links, activate incorrect links, and even become the tree's root.

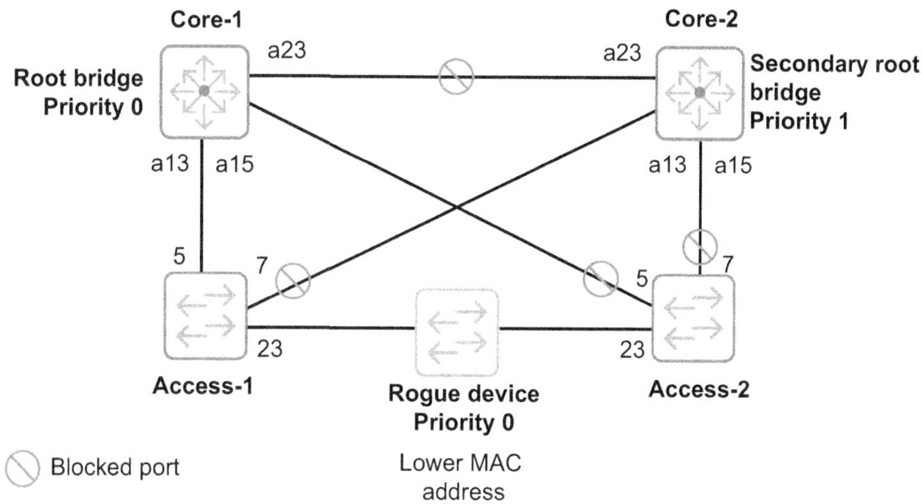


Figure 2-4 Vulnerability: Rogue device becomes root bridge

Figure 2-4 shows a rogue switch that has joined the spanning tree. The rogue switch has a priority of 0, and it happens to have a lower MAC address than the desired root bridge; therefore, Access-2 accepts its BPDUs as superior BPDUs.

A superior BPDU advertises "better" information for reaching the root. In this scenario, that better information is a root bridge with a lower ID. A BPDU with the current root bridge ID, but a lower root path cost is also a superior BPDU.

Based on the superior BPDU, Access-2 changes the port connected to the rogue device to its root port, and it advertises the superior BPDU to Core-1 and Core-2. Core-1 and Core-2 reconverge their topology based on the rogue device being the root. They block the high-speed link between them, creating a Denial of Service (DoS) attack.

## BPDU protection

AOS-Switches offer BPDU protection to prevent this situation from occurring in a network that uses MSTP or RSTP. This feature operates at the port level and is best implemented on edge ports, which should not be receiving BPDUs.

BPDU protection monitors a port for incoming BPDUs. If the port receives a BPDU, the switch shuts down the port, protecting the network from the rogue device. Figure 2-5 shows how BPDU protection could solve the issue of a rogue device (the problem you considered in Figure 2-4).

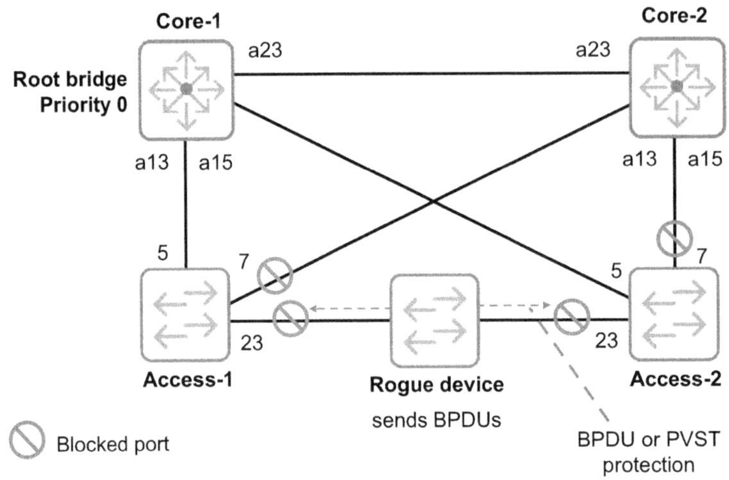


Figure 2-5 BPDU protection

## Configure BPDU protection

Use the command below to enable BPDU protection.

```
Switch(config)# spanning-tree <port_list> bpdu-protection
```

For example, when you implement BPDU protection on an access switch, you enable it on all ports except those providing switch-to-switch connections. You might enter:

```
Switch(config)# spanning-tree 1-4,9-28 bpdu-protection
```

You can use the following comment to determine whether BPDU protection has shut down a port.

```
Switch(config)# show spanning-tree bpdu-protection <port>
```

For example, the following command and output shows that BPDU protection has shut down port 23:

```
Switch(config)# show spanning-tree bpdu-protection 23
 Status and Counters - STP BPDU Protection Information
 BPDU Protection Timeout (sec) : 0
 BPDU Protected Ports : 1-4,9-26
  Port   Type       Protection State        Errant BPDUs
  ------ ---------- ---------- ------------ ------------
  23     100/1000T  Yes        BpduError    1
```

As you know, you can confirm that the port is down with this command:

```
Switch(config)# show interfaces brief
Status and Counters - Port Status
                  | Intrusion                             MDI    Flow   Bcast
  Port  Type      | Alert Enabled Status Mode            Mode   Ctrl   Limit
  ---- ---------  + ----- ------- ------ -------         ----   ----   -----
<output omitted>
  23   100/1000T  | No    No      Down   1000FDx         NA     off    0
  24   100/1000T  | No    No      Down   1000FDx         Auto   off    0
  25              | No    No      Down   .                      off    0
  26              | No    No      Down   .                      off    0
```

You can configure the amount of time the port remains disabled using a number of seconds that ranges from 0 to 65535. Configuring a value of zero (0) specifies an infinite time out period. In other words, the port remains disabled until manually re-enabled (such as with the interface <ID> enable command).

The command below configures a five-minute timeout for BPDU protection.

```
Switch(config)# spanning-tree bpdu-protection-timeout 300
```

The switch also logs an event when BPDU protection blocks the port.

## PVST protection

PVST protection is a similar feature for AOS-Switches that run spanning tree in RPVST+ mode. You should enable PVST protection on edge ports not expected to receive BPDUs. If the port receives a BPDU, the switch blocks the port and logs an event.

## BPDU protection versus BPDU filtering

Do not confuse BPDU protection with BPDU filtering.

BPDU filtering effectively disables spanning tree on a port. It drops all incoming BPDUs and also prevents the transmission of BPDUs on a port. The port also always remains in the forwarding state. Therefore, BPDU filtering, implemented on an edge port, would prevent a rogue switch taking over as root by dropping the rogue switch's BPDUs. However, because BPDU filtering forces the port into a forwarding state, it could allow loops to occur.

Edge ports that are vulnerable to rogue switches are often also vulnerable to situations such as these could create loops:

- Users connect an unauthorized switch that does not support spanning tree. The users loop ports together on that switch.
- Users loop wall jacks together.

BPDU filtering is generally best suited to disable spanning tree on trusted ports that you know will not create loops. For example, you have a distribution layer switch that is the root for a spanning tree. The switch routes traffic over redundant links to other distribution layer and core switches. You would implement BPDU filtering on the routed links to terminate the spanning tree.

### Configure BPDU filtering

Use the command below to enable BPDU filtering on a port.

```
Switch(config)# spanning-tree <port_list> bpdu-filter
```

For example, you would enter the following command to enable BPDU filtering on ports 23 and 24.

```
Switch(config)# spanning-tree 23,24 bpdu-filter
```

## Root guard

Root guard is an alternative to BPDU or PVST protection to protect your environment from rogue devices. It works when the switch operates in either MSTP or RPVST+ mode. Again, this feature helps ensure that the desired root bridge remains the root bridge. However, rather than blocking the port whenever the port receives BPDUs, root guard only blocks the port when the port receives superior BPDUs that could change the topology.

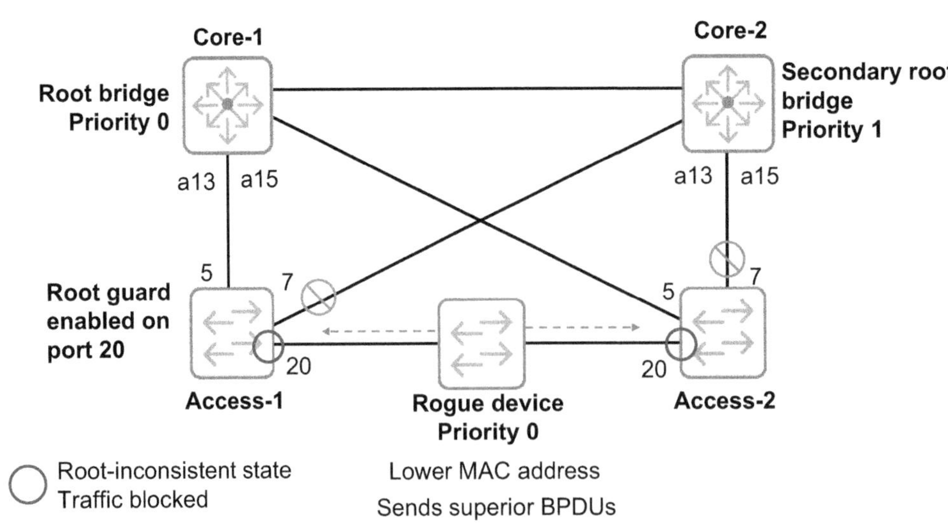


Figure 2-6 Root guard

You configure root guard on ports that should never receive BPDUs with information about the root—in other words, designated ports and generally designated ports at the network edge. For example, in Figure 2-6, you would enable root guard on all of the Access-1 switch ports except those that connect to the Core-1 and Core-2 switches. Likewise, you would enable root guard on all of the Access-2 switch ports except those that connect to the Core-1 and Core-2 switches. In this topology, Core-1 and Core-2 are the potential root switches. Access-1 and Access-2 switches should receive and act upon any BPDUs they receive on the ports that connect (directly or indirectly) to these switches.

You enable root guard on a port-by-port basis. With root guard enabled, the port will ignore any superior BPDUs it receives. It will not process RPVST+ topology change notifications it receives and will not propagate these changes to other ports.

If the switch simply ignored the superior BPDUs and remained in a forwarding state, it could allow a loop to form through the rogue root device. Therefore, root guard also changes the port's state to the root-inconsistent STP state if the port receives a superior BPDU. The port will not forward any traffic while it is in this state. Root guard will change the port state from root-inconsistent to its previous state when the port stops receiving superior BPDUs.

To configure root guard on port 20, for example, enter:

```
Switch(config)# spanning tree 20 root-guard
```

## BPDU throttling

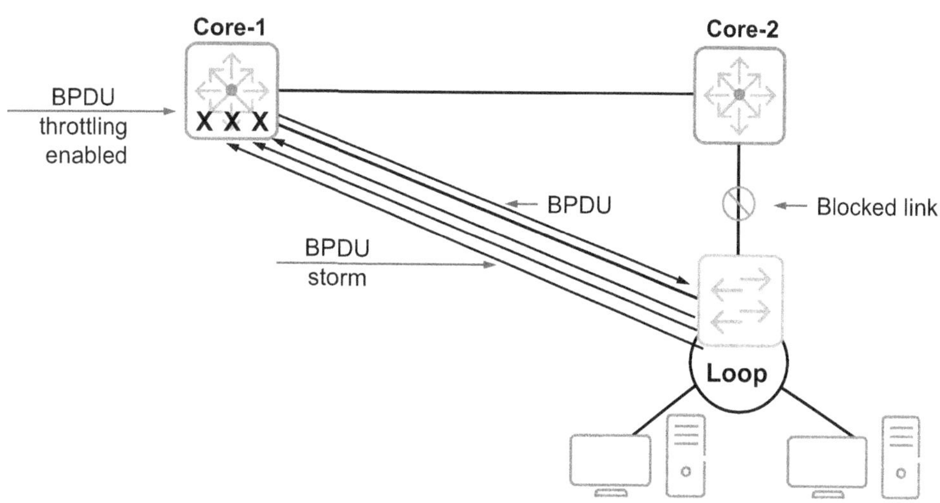


Figure 2-7 BPDU throttling

Figure 2-7 illustrates an MSTP BPDU storm that results from a loop in a hub that receives a single BPDU from a connected switch. When a BPDU storm bombards a switch on which spanning tree is enabled, the switch's CPU usage rises and makes the switch less manageable. This can make the broadcast storm even more damaging to the network and also more difficult to fix because managers cannot manage the switches and try to fix the problem. BPDU throttling eases CPU usage by limiting the rate at which BPDU packets reach the switch.

This protection is enabled by default when spanning tree is enabled on the switch unless you have already:

- Allowed v1 modules on Aruba 5400R zl2 Series Switches
- Enabled QinQ
- Enabled meshing

In each of the preceding cases, BPDU throttling is disabled and the switch generates a log message. Conversely, if spanning tree is enabled on the switch and you try to enable QinQ, meshing, or allow-v1-modules, the switch does not allow the new configuration and instead generates a log error message.

You also have the option to disable or re-enable BPDU throttling, using the switch's CLI. In addition, you can specify another throttle rate. BPDU throttling supports rates of 64, 128, and 256 packets per second (pps). The default throttle rate is 256 pps.

## STP loop guard

Occasionally, hardware or software failures can create a unidirectional link. This unidirectional link might prevent the flow of traffic—including BPDUs—from the designated port on the link, but allow traffic to flow from the nondesignated port. The nondesignated port realizes that it has stopped receiving BPDUs, which normally causes it to become a designated port. In the example shown in Figure 2-8, the access switch would also transition its alternate port to root port because it believes this port now gives it the best path to the root. In this case, though, the normal spanning tree behavior creates a loop. Traffic can flow from the access switch to the core switch 1, to core switch 2, and back to the access switch. A similar issue could occur if the Core-2 link stopped transmitting BPDUs to Access-1. Access-1 would transition the port to a designated port, as well as keeping its current root port.

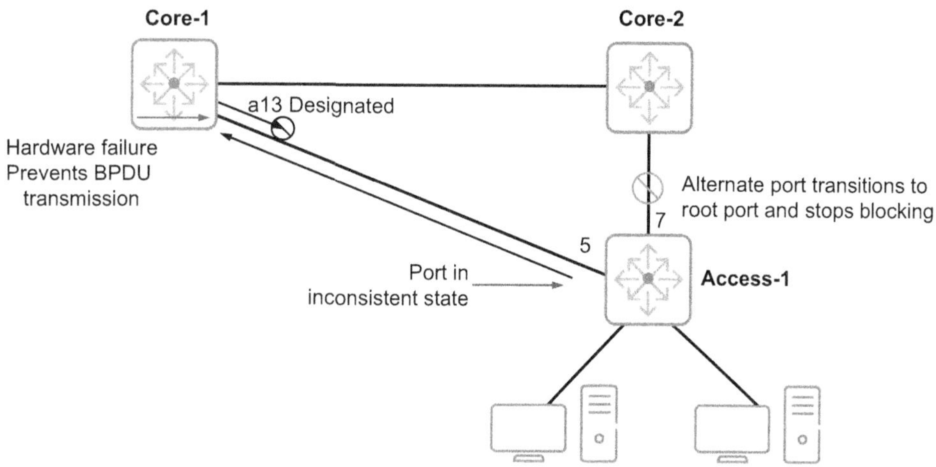


Figure 2-8 STP loop guard

STP loop guard prevents the loop from occurring by transitioning nondesignated ports to a loop inconsistent, rather than to a forwarding state, if they stop receiving BPDUs. In the loop inconsistent state, the nondesignated port prevents data traffic and BPDU transmissions through the link, thereby preventing a loop. If the root port transitions to a loop inconsistent state, the alternate port transitions to the root port, enabling the access switch to retain connectivity. When the nondesignated port again receives BPDUs from the link, it automatically transitions back to its former state.

You should typically use this protection on switch-to-switch links to prevent a root or an alternate port from changing states in the wrong circumstances.

## STP loop guard with MSTP

When you configure STP guard with MSTP, you enable STP loop guard on the port as a whole rather than on a specific MSTP instance. This makes sense because a port receives a single BPDU that contains information about multiple instances. However, loop guard detects inconsistencies and shuts down the port on an instance-by-instance basis.

Often the issue would cause the port as whole to shut down in any case. For example, in this network, Core-1 is root for instances 0 and 1, and Core-2 is root for instance 2. Access-1 implements loop guard on all interfaces that connect to the core switches. Then a hardware issue stops Access-1 from receiving the Core-2 BPDUs. These BPDUs are required to maintain the Alternate port status in instances 0 and 1 and the Root port status in instance 2. Therefore, Access-1 transitions to the loop inconsistent state in all of the instances. It now uses the link to Core-1 for all traffic.

However, you can see the per-instance behavior on the link between the core switches. On this link, Core-2 receives BPDUs from Core-1, but Core-1 also receives BPDUs from Core-2 because Core-2 is root in instance 2. You should implement loop guard on both sides of the link between the root switches. Then each switch can detect inconsistencies in the instances in which the other switch is root.

Consider what happens if a hardware issue makes the link unidirectional. Core-1 can still receive traffic from Core-2 and hear Core-2's BPDUs, but Core-2 cannot receive traffic from Core-1. When Core-2 detects that it no longer hears BPDUs from Core-1, it places the link to Core-1 in the loop inconsistent state in instances 0 and 1 and blocks traffic in those instances. However, it continues to keep the port open in instance 2 because the port is the designated port in that instance, and no change has occurred.

In this scenario, instance 2 does not have a loop. However, the unidirectional link that remains active in instance 2 could cause problems, depending on the network topology. For example, a server in a VLAN assigned to instance 2 connects to Core-1 and needs to reach a server in the same VLAN connected to Core-2. Core-1 believes that the link to Core-2 is forwarding traffic in this VLAN, but the traffic never actually reaches Core-2. It would be better if the core switches brought the unidirectional link down entirely so that Core-1 could failover to another switch-to-switch link for this instance. You will learn how to set up UDLD to prevent issues such as these later in this chapter.

## Loop protection

You will now explore a non-STP-related way to protect your network against loops. You will first consider why such a technology might be required and then learn how to implement it.

### Vulnerability: Edge loops in a network without spanning tree

Sometimes you have a network topology that does not require spanning tree to eliminate loops over switch-to-switch links. Examples include:

- A topology that uses link aggregations to connect access layer switches to a distribution layer or core VSF fabrics
- A topology that routes traffic between switches with all VLANs terminated on each switch

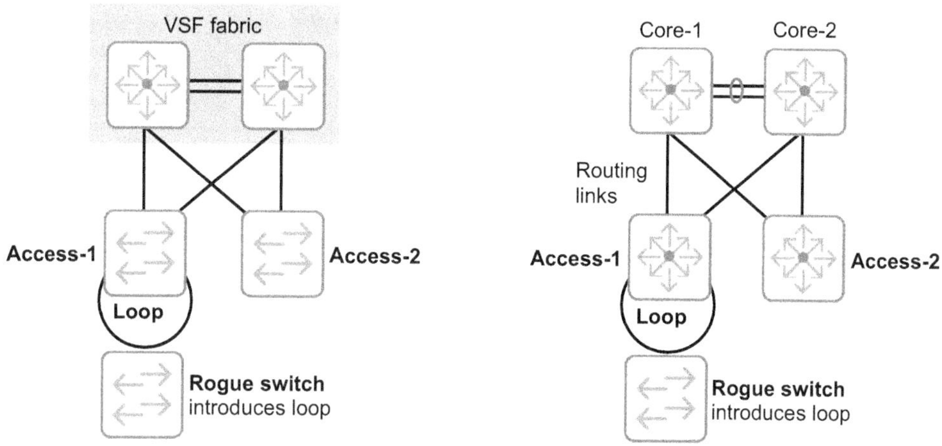


Figure 2-9 Vulnerability: Edge loops in a network without spanning tree

However, the access layer switches remain vulnerable to a variety of loop-causing incidents. As Figure 2-9 shows, employees who use spare Ethernet jacks to plug in personal devices such as unmanaged switches can inadvertently cause loops that in turn can bring your network down in an instant.

You can use loop protection on the edge ports to block these loops and prevent ill effects.

Note that loop protection is primarily intended to prevent loops on edge ports. Loop protection is not intended to provide convergence and fast failover for topologies with multiple redundant links. When you do not want to use spanning tree, you should prefer using technologies such as VSF and link aggregation to handle redundant switch-to-switch links.

## Vulnerability: Loops undetectable by spanning tree

You might also want to use loop protection on edge ports even when you are using RSTP, MSTP, or RPVST+.

Often, these spanning tree protocols can block loops introduced on the edge. For example, a user might connect two Ethernet jacks on the same switch together. The switch should detect its own BPDUs on the ports, causing spanning tree to block one of the ports. Even if you have configured the ports as spanning tree edge ports, the switch will automatically disable the edge port setting when it detects the BPDUs.

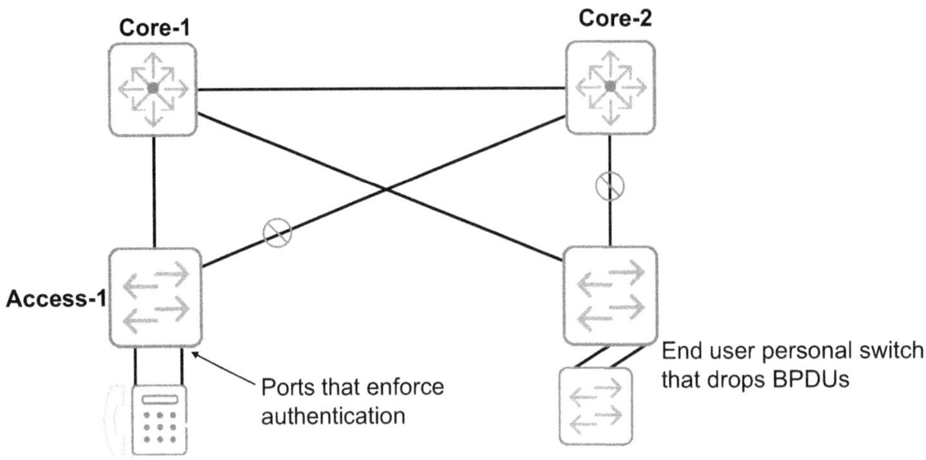


Figure 2-10 Vulnerability: Loops undetectable by spanning tree

However, spanning tree cannot protect your network from loops introduced by unmanaged devices that drop spanning tree packets—a situation shown in Figure 2-10.

In addition, spanning tree might fail to detect loops through edge ports that enforce client authentication (802.X, web, and MAC authentication). As you will learn in *Chapter 10: 802.1X Authentication* and *Chapter 11: MAC Authentication*, these authentication mechanisms can lock down the port to accepting traffic only from the authenticated device MAC address. Therefore, if the loop occurs through a port on which a device has already authenticated, the switch could drop the BPDUs and fail to detect the loop.

In such cases loop protection can help ensure that your edge network is loop free.

## Loop protection overview

The loop protection feature protects edge switches from downstream loops by transmitting loop protocol packets out of the ports or VLANs on which you have enabled it. You can enable loop protection in either port or VLAN mode (but not both).

Port mode is the typical mode, which you will examine first.

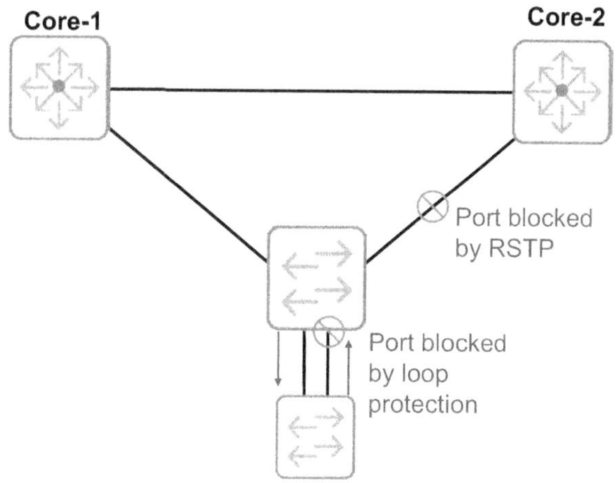


Figure 2-11 Loop protection

## Port mode

Loop protection uses port mode by default. In this mode, the enabled ports automatically send untagged loop protection packets at specified intervals of from 1 second to 10 seconds. (The default interval is 5 seconds.) When a loop-protection-enabled port receives a loop protocol packet, the port knows there is a downstream loop, in which case the port performs one of two receiver actions:

- send-disable
- no-disable

You can configure these actions on a per-port basis.

As Figure 2-11 shows, when you specify the send-disable option (which is enabled by default), the receiving port automatically disables the sending port, which remains disabled for a specified number of seconds. You can set the disable timer for values from 0 second to 604,800 seconds; when you set the value to 0 (which is the default value), the sending port remains disabled until you manually re-enable it. The no-disable option logs the loop but does not take action to eliminate it.

You configure timer and transmit intervals at the global level, rather than at the per-port level.

Loop protection includes a trap loop-detected feature that you can configure to trap loop-detection messages on the port and send the trapped messages via SNMP to a management station. Informed administrators can then investigate the reason for the loop and manually re-enable the disabled port. You configure the trap feature globally.

It is recommended that you enable loop protection on all edge ports on access layer switches. Please note that a port will only transmit loop protection packets when it is a member of an untagged VLAN. If only tagged VLANs are configured on the port, it will not transmit loop protection packets. Edge ports typically use untagged VLANs so that the port mode works will for them.

Loop protection is not recommended for managing redundant uplinks. Unlike a protocol such as RSTP or MSTP, loop protection does not give control over which link is blocked. In addition, it is not designed to provide fast failover if the topology changes.

## Configure loop protect in port mode

To enable loop protection in port mode on an AOS-switch, enter:

```
Switch(config)#loop-protect mode port
```

To enable protection for ports 1–26, type:

```
Switch(config)#loop-protect 1-26
```

You can use the command below to view the loop protection state on specific ports:

```
Switch(config)# show loop-protect 23,24

Status and Counters - Loop Protection Information

  Transmit Interval (sec)      : 5
  Port Disable Timer (sec)     : Disabled
  Loop Detected Trap           : Disabled
  Loop Protect Mode            : Port
  Loop Protect Enabled VLANs   :

        Loop    Loop     Detected Loop   Time Since Rx          Port
  Port  Protect Detected on VLAN  Count  Last Loop  Action      Status
  ----  ------- -------- -------  ------ ---------  ----------- --------
  23    Yes     Yes      NA       1      8s         send-disable Down
  24    Yes     No       NA       0                 send-disable Up
```

## VLAN mode

In port mode, loop protection always sends untagged packets. Sometimes, however, the other side of the link does not accept untagged packets. In this case, you must enable loop protection in VLAN mode.

You must still enable loop protection on the desired ports. You then enable loop protection on one or more of the VLANs tagged on those ports to tell the switch in which VLANs to transmit loop-protection packets. The loop-protection packet is forwarded only in the VLAN in which it is tagged so that it can only detect loops in that VLAN. It is best practice to enable loop protection on all of the VLANs carried by the protected ports to ensure that the switch can detect any loop.

Although the loop-protection feature detects loops within a particular VLAN, it responds just as it does when it is configured in port mode. If you have enabled the send-disable action, the port as a whole is disabled. For example, you have enabled loop protection on interface 1, which is tagged for VLANs 30 and 40. You also enabled loop protection on VLANs 30 and 40. If the switch receives a loop protection packet in VLAN 30, the entire sending port is disabled—not just VLAN 30.

The loop protection packets are always tagged. If you enable loop protection on a port that has an untagged membership in a protected VLAN, the port will not send out loop-protection packets on that VLAN. In other words, when loop protection operates in VLAN mode, you can only implement link protection on ports that carry at least one tagged VLAN.

### Configure loop protect in VLAN mode

To enable loop protection in VLAN mode, type:

```
Switch(config)#loop-protect mode vlan
```

To enable loop protection on interface 1, type:

```
Switch(config)#loop-protect 1
```

To enable loop protection on tagged VLANs 30 and 40, type:

```
Switch(config)#loop-protect vlan 30,40
```

## Unidirectional Link Detection (UDLD)

Unidirectional Link Detection (UDLD) is a Layer 2 protocol that allows AOS-Switches to monitor the physical status of a link. Typically, UDLD is used to monitor fiber optic links although it can be used to monitor copper-based links as well.

In the first example shown in Figure 2-12, two switches are connected through a fiber optic link. Because the fibers are connected correctly, the link is bidirectional: One fiber is used for sending frames from Switch 1 to Switch 2; the other fiber is used to send frames from Switch 2 to Switch 1.

In the second example shown in Figure 2-12, however, the fibers are cross-connected, creating a unidirectional link. That is, only one of the two directly connected switches can receive frames from the other directly connected switch. Because the physical connection is still up, however, the switches' normal detection feature may not indicate that the link is down.

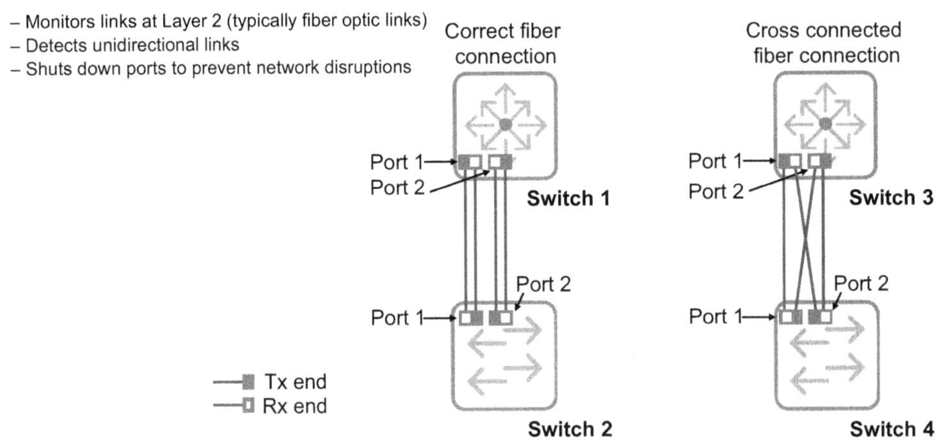


Figure 2-12 UDLD

Although cross-connected fibers are less common of a problem with current cables and transceivers, they still might occur, and you should protect against them. The same problem can occur on fiber optic links if one fiber breaks.

UDLD can also be used to monitor links between two switches that are not directly connected. For example, two switches, perhaps in different buildings, might be separated by a hub or a repeater, making it more difficult for the switches to verify the connection end-to-end. In fact, the switches might even be separated by other switches that do not run UDLD.

Such unidirectional links prevent switches from forwarding traffic as intended and can disrupt the operation of other network protocols. For example, they could cause a loop in an STP network. If an STP-enabled switch does not receive BPDUs on a link, it determines that it does not have a connection to a switch. With a unidirectional link, however, the switch might be able to forward traffic to the other switch even if it cannot receive the switch's BPDUs. This may cause the switch to open a blocked port, thereby creating a network loop.

When UDLD detects unidirectional links, it can shut down the affected ports, thereby safeguarding the network.

Vendors have developed several protocols for unidirectional link detection, providing similar capabilities. Unfortunately, the different implementations are not compatible. You can enable UDLD between two AOS-Switches. However, if you need to connect an AOS-switch to an HPE switch that supports the Comware operating system, use Device Link Detection Protocol (DLDP) instead. You can refer to your switches' *Basic Operation Guide* for more information on DLDP.

## UDLD frames

When you enable UDLD on a switch, it uses the protocol to identify the switch and the port on the other end of the protected link. You must, therefore, configure the ports on both switches to support UDLD. As Figure 2-13 shows, once the link is established, each switch port sends UDLD frames, which contain the following information:

- Port's own device ID and port ID
- Neighbor's device ID and port ID, which the switch receives through UDLD

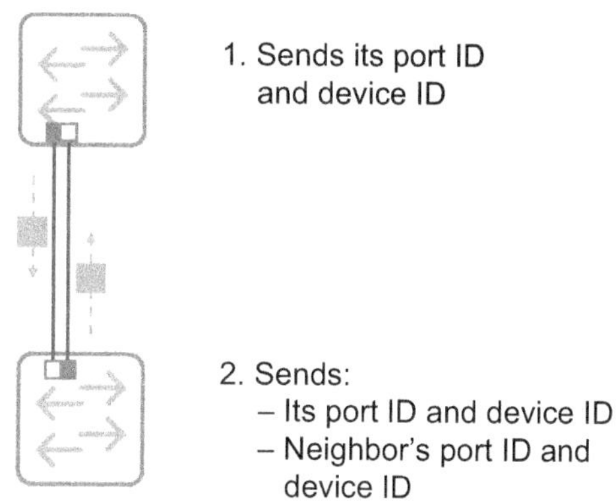


Figure 2-13 UDLD frames

When a port receives a UDLD frame, it checks it to ensure that the frame contains its own device ID and port ID. This is often referred to as the "echo" information. If the UDLD frame does not contain this "echo" information, the switch waits for the period of time determined by two settings on the switches:

- **link-keepalive interval**—This setting determines how frequently the switch sends a UDLD frame. The interval is set in 100 ms, and the default is 50 seconds, or 5 seconds. You can set the interval from 10 (1 second) to 100 (10 seconds). To change the default setting you use the following command:

  ```
  Switch(config)# link-keepalive interval <10-100>
  ```

- **link-keepalive retries**—This setting determines how many times the switch sends a UDLD frame before determining the link is down and blocking the port. The default is 5 retries. At the default settings, therefore, the switch will wait a total of 25 seconds if it does not receive a valid UDLD frame (5 seconds link-keepalive interval x 5 retries = 25 seconds).

If a port is blocked by UDLD, the switch records the event in its log or sends a Simple Network Management Protocol (SNMP) trap, if you have configured SNMP traps on the switch. The port will remain blocked until:

- The link is unplugged, disabled, or fixed.
- You disable UDLD on the port.

## Guidelines for configuring UDLD

When configuring UDLD, keep the following in mind:

- You must configure UDLD on a per-port basis.
- You must configure and enable UDLD on both ends of the link.
- To configure UDLD on an aggregated link, you must configure the feature on each port individually.
- Dynamic trunking (link aggregation) is not supported with UDLD.

---

**Note**

You can enable UDLD on dynamic link aggregations, and the feature might work. However, this mode of link aggregation is not recommended or supported for UDLD because UDLD requires every member of the link aggregation to support UDLD. In a dynamic link aggregation, a port might be selected that does not support UDLD.

---

### Configuring UDLD

Follow these steps to configure UDLD on AOS-Switches:

1. Enable UDLD on the desired interface or interfaces:

```
Switch(config)# [no] interface <port-list> link-keepalive
```

2. If you want, adjust the keepalive interval and retry time settings:

```
Switch(config)# link-keepalive interval <10-100>
Switch(config)# link-keepalive retries <2-10>
```

You specify the keepalive interval in 100 ms. For example, **link-keepalive interval 10** sets the interval to 1 second.

## Tagged or untagged UDLD frames

Sometimes you might want to implement UDLD on a port that is not an untagged member of any VLAN; it only has tagged assignments. By default, AOS-Switches send untagged UDLD frames on such ports. AOS-Switches will accept the untagged UDLD frames, but if you are using UDLD to monitor a link between two switches that are separated by a non-Aruba switch, the non-Aruba switch port may reject these frames.

To prevent this from happening, you can configure the port to send tagged UDLD frames:

```
Switch(config)# interface <ID>link-keepalive vlan <vlan_id>
```

You must configure the VLAN that will carry the UDLD frames to extend across all intervening devices. Otherwise, the switches cannot maintain the UDLD-protected link.

When you are setting up UDLD on ports in a link aggregation group (trunk) and you need to extend UDLD across intervening switches, you should assign a different VLAN for each port. For example, you need to configure UDLD on ports 4 and 5, which are in a link aggregation group (trunk) that supports tagged VLANs 4 and 5. You enter these commands:

```
Switch(config)# interface 4
Switch(eth-4)# link-keepalive vlan 4
Switch(eth-4)# interface 5
Switch(eth-5)# link-keepalive vlan 5
```

## View information about UDLD-enabled ports

To view UDLD information, use these commands:

```
Switch# show link-keepalive

Total link-keepalive enabled ports: 4

Keepalive Retries: 3 Keepalive Interval: 1 sec

Port    Enabled       Physical Keepalive   Adjacent        UDLD
                      Status   Status      Switch          VLAN
-------------------------------------------------------------------
1       Yes           up       up          00d9d-f9b700    200
2       Yes           up       up          01560-7b1600    untagged
3       Yes           down     off-line
4       Yes           up       failure
5       No            down     off-line

Switch# show link-keepalive statistics

Port:                   1

Current State:          up      Neighbor MAC Addr:     0000a1-b1-c1d1

Udld Packets Sent:      1000    Neighbor Port:         5

Udld Packets Received:  1000    State Transitions:     2

Port Blocking:          no      Link-vlan:             1
```

## Summary

This chapter has built on your knowledge of STP, RSTP, and MSTP, showing you how these protocols form just a part of your plan for data link layer redundancy. You have learned about RPVST+, and you know how to deploy it on AOS-Switches as required for interoperability with PVST+/RPVST+-based deployments. You also learned how to protect against rogue devices that try to exploit spanning tree to cause problems on the network. And you learned about loop protection, as a way to protect against loops. You explored how to use loop protection as an alternative to spanning tree and as an added protection with spanning tree.

Finally, you learned how UDLD can protect your environment from unidirectional Ethernet links, a problem that might occur on fiber links, from negatively affecting network connectivity.

## Learning check

1. What are some of the STP protections that you might want to enable on an edge port?
2. In what circumstances might you enable UDLD?
3. What are the advantages and disadvantages of having BPDU protection shut down a port as opposed to configuring a penalty period?
4. How can you check the status for BPDU protection or find out whether the feature has detected any issues?
5. Refer to Figure 2-14. You have configured loop guard on the Access-1 interfaces that connect to Core-1 and Core-2. Now assume that Access-1 stops receiving BPDUs from Core-2. Compare the traffic flow after loop guard detected an issue to the flow before the error occurred. Also consider what network administrators should do to resolve issues.

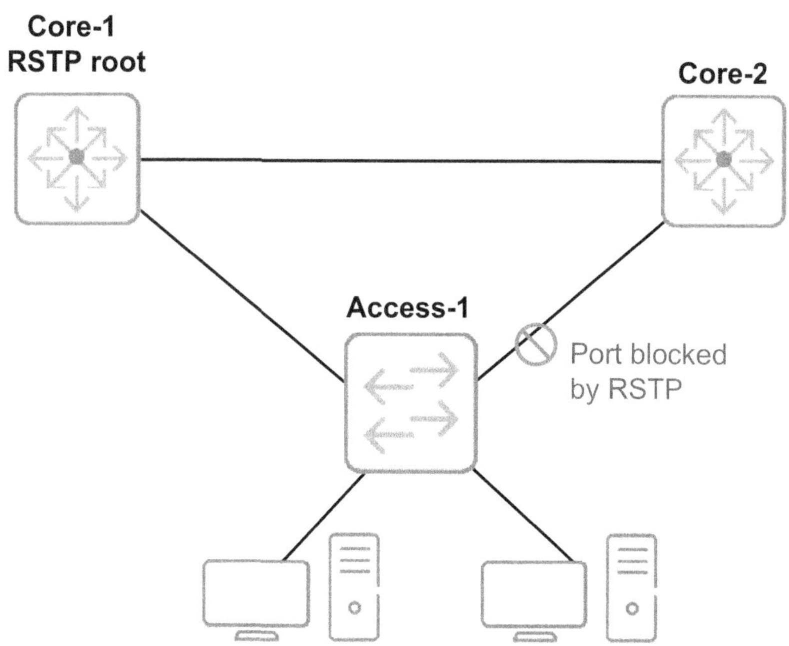


Figure 2-14 Loop guard example

6. Why might you want to implement loop protection on a switch that runs RSTP or MSTP?
7. How might you discover that loop protection has detected an issue?

# Answers

## MSTP versus RPVST+

What are advantages and disadvantages of RPVST+ as opposed to MSTP?

Use Figure 2-15 as a reference to compare RPVST+ and MSTP in terms of:

- Number of trees
- Number of BPDUs
- Traffic flow

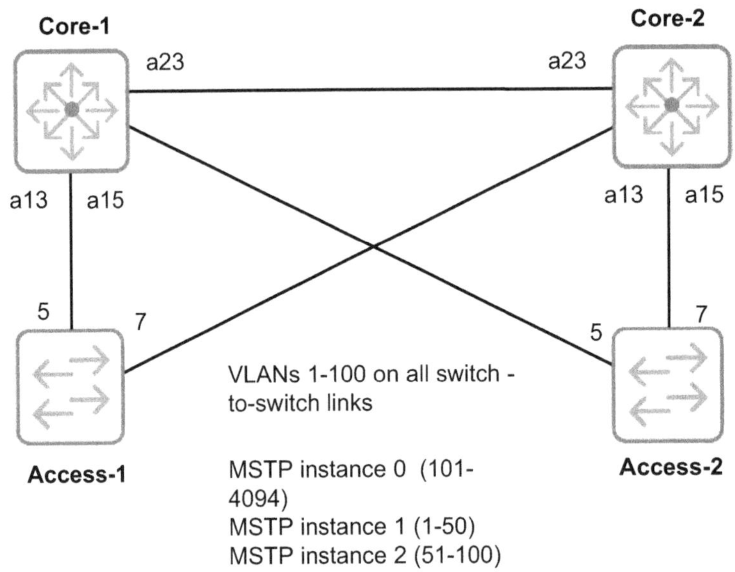


Figure 2-15 Answer: MSTP versus RPVST+

RPVST+ will generate 100 BPDUs, one for each VLAN, plus one RSTP BPDU. It will create 100 spanning trees, one for each VLAN. MSTP, on the other hand, generates only BPDU. It creates three spanning trees, one for each instance. The traffic flow established by RPVST+ and MSTP, though, could be quite similar, depending on how you assign VLANs to instances and load balance the root role. RPVST+, however, will place a much higher burden on the switches' processing power and memory.

- What would happen if you removed some VLANs from Access-1? How would MSTP and RPVST+ handle this differently?
- What could happen if the link between Core-1 and Core-2 fails? How would MSTP and RPVST+ handle this differently?

If you remove some VLANs from the Access-1 link, RPVST+ no longer considers that link when calculating the spanning trees for those VLANs. MSTP, however, still considers that link as part of the topology for all instances. With MSTP, the instance topology is created regardless of whether the links actually carry the VLANs associated with the instance.

This behavior could cause issues if the link between Core-1 and Core-2 fails. When the topology re-converges, the Access-1 links could be selected to connect Core-1 and Core-2 in the spanning trees for one or more instances. Because these links do not support all VLANs, traffic in the missing VLANs is blocked. RPVTP+ does not experience this issue because only links that actually support the VLAN can be selected to forward traffic in that VLAN's spanning tree.

For this reason, it is recommended that all switch-to-switch links in the MSTP region support all VLANs in use in the region. With MSTP, adding more VLANs to the link does not affect the number of BPDUs or spanning trees, so you do not need to worry about overburdening the switch, as with RPVST+.

## Learning check

1. What are some of the STP protections that you might want to enable on an edge port?

   You might enable BPDU protection or root guard on an edge port.

2. In what circumstances might you enable UDLD?

   You should enable UDLD on fiber optic links, which might become unidirectional if a physical issue occurs with one of the fibers. You could also enable UDLD on links for which the switch might not be able to use the physical status to determine whether it can reach the neighbor. For example, you could enable UDLD on a copper link that uses a repeater.

3. What are the advantages and disadvantages of having BPDU protection shut down a port as opposed to configuring a penalty period?

   Shutting down the port ensures that it stays down after the potential security issue is detected. An administrator must investigate the issue and make the decision to bring the port back up. This approach might be more appropriate for high security environments. A penalty period, on the other hand, can have the advantage of making the security feature easier to maintain. The switch will continue re-blocking the port for as long as the issue persists, but if the issue resolves on its own—for example, users remove the unauthorized switch and connect a legitimate device—the switch can open up the port without IT staff having to get involved.

4. How can you check the status for BPDU protection or find out whether the feature has detected any issues?

   You can use the **show spanning-tree bpdu-protection** command to check the ports on which BPDU protection is enabled, as well as to see whether the feature has detected errors on any ports. You can also check the log history on the switch for BPDU protection events. However, because you probably will not be checking every switch for such issues routinely, you might want to set up the switch to notify you of the event. You can configure the switch to send logged events or SNMP trap related to events to a centralized server.

5. Refer to Figure 2-16. You have configured loop guard on the Access-1 interfaces that connect to Core-1 and Core-2. Now assume that Access-1 stops receiving BPDUs from Core-2. Compare the traffic flow after loop guard detected an issue to the flow before the error occurred. Also consider what administrators should do to resolve issues.

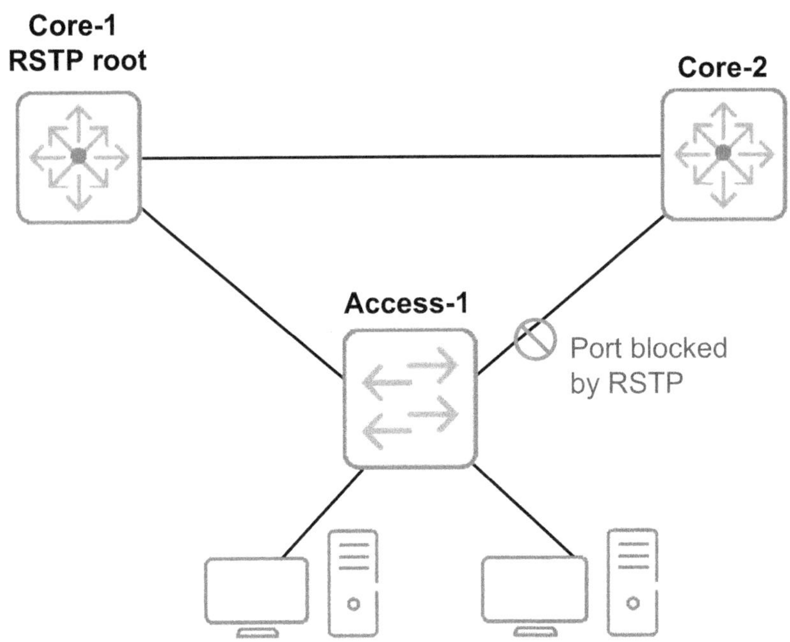


Figure 2-16 Answer: Loop guard example

The Access-1 port that connects to Core-2 is an alternate port. Normally if Access-1 stops receiving BPDUs on an alternate port, it transitions the port to designated and allows traffic forwarding on it. In this case, that behavior would cause a loop because Core-2 still can receive traffic from Access-1 and still has an active connection to Core-1. Loop guard, on the other hand, caused Access-1 to place the port in Inconsistent mode, which blocks traffic and prevents the loop.

The port was already blocking traffic before the issue, so in this case, the traffic flow is the same.

To resolve the issue, administrators should examine the link between Core-2 and Access-1. Usually, the link has a physical issue; the cable or transceiver should be replaced.

6. Why might you want to implement loop protection on a switch that runs RSTP or MSTP?

   Sometimes RSTP or MSTP can fail to detect a loop. For example, an unmanaged switch might not support spanning tree, but might not properly flood BPDUs. A switch that does run spanning tree could not detect a loop through this switch. Port-based authentication can also interfere with spanning tree. Loop protection can add an additional layer of protection.

7. How might you discover that loop protection has detected an issue?

   You can use the **show loop-protect** command if you suspect that loop-protect has shut down a port. You can also look for loop-protect events in the switch log. You can set up the switch to forward events to a syslog server or SNMP server.

# 3 Virtual Router Redundancy Protocol (VRRP)

EXAM OBJECTIVES

✓ Ensure redundancy for a network's default gateway by configuring VRRP on AOS-switches

✓ Establish load sharing of active routing in several different ways

✓ Use best practices for implementing VRRP with Multiple Spanning Tree Protocol (MSTP)

## Assumed knowledge

Before reading this chapter, you should have a basic understanding of:

- IP addressing
- Open Systems Interconnection (OSI) model
- Multiple Spanning Tree Protocol (MSTP) and Rapid Spanning Tree Protocol (RSTP)
- Link aggregation
- Virtual LANs (VLANs)
- Routing
- Switching

## VRRP use case

Most companies require redundancy for routing services at the distribution or core tier of a campus network. In this chapter, you will learn how to use Virtual Router Redundancy Protocol (VRRP) to provide redundancy for default gateway services.

In *Chapter 2: Data Link Layer Redundancy Technologies*, you focused on implementing technologies such as RSTP and MSTP that enhance Layer 2 redundancy and resiliency. These technologies ensure that endpoints across the network can reach each other even if a link or sometimes an entire device fails. However, MSTP on its own cannot provide redundancy for the default gateway service. Without additional measures, only one switch can route traffic for endpoints in each subnet, and if that switch fails, users cannot reach services in other subnets (see Figure 3-1).

You can add a second router to a subnet with relative ease. The challenge arises in ensuring that end-

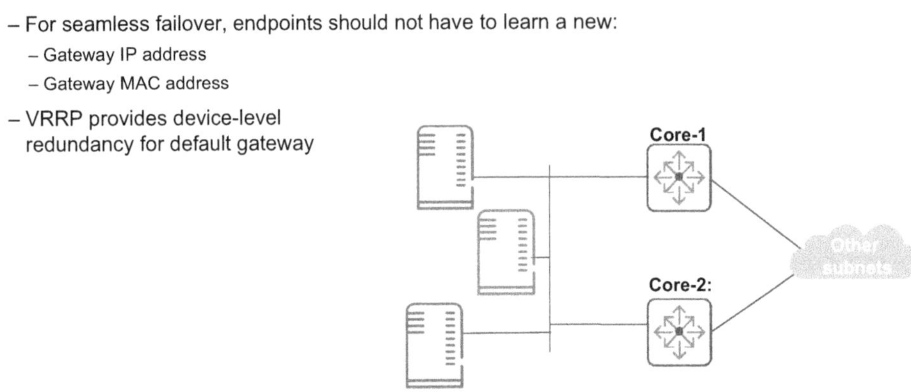


Figure 3-1 VRRP use case

points understand when they need to use that alternative default gateway. IPv4 does not provide a gateway discovery mechanism. Often endpoints learn their IP settings, including their default gateway address from a DHCP server; however, DHCP does not help the endpoints realize when one gateway is unavailable and they must switch to a new one. Clearly, endpoints with static IP settings have an even worse time responding. It would be difficult to deploy and maintain a solution for discovering an available gateway across all endpoints. Therefore, to provide the fastest, most seamless failover, a gateway redundancy protocol should ensure that:

- Endpoints can continue to use the same default gateway IP address during a failover situation. They can receive this address as usual from static settings or a DHCP server; you do not need to deploy a complicated, difficult to manage solution to all of the endpoints.
- Endpoints can continue to use the same default gateway MAC address during a failover situation. ARP table entries do not need to time out for failover to occur.

This chapter explains how to implement VRRP to meet these needs. VRRP allows multiple Layer 3 switches to act as default gateway that appears to endpoints as a single device. The protocol ensures that endpoints and other devices within a network can still reach other networks if a default gateway fails. VRRP can be an important part of a strategy for improving network reliability and ensuring that network services are always available to users.

Some AOS-switches also support Virtual Switching Framework (VSF) or backplane stacking, which can provide redundancy for default router services in addition to other services supported by the VSF fabric or stack. However, these technologies are not for everyone. Some companies prefer to keep the management and control plane for their default routers separate. Or the company might not have switches that support these technologies. In addition, you might sometimes want to have two VSF fabrics that implement VRRP together. No matter the reason, VRRP provides another option for providing redundancy for a subnet's default router.

## VRRP overview

VRRP is a standards-based protocol that provides automatic failover for gateways.

With VRRP, two or more routers are grouped together to form a virtual default gateway. The VRRP standard calls this virtual default gateway, a virtual router. This study guide uses that terminology, even when referring to routing switches. Using a single virtual IP address, the group of routers appears as a single default gateway to the endpoints in the subnet, as shown in Figure 3-2.

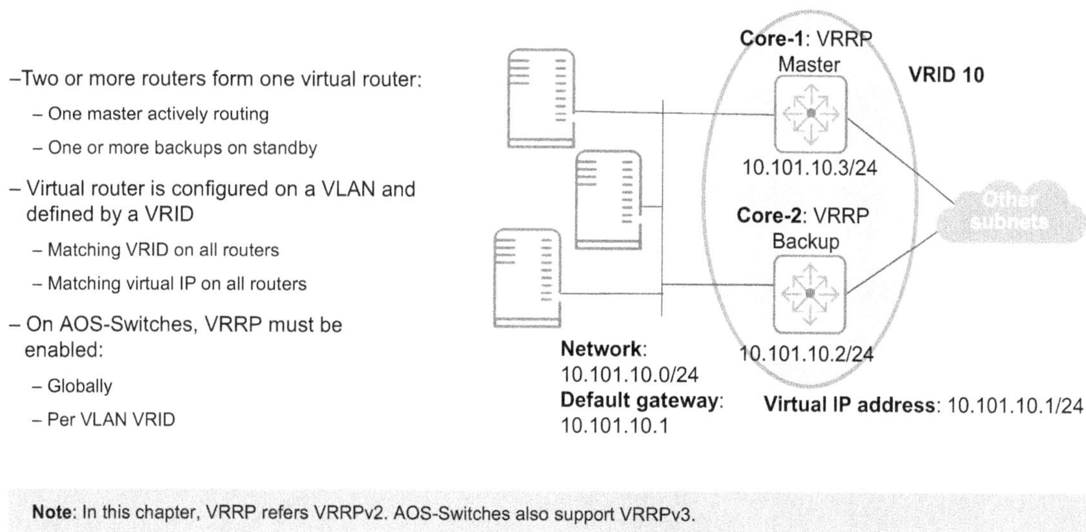


Figure 3-2 VRRP overview

One router in the group acts as the master and routes all traffic to other networks. The other routers in the group function as backups. If the master fails, VRRP enables a backup to become the new master.

The virtual router is tied to a VLAN interface, just as an IP address is. The virtual router also defined by a virtual router ID (VRID). For example, Core-1 and Core-2 run VRRP on VLAN 10, subnet 10.101.10.0/24. They are using 10 as the VRID. You can choose any value for the VRID that you like, but it must match on all the routers that you want to participate in the virtual router. The VRID is locally significant to the VLAN. You could use the same VRID on different VLANs. However, it is generally best practice to use a unique VRID on each VLAN to help you better track the VRIDs. Many administrators like to correlate the VRID with the third octet of a /24 subnet, as in the example shown in Figure 3-2.

The command for enabling VRRP for IPv4 globally on the switch is:

```
Switch(config)# router vrrp ipv4 enable
```

You must also enable VRRP individually on the VLAN VRID, as you will learn in a moment.

As a final note, you should understand that this chapter focuses on VRRP version 2. AOS-switches support VRRP version 2 and version 3. These versions operate similarly, but VRRP version 2 supports IPv4 only while VRRPv3 supports IPv4 and IPv6. You can set the VRRP version separately for each VLAN and virtual router instance. The VRRP version must match on all routers in the virtual router. The default version on AOS-switches is version 2.

## Controlling VRRP states

Members of a virtual router hold an election to determine which one will be the master. The router with the highest priority is elected master.

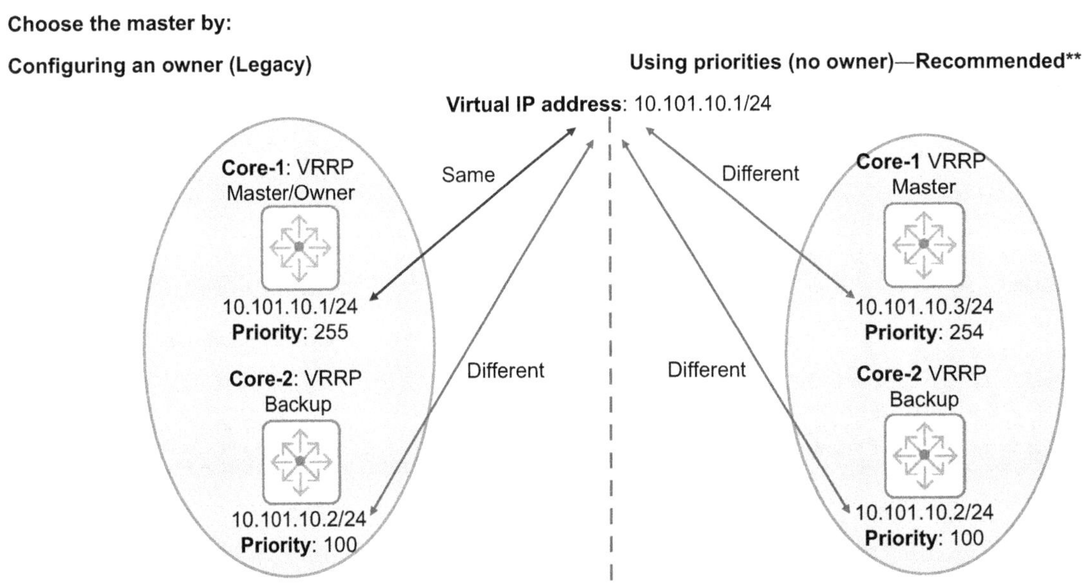


Figure 3-3 Controlling VRRP states

Refer to Figure 3-3 as you consider how a VRRP owner affects the virtual router.

### Controlling the states with a VRRP owner (legacy)

A virtual router can have an owner, which is a member that has the same actual IP address as the virtual IP address. The owner is always the master when it is available, automatically having a priority of 255, the highest possible value, without you assigning the priority. The 255 value, in fact, is reserved for VRRP owners.

To configure a device as the virtual router owner, simply set the virtual IP address to match the device's actual IP address. Although this setup is supported, it is not recommended for modern environments for reasons discussed throughout this chapter.

### Controlling the roles without a VRRP owner

You can also configure a virtual IP address that is the VRRP's virtual address alone—none of the routing devices within the group owns it. You configure the routers' priority to determine which router becomes master. The default value is 100, and you can set the value between 1 and 254. (Priority 0 is reserved for a master that has released its master responsibilities, and priority 255, for VRRP masters.)

In the example shown in Figure 3-3, Core-1 has a higher priority, so it is elected as the master.

If all the routers have the same priority number, the router with the highest IP address becomes the master. It is usually a good idea to set the priority manually, however. You can then predict and control which router becomes master during normal operation, giving you better knowledge of your network and control over the load-balancing strategies that you will examine in the "Considerations for setting up VRRP" section in this chapter.

Aruba recommends setting up VRRP in this way for several reasons that are discussed in more detail throughout this chapter.

## Configure VRRP

Use the following commands to configure VRRP without an owner for the example network shown in Figure 3-3:

Configure the switch's own IP address on the VLAN.

```
Core-1(config)# vlan 10
Core-1(vlan-10)# ip address 10.101.10.3/24
```

Create VRRP VRID 10 on VLAN 10.

```
Core-1(vlan-10) vrrp vrid 10
```

Set the virtual IP address.

```
Core-1(vlan-10-vrid-10)# virtual-ip-address 10.101.10.1
```

Set the priority so that Core-1 becomes Master in this VLAN.

```
Core-1(vlan-10-vrid-10)# priority 254
```

Enable the VRRP instance.

```
Core-1(vlan-10-vrid-10)# enable
```

If you have not already done so, return to the global configuration and enable VRRP globally.

```
Core-1(vlan-10-vrid-10)# exit
Core-1(vlan-10)# exit
Core-1(config)# router vrrp ipv4 enable
```

Complete the same steps on the Core-2 switch. In this example, you do not configure a priority on Core-2, but accept the default priority, 100.

```
Core-2(config)# vlan 10
Core-2(vlan-10)# ip address 10.101.10.2/24
Core-2(vlan-10) vrrp vrid 10
Core-2(vlan-10-vrid-10)# virtual-ip-address 10.101.10.1
Core-2(vlan-10-vrid-10)# enable
Core-2(vlan-10-vrid-10)# exit
Core-2(vlan-10)# exit
Core-2(config)# router vrrp ipv4 enable
```

You can use a **display** command to quickly verify that Core-1 is Master in VLAN 10 and the virtual IP address is 10.101.10.1.

```
Core-1(config)# display vrrp
 IPv4 Standby Information:
     Run Mode         : Standard
     Run Method       : Virtual MAC
 Total number of virtual routers : 1
 Interface VRID  State    Run    Adver    Auth     Virtual
                          Pri    Timer    Type     IP
 ----------------------------------------------------------------
 Vlan10    10    Master   254    1        None     10.101.10.1
```

If you want to view more detailed information about the VRRP settings, use the **show vrrp** command, as shown below:

```
Core-1(config)# show vrrp
VRRP Global Statistics Information
  VRRP Enabled              : Yes
<output omitted>
```

```
VRRP Virtual Router Statistics Information
 Vlan ID                  : 10
 Virtual Router ID        : 10
 Protocol Version         : 2
 State                    : Master
 Up Time                  : 4 mins
 Virtual MAC Address      : 00005e-00010a
 Master's IP Address      : 10.101.10.3
<output omitted>
```

If you use the **show vrrp** command to view the VRRP settings on Core 2 and find that Core-2's IP address is the Master IP address, both switches have formed separate VRIDs. Make sure that both the VRID and the virtual IP address on the switches match. (The Virtual IP address does not show in the output from **show vrrp**, but you can see it with the **display vrrp** command.)

## VRRP basic operation

You can now examine how the virtual router operates to route endpoints' traffic.

Figure 3-4 shows a simple network with VRRP enabled. Core-1 and Core-2 are configured to form a virtual router that acts as the default gateway. They share a virtual router identifier (VRID), a virtual IP address, and a virtual MAC address.

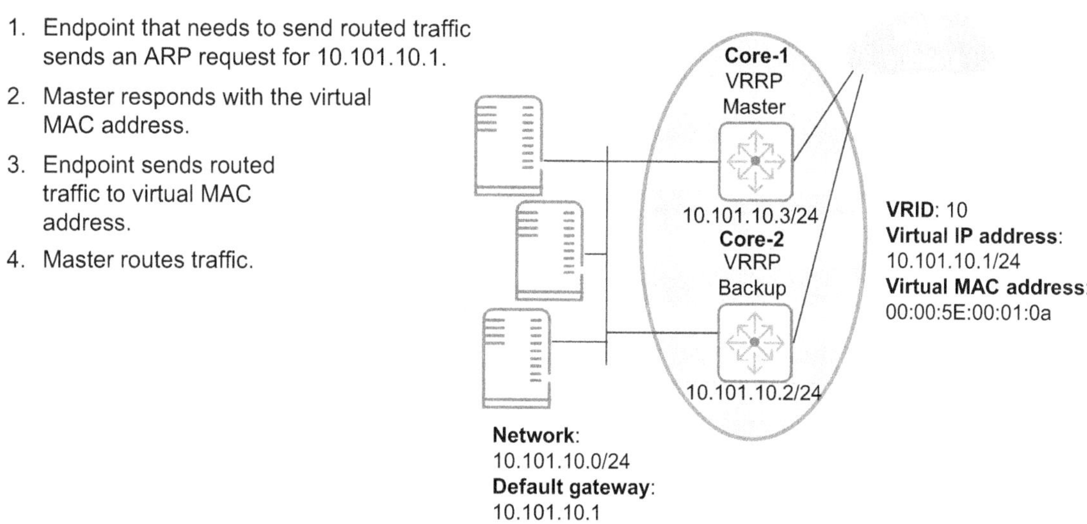


Figure 3-4 VRRP basic operation

With the virtual IP address and virtual MAC address, the virtual router always presents a consistent front to the endpoints for which it provides routing services—no matter which particular router is actually handling the services at the moment. Endpoints know only one IP address for their default gateway (configured statically or, more often, learned through DHCP). When an endpoint needs to learn the MAC address for its default gateway, it always sends an ARP request to that consistent virtual IP address. Similarly, it always addresses packets that need to be routed to the same destination MAC address.

All routers in the virtual router know the virtual IP address and virtual MAC address. However, only the master responds to ARP requests for the virtual IP address. Similarly, only the master accepts frames destined to the virtual MAC address. Just like any router, it decapsulates these frames and routes them.

Note that the backup router remains capable of routing, and it will route any traffic directed to its physical MAC address, but not its IP address. It simply does not listen for traffic on the virtual MAC address and does not respond to ARP requests for it. The backup router on a VLAN VRID can also route traffic that it receives from another interface into that VLAN.

Table 3-1 summarizes the main responsibilities of the VRRP master and the backup.

Table 3-1 Master and backup responsibilities

| VRRP state | Responds to ARP requests for the virtual IP address | Receives and routes frames destined to the virtual MAC address |
|---|---|---|
| Master | X | X |
| Backup | | |

## Choosing the virtual router settings

You configure the VRID and virtual IP address when you set up VRRP. Make sure that they match on all routers. The routers automatically calculate the virtual MAC address based on the VRID, as follows:

00:00:5E:00:01:VRID

**Note**

The virtual MAC address for IPv6 subnets is 00:00:5E:00:02:VRID.

# VRRP failover

In addition to handling routing, the VRRP master is responsible for transmitting VRRP advertisements, which it sends at every advertisement interval to multicast address 224.0.0.18. The default advertisement interval for VRRPv2 is 1 second, but you can raise this interval.

**Note**

By introducing *shorter* advertisement intervals, as low as 10 milliseconds, VRRPv3 allows much faster failover. This change is one of the few changes in VRRPv3 that applies to IPv4 as well as IPv6. However, AOS-switches, as of the publication of this study guide, supports a minimum of 1 second intervals even when using VRRPv3.

As Figure 3-5 shows, the virtual router's backup routers listen for the advertisements to determine whether the master is still up. After three advertisements are missed (and after a short skew time, which is explained in the "Supplemental information on electing the new master" section on p. x), the backup router with the next highest priority assumes the master role.

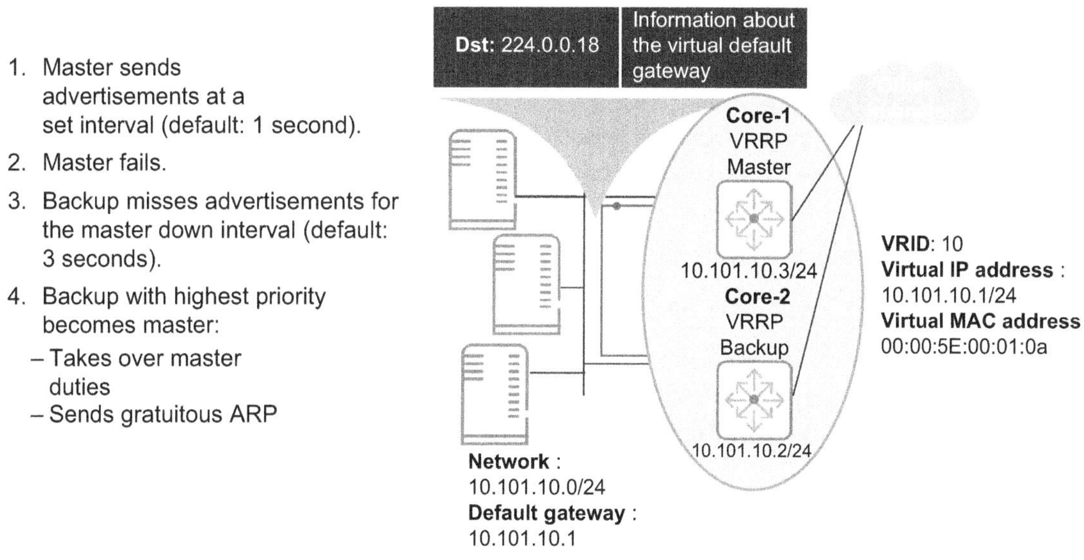


Figure 3-5 VRRP failover

The new master starts sending VRRP advertisements. It also begins responding to ARP requests to the virtual IP address. And it accepts frames destined to the virtual MAC address, which it then decapsulates and routes appropriately—in short, it assumes all the functions of a default router and the virtual router master. The new master also sends a gratuitous ARP response, which allows other switches to associate the virtual MAC address with the port they use to reach the new master. Table 3-2 summarizes these additional responsibilities.

As far as the actual endpoints are concerned, nothing has changed; they continue to send traffic they need routed to the same MAC address.

Table 3-2 Additional responsibilities of the master and backup

| VRRP state | Responds to ARP requests for the virtual IP address | Receives and routes frames destined to the virtual MAC address | Transmits virtual router advertisements | Listens for virtual router advertisements | Becomes master when the master down interval expires |
|---|---|---|---|---|---|
| Master | X | X | X | | |
| Backup | | | | X | X |

## Supplemental information on controlling the failover time

You can roughly determine the master down interval, and the failover time, by multiplying the master advertisement interval by three. At default settings, with an advertisement interval of 1 second, a virtual router recovers from a master failure in about 3 seconds. The default interval is the minimum one supported.

If you see that a router frequently changes between the backup and master role, you might have set too short of an advertisement interval; try raising the interval. You can set the interval with this command:

```
Switch(config)# vlan <ID> vrrp vrid <ID>
Switch(vlan-<ID>-vrid-<ID>)# advertise-interval <1-40>
```

Be careful to set the same interval on all routers participating in the virtual router. VRRP routers drop advertisements with an inconsistent interval indicated. If you set a different interval on your devices, they will not be able to form a VRRP router, and both routers will try to take the master role.

## Supplemental information on electing the new master

Skew time ensures that the remaining member with highest priority takes the master role. A VRRP backup router includes a very short skew time, which is inversely based on its own priority, in its master down interval. Each member has a different master down interval, and the member with the highest priority has the shortest interval. This member starts sending VRRP advertisements first and assumes the master role. The longer skew time of the other backup routers means that they hear the advertisements before their master down time expires. Therefore, they do not send advertisements themselves, which prevents them from competing in taking over as master.

Often the virtual router has only two members with a single backup router to take the master role. But if you do have a virtual router with more than two members, you should set the priority values relatively far apart (even if you do not particularly care which member becomes master), to prevent brief periods in which backups compete for the master role.

## Ping response behavior

When you are using the setup without an owner, by default, not even the Master will respond to pings for the virtual address. The Master will respond to ARP requests for the virtual IP addresses and route traffic successfully, but it will not respond to pings. If, for example, a network administrator tries to ping the virtual IP address to ensure a network device can reach its default gateway, the ping will fail.

Responding to pings must be enabled globally and on the VLAN. In the output below, you can see that responding to virtual IP ping addresses is enabled on VLAN 10, but not globally. Therefore, Core-1 will not respond to the pings. Note also that Core-1's mode is "Backup." This simply means that Core-1 does not own the virtual IP address; Core-1 is still the Master.

```
Core-1(config)# show vrrp config

VRRP Global Configuration Information

  VRRP Enabled                                : Yes

  Traps Enabled                               : Yes

  Virtual Routers Respond To Ping Requests : No

  VRRP Nonstop Enabled                        : No


 VRRP Virtual Router Configuration Information

  VLAN ID : 10

  Virtual Router ID : 10


  Administrative Status [Disabled] : Enabled

  Mode [Uninitialized] : Backup

  Priority [100] : 254

  Advertisement Interval [1] : 1

  Preempt Mode [True] : True

  Preempt Delay Time [0] : 0

  Respond To Virtual IP Ping Requests [Yes] : Yes

<-output omitted->
```

It can be useful to be able to ping the default gateway for troubleshooting purposes. To enable virtual IP pinging on VRRP globally, enter:

```
Core-1(config)# router vrrp virtual-ip-ping
```

## VRRP preemptive and nonpreemptive modes

VRRP failover provides continuity of services during the emergency situation of a total failure of the active router. But, eventually, the network returns to the normal operational topology, with the failed device once again being able to provide routing services. Depending on the type of problem that caused the original master to fail, the router might come back on its own, you might restore it by fixing failed links or power supplies, or you might replace the failed master with new hardware running the failed master's configuration.

You should understand how the restored master affects the VRRP operations. A new device joining the virtual router can also affect the operations similarly.

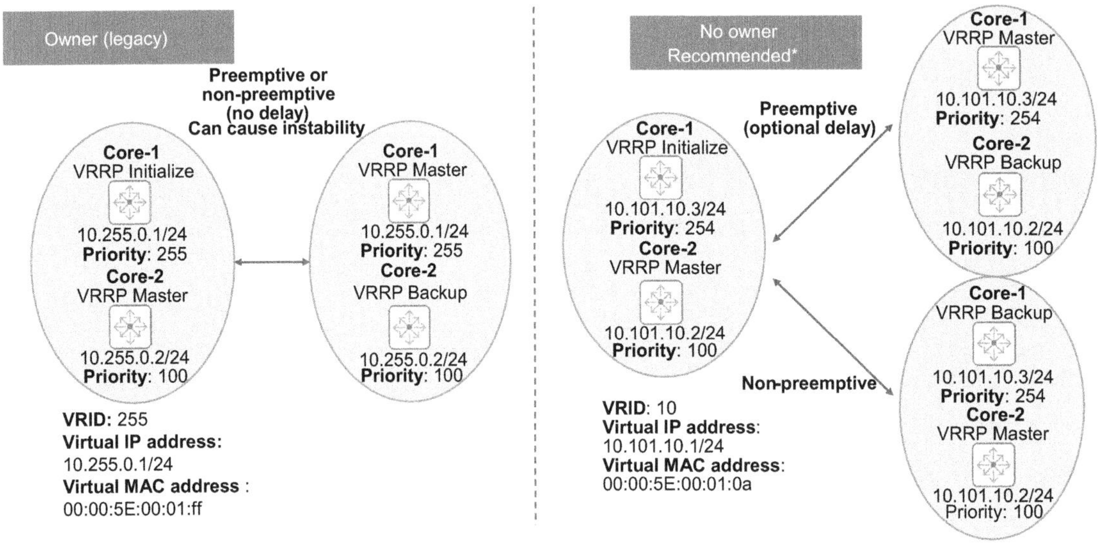


Figure 3-6 VRRP preemptive and non-preemptive modes

As Figure 3-6 shows, the operation depends on two factors:

- The preempt mode
- Whether the VRID has an owner or not

  When one of the VRRP routers owns the virtual IP address, it *always* takes over the master role *despite what you configure for the VRID's preempt mode.* In addition, any preemption delay that you configure does *not* take effect.

In other words, whether preempt mode is enabled or not matters when none of the routers own the virtual address.

- **Preempt mode**—When a router operates in preempt mode, it will take over the virtual router master role whenever it has a higher priority than the current Master. The router sees the advertisements with a lower priority and sends a preempt Master message telling the device with the lower priority to become a backup router. It also begins sending its own advertisements.

The preempt mode applies when you add a new router with a higher priority to the virtual router. It also applies when a failed master is restored. That router assumes the master role again because it has the higher priority.

You can configure a preemption delay, which allows the router with the higher priority to take over the master role but forces it to wait a certain amount of time after initializing its VRRP functions to do so. This delay allows the router to build up its routing table *before* taking over as the active router, preventing disruptions in service—you will learn more in *Chapter 5: Advanced Open Shortest Path First (OSPF).*

- **Nonpreempt mode**—If a router is using nonpreempt mode, the router does not attempt to take over the master role from an active master even if it has a higher priority. This behavior holds true whether the backup router with a higher priority is a new device or a former master that failed.

The preempt mode determines whether the router attempts to preempt the master role itself—not whether it accepts preemption from another router. Whether or not preempt mode is enabled on a router's VRRP instance, a Master will change to a Backup router in response to preempt master messages from a router with higher priority. Therefore, even if routers' preempt settings do not match, they can agree on the Master. However, you should generally match the preempt mode on the routers in the same VRID.

By default, AOS-switches operate in preempt mode with no delay. You can add a delay or disable preemption entirely with settings configurable per-VRID.

Use these commands to set the preempt mode and add or remove an optional delay:

```
Switch(config)# vlan <ID> vrrp vrid <ID>

Switch(vlan-<ID>-vrid-<ID>)# [no] preempt-mode

Switch(vlan-<ID>-vrid-<ID>)# [no] preempt-delay-time <1-600>
```

## Considerations for setting up VRRP

With your deeper knowledge of how VRRP works, you can now consider reasons for setting up VRRP in particular ways.

As one of your primary choices, you must determine whether you will set up the virtual router to have an owner or not. Why would you configure an owner? Why wouldn't you configure an owner? (You can compare your answers to those listed in the "Answers" section at the end of this chapter.)

## Load sharing routing within a subnet

A company might not want one router standing idle while another router bears the burden of routing all traffic for the network segment's subnet or subnets. VRRP provides several ways for you to distribute the routing functions across multiple devices.

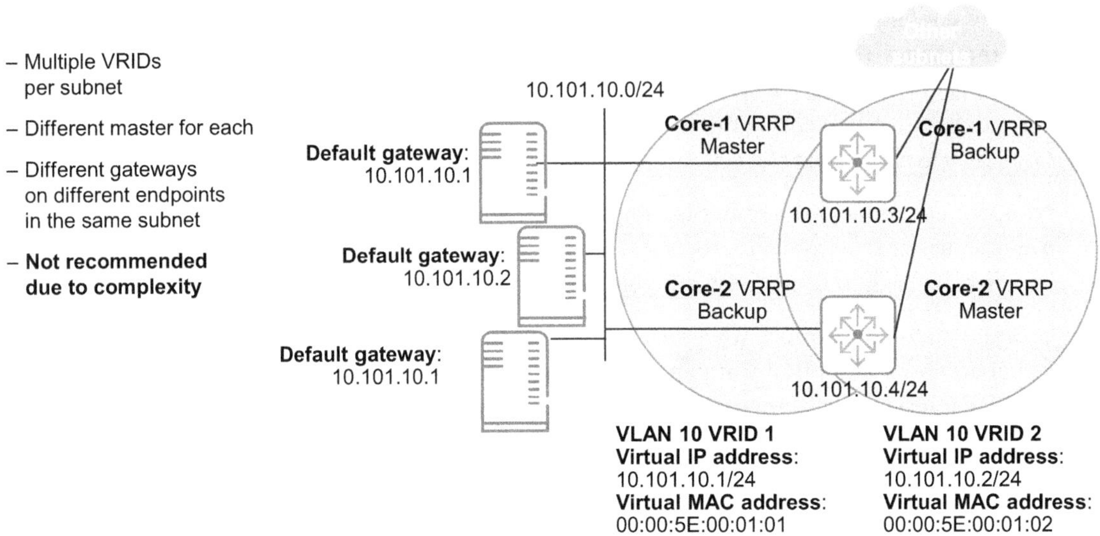


Figure 3-7 Load sharing routing within a subnet

As Figure 3-7 shows, the VRRP standard allows you to create multiple virtual routers on the same subnet, identifying each router with a different VRID. Because VRRP supports 255 VRIDs, you can theoretically create that many virtual routers on a subnet. Practically, you only need to create, at most, one virtual router per-router participating in VRRP. A different router acts as master in each virtual router while providing backup for the other virtual routers.

In the example shown in Figure 3-7, Core-1 is the master for virtual router 1 but the backup for virtual router 2. Core-2, on the other hand, is the master for virtual router 2 and the backup for virtual router 1.

Although VRRP permits this setup, you should understand why you should generally avoid using it. The primary drawback of this load-balancing strategy is that it features multiple virtual IP addresses. The load balancing depends on different endpoints in the same subnet using different virtual IP addresses for their default gateway. You either need to configure the default gateway addresses manually or the DHCP administrator needs to create different scopes. Both add needless complexity. In practice, the solution might not work as expected and can be difficult to troubleshoot.

If you need to load-balance routing capabilities within a subnet in a granular fashion, you should consider backplane stacking or VSF as an alternative to VRRP.

## Load sharing routing across different subnets

Typically, you can take a simpler approach to load balancing the routing functions. You configure a *single* VRID for each subnet, but you alternate the master role on different subnets.

In the example shown in Figure 3-8, Core-1 is the VRRP master on VLAN 10 but the backup on VLAN 20. Core-2, on the other hand, is the master for VLAN 20 and the backup for VLAN 10. Neither router owns the virtual IP address, but you have set priorities to control which router enters the master state during normal operation. (If necessary, you could also create a similar solution in which you alternate the owner role between subnets.)

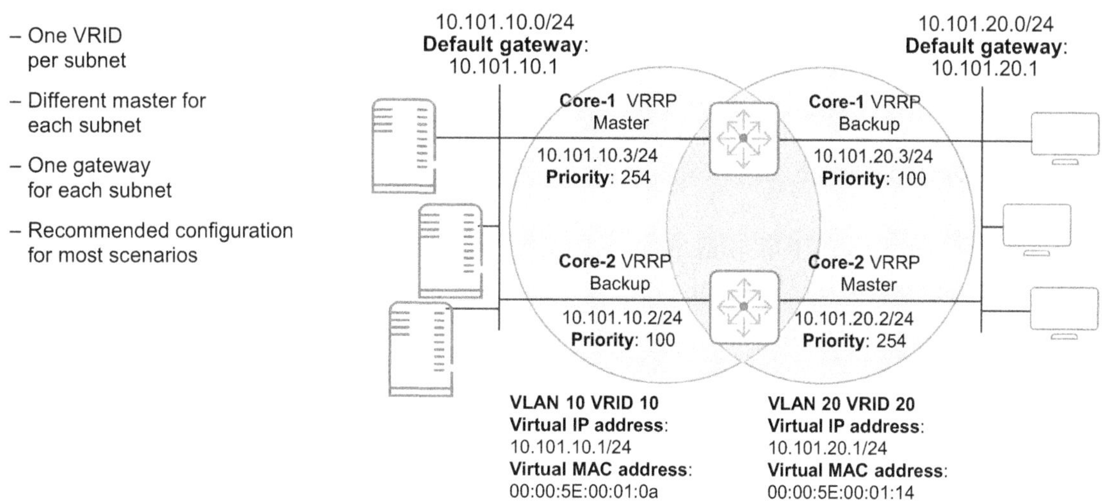


Figure 3-8 Load sharing routing across different subnets

This strategy might offer less fine-grained load sharing than using multiple virtual routers on the same subnet, but you do not have to worry about establishing more than one default gateway address per subnet. Aruba recommends this strategy for most deployments.

## Combining VRRP and MSTP

As Figure 3-9 shows, you can implement VRRP together with a data link layer redundancy protocol to provide a high level of network redundancy.

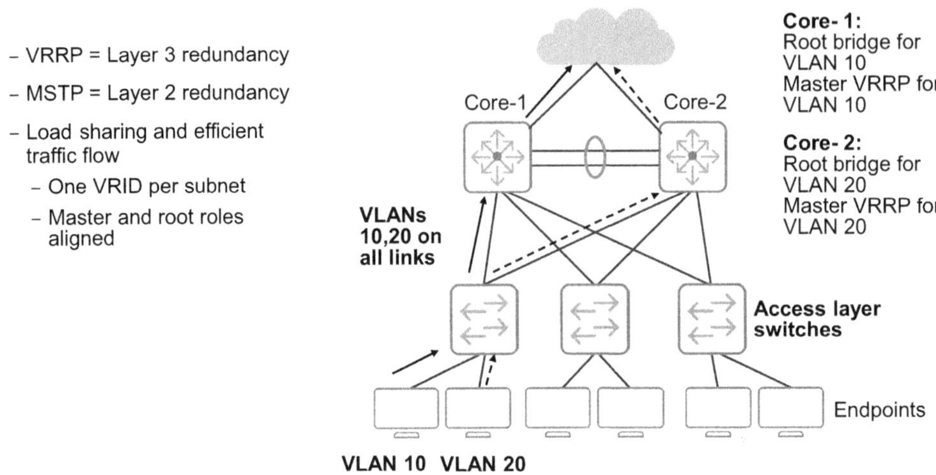


Figure 3-9 Combining VRRP and MSTP

When you implement VRRP in spanning tree topology, you should generally use MSTP. The benefits of MSTP, as opposed to RSTP, include:

- **Higher bandwidth (ability to utilize links more fully)**—Switch can use redundant links since each MSTP instance has a different active path. When a port belongs to multiple VLANs, it may be blocked in one MSTP instance, but forwarding in another instance.
- **Load balancing of the master role without overutilizing the link between the VRRP routers**—You might want to lower the burden on a single router by configuring different routers as the master in different subnets. In an RSTP topology, only one of the VRRP routers can be the root bridge with the active link to the downstream switches. That router must pass all traffic being routed in VLANs for which it plays the backup role over the link to the other VRRP router. That link can potentially become a bottleneck.

  When you use MSTP, on the other hand, you can create a topology in which downstream switches always forward traffic on the link to the master. You simply correlate the MSTP primary root bridge role in an instance with the VRRP master role for all VLANs mapped to that instance.

Now you will learn the basic steps for setting up a VRRP and MSTP solution on your network.

**Important**

Whether you are using MSTP or RSTP, you should create a direct link that carries all VLANs between the VRRP routers, ensuring that the routers receive each other's VRRP advertisements and prevent disruptive situations in which both routers attempt to route traffic. This link must provide high reliability; for example, you might use a link aggregation. If you cannot guarantee that this link always remains up, you must extend all VLANs on all switch-to-switch links. This strategy ensures that, even if the link between the VRRP routers goes down, the routers maintain connectivity in every VLAN no matter which blocked port transitions to the forwarding state.

In short, extending all VLANs on all switch-to-switch links is generally the best practice in MSTP and VRRP designs.

*Chapter 5: Backplane Stacking and Advanced Virtual Switching Framework (VSF)* explains how to use Virtual Switching Framework (VSF) instead of MSTP and VRRP, removing these limitations.

## Configure MSTP

- Create an MST instance for each redundant path. Because a VRID often includes two routing switches, you generally create two instances (as well as instance 0).
- Make sure that each core switch acts as the primary root bridge in one instance and the secondary root bridge in another.
  - Configure the bridge priority for each MST instance on the core switches to make the correct primary and secondary root assignments.
  - Leave the bridge priority at its default setting on access switches to ensure that the core switches have higher priority.
- Map a set of VLANs to each instance. You can simply map half of the VLANs to each instance, or you can look at the traffic load on each VLAN and attempt to create two sets of VLANs, each of which supports half of the traffic load.

## Configure VRRP

- Align the VRRP master state with the MSTP primary root role.
  - Each core switch should be the VRRP Master for the VLANs in the instance for which it is the root bridge. On each VLAN that is mapped to the instance for which the switch is the primary root, set a high VRRP priority such as 254.
  - Likewise, the VRRP backup state should correspond to the MSTP secondary root bridge. You can keep the default priority of 100 on the VLANs mapped to the instance for which the switch is the secondary root.

- This configuration ensures that each access layer switch transmits traffic to be routed in each VLAN directly to the Master. Also, if an uplink between an access switch and the VRRP master switch fails, the access switch can begin sending traffic to the backup VRRP router.

Tables 3-3 and 3-4 show how you might distribute MSTP root roles and VRRP master and backup states between the core switches in shown in Figure 3-9.

Table 3-3 MSTP instances

| MSTP instance | Mapped VLANs | Core Switch 1 role (normal operation) | Core Switch 2 role (normal operation) |
|---|---|---|---|
| 1 | 10 | Primary root (priority 0) | Secondary root (priority 1 or 4096) |
| 2 | 20 | Secondary root (priority 1 or 4096) | Primary root (priority 0) |
| 0 | All others | Primary root (priority 0) | Secondary root (priority 1 or 4096) |

Table 3-4 VRRP settings

| VLAN | VRID | Core Switch 1 state (normal operation) | Core Switch 2 state (normal operation) |
|---|---|---|---|
| 10 | 10 | Master (priority 254) | Backup (priority 100) |
| 20 | 20 | Backup (priority 100) | Master (priority 254) |

## Summary

This chapter introduced you to VRRP. This redundancy protocol, when implemented correctly and combined with data link layer redundancy protocols, increases fault tolerance on a network, allowing users to continue sending traffic, even if network links or devices fail.

## Learning check

1. What is a responsibility of a Backup router in a VLAN's VRRP instance?
   a. Respond to ARP requests for the VRRP virtual IP address
   b. Route traffic directed to the VRRP virtual MAC address
   c. Listen for the Master advertisements
   d. Respond to ICMP echo requests for the VRRP virtual IP address

2. What is a drawback to using multiple VRIDs in a VLAN for load-share routing *within* a subnet?
   a. This strategy can be complex because different endpoints in the same subnet must have different default gateway addresses.
   b. This strategy usually offers less fine-grained load-sharing than a strategy in which routers load share routing between subnets.
   c. This strategy does not permit companies to use DHCP to assign IP settings to endpoints.
   d. This strategy requires you to associate multiple virtual MAC addresses with a virtual router's virtual IP address.
3. A network administrator enters the **show vrrp vlan 10** command to verify that a switch (with hostname Core-2) is the backup router in VLAN 10 VRID 10. The following output is displayed:

```
Core-2(config)# show vrrp vlan 10

VRRP Virtual Router Statistics Information

Vlan ID                  : 10
Virtual Router ID        : 10
Protocol Version         : 2
State                    : Backup
Up Time                  : 4 mins
Virtual MAC Address      : 00005e-00010a
Master's IP Address      : 10.101.10.3
<output omitted>
```

   What is the virtual MAC address for VLAN 10 VRID 10? Why do you think that VRRP creates a virtual MAC address?
4. A network administrator tries to ping the VLAN 10 VRRP virtual IP address from a server in the same VLAN. The ping fails. What is the likely reason? Could the server still discover the correct MAC address for the virtual IP address?

   The following scenario applies to questions 5 and 6.

   A network administrator is configuring VRRP on a VLAN 20 on two routing switches named Core-1 and Core-2. The switches are connected in VLAN 20. The administrator first configures Core-1 with these commands:

```
Core-1(config)# vlan 20
Core-1(vlan-20)# ip address 10.101.20.3/24
Core-1(vlan-20) vrrp vrid 20
Core-1(vlan-20-vrid-20)# virtual-ip-address 10.101.20.1
Core-1(vlan-20-vrid-20)# enable
Core-1(vlan-20-vrid-20)# exit
Core-1(vlan-20)# exit
Core-1(config)# router vrrp ipv4 enable
```

The administrator next configures Core-2 with these commands:

```
Core-2(config)# vlan 20
Core-2(vlan-20)# ip address 10.101.20.2/24
Core-2(vlan-20) vrrp vrid 20
Core-2(vlan-20-vrid-20)# virtual-ip-address 10.101.20.1
Core-2(vlan-20-vrid-20)# priority 254
Core-2(vlan-20-vrid-20)# enable
Core-2(vlan-20-vrid-20)# exit
Core-2(vlan-20)# exit
Core-2(config)# router vrrp ipv4 enable
```

5. The administrator enabled VRRP on VLAN 20 on Core-1 before VRRP was enabled on Core-2, making Core-1 temporarily the Master. Under what circumstances would Core-2 preempt the role? If the setting that made this possible is disabled, what should you keep in mind when configuring VRRP?

6. When the administrator checks the VRRP settings, should the Master and Virtual IP addresses match on both the switches? If the correct addresses do not match, what could be the problem?

   The following scenario applies to questions 7 and 8.

   Figures 3-10 and 3-11 show an example network. In this network, most traffic flows from servers to clients. In Figure 3-11, MSTP instance 1 is mapped to VLANs 10-19, and MSTP instance 2 is mapped to VLANs 20-29. Assume that MSTP region settings match on all switches.

7. First, analyze the traffic flow for the network without MSTP. Then analyze the flow with MSTP. What are the differences in traffic flow?

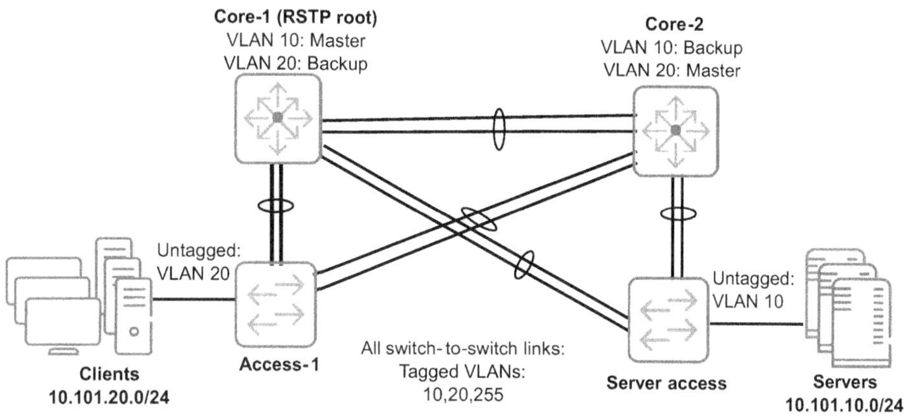


Figure 3-10 Traffic flow without MSTP

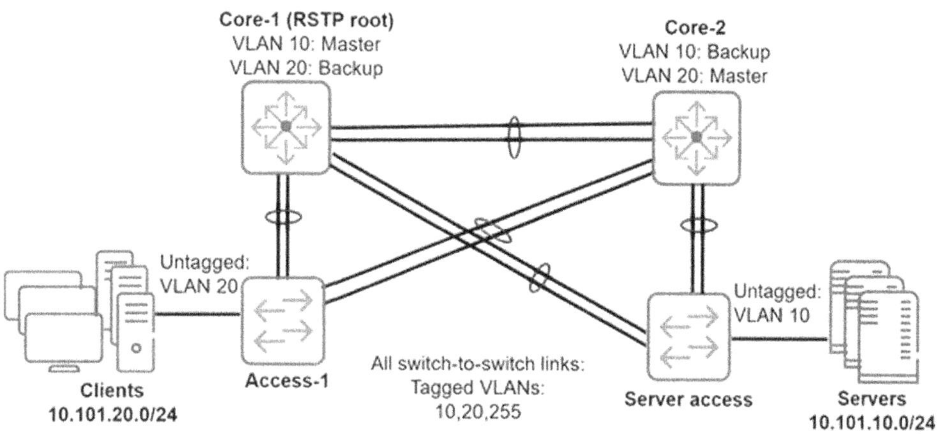


Figure 3-11 Traffic flow with MSTP

8. Now assume that you are planning to change the Users VLAN, which is currently VLAN 20, into two VLANs, one for employees and one for guests. You are also planning to add a second server VLAN in addition to VLAN 10. Each access switch still tends to support either clients or servers. Choose IDs for the new VLANs to support greater use of all uplinks on the access layer switches.

# Answers

## Considerations for setting up VRRP

As one of your primary choices, you must determine whether you will set up the virtual router to have an owner or not. Why would you configure an owner? Why wouldn't you configure an owner?

Whenever possible, you should select a virtual IP address that is not owned by any of the routers. This setup provides several advantages:

- You can more easily adjust the priority so that, for whatever reason, you can change which router acts as master during normal operation. You might also find it easier to adjust the master role to implement load balancing.
- You can configure a preempt delay, which, as you just learned, can prevent issues in which a VRRP router takes over as master before it has built its routing table.

Usually, you take the owner approach only to fit the needs of a legacy environment that did not use VRRP. Changing a subnet's default gateway IP address can require a great deal of work and introduce the chance of unplanned downtime, so you probably want to set the virtual IP address to match the current gateway IP address. You could change the current default gateway's actual IP address, which is the best choice in many circumstances (for reasons discussed above). However, you might be managing the default gateway on this IP address or have another reason to want to avoid changing it, at least temporarily.

Another reason for not using an owner exists (although an in-depth explanation of this reason is beyond the scope of this study guide). You can use tracks to adjust VRRP priorities dynamically, allowing a master to cede the role if it can no longer usefully route traffic.

If one VRRP device was the owner, it would have to lose all IP functions on the subnet to allow a backup router to take over as master. In some cases, though, a different sort of failure might make it desirable for the backup to assume active routing. For example, perhaps the current master loses its connection to an upstream router and can no longer route traffic to destinations behind that next hop. When none of the routers owns the address, you can configure a track on a VLAN or physical interface on an AOS-switch. If that interface goes down, the switch then lowers its priority, allowing the switch with the Backup role to take over.

## Learning check

1. What is a responsibility of a Backup router in a VLAN's VRRP instance?
    a. Respond to ARP requests for the VRRP virtual IP address
    b. Route traffic directed to the VRRP virtual MAC address
    **c. Listen for the Master advertisements**
    d. Respond to ICMP echo requests for the VRRP virtual IP address

2. What is a drawback to using multiple VRIDs in a VLAN for load-balance routing *within* a subnet?

   **a. This strategy can be complex because different endpoints in the same subnet must have different default gateway addresses.**

   b. This strategy usually offers less fine-grained load balancing than a strategy in which routers load balance routing between subnets.

   c. This strategy does not permit companies to use DHCP to assign IP settings to endpoints.

   d. This strategy requires you to associate multiple virtual MAC addresses with a virtual router's virtual IP address.

3. A network administrator enters the **show vrrp vlan 10** command to verify that a switch (with hostname Core-2) is the backup router in VLAN 10 VRID 10. The following output is displayed:

```
Core-2(config)# show vrrp vlan 10

VRRP Virtual Router Statistics Information

Vlan ID                  : 10
Virtual Router ID        : 10
Protocol Version         : 2
State                    : Backup
Up Time                  : 4 mins
Virtual MAC Address      : 00005e-00010a
Master's IP Address      : 10.101.10.3
<output omitted>
```

   What is the virtual MAC address for VLAN 10 VRID 10? Why do you think that VRRP creates a virtual MAC address?

   The virtual MAC address is 00005e-00010a. VRRP creates a standard MAC address based on the VRID. Endpoints direct traffic to their default router's MAC address, so it is important that the MAC address stays the same if the Master router fails, and the Backup takes over as the new Master.

4. A network administrator tries to ping the VLAN 10 VRRP virtual IP address from a server in the same VLAN. The ping fails. What is the likely reason? Could the server still discover the correct MAC address for the virtual IP address?

   The ping probably failed because VRRP, by default, does not permit the VRRP Master to respond to pings to the virtual IP address. However, the Master still responds to ARP requests, and the server can discover the correct MAC address for the virtual IP address. And the server can still direct traffic to the VRRP Master for routing. Even though the solution works without the Master responding to pings, this behavior might be confusing for you and other administrators, especially when you are troubleshooting. You should keep the behavior in mind and check the ARP tables on endpoints to determine whether the endpoints can reach their default gateway, rather than just use pings. You might also choose to always enable virtual IP pinging.

The following scenario applies to questions 5 and 6.

A network administrator is configuring VRRP on a VLAN 20 on two routing switches named Core-1 and Core-2. The switches are connected in VLAN 20. The administrator first configures Core-1 with these commands:

```
Core-1(config)# vlan 20
Core-1(vlan-20)# ip address 10.101.20.3/24
Core-1(vlan-20) vrrp vrid 20
Core-1(vlan-20-vrid-20)# virtual-ip-address 10.101.20.1
Core-1(vlan-20-vrid-20)# enable
Core-1(vlan-20-vrid-20)# exit
Core-1(vlan-20)# exit
Core-1(config)# router vrrp ipv4 enable
```

The administrator next configures Core-2 with these commands:

```
Core-2(config)# vlan 20
Core-2(vlan-20)# ip address 10.101.20.2/24
Core-2(vlan-20) vrrp vrid 20
Core-2(vlan-20-vrid-20)# virtual-ip-address 10.101.20.1
Core-2(vlan-20-vrid-20)# priority 254
Core-2(vlan-20-vrid-20)# enable
Core-2(vlan-20-vrid-20)# exit
Core-2(vlan-20)# exit
Core-2(config)# router vrrp ipv4 enable
```

5. The administrator enabled VRRP on VLAN 20 on Core-1 before VRRP was enabled on Core-2, making Core-1 temporarily the Master. Under what circumstances would Core-2 preempt the role? If the setting that made this possible is disabled, what should you keep in mind when configuring VRRP?

   Both the Virtual IP address and the Master IP address should match. If the Virtual IP address does not match, the switches will form different VRRP instances. This can occur due to a configuration error. If the Master IP address does not match, both switches have become Master. A communication issue, such as the VLAN not being tagged on switch-to-switch links, can cause this error. The error could also occur if the switches have different VRIDs on the VLAN, as well as different virtual IP addresses.

6. When the administrator checks the VRRP settings, should the Master and Virtual IP addresses match on both switches? If the correct addresses do not match, what could be the problem?

   Core-2 would preempt the Master role if the preempt mode is enabled. The preempt mode, which is enabled by default, permits a VRRP router with a higher priority to take over the Master role even if another router has already taken the Master role. If preempt mode is disabled, you should make sure to configure VRRP on the switch that you want to become Master before you configure the other switch.

   The following scenario applies to questions 7 and 8.

   Figures 3-12 and 3-13 show an example network. In this network, most traffic flows from servers to clients. In Figure 3-11, MSTP instance 1 is mapped to VLANs 10-19, and MSTP instance 2 is mapped to VLANs 20-29. Assume that MSTP region settings match on all switches.

7. First, analyze the traffic flow for the network without MSTP. Then analyze the flow with MSTP. What are the differences in traffic flow?

   Figures 3-12 and 3-13 show the traffic flow for both scenarios. As you see, RSTP used with VRRP creates unnecessary traffic between the core routers. Clients in VLAN 20 send their traffic to Core-2 for routing, but the RSTP topology forces the traffic to pass through Core-1 first. Using MSTP reduces unnecessary traffic between the core routers. It also provides some load sharing of traffic on the access layer uplinks. However, the access switches are primarily transmitting on one link and receiving on one link due to the VLANs that they support and the network traffic patterns.

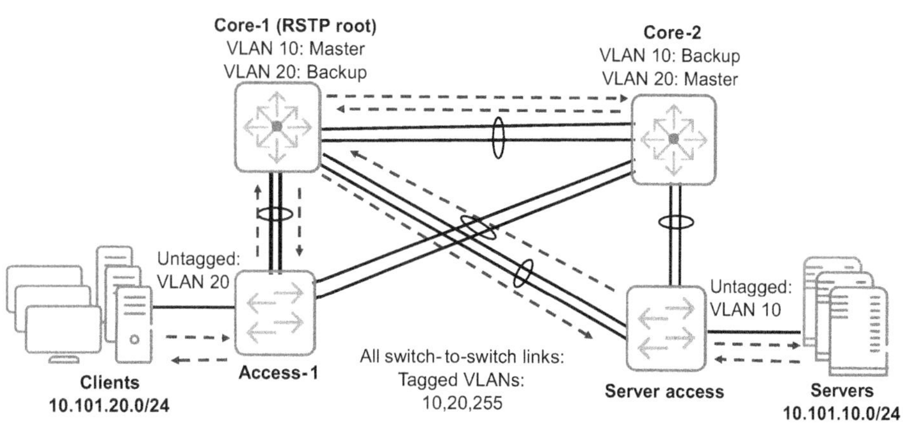


Figure 3-12 Answer: Traffic flow without MSTP

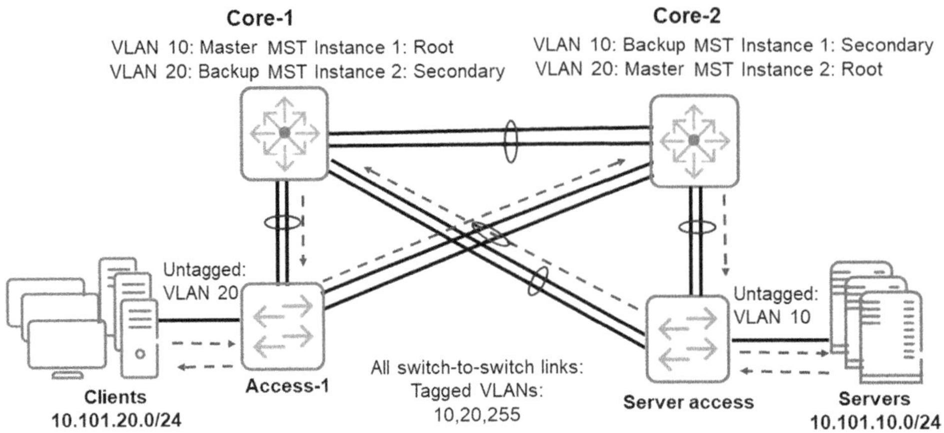


Figure 3-13 Answer: Traffic flow with MSTP

8. Now assume that you are planning to change the Users VLAN, which is currently VLAN 20, into two VLANs, one for employees and one for guests. You are also planning to add a second server VLAN in addition to VLAN 10. Each access switch still tends to support either clients or servers. Choose IDs for the new VLANs to support greater use of all uplinks on the access layer switches.

   To support more load sharing, you want each access switch to have one VLAN in one instance and another VLAN in the other instance. Instance 1 has VLANs 10–19, and instance 2 has VLANs 20–29. So you might keep VLAN 20 for the Employees VLAN and add VLAN 11 for the Guest VLAN. You might keep VLAN 10 for servers and add VLAN 21 for the second server VLAN. You can choose different IDs as long as each switch has one VLAN in each instance.

# 4 Aruba Backplane Stacking and Virtual Switching Framework (VSF)

EXAM OBJECTIVES

- ✓ Describe the three topologies supported with backplane stacking and the roles members play in the stack
- ✓ Explain how backplane stacking handles stack fragments
- ✓ Implement and manage an VSF fabric
- ✓ Describe what a split VSF stack is and configure the mechanisms designed to detect and remedy this problem

## Assumed knowledge

Before reading this chapter, you should have a basic understanding of:

- Aruba Virtual Switching Framework (VSF)
- IP addressing
- Open Systems Interconnection (OSI) model
- Multiple Spanning Tree Protocol (MSTP) and Rapid Spanning Tree Protocol (RSTP)
- Link aggregation
- Virtual LANs (VLANs)
- Routing
- Switching

## Introduction

This chapter focuses on two technologies that help you simplify your network architecture, operations, and management while providing a high level of redundancy and scalability:

- Aruba backplane stacking
- Aruba Virtual Switching Framework (VSF)

You should have a basic understanding of VSF before reading this chapter.

---

**Note**

You should check the Aruba website to determine which switch series currently support backplane stacking and VSF.

---

## Backplane stacking

The backplane stacking feature allows you to combine multiple switches to create a single logical virtual device. The stack operates as if it were a single switch with all the member switches providing ports.

A backplane stack provides the following benefits:

- Simplified management, allowing you to manage the stack from a single IP address.
- Scalability, enabling the network to handle increasing demands for faster processing and higher bandwidth
- Simplified deployment, allowing you to add switches to the network without configuring IP addresses and completing other tasks.
- Resiliency and redundancy, protecting the organization from link, power, or device failure

Backplane stacking is supported on:

- Aruba 3810 Switch Series
- Aruba 3800 Switch Series
- Aruba 2930M Switch Series
- Aruba 2920 Switch Series

If you want to run backplane stacking, you must purchase a stacking module and a stacking cable for the switch. For the stacking cable, you have the option of purchasing a .5 m, 1 m, or 3 m cable. For this reason, backplane stacking is intended for deployment between members that are relatively close together such as in the same closet. If you need to extend a logical switch fabric more widely, use VSF, which can have links that extend as far as supported by typical 10 GbE copper, 10 GbE fiber, or 40 GbE fiber.

## Backplane stacking topologies

When you implement backplane stacking, you can choose from three topologies: chain, ring, or mesh. As Figure 4-1, the topology you select depends on a number of factors:

- The switch model
- The number of switches you want to combine in a backplane stack
- The level of redundancy you want

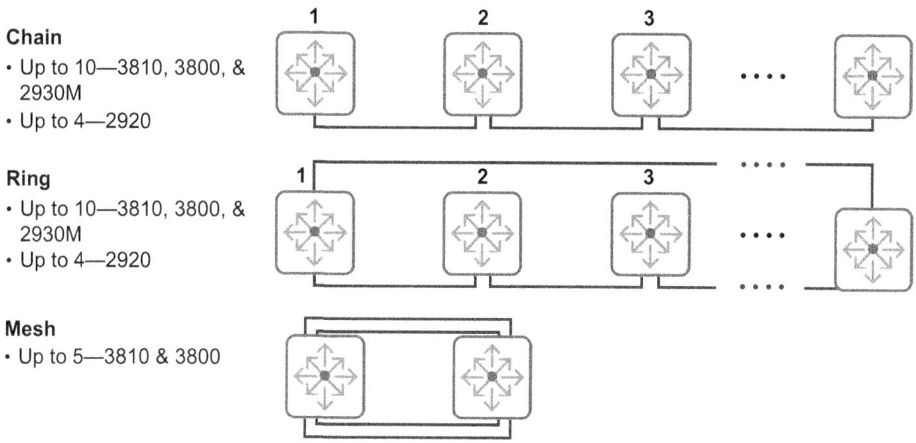


Figure 4-1 Backplane stacking topologies

### Chain topology

In a chain topology, each switch in the backplane stack is connected to another through a single cable, as shown in Figure 4-1. The chain topology is generally not recommended because a single failure (whether it is a switch, stacking module, or cable failure) disrupts communication among the switches in the backplane stack. Unless the failure occurs at the end of the chain, two stack fragments are created. One of the fragments becomes inactive to ensure that two virtual switches are not created. On the inactive fragment, the switches remain powered on, but all of switch ports in the inactive stack fragment are disabled and do not transmit network traffic.

You can combine up to ten 3810, 3800, 2930M Series switches in a chain topology. You can combine up to four 2920 Series switches in a chain topology.

### Ring topology

As the name suggests, each switch in a ring topology is connected to two switches, thereby forming a ring as shown in Figure 4-1. The ring topology provides a higher level of redundancy than the chain topology. A single failure in the switch, stacking module, or cable does not, therefore, disrupt communications within the backplane stack. If such a failure occurs, the ring topology becomes a chain topology. The switches can continue to function as a single virtual switch.

The ring topology supports the same number of members as the chain topology: ten 3810, 3800, or 2930M Series switches or four 2920 Series switches.

### Mesh topology

In a mesh topology, every switch in the stack is connected to every other switch, as shown in Figure 4-2. As a result, the mesh topology provides the highest level of redundancy because the stack can continue to function even if multiple failures occur.

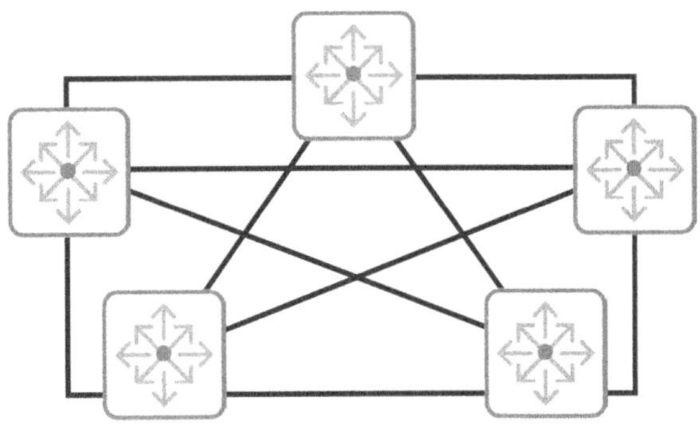

Figure 4-2 Mesh topology

The 2920 and 2930M Series switches do not support a mesh topology. For the 3810 or 3800 Series switches, the mesh topology supports fewer members. You can connect two to five switches in a mesh topology.

To set up the switches in a stack, you must purchase and install the appropriate stacking module and stacking cables for that switch. Check the Aruba web site for specific information about the stacking modules and cables.

## Roles in the backplane stack

Within the backplane stack, each switch fulfills one of the following roles:

- Commander
- Standby member
- Member

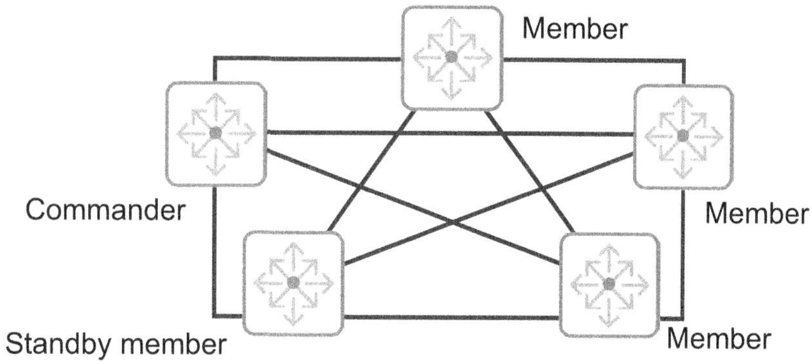


Figure 4-3 Roles in the backplane stack

As Figure 4-3 shows, each stack must have one commander and one standby member. Depending on the switch series and topology you use, you can combine up to 10 switches in a stack. The remaining switches function as members.

## Commander

The commander is responsible for:

- Managing the stack
- Responding to management requests for the stack
- Running all the routing and switching protocols for the entire stack
- Managing its own local subsystem and ports

Only one Commander is elected at any given time.

## Standby member

The standby member takes over management of the stack if the commander fails or if the network administrator forçes a failover. The standby member also manages its own local subsystem and ports.

Only one standby member is elected at any given time. If the standby member fails or becomes the commander (because the original commander failed), the member switches in the backplane stack elect a new standby.

### Members

Members do not participate in managing the stack. Each member must manage its local subsystems and ports to operate correctly as part of the stack.

## Configuring a backplane stack

Backplane stacking is enabled on 3810, 3800, 2930M, and 2920 switches by default. When a switch boots initially, it checks to see if a stacking module is installed. If the switch does not detect a stacking module, it disables the backplane stack feature. If you later install a stacking module, you must manually enable the backplane stacking feature.

There are two configuration options:

- **Deterministic**—Use this option if you want to control which switches function as the commander and standby member.
- **Plug-and-go**—Use this option if it does not matter which switches function as the commander and standby member.

### Deterministic configuration

To configure the switches so that you determine which switches function as the commander and standby member, complete these steps:

1. Power off all switches that will be part of the backplane stack.
2. Install the stacking modules in the switches and connect the stacking cables to create your stacking topology.
3. Configure the switch that you want to function as the commander.
    a. Power on the switch that you want to function as the commander.
    b. Ensure that stacking is enabled on the switch.

    ```
    Switch# show stacking
    ```

    c. If necessary, enable stacking:

    ```
    Switch(config)# stacking enable
    ```

    The switch automatically reboots.

    d. Display the switch's member ID.

    ```
    Switch# show stacking
    ```

e. If you want this switch to always function as the commander, configure the stacking priority. If all switches are booted simultaneously, the switch with the highest priority is selected as commander (see Figure 4-4)

```
Switch(config)# stacking member 1 priority 255
```

**Note**

If you add a switch to an existing backplane stack, that switch will not be elected commander or standby, no matter what priority you assign it. The current commander and standby member will continue to function, thereby preventing a system disruption and maintaining the stability of the backplane stack. In general terms, this means higher priority devices do not preempt switches that are currently acting as the commander or standby.

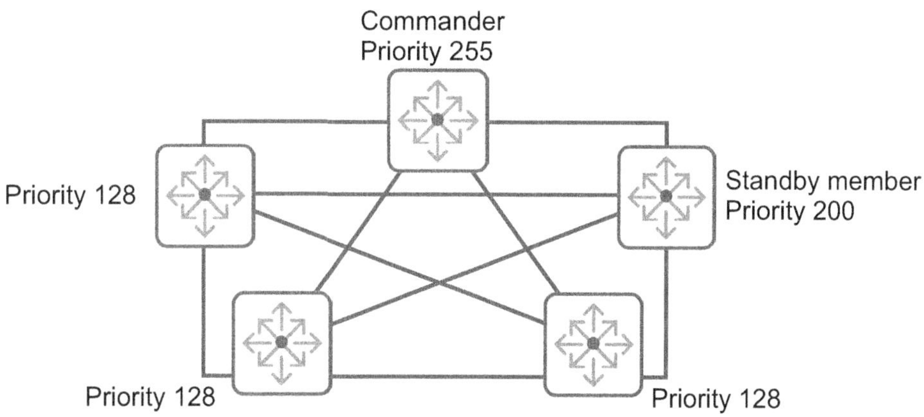


Figure 4-4 Deterministic configuration

4. Repeat the steps 3a to 3e on the switch that you want to function as the standby. When setting the priority, use a value that is lower than the priority you assigned the commander.
5. Power on the members, one at a time, and ensure that stacking is enabled on each switch.

   The member ID assigned to the switches is determined by the sequence in which they are booted.

## Plug-and-go installation method

If you do not care which switches function as the commander and standby member, complete these steps.

1. Power off all switches that will be part of the backplane stack.
2. Install the stacking modules in the switches and connect the stacking cables to create your stacking topology.

3. Power on the switches, one at a time. The order in which you power on the switches will determine which switch becomes the commander and the standby member. If you want to use the order in which switches are booted to determine which switch becomes commander and standby, complete these steps:
    a. First, power on the switch that you want to function as the commander.
    b. Second, power on the switch that you want to function as the standby.
    c. Power on the remaining switches, one at a time. The switches' member ID will be determined by the order in which they were booted and joined in the stack.
4. Ensure that stacking is enabled on each switch.

    ```
    Switch# show stacking
    ```

5. If necessary, enable stacking:

    ```
    Switch(config)# stacking enable
    ```

    The switch automatically reboots.
6. Determine the switch's member ID role in the stack.

    ```
    Switch# show stacking
    ```

## Election of the commander and standby member

If the stack is rebooted simultaneously, such as during a building power failure recovery, the members will undergo an election process. An election timer is set for 60 seconds, and if no new switches are discovered during that timeout period, the switches in the stack enter the election phase.

During the election process, for each group of switches that has the same stack ID, the following criteria is used for electing the commander:

- The switches with the highest stack revision are discovered.
- The switch with the highest configured priority is selected as the commander.
- If more than one switch has the same high priority, the switch that was the previous commander is selected.
- If none of the switches were previously the commander, the switch that was the standby member is selected.
- If none of the above conditions apply, the switch with the lowest MAC address is selected as the commander.

The commander then selects the standby member, using the same rules that were used to elect the commander.

## Stack operations

When the backplane stack is formed, the commander creates a stack ID, using its own MAC address hashed with time, and sends this stack ID to all the members of the stack. If the commander fails or if you manually force a failover and a new commander manages the stack, the stack ID does not change. The commander also assigns each switch a unique member ID.

Once the stack is formed, access to a member's console port redirects to the commander management plane. For remote access, managers can access the stack on IP addresses configured on a VLAN or loopback interface, just as they can with nonstacked switches.

To enable out-of-band access, managers can connect the commader's, standby's, and other members' OOBM ports in a management network. The IP addresses on the OOBM ports are different from other interfaces on the backplane stack because each member has its own MAC address on its OOBM port *and* its own OOBM IP address. The stack also has a global OOBM IP address. Managers can access the switch at any of the individual or global OOBM IP addresses; all requests are redirected to the commander. It is typical to access the stack at the global OOBM IP address, though.

By default, the global and individual OOBM IP addresses use DHCP. It is best practice to set the global OOBM IP address manually so that it remains constant if the commander fails and the standby member takes over. Otherwise, the new commander will send a new DHCP request and typically receive a new IP address.

It is recommended that you enable and configure OOBM on each member in the stack. As you will learn in the next section, this protects the stack if a problem interrupts the operation of the stack, creating two fragments that are of equal size.

The commander uses a stack revision to track the current stack topology. When the stack is created, the stack revision is stored in the configuration. Whenever a change is made to the stack—such as a new member is added—the stack revision is incremented and stored in the configuration.

To view information about the stack, you can enter the **show stacking** command. You will see output similar to the following:

```
Switch# show stacking
Stack ID : 00031cc1-de4d48c0
MAC Address : 1cc1de-4d48c9
Stack Topology : Mesh
Stack Status : Active
Uptime : 1d 2h 35m
Software Version : KA.15.05
Mbr
ID  Mac Address  Model                                  Pri  Status
--- ------------ -------------------------------------- ---- ------
1  1cc1de-4d48c0 Aruba J9574A 3800-48G-PoE+-4SFP+ Switch 250  Commander
2  1cc1de-4d8680 Aruba J9573A 3800-24G-PoE+-2SFP+ Switch 230  Standby
3  1cc1de-4e3180 Aruba J9574A 3800-48G-PoE+-4SFP+ Switch 128  Member
4  78acc0-3c2180 Aruba J9576A 3800-48G-4SFP+ Switch      128  Member
```

## Stack fragments

A backplane stack has built-in mechanisms to handle splits. You do not have to configure a protection mechanism. However, it is important that you enable and configure OOBM on each member of the stack.

If a link or a switch failure occurs, separating a stack into two groups, the smaller group, or fragment, becomes inactive by default (see Figure 4-5). All of the user ports on the switches in this stack fragment will be disabled. However, the OOBM and stack ports will be active, allowing you to manage the switches.

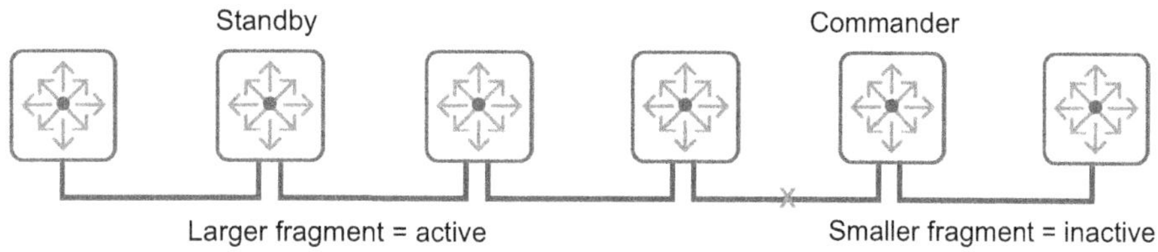


- Example—larger fragment (4 members) and smaller fragment (two members)
  - Larger fragment is active; smaller fragment is inactive.
  - Standby member becomes commander in the active fragment.
  - New commander keeps this role even after the stacks are reconnected.
- What happens if the two fragments are equal size (same number of members in each fragment)?
  - OOBM is enabled and configured on all members in stack:
    - Fragment that contains the Commander is active; other fragment is inactive
  - OOBM is not enabled and configured on all members in stack:
    - Both fragments are active

Figure 4-5 Stack fragments

The stack fragment that includes more switches will become the active stack and will inherit the MAC address and IP addresses assigned to the stack. This allows more of the user ports to remain operational.

What happens if the two stack fragments are the same size—meaning they have the same number of members? If OOBM is enabled and configured on all members in the stack, the fragment that contains the Commander is active. The other fragment is inactive.

If OOBM is not enabled and configured on all members, both fragments are active and will attempt to use the global IP addresses configured on the backplane stack. To protect the network from this problem occurring, you should ensure that OOBM is configured on all the switches.

When the two fragments are reconnected, the commander and standby of the active fragment retain those roles for the recombined stack. If the original commander was not in that fragment, then the stack will have a new commander when the stack is reformed. The switches in the Inactive fragment reboot and assume their new roles in the stack.

## Virtual Switching Framework (VSF)

The next section in this chapter focuses on VSF. To ensure that you have a basic understanding of VSF, take a few minutes to see if you can answer the following questions. You can refer to Figure 4-6, which shows both a physical and logical view of VSF, to help you answer these questions.

1. What are the benefits of implementing a VSF fabric?
2. What are the requirements for implementing VSF on a 5400R zl2 Series switch?
3. What are best practices for implementing VSF?
4. What is the maximum distance for a VSF link?

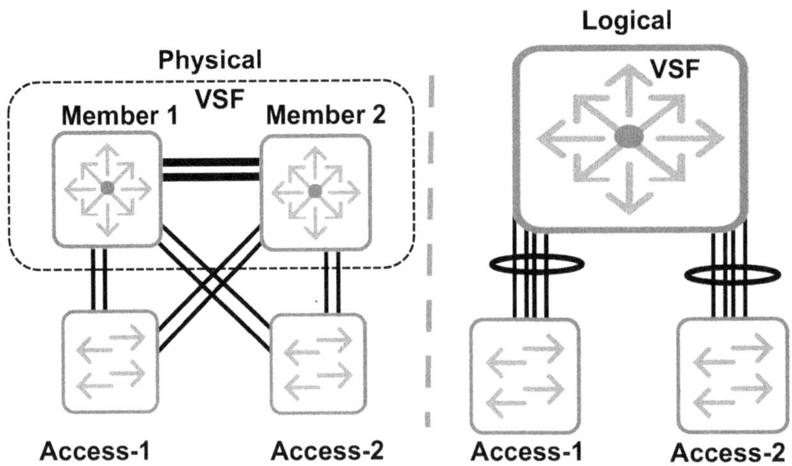


Figure 4-6 Virtual Switching Framework (VSF)

You will now review the plug-and-play VSF configuration and manual VSF configuration.

## Plug-and-play VSF configuration

Figure 4-7 provides an overview of the plug-and-play VSF configuration.

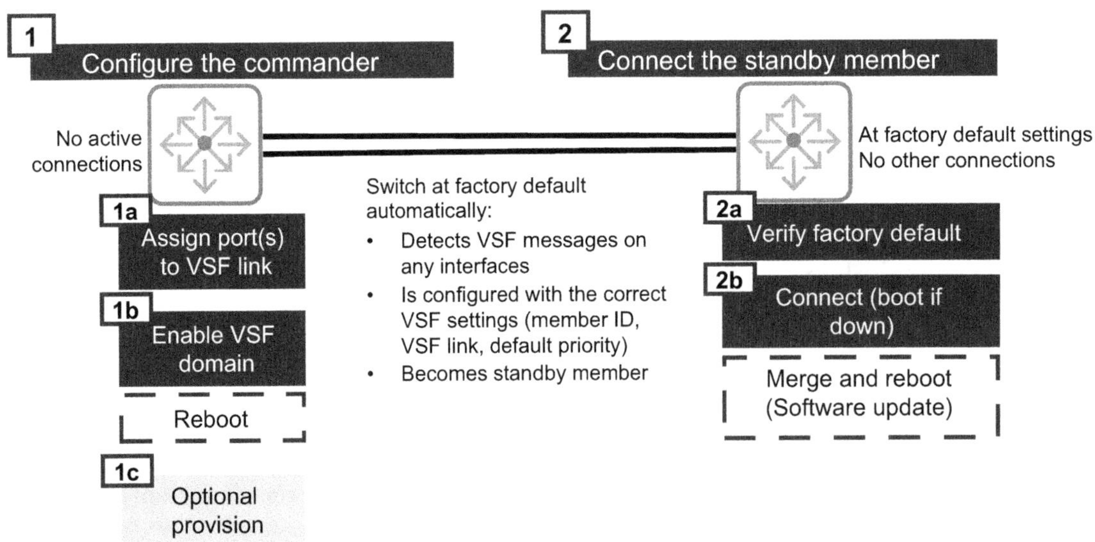


Figure 4-7 Plug-and-play VSF configuration

You will first configure the switch that you want to be commander. This switch might already by operating in your network. For example, a customer might have a 5400R switch at the network core and now wants to add redundancy to the core. You will set up a VSF fabric that uses the current 5400R switch as the commander, preserving all of the current configurations.

It is recommended that you create the VSF fabric during a scheduled network outage because:

- The switch that you are configuring as the commander must reboot during the process.
- You should remove any active links during the configuration process to prevent temporary issues (either by disconnecting cables or disabling ports).

Follow these simple steps to set up the fabric:

1. Configure the switch that you have selected as the commander:
    a. Create a VSF link. As you create the link, you specify:
        - The member ID—Typically, 1 for the commander, although it can be 2
        - The link ID—By default 1 as of software KB16.01.xxx
        - The interfaces assigned to the link—You should be aware of the guidelines for the switch you are configuring. The guidelines for the 2930F Series switches differ from the guidelines for the 5400R zl2 Series switches. Also, note that the interfaces lose their configuration when you add them to the VSF link. If you have disabled the interfaces, they will become enabled again. Do not cable these interfaces at this point.

    ```
    Switch(config)# vsf
    Switch(vsf)# member 1 link 1 a23,a24
    ```

    b. Enable VSF, specifying a unique domain ID for this fabric.

    ```
    Switch(vsf)# enable domain 1
    ```

    c. Enabling VSF saves the configuration and reboots the switch. The switch automatically adjusts the configuration so that it is valid for VSF mode, adding the VSF member ID to each interface ID. It is now the commander of a VSF fabric that consists of one member. (You will learn how to confirm this setup in the lab.)

    At this point, you can provision the standby member on the commander, if you want. The next section explains this option.

2. You are now ready to connect the standby member. You do not need to configure any settings on the standby member.
    a. Begin by making sure the switch has no active connections and is at factory default settings. It might be a new switch or one that you have reset to default settings. It will be taking its configuration from the commander, so it no longer needs the settings.
    b. Connect the standby member to the commander interfaces that you configured as part of the VSF link. Generally, the switch is powered down at this point; boot the switch.

c. When a switch that supports VSF is at factory default settings, it detects VSF messages on any of its interfaces and automatically uses those messages to configure itself with the correct VSF domain and link settings. A factory default switch that joins a VSF fabric always defers to the current commander, taking the standby role. The standby switch merges with the fabric and reboots.

If the standby member's software version does not match the commander's version, the commander updates the standby member, and the standby member reboots again. As the standby member reboots and joins the fabric, it takes its configuration from the commander. All of its interfaces are at factory default settings.

## VSF provisioning use cases

You may sometimes want to have more control over the process of forming a VSF fabric. For example, if you have multiple 5400R zl2 Series switches in your environment, you need to ensure that the right switch joins the VSF fabric.

You can use loose provisioning, in which you specify the member type. Type refers to model number, J9850A for a 5406R or J9851A for a 5412R. You can also use strict provisioning—in which you specify the standby member's type and MAC address (the switch's base MAC address). Strict provisioning controls which device is allowed to join the fabric; only the switch with the specified MAC address can join.

Provisioning also lets you configure the standby member's VSF priority and link name yourself rather have VSF do it automatically when the fabric forms. For example, you might want to preconfigure the standby member with VSF priority 1 so that you can be sure that the commander remains commander if both switches ever reboot at the same time.

You must first configure the switch's own VSF member ID and enable VSF on the switch. After the reboot, you can provision the other member with this command:

```
Switch(config)# vsf member <ID> type <type> mac-address <MAC address>
```

You might also want to preconfigure the standby member interfaces. Then when the standby member joins the fabric, it is immediately ready to support traffic. You can set the configuration up in advance. Someone can install the standby member, set up its connections, and then boot it up. The standby member joins the fabric, and its active connections are part of the proper link aggregations, eliminating dangers of loops.

To preconfigure the standby member interfaces, after provisioning the member on the commander, follow these steps:

1. Add interface modules on the standby member to the commander's configuration with this command:

   ```
   Switch(config)# module <standby member ID>/<module ID> type <module type>
   ```

2. Configure the interface settings just as you would for a module that was already installed in this switch.

If your only purpose in provisioning is to preconfigure the standby member settings, use loose provisioning, in which you only specify the device type. This provisioning method does not offer any extra control over the device that joins the fabric because VSF already prohibits switches of different models from merging in a fabric. But it does provide a place for preconfiguring the member settings.

You can combine the two use cases to both control which device can join the fabric and preconfigure that device's settings. In this case, use strict provisioning.

Table 4-1 summarizes the two types of provisioning.

Table 4-1: VSF provisioning

| Provisioning options | Required information |
|---|---|
| Strict | **Type + MAC** |
| Loose | **Type** |

## Configuring provisioning

You must set up provisioning in between enabling VSF on the commander and connecting the standby member.

When you begin configuring VSF, while VSF is still disabled, you can configure the settings for only *one* member, either member 1 or member 2. The switch becomes this member when you enable VSF, and the switch reboots. In other words, configuring a VSF link for member 1 is configuring this switch as member 1 and setting up its link. If you try to configure a setting for the other member at this point, you will see an error indicating that you have already set a different member ID for this switch. If you have accidently used the wrong ID and want to configure VSF settings with the other member ID, you would need to first remove the current member (with the **vsf member <ID> remove** command).

After you enable VSF and the switch reboots, the member settings that you configured automatically become bound to the switch's type and MAC address, as shown in the configuration in the figure. Note that if you enable VSF before configuring any member settings, the switch automatically becomes member 1 and starts using the default VSF priority and link name (the link interfaces are not defined). If you want to choose the member ID, set up the VSF link before enabling VSF.

After VSF is enabled, you can continue configuring this member's settings. At this point, you can also enter the **vsf member *<ID>* type** command to provision the other member. Specify the same type as this switch (otherwise, you will receive an error). If you want to use strict provisioning, also add the other member's MAC address. You can then use the **vsf member *<ID>* link** and **vsf member *<ID>* priority** commands to configure settings for the member that has not yet joined the fabric.

The member will accept these settings when it joins. If you used strict provisioning, only a switch with the correct MAC address is allowed to join. A switch with a different MAC address will reboot as if it is joining the fabric but fail to actually do so. You will see a message that the switch cannot join the VSF fabric because the fabric already has too many members (the preprovisioned member is counting as a member). With loose provisioning, any member of the correct type can join, and VSF automatically fills in its MAC address.

You should understand that after the VSF fabric has formed, the configuration includes settings for two members, each with the type and MAC address filled in. The end configuration looks the same whether you preprovisioned it or let VSF fill in the settings automatically. Therefore, the configuration is bound to the specific hardware. If one of the members fails and you want to replace it, you must first remove the failed member from the configuration with the **vsf member <*ID*> remove** command. You can then join the replacement switch.

## Manual VSF configuration

The plug-and-play setup provides the easiest way to establish a VSF fabric, but you can take other approaches as well. A manual configuration allows you to join two switches, neither of which is at the factory defaults. However, after the fabric forms, only the commander configuration remains.

Figure 4-8 provides an overview of the manual VSF configuration.

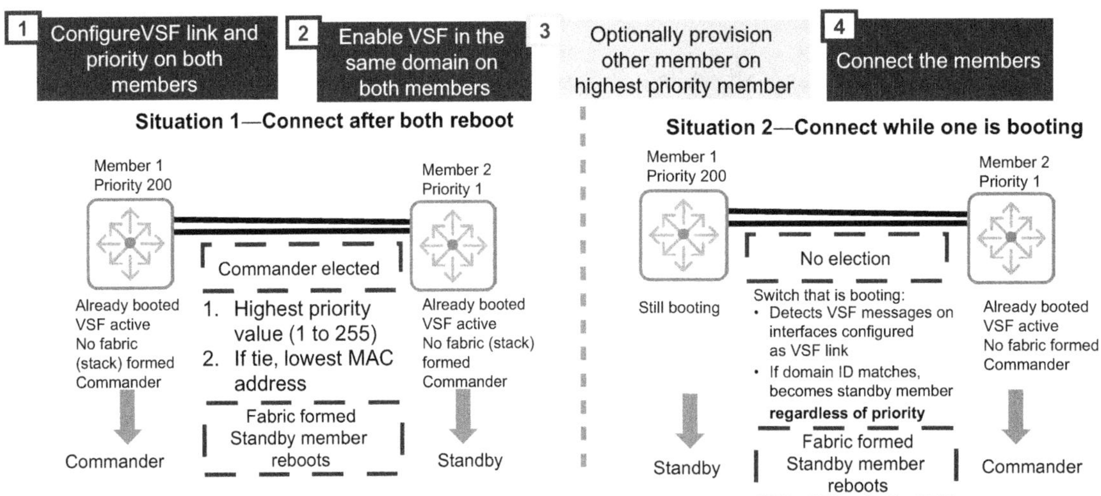


Figure 4-8 Manual VSF configuration

With the manual VSF configuration, you should begin by disconnecting both switches from all other devices *including from each other*. You then configure both members in a similar manner to configuring the commander for a plug-and-play setup. You assign ports to a VSF link, configuring one switch with member 1 link 1 and the other switch with member 2 link 1.

```
Member1(config)# vsf
Member1(vsf)# member 1 link 1 a23,a24

Member2(config)# vsf
Member2(vsf)# member 2 link 1 a23,a24
```

Before you enable the VSF domain, though, you should set a higher priority on the switch that you want to become commander. The VSF priority (values between 1 and 255, default 128) determines which switch will be elected commander; the switch with higher value wins.

```
Member1(vsf)# member 1 priority 255
```

Make sure to enable the VSF domain with the same ID on both switches.

```
Member1(vsf)# enable domain 1
Member1(vsf)# enable domain 1
```

After you configure these settings and enable the VSF domain on each switch, it reboots.

If you want to use the VSF priority to determine the commander, allow *both* switches to reboot while still disconnected. Verify that both switches have booted and are running VSF. Each switch should consider itself the commander of a VSF fabric.

If you want to provision the standby member settings on the commander, do that now. You should always provision only the switch that you intend to assign the higher priority and make commander. That is, you specify the type and optionally MAC address of the future standby member on the future commander. Although you can technically provision the other member on the switch that will become the standby member, these settings will have no effect. When the standby member merges with the commander's fabric, it takes the commander's settings in preference to its own. Even if you used strict provisioning on the future standby member, it does *not* check the commander MAC address against the provisioned MAC address.

You are now ready to connect the switches on the interfaces that you added to the VSF link. When the link comes up, the switches start to exchange VSF protocol messages. They verify that they are in the same VSF domain and hold an election. The switch with the higher priority becomes commander. If both switches have the same priority, the switch with the lower MAC address becomes commander.

The VSF fabric forms and begins using the commander configuration. The standby member reboots. When it comes back up, its interfaces are added to the fabric. You would need to configure those interfaces just as with the plug-and-play method.

Note that an election also occurs if both members boot at about the same time. For this reason, even if you use the plug-and-play configuration method, you might want to assign the switch that you want to be commander a higher priority than the other switch. Then, if both switches happen to reboot at the same time, the desired switch remains commander.

It is important for you to understand that an election for the master *only* occurs when two switches that are configured for VSF connect when both are fully booted or are booting at the same time. If a switch that is configured for VSF detects VSF messages on its VSF interfaces while it is booting, it checks the domain. As long as the domain matches its domain, it acts much like a switch at factory defaults. It defers to the current commander on the other side of the link *even if the current commander has a lower priority*, and the booting switch joins the VSF fabric as a standby member.

## Viewing the VSF fabric

You can confirm that the VSF fabric has established correctly with this command:

```
VSF-Switch# show vsf

 VSF Domain ID      : 1

 MAC Address        : 1c98ec-acd73f

 VSF Topology       : Chain

 VSF Status         : Active

 Uptime             : 0d 0h 24m

 VSF Oobm-MAD       : Disabled

 Software Version : KB.16.04.0000x

 Mbr

 ID  Mac Address    Model                             Pri    Status

 --- ------------   --------------------------------- ---    ---------

 *1  1c98ec-acc700  HP J9850A Switch 5406Rzl2         255    Commander

  2  1c98ec-aa8a00  HP J9850A Switch 5406Rzl2         100    Standby
```

The output above shows that two switches have joined the fabric. One switch is the commander, and the other switch is the standby member. If one of the switches had joined the fabric, but then failed or became disconnected, you would see “Missing” for the status.

## Implementing VSF on Aruba 2930F Series switches

Aruba 2930F Series switches support up to four switches in a VSF fabric. This configuration introduces a new role for VSF fabrics. If a VSF fabric includes three or more switches, one switch will be the commander, one will be the standby, and the remaining switches will assume the member role (see Figure 5-9).

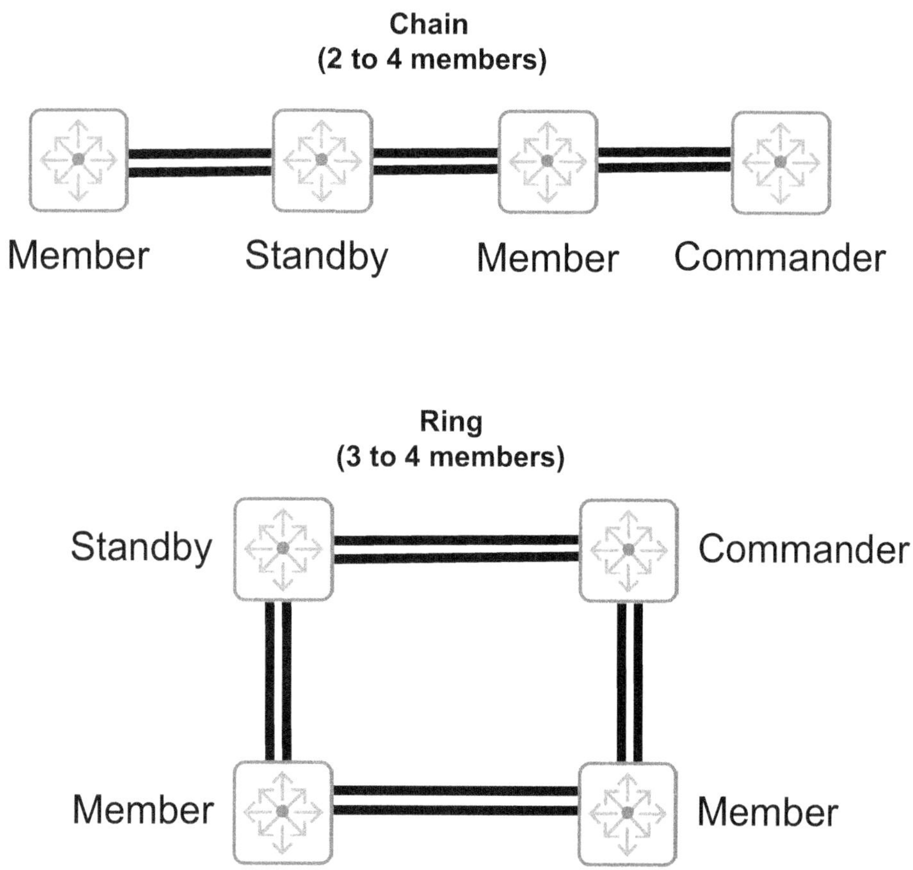


Figure 4-9 Implementing VSF on Aruba 2930F Series switches

## Commander

The commander provides the active control plane, which means that it handles protocol functions. Only the commander builds MAC forwarding tables, ARP tables, and routing tables. The commander also runs all IP routing protocols.

The commander provides the active management plane. Users and management solutions can connect through this plane to the CLI, Web user interface, and SNMP agent to manage the VSF fabric configuration. Note that, although the commander provides the only active management plane, you can connect to a console port on the standby switch and receive access to the CLI. The standby member proxies you to the commander management plane.

In addition to providing the device intelligence, the commander also has active physical interfaces, and it receives and forwards traffic.

### Standby

The standby member does not have its own active control and management functions. Instead, it receives the configuration for its interfaces from the commander. It also receives relevant portions of the MAC addressing tables and routing tables from the commander. It can then receive and forward traffic correctly.

The standby member retains the ability to take over the management and control functions if the commander fails. Therefore, even though the standby member does not have active management and control functions, it permanently receives copies of the current configuration and stores them. It also proxies the control plane so that it is ready to take over as the commander if necessary.

### Member

A member does not run networking protocols. The commander controls and programs the ports on members. Like the standby member, members receive relevant portions of the MAC addressing tables and routing tables from the commander. They can then receive and forward traffic correctly.

If the standby member must take over as commander, one of the members will assume the role of standby.

### Topologies

As Figure 4-9 shows, with 2930F Series switches, you have a choice of two topologies: ring and chain. As you learned earlier, the ring topology provides a higher level of redundancy than the chain topology and is, therefore, the recommended topology. If one link is severed, communications within the VSF continue. If such a failure occurs, the ring topology becomes a chain topology. The switches can continue to function as a single virtual switch.

### VSF links

As you learned in *Aruba Switching Fundamentals for Mobility*, VSF members connect to each other over a VSF link. Each VSF link consists of a logical VSF link defined on each member and is associated with up to eight physical interfaces.

Because 2930F Series switches support up to four switches in a VSF fabric, each switch supports two logical VSF links. This allows it to connect to two members as part of a chain or ring topology. VSF on these switches support two port speeds: 1 Gbps and 10 Gbps.

The switch automatically sets the VSF port speed when you first define a VSF link on a member. For example, interface 23 is a 1 Gbps port, and you enter this command:

```
Switch(config)# vsf member 1 link 1 23
```

If you check the running-config, you will see that the switch has added this configuration as well:

```
vsf port-speed 1G
```

On 2930F Series switches, you can add ports that support different speeds to the same VSF link. However, ports that do not match the global VSF port speed will have a down state. You can make the switch use the ports with the new speed by entering this command yourself:

```
Switch(config)# vsf port-speed <1G|10G>
```

If you enter this command to change the VSF port speed after the VSF fabric is formed, the switches will reboot.

You can use this behavior to upgrade the speed for the VSF link from 1 G to 10 G:

1. Complete this configuration during scheduled network maintenance time.
2. Add the new 10 Gbps interfaces to the VSF link. This example is for a fabric with two members.
   ```
   Switch(config)# vsf member 1 link 1 1/27,1/28
   Switch(config)# vsf member 2 link 1 2/27,2/28
   ```
3. Connect the new links.
4. Change the port speed.
   ```
   Switch(config)# vsf port-speed 10G
   ```
5. After the reboot, remove the old interfaces from the link configuration. Disconnect the links

You can use the **show vsf** command to view the VSF port speed. You can enter the **show vsf link detail** to see the ports assigned to the VSF link and their state (up or down).

## Configuring VSF on Aruba 2930F Series switches

Aruba 2930F switches support both plug and play and manual VSF configuration. No matter which type of deployment you are planning, begin with all of the switches disconnected.

Figure 4-10 provides an overview of the VSF configuration for Aruba 2930F switches.

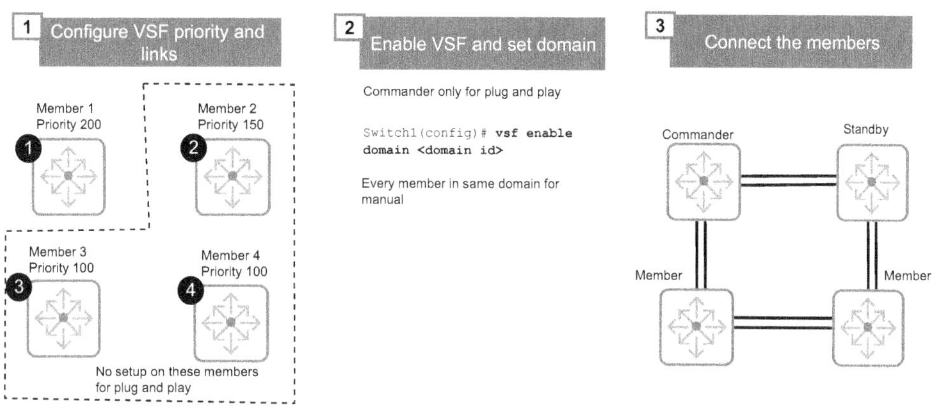


Figure 4-10 Configuring VSF on Aruba 2930F Series switches

If you are planning a plug-and-play deployment, configure the switch that you want to be commander as member 1. Set up its VSF links and set a high priority value such as 200 (default is 100). Then enable VSF and set the domain ID.

After the commander has fully rebooted, provision the other members on the commander; define each member with a unique ID and set its VSF links. This step is not strictly required for a two-member VSF fabric, but you should complete it if you want to create a fabric with more members. The factory default switches need to receive VSF messages from VSF links to join the fabric. Provisioning the links on all members will enable members that are not directly connected to the commander to join the fabric. If you want to control which member becomes the standby member, provision that member with a higher priority than default, but less than the commander, such as 150. If you want, you can then preconfigure all members' interfaces.

You can then connect the other switches. Make sure to connect the proper interfaces that you assigned to the VSF links.

For manual configuration, you configure the VSF link and priorities on every member, making sure to give each a unique member ID. As you recall, it is considered a best practice to assign the switch you intend to function as the commander member ID 1. You can then assign the standby member ID 2.

You should also assign these switches higher priorities. In the example shown in Figure 4-10, member 1 will be assigned a priority of 200, and member 2 a priority of 150. Members 3 and 4 will be assigned a lower priority, such as 100.

You the enable VSF on every switch with the same domain ID. After the devices reboot, you can connect the switches so that they can form a VSF fabric. The switches may reboot several times because the switches' roles may change more than once during the process of forming a VSF fabric. You can prevent this by powering off the switches and powering them on at the same time.

## Compare unicasts on backplane stacking and VSF forwarding

Both VSF and backplane stacking allow all members to forward traffic actively, but they handle the forwarding a bit differently. With both technologies, when a switch receives a unicast with a known destination MAC address, it can look up the egress port for that MAC address. If the egress port is local, the switch can simply forward the traffic out that port. Otherwise, it sends the traffic to the member with the egress port over the stacking or VSF links.

The two technologies differ in how they handle traffic with a link aggregation as the egress port. Backplane stacking uses the same load-balancing algorithm as link aggregations on a single switch to select a link. It includes all member links in the link aggregation in the selection process. The local switch has no preference, so it might end up forwarding the traffic to another member for forwarding. The switching links offer a great deal of bandwidth to handle this traffic.

VSF, on the other hand, always forwards unicasts on a local link in the link aggregation, if available. Only if no local link is available, does the VSF member forward the unicast over the VSF link for forwarding by another member. Typically, it is recommended that you balance links in the link aggregation across all members.

Figure 4-11 summarizes the differences in how backplane stacking and VSF handle unicasts.

**Backplane stacking**
**Unicasts**

Egress port determined on receiving switch

- Local port = Forward locally
- Port on other member = Forward over stacking links
- Link aggregation = Physical port selected with usual load balancing mechanism

**VSF**
**Unicasts**

Egress port determined on receiving switch

- Local port = Forward locally
- Port on other member = Forward over VSF links
- Link aggregation = Forward locally if possible

Figure 4-11 Compare unicasts on backplane stacking and VSF forwarding

## Compare flooding on backplane stacking and VSF forwarding

Backplane stacks and VSF fabrics also handle flooding broadcasts, multicasts, and unknown unicasts a bit differently. When a backplane stack member needs to flood traffic, its stacking module constructs a list of all the egress ports on all members that need to flood the traffic. For link aggregations, it adds a single link to the list, just as a switch not using backplane stacking would do. The selected link could be on the local member or another member. The backplane stack member then forwards the multicast directly over a stacking link to each member with at least one egress port in the list.

A VSF fabric member, on the other hand, floods the multicast to all members. Each member then determines by itself on which ports it needs to flood the multicast. Link aggregations have a designated forwarder. Only the designated forwarder floods broadcasts, multicasts, and unknown unicasts on that link aggregation, ensuring the traffic is not duplicated.

Figure 4-12 summarizes the differences in how backplane stacking and VSF handle flooded traffic.

**Backplane stacking**
**– Flooded traffic**

- Egress ports determined on receiving switch
  - Link aggregation = Physical port selected as usual
- Traffic forwarded over stacking links only to members with egress ports

**VSF**
**– Flooded traffic**

- Traffic flooded to other member(s) over VSF link
- Each member determines the egress ports for flooding
  - Link aggregation = Designated multicast forwarder

Figure 4-12 Compare flooding on backplane stacking and VSF forwarding

## Protection against split brain with MAD

As you know, you should attempt to create a resilient VSF link with multiple physical links that are connected on interfaces on different modules. However, some situations can still cause all of the physical links in the VSF link to fail, leading to a split fabric.

If a split occurs, the standby member loses contact with the commander. From the standby member point of view, the commander has failed, so the standby member becomes commander as well. Now multiple devices are active; in other words, the VSF has a split brain. Both devices use the same IP addressing and run the same protocols, which can cause issues with routing, for example. In addition, connectivity issues can occur because the devices cannot send data traffic between each other. If traffic arrives on one member and needs to be forwarded on another member, the traffic is now dropped.

To protect against a split-brain situation, you should enable Multi-Active Detection (MAD) on the VSF fabric (see Figure 4-13). When MAD is operating, the VSF link can fail without disrupting traffic. The standby still loses contact with the commander on the VSF link. However, the standby member can use MAD to detect that the commander is still up (you will see exactly how in just a moment). The standby member then becomes an inactive fragment and shuts down all of its interfaces. The commander remains up and an active fragment. The link aggregations all fail over gracefully to the links connected to the active fragment.

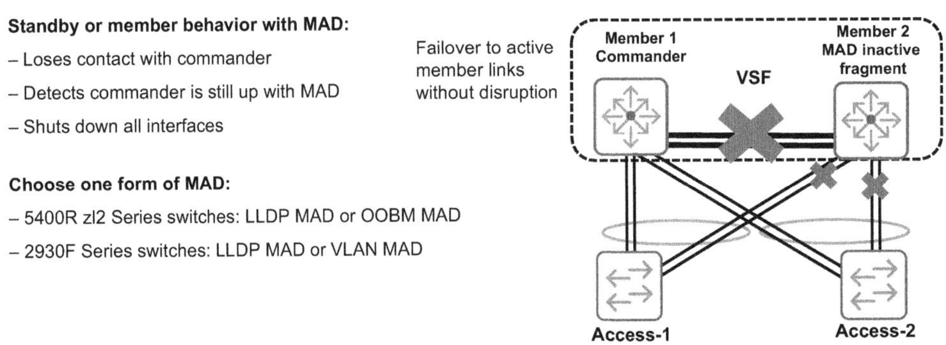


Figure 4-13 Protection against split brain with MAD

When the VSF link is restored, the standby member rejoins the fabric. Until that point, you have limited management control over the standby member.

VSF supports three types of MAD: OOBM, LLDP, and VLAN. You can configure one method on each VSF fabric. The 5400R zl2 switches support OOBM MAD and LLDP-MAD. The 5930F switches support LLDP-MAD and VLAN MAD.

## OOBM MAD

5400R zl2 switches support OOBM MAD, which uses the commander and standby member's OOBM ports to detect if the VSF link fails.

For OOBM MAD to work, the commander and standby member each require their own OOBM IP address, which is different from the global OOBM IP address for the VSF fabric as a whole. Management stations contact the VSF fabric OOBM IP address to manage the switch (see Figure 4-14). The individual member OOBM addresses, on the other hand, are dedicated to MAD.

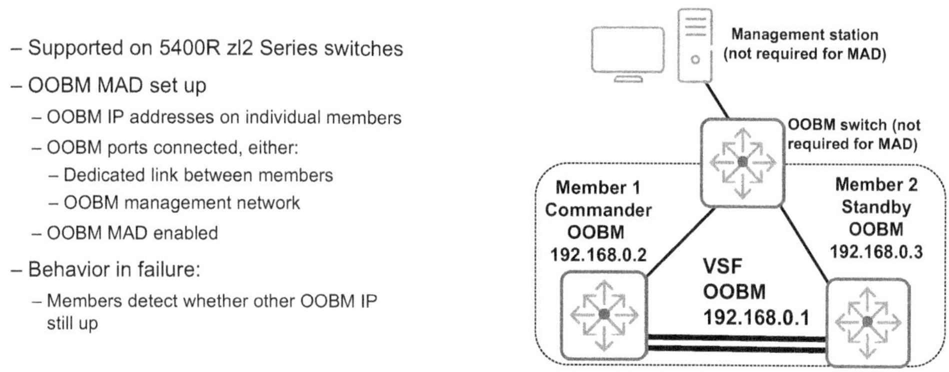


Figure 4-14 OOBM MAD

The OOBM ports can connect to a switch that connects to other devices such as management stations. Then you can use the OOBM ports for connecting the switches to an out-of-band management network, as well as for MAD. However, if you choose you can alternatively connect the OOBM ports directly together. In this latter case, the OOBM ports are dedicated to MAD (you cannot also manage the VSF fabric through them). After you have determined that the ports are set up correctly and the switches have IP addresses, you can enable OOBM MAD.

If a VSF link fails, the standby member can now attempt to contact the commander OOBM IP address. If successful, the standby member knows that the VSF link failed but that the commander is still up. The standby member can then become an inactive fragment and shut down all of its interfaces. (After the VSF link is restored, the member will automatically rejoin the fabric.)

## LLDP MAD setup

Both 5400R zl2 and 2930F Series switches support LLDP MAD. This form of MAD leverages an existing connection for detecting the other member's status if the VSF link fails. As Figure 4-15 shows, the connection must meet these criteria:

- It is a link aggregation that uses LACP.
- The link aggregation includes links on all members of the VSF fabric.
- LLDP is enabled on all of the links.

The device on the other side of the link is the MAD assistant. In addition to supporting the LACP link aggregation, the assistant must meet these requirements:

- It must have an IP address that is reachable by the VSF fabric.
- It must have an SNMPv2c community with read access (either read-only or read-write). SNMPv2c must also be enabled.

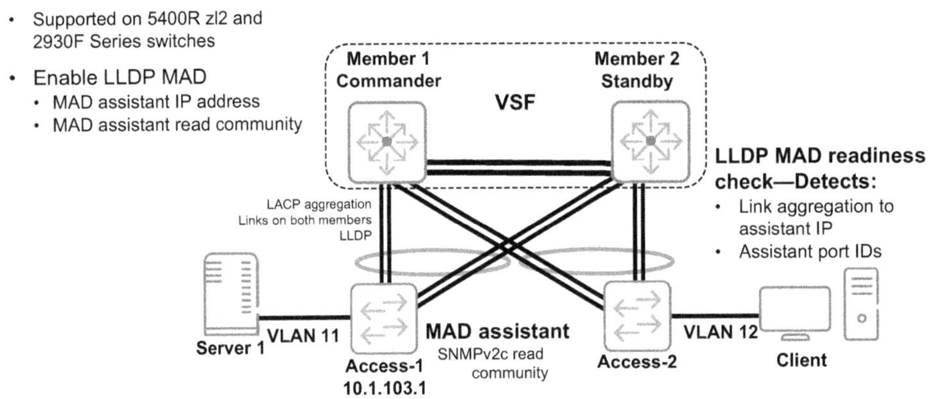


Figure 4-15 LLDP MAD setup

After you check these criteria, you can enable LLDP MAD, specifying the MAD assistant IP address and the SNMPv2 read community.

The VSF fabric then verifies that LLDP MAD is ready to operate. It detects the link aggregation on which it reaches the IP address specified for the MAD assistant and verifies that it has at least one link on each member in this aggregation. The VSF fabric then uses LACP to determine the port IDs that the assistant assigns to its side of the links and LLDP to verify the information. The fabric needs to know the port IDs, as the ports are identified in SNMP so that it can query their status about them in a VSF link failure situation.

When the fabric has collected all of this information, LLDP MAD is active and ready to detect a VSF link failure.

## LLDP MAD behavior

If the VSF link fails, the standby member sends a probe to the MAD assistant (an SNMP GET message). This probe queries the assistant for the status of all of its ports in the link aggregation using the port IDs detected earlier.

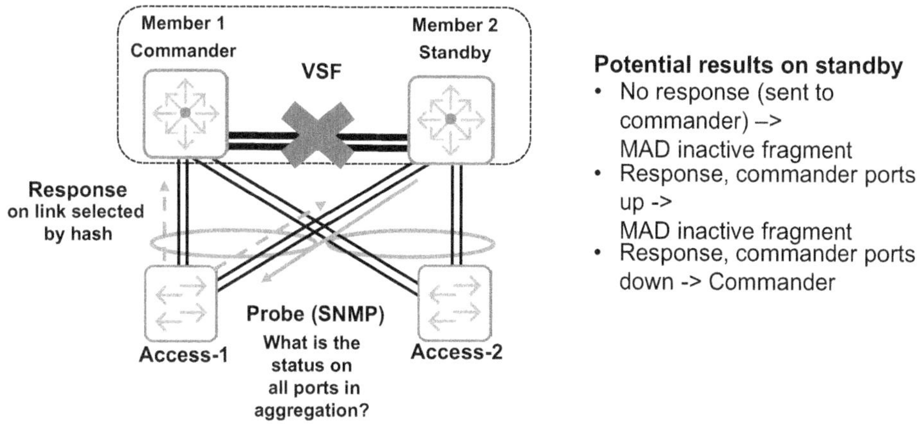


Figure 4-16 LLDP MAD behavior

The assistant selects an active link in the link aggregation and sends a probe response. As Figure 4-16 shows, one of three results occurs on the standby member:

- The standby member does not receive a probe response because the commander is still up, and the assistant sends the response on one of the links to the commander. When the standby member does not receive a timely response, it knows that the commander is up, and so it becomes a MAD inactive fragment and shuts down all interfaces.
- The standby member receives a probe response, and the response indicates that the links to the commander are still up. Again, the standby member becomes a MAD inactive fragment and shuts down all of its interfaces.
- The standby member receives a probe response, and the response indicates that the links to the commander are down. In this case, the standby member determines that the VSF link is down because the commander is down. The standby member becomes the new commander.

In all of these cases, MAD enables the active VSF fragment to continue forwarding traffic while the inactive one does not interfere.

## VLAN MAD

2930F Series switches support VLAN MAD, offering you an alternative to LLDP MAD. Figure 4-17 shows the setup for VLAN MAD.

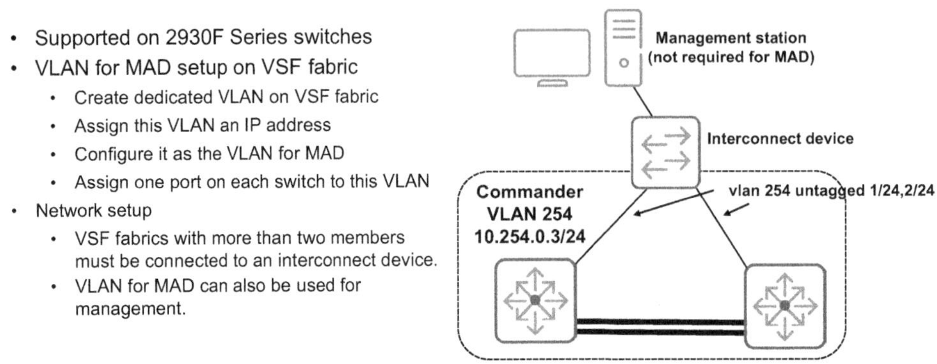


Figure 4-17 VLAN MAD

For VLAN MAD, you must first create a VLAN on the VSF fabric that is dedicated to MAD and then assign this VLAN an IP address. For example, you could create VLAN 254 for VLAN MAD and assign it the IP address 10.254.0.3/24.

```
Switch(config)# vlan 254 ip address 10.254.0.3/24
```

You then configure this VLAN as the VLAN dedicated to MAD.

```
Switch(config)# vsf vlan-mad 254
```

You must then assign one port on each switch in the VSF fabric to this VLAN. These ports should be configured as untagged members of the VLAN for MAD. In this example, ports 1/24 and 2/24 become untagged members of the VLAN.

```
Switch(config)# vlan 254 untagged 1/24,2/24
```

In a VSF fabric that contains more than two members, you must connect the ports assigned to the VLAN for MAD to an interconnect device, such as a nonproduction switch. You can then use the VLAN to manage the switches. This allows you to separate management traffic from production traffic.

If you have a two-member VSF fabric, you can instead configure the VLAN for MAD on a directly connected link between the two switches.

Be aware that, in both setups, from the point of view of the VSF fabric, the fabric is looped to itself. This "loop," however, must be maintained so that the switches can detect each other if the VSF link fails. The switch automatically applies BPDU filtering to the ports assigned to the VLAN configured for MAD. Do not disable this BPDU filtering and do not apply loop protection. Connect each member to just one interconnect switch on just one link.

You can verify the MAD configuration with the command below. During normal operation, when both members are connected on the MAD VLAN, and they can also reach each other over the VSF link, the connectivity status should be full. (If the status is not full, make sure that you have assigned the VLAN used for MAD on a port on both members and enabled both the ports.)

```
Access-1(config)# show vsf vlan-mad

 Multi-Active Detection VLAN status :

  VLAN ID                       : 254
  VLAN NAME                     : VLAN254
  VLAN MAD Connectivity Status : Full

  Port   Status   Member State
  -----  -------  ---------------
  1/24   Up       Commander
  2/24   Up       Standby
```

## VSF Fast Software Updates (FSU)

Beginning with version KB16.03, 5400R zl2 Series switches support Fast Software Updates (FSU). This feature is designed to minimize downtime for software updates on the VSF fabrics.

The process is simple and straightforward. You first download the new firmware into the primary or secondary flash on the VSF commander. Then enter the command to initiate FSU, specifying the location of the new firmware:

```
Switch(config)# vsf sequenced-reboot [primary | secondary]
```

The standby is updated first, while the commander continues normal operation. After the standby member is updated to the new software, it reboots as commander and takes over operation of the VSF fabric.

The old commander is then updated to the new firmware. It reboots and returns to the VSF fabric as a standby member.

# Summary

By enabling switches to operate as a single logical switch, backplane stacking and VSF enhance resiliency. For example, simple link aggregations replace complex spanning tree or routing topologies.

You learned how to set up backplane stacking and how a backplane stack operates both during normal circumstances and in case of the stack fragments. You learned best practices for using the OOBM network to prevent a split brain in case the stack breaks into two fragments of equal size.

You reviewed several strategies for establishing a VSF fabric so that you can choose the method that works best for you—whether the simple plug-and-play setup or a manual configuration, both with or without provisioning. You also understand when the VSF priority controls, which switch becomes controller, and when the existing controller maintains the role regardless of priority.

In addition, you examined the components and operation of a VSF fabric. The controller provides the active management and control planes, but both members contribute forwarding planes and can actively forward traffic on the most efficient path. If a link or even a member fails, VSF permits seamless failover helping customers maintain business continuity for network services.

## Learning check

1. What is a split VSF stack?
    a. It is the creation of two separate VSF virtual devices, each unaware of the other, in the event that members in an VSF virtual device cannot communicate.
    b. It is a mechanism that prevents address conflicts by permitting only one VSF virtual device to be active and tries to re-establish both the failed link and the VSF virtual device.
    c. It is a piece of software that allows an administrator to upgrade the VSF virtual device without disrupting the services it provides.
    d. It is a process that supports version rollback, which allows a user to go back to the previous software version.
2. What role do members play in a mesh topology implemented with backplane stacking?
    a. Members manage their local subsystems and ports to operate correctly as part of the stack.
    b. Members are responsible for responding to management requests for the stack.
    c. Members take over management of the stack if the commander fails or if the network administrator forces a failover.
    d. Members run all the routing and switching protocols for the entire stack.
3. How does backplane stacking handle stack fragments in the event of a link or switch failure?
4. Compare plug-and-play setup for VSF with manual setup.
5. What is the value in pre-provisioning a member before establishing VSF?

# Answers

## Virtual Switching Framework (VSF)

1. What are the benefits of implementing a VSF fabric?

   A VSF fabric increases redundancy and resiliency while simplifying design. Because the switches in a VSF fabric are logically the same switch, you can connect them to another switch, VSF fabric, or backplane stack with a link aggregation. It then becomes simple to create a resilient topology that logically has no loops, removing the need for spanning tree. This topology tends to be more stable than a spanning tree-based topology, and it recovers from a failed link much more quickly. Link aggregations also provide more granular load balancing of traffic than spanning tree.

   VSF also makes it simpler to provide redundancy for Layer 3 services. For example, rather than configure VRRP between two routing switches to provide redundancy for a default gateway, you can make the default gateway a VSF fabric.

2. What are the requirements for implementing VSF on a 5400R zl2 Series switch?

   The switches must be the same switch model. The software version should be KB.16.01 or higher. The switches must have v3 modules, and support for v2 modules must be disabled. The switches should only have one management module; if a switch has a redundant management module, that module is disabled when the switch becomes part of a VSF fabric.

3. What are best practices for implementing VSF?

   Best practices include:

   - Creating balanced link aggregations with the same number of links on each member
   - Planning sufficient bandwidth for the VSF link and using interfaces on different modules for these links
   - Configuring a form of MAD, whether OOBM MAD or LLDP MAD, to prevent split-brain situations if the VSF link fails

4. What is the maximum distance for a VSF link?

   VSF uses normal 1 GbE, 10 GbE, or 40 GbE cables, depending on the speed requirements for the model. The maximum lengths are the same as those for any such link, so VSF fabrics can extend across closets and sites.

## Learning check

1. What is a split VSF stack?
   a. **It is the creation of two separate VSF virtual devices, each unaware of the other, in the event that members in an VSF virtual device cannot communicate.**
   b. It is a mechanism that prevents address conflicts by permitting only one VSF virtual device to be active and tries to re-establish both the failed link and the VSF virtual device.
   c. It is a piece of software that allows an administrator to upgrade the VSF virtual device without disrupting the services it provides.
   d. It is a process that supports version rollback, which allows a user to go back to the previous software version.
2. What role do members play in a mesh topology implemented with backplane stacking?
   a. **Members manage their local subsystems and ports to operate correctly as part of the stack.**
   b. Members are responsible for responding to management requests for the stack.
   c. Members take over management of the stack if the commander fails or if the network administrator forces a failover.
   d. Members run all the routing and switching protocols for the entire stack.
3. How does backplane stacking handle stack fragments in the event of a link or switch failure?

   The larger stack fragment remains active. If this fragment does not include the commander, the standby member becomes commander. If this fragment does not include either the commander or the standby member, a new commander is elected. Any smaller fragments become inactive, and members in these fragments shut down all of their frontplane ports. The OOBM ports remain active so that managers can reach the fragment.

   No extra configuration is required for this functionality. However, it is recommended that stack members connect together on their OOBM ports so that managers can reach the fragment and to prevent both fragments from remaining active if the split results in equal size fragments.
4. Compare plug-and-play setup for VSF with manual setup.

   Plug-and-play setup tends to be simpler because you only need to configure VSF settings on one of the switches. Plug-and-play set up requires the switch joining the fabric to be at factory defaults. With manual setup, the switch that is not elected commander can be running a nondefault configuration, but it will lose this configuration when it joins the fabric.

   Both types of setup allow preprovisioning of member settings on the commander before the member joins the fabric.

5. What is the value in preprovisioning a member before establishing VSF?

   Preprovisioning lets you set up the interfaces on all members before the members join. If you are using plug-and-play setup, you can cable the noncommander in advance and then simply power them on. Preprovisioning is also required for a plug-and-play set up for a fabric with more than two members. Otherwise, members can automatically set up their VSF links to the commander when they receive the commander messages, but they cannot set up their links between each other.

   Strict preprovisioning, in which you provision the MAC address for each member as well as the model number, gives you more control over which devices can join the fabric. You can also assign each particular switch its member ID and priority.

# 5 Advanced Open Shortest Path First (OSPF)

EXAM OBJECTIVES

- ✓ Deploy AOS-Switches in single-area and multi-area Open Shortest Path First (OSPF) systems
- ✓ Use area definitions and summaries to create efficient and scalable multiple area designs
- ✓ Advertise routes to external networks in a variety of OSPF environments
- ✓ Promote fast, effective convergence during a variety of failover situations
- ✓ Use virtual links as required to establish nondirect connections to the backbone
- ✓ Implement OSPF authentication

## Assumed knowledge

Before reading this chapter, you should have a basic understanding of:

- Aruba Virtual Switching Framework (VSF)
- IP addressing
- Open Systems Interconnection (OSI) model
- Multiple Spanning Tree Protocol (MSTP) and Rapid Spanning Tree Protocol (RSTP)
- Link aggregation
- Virtual LANs (VLANs)
- IP routing, including static routing and basic understanding of OSPF
- Switching

## Introduction

In this chapter, you will learn how to implement OSPF routing in multiple area designs. You will examine several advanced scenarios and learn ways to configure OSPF to meet their needs.

## OSPF overview

A very simple campus might have a single core switch that routes all traffic for the campus and uses a default route to send traffic out to the Internet. However, many companies have multiple routers and routing switches which need to send traffic across the campus. The routing devices use routes to tell them how to forward traffic to each destination network. Static routes quickly become too time-consuming and error-prone to manage, particularly in a complex or redundant topology. A dynamic routing protocol, on the other hand, enables routers to discover routes automatically and to automatically update the routes when the topology changes.

OSPF, an open standard routing protocol, is the typical choice for enterprise private networks. As an Interior Gateway Protocol (IGP), OSPF facilitates the exchange of routing information among routers under the same organizational control or in other words within the same autonomous system (AS).

OSPF is a link-state protocol. Rather than advertise routes themselves, routers advertise information about their connected Layer 3 interfaces, also called links, and the cost (or metric) associated with that interface. These link-state advertisements (LSAs) propagate across participating routers. Routers use the advertisements to construct a topology of the network, consisting of all the known links, the routers connected to the links, and the associated costs. Using the topology, routers calculate their own lowest cost route to each destination subnet.

Link-state protocols such as OSPF tend to choose better routing paths and to converge faster than distance-vector protocols such as Routing Information Protocol (RIP).

## Basic OSPF setup

You will now review the basic steps for setting up OSPF, which are listed in Figure 5-1.

1. Enable OSPF.
2. Create an area.
3. Enable OSPF on VLAN interfaces and place in the area:
   - Enables the switch to find OSPF neighbors on the same subnet
   - Enables the switch to advertise the VLAN's subnet as a link

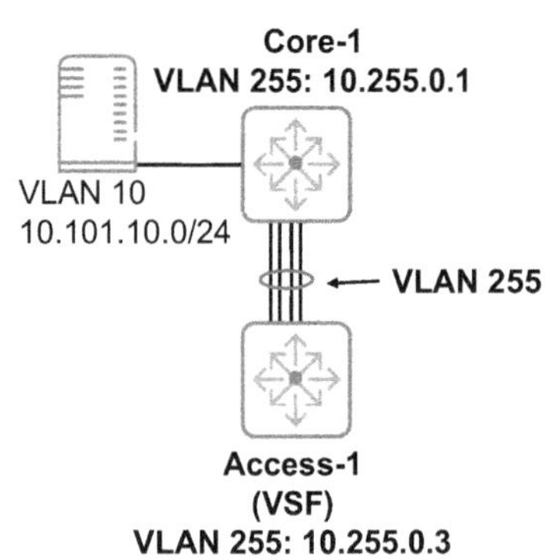


Figure 5-1 Basic OSPF setup

Of course, configuring OSPF to meet your organization's needs has many more nuances—many of which are covered in this chapter. However, these basic steps can get your AOS-Switches routing traffic across the network:

1. Enable OSPF.
2. Create an area.

   OSPF uses areas to segment the network into smaller, more manageable pieces and to enable route aggregation. For the initial configuration, you will simply use one area, area 1. You will then learn about multiple area solutions.

3. Enable OSPF on Layer 3 interfaces. For AOS-Switches, these are VLAN interfaces. Enabling OSPF on an interface has two effects.

   - The routing switch sends OSPF messages on the interface and can form neighbor relationships with other routers on the same interface. Neighbors that fully exchange their topology information are called fully adjacent.
   - The routing switch advertises this interface in OSPF. For example, if the interface is associated with IP address 10.255.0.1/24, the routing switch advertises that it has a link to 10.255.0.0/24.

   VLANs that need to be advertised in OSPF include:

   - Those that connect routing switches (like VLAN 255 on Access-1 and Core-1)
   - Those that support endpoints (like VLAN 10 on Core-1)

     If you are only enabling OSPF on the VLAN because you want to advertise its subnet, and you do not want the switch to form adjacencies with other routers or routing switches on the VLAN, configure the VLAN as a passive OSPF interface.

   When you enable OSPF on a VLAN, you also specify the VLAN's OSPF area. The area ID must match on all OSPF routing switches connected on the same VLAN or subnet.

An optional step, but one that you should typically perform is setting a router ID. The router ID does not have to be a valid IP address on the switch, but you often should use an IP address on a loopback interface.

After you complete these steps, your routing switches will automatically create a topology of your network and learn routes to every subnet within it. If a link fails, the routing switches inform each other of the change and learn new routes.

## Background information on OSPF

This section provides background material on basic OSPF concepts. You can use this section as a review or to increase your knowledge of OSPF by exploring how OSPF routers discover neighbors and advertise links in more depth.

## Router IDs

At various points, this explanation will refer to a routing switch's OSPF router ID. The router ID identifies the router uniquely within the OSPF system. As Figure 5-2 shows, this ID has the format of an IP address, and it can be an IP address on one of the routing device's interfaces. However, you can also set an ID manually, and this ID does not necessarily need to match an IP address on the router.

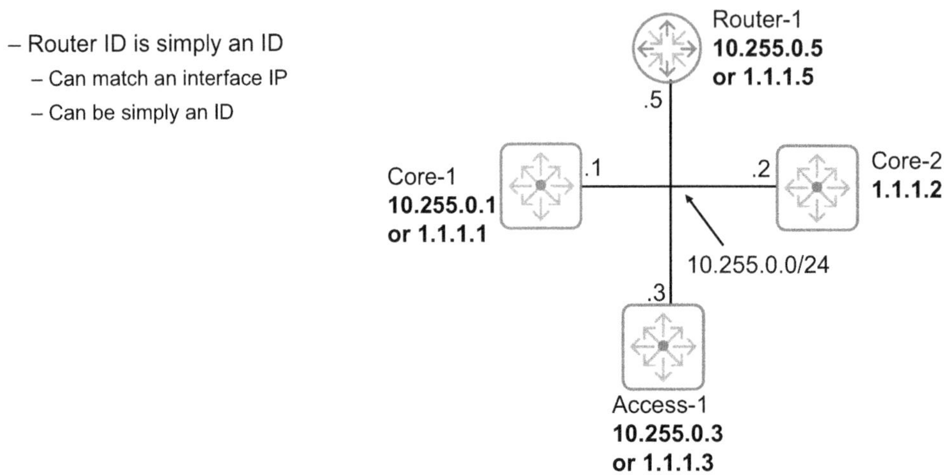


Figure 5-2 Router IDs

Figures 5-2 to 5-8 use a very simple topology in which the routers connect on a single shared subnet (for example, through a Layer 2 switch, which is not shown). Each router has a router ID that matches their IP address on that subnet. (For more complex topologies, you should consider setting the router ID to match a loopback interface ID. This ensures that the associated IP address is always reachable, even if some of the router's links fail.)

## Neighbors

Now, you will review how an OSPF router discovers its neighbors. The router sends out hellos on each OSPF interface. (An OSPF interface is a Layer 3 interface with an IP address on which OSPF is enabled. On AOS-Switches, the Layer 3 interface is a VLAN.) The hello includes information about the router's OSPF settings on the interface, as well as a list of neighbors discovered on the interface. The neighbor list is empty until the router receives hellos from neighbors. The hellos are destined to a multicast IP address, 224.0.0.5, the standard OSPF multicast address for all routers. Therefore, all other OSPF routers in the same subnet will hear the hello.

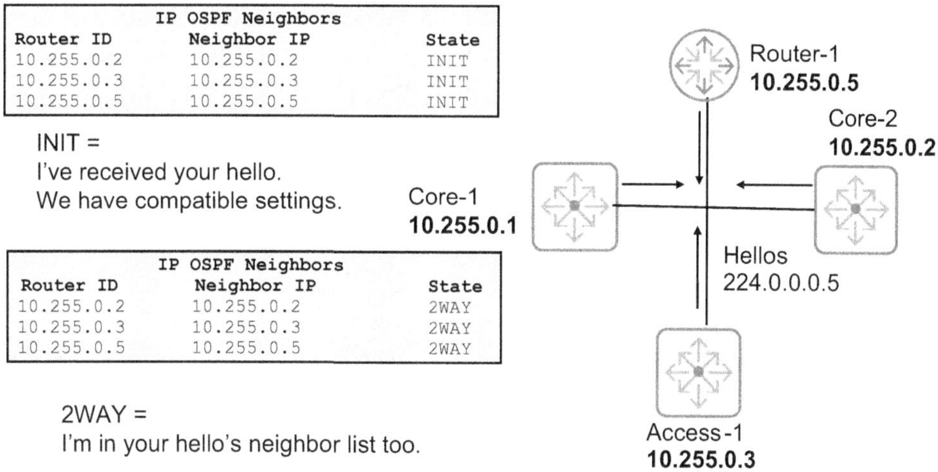


Figure 5-3 Neighbors

A receiving router checks the settings in the hello to make sure that they match its own settings on the interface. Table 5-1 presents the settings that must match for the router to accept the hello. Note that these settings might be mismatched initially or configuration changes might cause these settings to change after neighbors already have an established relationship. Routers continue to transmit hellos periodically, so the neighbor will receive the hello with the mismatched settings and remove the neighbor relationship.

But assuming that the settings match, the router adds the neighbor that sent the hello as an OSPF neighbor in the INIT state. It also adds the neighbor's router ID in the neighbor list included in its hellos. When an OSPF router receives a hello with its own ID in this list, it knows that it has bidirectional connectivity with the neighbor. It moves the neighbor to 2WAY state (see Figure 5-3).

Table 5-1 Settings that must match on OSPF neighbors

| Setting |
| --- |
| Network address and mask |
| Area ID |
| Area type (OSPF defines different types of areas covered in other training) |
| Authentication method and key if authentication is used |
| Network type |
| Hello timer |
| MTU (default on AOS-Switches is the standard Ethernet maximum 1500 bytes. You can increase the Maximum Transmission Unit [MTU] by enabling jumbo frames on the VLAN.) |

## Adjacency

The 2WAY state is sufficient for some OSPF neighbors. But an OSPF router must establish full adjacency with certain neighbors.

To achieve full adjacency, OSPF neighbors send unicasts to describe their databases to each other and exchange LSAs until their link-state databases (LSDBs) match. In this way, information about the complete topology spreads from neighbor to neighbor throughout the network.

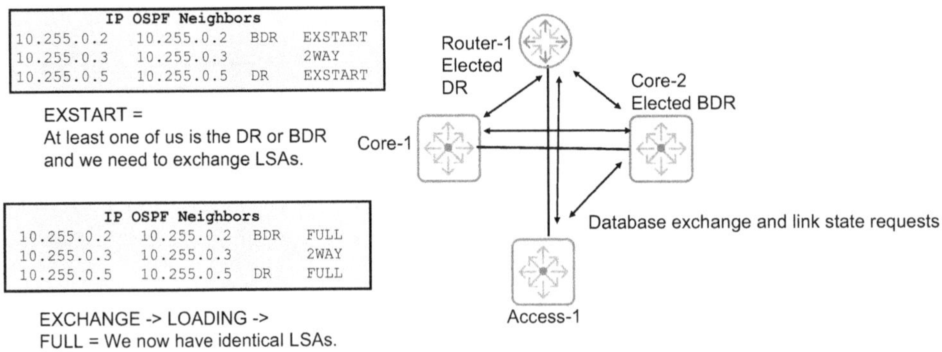


Figure 5-4 Adjacency

As Figure 5-4 shows, OSPF routers must establish full adjacency with:

- The single neighbor on a point-to-point interface
- The Designated Router (DR) and Backup Designated Router (BDR) of a broadcast or non-broadcast multi-access (NBMA) network

  The DR for a subnet running OSPF (called an OSPF link) is elected based on the priority advertised in the hello (higher priority value wins) and, in the case of a tie, higher router ID.

  When a link has many routers, the DR and BDR roles reduce the number of adjacencies on routers and allow routers to listen for Link State Updates (LSUs) from a single source. If an interface goes down and comes back up, the router can quickly achieve adjacency with just two routers. Although every router on a broadcast link does not necessarily achieve full adjacency, all routers still have identical LSDBs because everyone achieves full adjacency with the DR and BDR.

  An Enternet network such as a VLAN is an example of a broadcast network. However, you can design your network such that a VLAN acts more like a point-to-point link. When a link has only two routers, which devices take the DR and BDR role do not usually matter.

Table 5-2 lists the possible roles for OSPF routers on broadcast networks.

Periodic hellos (every 10 seconds, by default) maintain the 2WAY or FULL state. If the OSPF router misses for hellos from a neighbor, it moves the neighbor to down. You will learn about how OSPF routers detect that neighbors are down in more detail later.

Table 5-2 Roles for routers on broadcast networks

| Role | Description |
|---|---|
| Designated Router (DR) | Achieves adjacency with all other routers on the network<br>Advertises Type 2 (Network) LSAs<br>Receives Link State Updates (LSUs) from other routers (and sends its own LSUs)<br>Advertises LSUs on the all routers multicast address, 224.0.0.5 |
| Backup Designated Router (BDR) | Achieves adjacency with all other routers on the network<br>Receives LSUs from other routers (and sends its own LSUs to the DR)<br>Takes over other DR roles if the DR fails |
| Other | Achieves adjacency with the DR and BDR<br>Has 2WAY relationship with other routers<br>Sends LSUs to 224.0.0.6 (on which the DR and BDR listen) |

## LSAs

You will next review what is in the LSDB and how routers use that information to create a topology of the OSPF area.

An OSPF router generates a Router LSA, or Type 1 LSA, with information about its own OSPF networks, or links, and the cost of using those links. Figure 5-5 shows a summarized view of just some of the critical information in the LSA; the real LSA has many fields.

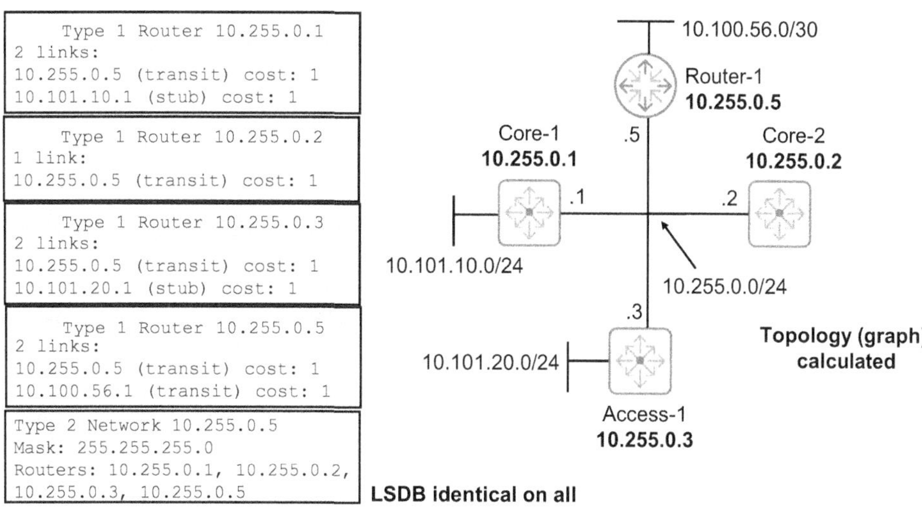


Figure 5-5 LSAs

The DR on a broadcast or NBMA transit network also generates a Network, or Type 2, LSA with information about all the routers on that network. This allows routers throughout the system to determine which routers are available on a network. A stub network, which is a network with just one OSPF router on it, does not require a Type 2 LSA. The Type 1 LSA of the single router on that network is enough to advertise the stub network's location.

The cost in an LSA generally relates to the bandwidth with higher bandwidth links having a lower cost. However, administrators can set the cost as they choose. The router labels itself as the advertising router for these LSAs, using its router ID.

For example, the routers shown in the Figure 5-5 have learned that:

- Core-1 (10.255.0.1) connects to:
  - 10.255.0.0/24 (same network as Router-1, Core-2, and Access-1)

    This transit link is identified by the IP address of the DR on the link, Router-1 in this example.
  - 10.101.10.0/24

    This stub link is identified by Core-1's own IP address on the link.
- Core-2 (10.255.0.2) connects to:
  - 10.255.0.0/24 (same network as Router-1, Core-1, and Access-1)
- Access-1 (10.255.0.3) connects to:
  - 10.255.0.0/24 (same network as Router-1, Core-1, and Core-2)
  - 10.101.20.0/24
- Router-1 (10.255.0.5) connects to:
  - 10.255.0.0/24 (same network as Core-1, Core-2, and Access-2)
  - 10.100.56.0/30

The DR in the transit broadcast network has also sent out network LSAs for the network indicating which routers connect to it.

Table 5-3 provides information about LSA types. You already learned about Type 1 and 2 LSAs. You will learn about LSA types 3 to 7 in the rest of this chapter.

Table 5-3 also lists extended or opaque LSAs, which enable features such as OSPF graceful restart and traffic engineering. Routers only advertise opaque LSAs to neighbors that indicate that they are opaque capable during adjacency establishment. You will learn about graceful restart later in this chapter. Other opaque LSAs are beyond the scope of this study guide. As presented in Table 5-3, some LSAs have special functions in OSPFv3, which is the OSPF version for IPv6 routing. OSPFv3 is also beyond the scope of this study guide.

Table 5-3 LSA types

| Type | Name | Information advertised | Advertised by | Scope |
|---|---|---|---|---|
| 1 | Router | The OSPF links on a routing device (transit and stub networks) | Each OSPF routing device | Area |
| 2 | Network | The routers on broadcast or NBMA networks | DR for the network | Area |
| 3 | Summary | Routes to networks (or aggregated ranges of networks) in another area (copied from or into the backbone area) | ABR | Area |
| 4 | ASBR | Route to an ASBR | ABR | All non-stub areas |
| 5 | External (or ASE) | Routes imported into OSPF from another routing protocol or method | ASBR | All non-stub areas |
| 6 | Multicast group membership<br>Not generally used | Multicast groups desired on this router's networks<br>Not generally used | Multicast OSPF capable router (DR in broadcast networks) | Area |
| 7 | NSSA external | Routes imported into OSPF from another routing protocol or method | ASBR | NSSA |
| 8 | Intra area prefix (OSPFv3 only) | OSPFv3, the network prefixes associated with stub and transit networks in Type 1 and 2 LSAs | Each OSPF routing device (that is capable) | Area (OSPFv3) |
| 9 | Opaque link-local | Extensions (such as graceful restart) | Each OSPF routing device (that is capable) | Link |
| 10 | Opaque area-local | Extensions (such as traffic engineering) | Each OSPF routing device (that is capable) | Area |
| 11 | Opaque AS | Extensions | ASBR (that is capable) | All non-stub areas |

## SPF algorithm

Within an OSPF area, the Type 1 and Type 2 LSAs give each router enough information to create a topology (sometimes called a directed graph) a bit like the one shown in Figure 5-6. That is, they know which routers connect to other routers by the links that they share, and they know which routers offer gateways to which stub networks, which are networks advertised by only that router.

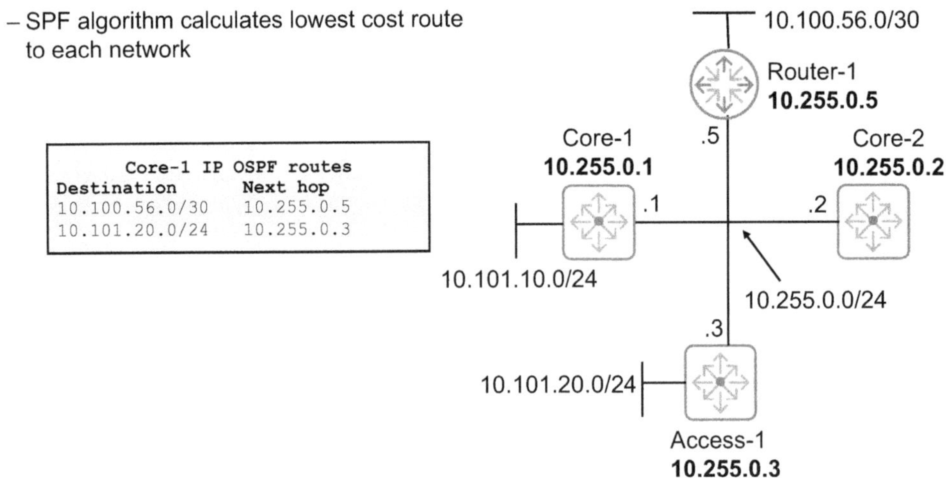


Figure 5-6 SPF algorithm

Each router then calculates the best route to each network—each advertised link—based on this topology. Specifically, they run the shortest path first (SPF), or Dijkstra, algorithm, which determines the lowest cost path between the router and the network. For example, in Figure 5-6, Core-1 has learned that it has a route to 10.100.56.0/30 through next hop 10.255.0.5 (the actual Router-1 IP address on the transit network, not the router ID, although they are the same in this instance). You will explore more complicated topologies with multiple possible paths later in this chapter.

## LSUs

LSAs have an age, and they age out of the database when the LSA reaches the max age (standard 1800 seconds). Routers periodically re-advertise the LSAs that they have generated to reset the age and maintain them. If a router needs to withdraw one of its LSAs, it can flush it from the system by re-advertising the LSA with an age set to the max age.

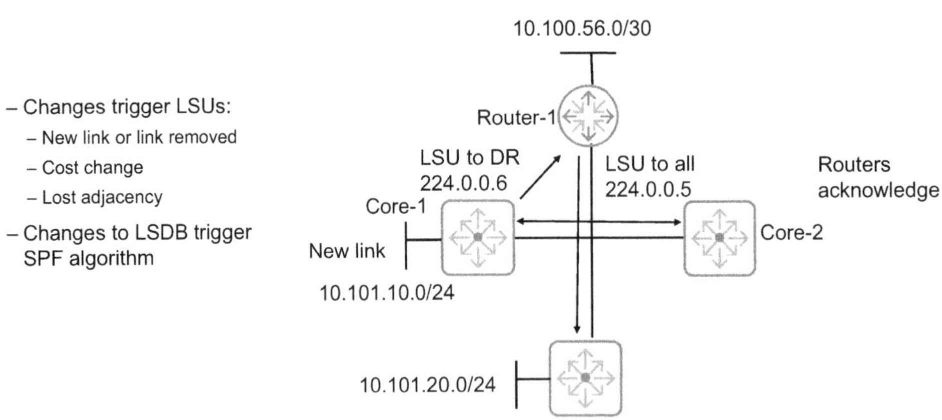


Figure 5-7 LSUs

But an LSA aging out is not the typical way that routers learn about changes to the topology; this would be far too slow. Instead, if a router needs to change information in one of its LSA, it sends an LSU and waits for an acknowledgment. For example, Core-1 in Figure 5-7 adds a new link to 10.101.10.0/24, so it adds that new link to its Type 1 (router) LSA and sends an LSU for that LSA. As you see Figure 5-7, the DR in a broadcast network is responsible for forwarding the information on the Ethernet network. In a larger system, the routers that receive the LSU would then flood it out on other OSPF interfaces until the LSU floods across the entire system.

If Router-1, the DR, lost adjacency with Access-1, it would update the Network LSA and send an LSU. Then the other routers would know that Access-1 is no longer available on the 10.255.0.0/24 subnet, and they could adjust routes accordingly.

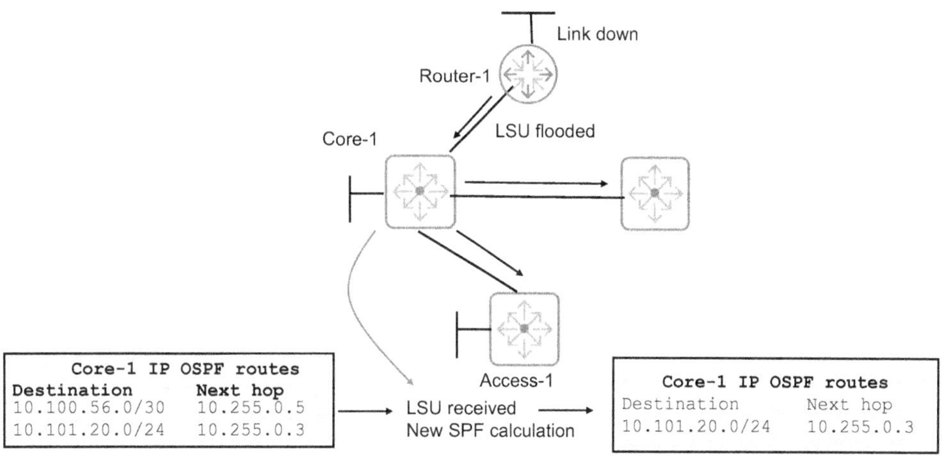


Figure 5-8 LSUs

Or, in another example, a stub link goes down on Router-1 (see Figure 5-8). The router updates its router LSA to indicate that it has fewer links. In this example, the system has a topology with multiple Layer 3 hops. Neighbors still flood the LSU between each other (and send acknowledgments) until the LSU propagates throughout the system. The routers also update the appropriate LSA in their LSDBs.

LSUs and changes to the LSDB trigger the router to rerun the SPF algorithm so that it can calculate new best routes. In the example shown in Figure 5-8, the change to the topology causes Core-1 to remove a route to a destination that is no longer available. In a more complex and redundant topology—such as the ones you will explore later—the router might find a new next hop for the route.

## Configure OSPF for a one area topology

You will now review the steps for setting up OSPF for a one area topology. To help you understand these configuration steps, you will review how to configure OSPF for a simple network, which is shown in Figure 5-9. In this example network, Access-1, Core-1, Core-2, and Router-1 are all on the 10.255.0.0/24 subnet. Router-1 is an HPE Comware router. (For information about HPE routers that run the Comware OS, visit http://www.hpe.com.) You will see the relevant running-config for this router, but you will not be provided with step-by-step configurations for it.

Note that this topology does not provide the redundancy recommended for a real-world network; it is a simplified topology for the purposes of illustration. You will learn more about adding redundant links later in this chapter.

Initially, Access-1, Core-1, Core-2, and Router-1 are not connected. The steps outlined in the "Enable OSPF" section will indicate when the switches become connected.

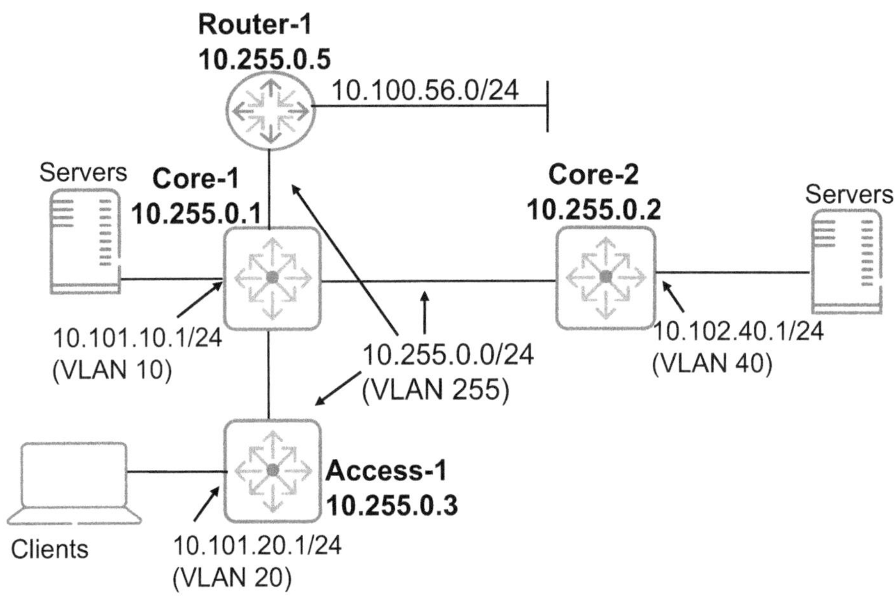


Figure 5-9 Example topology

### Router-1 partial configuration

The portion of the Router-1 configuration that is related to OSPF is shown below:

```
sysname Router-1
#
ospf 1 router-id 10.255.0.5
 area 0.0.0.1
  network 10.100.0.0 0.0.255.255
  network 10.255.0.0 0.0.0.255
#
interface GigabitEthernet1/0
ip address 10.100.56.1 255.255.255.0
#
interface GigabitEthernet2/0
 description To-Core-1
 ip address 10.255.0.5 255.255.255.0
 ospf dr-priority 200
```

### Enable OSPF

You will begin by enabling OSPF on the AOS-Switches and connecting the routing devices in VLAN 255 so that they can become OSPF neighbors.

*Core-1*

To enable OSPF and set the router ID on the Core-1 switch shown in Figure 5-9, complete the following steps:

1. Access the Core-1 terminal session and move to global configuration mode.
2. Create OSPF area 1.

   ```
   Core-1(config)# router ospf area 1
   ```

3. For this scenario, you want to use the 10.255.0.1 IP address as the router ID for Core-1. To set the ID manually, enter:

   ```
   Core-1(config)# ip router-id 10.255.0.1
   ```

4. Enable OSPF.

```
Core-1(config)# router ospf enable
```

5. Enable OSPF on VLAN 255 so Core-1 can establish neighbor relationships with other routing devices on the VLAN.

```
Core-1(config)# vlan 255 ip ospf
```

6. You can verify that OSPF is running on the interface with this command:

```
Core-1(config)# show ip ospf interface vlan 255
 OSPF configuration and statistics for VLAN 255

 OSPF Interface Status for 10.255.0.1
  IP Address       : 10.255.0.1          Status   : enabled
  Area ID          : 0.0.0.1
<-output omitted->
```

*Access-1*

7. Open a terminal session with Access-1 and move to global configuration mode context.
8. Configure OSPF area 1.

```
Access-1(config)# router ospf area 1
```

9. Set the router ID to 10.255.0.3.

```
Access-1(config)# ip router-id 10.255.0.3
```

10. Enable IP routing and OSPF globally.

```
Access-1(config)# ip routing
Access-1(config)# router ospf enable
```

11. Enable OSPF on VLAN 255.

```
Access-1(config)# vlan 255 ip ospf
```

*Core-2*

12. Open a terminal session with Core-2 and move to global configuration mode context.
13. Configure OSPF area 1.

```
Core-2(config)# router ospf area 1
```

14. Set the router ID to 10.255.0.2.

```
Core-2(config)# ip router-id 10.255.0.3
```

15. Enable IP routing and OSPF globally.

```
Core-2(config)# ip routing
Core-2(config)# router ospf enable
```

16. Enable OSPF on VLAN 255.

```
Core-2(config)# vlan 255
Core-2(vlan-255)# ip ospf
```

17. In this scenario, you want Core-2 to have a higher priority for becoming elected DR. Set the priority with this command:

```
Core-2(vlan-255)# ip ospf priority 200
Core-2(vlan-255)# exit
```

You will now connect all of the devices as shown in Figure 5-9.

*Core-1*

18. Access-1, Core-1, Core-2, and Router-1 should now become OSPF neighbors on VLAN 255, as shown in the output below:

```
Core-1(config)# show ip ospf neighbor

 OSPF Neighbor Information

  Router ID   Pri  IP Address  NbIfState  State   QLen   Events  Status
  ----------  ---  ----------  ---------  ------  -----  ------  -----
  10.255.0.2  200  10.255.0.2  BDR        FULL    0      6       None
  10.255.0.3  1    10.255.0.3             2WAY    0      8       None
  10.255.0.5  200  10.255.0.5  DR         FULL    0      7       None
```

19. You can see more detailed information about a neighbor with this command:

```
Core-1(config)# show ip ospf neighbor 10.255.0.2
 OSPF Neighbor Information for neighbor 10.255.0.2

  IP Address   : 10.255.0.2
  Router ID    : 10.255.0.2   State                      : FULL
  Interface    : vlan-255     Designated Router          : 10.255.0.5
  Area         : 0.0.0.1      Backup Designated Router   : 10.255.0.2
  Priority     : 1            Retransmit Queue Length    : 0
  Options      : 0x42         Neighbor Uptime            : 0h:0m:34s
  Events       : 6            Dead Timer Expires         : 36 sec
```

20. The output shows that the routing devices on VLAN 255 1 have automatically discovered each other. They did so by sending hellos. You can also see that:
    - VLAN 255 has a DR and BDR. Router-1 is the DR, and Core-2 is now the BDR.
    - Core-1 achieves full adjacency with only the DR and BDR. It has a 2WAY status with Access-1.
    - The state for this neighbor is Full, which means that Access-1 and Core-2 have achieved full adjacency. They have exchanged all LSAs in their database with each other.
21. Think about what you learned earlier to explain why Router-1 became DR.

    When you first enable OSPF on a broadcast interface such as a VLAN, the interface enters a waiting period during which it listens for hellos indicating the current DR and BDR. If the network does not already have devices fulfilling these roles or if different devices' hellos indicate different DRs and BDRs, an election is held. Router-1 and Core-2 tie for the highest priority. Router-1 has the higher IP address. Therefore, Router-1 became DR.

## Advertise VLAN 10, 20, and 30 and explore LSA updates (LSUs)

As you learned earlier, OSPF routers send each other topology information in LSAs.

You will now add VLAN 10 as another OSPF interface on Core-1 in the network topology shown in Figure 5-10. For illustrative purposes, the steps will show how the LSU for this new link propagates across the system. (Enabling the debug messages and viewing the LSA is not part of the typical configuration process). You will also configure Access-1 to advertise the 10.101.20.0/24 subnet by enabling OSPF on this interface and Core-2 to advertise VLAN 30.

While you complete this configuration, you will view the associated LSUs. You will then see the routes that the OSPF routing devices have learned.

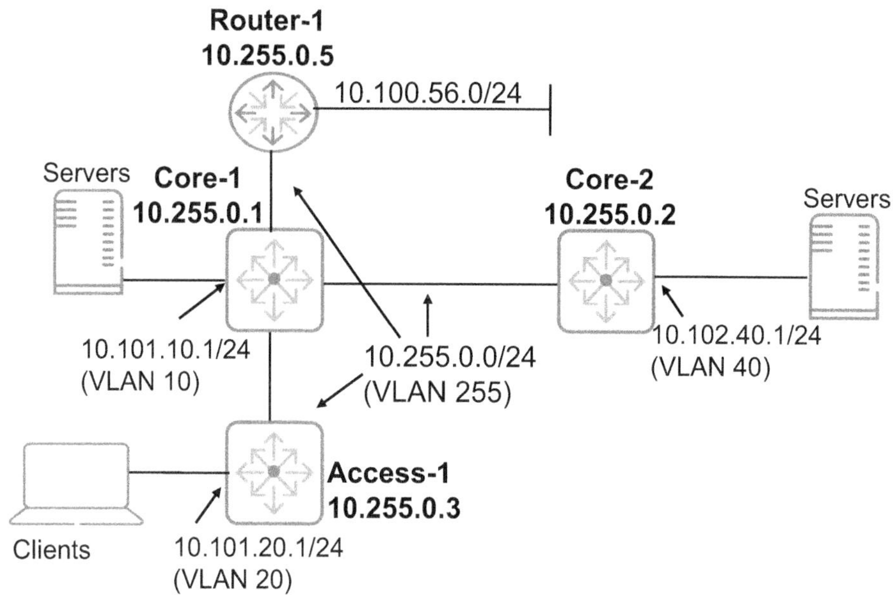


Figure 5-10 Configure OSPF for a one area topology

*Access-1*

22. Access the Access-1 terminal session.
23. Enable debugging of OSPF LSUs and set the debugging destination to the terminal session.

```
Access-1(config)# debug ip ospf packet lsu
Access-1(config)# debug destination session
```

*Core-1*

24. Access the Core-1 terminal session.
25. Enable debugging of OSPF LSUs and set the debugging destination to the terminal session.

```
Core-1(config)# debug ip ospf packet lsu
Core-1(config)# debug destination session
```

26. For the purposes of this scenario, assume that Core-1 already has VLAN 10 configured on it with IP address 10.101.10.0/24. It connects to several devices in this VLAN and acts as the default router for it.
27. Enable OSPF on VLAN 10. Enable it in passive mode because Core-1 is the only router on this interface, and it does not need to establish adjacency with any other routers.

```
Core-1(config)# vlan 10 ip ospf passive
```

28. Example output on Core-1, showing how Core-1 begins to advertise this new link, is shown below:

```
0000:01:30:47.14 OSPF eRouteCtrl:OSPF SEND: 10.255.0.1 -> 224.0.0.6: Version 2,
   Type LS Update (4), Length 76 ret 96
0000:01:30:47.27 OSPF eRouteCtrl:    Router ID 10.255.0.1, Area 0.0.0.1,
   Authentication <None> (0)
0000:01:30:47.38 OSPF eRouteCtrl:     Authentication data: 00000000 00000000
0000:01:30:47.45 OSPF eRouteCtrl:     Number of Link State: 1:
0000:01:30:47.52 OSPF eRouteCtrl:     LS RTR:10.255.0.1 [10.255.0.1] Age 0 Sequence
   8000000e CkSum e486 Length 48 Options <E DC> (22)
0000:01:30:47.72 OSPF eRouteCtrl:     Type TRANS (2) ID 10.255.0.5 Data 10.255.0.1
   NbTOS 0 Cost 1
0000:01:30:47.82 OSPF eRouteCtrl:    Type STUB (3) ID 10.101.10.0 Data
   255.255.255.0 NbTOS 0 Cost 1
0000:01:30:47.93 OSPF eRouteCtrl:OSPF RECV: 10.255.0.5 -> 224.0.0.5: Version 2,
   Type LS Update (4), Length 76 ret 0
<output omitted>
```

29. Turn debugging off.

```
Core-1(vlan-10)# exit
Core-1(config)# no debug ip ospf
```

*Access-1*

30. Example output on Access-1 is shown below.

```
0000:06:44:57.77 OSPF eRouteCtrl:OSPF RECV: 10.255.0.5 -> 224.0.0.5: Version 2,
   Type LS Update (4), Length 76 ret 0
0000:06:44:57.77 OSPF eRouteCtrl:    Router ID 10.255.0.5, Area 0.0.0.1,
   Authentication <None> (0)
0000:06:44:57.77 OSPF eRouteCtrl:   Authentication data: 00000000 00000000
0000:06:44:57.77 OSPF eRouteCtrl:   Number of Link State: 1:
0000:06:44:57.77 OSPF eRouteCtrl:   LS RTR:10.255.0.1 [10.255.0.1] Age 1 Sequence
   8000000e CkSum e486 Length 48 Options <E DC> (22)
0000:06:44:57.77 OSPF eRouteCtrl:   bits 0x0 <> #links 2:
0000:06:44:57.77 OSPF eRouteCtrl:   Type TRANS (2) ID 10.255.0.5 Data 10.255.0.1
   NbTOS 0 Cost 1
0000:06:44:57.77 OSPF eRouteCtrl:    Type STUB (3) ID 10.101.10.0 Data
   255.255.255.0 NbTOS 0 Cost 1
```

31. Turn debugging off.

```
Access-1(config)# no debug ip ospf
```

32. You are now ready to advertise VLAN 20, 10.101.20.0/24, on Access-1. Again, assume that Access-1 already connects to devices in VLAN 20, has IP address 10.101.20.1/24 on this VLAN, and acts as the default router for it.

```
Access-1(config)# vlan 20
Access-1(vlan-20)# ip ospf passive
```

*Core-2*

33. Follow the same steps on Core-2, which already connects to devices in VLAN 40, has IP address 10.102.40.1/24 on this VLAN, and acts as the default router for it.

```
Core-2(config)# vlan 40
Core-2(vlan-40)# ip ospf passive
```

*Router-1*

34. Although you did not track it, Access-1 and Core-2 sent LSUs adding their new OSPF subnets to their Router LSAs. The command output below shows how Router-1 (as well as other devices) has learned routes to the subnets behind the other routers.

    Core-1 is the next hop for 10.101.10.0/24, Access-1 is the next hop for 10.101.20.0/24, and Core-2 is the next hop for 10.102.40.0/24.

```
<Router-1> display ospf routing

OSPF Process 1 with Router ID 10.255.0.5

                 Routing Table


Routing for network

Destination      Cost   Type      NextHop      AdvRouter    Area

10.255.0.0/24    1      Transit   0.0.0.0      10.255.0.5   0.0.0.1

10.101.10.0/24   2      Stub      10.255.0.1   10.255.0.1   0.0.0.1

10.100.56.0/24   1      Stub      0.0.0.0      10.255.0.5   0.0.0.1

10.101.20.0/24   2      Stub      10.255.0.3   10.255.0.3   0.0.0.1

10.102.40.0/24   2      Stub      10.255.0.2   10.255.0.2   0.0.0.1

Total nets: 5

Intra area: 5  Inter area: 0  ASE: 0  NSSA: 0
```

## Consider a topology with a dedicated VLAN per link

The topology in the configuration example outlined in the previous section extended VLAN 255 across multiple routing switch links so that you could examine a network with multiple OSPF routers. Often, though, it is better practice to dedicate a separate VLAN and subnet to each link between routing devices, as shown in Figure 5-11. Doing so ties the status of the OSPF interface to the physical link status, which enables faster convergence in redundant topologies, as you will explore in more detail later.

This topology also enables you to avoid running spanning tree on the links between routers. When every switch-to-switch link has a VLAN and subnet dedicated to it, there are no loops in the broadcast domain, and spanning tree is not required. (The VLANs could be tagged on the links, or but they could be untagged. As long as the tagging, or lack of tagging, matches on both sides of the link and every link has a unique VLAN, it does not matter.)

This VLAN design lets the routing protocol handle failover rather than spanning tree as well as the routing protocol, which could slow down convergence. The design also ensures that the status of the link corresponds with the status of the Layer 3 VLAN. If the link goes down, the OSPF interface goes down immediately, so failover can occur quickly.

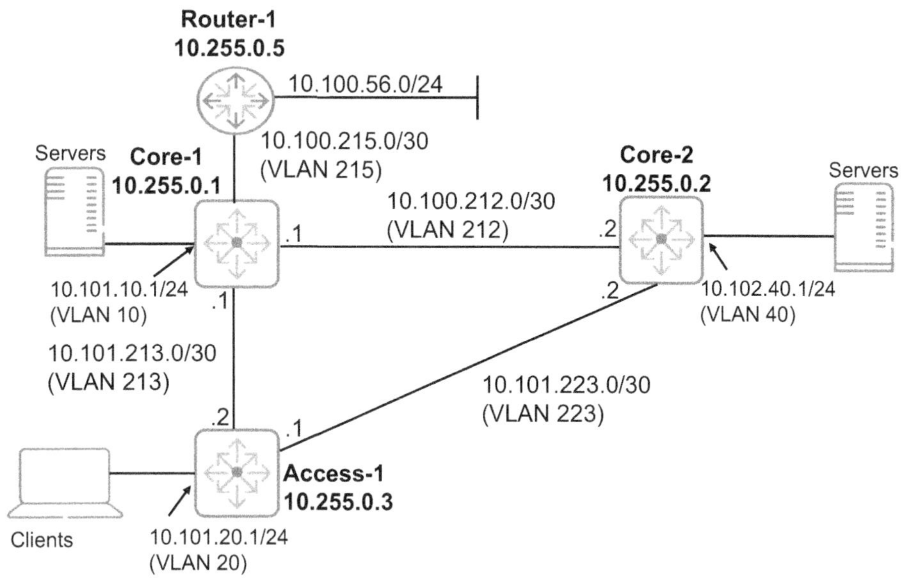


Figure 5-11 Topology with dedicated VLANs per link

## Review basic OSPF concepts

You will now take a few minutes to review basic OSPF concepts before you consider a more complex OSPF topology. You will find answers to these questions in the "Answers" section at the end of this chapter.

### Neighbors and adjacency

1. How do OSPF neighbors discover each other? Which settings must match in order for neighbors to establish a relationship?
2. Which type of OSPF network is an AOS-Switch's VLAN interface?
3. A broadcast network or an NBMA network can support multiple OSPF routers, one of which is the DR and one of which is the BDR. How are the routers with these roles selected?
4. Which routers in a broadcast network establish adjacencies with each other?

### Router IDs

5. How does an OSPF router determine its router ID if it is not set manually?
6. Does the router ID have to match an IP address on the router?
7. If you do use an IP address on the router for the router ID, what type of interface is recommended for supporting the address?

### LSAs, SPF algorithm, and LSUs

8. How do OSPF routers learn routes within an OSPF area? (Hint: Do they learn specific routes, or do they calculate them?)
9. Describe a router LSA (a Type 1 LSA). What information does it contain, and which OSPF routers transmit them?
10. Describe a network LSA (a Type 2 LSA). What information does it contain, and which OSPF routers transmit them?
11. A router might run OSPF on a network for which it is the only router. How does a router identify such a network in a Type 1 LSA? Does the router transmit a Type 2 LSA for that network?
12. A routing switch is running OSPF and is part of an OSPF AS. The network administrator configures a new VLAN on the switch, connects interfaces in the VLAN, and enables OSPF on it. What does the switch do to advertise the network? How is the LSU propagated? (Assume that all OSPF routers are in the same area.)
13. How does a router calculate the cost for an intra-area OSPF route? What is the default metric for a VLAN interface on an AOS-Switch?
14. What other types of changes can cause a router to generate an LSU?
15. What does receiving an LSU trigger an OSPF router to do?

## OSPF multi-area overview

You will now learn about dividing OSPF ASs into multiple areas. In addition to learning how to establish multiple areas, you will learn *why* you would want to do so. You will explore the differences between intra-areas OSPF routes and inter-area OSPF routes, as well as the LSAs that help to propagate routing information across the area boundaries.

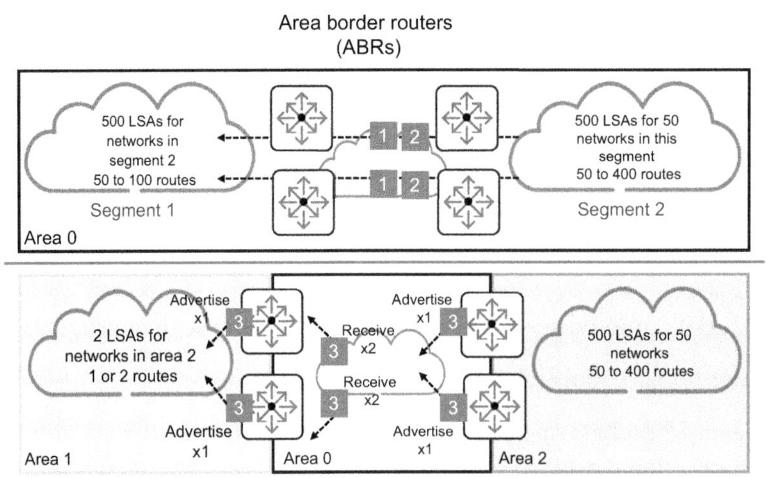


Figure 5-12 OSPF multi-area overview

Figure 5-12 shows an OSPF network, which consists of two segments, Segment 1 and Segment 2. These segments might be a campus LAN and a data center, a campus LAN and a large branch office, buildings in a large three tier-campus topology, or any other segments within a larger network. Segment 1 and Segment 2 each represent many routing switches, which ultimately connect to two core routing switches. These core routing switches connect through a network backbone, which might also include more routers and routing switches. Figure 5-12 shows only two segments for simplicity, but a large enterprise network might have several such segments.

Every OSPF router in an area must maintain LSAs from every other router in the area in its LSDB. Figure 5-12 shows how a single-area implementation forces each of these Type 1 and 2 LSAs to propagate across the system. In addition, Figure 5-12 only shows LSAs associated with Segment 2. Each OSPF routing device would also maintain LSAs for routers and networks in Segment 1 and the backbone.

As a domain grows, the LSDB becomes excessively large and difficult to process. The shortest path algorithm also becomes complicated, and the OSPF routing switch must dedicate valuable processing resources to running it. Often this resource consumption comes with little value. As shown in Figure 5-12, networks often feature aggregation such that one segment connects to another through a few core devices. With only two exit points from Segment 1 towards Segment 2, the routing switches in Segment 1 have no reason to maintain so much granular information about networks in Segment 2.

Modern routers and routing switches often do have the power to handle large LSDBs and many calculations. However, there is no reason to burden the devices, network administrators, and support staff with the large, complex LSDBs and routing tables when most of the routes will use the same one or two next hops.

In addition, suppose that two routing switches in Segment 2 provide a connection to the subnet A. One of those switches has a flapping interface. It loses its connection to subnet A and sends an LSU withdrawing that subnet from its list of links. Every routing switch in the network backbone and Segment 1 receives this LSU, adjusts the LSDB, and reruns the Dijkstra algorithm on the topology. However, these routers still reach subnet A through the same core routing switches. When the flapping interface comes back up, the switch sends another LSU, which propagates throughout the entire network, causing every OSPF router to recalculate shortest paths, again without any significant change.

OSPF areas segment the domain into more stable and manageable pieces. Each OSPF routing device maintains the LSDB and runs the shortest path algorithm only for its own areas. OSPF routers called area border routers (ABRs) forward information necessary for routing between areas. As you see in Figure 5-12, the ABRs act as bottlenecks for LSAs. Type 1 and Type 2 LSAs do not flow across area boundaries. You will also learn about the Type 3 LSAs that do flow between areas in this chapter.

In the simplest configuration, a multi-area design decreases LSDB size dramatically and increases stability—routers do not have to rerun the shortest path algorithm as often—but does not greatly affect the number of routes. OSPF, however, provides options for further optimizing the LSDB and routing table sizes. As you will see, you can aggregate advertisements of networks in between areas, simplifying the routing table. You can also control routes at this boundary, filtering them if you so desire. These benefits still apply even for powerful routers that could support very large areas.

## ABRs

In the "OSPF multi-area overview" section, you saw how each OSPF area defines an isolated region beyond which Type 1 and Type 2 LSAs and shortest path topologies do not extend. However, some routing information must flow between the areas. ABRs are responsible for forwarding this information.

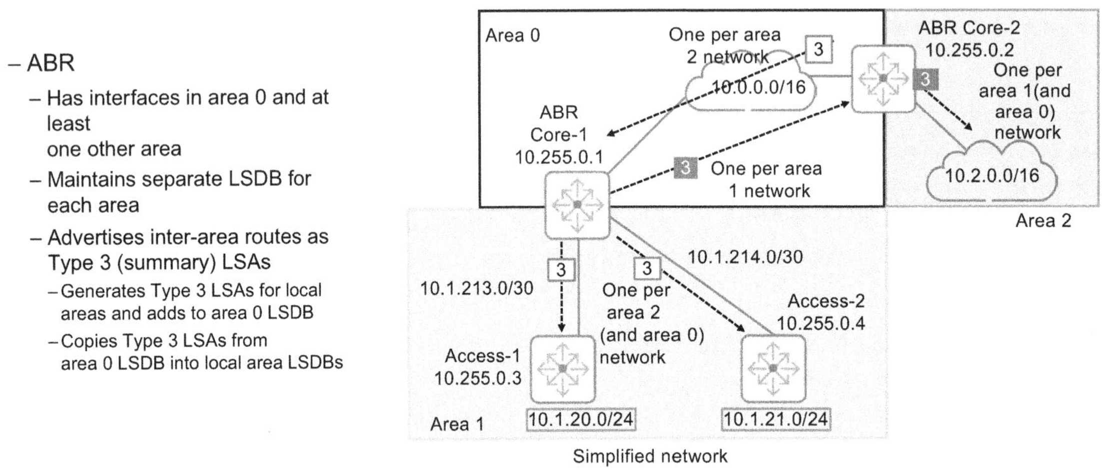


Figure 5-13 ABRs

ABRs have interfaces in at least two areas, one of which is area 0 (see Figure 5-13). Area 0 is the backbone area, and OSPF design requires all areas to connect to this backbone (you will explore an exception later in this chapter).

As a member of multiple areas, the ABR maintains multiple LSDBs, one for each area. In the example shown in Figure 5-13, Core-1 is an ABR. It synchronizes Type 1 and Type 2 LSAs with other OSPF routing devices in area 1. Figure 5-13 shows just two other routing devices, Access-1 and Access-2, for simplicity, but in the real world, the area would usually have many more routing devices. Access-1 and Access-2 reside entirely within area 1 and are called internal routers. Core-1, Access-1, and Access-2 have identical area 1 LSDBs.

The ABR follows the same process in area 0, exchanging Type 1 and Type 2 LSAs and synchronizing its area 0 LSDB with routers such as Router-1 and Core-2.

In each area, the ABR also creates Type 3, or summary LSAs, which advertise routes that it knows in *other* areas. The sections that follow elaborate on how the ABR conducts this advertisement.

### Type 3 LSAs generated in area 0

The ABR creates a Type 3, or summary LSA, for each network in *area 1*. It places these Type 3 LSAs in its LSDB for *area 0*. The ABR can then advertise its routes to area 1 networks to other routers in area 0.

For example, Core-1 shown in Figure 5-13 has an inter-area route to 10.101.20.0/24. It learned about this network from Access-1's Type 1 LSA, contained in its area 1 LSDB. From that LSDB, Core-1 was able to generate an *intra-area* route to 10.101.20.0/24. ABR-A generates a Type 3 LSA for 10.101.20.0/24 and places the Type 3 LSA in its area 0 LSDB. Other area 0 routers, such as Core-2, receive Core-1's Type 3 LSA and add it to their area 0 LSDB. They can then calculate an inter-area route to 10.101.20.0/24.

In addition to the network address, the Type 3 LSA includes a metric, which enables routers to select the best inter-area route when multiple ABRs advertise a Type 3 LSA with the same network ID. (You will learn more about influencing the inter-area route calculation later in this chapter.)

### Type 3 LSAs generated in non-backbone areas

Core-1 shown in Figure 5-13 also generates Type 3 LSAs to advertise into non-backbone areas.

First, just as Core-1 advertised a Type 3 LSA for each area 1 network to routers in area 0, the ABR advertises a Type 3 LSA for each area 0 network to routers in area 1.

The ABR also advertises a Type 3 LSA for each *inter-area* route that it has learned from Type 3 LSAs advertised by other ABRs in area 0. For example, Core-2 shown in Figure 5-13 has generated Type 3 LSAs for each network in area 2 and advertised them in area 0. Using these LSAs, Core-1 has calculated an inter-area route to each area 2 network. Now, Core-1 generates Type 3 LSAs for these routes and advertises them in area 1, using the metric in the routing table. (It does *not* advertise these LSAs in area 0 because the inter-area routes' next hops are in area 0. The original ABR, which always resides in area 0, has already advertised these LSAs in area 0.)

If Core-1 shown in Figure 5-13 connected to another area, such as area 3, it would place Type 3 LSAs for each area 3 intra-area route in the area 0 LSDB and the area 1 LSDB. In other words, for each area, an ABR creates Type 3 LSAs with routes to *other* areas to which the ABR connects. Remember, though, that the inter-area routes always pass through area 0 even if the same ABR supports multiple non-backbone areas. That is, you cannot configure an OSPF router with area 1 and area 3 and expect the router to advertise area 3 networks in area 1 and area 1 networks in area 3. The router must have interfaces in area1, area 3, *and* area 0.

Figure 5-13 shows how internal routing switches Access-1 and Access-2 in area 1 receive the Type 3 LSAs for area 0 and area 2. Note that, although area 1 routers learn routes to area 2, the Type 3 LSAs themselves do not cross area boundaries. Instead, Core-2, connected to area 2 and area 0, generates Type 3 LSAs for area 2 in area 0. It is the advertising router for these LSAs. Core-1 receives these LSAs in area 0 and generates *new* Type 3 LSAs for advertising these routes into area 1, and it is the advertising router for these new LSAs.

## Need for route aggregation between areas

Simply dividing an AS into multiple areas begins to decrease the size of OSPF routers' LSDBs and to reduce the complexity of SPF calculations. However, to achieve the true benefits of multiple areas, you should further reduce the number of LSAs advertised between areas.

In the example network shown in Figure 5-14, both area 1 and area 2 have only two exits toward the network backbone and other areas. Internal area 1 routers and backbone routers might benefit from some level of detail in the information that they receive about area 2. For example, each ABR's Type 3 LSAs reflect the metrics of reaching the network in question, enabling routers in other areas to select the best ABR for reaching each network in area 2.

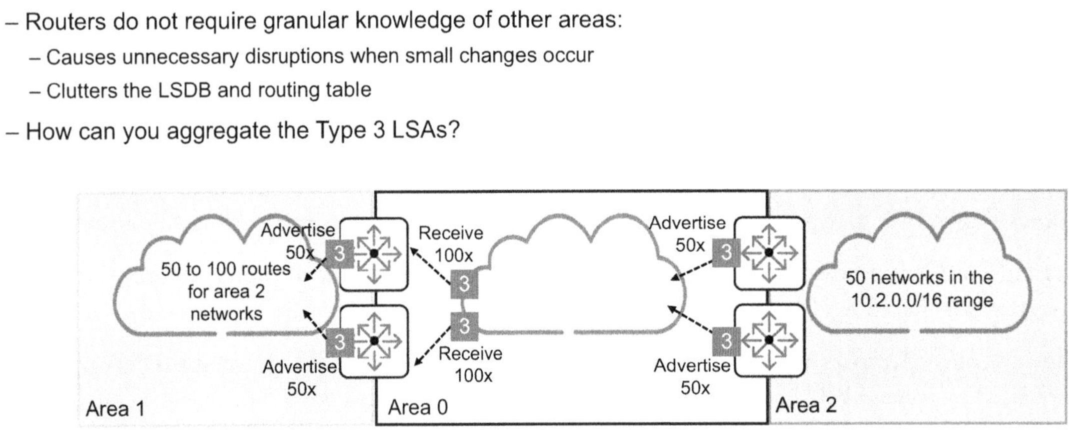


Figure 5-14 Need for route aggregation between areas

However, with only two entry points into area 2, routers (and, in particular, internal area 1 routers) are probably receiving too granular an amount of information about every subnet. This information clutters the routers' LSDB and routing tables.

In addition, small changes in the area 2 topology shown in Figure 5-14 could flood LSUs through the backbone and area 1, causing routers to rerun the SPF algorithm. For example, network 10.102.40.0/24 in area 2 becomes unavailable. The two area 2 ABRs withdraw their Type 3 LSA for that specific network in area 0, and then the two area 1 ABRs do the same in area 1. However, the area 1 routers have no other path to this network. It might be simpler not to inform routers beyond area 2 of the small change. If they continue to forward traffic for this network, the area 2 ABRs simply drop it.

You need to aggregate the Type 3 LSAs to hide the unnecessary information and to smooth over small changes, thereby gaining the true benefits of a multiple area OSPF configuration.

---

**Note**

Although the example shown in Figure 5-14 focuses on aggregating advertisements for area 2 networks, you would aggregate summaries of area 1 or area 0 networks for similar reasons.

---

## Aggregating summaries

You can configure an ABR to aggregate its summary routes. Rather than generate a Type 3 LSA for every network in an area, it generates a few Type 3 LSAs, each of which includes many networks in its range. In other words, the Type 3 LSA advertises a network with a shorter prefix length such as a /20 or a /16 subnet that includes many /24 subnets.

You configure the area summaries on the ABR that connects to the area for which you aggregating the summaries. For example, in the network shown in Figure 5-15, you configure area summaries for area 2 on the two ABRs on the right.

These ABRs then advertise the summaries to other backbone routers and ABRs in area 0. The other ABRs can then copy them into their own areas. In the example shown in Figure 5-15, the aggregated summary 10.102.0.0/16 shows up as a route on ABR A and on internal routing switches in area 1.

If you create area summaries for area 1 on the ABRs shown on the left in Figure 5-15, those summaries aggregate area 1 networks. The area 1 ABRs advertise them into area 0 and other ABRs re-advertise them into area 2.

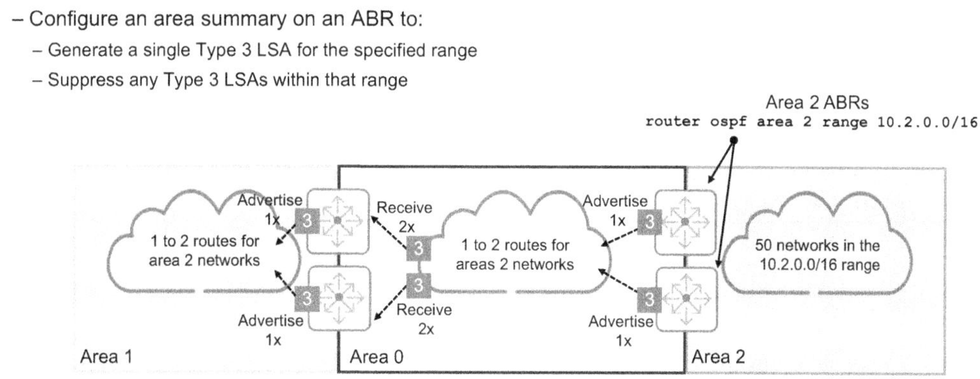


Figure 5-15 Aggregating summaries

Figure 5-15 shows how area summaries drastically reduce the number of LSAs associated with area 2. In this example, a single summary includes all of the networks in the area.

You enter the AOS-Switch command for creating this area summary in the OSPF configuration mode context:

```
Switch(ospf)# area 2 range 10.102.0.0/16 [type summary cost metric]
```

When you enter this command, the ABR automatically suppresses the generation of individual Type 3 LSAs for subnets within the specified network. However, it *continues* to advertise individual Type 3 LSAs for networks that do not fall into the range. This is why it is recommended to assign an area contiguous IP addresses within a binary block. Then you can easily aggregate the routes.

In Figure 5-15, the ABRs for area 1 now receive *one* Type 3 LSA with the aggregated summary from *each* of the two ABRs that connect to area 2. Each area 1 ABR selects the best LSA for the summary range and creates an inter-area route to 10.102.0.0/16 through the best next-hop.

Each area 1 ABR then generates an area 1 Type 3 LSA to advertise this inter-area route to routers in area 1. The internal area 1 routers now have two LSAs for all area 2 networks, and they learn routes to only the one aggregated network (up to two routes if the ABRs advertise equal metrics and the internal routers support Equal-Cost Multi-Path [ECMP]).

Usually, you want to create as few area summaries as possible. Sometimes, though, you need to create more summaries. For example, areas might have grown organically and without advance planning, creating noncontiguous ranges or ranges that do not fit neatly within a CIDR subnet. For example, area 2 might include networks in the 10.102.0.0-10.102.255.255 range as well as 10.103.20.0-10.103.23.255. Area 3 includes networks in the 10.103.0.0-10.103.19.255 range and the 10.103.30.0-10.103.39.255 range. You cannot simply use 10.102.0.0/15 for the area 2 summary and 10.103.0.0/16 for the area 3 summary, due to the noncontiguous and overlapping ranges. Instead, you would need to use several area summaries for area 2 and several summaries for area 3.

**Important**

Examples throughout this chapter use the /16 prefix length for summary ranges to illustrate the concept in a simple way. When you create a range for your area, choose an appropriate range. For example, your area might include 16 /24 subnets, 10.1.0.0/24 to 10.1.15.0/24. This is equal to the 10.1.0.0/20 network, and you should specify that in the **area <ID> range** command.

## Area 1 routers' routing tables

After you configure area summaries on an area's ABR, you can see the summaries in the routing tables for routers *not* connected to that area.

Below you see the route to 10.102.0.0/16 for an internal router in area 1. Other routes have been removed for clarity. As you see, the internal router has learned the route through the ABR.

```
Access-1# show ip route

                                IP Route Entries

Destination     Gateway         VLAN  Type     Sub-Type    Metric    Dist.
--------------- ------------ ---- ------- ---------- -------- -----
10.102.0.0/16  10.101.213.1  1213  ospf     InterArea   3         110
```

## Area 1 routers' LSDB

Below are examples of Type 3 LSAs associated with the aggregated summary route. You can see the summary LSAs for the aggregated area 2 routes on an internal router in area 1. Note that the LSAs are associated with area *1* (not 2 or 0) because the area 1 ABR generated new summary LSAs for this area. The advertising router is the area 1 ABR (but the original aggregation was configured on the area 2 ABR).

```
InternalArea1# show ip ospf link-state type summary

 OSPF Link State Database for Area 0.0.0.1

                                  Advertising
  LSA Type  Link State ID  Router ID   Age  Sequence #  Checksum
  --------- -------------- ----------- ---- ----------- --------
  Summary   10.102.0.0     10.255.0.1  888  0x8000000a  0x00000d9e

InternalArea1# show ip ospf link-state detail type summary


 OSPF Link State Database for Area 0.0.0.1
LSA Age                           : 1235
LSA Type                          : 0x3 (Summary)
Advertising Router                : 10.255.0.1
Link State ID                     : 10.102.0.0
LSA Sequence                      : 0x80000007
LSA Checksum                      : 0x139b
LSA Option Bits                   : E=1 MC=0 N/P=0 EA=0 DC=0
LSA Metric                        : 2
Network Mask                      : 255.255.0.0
```

## Filtering inter-area routes

Remember that failing to configure an area summary for a specific range makes the routing switch continue to advertise the individual routes. If you want to *stop* advertisement of certain routes to certain networks entirely, you must configure a nonadvertised area summary on the ABR.

For example, suppose a company has a strict security policy for one of the sites that makes up OSPF area 2 (see Figure 5-16). The policies allow only local access to high-security subnets 10.102.128.0/17; devices in other areas can reach subnets 10.102.0.0/17. Of course, a firewall can filter out prohibited traffic, but, in this case, you want to prevent any routing of traffic from other areas to the restricted networks.

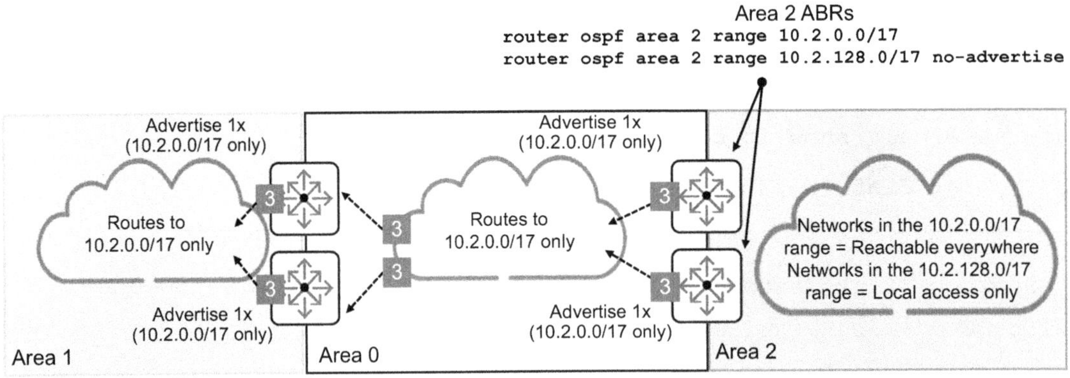


Figure 5-16 Filtering inter-area routes

Therefore, you configure two area summaries on the area 2 ABRs shown in Figure 5-16—one for 10.102.0.0/17 and one for 10.102.128.0/17. ABRs advertise the first but not the second.

Note that the filtering occurs at the area 2 boundary; you cannot apply the filtering to some areas and not others. For example, you *cannot* use this configuration to block inter-area routes to the area 2 subnets in area 1 but allow them in area 0.

The commands for configuring this example are:

```
Core-2(config)# router ospf
Core-2(ospf)# area 2 range 10.102.0.0/17 [type summary cost metric]
Core-2(ospf)# area 2 range 10.102.128.0/17 no-advertise
```

To enable the advertisement again, configure the same summary but without the no-advertise option.

```
Core-2(ospf)# area 2 range 10.102.0.0/17 [type summary cost metric]
```

Simply removing the nonadvertised summary would enable the advertisement of individual routes without aggregation.

## Review multi-area OSPF concepts

You will now take a minute to review what you have learned about multi-area OSPF topologies.

Refer to Figure 5-17 to answer these questions. Note that the real-world network would have many more routing switches in area 1 and area 2, configured much like Access-1 and Access-2. Figure 5-17 does not show these switches for the purposes of simplicity.

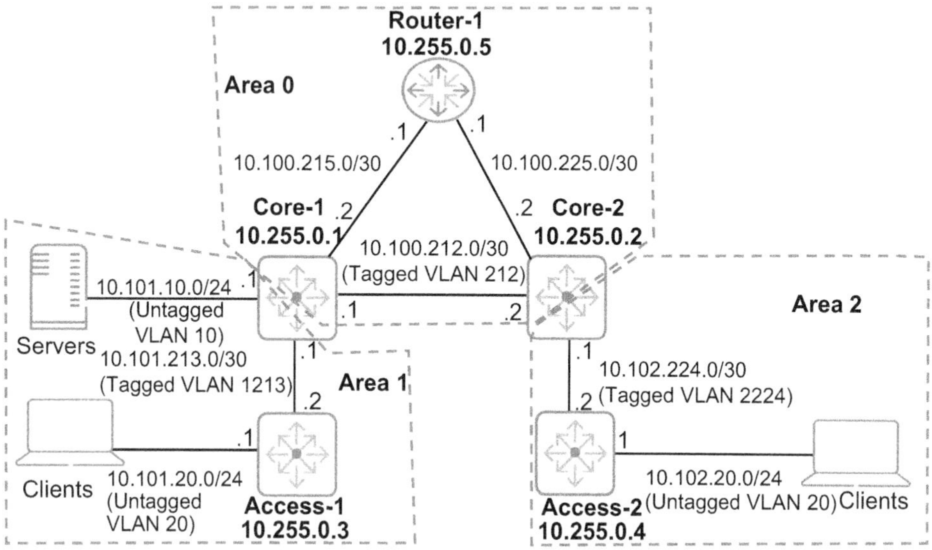


Figure 5-17 Review multi-area OSPF concepts

## Multi-area design without aggregation

First, you will review the advertisement of inter-area routes in a multi-area network with no aggregation. You will also review how LSUs propagate across the AS.

1. Why would Core-1 shown in Figure 5-17 generate the summary LSA (Type 3) for 10.101.20.0/24, a network connected to Access-1? In which area would Core-1 generate the LSA?
2. Which summary LSAs would Core-1 advertise in area 1?
3. Access-1 and Core-2 are in different areas but have the same OSPF routes. Why?
4. Suppose that Router-1 shown in Figure 5-17 loses its connection to Core-2, causing the 10.100.225.0/30 link to go down. If you entered the **show ip ospf spf-log** command on Access-1 before and after this issue occurred, you would find that Access-1 ran the SPF algorithm after the link failure. Why would Access-1 need to run the SPF algorithm when a link went down in a different area?

## Reviewing aggregation

5. Area 2 includes networks in the 10.102.0.0 to 10.102.255.0 range, so you would use the 10.102.0.0/16 range to summarize it.
    - Where would you configure this summary range?
    - What changes would occur in the OSPF system after you configured this range?

6. What would occur after you configured the 10.100.0.0/16 summary range in area 0 on Core-1?

Figure 5-18 summarizes what you have learned about the proper places to configure aggregation and the effect of creating the ranges.

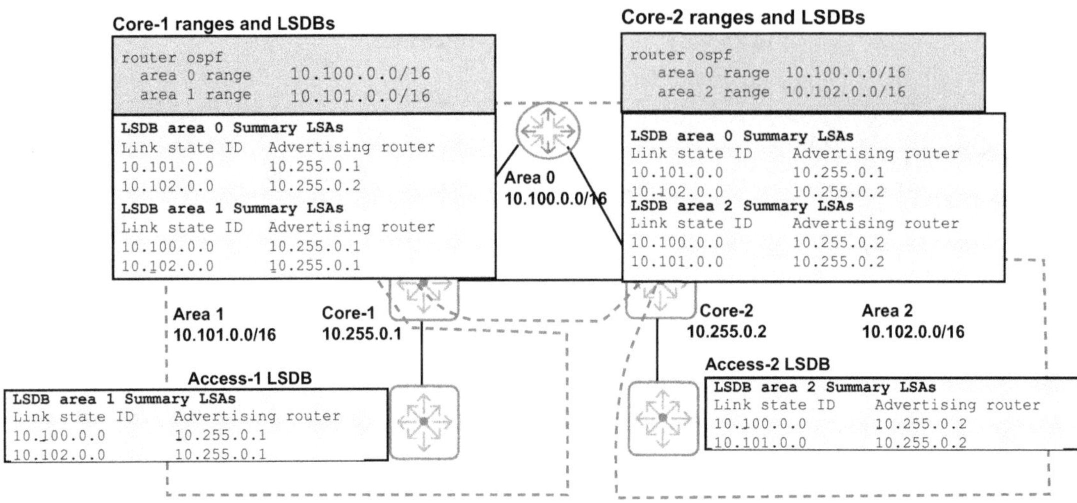


Figure 5-18 Reviewing aggregation

7. Now, consider the same scenario from question 4, but with the aggregations shown in Figure 5-18. Router-1 loses its link to Core-2, causing the 10.100.225.0/30 network to go down. Would Access-1 receive an LSU and have to rerun the SPF algorithm?

8. When you configure an aggregation for an area on an ABR, you have the option to set the cost or not. If you do not set the cost, the ABR takes the cost from the highest cost route that it knows within that range. If you do not set the cost, what are the implications for the stability of the aggregated route? For example, in the topology shown in Figure 5-18, assume that you have configured the 10.101.0.0/16 summary on Core-1 without a cost. A VLAN interface on Access-1 goes down. Why could this cause Core-2, in another area, to receive an LSU and rerun the SPF algorithm?

9. How would you troubleshoot if Access-1 was not receiving the proper aggregated routes from area 2? What if Access-1 used to receive both the 10.100.0.0/16 route and the 10.102.0.0/16, but was then only receiving the 10.100.0.0/16 route?

## OSPF external routes

In this section, you will learn when an OSPF AS might require external routes. You will earn how to redistribute these routes into the OSPF AS, how the OSPF routers advertise and learn the external routes, and how you can use area definitions to filter the external routes.

## Need for redistributing external routes into OSPF

Sometimes the OSPF AS needs to learn routes to networks outside the OSPF AS. As you have learned, OSPF is a link-state protocol. OSPF routers advertise network interfaces that run OSPF, and ABRs advertise inter-area routes. But sometimes an OSPF router has other routes in its IP routing table (a static route, for example), and you want the router to advertise those routes to its OSPF neighbors.

Examples include:

- A company uses OSPF internally. One or two of the company's routers connect to an ISP. They have static default routes to this ISP and need to communicate the default route to the rest of the OSPF AS.
- You are upgrading a network from RIP to OSPF. During the upgrade, some segments of the network will continue to run RIP. The OSPF AS needs to know about the networks in the RIP segment, just as the devices running RIP need to know about the networks in the OSPF segment.
- Often you make stub networks (networks with just one OSPF router) passive OSPF interfaces. However, you might choose instead to *not* enable OSPF on the stub network interfaces at all. You can redistribute connected routes into OSPF so that the router can advertise routes to these networks.

You can make any of these types of routes available to OSPF by redistributing (or importing) the routes into OSPF. In detail, you can redistribute these routes:

- Static routes
- Any routes discovered by another routing protocol supported on the routing switch, which might include:
  - RIP
  - Border Gateway Protocol (BGP)
  - Connected routes on which OSPF is not enabled

You redistribute routes by type (static, specific routing protocol, or directly connected). By default, the OSPF process receives all routes discovered by the router through the specified mechanism. You can filter the redistributed routes using route maps, but the use of route maps is beyond the scope of this study guide.

Table 5-4 summarizes the options for redistributing external routes into OSPF.

Table 5-4 Redistributing external routes into OSPF

| Options for routes redistributed into OSPF | Example use case |
|---|---|
| Static | The OSPF router needs to advertise its default static route through an ISP router to the OSPF domain. |
| Another routing protocol supported by the device | During a migration from RIP to OSPF, OSPF segments need to learn about RIP segments. |
| Directly connected | You do not want to configure connected stub networks as passive OSPF interfaces. |

## External routes and ASBRs

As Figure 5-19 shows, the router on which you redistribute the routes is called an Autonomous System Border Router (ASBR) because it communicates routing information between the OSPF AS and other routing processes. A redistributed route becomes an *external* OSPF route, which is sometimes referred to as an AS external (ASE) route. All of the routes calculated from Type 1, Type 2, and Type 3 LSAs, including both intra-area and inter-area routes, are *internal* OSPF routes.

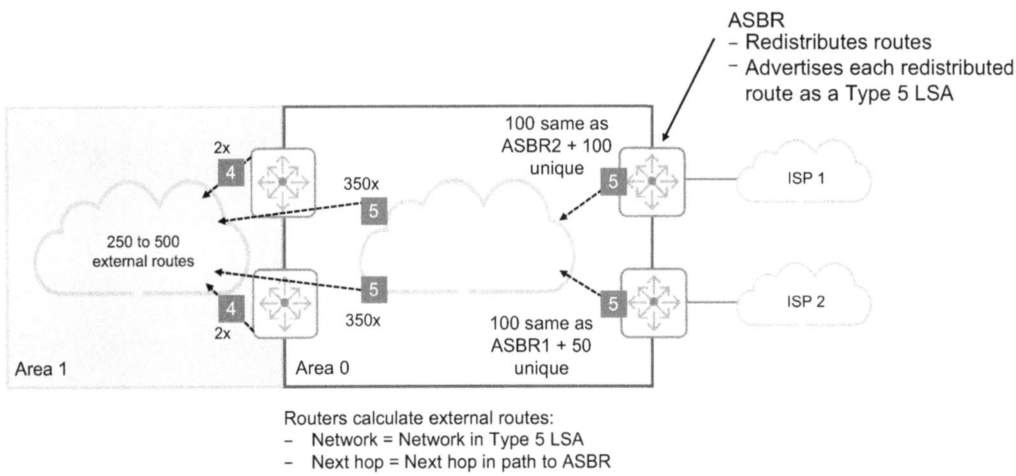


Figure 5-19 External routes and ASBRs

ASBRs advertise external routes in Type 5 LSAs. The LSA includes the network address for the redistributed route, the router ID of the advertising ASBR, and the metric, which you assign when you redistribute the route into OSPF.

OSPF routers propagate the Type 5 LSA in LSUs throughout the entire AS, making Type 5 LSAs different from Type 1, Type 2, and Type 3 LSAs. (Remember: although Type 3 LSAs advertise inter-area routes, each area has its own set of Type 3 LSAs.)

To calculate an external route from the Type 5 LSA, a router refers to the LSA's advertising ASBR. The router has calculated a shortest path to each ASBR. The forwarding interface and next hop for that path become the forwarding interface and next hop for all external routes advertised by that ASBR.

In other words, routers do *not* add the external networks to the directed graph for the shortest path algorithm. Instead, they add them to a list of networks for which the advertising ASBR is the gateway. Therefore, changes to the particular external networks advertised by an ASBR do not affect the area topology.

## Example OSPF external routes in routing tables

You will now consider examples of external OSPF routes. The routes belong to a router in area 0 that has learned them from an ASBR (see Figure 5-19).

All routes except the external OSPF ones have been removed for clarity. Of course, in an actual enterprise environment, more external routes would be included as well.

Examples of Type 5 LSAs are also provided. (These LSAs are using type 2 metrics, which are the default. You will learn more about the differences between type 1 and type 2 metrics a bit later.) Note that:

- These LSAs are not associated with an area in the LSDB; they extend across the AS.
- The LS ID and the network mask indicate the external network in the route.
- The metric is the metric advertised by the ASBR.

### External route

The command output below shows an external route on a routing AOS-Switch. As you see, the OSPF sub-type is External2 (the 2 indicates a type 2 metric). Note that AOS-Switches use the standard OSPF administrative distance for both internal and external OSPF routes.

```
Area1ABR# show ip route

                              IP Route Entries

 Destination      Gateway       VLAN  Type    Sub-Type   Metric   Dist.
 ---------------  ------------  ----- ------- ---------- -------- -----
 172.16.0.0/16    10.100.212.2  1012  ospf    External2  10       110
```

### AOS-Switch Type 5 LSA

You must use a different command to view the external LSAs.

```
Switch# show ip ospf external-link-state
      OSPF Process 1 with Router ID 10.255.0.1
                 Link State Database

    Type        : External
    LS ID       : 172.16.0.0
    Adv Rtr     : 10.255.0.2
    LS Age      : 217
    Len         : n/a
    Options     :
    Seq#        : 0x80000004
    Checksum    : 0x7369
    Net Mask    : n/a
    TOS 0  Metric: 10
    E Type      : 1
    Forwarding Address : 0.0.0.0
    Tag         : 0
```

## Summary ASBR advertisements

When a router receives a Type 5 LSA from an ASBR in the same area, it can use the area's topology to calculate the shortest path to that ASBR, the ASBR route. The next hop in this route becomes the next hop for all external networks for which that ASBR is the gateway.

Routers in different areas from the ASBR also receive the Type 5 LSA, but they might need help determining how to reach the ASBR. The Type 5 LSA indicates the advertising ASBR by router ID. You have learned how to make router IDs routable. However, because OSPF does not *require* routable router IDs, it must provide another mechanism for informing routers in other areas how to reach the ASBR.

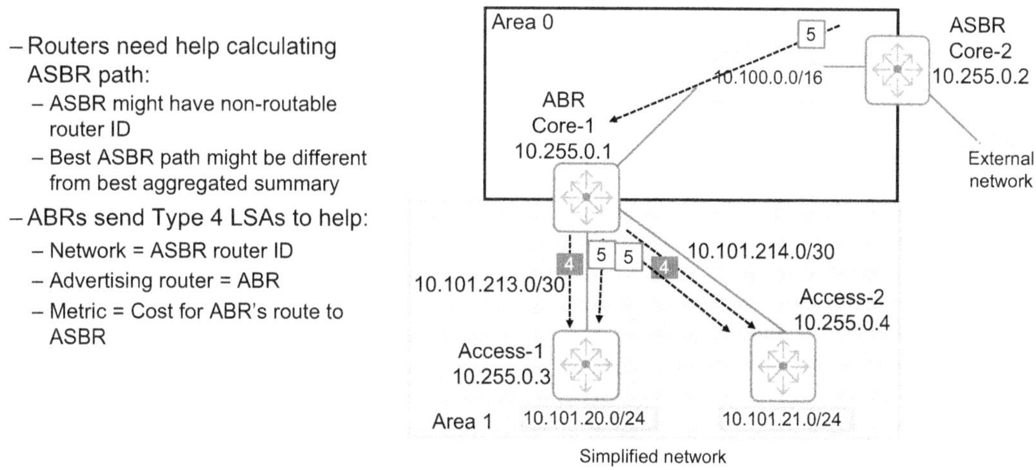


Figure 5-20 Summary ASBR advertisements

Also, even if OSPF did require routable router IDs, an OSPF router in another area might not want to use its typical inter-area routes to reach the ASBR. In areas with multiple ABRs, the ABR with the lowest cost for the broader area range might not provide the best path to the ASBR within the area.

OSPF defines the Type 4 summary LSA so that the routers in other areas can learn the best ABR through which to reach particular ASBRs. For each area, an ABR generates one Type 4 LSA for each ASBR that it can reach in *another* area. As the metric for this LSA, the ABR specifies the cost for its shortest path to the ASBR. For example, in Figure 5-20, Core-1 would specify its cost for reaching Core-2.

Internal routers that receive the Type 4 LSAs use them to select the best path to each ASBR in other areas. In this example, the choice is simple because area 1 has only one ABR. However, you will examine more complex topologies later in this chapter.

## Example OSPF external routes (ASBR in another area)

You will now review examples of an external OSPF route learned by an internal area 1 router from the ASBR in area 0.

You can see those Type 4 LSAs in the "Routing table" section that follows. You can also see the Type 5 LSA in the router's LSDB. Note that the Type 5 LSA matches the one in area 0, and the advertising router remains the ASBR that redistributed the route. Type 5 LSAs extend across the AS. The ABR is the advertising router for the Type 4 LSA, on the other hand.

### Routing table

```
InternalArea1# show ip route
                        IP Route Entries
  Destination     Gateway        VLAN  Type    Sub-Type   Metric  Dist.
  --------------- ------------   ----  ----    ---------  ------  -----
  10.100.0.0/16   10.101.213.1   1213  ospf    InterArea  3       110
  10.102.0.0/16   10.101.213.1   1213  ospf    InterArea  3       110
  172.16.0.0/16   10.101.213.1   1213  ospf    External2  10      110
```

### Type 4 LSA

```
InternalArea1# show ip ospf link-state type as-summary
 OSPF Link State Database for Area 0.0.0.1
                              Advertising
  LSA Type   Link State ID  Router ID    Age  Sequence #  Checksum
  ---------- -------------- ------------ ---- ----------- --------
  AsbSummary 10.255.0.2     10.255.0.1   144  0x80000001 0x00002a50

InternalArea1# show ip ospf link-state detail type as-summary
OSPF Link State Database for Area 0.0.0.1

LSA Age                         : 496
LSA Type                        : 0x4 (AS Boundary)
Advertising Router              : 10.255.0.1
Link State ID                   : 10.255.0.2
LSA Sequence                    : 0x80000006
LSA Checksum                    : 0x4893
LSA Option Bits                 : E=1 MC=0 N/P=0 EA=0 DC=0
LSA Metric                      : 100
Network Mask                    : 255.255.255.255
```

### Type 5 LSA

```
InternalArea1# show ip ospf external-link-state detail
OSPF Process with Router ID 10.255.0.3
                 Link State Database

    Type       : External
    LS ID      : 172.16.0.0
    Adv Rtr    : 10.255.0.2
    LS Age     : 565
    Len        : n/a
    Options    :
    Seq#       : 0x80000009
    Checksum   : 0x696e
    Net Mask   : n/a
    TOS 0  Metric: 10
    E Type     : 1
    Forwarding Address : 0.0.0.0
    Tag        : 0
```

## Need for eliminating excessive external routes

The internal routers in some OSPF areas often do not require all of the external routes.

Remember the primary benefit of individual Type 4 and Type 5 LSAs. The Type 5 LSAs help routers choose the best ASBR for reaching a particular external network. If that ASBR is in another area, Type 4 LSAs further help the routers choose the best ABR for reaching that ASBR. (Depending on the external metric type, the Type 4 LSA might also help the routers select the best ASBR). You should examine each non-backbone area and determine whether routers in the area truly need to choose between paths for particular external networks.

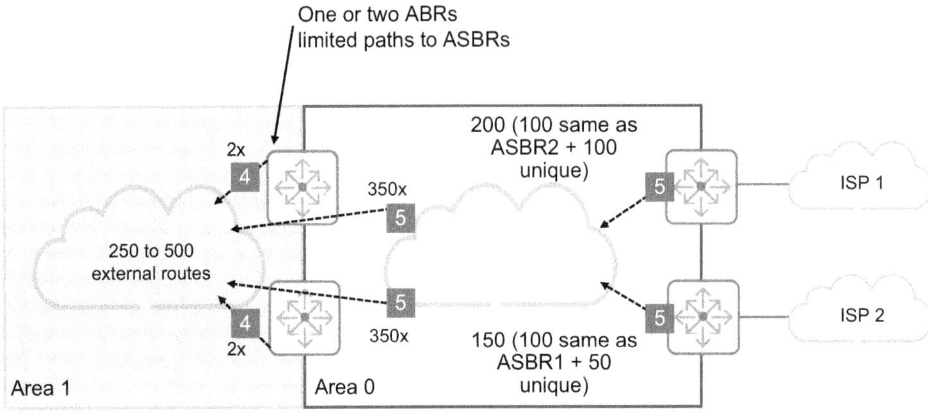


Figure 5-21 Need for eliminating excessive external routes

First, consider whether the area includes any ASBRs. If it does not, then all external traffic must pass through the area's ABRs. The number of ABRs in the area restricts the number of paths for external routes. If the area has only one ABR, the area has only one path for external traffic. A default route through the ABR provides the same benefit as individual external route advertisements much more efficiently.

If the area has multiple ABRs, as shown in Figure 5-21, internal routers *might* benefit from choices for external paths. As you learned, these choices extend not just to choosing the best ASBR but also the best ABR for reaching a particular ASBR. You need to assess, however, whether the internal routers truly receive a benefit from this level of detail and choice. In many cases, the ABRs offer roughly equivalent paths to the external networks, so the internal routers can receive the same benefit from a default route advertised by both.

## Using stub areas to eliminate external routes

To eliminate external routes and advertisements from an area, define the area as a stub area (see Figure 5-22). ABRs for stub areas do not forward Type 4 or Type 5 LSAs into those areas, and internal routers in those areas do not generate or accept them. You must define the stub area setting on each OSPF routing device within the stub area as well as the ABR. Otherwise, the devices cannot become neighbors and establish adjacency.

When you activate this option on the ABR, it automatically generates a default route, which it injects as a Type 3 LSA into the stub area. As usual, the ABR assigns a metric to the default route, and you can manipulate metrics to set up one ABR as a preferred exit for external traffic.

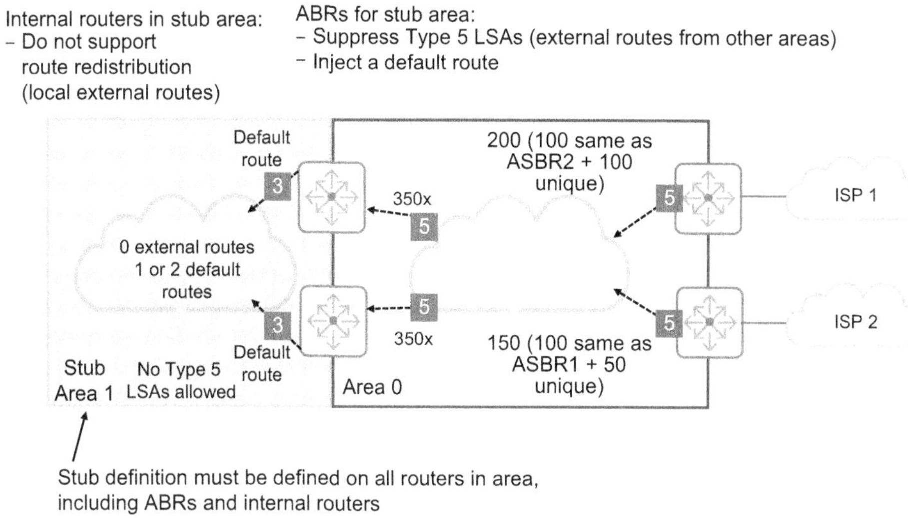


Figure 5-22 Using stub areas to eliminate external routes

Note that, although Type 3 LSAs for inter-area routes are not shown in Figure 5-22, the stub area acts like a normal area in this respect. It receives summary LSAs for other areas through ABRs; the summary LSAs include individual or aggregated routes as configured on the ABRs. Therefore, internal routers in the stub area can continue to select the best path for inter-area traffic, based on the cost of the summary routes advertised by the ABRs.

The OSPF command for configuring a stub area and the default metric is:

```
Switche(ospf)# area <ID> stub <metric>
```

Note that you must set the metric when you configure the area as a stub on internal routers as well as on ABRs. However, only ABRs advertise the default route.

## Stub internal area 1 router routing table

With area 1 defined as a stub, the internal router receives a single default route from each ABR instead of the external routes (it selects the lowest-metric default route). The default route is considered an inter-area OSPF route, and the router still has two other inter-area routes.

Below is an example. Only inter-area routes are shown although the router actually has other routes.

```
InternalArea1# show ip route ospf

                    IP Route Entries

 Destination     Gateway         VLAN  Type  Sub-Type   Metric  Dist.
 --------------- --------------- ----- ----  ---------  ------  -----
 0.0.0.0/0       10.101.213.1    1213  ospf  InterArea  2       110
 10.100.0.0/16   10.101.213.5    1213  ospf  InterArea  3       110
 10.102.0.0/16   10.101.213.5    1213  ospf  InterArea  3       110
```

## Need for eliminating all inter-area and external routes

In the example network shown in Figure 5-23, area 1 is a stub area. All traffic destined to it terminates there. In addition, the area has only one exit for all nonlocal traffic, including traffic destined to the backbone, to other OSPF areas, and to the ISP. In such an environment, the internal area 1 routers do not gain a benefit from multiple inter-area routes.

You can configure the OSPF system to suppress all inter-area routes in this area in addition to all external routes.

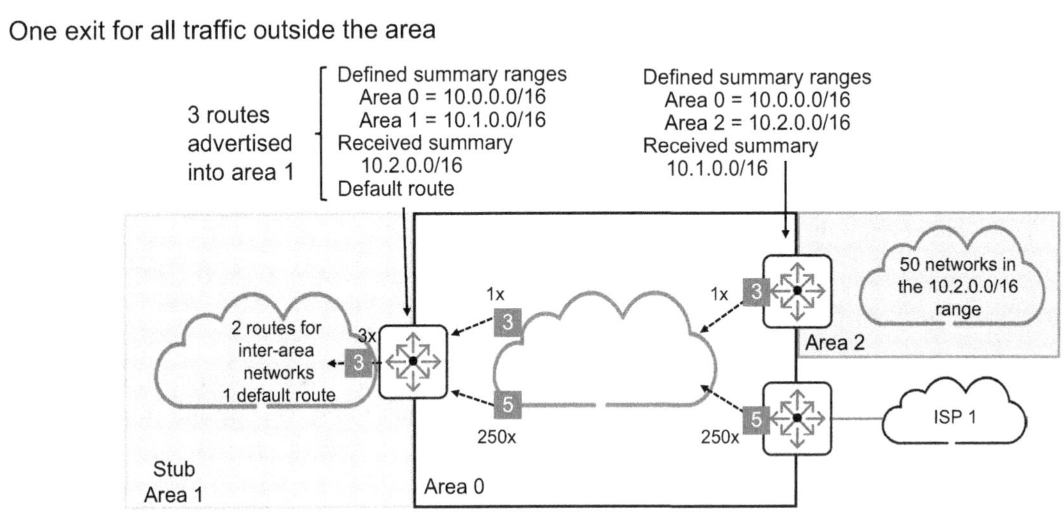


Figure 5-23 Need for eliminating all inter-area and external routes

## Using totally stub areas

You define a totally stub area by configuring the ABR or ABRs connected to that area to suppress summaries.

You enter this OSPF command on all ABRs that connect to the area:

```
Switch(ospf)# area <ID> stub no-summary <metric>
```

This command suppresses all external route advertisements as normal for a stub area. It also prevents the ABR from generating nonaggregated summary routes for this area. For example, the ABR shown in Figure 5-24 would not generate area 1 summary LSAs for the routes that the ABR knows to area 0 and area 2 networks. Instead, the internal routers in area 1 use the default route to reach the other areas.

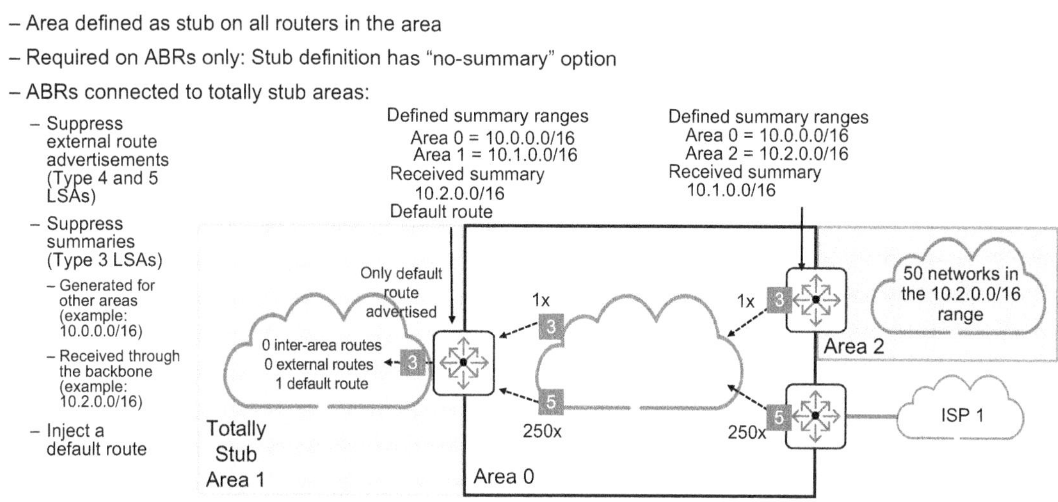


Figure 5-24 Using totally stub areas

### Internal area 1 router routing table

The output from the **show ip route ospf** command shows how the internal router in totally stub area 1 now has only one inter-area route (the default route) and no external routes. (It still maintains all intra-area routes, but these are not shown below.)

```
InternalArea1# show ip route ospf

                    IP Route Entries

  Destination    Gateway        VLAN  Type   Sub-Type   Metric     Dist.
  -------------  ------------- ----- ------ ---------- ---------- -----
  0.0.0.0/0      10.101.213.1  1213  ospf   InterArea  2          110
```

## Need for advertising local external routes in a stub area

A stub or totally stub area might have its own local connection to an external network. The area would still benefit from a suppression of external routes from other sources (see Figure 5-25). You should define the area such that the internal OSPF routers receive the local external routes but not external routes from other areas.

Remember that any redistributed route is defined as an external route. Therefore, you would encounter a similar issue if you decided to redistribute connected routes into OSPF rather than configure the associated VLANs as passive OSPF interfaces.

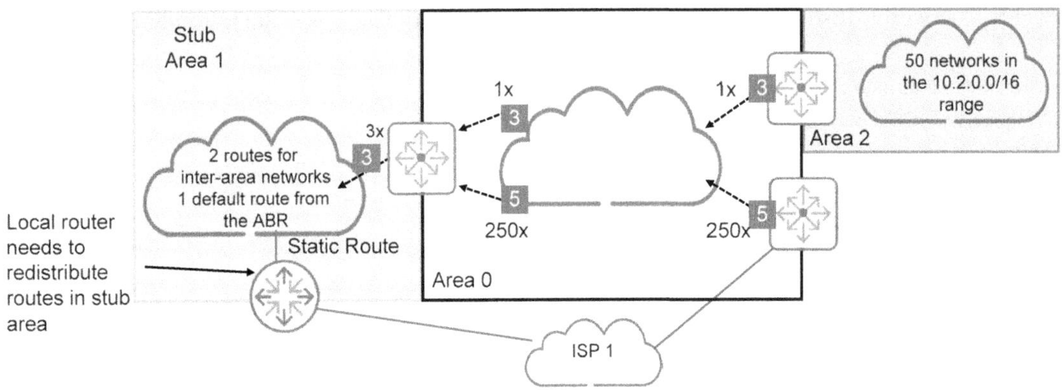


Figure 5-25 Need for advertising local external routes in a stub area

## Using NSSAs

A not so stubby area (NSSA) furnishes the solution for this problem. You must define this area type on every OSPF router in the area.

The OSPF command is:

```
Switch(ospf)# area <ID> nssa <metric> [no-summary]
```

An NSSA acts like a stub area or totally stub area (depending on whether the ABR uses the **no-summary** option). As Figure 5-26 shows, however, the area permits external routes that are advertised in OSPF by a local ASBR. These external routes are carried in Type 7 LSAs.

Of course, you must configure the local ASBR to redistribute routes, advertise a default route, or both, as you learned in the section on configuring ASBRs and external routes. Like other ASBRs, the NSSA ASBR assigns a metric (type 1 or type 2) to the external routes that it advertises in OSPF, which you can adjust to influence route selection.

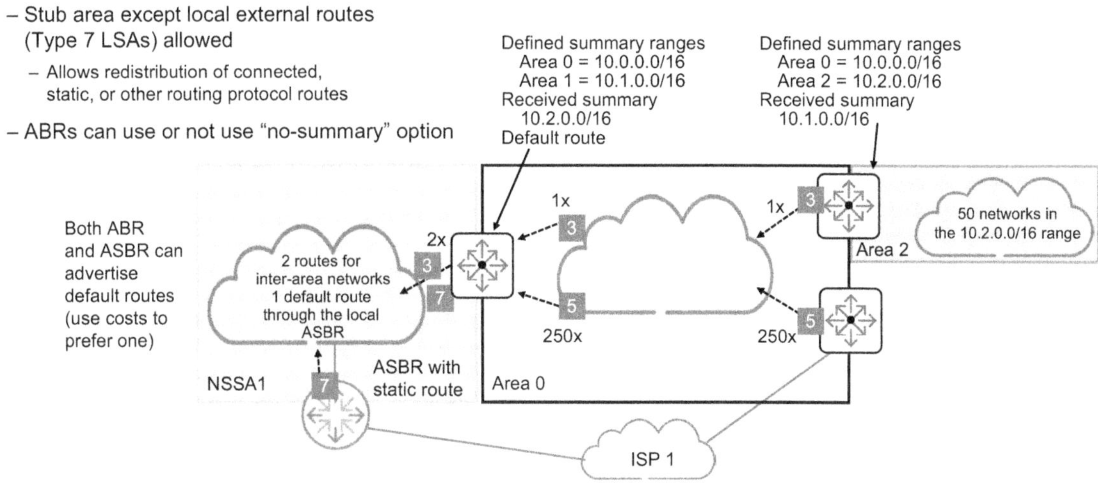


Figure 5-26 Using NSSAs

The ABR injects the Type 7 LSAs into other areas as Type 5 LSAs that it appears to originate (see Figure 5-26). The ABR still filters Type 5 LSAs from other areas and does not advertise them in this area. It also continues to advertise a default route in the NSSA, but as a Type 7 LSA rather than a Type 3 one. If the NSSA's ASBR advertises a default route as well, you must adjust metrics such that your routing devices prefer the route that you want them to prefer.

## Review external route advertisement

You will now consider several questions related to OSPF external routes. For each of these questions, refer to the scenario that follows.

### Scenario

As shown in Figure 5-27, Access-1, Access-2, Core-1, and Core-2 form an OSPF AS. Assume that all of these AOS-Switches have the addressing shown in Figure 5-27 and have achieved adjacency. Area 1 and area 2 are normal areas. (The AS would actually have many more routing devices, but the topology is simplified for this scenario.)

The company then acquires a new site, which is currently using different routing. Core-2 will act as a gateway between the company's existing OSPF network and the new site. Core-2 connects to Router-2 on the 192.168.26.0/24 network. Router-2 is outside of the OSPF AS and provides connectivity to networks in the 192.168.24.0/21 range. Router-2 already has static routes for reaching the networks in the OSPF AS. The network administrator enters this static route on Core-2:

```
Core-2(config)# ip route 192.168.24.0/21 192.168.26.1
```

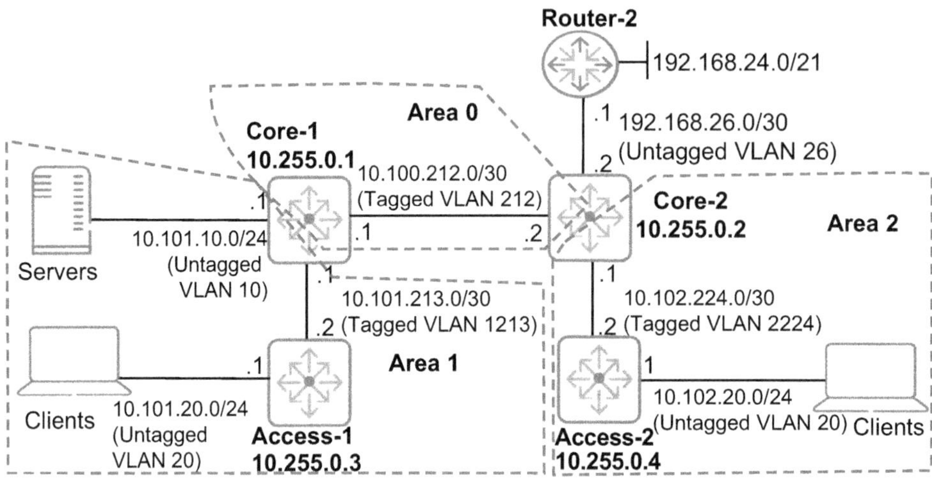


Figure 5-27 OSPF external routes

## Questions

Answer the questions below, based on this scenario. Answers are provided at the end of this chapter.

*External route advertisement*

1. What must the network administrator do to make Core-2 advertise the 192.168.24.0/21 route to the other AOS-Switches?

Assume that the administrator completes this step and answer the next questions.

2. Which switch or switches receive the external LSA and learn the route to the external network?
3. Access-1 receives a Type 4 LSA with a link state of 10.255.0.2 (Core-2's router ID). Which routing switch advertised this LSA to Access-1?

*Stub areas*

Now, the network administrator defines area 1 as a stub area. Answer the next questions.

4. On which switches, must the administrator configure area 1 as a stub area?
5. During the process of configuring area 1 as a stub area, what could occur? What are the implications for changing the type of area in a live network?
6. After area 1 is defined as a stub, what switch or switches experience changes in their routing tables? What old routes are no longer present? Which new route is present?

*Totally stub areas*

Now, the network administrator wants to define area 1 as a totally stub area.

7. Where should the administrator specify the **stub no-summary** option for area 1?
8. The administrator completes this step. Underline the correct effect or effects.
    - Core-1 stops advertising the area 1 range to Core-2
    - Core-1 stops advertising inter-area routes into area 1
9. Core-1 no longer advertises a route to 10.102.0.0/16 to area 1 routers. Does the Core-1 switch still have an LSA for this network? Can Access-1 still reach networks in 10.102.0.0/16?

# Best route selection in redundant OSPF network

You will now explore redundant OSPF networks. You will begin by exploring how to predict and control path selection in complex and redundant networks. You will also examine redundant topologies and apply what you have learned about multi-area OSPF systems to determine how you can control which paths are selected in various scenarios.

## Setting interface cost

Link cost provides the basis for route selection within OSPF. To ensure that your routing switches select the best routes, you must remember to assign the VLAN interfaces logical costs, typically based on their bandwidth. By default, a VLAN interface has a cost of 1. Because every VLAN interface has the same cost, route selection becomes a matter of hop count, rather than true lowest cost path.

When you follow the approach of assigning a unique VLAN and subnet to each link between OSPF routing switches, you can correlate the VLAN interface with the bandwidth of that link. Choose a base bandwidth to set to 1, setting this bandwidth well above the maximum bandwidth used in your network for future proofing. Then divide that base bandwidth by the bandwidth of the link or link aggregation associated with the VLAN. Table 5-5 presents some examples.

Table 5-5 Configuring cost for VLAN interfaces dedicated to router-to-router links

| Bandwidth on the link | Cost |
|---|---|
| 1000 Gbps | 1 |
| 100 Gbps | 10 |
| 20 Gbps | 50 |
| 10 Gbps | 100 |
| 4 Gbps | 250 |
| 2 Gbps | 500 |
| 1 Gbps | 1000 |
| 100 Mbps | 10,000 |

You can use this command to set the cost on a VLAN interface:

```
Switch(config)# vlan <ID> ip ospf cost <cost>
```

## Best practices for networks with redundant ABRs

For simplicity, you have been concentrating on OSPF systems that have simple paths. When you are using technologies such as VSF which build redundancy and resiliency into the logical device acting as ABR, a topology such as this might be adequate. Sometimes, though, you need to plan redundant designs more like those shown in Figure 5-28.

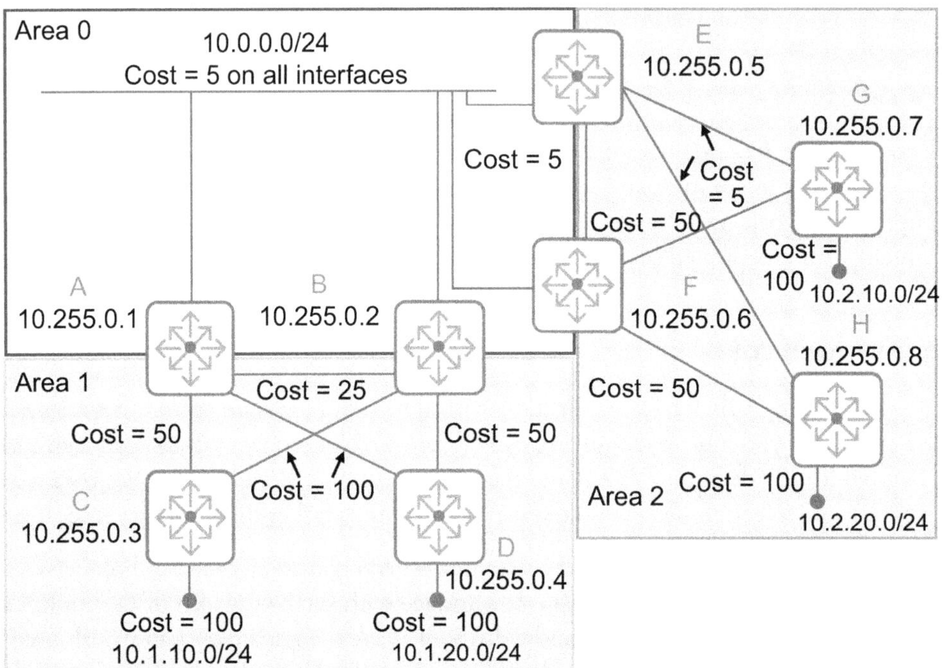


Figure 5-28 Best practices for networks with redundant ABRs

When an OSPF area has multiple ABRs, you need to follow a couple of best practices.

First, you should make sure mirror the configuration on both ABRs. For example, both should define the area in the same way. Of course, it is required that both define the area as normal, as stub, or as NSSA. But also check the **no-summary** option for a stub area or NSSA. If you define this option on one ABR, define it on the other ABR too for consistent behavior.

You should also configure exactly the same summary range or ranges for the area on both routers. Although you are allowed to configure different summary ranges on different ABRs, doing so can lead to potential routing loops. This is because the ABRs advertise those ranges in Type 3 LSAs in area 0, and they can learn them from each other in area 0. However, they will not learn an inter-area route through the other ABR for an identical range that they are already advertising themselves—which is the desired behavior during normal operation.

The following example illustrates how summary ranges should be configured. For example, area 1 shown in Figure 5-28 includes routes in the 10.1.0.0/19 range, but the range might have some gaps. The area might not yet be using 10.1.31.0/24 network. If both ABR-A and ABR-B advertise a 10.1.0.0/19 summary, this gap does not matter. The two ABRs advertise the same 10.1.0.0/19 summary in area 0 and do not learn routes to 10.1.0.0/19 through each other. If a device in area 2 attempts to reach an address in 10.1.31.0/24, the packet reaches either ABR-A or ABR-B. The ABR does not have a route that matches that destination network, so it drops the packet to the invalid destination.

However, if the administrator configured different summary ranges for area 1 on ABR-A and ABR-B, the behavior would be different. For example, maybe the administrator configured 10.1.0.0/19 an ABR-A and 10.1.0.0/16 on ABR-B. Now, ABR-A learns a route to 10.1.0.0/16 through ABR-B, and ABR-A learns a route to 10.1.0.0/19 through ABR-A. Perhaps a device in area 2 attempts to reach an address in 10.1.31.0/24. Now, the packet reaches ABR-A. ABR-A matches the destination to the 10.1.0.0/16 route through ABR-B. When ABR-B receives the packet, it matches the destination to the 10.1.0.0/19 route through ABR-A. The ABRs continue to route the packet back and forth between each other.

To provide the best consistency and lowest chance of routing loops, configure the same summary ranges on both ABRs. You can set a different cost for the range on each ABR, if you want to prefer one over the other, though.

As a second best practice, make sure that the redundant ABRs can reach each other through both area 0 and the area that they share in common. For example, ABR-A and ABR-B should connect in both area 1 and area 2.

Remember that OSPF routers only use links within an area as part of the topology for that area; links assigned to area 0 are essentially invisible to the area 1 SPF algorithm. This means that an area 0 link between ABR-A and ABR-B is not available for area 1 intra-area routes. Without a link in area 1 between each other, the ABRs would send area 1 traffic destined to the other switch through an access switch rather than through the network backbone. You should also keep this in mind for areas with more complex topologies; they should never allow one segment of an area to become disconnected from another segment.

To meet this criterion, you could plan different physical links between the ABRs, as shown in Figure 5-28. But often you want to create a single logical link (such as a link aggregation) between the ABRs. In this case, you have two options. You can assign two VLANs to that logical link and place one VLAN in area 0 and one VLAN in area 1. Alternatively, you can assign a single VLAN to the logical link and assign two IP addresses to that VLAN. You would enable OSPF in area 0 on one IP address and OSPF in area 1 on the other IP address.

## Choosing best inter-area routes

You have seen how ABRs advertise inter-area routes in Type 3 LSAs. When an area has a single ABR, internal routes send all inter-area traffic to the next hop closest to that ABR. When an area has multiple ABRs and redundant paths, though, you need to understand how routers calculate inter-area routes in more detail.

You will begin by looking at how routers choose the best route for inter-area traffic. This discussion assumes that area 1 and area 2 are normal, stub, or NSSA areas, but not totally stub or totally stub NSSAs. The totally stub areas do not receive Type 3 LSAs, except a default route, so the routers in those areas cannot choose best paths for inter-area traffic based on anything except the cost in the default route.

A Type 3 LSA advertises a *route* to the network. The routers that receive these advertisements do *not* create a topology of the networks in other areas. Instead, they treat the ABR as a gateway to all of the networks which the ABR advertises in Type 3 LSAs. That is, those networks are leaves hanging off the ABR in the shortest path tree.

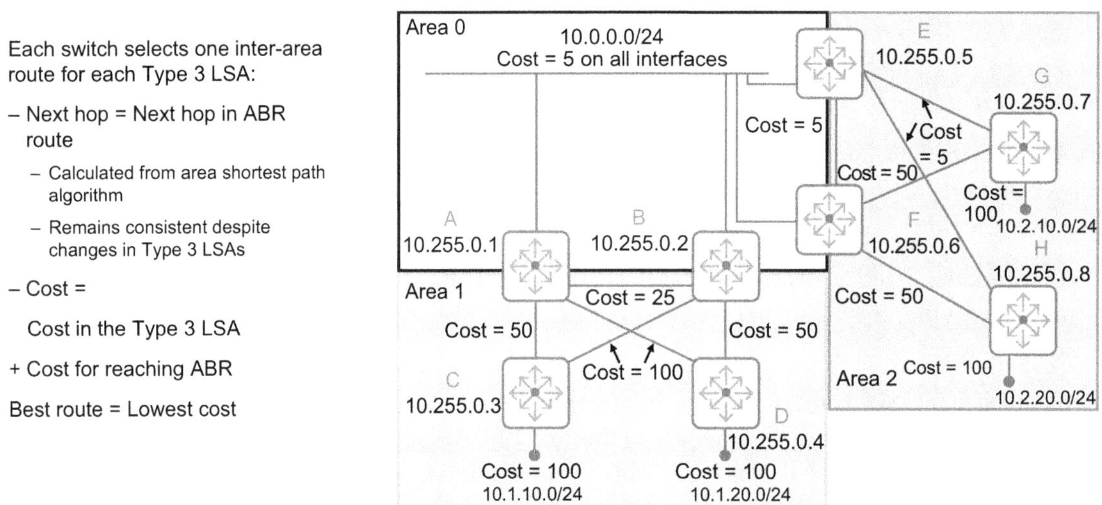


Figure 5-29 Choosing best inter-area routes

Each router determines the shortest path to the ABR or ABRs advertising Type 3 LSAs to it. It calculates this path as normal for inter-area routes by applying Dijkstra's algorithm to the area in which the router connects to the ABR. The next hop for reaching the ABR becomes the next hop for all inter-area routes advertised by that ABR in Type 3 LSAs.

If a router receives multiple Type 3 LSAs for the same network, as it does when the area includes multiple ABRs, it learns multiple inter-area routes for that network. It uses the metric to choose between the routes. The metric for each inter-area route consists of:

- Metric advertised in the Type 3 LSA, which the ABR copies from its metric for the route in question
- Metric for reaching the advertising ABR (from area shortest path topology)

Because each ABR advertises the cost of its own route to the network, cost increments across the complete system. First, consider a situation without route aggregation for the purposes of illustration (see Figure 5-29).

ABR-E advertises 10.2.20.0/24 as a Type 3 LSA with metric 105 in area 0, and ABR-F advertises this route with metric 150. ABR-A adds 5 to each of these metrics because that is its cost for reaching each of the routers. It selects ABR-E as offering the best route and adds an inter-area route with metric 110 to its OSPF table. When ABR-A generates an LSA for 10.2.20.0/24 in area 1, it advertises metric 110. Router C adds its metric for reaching ABR-A to 110, assigning the inter-area route to 10.2.20.0/24 a metric of 160.

Inter-area routing in OSPF combines the best aspects of link-state and distance-vector routing. Router C, for example, uses link-state routing to determine its shortest path to its two ABRs. It can then use those same two paths for all routes to other areas without considering the link states of networks in those areas. Even though Router C only knows a small part of the topology, traffic that it routes toward other areas still receives the benefits of link-state routing across the complete path. For example, Router C sends traffic to 10.2.20.0/24 on its shortest path to ABR-A. ABR-A, in turn, routes the traffic using the shortest path to ABR-E, which it has calculated from its detailed area 0 topology. Finally, ABR-E routes the traffic using the best path calculated by the detailed area 2 topology. In each area, routers maintain just the local segment of the complete path for inter-area traffic.

Also, consider how the area boundaries enhance stability. When an OSPF router receives an update for a Type 3 LSA, it does not run the complete shortest path algorithm. Instead, it adjusts the networks behind each ABR, as indicated by the update, and adds a new inter-area route, removes an inter-area route, or selects a different inter-area route (due to a cost change), as appropriate. The router *does not*, on the other hand, need to recalculate the path to the ABR, which is the only segment of the path with which it is concerned.

Some loss of information is introduced by route aggregation at the area boundaries; however, the simplicity is typically worth this loss. For example, in this topology, network administrators might configure an aggregated range of 10.2.0.0/16 for area 2 on ABR-E and ABR-F. They can assign cost 105 to this range on ABR-E, but cost 150 to the range on ABR-F. ABR-A can still choose the route through ABR-E as the lowest cost route. In this example, ABR-A and ABR-B have the same cost to reach ABR-E, so they advertise the same cost for the 10.2.0.0/16 route into area 1. However, ABR-B, for example, had a better cost path to ABR-E, it would advertise a lower cost route, and internal routers in area 1 would direct their area 2 traffic to that ABR.

You could also use multiple area summaries when an area has multiple ABRs, and you want to prefer one ABR for one segment of the area but another ABR for another segment. This approach is more complicated, however. You must also take care to configuring matching summaries on each ABR (although the costs would not match). Otherwise, you can accidentally introduce routing loops.

## Options for external route metrics

You will next consider how OSPF routers choose the best external route in networks with redundant ASBRs, as well as redundant paths to the ASBRs.

Every external route advertised in a Type 5 LSA has two important properties: the metric-type, which is type 1 or type 2, and the metric. The ASBR that advertises the Type 5 LSA chooses the metric type and sets the metric. Figure 5-30 shows the AOS-Switch settings that you use to control these properties for all routes redistributed into OSPF on this router:

```
Switch(ospf)# metric-type <type1 | type2>
```

```
Switch(ospf)# default-metric <cost>
```

If you are using NSSAs, you can set the metric type for the NSSA's external routes with this OSPF command:

```
Switch(ospf)# area <ID> nssa <default route cost> metric-type <type1 | type2>
```

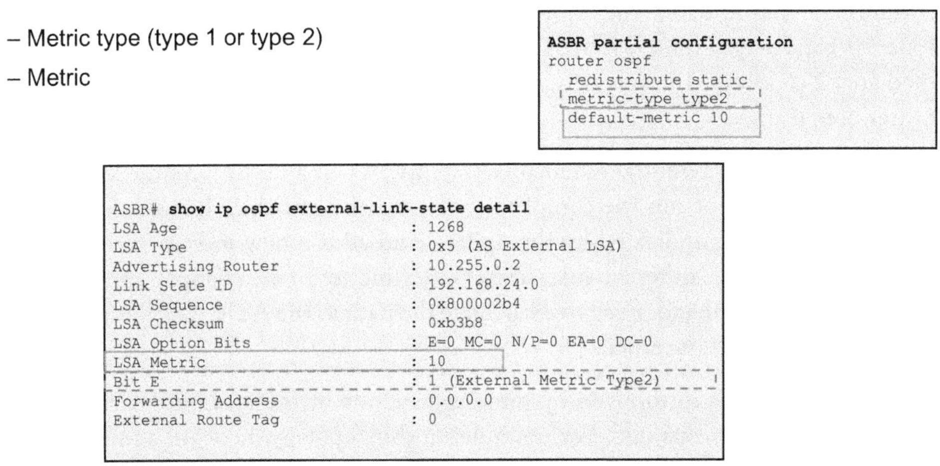


Figure 5-30 Options for external route metrics

## Choosing between external routes to the same network: Type 2 metric

You will now examine how OSPF routers use the metric to choose which external route to install in the routing table when they receive multiple LSAs for the same external route. (In the example shown in Figure 5-31, area 1 is a normal area. Routers in stub areas and totally stub areas do not receive external routes, so the considerations discussed in this section do not apply to them. Instead, routers in stub and totally stub areas select a default route, advertised by their ABR or ABRs, for this traffic.)

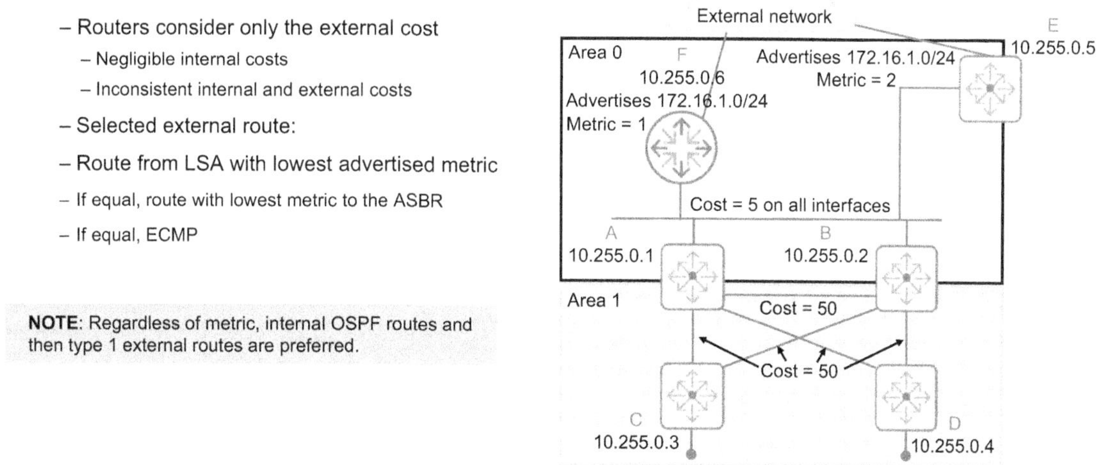


Figure 5-31 Choosing between external routes to the same network: Type 2 metric

Type 5 LSAs use type 1 and type 2 metrics. When routers examine a type 2 metric, which is the default, they consider only the metric advertised by the ASBR. OSPF follows this high-level process to choose the best external route:

1. The router uses the Type 5 LSA to calculate the external route, setting the correct forwarding interface, and next hop for the shortest path to the advertising ASBR.
   - If the router is in the same area as the ASBR, it knows the correct forwarding interface and next hop from the area's shortest path topology. ECMP routing might apply.
   - If the router is in a different area from the ASBR, it calculates a metric for the ASBR route by incrementing the metric in the Type 4 LSA with the metric for reaching the advertising ABR. If multiple ABRs advertise a Type 4 LSA to the same ASBR, the router chooses the ASBR route with the lower *total* cost.
   - A router might have multiple equal cost paths to an ASBR. Multiple ABRs might offer the router an equal cost path to the ASBR, and the router has a different next hop for each ABR. Or, the router might have multiple equal cost paths to one ABR.
   - The best path might not match the IP route to the ASBR's IP address in the routing table. For example, the ABRs shown in Figure 5-31 advertise the same cost to the ASBRs. However, in Figure 5-31, router A and router B might advertise the same cost for the area 0 summary. However, ABR-B advertises a better Type 4 LSA for ASBR-E. Therefore, the internal area 1 routers will use their best path to router B to calculate the path to the ASBR, rather than load-balance over the link to both ABRs.
2. The router sets the external route's metric equal to the metric advertised in the Type 5 LSA. The advertising ASBR added this metric when it redistributed the route into OSPF.

3. When the OSPF routing table already includes an external (type 2) OSPF route to this network, the router selects the route with the lower metric.
4. If both routes have the same metric, the router examines the metric for the forwarding path to the ASBR. It selects the route associated with the ASBR to which it has a lower cost path.
5. If forwarding paths to the ASBRs have equal costs and the router supports ECMP, the router installs multiple routes in the OSPF routing table. (Otherwise, it uses another mechanism such as the router ID to break the tie.)

When all ASBRs use type 2 metrics, an OSPF router will always select the external route through the ASBR that advertises the lowest metric for it, *even if the router is closer to another ASBR that advertises the same route*. However, if multiple ASBRs advertise the route with the same metric, other routers do take the cost of reaching the ASBR into account.

The reasoning behind this behavior is that the cost of reaching the ASBR through the OSPF AS is often negligible compared to the cost of reaching the external network. In addition, the ASBR might not be assigning metrics to the external routes that correspond to the metrics used in the OSPF AS. In other words, a metric of 10 for the external route might not mean the same thing that a 10 metric on an OSPF link means, in terms of how strongly the company prefers using a particular path.

---

**Note**

Figure 5-31 examines the selection process when OSPF is choosing between identical *external* OSPF routes. Usually, a network advertised in a Type 5 LSA should not be associated with an internal OSPF route, but a misconfiguration could cause this situation to occur. In that case, the OSPF always prefers internal (intra-area and then inter-area) routes.

And, of course, the router uses administrative distance to choose between the OSPF route and routes learned through other means.

---

## Learning check

Refer to Figure 5-32 as you answer the following questions:

1. Which ASBR does router C, in area 1, select to reach the external route, 172.16.1.0/24?
2. What is the next hop in router C's external route to 172.16.1.0/24? (This router supports ECMP.)

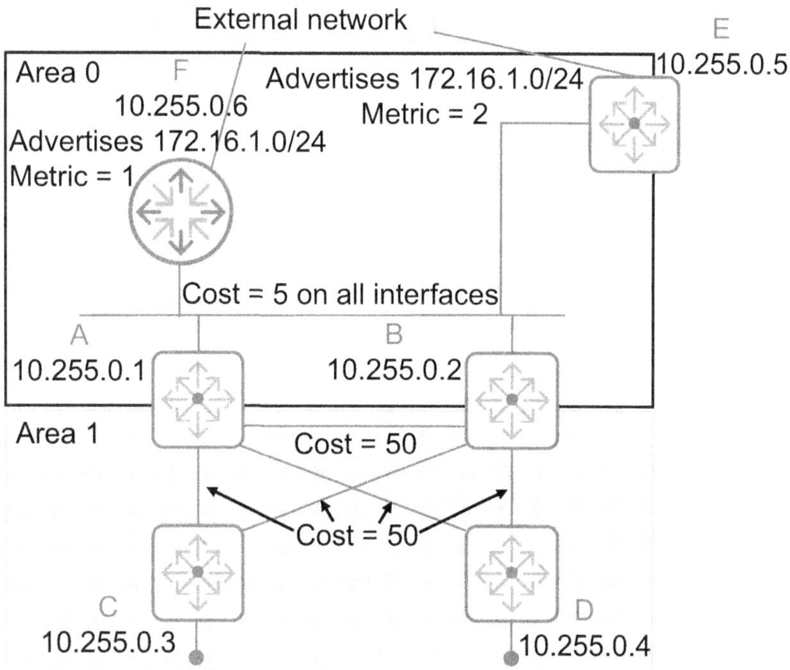


Figure 5-32 Choosing between external routes to the same network: Type 2 metric

Figure 5-33 shows a slightly different topology in which the ABRs have different costs to the ASBRs. Refer to Figure 5-33 as you answer the following questions:

3. Which ASBR does router C, in area 1, select to reach the external route, 172.16.1.0/24? Is this the same ASBR as it selected in the topology shown in Figure 5-32?
4. What is the next hop in router C's external route to 172.16.1.0/24? (This router supports ECMP.) Is this the same next hop used for this route in the previous topology?

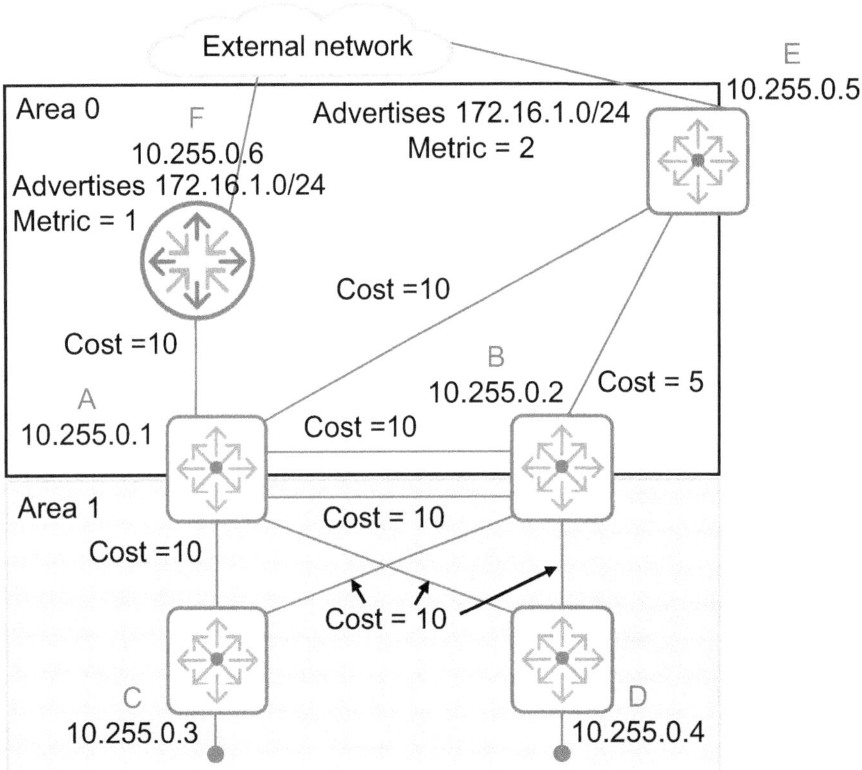


Figure 5-33 Choosing between external routes to the same network: Type 2 metric

## Choosing between external routes to the same network: Type 1 metric

Sometimes the cost of reaching the ASBR is not negligible. In that case, you might want routers to take the cost of reaching the ASBR into account when selecting the ASBR for a particular external network (as opposed to the path to the already selected ASBR). Use a type 1 metric, which signals routers to add the cost of reaching the ASBR to the metric advertised in the Type 5 LSA. You should also ensure that ASBRs redistribute the external routes with metrics that make sense when compared to costs used within the OSPF process. For example, the total metric for the LSA received from ASBR F is 21:

1 (external metric) + 20 (metric of lowest cost path to ASBR F)

The total metric for the LSA received from ASBR E is 17:

2 (external metric) + 15 (metric of lowest cost path to ASBR E)

Therefore, router C selects ASBR E. In this topology, router C makes a different choice when the ASBR use type 1 metrics versus type 2 metrics because the cost of its path to ASBR E is enough lower to counteract the higher metric advertised by ASBR E.

- Routers consider both internal and external costs
  - Should use similar scale
- Selected route:
  - Route from LSA with lowest Advertised metric + Metric for reaching ASBR
  - If equal, ECMP

**NOTE**: Regardless of metric, internal OSPF routes are preferred.

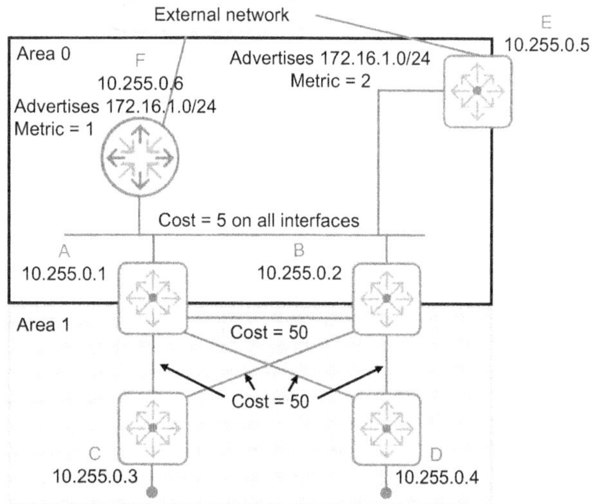


Figure 5-34 Choosing between external routes to the same network: Type 1 metric

In more detail, an OSPF router chooses between type 1 external routes to the same network as follows (see Figure 5-34):

1. The router uses the Type 5 LSA to calculate the external route, setting the correct forwarding interface, and next hop for the path to the advertising ASBR.
2. The router sets the external route's metric equal to:

   The metric advertised in the Type 5 LSA + The metric for the forwarding path to the advertising ASBR.
3. When the OSPF routing table already includes an external (type 2) OSPF route to this network, the router selects the route with the lower metric.
4. If both routes have the same metric, the router installs multiple routes in the OSPF routing table. (Otherwise, it uses a mechanism such as router ID to break the tie.)

## Learning check

Refer to Figure 5-35 as you answer the following questions:

1. Which ASBR does router C, in area 1, select to reach the external route, 172.16.1.0/24? Is this choice different from the choice when ASBRs use type 2 metrics?
2. What is the next hop in router C's external route to 172.16.1.0/24? (This router supports ECMP.)

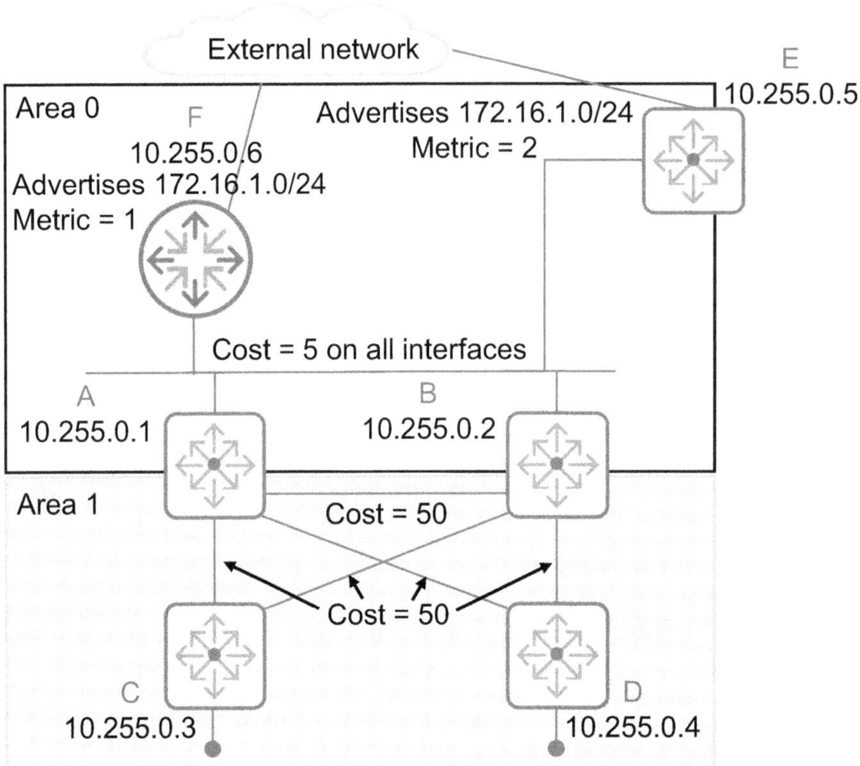


Figure 5-35 Choosing between external routes to the same network: Type 1 metric

Consider the effects of advertising type 1 LSAs is a topology with different costs on different links. Refer to Figure 5-36 as you answer the next questions.

3. Which ASBR does router C, in area 1, select to reach the external route, 172.16.1.0/24? Is this choice different from when the ASBRs use type 2 metrics?

4. What is the next hop in router C's external route to 172.16.1.0/24? (This router supports ECMP.)

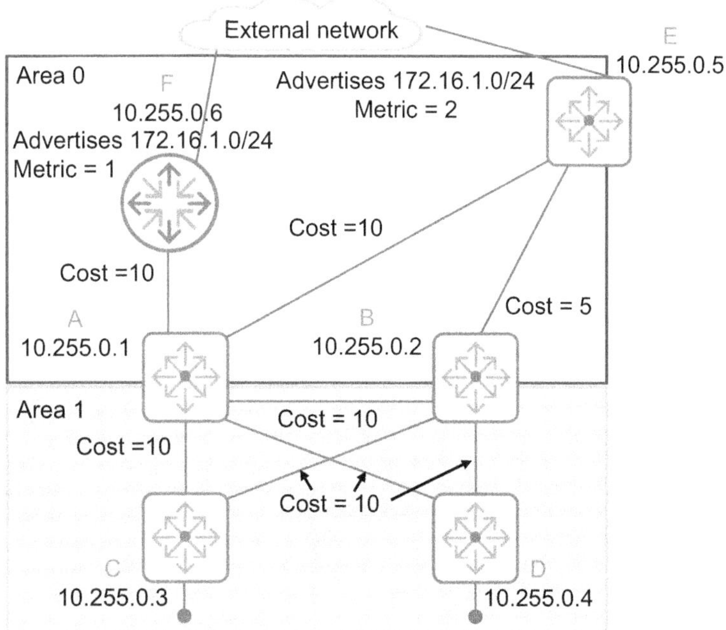


Figure 5-36 Choosing between external routes to the same network: Type 1 metric

## Review factors that affect OSPF route selection

Before moving on, take a moment to review what you have learned.

Consider Router C, an internal router in area 1, as shown in Figure 5-37. Area 1 is a stub area with two ABRs, Router A and Router B. For intra-area routes such as that to 10.1.20.0/24, link costs alone determine the best path and selected next hop. In other words, if the cost of the C-to-B link + the B-to-D link is less than the cost of the C-to-A + the A-to-D link, C will use B as the next hop. If the costs are the same, C will learn two routes and use a hash to assign conversations to each.

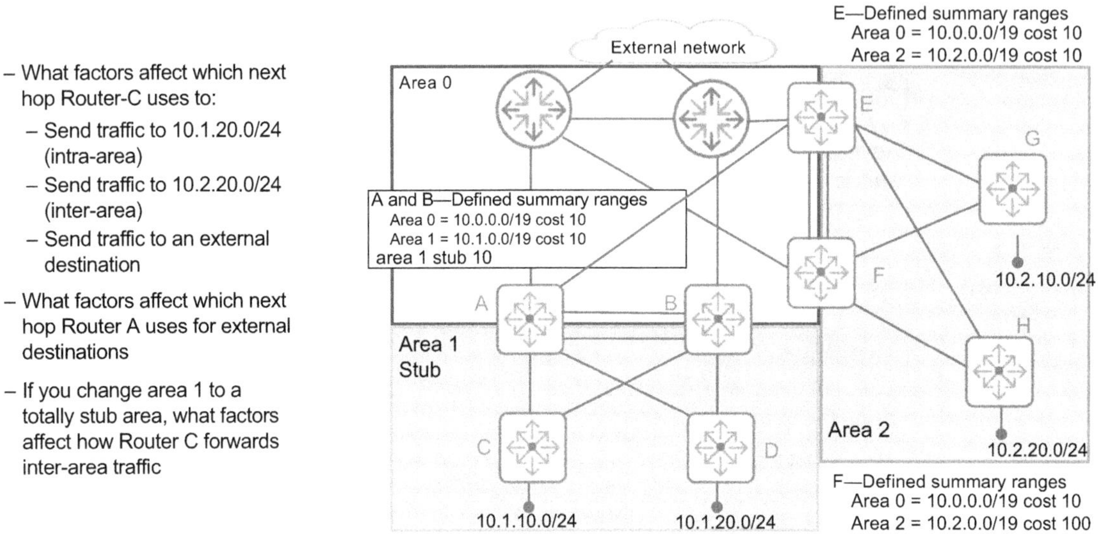


Figure 5-37 Review factors that affect OSPF route selection

Link costs also play a large factor in determining how C shown in Figure 5-37 forwards inter-area traffic such as that destined to 10.2.20.0/24. Remember, though, that C is using 10.2.0.0/19 route for all traffic destined to area 2 (10.2.0.0 to 10.2.31.255). You need to consider the link costs from C to its ABRs and then from those ABRs to the area 2 ABRs. At that point, you add the cost of the 10.2.0.0/19 summary that the area 2 ABR advertises. In other words, the cost set for the summary range on the area 2 ABR influences the path for the inter-area traffic destined to that area, but a router's cost for reaching that ABR is also taken into account.

Because this is a stub area, Router C shown in Figure 5-37 uses a default route to reach external destinations. It chooses the default route based on the metric advertised by the ABR and the cost for reaching the ABR. The next hop is the next hop in the best path to the advertising ABR. So the next hop for the default route is affected by link costs within area 1 and the cost set in the **area 1 stub** command on the ABRs.

More factors affect Router A's choice of next hop for routes to external destinations. The metric type (1 or 2) advertised by the ASBRs plays a role, as does the advertised metric itself. Link costs within area 0 can also affect the choice. If ASBRs use type 1 LSAs, these costs are incremented with the advertised metric when Router A chooses the best of two external LSAs for the same destination. Even if ASBRs use type 2 LSAs, the area 0 costs will still affect Router A's best path to the ASBR that advertises the best LSA.

As a final review, suppose that you change area 0 shown in Figure 5-37 to a totally stub network. In this case, Router C uses its default route for both inter-area and external OSPF routes. Therefore, the ways to influence how Router C forwards inter-area traffic are to manipulate the link costs within area 1 and the cost in the **area 1 stub** command on the ABRs.

## OSPF failover and convergence

You will now explore how to ensure that OSPF systems with redundant links provide the required level of fast convergence. You will learn how features such as bidirectional forwarding detection (BFD) and OSPF graceful restart can speed convergence.

In a topology with redundant links (as shown in Figure 5-38), OSPF automatically handles reconvergence if a link fails. You should consider, though, how your design and configuration can affect how long reconvergence will take. Factors that affect whether connectivity is disrupted and for how long include:

- How quickly neighbors on a failed link detect lost connectivity
- How quickly routers can generate and transmit LSUs in response to the problem and how quickly their neighbors can process LSUs
- How many routers have to rerun the shortest path algorithm and how much of the algorithm they have to run
- How far LSUs withdrawing LSAs need to propagate (the more routers that need to receive and generate updates, the longer it takes for the system to converge)

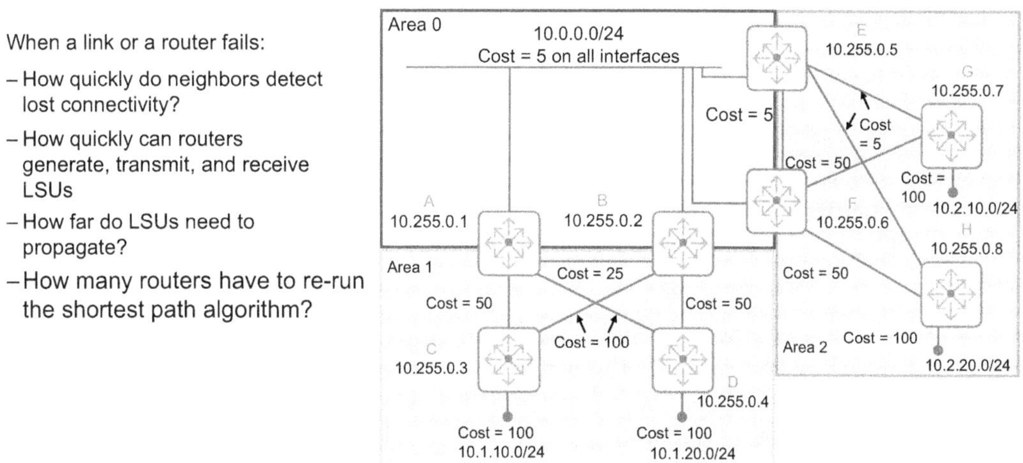


Figure 5-38 Review factors that affect OSPF route selection

Set aside the first factor for a moment. (You will look at ways to speed lost neighbor detection later in this chapter.) For the next factor, the default timers often provide sufficiently speedy LSU generation and propagation. When very fast convergence is required, you can adjust OSPF timers such as the LSA generation interval. However, in most cases, you should leave the intervals at their defaults; tuning them is beyond the scope of this study guide.

For the third and fourth questions, consider how what you have learned about multi-area designs helps to stabilize the system and enhance convergence.

Area borders act as boundaries for changes, and often LSUs generated by a change within the area will not prompt LSUs for other areas. In addition, only changes within the OSPF area cause a router to rerun the full shortest path algorithm. Updates to summary, summary-ASBR, and external LSAs require just a partial rerun. The router simply adds a new network to the list of networks reachable behind the ABR, removes a network from the list, or adjusts the cost for reaching the network. The router does not need to recalculate and run the shortest path algorithm because it cares only about the segment of the inter-area path between itself and the proper ABR for reaching the inter-area network. Those paths have not changed.

For example, assume Router B shown in Figure 5-38 loses its link to Router C. Routers in area 1 learn this information, and Router D and B begin route all traffic to 10.1.10.0/24 through Router A. However, Router A and Router B still have a route to this network, so they do not withdraw its Type 3 LSA for the subnet. It might need to update the cost, but usually, it will not even need to do that because it is aggregating the area 1 summaries anyway. As far as routers in area 0 and area 2 are concerned nothing has changed. As you see, changes and any attendant disruptions are isolated to area 1.

## Detecting failed neighbor relationships

In a well-designed OSPF AS with proper area boundaries, the time to detect failed neighbor relationships often determines how seamlessly OSPF routes fail over.

Consider a situation in which an OSPF router has lost its connection to the next-hop in one of its routes. Either a link has failed or the neighbor as a whole has failed. To remove the invalid route and begin using an alternate, the OSPF router must detect the failure of the next hop neighbor in the primary route. Often the detection of the problem makes up the bulk of the time required for routes to failover.

When two neighbors have a point-to-point connection on a direct link, the status of the interface correlates rather well to the status of the neighbor. If the neighbor fails, the interface with the direct connection goes down. The router can immediately remove any routes through that interface. Similarly, when a VLAN interface is dedicated to a single physical link, the failure of that link brings the VLAN interface down. The routing switch can then remove any routes through that interface. In either case, the time to detect the Link Layer problem affects the time for detecting the failed neighbor relationship. This time varies depending on the media and is acceptable for many companies' needs.

Figure 5-39 shows a topology with a design with direct links between routing devices. Each link has a different VLAN and subnet dedicated to it, enabling fast convergence.

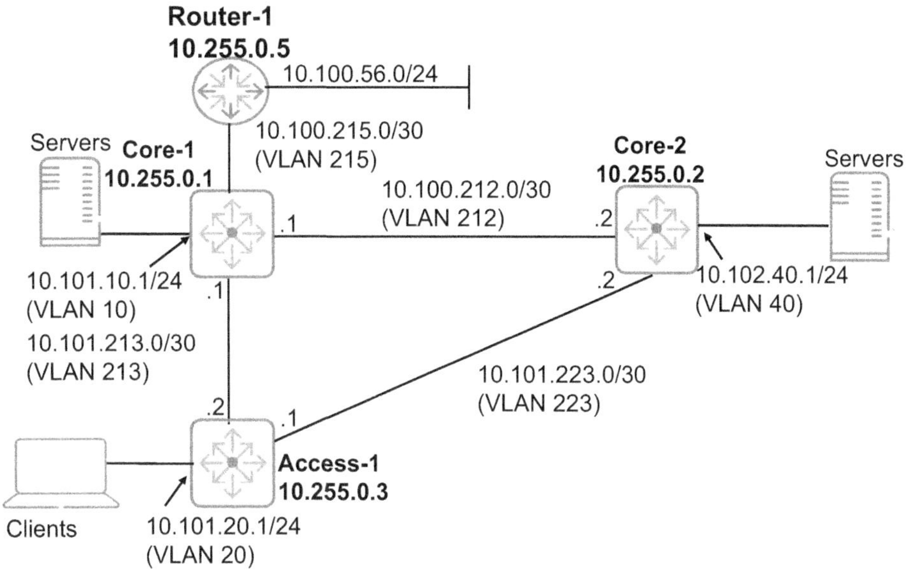


Figure 5-39 Topology with dedicated VLANs

However, sometimes the status of an OSPF interface and the status of an OSPF neighbor do not directly correlate. Examples relevant to AOS-Switches include:

- The neighbors connect on a broadcast network such as a VLAN but the VLAN has multiple links, and possibly multiple neighbors, associated with it.
- The neighbors do not have a direct Layer 2 connection. For example, a non-routing switch intervenes between two OSPF neighbors.
- The neighbors have a direct Layer 2 connection, but problems occur at Layer 3. For example, a misconfiguration has prevented one of the neighbors from implementing OSPF on the network.

Table 5-6 summarizes how to detect a failed neighbor relationship.

Table 5-6 Detecting failed neighbor relationships

| Type of link to neighbor | Time for removing neighbor relationship depends on | Typical times |
|---|---|---|
| Ethernet dedicated VLAN on direct links | Time for detecting Layer 2 issue and bringing the VLAN interface down | Under 1 second |
| Ethernet with indirect links:<br>• Multiple routing devices on the network<br>• Intervening Layer 1 or Layer 2 devices | Interface OSPF dead timer | • 40 seconds (default)<br>• 4 seconds (minimum) |

In those cases, the OSPF router must rely on the OSPF timers to determine the neighbor status. That is, if the dead time expires without a hello from the neighbor, the router considers the neighbor down and removes routes using that neighbor as a next hop from the routing table. The OSPF dead timer is always four times the hello timer. Because the default hello timer is 10 seconds, the default dead timer is 40 seconds, which is far too long for contemporary networks.

You can adjust the hello and dead timers, but the lowest standard hello timer is 1 second, making the lowest dead timer 4 seconds, still too long for many contemporary networks.

## Using BFD to speed OSPF failed neighbor detection

BFD provides a standard, reliable mechanism for detecting failed neighbors in any of the cases you examined in the "Detecting failed neighbor relationships" section.

BFD tests the connectivity between two IP addresses in a BFD session. BFD reports when connectivity is lost. The router (or routing switch) can then use that information to take the appropriate actions, depending on the functions to which you have tied BFD.

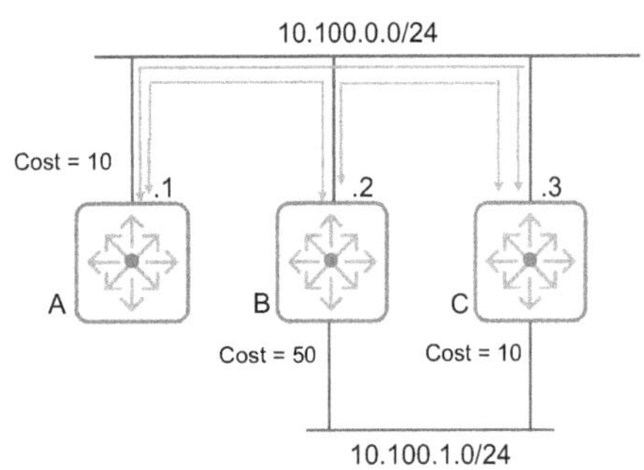


- Enable BFD globally
- Enable OSPF BFD on VLAN interface

BFD sessions on A

| IP source | IP destination |
|---|---|
| 10.100.0.1 | 10.100.0.2 |
| 10.100.0.1 | 10.100.0.3 |

BFD sessions on B

| IP source | IP destination |
|---|---|
| 10.100.0.2 | 10.100.0.1 |
| 10.100.0.2 | 10.100.0.3 |

BFD sessions on C

| IP source | IP destination |
|---|---|
| 10.100.0.3 | 10.100.0.1 |
| 10.100.0.3 | 10.100.0.2 |

Figure 5-40 Using BFD to speed OSPF failed neighbor detection

When you enable OSPF BFD on an OSPF interface, BFD assumes responsibility for testing connectivity to the neighbor. If the BFD session fails, the switch removes the BFD neighbor relationship, enabling the switch to remove all LSAs through that neighbor and update routing paths. (The interface still sends out OSPF hellos, but BFD will generally detect any problems first).

For example, in Figure 5-40, three routing switches connect on subnet 10.100.0.0/24. Switch B and Switch C also connect to network 10.100.1.0/24. Switch A is using Switch C as the next hop for 10.100.1.0/24 because Switch C has the lower cost link on this network. If Switch C's link on

10.100.0.0/24 fails, and Switch A is not using BFD, Switch A continues sending traffic to 10.100.1.0/24 through 10.100.0.3 until its neighbor relationship times out. Because 10.100.0.3 is no longer up, this traffic does not reach its destination. With BFD, Switch A quickly detects that 10.100.0.3 is no longer available. BFD removes the neighbor relationship, causing Switch A to lose adjacency with Switch C. Switch A can then immediately start using Switch B as the next hop to 10.100.1.0/24 instead.

Here, you see the events associated with the BFD function on Switch A in the example shown in Figure 5-40.

```
I 07/21/17 04:50:23 05080 bfd: AM1: Session 1 under OSPF changed to DOWN.
W 07/21/17 04:50:23 05076 bfd: AM1: BFD session 2 error NeighborSessionDown.
E 09/02/17 04:50:23 02703 OSPF: AM1: ADJCHG: Neighbor with Router ID 10.100.0.3
            on vlan-100 moved to Down state - adjacency lost.
```

On Aruba 5400R switches, BFD is supported with v3 modules and above. You can only enable BFD if you have disabled v2 modules with this command and rebooted the switch:

```
Switch(config)# no allow-v2-modules
```

Then enter this command to enable BFD globally:

```
Switch(config)# bfd enable
```

You must also enable OSPF BFD on the individual VLAN interfaces with this command:

```
Switch(config)# vlan <ID> ip ospf <all | IP address> bfd
```

The **all** keyword tells the switch to enable OSPF BFD on all IP addresses configured on the VLAN. If a VLAN is multi-netted, you can specify an IP address to configure BFD on just that IP address.

Because AOS-Switches use active mode, the interface automatically attempts to establish a BFD session with each OSPF neighbor on that interface. It transmits a unicast BFD control packets on UDP port 3784 to each neighbor. As you see in Figure 5-40, a BFD session is point-to-point. In this example, the 10.100.0.0/24 network has three OSPF routers, each of which implements OSPF BFD. Each router will attempt to establish a session with each of its two neighbors for six total BFD sessions on the network.

To establish a BFD session, the neighbors simply determine that both support BFD and negotiate timers.

---

**Note**

If an OSPF neighbor does not support BFD, the switch continues to try to establish a BFD session with that neighbor. It lists the session as down, but, because the session was never up, the down state does not cause the switch to tear down the neighbor relationship.

---

## BFD control messages and asynchronous mode

Each neighbor in the session has its own active Tx timer, which determines how often it transmits BFD control packets. You do not configure the active Tx timer manually. Instead, this timer derives from the Min Tx and Min Rx timers, which are configurable intervals on each OSPF interface. An interface's active Tx timer in a particular BFD session is the *larger* of two values: its Min Tx timer (the Tx timer that the interface wants to use) and its *neighbor's* Min Rx timer (the smallest interval at which the neighbor can receive control packets). In the example shown in Figure 5-41, the active Tx timer for A's session to B at 10.100.0.2 is 3 because B's min Rx timer, 3, is higher than A's min Tx timer, 2. B's active Tx timer on its side is also 3 (B's min Tx timer, 3, is higher than A's min Rx timer, 2). Similarly, A negotiates an active Tx timer of 2 for its session with C, and C also negotiates an active Tx timer of 2 for this session.

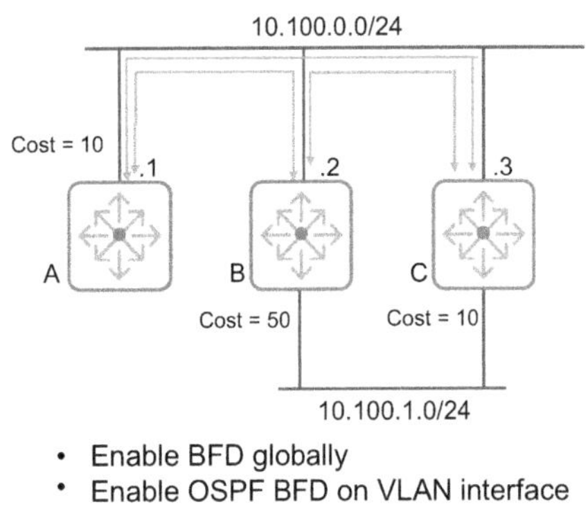


OSPF BFD settings on A, B, and C VLAN 100

| | Min Tx | Min Rx | Detect multiplier |
|---|---|---|---|
| A | 2 | 2 | 3 |
| B | 3 | 3 | 3 |
| C | 1 | 1 | 3 |

BFD sessions on A

| IP source | IP destination | Active Tx timer | Detect timer |
|---|---|---|---|
| 10.100.0.1 | 10.100.0.2 | 3 | 9 (3x3) |
| 10.100.0.1 | 10.100.0.3 | 2 | 6 (2x3) |

Figure 5-41 BFD control messages and asynchronous mode

Each neighbor in the session also has its own detect timer, which determines how long the interface can go without receiving a control packet from the neighbor before taking the session down. When the session goes down, the switch tears down the OSPF neighbor relationship even if the dead timer has not yet expired.

The detect timer derives from the detect multiplier configured on the interface multiplied by the *neighbor's* active Tx timer, which in turn is the larger of the neighbor's Min Tx timer or this interface's Min Rx timer. In the example shown in Figure 5-41, the neighbor's active Tx timer is the same as A's active Tx timer. The neighbor's timer multiplied by the detect multiplier, which is 3 in this example, sets the detect time. You can set the interface's Min Rx timer to 0 if you do not want the switch to track control messages; in this case, the switch will not tear down the session if it fails to receive control messages from the peer.

In short, an interface's Min Tx timer determines how quickly a neighbor can detect a control message timeout. The interface's Min Rx timer determines how quickly *this* interface can detect a neighbor no longer sending control messages. However, the neighbor values will also affect these settings, if they are larger. The detect multiplier also affects how quickly this interface detects failed neighbors; the default is 5, and you can lower it to 4 or 3 if you have a reliable link that loses little traffic. If you set the Min Tx and Min Rx timers to the minimum value (1 second), do not set the detect multiplier lower than 3.

The active Tx timer and detect time on the two neighbors in a BFD session do not have to match. However, they often do.

When the switch uses the control message timeout alone to determine when a session fails, it operates in asynchronous mode. In this mode, BFD does not provide subsecond detection of issues, which is often what you want from BFD. Therefore, you should usually enable OSPF BFD to operate in echo mode.

Enter this command to set the timers on a VLAN interface (the intervals are in seconds):

```
Switch(config)# vlan <ID> bfd min-transmit-interval <1-20> min-receive-
    interval <0-20>  detect-multiplier <1-5>
```

The min-transmit-interval sets the Min Tx timer. The min-receive-interval sets the Min Rx timer. The default values are 3 for the intervals and 5 for the multiplier. Note that the default settings for these intervals and the detect multipliers are not those shown in Figure 5-41; those settings were selected for purposes of illustrating concepts.

## BFD echo mode

In echo mode, control messages still maintain the BFD session but echo messages, which are transmitted at subsecond intervals, allow BFD to respond to issues much more quickly. As Figure 5-42 shows, the interface implementing BFD sends an echo message to the other side of the session. The other side of the session simply echoes the message back without processing it. If the interface does not receive its echo message back, BFD takes down the session and the OSPF neighbor relationship. (The switches still exchange control messages in echo mode, but these become less important for determining when the session has failed.)

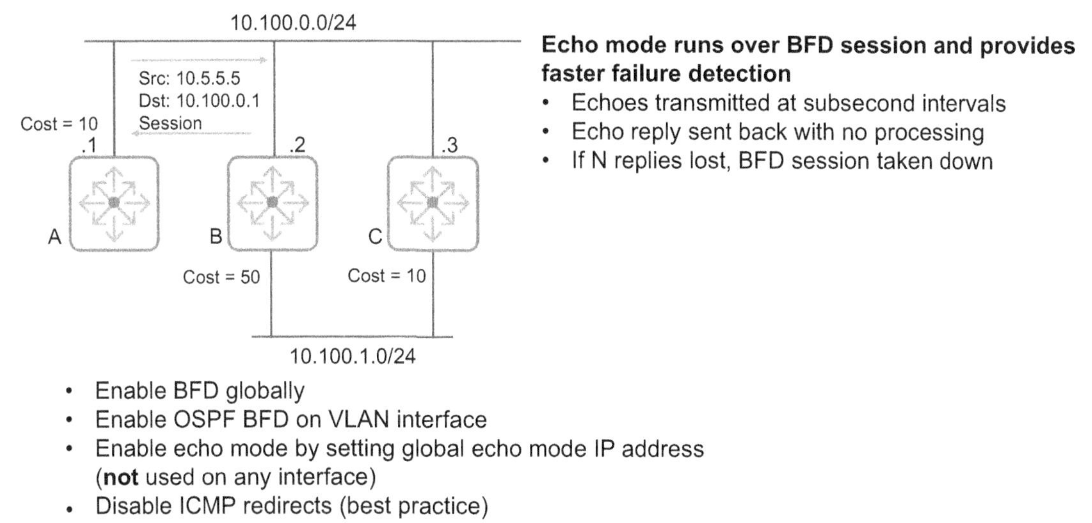


Figure 5-42 BFD echo mode

The switch transmits echo messages at the minimum echo receive interval that its *neighbor* supports. You configure the echo receive timer with this command:

```
Switch(config)# vlan <ID> bfd min-echo-receive-interval <ms>
```

If you do not want an individual VLAN interface to allow the *neighbor* to use echo mode, set the min-echo-receive interval to 0.

By default, AOS-Switches support echoing echo messages back to their BFD neighbors at a 500 ms interval. However, they will *not* send echo messages themselves until you set a global BFD echo source for the packets, which is *not* set by default. Until you set the address, the BFD session will have echo mode disabled. You should choose a unique "dummy" IP address that is *not* used on this device.

```
Switch(config)# bfd echo-src-ip-address <IP address>
```

The switch uses this as the source for the echo packets. The destination is the switch's own IP address, and the neighbor can quickly echo the packet back. Setting the source IP address to a different subnet ensures that the neighbor does not have to process the packet and send Internet Control Message Protocol (ICMP) redirects. It is also best practice to disable ICMP redirects on the switches that use BFD in echo mode.

After you set the global echo IP address, the switch automatically uses echo mode on every VLAN on which you have enabled OSPF BFD, as long as the neighbor also allows.

## The need for graceful restart

Next, consider situations in which an OSPF system includes routers that also implement other protocols for high availability. In this study guide, you have explored several ways to ensure redundancy of the default router (or routing switch).

- VSF (preferred when possible)
- Virtual Router Redundancy Protocol (VRRP)

However, simply ensuring that the default gateway functions are maintained does not ensure that failure of the VSF commander or VRRP master does not disrupt the routing system as a whole. When you use VSF, OSPF graceful restart ensures nonstop routing as the standby member takes over as commander. (You will examine strategies for speeding convergence in systems that use VRRP later in this chapter.)

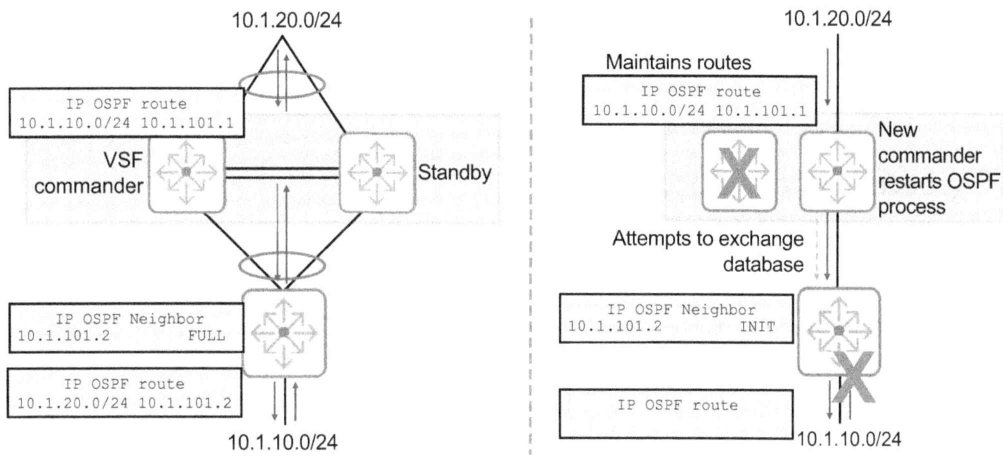


Figure 5-43 The need for graceful restart

Figure 5-43 shows why graceful restart is necessary.

The commander of the VSF fabric maintains routing tables and routing protocol information in its control plane. (In a chassis switch, the commander's primary management module maintains this information.) The commander proxies this information to other members' control planes, but if the commander fails, the routing processes must restart on the new commander.

The VSF members have routes proxied to the forwarding information databases (FIBs) in their control planes (or the control planes of their LPUs, in the case of chassis-based switches). They can continue to route traffic with these stale routes until the new commander builds the routes in its own control plane—and, when the VSF fabric is using static routes or Routing Information Protocol (RIP) routes, they do seamlessly.

However, standard OSPF does not allow OSPF neighbors to entirely resynchronize the LSDBs without tearing down the old adjacency relationship. Therefore, when the new commander tries to re-establish adjacency, the VSF fabric's neighbors take down the neighbor relationship and send out LSUs as if the fabric were no longer available. Routes reconverge away from VSF fabric—even though the fabric is perfectly capable of routing the traffic—causing unnecessary disruption to the traffic flow and possible interruption to service.

OSPF graceful restart, on the other hand, enables the VSF fabric to ask its neighbors to maintain the neighbor and/or adjacency relationship undisturbed while the new commander restarts the OSPF process. Thus, traffic continues toward its destination undisturbed.

An OSPF router or routing switch that has redundant management modules should also implement OSPF graceful restart. The failover of the primary management module to the standby module is analogous to the failover of the VSF commander to the standby member. Although the OSPF router or routing switch can use its stale routes to forward traffic, it must also send OSPF graceful restart requests to inform its neighbors not to drop its LSAs while the new management module rebuilds the adjacencies.

Note that OSPF graceful restart also helps to maintain routing system stability in *any* circumstance in which an OSPF router must restart its OSPF processes, including when a network administrator restarts the process for maintenance purposes (such as applying configuring a new router ID).

## OSPF graceful restart process

Now that you understand when and why graceful restart is required, you can examine the IETF standard graceful restart process. Refer to Figure 5-44 as you review this process.

1. The switch configured to support graceful restart, or the GR Restarter, determines that it needs to restart its OSPF process. As you learned, this often occurs when a new VSF member takes over the commander role or when a redundant management module takes over.

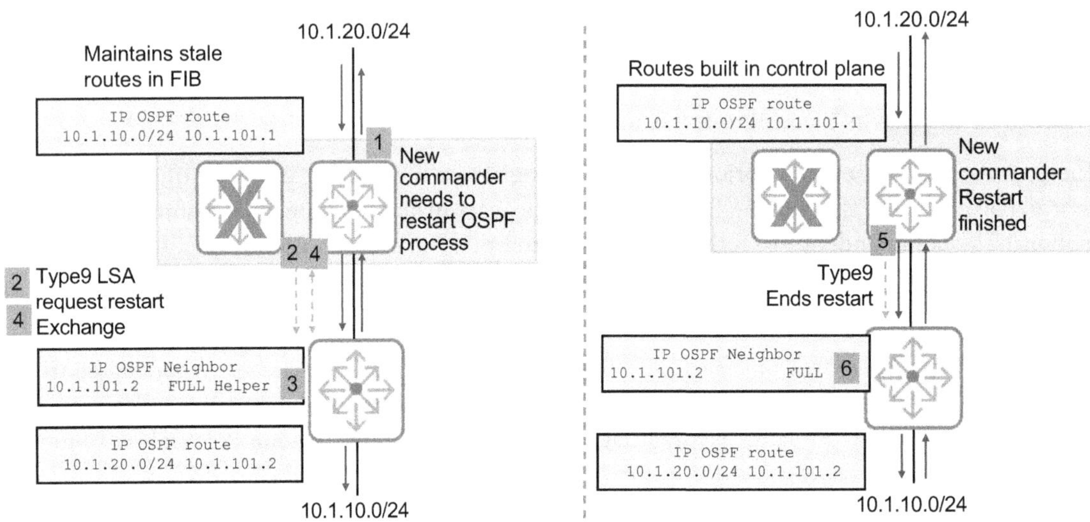


Figure 5-44 OSPF graceful restart process

2. The GR Restarter sends a Type 9 opaque LSA, or grace LSA, to its neighbors, which requests that the neighbors transition to graceful helper mode. The LSA includes:
   - A grace period timer, which specifies how long the neighbors stay in graceful helper mode
   - A graceful restart reason:
     - 0 = Unknown
     - 1 = Software restart
     - 2 = Software upgrade
     - 3 = Failover from an active to a standby management module, or, for VSF, failover from commander to standby
   - The GR Restarter's IP address

3. The neighbors, which must be configured as IETF standard GR Helpers, place the GR Restarter in graceful restart mode. In this mode, they behave as if they have full adjacency with the GR Restarter no matter what is actually occurring. Therefore, the GR Helpers continue routing traffic to the GR Restarter and maintain LSAs from it, trusting that the GR Restarter can truly continue to route traffic with its stale routes.

4. During this time, the GR Restarter is establishing neighbor relationships and adjacencies with the GR Helpers. As always during this process, the switch obtains LSAs advertised by OSPF routing devices throughout the area. Some of these LSAs were advertised by itself (or the previous VSF commander); the Restarter labels those LSAs as stale.

5. After the GR Restarter has established adjacency with all of its neighbors, it sends a grace LSA, requesting that the Helpers leavehelper mode (the grace period time is set to 0).

6. The GR Helpers leave helper mode. However, because they have achieved adjacency with the GR Restarter, they continue to route traffic to it without interruption.

The GR Restarter has continued routing traffic with stale routes. However, it must ensure the truth of what it asked the GR Helpers to trust: it knows the correct routes and the topology that it advertised before the restart remains accurate. During and after the process of establishing adjacency, the GR Restarter recalculates routes, changes stale routes to active routes, and determines whether any updates are necessary.

- The GR Restarter calculates routes from the LSAs that it received from OSPF neighbors. The new routes replace the stale routes. If any stale routes remain, they are deleted as no longer valid. The GR Restarter now knows that it is routing traffic with the most up-to-date information.
- The GR Restarter generates its own LSAs and compares them to its own stale LSAs, which it received from the Helpers. Unless its connections have changed, the GR Restarter's LSAs will match its stale LSAs. The GR Restarter removes the stale designation from those LSAs and takes no further action (its neighbors already know the LSAs).
- If the GR Restarter has generated any new LSAs, it advertises them to neighbors as normal in an LSU message. Similarly, if any stale LSAs remain (no matching current LSA), the GR Restarter deletes those LSAs and withdraws them in an LSU message.

The GR Restarter and the GR Helpers now know the proper LSAs, network topology, and routes. Throughout the process, all of the OSPF routing switches continued routing traffic with stale routes, only removing the routes if they were demonstrated to be truly invalid. Because the stale routes typically prove to be valid, the routing switches typically transition seamlessly from routing with stale routes to routing with active routes.

> **Note**
> The OSPF graceful restart standard dictates that GR Helpers must leave helper mode if the topology changes in a way that would affect the GR Restarter. That is, the GR Helper generates or receives an LSA that it would normally send to the GR Restarter. This provision prevents routing loops.

## Implementing OSPF graceful restart

Now that you understand why you need to enable OSPF graceful restart, doing so is simple. Configure VSF fabrics, as well as routing devices that must support nonstop routing during management module failover, as GR Restarters. As a best practice, you could also enable the restarter function on other routing devices that support it, protecting the network in case an administrator accidentally restarts the OSPF process in a live environment.

All neighbors of the GR Restarters must act as GR Helpers. As a best practice, you should generally ensure that all OSPF routing devices in the AS support this function.

### Configuration process

AOS-Switches can act as GR restarters when they have redundant Main Processing Units (MPUs) and the main MPU fails or when they are part of a VSF fabric and the commander fails. To enable the graceful restart functions, follow these steps:

1. Enable nonstop routing for OSPF.

```
SwitchRestarter(config)# router ospf
SwitchRestarter(ospf)# nonstop
```

2. Adjust the restart interval (default 120 seconds). The time should exceed the time required for the new management module or commander to achieve adjacency with its neighbors.

```
SwitchRestarter(ospf)# restart interval <1-800>
SwitchRestarter(ospf)# exit
```

3. Increase the redundancy rapid switchover time so that it exceeds the restart interval.

   After this timer expires, the switch removes any stale routes—that is, routes not recalculated from the reconstructed LSDB. The restart interval dictates the amount of time that the switch promises its neighbors that it can continue to route traffic while it achieves adjacency and reconstructs the LSDB. Therefore, the rapid switchover time must exceed the restart interval. (For example, exceed the restart interval by 3 seconds.)

   The default rapid switchover time of 90 seconds does *not* exceed the default restart interval of 120 seconds, so you must complete this step even if you did not adjust the restart interval.

   ```
   Switch(config)# redundancy rapid-switchover <0-2147483647>
   ```

All AOS-Switches that support OSPF automatically act as GR Helpers.

## Implementing OSPF and VRRP

As you have learned, you should use VSF to provide redundancy for the default router role whenever possible. VSF provides redundancy while allowing the VSF fabric to act as a single entity in the routing protocol, making implementing VSF with OSPF almost as easy as implementing OSPF without redundancy. However, sometimes customer requirements might force you to implement OSPF and VRRP. You need to design the solution carefully to ensure that the OSPF and VRRP functions work well together.

When a router implements VRRP and OSPF on the same interface, it uses its actual IP address to run OSPF. However, the protocol interoperations can cause complexities. To minimize these complexities, you should avoid running OSPF and VRRP on the same interfaces.

First, connect VRRP routers to upstream OSPF routers on their own networks and do *not* run VRRP on these networks, as shown in Figure 5-45. This design helps an upstream router to immediately determine when it loses connectivity to a VRRP router.

Second, do not establish OSPF adjacencies on the interfaces that run VRRP. Because VRRP provides redundancy for default gateway services, VRRP runs on directly connected networks, which are generally stub networks. You can redistribute the directly connected networks as external networks. (Make sure to set up the area as a normal area or an NSSA.) You could alternatively configure the interfaces as passive OSPF interfaces.

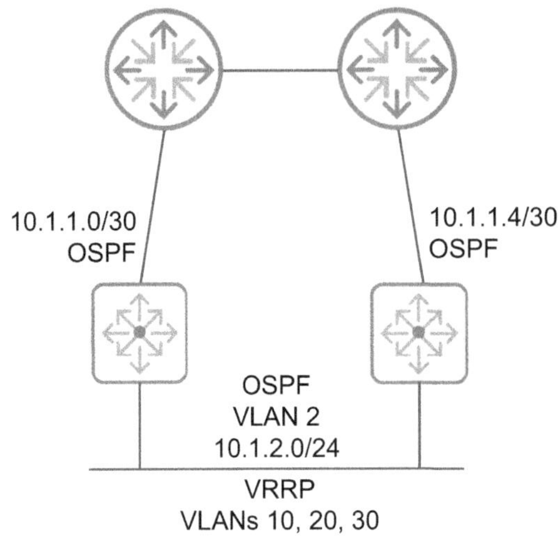


Figure 5-45 Implementing OSPF and VRRP

One exception applies: You should create one OSPF adjacency between the VRRP routers. These routers should exchange routes with each other to prevent routing issues in failover situations. For example, one of the routers might lose its connection to the network core. However, it is still the VRRP master for one or more networks. It needs a backup path to the network core, and its adjacency with the other VRRP router provides this path. (An alternative strategy is using a VRRP track to reduce the VRRP priority if the switch loses its upstream connection, but this study guide does not cover tracks.)

Third, choose the VRRP design in which none of the VRRP routers own the virtual IP address. Otherwise, when the VRRP Owner fails and comes back up, it immediately takes over routing on the interfaces for which it owns the VRRP address. However, it has not yet established adjacencies with upstream OSPF routers, disrupting connectivity on those VLANs. By configuring a virtual IP address that none of the VRRP routers owns, you can prevent this problem. Either disable preempt mode or set a preempt mode delay time that is longer than the time required to establish adjacency with all neighbors and calculate the OSPF routes (generally, two or three minutes).

# Virtual links

Finally, you will look at several additional features for OSPF, beginning with virtual links.

## Example situations that require virtual links

- Area expands and needs to be segmented, but new segment cannot connect to area 0 (shown below)
- Area requires a redundant link to backbone but no connection to area 0 ABR available

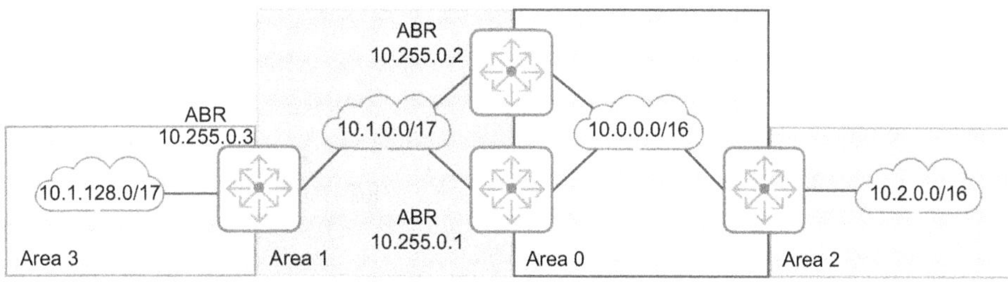


Figure 5-46 Example situations that require virtual links

Well-designed OSPF systems should ensure that you can always connect new areas directly to the backbone. However, sometimes the company expands in unexpected ways, and you cannot meet this requirement.

For example, in the scenario shown in Figure 5-46, the company needs to expand to new sites (10.1.128.0/17). Routers in area 1 are available for connecting to the new routers. However, area 1 has grown so large that you would prefer to establish the new sites in area 3. However, the rules of OSPF prevent you from creating the new area because this area would need to connect directly to routers in area 0, not area 1.

Similar issues can arise when you need to add a redundant link between an area and the backbone area 0. As you have learned, you can create link aggregations between internal area routers and the ABR, which might be one router or, for even better redundancy, two physical routing switches in a VSF fabric. You can also connect internal area routers to two ABRs in area 0. You should choose one of these solutions whenever possible.

In this case, however, a second connection between a particular site and an ABR at the backbone is not available. You must establish the link through a transit site.

## Virtual link

You can use a virtual link to resolve both of these issues.

You establish the virtual link across a transit area (area 1, in the example network shown in Figure 5-47). A routing device on the border between the non-backbone connected area and the transit area uses the virtual link to connect to an ABR between area 0 and the transit area. A virtual link acts like a shared network interface, allowing the two OSPF routing devices to exchange hellos and establish adjacency. Logically, the virtual link acts as a point-to-point OSPF network on which both ABRs have an interface.

In the example shown in Figure 5-47, you would also configure a virtual link between ABR 10.255.0.3 and ABR 10.255.0.2 for redundancy.

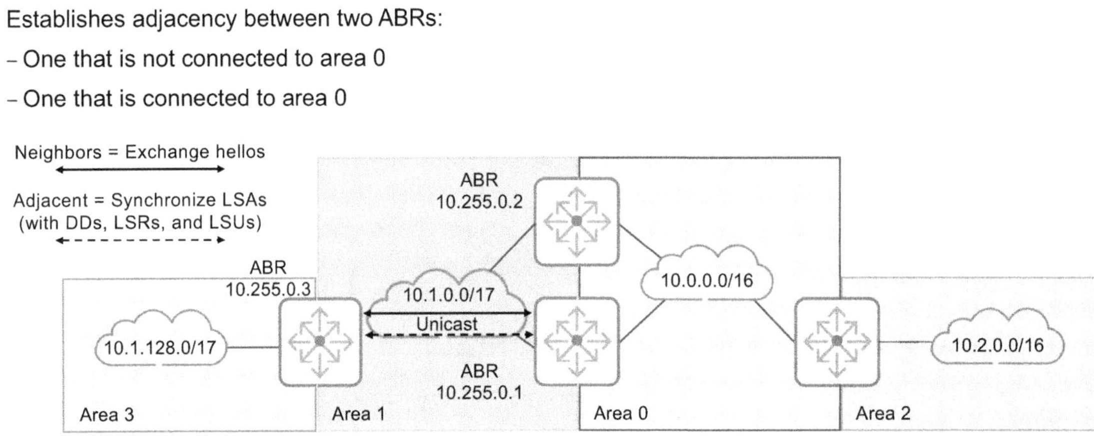


Figure 5-47 Virtual link

Note that you should *not* generally rely on virtual links as part of your design because they introduce complexity. They also negate some of the benefits of multi-area designs by leaking backbone routing information into non-backbone areas. Instead, use virtual links as a patch when you have no other way to create the necessary link to the backbone at the current time.

## Virtual link configuration process

The process for adding the virtual link is outlined below. Before completing these steps, you should configure the basic OSPF settings on all of the routers involved in the solution. The section below provides more detailed steps.

1. Make sure that the transit area is not defined as a stub area or NSSA.
2. Configure the virtual link on the ABR that does not connect to area 0.
    a. As mentioned above, this ABR should have its basic OSPF settings defined:
        - Router ID
        - The area without the direct connection to the backbone (area 3 in the example)
        - The transit area (area 1 in the example)
        - OSPF enabled on the appropriate interfaces in each area
        - Any other settings required for the OSPF solution (such as aggregated area summaries)

b. In the transit area (area 1 in the example shown in Figure 5-47), configure a virtual link. Specify the router ID of the device at the other end of the link.

```
NonbackboneABR(config)# router ospf
NonbackboneABR(ospf)# area 1 virtual-link 10.255.0.1
```

3. Configure the virtual link on the ABR that connects to area 0.

a. Again, this ABR should have its basic OSPF settings defined:

- Router ID
- Area 0
- The transit area (area 1 in the example)
- OSPF enabled on the appropriate networks in each area
- Any other settings required for the OSPF solution

b. In the transit area, configure a virtual link, specifying the router ID of the device at the other end of the link.

```
BackboneABR(ospf)# area 1 virtual-link 10.255.0.3
```

**Note**
Note that the OSPF routing devices have connectivity within the transit area. As always, if you want to be able to ping the router ID, use an IP address on loopback interface that runs OSPF.

4. You must check consistency for the typical settings required for two OSPF routers on a link to achieve adjacency. These settings include the OSPF timers. (The virtual link does not have a network associated with it, so you do not have to check consistency for its type.)

## OSPF authentication

You can implement authentication for OSPF processes on particular router or routing switch interfaces. When an OSPF interface implements authentication, it includes authentication data in all OSPF packets that it transmits. It also checks this data in all OSPF packets that it receives and rejects any packets that fail the check. In other words, only OSPF routers configured with the same authentication keys can establish neighbor relationships.

- Choose authentication type per-area:
  - Null—Provides no authentication
  - Simple—Protects against misconfigurations
  - Cryptographic—Protects against unauthorized routers
- Simple authentication
  - Password per-interface
  - Must match with neighbors on the same interface
- Cryptographic:
  - Global key chains
  - Set the MD5 key chain per-interface
  - Key ID and key secret in associated chain must match with neighbors on the same interface

```
Switch-1(config)# key-chain chain1
Switch-1(config)# key-chain chain1 key 1 key-string password101
Switch-1(config)# key-chain chain2
Switch-1(config)# key-chain chain2 key 1 key-string password102
Switch-1(config)# vlan 101
Switch-1(vlan101)# ip ospf md5-auth-key-chain chain1
Switch-1(vlan101)# vlan 102
Switch-1(vlan102)# ip ospf md5-auth-key-chain chain2
```

```
Switch-2(config)# key-chain chain1
Switch-2(config)# key-chain chain1 key 1 key-string password101
Switch-2(config)# vlan 101
Switch-2(vlan101)# ip ospf md5-auth-key-chain chain1
```

```
Switch-3(config)# key-chain chain1
Switch-3(config)# key-chain chain1 key 1 key-string password102
Switch-3(config)# vlan 102
Switch-3(vlan102)# ip ospf md5-auth-key-chain chain1
```

Figure 5-48 Virtual link configuration process

A packet's authentication field specifies the type (as the AuthID), so receiving routers know how they are expected to authenticate the packet. They only accept packets that are using the same authentication type configured on their interface. As shown in Figure 5-48, for each area, you can choose from several authentication options:

- Null—The default authentication type, in which OSPF interfaces do not enforce authentication. The OSPF packets have an authentication field, but the field does not include any data. An OSPF interface implementing null authentication does not examine the authentication field but process all valid OSPF packets.
- Simple—The OSPF interface places the authentication key in every packet's OSPF header. Other OSPF routers, also implementing this type, examine this field. They only accept OSPF packets for which the field matches their own key.

  Because packets include the key in plaintext, anyone who can collect an OSPF packet transmitted on the network can learn the key. You should use this form of authentication only if you primarily aim to eliminate misconfigurations and routers inadvertently connecting on the wrong networks. You should not use it to secure your OSPF system from unauthorized routers and hackers.
- Cryptographic (MD5)—The OSPF interface hashes the OSPF packet data and the key. It then places the hash at the end of the packet. The authentication field includes the key ID, a length for the hash, and a cryptographic sequence number; however, it does not include the key itself, protecting it from eavesdroppers.

  A router receiving the OSPF packet hashes the packet with its secret key, identified by the key ID. If the hash matches, the router knows that the transmitting router has the correct secret key for this key ID, so it accepts the packet.

  The cryptographic sequence number provides a degree of protection against replay attacks. An OSPF interface only accepts packets with a sequence number equal to or higher than the number for the most recent accepted OSPF packet from this neighbor. The sequence number might be a counter but is usually based on the system clock. In either case, the number is always increasing.

If a hacker obtains a legitimate OSPF packet and attempts to retransmit it later, the packet's cryptographic sequence number is no longer valid, and the other routers on the network reject it. A hacker could replay a packet in the window before the legitimate neighbor sends a packet with a higher sequence, but this window is quite small.

Cryptographic authentication provides authenticity, ensuring that only OSPF interfaces configured with the same key can communicate. It does not provide privacy: the contents of the packet are not encrypted.

All Aruba routers and routing switches support MD5 for the cryptographic hashing algorithm.

## Simple authentication configuration

To set up simple authentication on an AOS-Switch that supports routing, access each interface on which you want to enforce this form of authentication. Enable authentication and set the password with this command:

```
Switch(<vlanID>)# ip ospf [IP address] authentication-key <password>
```

The password can have up to eight characters and must match the password on any OSPF neighbors on this interface.

You only need to set the IP address if the VLAN supports multiple IP addresses, and you want to specify different settings for each. The neighbors on the interface must match.

For example, you might enter these commands:

```
Switch-1(config)# vlan 100
Switch-1(vlan100)# ip ospf authentication-key key100
Switch-1(vlan100)# vlan 101
Switch-1(vlan101)# ip ospf authentication-key key101

Switch-2(config)# vlan 100
Switch-2(vlan100)# ip ospf authentication-key key100

Switch-3(config)# vlan 101
Switch-3(vlan101)# ip ospf authentication-key key101
```

## MD5 authentication configuration

Enter these commands to set up MD5 authentication on an AOS-Switch that supports routing:

1. Configure one or more MD5 key chains from the global configuration mode context. You must first configure the chain. You can then add one or more keys to it.

   ```
   Switch(config)# key-chain <chain name>
   ```

   ```
   Switch(config)# key-chain <chain name> key <key ID> key-string
      <password>
   ```

2. Access each interface on which you want to enable MD5 authentication. Enable this form of authentication and select the key chain.

   ```
   Switch(vlanID)# ip ospf md5-auth-key-chain <chain name>
   ```

The chain name is locally significant. The key ID and key secret must match the key ID and key secret set on neighbors on the same VLAN interface. If the chain has multiple key IDs, only one needs to match. This enables key rotation.

# Summary

In this chapter, you have learned how to implement more complex OSPF systems. You know why you might need to divide an OSPF AS into multiple areas, how to establish the areas, and how the area borders affect LSA propagation. You understand how OSPF routers use metrics to select inter-areas routes, and you can aggregate and filter routes between areas.

You also know when and how to redistribute external routes into OSPF. You understand how routers calculate external routes using the best path to the ASBR, and external type 1 and type 2 metrics help them choose between identical external routes. You can also aggregate external networks with ASBR summaries, as well as eliminate the external routes from stub areas entirely.

You know which types of areas benefit from being defined as stub areas and from being defined as totally stub areas. You can also set up an NSSA to allow local external routes within a stub area.

You also explored strategies and technologies for enhancing OSPF convergence. In particular, you learned when and how to use BFD to speed the detection of a failed neighbor. You can also use OSPF graceful restart to ensure seamless failover of an OSPF process on a VSF fabric or routing device with redundant management modules.

You examined several situations when a virtual link might be necessary, and you practiced creating such a link.

Finally, you learned how to implement OSPF authentication to minimize misconfigurations as well as to provide some protection against hackers.

## Learning check

1. A router needs to choose between the same external route advertised by two ASBRs. ASBR 1 advertises a type 2 metric of 10, and ASBR 2 advertises a type 2 metric of 20. How does the router choose which ASBR's LSA to prefer?
   a. Based on the highest metric
   b. Based on the lowest metric
   c. Based on the highest total of the metric plus the path cost to the ASBR
   d. Based on the lowest total of the metric plus the path cost to the ASBR
2. An OSPF router has an Ethernet link to another OSPF router; however, the link is indirect. The router needs to detect a failed neighbor in under a second. What feature meets these needs?
   a. BFD echo mode
   b. BFD without echo mode
   c. OSPF dead timer
   d. Graceful restart
3. What are advantages of designing an OSPF AS to use multiple areas?
4. An OSPF AS currently uses one area. The network administrator is configuring the AS to use multiple areas and changes the area ID for a VLAN on one routing switch. What will happen to the neighbor relationships on the VLAN? If this issue occurred accidentally, how could you troubleshoot the issue?
5. A network administrator creates an area range 10.100.0.0/17 with the **no-advertise** option. How is this different from not creating the aggregated summary at all?

## Answers

## Review basic OSPF concepts

### Neighbors and adjacency

1. How do OSPF neighbors discover each other? Which settings must match in order for neighbors to establish a relationship?

   They send hellos on any interface that runs OSPF and discover each other automatically. Settings that must match include the network address and subnet mask, the network type, the hello and dead timer settings, the area ID, and the area type (areas are discussed in more detail later).

2. Which type of OSPF network is an AOS-Switch's VLAN interface?

   This is broadcast network.

3. A broadcast network or an NBMA network can support multiple OSPF routers, one of which is the DR and one of which is the BDR. How are the routers with these roles selected?

   When you first enable OSPF on a broadcast interface such as a VLAN, the interface enters a waiting period during which it listens for hellos indicating the current DR and BDR. If the network does not already have devices fulfilling these roles or if different devices' hellos indicate different DRs and BDRs, an election is held. The device with the highest DR priority on the interface wins the election. If multiple devices tie for the highest priority, the device with the higher IP address wins the election and becomes DR. The device with the next highest priority (or IP address, as tiebreaker) becomes BDR.

4. Which routers in a broadcast network establish adjacencies with each other?

   All routers establish an adjacency with the DR and with the BDR. They do not establish an adjacency with other routers.

## Router IDs

5. How does an OSPF router determine its router ID if it is not set manually?

   If you do not manually specify a global IP router ID, the AOS-Switch uses the lowest IP address on the lowest numbered routing interface. (This would be loopback interface 0, if you have configured that interface.)

6. Does the router ID have to match an IP address on the router?)

   No. However, many administrators choose to use an IP address on the router so that they can contact the router ID. This approach can help in troubleshooting and administration.

7. If you do use an IP address on the router for the router ID, what type of interface is recommended for supporting the address?

   It is recommended that you use a loopback interface so that a link failing does not make the address become unavailable.

## LSAs, SPF algorithm, and LSUs

8. How do OSPF routers learn routes within an OSPF area? (Hint: Do they learn specific routes, or do they calculate them?)

   They do not advertise specific routes. Instead, use LSAs from their neighbors to create a topology of the network. Then they run an algorithm (Djikstra's algorithm) on that topology to calculate the lowest cost path to each network.

9. Describe a router LSA (a Type 1 LSA). What information does it contain, and which OSPF routers transmit them?

   Every OSPF router transmits a router LSA. This LSA identifies the router by router ID and lists all the links (networks) that run OSPF on that router. Every link has a cost, which is typically related to the bandwidth.

   You can compare OSPF to a map. The router LSA identifies a city and lists all the roads coming out of the city.

10. Describe a network LSA (a Type 2 LSA). What information does it contain, and which OSPF routers transmit them?

    A Type 2 LSA describes a broadcast network or an NBMA network and lists the router IDs for all routers on that network. The DR for the network transmits this LSA.

    In the map analogy, the network LSA identifies a road and lists all the cities connected to that road.

11. A router might run OSPF on a network for which it is the only router. How does a router identify such a network in a Type 1 LSA? Does the router transmit a Type 2 LSA for that network?

    The router identifies this type of network as a stub network. It does not transmit a Type 2 LSA for that network; a Type 2 LSA is only required for broadcast and NBMA networks which might have multiple routers attached.

12. A routing switch is running OSPF and is part of an OSPF AS. The network administrator configures a new VLAN on the switch, connects interfaces in the VLAN, and enables OSPF on it. What does the switch do to advertise the network? How is the LSU propagated? (Assume that all OSPF routers are in the same area.)

    The switch sends an LSU for its Type 1 LSA, adding the new link to its list of links. It sends the LSUs on all VLAN interfaces on which OSPF is enabled (except ones on which OSPF is passive). On each interface, the switch directs the LSU to the multicast IP address for the DR. The DR then distributes the LSU on the multicast IP address for all OSPF routers. The routers then advertise the LSU out other interfaces in the same area in a similar manner. No matter what its role, it sends the LSU out on all other links (that are in the same area). In this way, the LSU propagates across the OSPF AS.

13. How does a router calculate the cost for an intra-area OSPF route? What is the default metric for a VLAN interface on an AOS-Switch?

    It increments the costs for each link in the path. It knows the cost for each link from the LSAs. The default metric for a VLAN interface is 1.

14. What other types of changes can cause a router to generate an LSU?

    Such changes include a new network that runs OSPF, a change to the cost for a connected network, and a change to the router ID.

15. What does receiving an LSU trigger an OSPF router to do?

    In addition to propagating the LSU, the router runs the SPF algorithm to recalculate routes based on the new information.

## Review multi-area OSPF concepts

### Multiple area design without aggregation

1. Why would Core-1 shown in Figure 5-17 generate the summary LSA (Type 3) for 10.101.20.0/24, a network connected to Access-1? In which area would Core-1 generate the LSA?

   It would generate this summary LSA because it is the ABR. The ABR has the responsibility of generating a Type 3 LSA for each OSPF network in the area.

   It generated the LSA is in the area 0 LSDB. Remember the summary LSA for a network is never advertised in that network's area, which has router and network LSAs for that purpose. The summary LSA is advertised in the backbone area (and from there into other areas).

2. Which summary LSAs would Core-1 advertise in area 1?

   It advertised summary LSAs for routes to networks in area 0 and area 2.

3. Access-1 and Core-2 are in different areas but have the same OSPF routes. Why?

   Creating the area boundaries reduces LSAs and reduces the complexity of the directed graph (network map) that the routers use to calculate routes. However, although area boundaries enable you to aggregate routes, the aggregation does *not* occur automatically.

4. Suppose that Router-1 shown in Figure 5-17 loses its connection to Core-2, causing the 10.100.225.0/30 link to go down. If you entered the **show ip ospf spf-log** command on Access-1 before and after this issue occurred, you would find that Access-1 ran the SPF algorithm after the link failure. Why would Access-1 need to run the SPF algorithm when a link went down in a different area?

   When the Router-1 link goes down in area 0, Core-1 lost its route to it. Because Core-1 was advertising the individual route in area 0, it had to withdraw its LSA for that specific route. Therefore, Access-1 received an LSU and had to rerun the SPF algorithm for partial topology recalculations.

   As you see, failing to aggregate the routes is causing some instability and preventing the AS from fully benefiting from the area boundaries.

## Reviewing aggregation

5. Area 2 includes networks in the 10.102.0.0 to 10.102.255.0 range, so you would use the 10.102.0.0/16 range to summarize it.
   - Where would you configure this summary range?
   - What changes would occur in the OSPF system after you configured this range?

   You configured the 10.102.0.0/16 summary range in *area 2*. The changes occurred in the area 0 LSDB and area 1 LSDB. The many LSAs for routes in that range were replaced by a single route. You saw the change in the routing table on Access-1, which is in area 1.

6. What would occur after you configured the 10.100.0.0/16 summary range in area 0 on Core-1?

   After you configure the 10.100.0.0/16 summary for area 0, Core-1 will start advertising an LSA for that route in area 1, rather than the individual 10.100.0.0/16 routes. You will see the aggregated route in area 1 on Access-1.

7. Now, consider the same scenario from question 4, but with the aggregations shown in Figure 5-18. Router-1 loses its link to Core-2, causing the 10.100.225.0/30 network to go down. Would Access-1 receive an LSU and have to rerun the SPF algorithm?

   Now, Access-1 does not receive an LSA or run the SPF algorithm. The change does not alter the summary LSA advertised by Core-1, so the internal area 1 switch is insulated from the change in other areas.

8. When you configure an aggregation for an area on an ABR, you have the option to set the cost or not. If you do not set the cost, the ABR takes the cost from the highest cost route that it knows within that range. If you do not set the cost, what are the implications for the stability of the aggregated route? For example, in the topology shown in Figure 5-18, assume that you have configured the 10.101.0.0/16 summary on Core-1 without a cost. A VLAN interface on Access-1 goes down. Why could this cause Core-2, in another area, to receive an LSU and rerun the SPF algorithm?

   That VLAN interface could be the highest cost interface and the furthest from Core-1. Because Core-1 is using its highest cost route in the area 1 summary range to set the summary cost, if it loses this route, it must change the cost. This change would cause Core1 to send an LSU into area 0, which Core-2 would receive. This behavior might not bother you, or you might want to prevent such changes by setting a static cost.

9. How would you troubleshoot if Access-1 was not receiving the proper aggregated routes from area 2? What if Access-1 used to receive both the 10.100.0.0/16 route and the 10.102.0.0/16, but was then only receiving the 10.100.0.0/16 route?

   You would check Core-2, which is responsible for aggregating these routes.

   If an internal router used to receive the aggregated inter-area route and no longer receives any route, an issue is occurring somewhere on the connection to the local ABR or between the local ABR and the advertising ABR. In this case, it is probably the latter because the local ABR is still advertising other inter-area routes.

## Review external route advertisement

### External route advertisement

1. What must the network administrator do to make Core-2 advertise the 192.168.24.0/21 route to the other AOS-Switches?

   The administrator must redistribute static routes into OSPF. The command is:

   ```
   Core-2(config)# router ospf redistribute static
   ```

Assume that the administrator completes this step and answer the next questions.

2. Which switch or switches receive the external LSA and learn the route to the external network?

   All OSPF switches learned the LSA and route (Core-1, Access-1, and Access-2). External routes are advertised in all areas.

3. Access-1 receives a Type 4 LSA with a link state of 10.255.0.2 (Core-2's router ID). Which routing switch advertised this LSA to Access-1?

   Core-1 advertised it. The ABR is responsible for advertising ASBRs in one area to internal routers in another area.

### Stub areas

Now, the network administrator defines area 1 as a stub area. Answer the next questions.

4. On which switches, must the administrator configure area 1 as a stub area?

   The administrator must define the stub area on all switches in the area (Core-1 and Access-1).

5. During the process of configuring area 1 as a stub area, what could occur? What are the implications for changing the type of area in a live network?

   As you configure the stub area definition, the OSPF routing switches will temporarily lose their neighbor relationships because OSPF routers cannot become adjacent when they define the area differently. You should not make changes of this type in a live network.

6. After area 1 is defined as a stub, what switch or switches experience changes in their routing tables? What old routes are no longer present? Which new route is present?

   Internal routers in the stub area—in this scenario, Access-1—experience a change. The external route is no longer present. The table now has a default route, which is an inter-area OSPF route. The next hop is Core-1, as the directly connected ABR.

### Totally stub areas

Now, the network administrator wants to define area 1 as a totally stub area.

7. Where should the administrator specify the **stub no-summary** option for area 1?

   The administrator should define this option on Core-1, the ABR. Other routing devices (Access-1) can continue to use just the stub option.

8. The administrator completes this step. Underline the correct effect or effects.

   - Core-1 stops advertising the area 1 range to Core-2
   - Core-1 stops advertising inter-area routes into area 1

9. Core-1 no longer advertises a route to 10.102.0.0/16 to area 1 routers. Does the Core-1 switch still have an LSA for this network? Can Access-1 still reach networks in 10.102.0.0/16?

   Core-1 still knows the summary LSA for 10.102.0.0/16 in area 0, and it still knows a route to this network. It has just removed the summary from its area 1 LSDB.

   Access-1 can still reach these networks using the default route.

## Learning check for "Choosing between external routes to the same network: Type 2 metric"

1. Which ASBR does router C, in area 1, select to reach the external route, 172.16.1.0/24?

   Router C selects router F as the ASBR for 172.16.1.0/24 because this router advertises the lowest metric.

2. What is the next hop in router C's external route to 172.16.1.0/24? (This router supports ECMP.)

   Router C has the same cost to reach the ASBR through both ABRs, router A and router B. Therefore, it learns two routes to 172.16.1.0/24, one through each ABR.

The next questions refer to a different topology.

3. Which ASBR does router C, in area 1, select to reach the external route, 172.16.1.0/24? Is this the same ASBR as it selected in the topology shown in Figure 5-32?

   Router C still selects ASBR F because this ASBR advertises the lowest cost for the external route. With type 2 metrics, the router always selects the ASBR that advertises the lowest cost regardless of the cost of reaching that ASBR.

4. What is the next hop in router C's external route to 172.16.1.0/24? (This router supports ECMP.) Is this the same next hop used for this route in the previous topology?

   Router C learns just one route to 172.16.1.0/24 because it has a single lowest cost path to the ASBR through ABR A. This is different from the previous topology because ABR A offers a lower cost path to ASBR F in this topology.

## Learning check for "Choosing between external routes to the same network: Type 1 metric"

1. Which ASBR does router C, in area 1, select to reach the external route, 172.16.1.0/24? Is this choice different from the choice when ASBRs use type 2 metrics?

   The total metric for the LSA received from ASBR F is 56:

   1 (external metric) + 55 (metric of lowest cost path to ASBR F)

   The total metric for the LSA received from ASBR E is 57:

   2 (external metric) + 55 (metric of lowest cost path to ASBR E)

   Therefore, router C selects ASBR F. In this topology, router C's choice is the same with type 1 and type 2 metrics. Because router C has the same cost for reaching both ASBRs, the external metric still remains the deciding factor.

2. What is the next hop in router C's external route to 172.16.1.0/24? (This router supports ECMP.)

   Router C has the same cost to reach the ASBR through both ABRs, router A and router B. Therefore, it learns two routes to 172.16.1.0/24, one through each ABR.

The next questions refer to a different topology.

3. Which ASBR does router C, in area 1, select to reach the external route, 172.16.1.0/24? Is this choice different from when the ASBRs use type 2 metrics?

   The total metric for the LSA received from ASBR F is 21:

   1 (external metric) + 20 (metric of lowest cost path to ASBR F)

   The total metric for the LSA received from ASBR E is 17:

   2 (external metric) + 15 (metric of lowest cost path to ASBR E)

   Therefore, router C selects ASBR E. In this topology, router C makes a different choice when the ASBR use type 1 metrics versus type 2 metrics because the cost of its path to ASBR E is enough lower to counteract the higher metric advertised by ASBR E.

4. What is the next hop in router C's external route to 172.16.1.0/24? (This router supports ECMP.)

   In this case, ABR B offers Router C a lowest cost path to ASBR E. ABR B is the next hop in this path, so Router C learners one external route, in which ABR B is the next hop.

## Learning check

1. A router needs to choose between the same external route advertised by two ASBRs. ASBR 1 advertises a type 2 metric of 10, and ASBR 2 advertises a type 2 metric of 20. How does the router choose which ASBR's LSA to prefer?

   a. Based on the highest metric

   **b. Based on the lowest metric**

   c. Based on the highest total of the metric plus the path cost to the ASBR

   d. Based on the lowest total of the metric plus the path cost to the ASBR

2. An OSPF router has an Ethernet link to another OSPF router; however, the link is indirect. The router needs to detect a failed neighbor in under a second. What feature meets these needs?

   **a. BFD echo mode**

   b. BFD without echo mode

   c. OSPF dead timer

   d. Graceful restart

3. What are advantages of designing an OSPF AS to use multiple areas?

   OSPF areas segment the domain into more stable and manageable pieces. Each OSPF routing device maintains the LSDB and runs the shortest path algorithm only for its own areas. A multi-area design decreases LSDB size and increases stability—routers do not have to rerun the SPF algorithm as often. It also lets you aggregate advertisements of networks in between areas, simplifying the routing table and further increasing stability. You can also control routes at this boundary, filtering them if you want. These benefits still apply even for powerful routers that could support very large areas.

4. An OSPF AS currently uses one area. The network administrator is configuring the AS to use multiple areas and changes the area ID for a VLAN on one routing switch. What will happen to the neighbor relationships on the VLAN? If this issue occurred accidentally, how could you troubleshoot the issue?

   The switch loses its neighbor relationships on the VLAN because its area ID does not match the area ID of its neighbors. Matching area ID is just one of the parameters that must match on OSPF routing devices for them to become neighbors. After you move all of the routing devices on the VLAN to the same area, they will become neighbors again.

   If you accidentally placed AOS-Switches in the same VLAN but in different area, you could troubleshoot by viewing the OSPF neighbors on a switch and seeing that it does not have the expected neighbors. You could then look at OSPF statistics and see that the switch is receiving errors. You could then debug OSPF events and see the mismatch when a neighbor's hello arrives—in this case, the area ID mismatch.

5. A network administrator creates an area range 10.100.0.0/17 with the **no-advertise** option. How is this different from not creating the aggregated summary at all?

   When you set the **no-advertise** option for the aggregated summary on an ABR, the ABR no longer advertises any routes in this range, including the summary. Routers in other areas cannot reach the networks within the range if this is the only ABR. If you removed the aggregated summary, on the other hand, the ABR would advertise the individual routes in the range.

# 6 Internet Group Management Protocol (IGMP)

EXAM OBJECTIVES

✓ Use Internet Group Management Protocol (IGMP) to optimize forwarding of multicast traffic within virtual LANs (VLANs)

✓ Describe the differences between IGMP and IGMP snooping

## Assumed knowledge

Before reading this chapter, you should have a basic understanding of:

- IP addressing
- Open Systems Interconnection (OSI) model
- Multiple Spanning Tree Protocol (MSTP) and Rapid Spanning Tree Protocol (RSTP)
- Link aggregation
- Virtual LANs (VLANs)
- Routing
- Switching

## Introduction

Enterprises need networks that can deliver a variety of multicast services to the right destinations. In this chapter, you learn about multicast traffic and how to use IGMP to control it.

## Multicast overview

You are familiar with unicast traffic, which is directed to a unique destination device, and with broadcast traffic, which every device in a subnet/VLAN (broadcast domain) receives and processes. IPv4 defines a third type of traffic, multicast traffic, which flows from one source to multiple destinations.

The multicast source includes the multicast address as the destination IP address for the packet. Because multiple receivers can listen for the same address, switches might need to flood the packet on multiple interfaces. As Figure 6-1 shows, any source that is listening for that address processes the packet. Because multiple IPv4 nodes listen for the same multicast address, this address is often referred to as a *group address.*

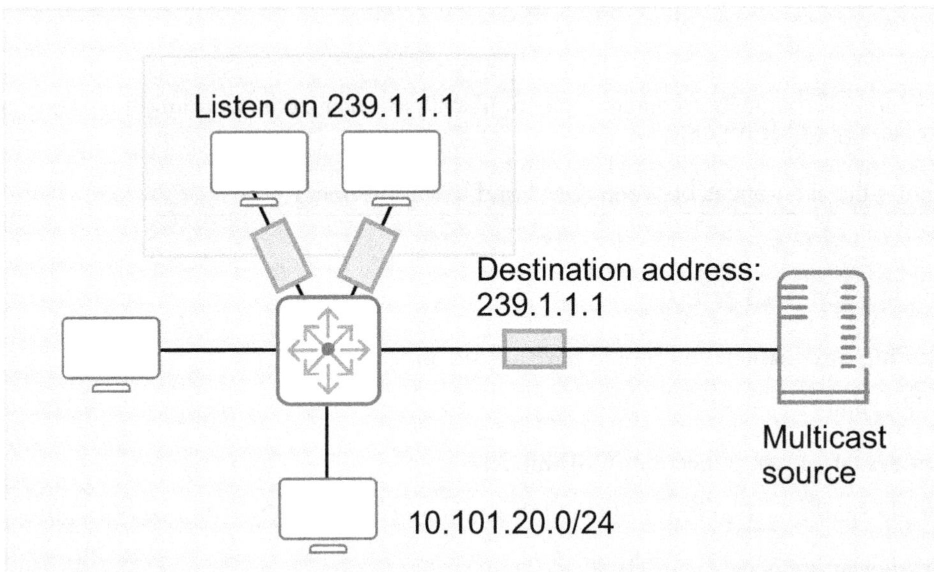


Figure 6-1 Multicast overview

Multicast addresses fall within the 224.0.0.0/4 range (224.0.0.0 to 239.255.255.255). Internet Assigned Numbers Authority (IANA) has assigned specific multicast addresses to some protocols. For example, Open Shortest Path First (OSPF) routers communicate with each other on multicast address 224.0.0.5 and 224.0.0.6. As shown in Table 6-1, IANA has assigned other addresses to specific organizations. Some applications, such as applications that use Session Announcement Protocol (SAP), can dynamically select multicast addresses from a certain range. Finally, individual organizations can define administratively scoped multicast addresses in the 239.0.0.0/8 range as they want; these multicasts should not leave the administrative domain.

Depending on the type of application, the multicast source and multicast receivers might be statically configured to stream to, and listen for, a specific multicast address. Or they might negotiate the address dynamically. Determining the multicast address to use is the application's responsibility; the network infrastructure must simply ensure that the traffic reaches its destination.

Table 6-1 provides information about the purposes for various multicast address ranges. This information is for your reference only and is taken from Request for Comments (RFC) 1112. You can refer to IANA for the latest assignments.

Table 6-1 Multicast addresses

| Multicast address range | Purpose |
|---|---|
| 224.0.0.0 to 224.0.0.255 | Local Network Control Block<br>IANA assigns these addresses to specific protocols (such as OSPF) for communications within a subnet. These multicasts must never be suppressed within a subnet and never be routed outside the subnet. |
| 224.0.1.0 to 224.0.1.255 | Internetwork Control Block<br>IANA assigns these addresses to specific protocols for communications globally. These multicasts must never be suppressed and may be routed. |
| 224.0.2.0 to 224.0.255.255 | AD-HOC Block I<br>The AD-HOC Block I, II, and II addresses were intended for multicasts that could be routed throughout the Internet but did not fit in the Internetwork Control Block. They are not typically used. |
| 224.1.0.0 to 224.1.255.255 | Reserved |
| 224.2.0.0 to 224.2.255.255 | SDP/SAP Block<br>These addresses are dynamically selected by applications that use Session Announcement Protocol (SAP) to do so. |
| 224.3.0.0 to 224.4.255.255 | AD-HOC Block II |
| 224.5.0.0 to 224.251.255.255 | Reserved |
| 224.252.0.0 to 224.255.255.255 | DIS Transient Groups |
| 225.0.0.0 to 231.255.255.255 | Reserved |
| 232.0.0.0 to 232.255.255.255 | Source-Specific Multicast Block<br>These addresses are used for source-specific multicasting (SSM), in which hosts not only listen for a specific multicast address but also for a specific source. |
| 233.252.0.0 to 233.255.255.255 | AD-HOC Block III |
| Scoped addresses | |
| 233.0.0.0 to 233.251.255.255 | GLOP Block<br>These addresses are assigned to organizations based on their autonomous system (AS) number. |
| 233.252.0.0 to 233.255.255.255 | AD-HOC Block III |
| 234.0.0.0 to 234.255.255.255 | Unicast-Prefix-based IPv4 Multicast Addresses<br>These addresses are automatically allocated to organizations based on their public IP address. |
| 235.0.0.0 to 238.255.255.255 | Reserved |
| 239.0.0.0 to 239.255.255.255 | Organization-Local Scope<br>These addresses are intended for organizations to use locally and should not be routed outside of the administrative domain. |

## Multicast uses

Latest generation network applications often feature more collaborative components, making them well-suited for multicast traffic. Applications that often rely on multicasting include:

- Unified communications and collaboration applications such as:
  - IP voice conference calling
  - Video conferencing
  - Telepresence
  - Video streaming applications
  - Virtual classroom applications
  - Stock ticker tape streaming applications

IT administrators might also assign servers or endpoints to multicast groups so that they can deliver patches, software updates, and other controls to a targeted group.

Multicasting presents two primary challenges to network administrators:

- Multicast traffic for sophisticated applications, particularly multimedia applications, can consume a great deal of bandwidth, particularly when it is copied for distribution to multiple locations. In fact, even copying multicasts can consume processing power on network infrastructure devices. To maintain a high-performing network environment, administrators must implement multicast control technologies properly to minimize unnecessary flooding and duplication. Not only do administrators need to preserve bandwidth, but they also need to protect endpoint functionality. An endpoint NIC must process the multicasts that it receives, even if it is not listening for that multicast, which can consume CPU cycles.
- Users and devices that require specific multicast traffic often connect in a variety of locations. Network administrators might need to route the traffic across multiple VLANs and even campus LAN sites.

You will learn about meeting this first challenge in this chapter. Then, in *Chapter 7: Protocol Independent Multicast* you will build on that knowledge and learn about multicast routing.

## Multicast flooding within VLANs

By default, in an Ethernet network, switches flood multicasts on all ports in a VLAN, or broadcast domain. For example, Figures 6-2, 6-3, and 6-4 show that the switches flood multicast frames to all the devices within a VLAN. In Figure 6-2, you see that the Core VSF, Access 1, and Access 2 switches flood multicast packets with the destination address of 239.1.1.1 to all the devices in VLAN 20—even though only Client 3 wants the multicast packets.

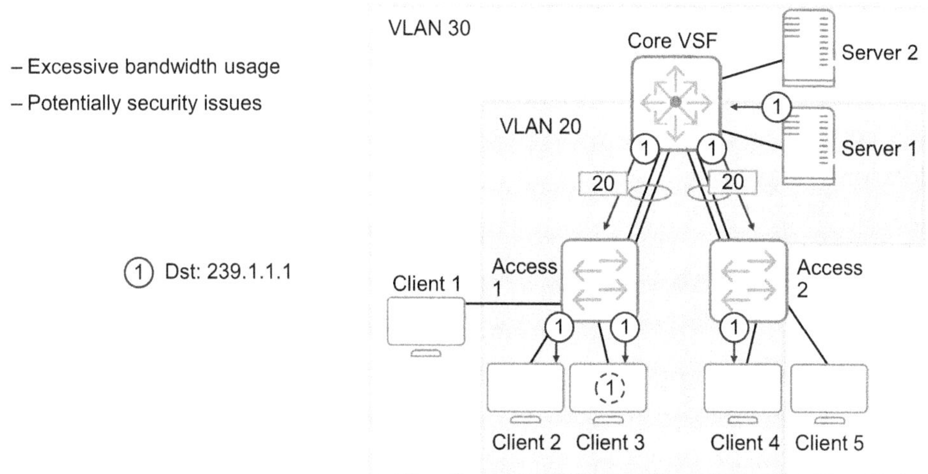


Figure 6-2 Multicast flooding within VLANs

Likewise, the switches flood multicast packets with the destination 239.2.2.2 to all devices in VLAN 20 (Figure 6-3).

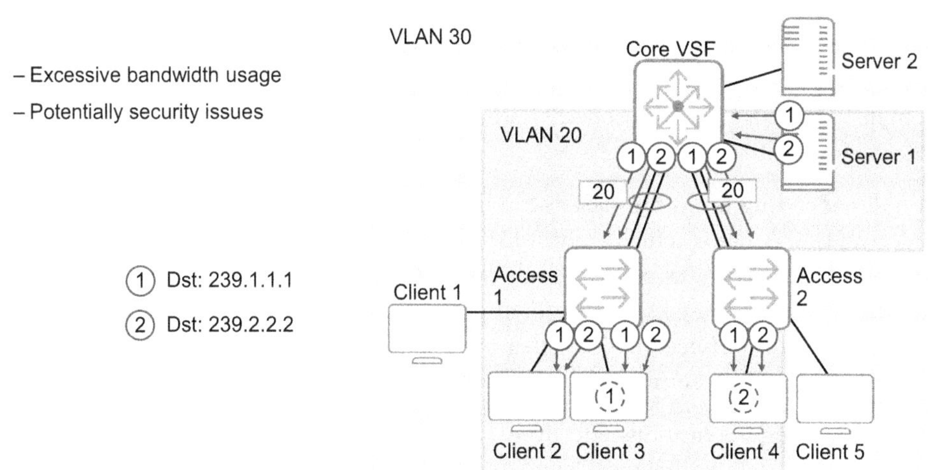


Figure 6-3 Multicast flooding within VLANs

Figure 6-4 illustrates how the switches flood multicast packets in VLAN 30 if the server sends out the packets in that VLAN.

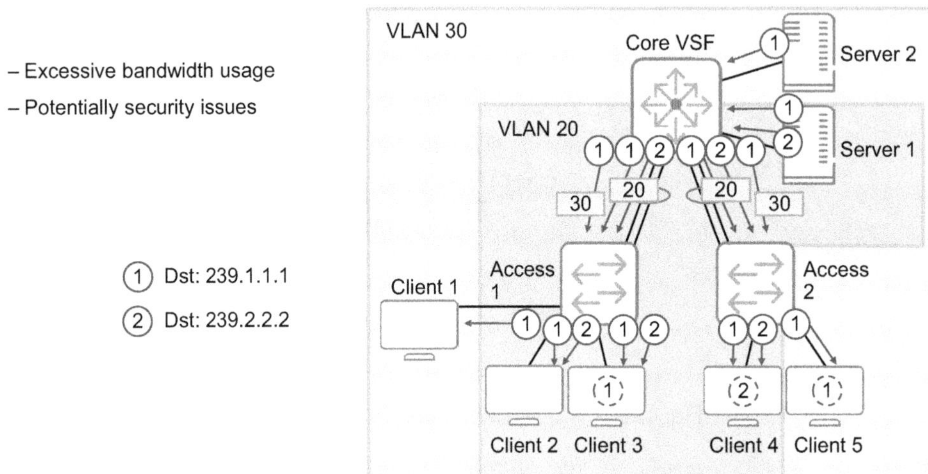


Figure 6-4 Multicast flooding within VLANs

Thus, although multicasts should target only the specific devices that require them, they act like broadcasts, creating congestion for an entire subnet. Contemporary unified communications and collaboration applications, such as video-conferencing applications, often involve high bandwidth streams of multicast traffic. If all edge ports must carry traffic for all multicast groups within the VLAN, overall performance quickly suffers.

In addition, broadcasting multicast packets can introduce security issues because every endpoint in a subnet receives traffic that is actually meant for a particular group. For example, even if most users would not know how to eavesdrop on the multicast traffic from a neighboring meeting room's video conference that shows up unnecessarily on their ports, some users might—which could violate privacy regulations. Finally, service providers that provide for-pay services must limit multicast traffic to the properly registered receivers so that they can track who actually uses the services.

To deploy multicasting applications effectively, you must enable the switches to suppress specific multicasts on ports that do not require them.

## IGMP use cases

You will now learn how switches use IGMP to suppress unnecessary multicasts and optimize forwarding of multicasts within VLANs.

IGMP is a Layer 3 protocol, originally developed to allow hosts to inform their multicast router which multicasts the router should forward into the subnet. For this use case, the router only cares whether any host requires multicasts in a particular group; it does not care how many hosts require the multicasts or where within the Layer 2 topology the hosts are located.

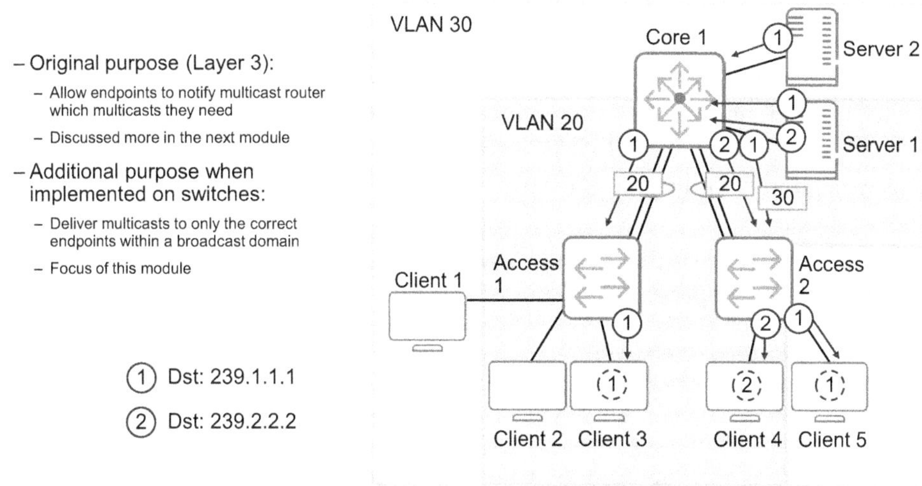


Figure 6-5 IGMP use cases

When a switch or a routing switch implements IGMP, IGMP can also act at Layer 2 to fulfill another purpose, which is the focus for this chapter. The switch can discover which specific hosts within the VLAN require multicasts for various multicast groups and, therefore, which physical interfaces must forward the traffic. Figure 6-5 shows the traffic flow for multicasts with IGMP (or IGMP snooping) operating on all of your switches.

Server 1 is transmitting multicasts to 239.1.1.1 in VLAN 20. These multicasts flow to Core-1, Access-1, and Client 3, the only device that wants them in this VLAN. Similarly, the multicasts to 239.2.2.2 only flow to the client listening for them, Client 4. The same process occurs in VLAN 30; multicasts only flow on the path toward clients that need them. Unnecessary multicasts are removed, reducing congestion.

---

**Note**

The IGMP functions fulfilled by switches are sometimes called IGMP snooping because switches traditionally did not generate IGMP messages, but only listened for the ones sent by routers and hosts.

Routing AOS-Switches, though, can fulfill all the IGMP functions of both a multicast router and a switch. You enable IGMP without distinguishing between IGMP (Layer 3) and IGMP snooping (Layer 2). However, whether the VLAN has an IP address *does* affect the functionality, as you will learn in this chapter.

---

## IGMP queriers

A routing switch that implements IGMP, called an IGMP querier, sends periodic queries, asking hosts for which multicast groups they want to listen. As Figure 6-6 illustrates, the queries are directed to multicast address 224.0.0.1, and all IGMP-capable devices listen on this address. Figure 6-7 illustrates how they respond with the groups for which they want to receive traffic.

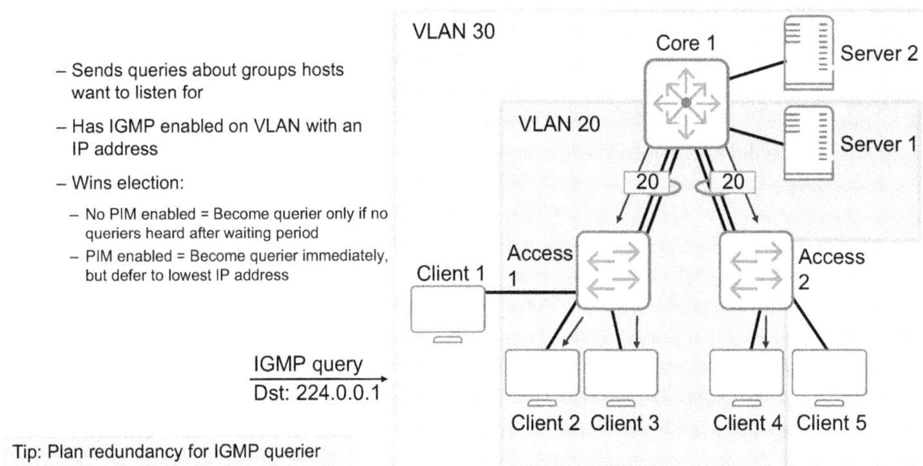


Figure 6-6 IGMP queriers

Generally, the default router for a VLAN should act as the IGMP querier.

## Enabling IGMP

You enable IGMP on a per VLAN basis. In Figure 6-6, the Core VSF is running IGMP in VLAN 20 only. If you want the benefits of IGMP in VLAN 30, you must enable it on that VLAN as well.

Enter this command to enable IGMP on a VLAN:

```
Switch(config)# vlan <ID> ip igmp
```

Once IGMP is enabled on a VLAN, the IGMP querier function is enabled by default, as long as the switch has an IP address in that VLAN. You can disable and re-enable this function with this command:

```
Switch(config)# [no] vlan <ID> ip igmp querier
```

Note that if you disable IGMP on a VLAN and then later re-enable IGMP on that VLAN, the switch restores the last-saved IGMP configuration for that VLAN.

You can see the IGMP status on an AOS-Switch with this command:

```
Switch# show ip igmp
 IGMP Service Protocol Info

  Total VLANs with IGMP enabled                : 1
  Current count of multicast groups joined     : 0

  IGMP Filter Unknown Multicast: Disabled
  IGMP Filter Unknown Multicast Status: Disabled

  VLAN ID : 1
  VLAN Name : DEFAULT_VLAN
  IGMP version : 2
  IGMP is not enabled

  VLAN ID : 20
  VLAN Name : Users
  IGMP version : 2
  Querier Address : 10.101.20.1
  Querier Port : trk13
  Querier UpTime : 0h 10m 9s
  Querier Expiration Time : 0h 3m 34s
  Active Group Addresses Type      Expires    Ports          Reports  Queries
  ------ --------------- --------- ---------- ----------     -------  -------


  20     239.1.1.1       0h 2m 39s 0h 45m 27s 10.101.20.20         |  Filter
  20     239.255.255.250 0h 2m 41s 1h 54m 5s  10.101.20.20         |  Filter
  20     239.255.255.254 0h 2m 36s 1h 54m 6s  10.101.20.21         |  Filter
```

## Multiple IGMP queriers and elections

Just as you need to consider redundancy for the default gateway, you should consider how you will provide redundancy for the IGMP querier role. In the example shown in Figure 6-6, the core is a VSF fabric, which has built-in redundancy.

If you are using a protocol such as Virtual Router Redundancy Protocol (VRRP), you should usually implement a backup IGMP querier. Simply enable the querier function on both VRRP devices. Even if you do not have redundancy for routing within the VLAN, though, you can still create a backup IGMP querier. Just add an IP address on the VLAN to one of the nonrouting switches and enable IGMP.

Only one device acts as the IGMP querier within the VLAN. Other querier-capable switches become IGMP listeners. As you will see, a listener continues to use IGMP to learn the multicast traffic that endpoints desire in the interface, just like the querier. It simply refrains from sending queries itself. The listener also takes over as the querier if it fails to hear a query within two times the querier interval.

The AOS-Switch behavior in determining whether to act as IGMP querier or listener differs based on whether the switch is also implementing a multicast routing protocol such as PIM. You will learn about PIM in the *Chapter 7: Protocol Independent Multicast* but the behavior with PIM enabled is described in the next section for your reference.

## Behavior without PIM enabled

When you enable IGMP on a switch VLAN with an IP address, the querier capability is enabled by default. However, based on the presumption that a multicast router will act as IGMP querier, the switch does not attempt to become querier immediately. Instead, it listens for IGMP queries for a waiting period equal to twice the IGMP querier interval. If it hears any queries in this period, it becomes an IGMP listener. If it does not, it becomes the querier. However, if the switch later hears a query from another device, it disables the querier function and defers to that device.

If you enable IGMP on two AOS-Switches that are not running PIM, the first switch on which you enable IGMP becomes the querier.

## Behavior with PIM enabled

When an AOS-Switch has PIM and IGMP enabled on a VLAN, it uses the IGMPv2 rules for its querier functions. As soon as IGMP is enabled, the switch begins to send IGMP queries at the designated interval. If it ever hears a query from another querier with a lower IP address, it stops sending queries and becomes an IGMP listener. In other words, the switch running IGMP and PIM with the lowest IP address becomes querier, possibly pre-empting the role from another switch.

IGMP operates separately from VRRP. That is, if two routing switches implement VRRP and IGMP in VLAN 20, either the VRRP backup or the VRRP master could be elected as the IGMP querier regardless of its VRRP role. This is because the switches use their actual IP addresses for the election (the VRRP master does not use its virtual address).

## Building membership tables with IGMP reports

As Figure 6-7 shows, when an IGMP host such as a computer receives an IGMP query, it sends an IGMP membership report that lists the multicast groups for which it wants to receive traffic. This report is multicast to 224.0.0.2. Note also that multicast receivers do not need to wait for an IGMP query to send a report. They can send a report for a group as soon as they want to join it—for example, as soon as a user starts the multicast application. This group-specific report is destined to the multicast address in question. For example, if the application wants to listen for 239.1.1.1, the endpoint sends the IGMP report to 239.1.1.1.

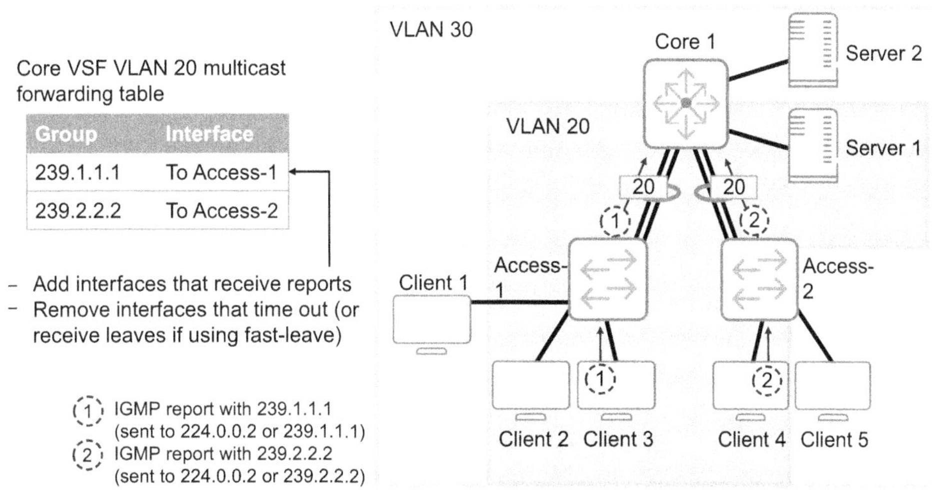


Figure 6-7 Building membership tables with IGMP reports

Any network infrastructure device that implements IGMP, whether or not it is the active querier, uses both of these types of reports to construct multicast forwarding tables.

When the switch receives the first report for a particular multicast group on a VLAN interface, it adds a table for that group to the VLAN. Each VLAN that implements IGMP has its own forwarding tables. Because the switch implements IGMP at Layer 2, as well as Layer 3, the physical interface on which the switch received the report becomes a forwarding interface for that group. If the switch receives another membership report on a different physical interface, it adds that interface to the forwarding table as well.

You can view the IGMP groups discovered on an AOS-Switch with this command:

```
Switch# show ip igmp group

 IGMP Group Address Information

  VLAN ID Group Address   Expires   UpTime      Last Reporter | Type
  ------- --------------- --------- ----------- ------------- + ------
  20      239.1.1.1       0h 2m 39s 0h 45m 27s  10.101.20.20  | Filter
  20      239.255.255.250 0h 2m 41s 1h 54m 5s   10.101.20.20  | Filter
  20      239.255.255.254 0h 2m 36s 1h 54m 6s   10.101.20.21  | Filter
```

The group membership entries do not persist indefinitely. Instead, the switch also sets a timer for the group membership, which it resets every time that its query produces another report. If the timer expires, the switch removes the group membership from the interface.

However, IGMPv2 defines a faster way for an interface to leave a group. When a host no longer requires multicast traffic in a particular group, it can send an IGMP leave group message. The IGMP querier instantly sends one or more queries for the multicast group in question. This allows another IGMP host connected to the same interface to send a membership report indicating that it still wants to receive the multicasts. (Remember that IGMP on AOS-Switches detects which multicast groups are required on both VLAN interfaces and individual physical interfaces within the VLAN. When fast-leave mode is enabled on a physical interface, the switch can immediately remove the interface from a multicast cast group table when it receives a leave for that group. You will learn more about when AOS-Switches enable fast leave mode later.)

## Supplemental information on how AOS-Switches handle reports

In the example shown in Figure 6-7, only one IGMP host in VLAN 20 wants to join the 239.1.1.1 group, and, as you see, the Core VSF receives only one membership report. Even if multiple hosts on Access-1 wanted to join this group, though, they would all receive the membership report from the first host to submit the report because this report is a multicast. Those hosts would then suppress their own reports, and a single report still flows to the Core VSF. (This behavior is a bit different when Access-1 also implements IGMP, as you will see later.)

IGMP defines this behavior because it was originally designed to inform multicast routers if at least one host in the subnet requires multicasts in the subnet. How many hosts required the multicasts did not really matter. Because routing AOS-Switches also implement IGMP at Layer 2 and need to discover on which physical interfaces to forward traffic, they alter this behavior a bit. The Core VSF switch, which implements IGMP, suppresses the membership reports that it receives on each physical interface and does not forward them on other physical interfaces in the VLAN. This behavior prevents hosts on Access-2 from hearing the membership reports from hosts on Access-1. In this way, the Core VSF can receive a report on the Access-2 link—for example, if any hosts connected to that switch wanted to listen on 239.1.1.1.

## Filtering traffic based on membership tables

The multicast group table filters traffic for multicasts destined to that address. Rather than forward these multicasts on all ports, the switch forwards multicasts only on ports listed in the table.

In the example shown in Figure 6-8, the Core VSF is the only switch running IGMP, and it is the IGMP querier. Based on the membership reports that it has received in VLAN 20, it has created two forwarding tables, one for 239.1.1.1 and one for 239.2.2.2.

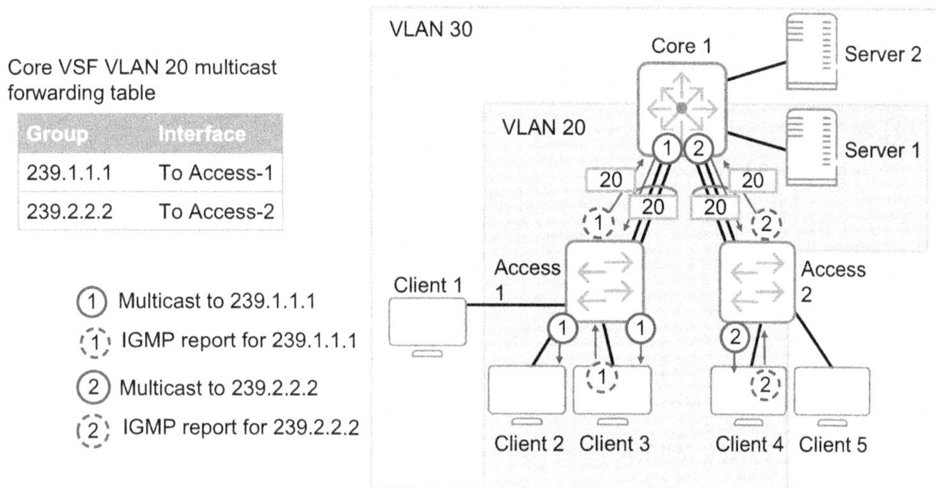


Figure 6-8 Filtering traffic based on membership tables

You also see that the table controls how the switches forward the multicasts. Now the Core VSF sends multicasts for 239.1.1.1 only to Access-1, which supports a host in that group. And it sends multicasts for 239.2.2.2 only to Access-2, which has a host in that group.

Figure 6-8 shows one issue for a design that uses Layer 3 switches at the core (or distribution layer) and Layer 2 switches at the access layer. The Core VSF is filtering multicasts, but the access layer switches are not. Access-1, for example, sends a multicast to Client-2, which is not listening for this group.

## IGMP snooping

IGMP snooping solves this issue.

As Figure 6-9 shows, IGMP snooping allows a switch acting at Layer 2 on a VLAN—it has no IP address—to partially implement IGMP. These switches do not act as IGMP queriers or backup queriers, but they can still use hosts' IGMP messages to create efficient multicast forwarding tables.

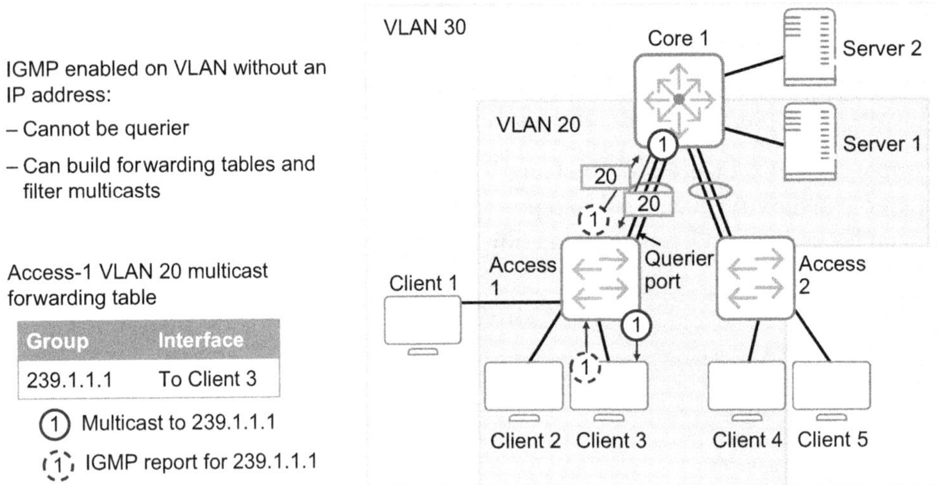


Figure 6-9 IGMP snooping

The IGMP snooping switch eavesdrops on IGMP traffic, using what it learns to determine which ports require specific multicast traffic. It stores this information in a table, creating one table for each VLAN interface on which IGMP snooping is enabled.

To create the table, the switch follows these basic rules, which allow it to discover necessary information about group memberships without disturbing IGMP communications between multicast receivers and their default routers:

1. The switch tracks the ports that receive IGMP general queries.

   AOS-Switches call these ports, querier ports.

   The switch needs to identify router or querier ports so that it knows on which ports to forward IGMP reports and also so that it can forward all received multicasts out this port. In Figure 6-9, the link aggregation to the Core VSF is the querier port.

2. When the switch receives a multicast receiver's IGMP report, it maps the incoming port to the group in the report in the appropriate VLAN IGMP snooping table. Or if the port is already mapped to that group, the switch resets the dynamic port member aging timer for that port and group.

   When hosts hear IGMP reports from other hosts in the same group, they typically suppress their own reports to minimize floods or reports. However, the IGMP snooping switch requires more granular information about the receivers on each port. Therefore, the switch only forwards IGMP reports on router or querier ports. Other hosts, not hearing the report, send their own reports, and the switch can learn their group memberships.

The snooping switch minimizes floods of reports to the IGMP querier by forwarding a report only when it creates the initial entry for a multicast group in its IGMP snooping table (rather than every time it adds a new port to the entry).

3. Inactive group memberships time out. How the switch handles leave messages depends on the fast-leave setting, which you will examine in a moment.

Following these rules, the IGMP snooping switch builds up a table such as the one in Figure 6-9. When the switch receives multicast packets for a particular group on a router port, it forwards them only on the ports mapped to the group.

### Configuring IGMP snooping

Remember that an AOS-Switch's VLAN interface controls both Layer 2 and Layer 3 functions. You can enable IGMP whether or not the VLAN has an IP address. When the VLAN does not have an IP address, entering the **vlan <ID> ip igmp** command enables IGMP snooping.

## How AOS-Switches handle unknown multicasts

Sometimes an IGMP or IGMP snooping switch receives a multicast for a group for which the switch does not have a filtering table. Called "unknown multicasts," these multicasts can occur when:

- The multicast source is directly connected to this switch, and it starts streaming before any clients join the group.
- A multicast source is streaming, and another switch in the path between the source and this switch does not support IGMP.
- The switch has removed a multicast group filtering table because the last member left the group. However, a multicast router forwarding the traffic has not yet received the leave, so it continues to forward the multicasts.

As Figure 6-10 shows, AOS-Switches operate in data-driven (or smart) mode. They filter all multicasts for which they do not have a multicast table. If no host has joined the group, and the switch receives multicasts, then the switch drops them.

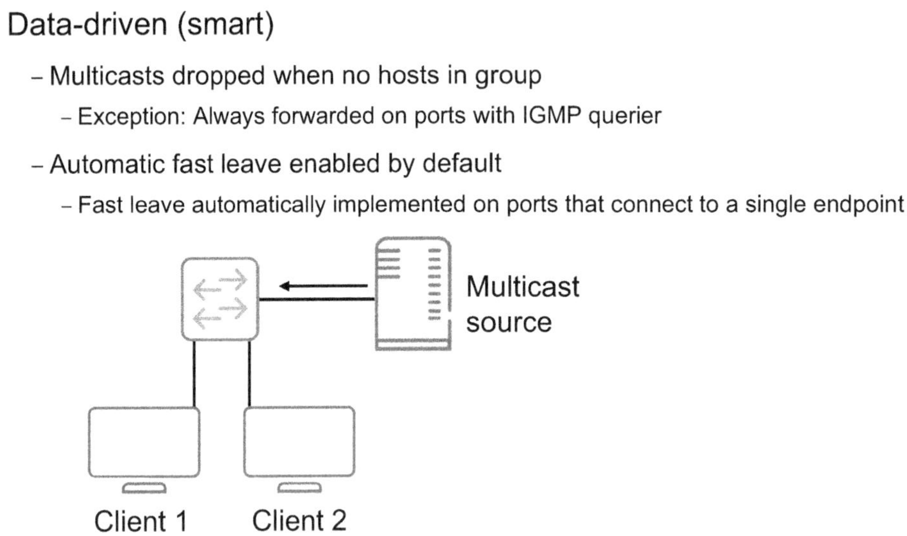


Figure 6-10 How AOS-Switches handle unknown multicasts

One exception applies: an IGMP snooping switch does forward both unknown and known multicasts on any port on which it has heard IGMP queries. (This behavior is required so that a multicast stream can reach the multicast router.) In fact, by default, the switch forwards unknown multicasts that arrive on one VLAN on any port on which it has heard queries in *any* VLAN.

If you want to change this behavior and restrict the forwarding to the querier ports for that specific VLAN, you must enter this command:

```
Switch(config)# igmp filter-unknown-mcast
```

*After a reboot*, the switch starts to filter the unknown multicasts.

It is important that you understand that the **igmp filter-unknown-mcast** command has no effect on how the data-driven switch behaves with nonquerier ports. The switch always filters unknown multicasts on these ports.

## Data-driven mode and fast leave

In typical IGMP behavior, when a host sends a leave message, the IGMP querier quickly sends two queries specific for that group to determine if another host also needs the multicasts. It then waits for a timeout period, and if it receives no response, it removes the host's interface from the forwarding table. Fast leave allows a switch to immediately remove an interface from the multicast group forwarding table when a host sends a leave message rather than waiting for the timeout period. When a port has fast leave enabled on it, the switch automatically determines when to use fast leave. It uses fast leave when it detects that the port connects to only one endpoint; it does not use fast leave when it connects to multiple devices.

Switches that operate in data-driven (smart) mode enable fast leave on all ports by default. You should generally keep the default mode. However, if necessary, you can enable or disable automatic fast leave on ports with this command (remember automatic fast leave being enabled does not necessarily mean that fast leave is used; it means that the switch detects whether to use fast leave based on the type of port):

```
Switch(config)# vlan <ID> ip igmp fastleave <port_ID_list>
```

You can also enable forced fast leave on a port, which enables fast leave regardless of whether the port connects to multiple devices or not. You should generally only enable forced fast leave if you know that the port connects to multiple devices, but only one IGMP host. You can enable forced fast leave with this command:

```
Switch(config)# vlan <ID> ip igmp forcedfastleave <port_ID_list>
```

As you see, both the fast leave and forced fast leave settings apply to a VLAN and an interface. The interface must carry traffic in that VLAN for the command to work.

## Nondata-driven mode (legacy)

Some older AOS-Switches operate in nondata-driven mode. (Refer to the switch documentation). These switches filters multicasts in a VLAN only if it has a table for that multicast group—in other words, if at least one host has joined the group for known multicast groups. If the switch happens to receive multicasts for an unknown multicast group, it floods rather than filters the multicasts.

Switches that use nondata-driven mode have fast leave *disabled* by default. They need to maintain the multicast group forwarding table for a period after the last host has left the group so that they can continue to filter multicasts until the multicasts stop arriving. You should leave fast leave disabled.

Sometimes nondata-driven switches need an extra buffer of time to maintain the multicast forwarding table after the last host has left so that they can filter multicasts from a source that continues streaming. You can add a delay time for postponing the deleting of the table with this command:

```
Switch(config)# igmp delayed-flush 0-255
```

# Summary

This chapter introduced you to IGMP, a technology that enables a network infrastructure to better support the multicast traffic that is becoming more and more ubiquitous. You can implement IGMP and IGMP snooping to reduce excessive multicasts.

## Learning check

1. How do AOS-Switches treat multicast traffic at the factory default settings?
   a. They forward the multicasts on interfaces that connect to other switches, but drop them on edge ports.
   b. They drop the multicasts.
   c. They forward the multicasts only on interfaces that have received IGMP reports for destination group.
   d. They flood traffic throughout the VLAN in the same manner as a broadcast.
2. A network administrator wants to ensure that multicasts in VLAN 4 are only forwarded to devices listening for those multicasts. Layer 2 access switches support VLAN 4, and a core switch routes traffic for VLAN 4. On which devices should the administrator enable IGMP?
   a. On the core switch only
   b. On the core switch and all access switches
   c. On the core switch and just one of the access switches
   d. On the access switches only
3. An AOS-Switch is connected to two endpoints in the same VLAN. One of the endpoints starts to send multicasts. The other endpoint does not want to listen to this multicast group. Compare what occurs when the switch has IGMP disabled (default setting) with what occurs after the administrator enables IGMP.
4. A network administrator enables IGMP on VLAN 20 on an AOS-Switch. The switch has the configuration on VLAN 20 shown below. Does the switch immediately start sending IGMP queries or not? Explain why or why not.

```
vlan 20
   name "Users"
   untagged 1/1,2/1
   ip address 10.101.20.1 255.255.255.0
   ip helper-address 10.101.10.10
   ip igmp
   ip ospf 10.101.20.1 passive
   ip ospf 10.101.20.1 area 0.0.0.1
   exit
```

# Answers

## Learning check

1. How do AOS-Switches treat multicast traffic at the factory default settings?
   a. They forward the multicasts on interfaces that connect to other switches, but drop them on edge ports.
   b. They drop the multicasts.
   c. They forward the multicasts only on interfaces that have received IGMP reports for destination group.
   **d. They flood traffic throughout the VLAN in the same manner as a broadcast.**
2. A network administrator wants to ensure that multicasts in VLAN 4 are only forwarded to devices listening for those multicasts. Layer 2 access switches support VLAN 4, and a core switch routes traffic for VLAN 4. On which devices should the administrator enable IGMP?
   a. On the core switch only
   **b. On the core switch and all access switches**
   c. On the core switch and just one of the access switches
   d. On the access switches only
3. An AOS-Switch is connected to two endpoints in the same VLAN. One of the endpoints starts to send multicasts. The other endpoint does not want to listen to this multicast group. Compare what occurs when the switch has IGMP disabled (default setting) with what occurs after the administrator enables IGMP.

   When IGMP is disabled, the switch floods the multicasts, and the second endpoint receives them even though it does not need them. After the administrator enables IGMP, the switch stops flooding the multicasts except on ports that have received an IGMP join. Therefore, the second endpoint no longer receives the multicasts. AOS-Switches operate in data-driven mode, so the switch will filter the multicasts entirely if no hosts have joined the group.
4. A network administrator enables IGMP on VLAN 20 on an AOS-Switch. The switch has this configuration on VLAN 20 shown below. Does the switch immediately start sending IGMP queries or not? Explain why or why not.

```
vlan 20
   name "Users"
   untagged 1/1,2/1
   ip address 10.101.20.1 255.255.255.0
```

```
ip helper-address 10.101.10.10
ip igmp
ip ospf 10.101.20.1 passive
ip ospf 10.101.20.1 area 0.0.0.1
exit
```

The switch will not send IGMP queries immediately. The switch has IGMP enabled and an IP address on VLAN 20. However, it does not have multicast routing and PIM enabled on this VLAN. Therefore, it will wait for a timeout period to hear if another device (such as a multicast router) is sending queries before starting to send queries itself. After this period expires, and if the switch has not heard any IGMP queries, it will start to send them itself. Although the switch does not immediately start sending queries, it can immediately start filtering multicasts.

# 7 Protocol Independent Multicast (PIM)

EXAM OBJECTIVES

✓ Distinguish between Protocol Independent Multicast Dense Mode (PIM-DM) and Protocol Independent Multicast Sparse Mode (PIM-SM)

✓ Implement PIM-DM and PIM-SM to route multicast traffic

## Assumed knowledge

Before reading this chapter, you should have a basic understanding of:

- Internet Group Management Protocol (IGMP)
- IP addressing
- Open Systems Interconnection (OSI) model
- Multiple Spanning Tree Protocol (MSTP) and Rapid Spanning Tree Protocol (RSTP)
- Link aggregation
- Virtual LANs (VLANs)
- Routing
- Switching

## Introduction

In this chapter, you will be introduced to Protocol Independent Multicast (PIM), which allows switches to determine which interfaces should receive multicast traffic.

## Multicast routing use cases

In *Chapter 6: Internet Group Management Protocol (IGMP)*, you learned how only devices in VLAN 10 receive multicasts from a source in VLAN 10. If you want hosts in VLAN 20 to receive multicasts in the same group, you must add another multicast source to VLAN 20. Sometimes companies want to isolate multicasts within a VLAN, but sometimes it would be more efficient to allow a single multicast source to transmit to devices in multiple VLANs. Multicast routing enables a source in one VLAN to stream to receivers in multiple VLANs.

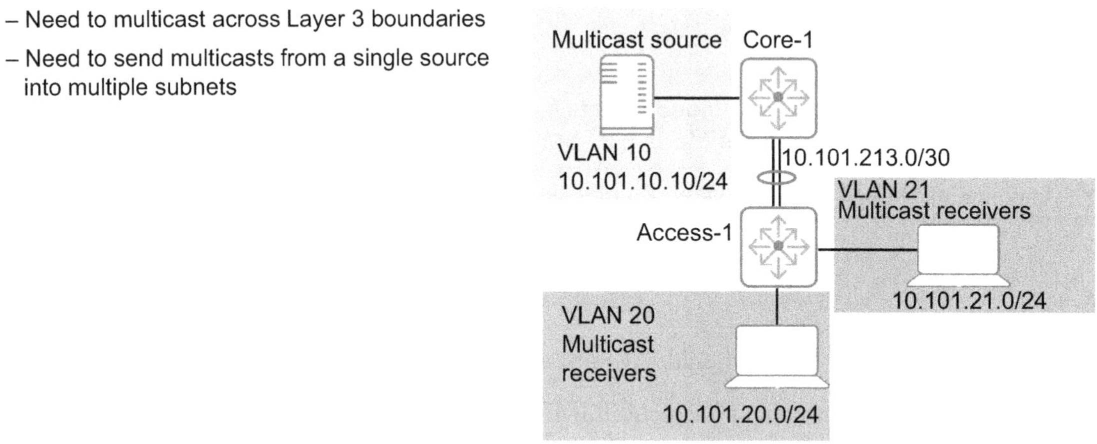


Figure 7-1 Multicast routing use cases

Multicast routing is also useful when the multicast source is in a different location from the multicast receivers, as shown in Figure 7-1.

**Note**

If you want to route multicast traffic into a VLAN, it is recommended that you avoid multinetting on that VLAN (configuring more than one subnet).

## Multicast routes

You understand how unicast routes direct traffic for a specific destination to a next hop. Due to the nature of multicasting, multicast routes function a bit differently. Figure 7-2 summarizes these differences.

| | Traffic from: | And destined to: | Is forwarded on: |
|---|---|---|---|
| Unicast route | Any | Destination network | Forwarding interface to next hop |
| Multicastroute | Source (S) (received on correct upstream interface) | Multicast group address (G) | Downstream interfaces |

Standard multicast route notation: (S,G)
(10.101.10.10,239.1.1.1)

```
Switch# show ip pim mroute 239.1.1.1 10.101.10.10
 IP Multicast Route Entry
  Group Address   : 239.1.1.1
  Source Address  : 10.101.10.10
 <output omitted>
 Downstream Interfaces
  VLAN State        Up Time (sec)       Expire Time (sec)
  ---- ---------- ------------------ ------------------
  1213 forwarding 216                 0
```

Figure 7-2 Multicast routes

Instead of a unicast destination network such as 10.101.20.0/24, the multicast route is directed toward a multicast group such as 239.1.1.1.

Instead of a next hop, the multicast route has downstream interfaces. Many endpoints across many subnets might need to receive multicasts; therefore, the forwarding path takes the shape of a tree with many leaves (endpoints), all of which require the traffic. In keeping with that tree shape, the multicast routing table entry can feature multiple downstream interfaces rather than a single forwarding interface to a next hop.

In addition, unlike for most unicast routes, the source matters for multicast routes. A multicast route must track the upstream interface that is closest to the source so that the router can verify that the multicasts are arriving on the correct interface. It can then drop multicasts that arrive on the wrong interface, preventing multicasts from looping through the network. An active multicast route is called an (S, G) route because it includes both the source IP address (S) and the destination multicast group address (G). Multicast routing devices create an (S, G) route after they receive a multicast from a source to a group. For example, the (10.101.10.10, 239.1.1.1) route refers to traffic from 10.101.10.10 to 239.1.1.1.

You will learn more about (S, G) routes and another type of route called a (*, G) route as you see multicast routing in action during the lab.

## Discovering multicast routes

Now that you understand the anatomy of a multicast route, you will consider how the route is created.

Forwarding paths can change because destinations that require multicasts frequently change. For example, a user might close the application that receives a multicast video stream, causing the endpoint to leave the multicast group. Routers and routing switches require a way to discover which destination devices require which multicast traffic. Unicast routing protocols such as Open Shortest Path First (OSPF) enable routers to discover the next hop for unicast routes dynamically.

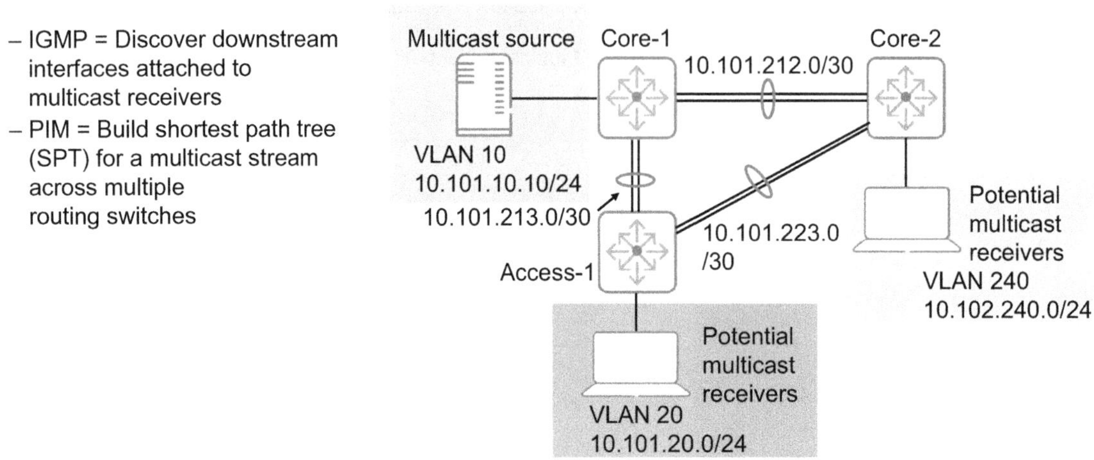


Figure 7-3 Discovering multicast routes

As Figure 7-3 shows, routers dynamically discover the downstream interfaces for multicast routes with two protocols working together.

- Chapter 6: Internet Group Management Protocol (IGMP)—You learned in *Chapter 6: Internet Group Management Protocol (IGMP)* about how endpoints use IGMP to inform infrastructure devices that they want to listen for specific multicast groups. In that chapter you focused on IGMP and IGMP snooping's filtering functions, but IGMP also informs a subnet's multicast router which multicasts the router must forward into the subnet. The router can then make sure that the corresponding interface (VLAN on AOS-Switches) is listed as a downstream interface in any multicast routes for the group in question.
- PIM—On its own, IGMP allows multicast routers to discover downstream interfaces attached to multicast receivers, but not downstream interfaces attached to other multicast routers that need the traffic. For example, Access-1 can learn VLAN 20 as a downstream interface for multicast group 239.1.1.1, but Core-1 cannot use IGMP to learn that it should forward these multicasts to Access-1. PIM allows multicast routers to communicate with each other about which multicast traffic they need. The system of multicast routing switches, each with a multicast route for a particular group, together compose the shortest path tree (SPT) for a particular multicast stream, as identified by source and group.

It is important that you understand that IGMP alone is never enough to provide multicast routing even if the multicast source and multicast receivers are connected to VLANs on the same multicast routing switch. This switch must still have multicast routing enabled and run PIM on the VLAN interfaces to route multicast traffic from one subnet to another.

## PIM-DM versus PIM-SM

The routing switches can construct the multicast routing tree in one of two modes: PIM-DM or PIM-SM.

- PIM-DM—PIM-DM dynamically creates the multicast routing tree, when a source begins streaming traffic for a multicast group. VLAN interfaces on which PIM-DM is enabled flood multicasts to all neighbors until the neighbors indicate that they do not need them by sending a prune. Prune is the term that PIM uses for a leave message. In addition, the upstream neighbor sets a timer for the pruned interface. When the timer expires, the interface reverts to the default behavior—forwarding multicasts until explicitly requested not to. (However, as you will learn later, PIM-DM can use state refreshes to prevent the timer from expiring.)

  This mode works best in environments with high bandwidth and high tolerance for congestion, such as a high-speed Ethernet network. Because the PIM-DM routers automatically create the multicast routing tree for a particular stream when that stream begins, PIM-DM is quite simple to set up.

- PIM-SM—PIM-SM builds the multicast routing tree for a group in advance and then forwards multicasts on that tree when a source begins to stream to that group. PIM-SM-enabled routing interfaces must specifically indicate that they want to receive multicast traffic in a particular group by sending a join for the tree. The interface must then periodically refresh its join. If its upstream neighbor does not receive joins, it reverts to its default behavior—not forwarding traffic.

  Because PIM-SM establishes efficient forwarding paths, it is well-suited for a lower-bandwidth environment, such as one built on WAN links. PIM-SM also gives you more control over which multicast groups are routed.

  PIM-SM has more configuration options and tends to be more complex to set up than PIM-DM.

You should check your AOS-Switch to determine which PIM modes it supports. If the AOS-Switch supports both PIM-DM and PIM-SM, it can support only one mode concurrently. All multicast routing switches in the network must also agree and run the same type of PIM.

## PIM-DM

You will now learn how PIM-DM works and how to configure this protocol on AOS-Switches.

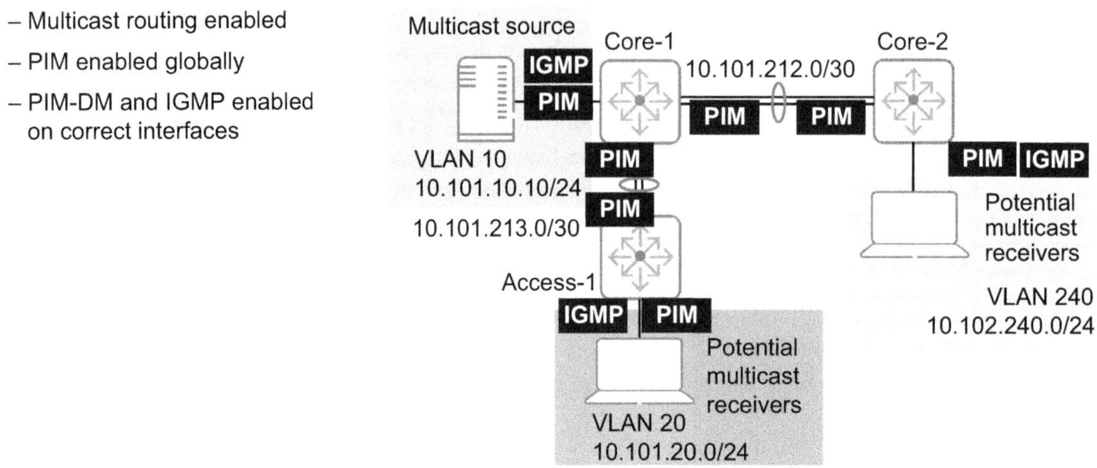


Figure 7-4 PIM-DM

PIM-DM must be enabled on all VLAN interfaces between the multicast sources and the multicast receivers.

- Interfaces on which multicast sources reside.
- Interfaces on which multicast receivers reside (IGMP-enabled interfaces).
- Interfaces between all routers and routing switches that connect sources and receivers.

Figure 7-4 shows the interfaces on which you would enable PIM-DM, as well as the interfaces on which you must enable IGMP, in an example network. Note that you should also enable IGMP on the server VLAN; although IGMP is not strictly required in the source VLAN, it enables Core-1 to filter multicasts within that VLAN.

You should begin by ensuring that unicast routing is in place. You must then enable both multicast routing and PIM-DM globally. Finally, you can enable PIM-DM on the VLAN interface, as shown below:

```
Switch(config)# ip multicast-routing
Switch(config)# router pim enable
Switch(config)# vlan <ID> ip pim-dense
```

PIM-DM interfaces automatically discover neighbors on the same subnet by transmitting and listening for hellos. PIM-DM routers communicate on multicast address 224.0.0.13.

Figure 7-5 shows a more complex system. Note that Core-2 must support PIM even though it does not directly connect to any subnets with multicast sources or receivers.

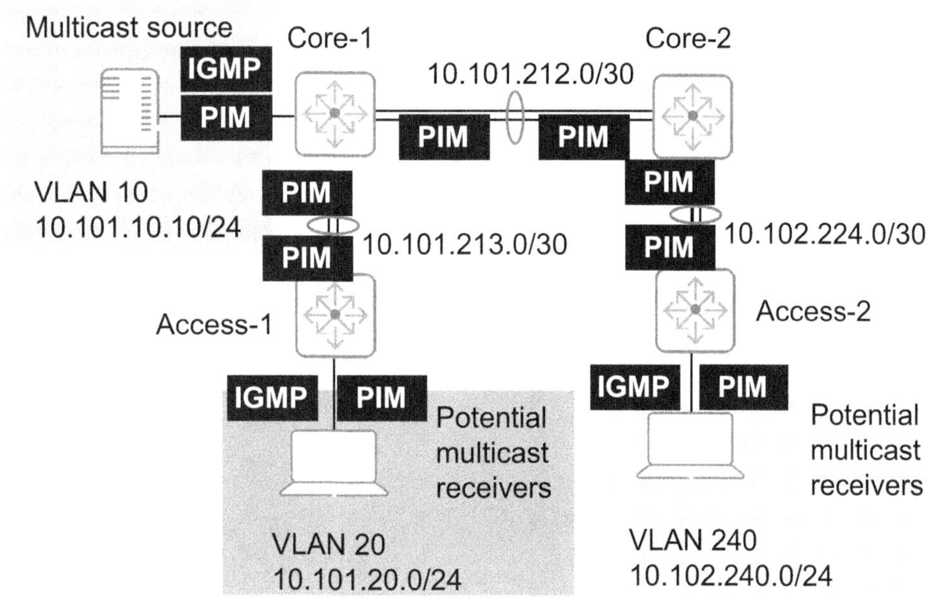


Figure 7-5 PIM and IGMP in a more complex system

## PIM-DM operation: flooding and pruning

When a multicast source begins to transmit, the source's default router receives the multicasts. The VLAN interface on which the multicasts arrive should be enabled for PIM-DM. The router then floods the multicasts on every PIM-DM interface, including the following:

- Interfaces that connect to PIM-DM neighbors.

  In the example shown in Figure 7-6, these neighbors are Core-2 and Access-1.

- Interfaces that connect to receivers that have requested the multicast using IGMP.

  In the example shown in Figure 7-6, Core-1 does not have any interfaces with directly attached multicast receivers.

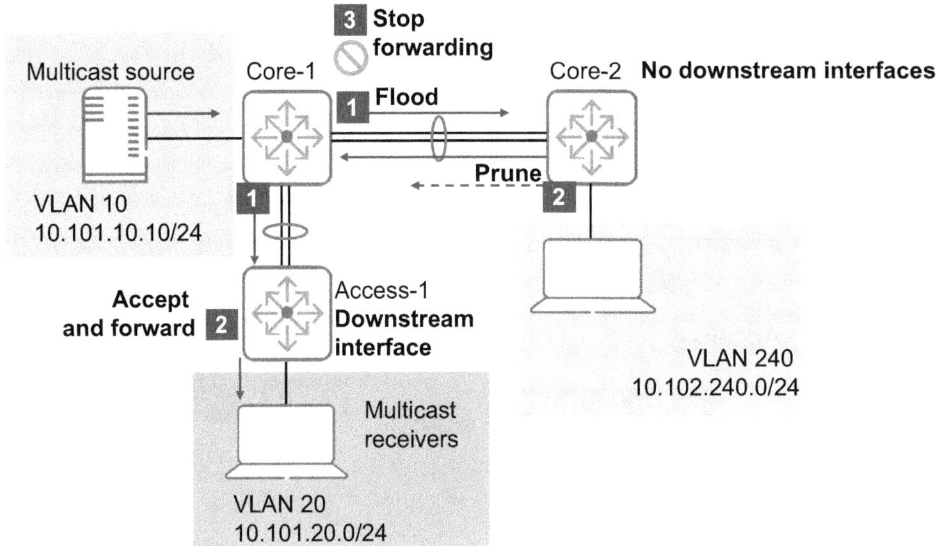


Figure 7-6 PIM-DM operation: flooding and pruning

The downstream multicast routers follow the same steps to flood the multicast. In the simple network shown in Figure 7-6, Access-1 and Core-2 do not have any neighbors except Core-1. Access-1 has learned that VLAN 20 is a downstream interface for this group from IGMP. Core-2, though, does not have any multicast receivers for this group on VLAN 40, its only other PIM-DM interface.

Because Access-1 has one downstream interface, it continues to accept the traffic from Core-1. Because Core-2 has no downstream interfaces, it prunes itself from the tree by sending a prune (leave) message on the upstream interface. The upstream neighbor removes the interface on which it receives the message from the downstream interfaces for this route.

Note that Core-2 still maintains the multicast route [the (S, G) entry), which it can use to receive multicasts later, if necessary.

## PIM-DM operation: grafts

After pruning, Core-1 in the example network shown in Figure 7-7 is forwarding multicast traffic to Access-1 only, which forwards the traffic to receivers in VLAN 20.

Because group memberships change all the time, the SPT can change as well. First, PIM-DM operates on preferring forwarding unnecessary multicast traffic over failing to forward necessary traffic. Therefore, prune messages expire, and the routing switch that had received the prune message begins forwarding multicast traffic again.

In addition, group members leave groups. For example, if all of the multicast receivers in VLAN 20 left the group, then Access-1 would send a prune message to Core-1, stopping the flow of traffic.

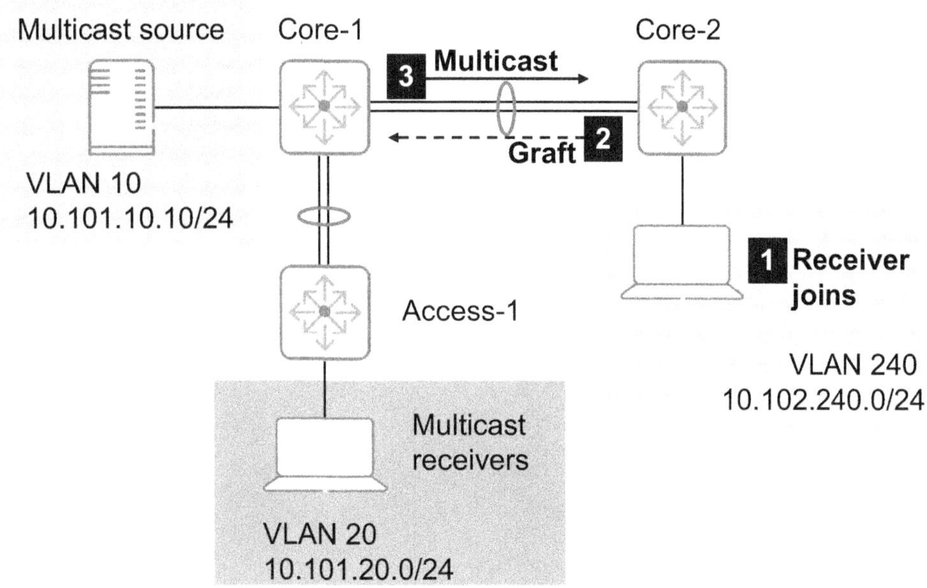


Figure 7-7 PIM-DM operation: grafts

Figure 7-7 shows another change in the situation: a multicast receiver for this group becomes active in VLAN 40 connected to Core-2. (Perhaps a user starts a multicast video streaming application.) The host sends an IGMP report for this group, and Core-2 adds VLAN 40 as a downstream interface for its (S, G) multicast route for this multicast stream. Eventually, the prune message would expire, and Core-2 would receive traffic again. However, PIM-DM provides a faster method of pulling the multicast traffic down. Core-2 sends a graft message on the upstream interface, requesting to be added to the tree.

Core-1 adds the interface that connects to Core-1 back to the (S, G) multicast route's list of downstream interfaces. Core-2 begins to receive the traffic again, and it forwards it to the receiver.

## Interpreting PIM-DIM (*, G) entries

When you are monitoring and troubleshooting a multicast routing solution, you do not have an illustration that traces multicasts for you. It can be helpful for you to understand more about the multicast route entries, how to interpret them, and how the routing switch uses them to forward traffic.

- (*,G) entry indicates router wants the multicast traffic
- (*, G) entry created when both:
  - PIM and IGMP are enabled on the VLAN
  - IGMP discovers multicast receivers for the group address

```
Access-1(config)# show ip igmp group

 IGMP Group Address Information

  VLAN ID  Group Address    Expires        UpTime         Last Reporter    | Type
  -------  ---------------  -------------  -------------  ---------------  + ------
  20       239.1.1.1        0h 2m 39s      0h 45m 27s     10.101.20.10     | Filter
  30       239.2.2.2        0h 1m 13s      0h 30m 34s     10.101.30.11     | Filter
```

```
Access-1# show ip pim pending
Join Pending

   Group 239.1.1.1
      (*,G) Pending
         Incoming VLAN:   20

  Group 239.2.2.2
       (*,G) Pending
          Incoming VLAN:   30
```

Figure 7-8 Interpreting PIM-DIM (*, G) entries

Refer to Figure 7-8 as you consider (*, G) entries.

As soon as PIM-DM is enabled on a switch VLAN interface, the switch creates a (*, G) entry for each group membership discovered by IGMP on that VLAN. This entry specifies the downstream interfaces from which a tree can be formed when multicasts begin to arrive from a particular source.

When you use PIM-DM, the (*, G) entry essentially acts as a placeholder, listing the downstream interfaces that require multicasts in this group, as discovered by IGMP. The framework of the tree that delivers these multicasts is not filled in. For example, no upstream interface is specified (the routing switch does not know where multicasts will arrive).

The (*, G) entry exists only as a pending route; it is not an active route forwarding multicasts. The (*, G) entry remains in the PIM routing table for as long as an IGMP membership for the group exists on at least one interface. This signals to the routing switch that it should stay part of the multicast routing tree for any multicast stream to this group, regardless of whether it needs to forward the traffic to any downstream PIM-DM neighbors.

To view (*, G) routes, enter the **show ip pim pending** command. To view information about IGMP groups, enter **show ip igmp group**.

## Interpreting PIM-DM (S, G) entries

When the switch receives a multicast on the proper upstream interface for the source, it creates an (S, G) entry, as shown in Figure 7-9. It uses this entry to route the multicast traffic on the correct interface or interfaces.

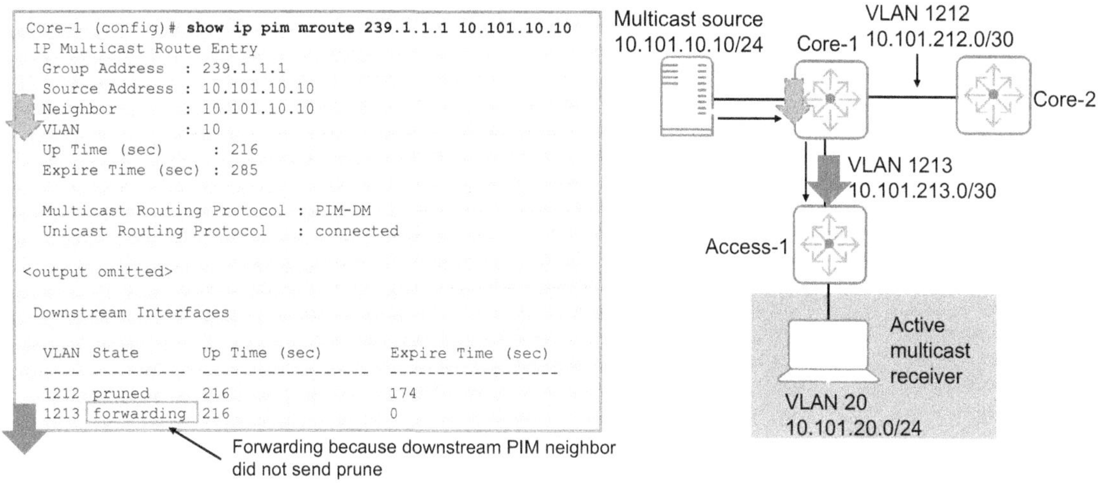


Figure 7-9 Interpreting PIM-DM (S, G) entries

The (S, G) entry includes the following:

- The source for the incoming multicasts.
- The upstream interface on which the multicast arrived.

  You will learn in a moment how the switch checks the validity of this interface. It will not add the route if the upstream interface is invalid.

- The downstream interfaces.

  Initially, the downstream interface includes all PIM-DM interfaces set to a forwarding state. The switch maintains the forwarding state unless a neighbor sends a prune on that interface. The switch also always maintains the forwarding state for interfaces discovered by IGMP as long as they are in the (*, G) entry associated with this group.

  As you see, if the interface receives a prune, the switch maintains the interface in the list, but places it in the pruned state and does not forward multicasts on it.

If the (S, G) entry has downstream interfaces or if the source is connected directly to the routing switch, the routing switch adds the (S, G) entry to its active multicast routing table. The routing switch then uses the (S, G) entry to forward multicasts.

You can see a shortened version of the multicast route with this command:

```
Switch# show ip mroute
 IP Multicast Route Entries

  Total number of entries: 1

  Group Address    Source Address  Neighbor        VLAN
  ---------------- --------------- --------------- ----
  239.1.1.1        10.101.10.10    10.101.213.1    1213
```

In the shortened version, VLAN indicates the incoming or upstream VLAN for the traffic.

It can be useful to view the complete entry by specifying the multicast group and the source IP address. The full output for the example (S, G) entry in Figure 7-9 is as follows:

```
Core-1(config)# show ip mroute 239.1.1.1 10.101.10.10

 IP Multicast Route Entry

  Group Address  : 239.1.1.1
  Source Address : 10.101.10.10
  Neighbor       : 10.101.10.10
  VLAN           : 10
  Up Time (sec)     : 216
  Expire Time (sec) : 285

  Multicast Routing Protocol : PIM-DM
  Unicast Routing Protocol   : connected

  Metric       : 1
  Metric Pref  : 0
  Assert Timer : 0
  RP tree      : No
```

```
Downstream Interfaces

 VLAN State       Up Time (sec)       Expire Time (sec)
 ---- ---------- ------------------ ------------------
 1212 pruned      216                194
 1213 forwarding 216                0
```

Figure 7-9 shows how this entry corresponds to traffic flow. You can continue to trace the flow through Access-1, as shown in Figure 7-10.

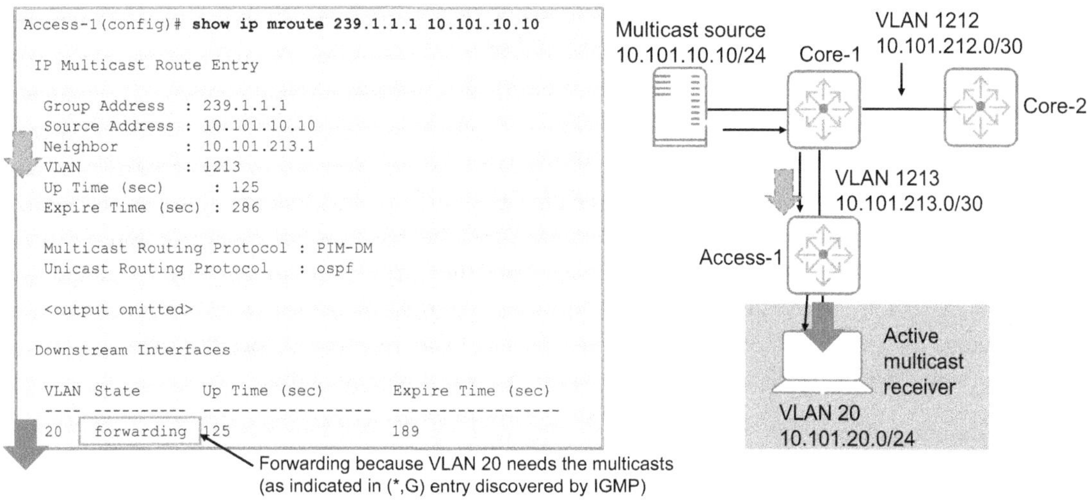


Figure 7-10 Interpreting PIM-DM (S, G) entries

## Using state refreshes to minimize flooding

Prunes periodically time out, causing PIM-DM-enabled interfaces to begin again to flood multicasts to neighbors that had sent prune messages. If the neighbor still does not require the traffic, it must send another prune message. These bursts of unnecessary traffic can contribute to congestion.

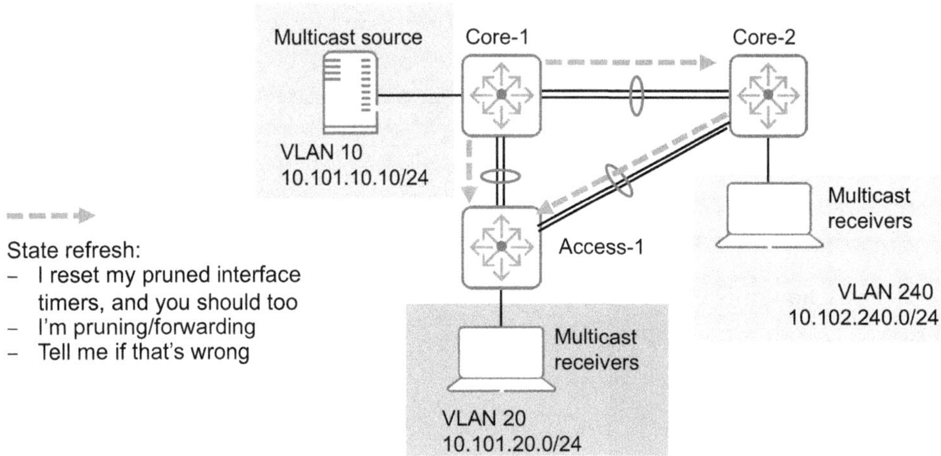


Figure 7-11 Using state refreshes to minimize flooding

As Figure 7-11 shows, AOS-Switches automatically take measures to prevent the prune state from timing out. The switch connected to the source does this through state refresh messages. It floods a refresh message on all PIM-DM interfaces. The state refresh message indicates information about the state of the interface that transmits the message, whether pruned or forwarding. It propagates throughout the system, triggering all PIM-DM routing switches to send joins and prunes only if they need to change the current state of the upstream interface. The routing switches can then also refresh their prune states with confidence without needing to flood multicast traffic.

In more detail, receiving a state refresh message triggers the PIM-DM interface to take these actions:

1. Drop the message unless it has arrived from the reverse path forwarding (RPF) upstream neighbor.
2. For messages from the proper upstream neighbor:
   a. Check the indicated state of the upstream interface and determine whether it matches this routing switch's requirements.
      - If the indicated state is pruned and this routing switch has no downstream interfaces for the (S, G) entry, the indicated state is correct. Similarly, if the indicated state is forwarding and this routing switch does have downstream interfaces on which it must forward traffic, the state is correct.
      - If the indicated state is pruned, and this switch requires the multicasts, the switch sends an (S, G) join upstream to alter the state. Similarly, if the indicated state is forwarding, but this switch does not have an active entry forwarding multicast traffic downstream, the switch sends an (S, G) prune upstream.
   b. Reset all of its pruned interface timers.

      The switch can safely reset all of the timers because its downstream neighbors will correct any mistakes on receipt of the state refresh message, just as this routing switch did.

c. Forward the state refresh message (with one less value in the time to live [TTL]) on all interfaces with PIM-DM neighbors except the interface on which it received the message.

   The TTL prevents the state refresh message from endlessly looping through the PIM-DM domain.

AOS-Switches automatically support state refresh messages, but only the routing switch connected directly to the unicast source initiates state refresh messages. All other PIM routers in the network only propagate these state-refresh messages.

You can configure the interval in seconds (10 to 300) between successive state refresh messages. The default setting is 60 seconds. You should keep the interval below the PIM-DM prune expiry time to prevent periodic unnecessary floods of traffic.

```
Switch(config)# router pim state-refresh [10-300]
```

## Understanding the relationship between the PIM-DM tree and the unicast routing table

Up until now, you have examined a simple network with just one path for multicasts. However, networks often feature redundant links and loops such as those shown in Figure 7-12. Because PIM-DM routing switches flood multicasts on all PIM-DM interfaces except the one on which the multicasts arrived, they run the risk of looping multicasts. PIM-DM automatically deals with this situation, so you can use the protocol in redundant network designs without worry. PIM-DM prunes the forwarding paths into a loop-free tree, rooted at the multicast source with the lowest cost path to each receiver subnet. (Note that you are looking at redundant Layer 3 links; loops at Layer 2 must be eliminated by a protocol such as spanning tree.)

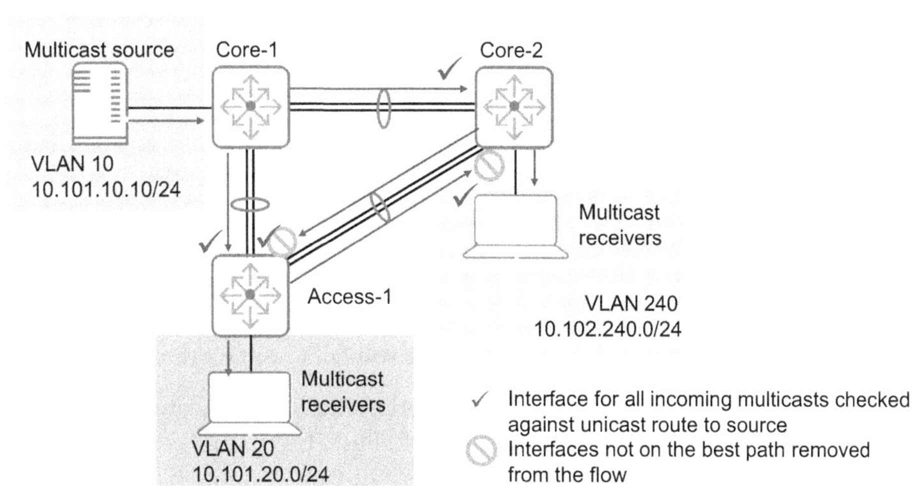


Figure 7-12 Understanding the relationship between the PIM-DM tree and the unicast routing table

Although PIM operates independently from unicast routing protocols, it uses the unicast routing table for this purpose. This process occurs as follows:

1. The multicast source's default router sends the multicasts to all PIM neighbors. In this example, Core-1 sends multicasts to Access-1 and Core-2.
2. The PIM neighbors run an RPF check on the traffic, which verifies that the upstream interface on which the traffic arrives is the forwarding interface for the unicast route to the source.
3. If the multicast passes the RPF check, the routing switch accepts it and sets the RPF flag for the (S, G) entry with that upstream interface. This flag allows the switch to accept future multicasts on this interface without the processing overhead of running the RPF check again.
4. The routing switch then forwards the multicast on all PIM-DM interfaces.

   As you see, this means that Core-2 sends multicasts to Access-1 and Access-1 sends multicasts to Core-2. However, the routing switches do not accept these multicasts because they do not pass the RPF check. They also exchange assert messages, which enable them to choose which routing switch has a better path to the source. The switch that loses removes this interface from its downstream interface list. It now knows that, for this source, its neighbor is upstream to it. It switches also send a prune to the routing switch that won, telling that switch to stop sending the multicasts to it—because it has a better upstream interface. In short—the multicast routing switches stop sending the unnecessary traffic to each other.

In this way, PIM-DM creates a multicast tree that imitates the forwarding paths for unicast traffic. In other words, 10.101.10.10 is sending multicasts, for which receivers in 10.101.20.0/24 are listening. This traffic follows the same path as unicast traffic from 10.101.10.10 to a client in 10.101.20.0/24. If receivers in 10.102.40.0/24 start listening, that traffic follows the same path as unicast traffic from 10.101.10.10 to 10.102.40.0/24.

If you ever have an issue in which multicasts are not following the path that you expect, you should remember to check the unicast routing table, as well as that PIM-DM is enabled on the correct interfaces.

You should also understand that the PIM-DM router must receive the multicasts on the forwarding interface for the unicast route to the source. If PIM-DM is not enabled on that interface, the router does **not** accept the traffic on the second best route. For example, you enable PIM-DM on the link between Core-1 and Core-2, as well as on the link between Core-2 and Access-1. But you do not enable PIM-DM on the link between Core-1 and Access-1. However, Access-1's route to the multicast source's subnet is through the link to Core-1. Access-1 will drop all multicasts because they are arriving on the wrong interface, and multicast receivers will fail to receive the traffic.

This is also why you needed to enable PIM-DM on VLAN 1212 between Core-1 and Core-2. Core-2 can reach 10.101.10.0/24 through VLAN 1212 or 212, but VLAN 1212 offers the better route. If the multicasts arrived on VLAN 212, but not VLAN 1212, Core-2 would have dropped them. You could enable PIM-DM on VLAN 212 for additional redundancy, which would also add to the bursts of bandwidth consumption. Remember that PIM-SM, covered in other Aruba training, helps to minimize bandwidth usage for multicast routing.

In short, be careful to enable PIM-DM on the correct interfaces.

## Understanding how a multicast forwarder is elected

Figure 7-13 shows a different scenario: the company has two switches performing routing for VLAN 20. It has chosen this solution rather than a Virtual Switching Framework (VSF) fabric, which is typically recommended. The switches run Virtual Router Redundancy Protocol (VRRP) and also PIM-DM. Just as only one of the redundant switches can act as the active VRRP master, only one of the switches can forward multicasts. Otherwise, endpoints could receive duplicate copies of the multicasts, causing errors.

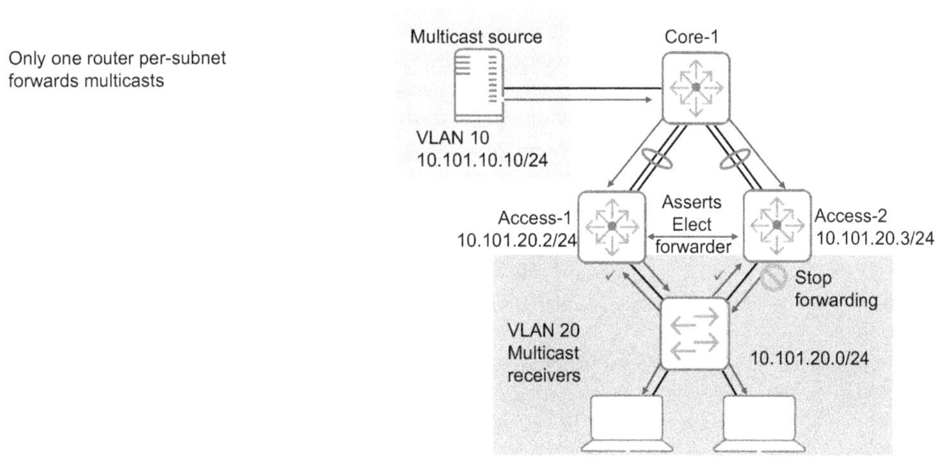


Figure 7-13 Understanding how a multicast forwarder is elected

When Access-1 and Access-2 shown in Figure 7-13 receive multicasts from Core-2, they flood the multicasts to each other. As you saw in the "Understanding the relationship between the PIM-DM tree and the unicast routing table" section, the RPF fails, and the switches send an assert. You will now look at that assert in more detail.

The PIM routing switches examine each other's asserts to elect a multicast forwarder for the interface. The assert includes the (S, G) entry under dispute and information about the PIM routing switch's unicast path to the source. The routing switch with the more favorable path becomes the multicast forwarder, as determined first by administrative distance (preference) and then, if the administrative distance ties, by metric or cost. If the metric ties as well, the routing interface with the higher IP address is elected.

In the example shown in Figure 7-13, both switches have OSPF routes (preference 10) to the multicast source and both have the same cost for the route. However, Access-2 has the higher IP address. Therefore, Access-2 is elected multicast forwarder for VLAN 20.

Access-1 removes this VLAN from its list of downstream interfaces in its (S, G) entry. It also sends a prune to Access-2. Access-2 continues to forward multicasts in VLAN 20 because multicast receivers connect in this VLAN. However, the prune would be important if this VLAN did not include receivers; it would stop routing switches from looping traffic across redundant paths.

If you are using a design such as this, you might want to pay attention to the actual IP addresses that you assign to the routing switches. To load balance the Master and multicast forwarder role on different VLANs, assign one switch a higher IP address and VRRP priority on some VLANs and the other switch a higher IP address and VRRP priority on other VLANs.

## PIM-SM

You will now examine PIM-SM. Because PIM-SM does not flood traffic whenever a source starts to send multicasts, it can be the better choice for larger environments.

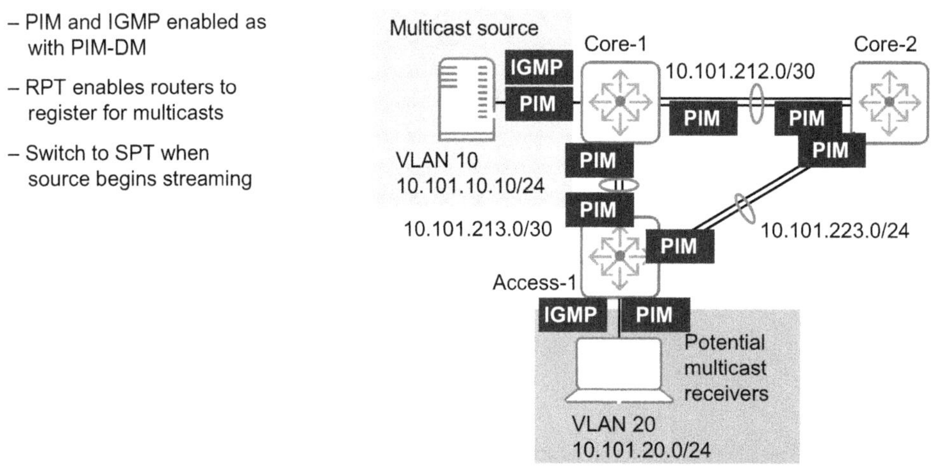


Figure 7-14 PIM-SM

PIM-SM involves a little more setup than PIM-DM because PIM-SM routing switches cannot assume that they are part of the initial multicast routing tree for all traffic. Instead, PIM-SM routing switches must explicitly join that tree, and you must configure them to do so (see Figure 7-14).

Configuring PIM-SM is similar to configuring PIM-DM in some ways. For example, you must enable PIM-SM on every interface between multicast sources and receivers, including the following:

- VLAN interfaces on which multicast sources reside
- VLAN interfaces on which multicast receivers reside (IGMP-enabled interfaces)
- VLAN interfaces between all routers and routing switches that connect sources and receivers

As with PIM-DM, PIM SM-enabled interfaces exchange hellos on 224.0.0.13. In addition to establishing neighbor relationships, PIM interfaces in broadcast or multiaccess networks elect a designated router (DR). The DR is responsible for forwarding multicasts and is selected according to priority (higher priority is preferred) and by address. The same best practice as for Multiple Spanning Tree Protocol (MSTP) and VRRP apply—load balance DR responsibilities across VLANs by setting a higher priority on one routing switch in one VLAN and another routing switch in the other.

**Note**

PIM-SM uses the same multicast address as PIM-DM, 234.0.0.13, which helps to explain why you cannot implement PIM-SM and PIM-DM in the same domain. PIM-enabled routing switches operating in one mode would expect certain behavior from neighbors operating in another, leading to the failed establishment of the multicast forwarding tree.

## RPT

PIM-SM routers must explicitly join multicast forwarding trees for traffic that receivers on their subnets require. However, with no knowledge of the source address, the routing switches have no way of knowing where to direct their joins. Similarly, the DR for the source would not know where to direct the multicast traffic. Without these joins, the DR has no way of discovering which PIM-SM routing switches require the traffic.

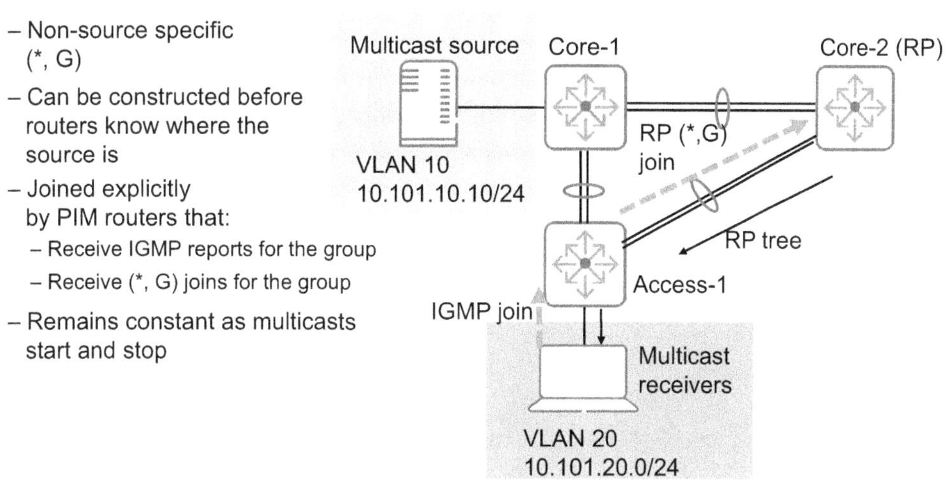


Figure 7-15 RPT

To avoid this problem, the routing switches that are interested in a particular multicast group direct their joins to a router selected as the rendezvous point (RP) and establish an RP tree (RPT) rooted at that device. The source's DR also directs multicast traffic to the RP. Thus, the RPT connects the multicast traffic to the devices that need it. Depending on where the source resides, the RP might not provide the *best* root for tree, but what is most important is that it provides a well-known root. (You will see later how PIM-SM enables devices to establish more efficient paths after traffic starts to flow.)

As you see in Figure 7-15, interested multicast receivers begin the process of establishing the RPT by sending IGMP reports for the group in question. The IGMP join triggers the DR to join the RPT, sending a (*, G) join toward the RP.

As with PIM-DM, the (*, G) entry is called a pending PIM route on the AOS-Switches. A PIM routing device such as Access-1 creates a (*, G) entry for the groups that IGMP informs it clients want. However, unlike the PIM-DM (*, G) entry, this (*, G) entry has an upstream interface, which enables the PIM routing switch to explicitly join the tree. The switch discovers the upstream interface by looking up the forwarding interface in the unicast route to the RP.

The PIM-SM upstream interface transmits a join message, asking the upstream neighbor to add this interface as a downstream interface in the RPT tree. The upstream neighbor adds the interface in the (*, G) entry in question. It then discovers the upstream interface and sends a join message out that interface. The join messages travel up the tree in this manner until they reach the RP.

The RPT, which will forward multicasts, follow the reverse flow of the RPT joins.

## Behavior as source begins forwarding

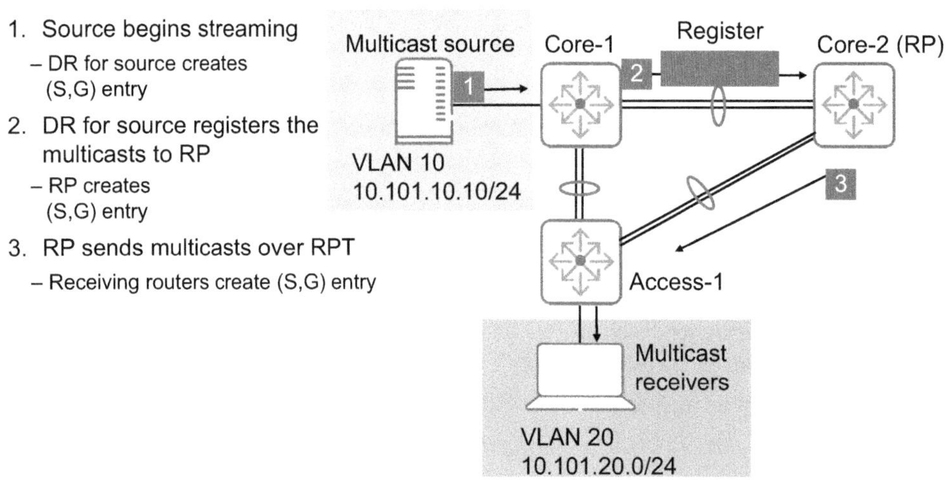


Figure 7-16 Behavior as source begins forwarding

Figure 7-16 shows an RPT that is ready to deliver multicast traffic from the RP to all PIM routing switches connected to receivers for the group. The RP simply needs to receive the traffic.

When a source begins to forward multicast traffic for this group, this process occurs:

1. The default router for the source's subnet receives the traffic. This router is called the DR. (If more than one PIM router exists on the subnet, the DR is elected as you learned with PIM-DM.)
2. The DR registers with the RP. The unicast register messages encapsulate the multicast traffic.
3. The RP decapsulates the multicast traffic and forwards it on the RPT multicast tree.

To forward this traffic, the DR, the RP, and any other routing switches in the path use (S, G) entries, which specify the active source and the multicast destination. Each router creates the (S, G) entry as soon as it receives multicast traffic on the RPT, copying the downstream interfaces from the (*, G) entry into the new entry. The DR also includes the tunnel on which it sends register messages as downstream interfaces.

The upstream interface depends on whether the routing switch uses the RPT or the SPT. The RPT initially forwards the traffic as shown in the figure above, and the (S, G) routes used for this forwarding have an RPT bit, indicating that the RPT is being used. However, you will almost never see an (S, G) entry with the RPT bit because the PIM-SIM routing switch quickly transitions to a more efficient tree.

Consider this point.

A more efficient traffic flow would have the DR as the root of the multicast forwarding tree. For example, in this network, multicasts flow from the source to Core-1 (the DR), which tunnels them in unicast messages to Core-2 (the RP). Core-2 then forwards the multicasts to Access-1. If Core-1 could forward the traffic directly to Access-1, the multicast stream would consume less bandwidth. Core-1 and Core-2 would also not need to encapsulate and decapsulate the multicasts, which would impose less of a burden on the DR and RP.

## Switching to SPT

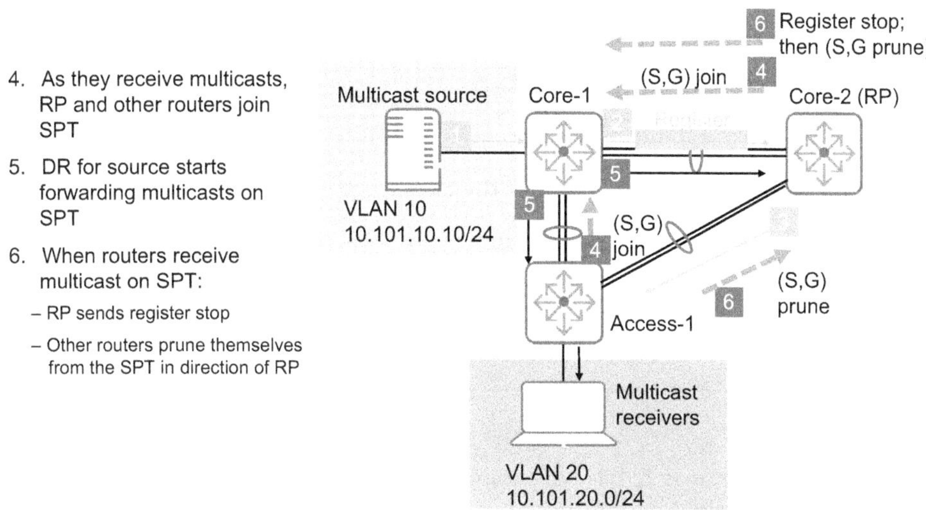


Figure 7-17 Switching to SPT

PIM-SM allows routing devices to transition from the RPT to the SPT with the DR at the root.

The arrival of the first multicast packet in a group triggers a switch from the RPT to the SPT on the DR, RP, and any PIM-SM routing device that forwards traffic into a VLAN for IGMP hosts.

To switch to the SPT, the PIM-SM routing devices perform these tasks outlined in Figure 7-17 and described in more depth below. (The numbering in Figure 7-17 continues from Figure 7-16.)

4. The PIM-SM router determines the upstream interface for the SPT, using RPF to discover the forwarding interface for the shortest path to the source. It then sends an (S, G) join on this interface.

   At this point, to ensure that traffic flow continues uninterrupted, the switch continues to accept traffic on the upstream interface for the RPT.

5. The DR receives the (S, G) joins and adds the receiving interfaces to the downstream interface list for its (S, G) entry. Now it starts forwarding multicasts on the SPT. It continues sending multicasts in register packets too in case some devices have not yet joined the SPT.

6. The RP and DRs for receivers monitor the incoming interface for multicast traffic to determine when they can set the SPT bit.

   The SPT bit prevents the routing switch from accepting multicasts on any interface except the correct upstream for the SPT, preventing duplication of multicast streams. Routing switches can set this bit when they are certain that the SPT has been established above them—that is, they can receive traffic on the correct interface for this tree.

   Routing switches can determine that the upstream SPT has been established in a few different ways, which include:

   - The switch receives a multicast on the correct upstream interface for the (S, G) entry.
   - The switch is the DR so, as the root of the SPT, it sets the SPT bit immediately.
   - The upstream interface for the RPT and the SPT are the same, so the switch cannot ever determine whether the upstream SPT has been established—but does not care because it is receiving traffic in the same way in either case. This switch can set the SPT bit immediately.

---

**Note**

In reality, the behavior is a bit more nuanced because, in a multiaccess network, the upstream interface might be the same but the neighbor is different. However, this basic description suffices for our purposes.

---

7. When a PIM-SM routing device sets the SPT bit:

   - A non-RP routing switch sends an RPT (S, G) prune on the upstream interface for the RPT (unless that is the same as for the SPT). It no longer needs multicasts on this path.

Note that the PIM-SM routing switch does not prune itself from the RPT; it maintains its (*, G) entry and its place in the RPT so that it can continue to receive multicasts in this group from other sources. Rather this prune removes the routing switch from the RPT *for the specific source.*

- The RP sends register stop messages. These messages request that the DR to stop sending the encapsulated multicast messages because it can receive the multicasts on the SPT more efficiently. In the example shown in the Figure 7-17, the RP also prunes itself from the SPT because it no longer has downstream interfaces in this tree after Access-1 pruned itself. But the RP could remain part of the SPT, depending on the topology.

Thus, PIM routing switches always ensure that the SPT has been established upstream of them before they prune themselves from the RPT. This process ensures that the multicast stream is never interrupted.

This process can occur very quickly. Once the SPT is established, it resembles the PIM-DM tree. Traffic flows from the source to the destination following the best path, as calculated by the unicast routing table.

You can disable and enable the switch to the SPT with this command:

```
Switch(config)# [no] router pim spt-threshold
```

However, it is generally recommended that you leave the default behavior of enabled.

## Specifying the RP

You now have a basic idea of how PIM-SM routers join an RPT in order to receive initial multicasts and then switch to an SPT for more efficient traffic flow. Besides enabling PIM-SM on the proper interfaces, the most important step for configuring the system is specifying the RP or RPs.

A PIM-SM router must have the correct RP address for every multicast address for which it needs to forwards traffic. Otherwise, the router cannot receive the stream. And every PIM-SM router in the domain must always select the same RP for the same multicast addresses. Clearly, if some routers that need a particular type of multicast traffic established an RPT to one RP, and the DR then registers to another RP, the traffic will go astray.

It is recommended that you select core routers for RPs, which encourages devices to establish the RPT over backbone links. Traffic would need to flow over these links in any case, so placing the RP there does not redirect the traffic to an area that might not otherwise have to support it. For example, in this scenario, Core-1 or Core-2 is the natural choice for the RP because all other PIM-SM devices connect directly to it.

In addition, because RPs might need to store many multicast route entries and handle a great deal of multicast traffic, you should also select high-performance routing switches capable of meeting the needs.

When the PIM-SM routing switches meet these criteria, you should also try to place them as near multicast sources as possible, which makes the transition to the SPT more efficient.

You can either specify a single RP for all multicast groups, or you can configure the bootstrap mechanism, which enables the PIM-SM domain to elect an RP for each group dynamically.

### Manual

When you set the RP address manually, you must set the same, single RP on every device. Because the domain will have only one RP, you should generally select the PIM-SM routing device that is the fewest hops from most other routers or has the highest bandwidth and throughput capabilities. If you have a relatively small core and you know that multicast traffic will be originating from a specific location, you could alternatively set the DR for that location as the RP.

Enter this PIM command to specify the static RP:

```
Switch(pim)# rp-address <IP address> [group-address/group-mask] [override]
```

You must enter the command on *every* PIM-SM router and routing switch in the domain; PIM neighbors do *not* advertise static RPs to each other. The group address and group mask settings are optional. Specify these to limit the RP to supporting the multicast addresses included in that range. For example, if you specify 239.0.0.0/8, the RP can only support multicasts between 239.0.0.0 and 239.255.255.255.

You can only define one manual RP address on each AOS-Switch per range, which makes the manual option less conducive to redundancy than the bootstrap option. The **override** option dictates whether the manual RP address takes precedence over one sent by bootstrap.

### Bootstrap

The bootstrap mechanism is typically recommended over a manual configuration. Not only is it simpler to set up, it enables more than one RP to operate in the system. Each RP supports different multicast groups. Therefore, the burden of the role is load-balanced. The system also has greater redundancy because, if one RP fails, another RP can be selected to support the multicast groups that the failed RP used to support.

To determine how many PIM-SM devices to configure as Candidate RPs (C-RPs), you should consider the size of your network and the number of multicast receivers. In an environment with thousands of receivers, you should configure several RPs, which load balance groups between them.

Finally, keep in mind that, if you configure an RP address on a PIM-DM routing device manually, and the routing device also receives RP addresses through the bootstrap mechanism, the manual configuration overrides the bootstrap message. For consistency, you should *not* configure an address manually if you plan to use bootstrap.

## Bootstrap mechanism

Instead of specifying an RP on all PIM-SM devices, you can set up the bootstrap mechanism. With this approach, you configure each device with its role and make no configurations at all on devices that do not require a role:

- C-RPs are PIM-SM devices that can act as RPs. In the pool of C-RPs, only one is elected the RP for a particular group. However, multiple RPs can be active at once, each supporting a different group.
- A Bootstrap Routers (BSR) is a PIM-SM device that distributes information about RPs to other PIM-SM devices in the domain. You can configure a pool of Candidate BSRs (C-BSRs). Only one BSR is active while the others function as backups.

In more detail, C-BSRs use their bootstrap messages, which they begin to send as soon as they are configured with the role, to elect the active BSR. That is, when a C-BSR receives a bootstrap message with a higher priority than its own, it suppresses its messages. If the priority is the same, the C-BSR defers to the C-BSR with a higher IP address. Thus, after all C-BSRs have heard each other's messages, only the C-BSR with the highest priority or tied highest priority and highest IP address, remains active.

> **Note**
> The C-BSR uses the IP address of the interface that you specify with the C-BSR command. PIM-SM must be enabled on this interface or the BSR cannot send messages.

The C-BSRs continue to listen for the BSR's periodic messages. If the hold time expires without a message, the C-BSRs become active again, electing a new BSR.

C-RPs send C-RP advertisements to the active BSR. The advertisements include the RP's IP address, the range of multicast addresses that it supports, and its priority for each range. The BSR compiles the information as an RP set, which it advertises to all PIM-SM routing devices in the domain.

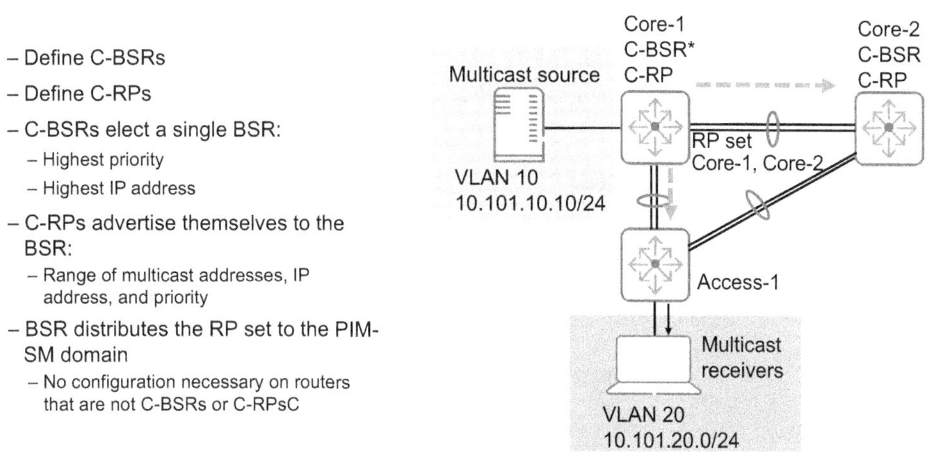


Figure 7-18 Bootstrap mechanism

For example, in Figure 7-18 both Core-1 and Core-2 are configured as C-BSRs. Both Core-1 and Core-2 are configured as C-RPs. Example commands are listed below:

```
Core-1(config)# router pim
Core-1(pim)# bsr-candidate source-ip-vlan 1212
Core-1(pim)# bsr-candidate priority 250
Core-1(pim)# rp-candidate source-ip-vlan 1212

Core-2(config)# router pim
Core-2(pim)# bsr-candidate source-ip-vlan 1212
Core-2(pim)# rp-candidate source-ip-vlan 1212
```

For the source VLAN in these commands, you must choose a VLAN has PIM-SM enabled on it. You should choose a VLAN that offers as much redundancy as possible (for example, it is carried on a link aggregation).

In the example shown in Figure 7-18, Core-1 is elected as BSR because it has the higher priority. It is also a C-RP. Core-2 is also a C-RP, and it advertises itself as such to Core-1. Both C-RPs are configured with priority 100, and neither is limited in the groups that it supports. Core-1 would send bootstrap messages with this RP set:

- Core-1's C-RP IP address for 224.0.0.0/4 priority 100
- Core-2's C-RP IP address for 224.0.0.0/4 priority 100

Remember that you only need to enter the **rp-candidate** command on the routers that you actually want to act as C-RPs, not on the C-BSRs. The C-RPs automatically advertise themselves to the BSR. In this example, you entered the **rp-candidate** command on the C-BSRs because you wanted your core switches to be able to perform both the BSR and RP roles.

## Selecting an RP from the RP set

To view the RPs that are manually configured on the AOS-Switch, as well as the ones received from the BSR, enter this command. Example output is provided.

```
Switch# show ip pim rp-set
 Status and Counters - PIM-SM Static RP-Set Information

  Group Address   Group Mask      RP Address      Override
  --------------- --------------- --------------- --------

 Status and Counters - PIM-SM Learned RP-Set Information

  Group Address   Group Mask      RP Address      Hold Time Expire Time
  -------------   -----------     -------------   --------- -----------
  224.0.0.0       240.0.0.0       10.101.212.1    150       144
  224.0.0.0       240.0.0.0       10.101.212.2    150       144
```

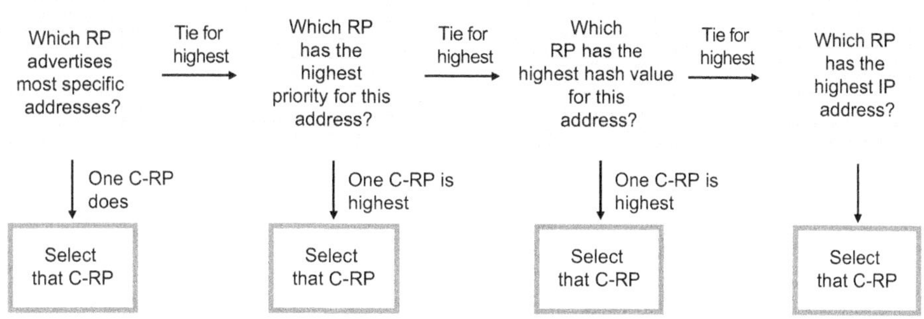


Figure 7-19 Selecting an RP from the RP set

PIM-SM routing devices that have identical RP sets—which they should—always select the same RP for the same multicast address, following the rules outlined in Figure 7-19 and explained in more depth below:

1. Select the RP that advertises the most specific range of multicast addresses that includes the desired address.
2. If more than one C-RP advertises a range of the same specificity, select the C-RP configured with the highest priority.
3. If more than one C-RP is configured with the highest priority, a hash function generates a series of mask length values that are individually assigned to the set of eligible C-RPs. If the hash function matches a single RP candidate to a longer mask length than the other candidates, that candidate is selected to support the group.
4. If the hash function matches the longest mask length to multiple RP candidates, the C-RP that has the highest IP address is selected to support the group.

The PIM-SM devices store the RP set, but only calculate an RP when they need to join an RPT for a group (when a connected IGMP host sends a report for the address or when a downstream neighbor sends a (*, G) join). This behavior preserves memory and processing power.

Now that you understand how PIM-SM routing devices select the RP, you can consider ways to affect the selection by adding options to the candidate RP configuration.

## Group prefixes

Perhaps one of your PIM-DM routers is closer to the multicast sources for a specific multicast address or range of addresses, so you want other routers to prefer it as the RP for those addresses. Tell the RP to advertise that specific address or range with this PIM configuration command:

```
Switch(pim)# rp-candidate group-prefix <group address/prefix>
```

For example, enter:

```
Switch(pim)# rp-candidate group-prefix 239.255.0.0/16
```

As long as other candidate RPs are advertising a less specific range, this switch is the preferred RP for multicast groups in the 239.255.0.0/16 range, regardless of priority.

You can enter the command multiple times to advertise multiple ranges.

You should keep in mind that the **source-ip-vlan** <*ID*> option is required the first time that you enter the **rp-candidate** command. If you specify a group-prefix option the first time that you enter the command, the switch *only* supports the specified range.

But if you first enter the **rp-candidate source-ip-vlan <ID>** command without any group-prefix range, the switch automatically supports all multicast groups (224.0.0.0/4). For example, you enter this command:

```
Switch(pim)# rp-candidate source-ip-vlan 1212
```

You will see this in the running-config:

```
router pim
   rp-candidate
   rp-candidate source-ip-vlan 1212
   rp-candidate group-prefix 224.0.0.0 240.0.0.0
```

Later you might enter a specific range such as the following:

```
Switch(pim)# rp-candidate group-prefix 239.255.0.0/16
```

Then the switch advertises *both* ranges. This lets you create scenarios in which various RPs are preferred for different specific ranges, but they can all support any group if the preferred RP for that group goes down.

### Priority

As indicated above, when no RP advertises a more specific range into which the multicast group falls, priority comes into play. You can set the priority with this command:

```
Switch(pim)# rp-candidate priority <0-255>
```

A single priority applies to all ranges advertised by the RP.

### Load balancing

If you want to load-balance the role roughly evenly over multiple active RPs, you should explicitly set the same priority on each C-RP because different models of switches use different default priorities. After you set up each C-RP in this way, the hash algorithm will automatically allocate multicast addresses among the various C-RPs in a more or less equal fashion.

Consider this statement in more detail.

As you just learned, the hash algorithm assigns each RP a value for a block of multicast addresses. The length of the range of addresses that produce the same value for the same RP depends on the length of the mask that is advertised by the BSR. When PIM-SM devices use the hash algorithm to select an RP for a particular multicast address, they apply an AND function on the multicast address and the mask (much as an IP address is combined with a mask to produce a network address). Therefore, a 32-bit mask would result in a different value for each multicast address. With a 31-bit mask, the hash would produce the same value for two addresses in a row (because the 31-bit mask reduces two addresses to the same value), and a 24-bit mask would produce the same result for 256 addresses.

You can set the hash length on the BSR to control the size of the blocks of addresses that are always assigned to the same RP. The smaller the size (the longer the hash length), the more likely it is that multicast addresses will be distributed equally among the C-RPs. If the BSR advertises a shorter hash that produces large blocks of addresses, the same RP might happen to be selected for a preponderance of the multicast addresses—particularly, if server administrators select multicast addresses in a row.

The default mask length is 30, which produces the same hash for blocks of four addresses. In other words, the PIM-SM domain will elect the same RP for multicast group 239.255.0.0, 239.255.0.1, 239.255.0.2, and 239.255.0.3. A different hash is produced for 239.255.0.4-239.255.0.7, so a different RP can be elected. The more multicast addresses that are used, the higher the likelihood that they will be distributed more or less equally.

To configure the hash algorithm on the C-BSRs, use this PIM configuration command:

```
Switch(pim)# bsr-candidate hash-mask-length <1-32>
```

## Summary

This chapter introduced you to how PIM-DM builds SPTs by flooding multicast traffic and then pruning back branches when there are no receivers. You can now configure PIM-DM to route multicasts from one subnet to another. You also learned how PIM-SM uses an RPT to initially forward multicasts, but then switches to an SPT that resembles the SPT used by PIM-DM. You know how to use the bootstrap mechanisms to create an RP set so that PIM-SM functions correctly.

## Learning check

1. What is one advantage of PIM-DM as compared to PIM-SM?
   a. PIM-DM uses bandwidth more conservatively.
   b. PIM-DM tends to be simpler to set up.
   c. PIM-DM is designed for routing across WAN links.
   d. PIM-DM does not require the use of IGMP.
2. A network administrator is configuring a multicast routing solution. Potential multicast receivers are in VLAN 5. What must the administrator enable on this VLAN?
   a. PIM-DM only
   b. PIM-DM and IGMP
   c. IGMP only
   d. PIM-DM and PIM-SM
3. A multicast stream has been enabled between the server and the client shown in Figure 7-20.

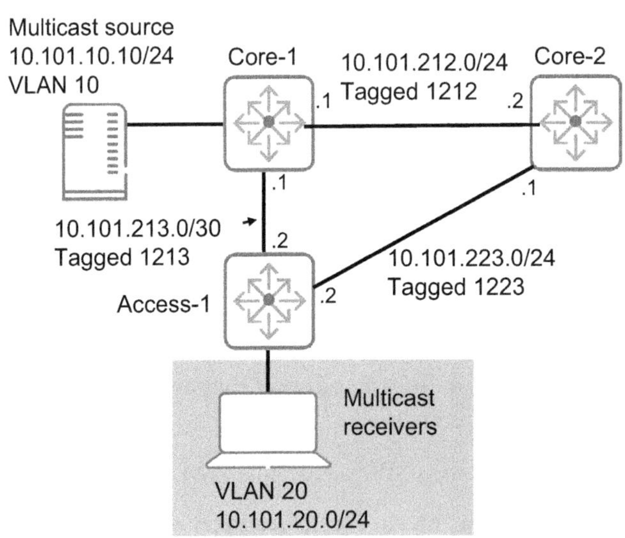


Figure 7-20 Multicast flow

Review the multicast routes on Core-1 and Access-1 after this multicast stream starts. Then answer the questions that follow:

### Access-1

```
Access-1# show ip mroute
 IP Multicast Route Entries

  Total number of entries : 1

  Group Address    Source Address  Neighbor        VLAN
  ---------------  --------------- --------------- ----
  239.1.1.1        10.101.10.10    10.101.213.1     1213

Access-1(config)# show ip mroute 239.1.1.1 10.101.10.10

 IP Multicast Route Entry

  Group Address  : 239.1.1.1
  Source Address : 10.101.10.10
  Neighbor       : 10.101.213.1
  VLAN           : 1213
  Up Time (sec)     : 343
  Expire Time (sec) : 194

  Multicast Routing Protocol : PIM-DM
  Unicast Routing Protocol   : ospf

  Metric       : 2
  Metric Pref  : 110
  Assert Timer : 0
  RP tree      : No

 Downstream Interfaces

  VLAN State      Up Time (sec)      Expire Time (sec)
  ---- ---------- ------------------ ------------------
  20   forwarding 343                176
  1223 pruned     343                0
```

### Core-1

```
Core-1(config)# show ip pim mroute 239.1.1.1 10.101.10.10
 IP Multicast Route Entry
  Group Address  : 239.1.1.1
  Source Address : 10.101.10.10
  Neighbor       : 10.101.10.10
  VLAN           : 10
  Up Time (sec)     : 216
  Expire Time (sec) : 285

  Multicast Routing Protocol : PIM-DM
  Unicast Routing Protocol   : connected

  Metric       : 1
  Metric Pref  : 0
  Assert Timer : 0
  RP tree      : No

 Downstream Interfaces

  VLAN State      Up Time (sec)      Expire Time (sec)

  ---- ---------- -------------      ----------- -----

  1212 pruned     216                174

  1213 forwarding 216                0
```

Describe the multicast route entries that you see on Core-1 and Access-1.

What is the meaning of the VLAN column in the output for the **show ip mroute** command? Which command shows the list of downstream interfaces? Relate what you see in the entries to the multicast flow in Figure 7-20.

4. A network administrator is monitoring the multicast routes on a switch that implements PIM-DM. The administrator sees this output:

```
Core-1(config)# show ip pim mroute 239.1.1.1 10.101.10.10
 IP Multicast Route Entry
  Group Address  : 239.1.1.1
  Source Address : 10.101.10.10
 <output omitted>
 Downstream Interfaces
  VLAN State      Up Time (sec)      Expire Time (sec)
  ---- -----      -------------      -----------------
  1212 pruned     216                174
  1213 forwarding 216                0
```

After about a minute, the administrator checks the route again and sees that the expire timer for VLAN 1212 has gone up rather than down. What explains this behavior?

5. Discuss strategies that you could use to troubleshoot a multicast routing solution that is not functioning correctly.

# Answers

## Learning check

1. What is one advantage of PIM-DM as compared to PIM-SM?
   a. PIM-DM uses bandwidth more conservatively.
   **b. PIM-DM tends to be simpler to set up.**
   c. PIM-DM is designed for routing across WAN links.
   d. PIM-DM does not require the use of IGMP.

2. A network administrator is configuring a multicast routing solution. Potential multicast receivers are in VLAN 5. What must the administrator enable on this VLAN?
   a. PIM-DM only
   **b. PIM-DM and IGMP**
   c. IGMP only
   d. PIM-DM and PIM-SM

3. Describe the multicast route entries that you see on Core-1 and Access-1.

   What is the meaning of the VLAN column in the output for the **show ip mroute** command? Which command shows the list of downstream interfaces? Relate what you see in the entries to the multicast flow in Figure 7-20.

   Core-1 and Access-1 both have a (10.101.10.10, 239.1.1.1) route. The VLAN listed in the **show ip mroute** command output is the upstream VLAN. It was VLAN 10 on Core-1, which connects directly to the source in that VLAN. The upstream VLAN was VLAN 1213 on Access-1, which received the multicasts from Core-1 on that VLAN.

   To see the downstream interfaces, you must look at the detailed route with the **show ip [pim] mroute 239.1.1.1 10.101.10.10** command.

   On Core-1, the downstream interface list includes both interfaces with PIM neighbors. VLAN 1212, which connects to Core-2, was pruned. VLAN 1213, which connects to Access-1, is forwarding.

   In Access-1's multicast route, the downstream interface list includes just VLAN 20, which has the multicast receiver. Access-1 knew that it needed VLAN 20 in its downstream interface list from the (*, G) route.

   You can use either the upstream interfaces in reverse or the forwarding downstream interfaces to trace the flow in the figure. The flow is from server to Core-1 on VLAN 10, from Core-1 to Access-1 on VLAN 1213, and from Access-1 to clients on VLAN 20. While the flow is simple in this example, understanding how to relate multicast route output to the flow of multicasts can help you to troubleshoot in more complicated topologies.

4. A network administrator is monitoring the multicast routes on a switch that implements PIM-DM. The administrator sees this output.

   After about a minute, the administrator checks the route again and sees that the expire timer for VLAN 1212 has gone up rather than down. What explains this behavior?

   The timer periodically resets because the DR for this multicast traffic periodically sends a state refresh message. The state refresh message specifies the state for interfaces (forwarding or pruning) and indicates that neighbors should send a response if they want to change the interface's state. They should also pass on the message with the state for their interfaces and reset their timers. The state refresh message floods through the PIM-DM domain and enables all PIM-DM routers to reset their timers with confidence that their interfaces are in the correct state. This means that Core-1 will never start flooding these multicasts on VLAN 1212 unless a PIM-DM router on this VLAN needs the multicasts.

5. Discuss strategies that you could use to troubleshoot a multicast routing solution that is not functioning correctly.

   You can take many approaches. A first step is often determining how far the multicasts are reaching.

For PIM-DM, you can use the **show ip [pim] mroute** command on each PIM-DM switch in the flow. If any multicasts have reached the switch, you should see a route with the IP address of the source. You should check the upstream interface listed in that route. If the route does not have an upstream interface, the switch cannot use it. (As you will examine in more detail at the end of this chapter, a switch might fail to discover a valid upstream interface because it does not have a route to the source or because the correct VLAN interface for reaching the source does not have PIM enabled on it.)

The route might also lack an upstream interface because the switch does not have any downstream interfaces for the route—so it has pruned itself. Check the downstream interfaces in the route and make sure that the switch is forwarding on the interfaces that you expect. An interface might be missing from the list because PIM-DM is not enabled on it. On a switch that connects to multicast receivers, make sure that IGMP, as well as PIM-DM, is enabled on the multicast receivers' VLANs. Otherwise, the switch cannot learn that it should forward multicasts on those VLANs.

You can use **show ip igmp** commands to examine and troubleshoot the IGMP functions. You can also use Wireshark to look for the type of IGMP messages that you examined in Lab 6.1.

You can use **show ip pim** commands to see whether switches have PIM-DM enabled on the correct interfaces and whether they have discovered each other as neighbors.

You can take similar strategies with PIM-SM. In addition, you should check that the switch not receiving the multicast traffic has the correct RP address for the multicast group in question. You should also check that the switch has a route to the RP address.

# 8 Border Gateway Protocol (BGP)

EXAM OBJECTIVES

✓ Establish and monitor Border Gateway Protocol (BGP) sessions between your routers and Internet Service Provider (ISP) routers

✓ Advertise an Internet Protocol (IP) block to multiple ISP routers

✓ Configure a BGP router to advertise a default route in Open Shortest Path First (OSPF)

## Assumed knowledge

- IP addressing
- Open Systems Interconnection (OSI) model
- Multiple Spanning Tree Protocol (MSTP) and Rapid Spanning Tree Protocol (RSTP)
- Link aggregation
- Virtual LANs (VLANs)
- Routing, including OSPF
- Switching

## Introduction

This chapter introduces you to Border Gateway Protocol (BGP), a powerful routing protocol designed for Internet Service Providers (ISPs) and very large enterprise networks. BGP is well suited to these use cases because it permits administrators to manipulate and even add attributes to route advertisements. However, this chapter does not teach you about all the aspects of the protocol or all the ways in which you can manipulate BGP route advertisements and route selection. Rather this chapter is intended to train you to configure BGP for a specific use case: a company with a multihomed ISP connection.

## BGP use case: Multihomed ISP connections

You will now examine the BGP use case that is the focus of this chapter. For your reference, this section also introduces other use cases for BGP that are beyond the scope of this study guide. Finally, you will begin to learn ways in which BGP differs in design from routing protocols such as Router Information Protocol (RIP) and Open Shortest Path First (OSPF)—an exploration that you will continue throughout the chapter.

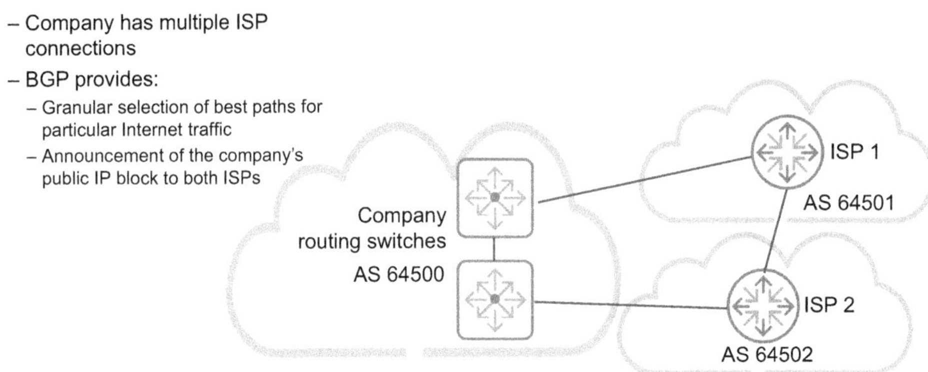


Figure 8-1 BGP use case: Multihomed ISP connections

Figure 8-1 shows the primary use case that you will examine in this chapter: a company needs to communicate with multiple ISP routers. You must understand when this scenario and similar scenarios call for BGP, as well as when they do not.

You do not need to implement BGP simply to connect to an ISP. You only need to do so when the company specifically needs to communicate routing information with the ISP. Typically, a company with a single connection to an ISP does not require BGP.

- The ISP handles announcing the block of public IP addresses assigned to the company.
- The company's routers use a default route for reaching all public IP addresses.

---

**Note**
This chapter refers to "BGP routers" as shorthand for routing AOS-Switches that support BGP.

---

When the company has multiple connections to the same ISP, it might benefit from communicating routing information with the ISP.

- The company router can discover more granular information about which connection offers the best route to particular external networks.
- In some special cases, the company might need to advertise different IP blocks over different connections.

Figure 8-1 shows a use case in which BGP might become even more useful: the company router is multihomed to different ISPs.

- Again, the company router can discover which connection offers the best connection for particular traffic.
- The company router might need to announce the company's public IP address block to the second ISP. That ISP can then propagate this advertisement throughout the Internet, enabling external devices to reach the company over the best path, which might include either ISP.

  Alternatively, *both* ISPs might be able to handle advertising the block of addresses. The company would need to discuss the proper solution with both ISPs. If the ISPs handle announcing the company's addresses, the company might not need to implement BGP at all. You should assess whether the benefit of selecting the particular connection for particular external routes outweighs the complexities of implementing BGP.

Figure 8-1 shows a design in which a different router connects to each ISP. This design offers better resiliency than a design in which a single router connects to both ISPs; however, it can be slightly more complex because it requires two BGP routers, which communicate with each other as well as the ISP routers.

You can alternatively use Virtual Switching Framework (VSF) to combine two physical AOS-Switches that support BGP, such as Aruba 5400R zl2 Series switches. You can then connect to the two ISPs on different physical chassis, but still retain the simplicity of a single (logical) BGP router for both connections.

### Other BGP use cases

BGP is designed specifically to communicate routes between organizations controlled by different entities and scales to hundreds of thousands of routes. For these reasons, ISPs use BGP to communicate routes with other ISPs, and BGP underlies all Internet routing.

For the same reasons, large enterprises that have outgrown a routing protocol such as OSPF (or Intermediate System to Intermediate System [IS-IS]) can implement BGP. The enterprise can segment itself into multiple OSPF autonomous systems and use BGP to communicate routes between these autonomous systems in a scalable manner.

Implementing a complete BGP solution in use cases such as these is beyond the scope of this study guide.

## BGP AS

BGP is an external gateway protocol (EGP) used to connect different autonomous systems, between a company and an ISP, multiple ISPs, or even segments within a large private network.

**Note**

Do not confuse the fact that BGP is an external gateway protocol (EGP) with a deprecated routing protocol, which is also called EGP.

The Autonomous System (AS) forms the fundamental building block of BGP, and each organization such as a company or ISP generally has its own AS, identified by a unique number. BGP originally supported only 16-bit AS numbers, ranging between 0 and 65535.

Because 16-bit numbers allow for only 65535 unique numbers, Request for Comments (RFC) 4893 establishes 32-bit AS numbers, increasing the range of AS numbers to 4 billion. (AOS-Switches support 16-bit AS numbers, as of the publication of this study guide.)

When a company determines that it needs to run BGP in a multihome scenario, it must obtain a valid public AS from the proper regional authority (see Table 8-1).

Table 8-1 BGP AS 16-bit numbers

| Purpose | AS numbers |
|---|---|
| Reserved | 0 and 65535 |
| Public IANA-assigned | 1-64495 |
| Documentation and examples | 64496-64511 |
| Private | 64512-65534 |

As Figure 8-2 shows, BGP operates in one of two forms depending on the autonomous systems to which the communicating neighbors belong.

- Neighbors in different autonomous systems communicate with exterior BGP (eBGP).
- Neighbors in the same AS communicate with interior BGP (iBGP).

The same router might use eBGP with one neighbor and iBGP with another.

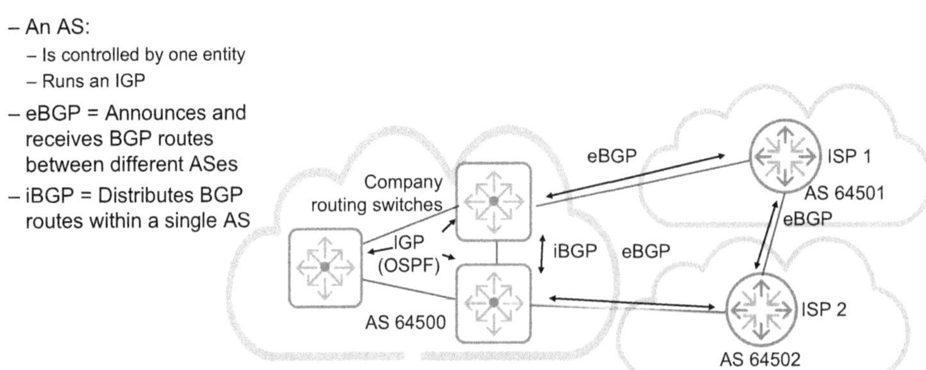


Figure 8-2 BGP AS

It is important that you understand that iBGP is not the only routing protocol that operates within the AS. The AS also runs an interior gateway protocol (IGP) such as OSPF, RIP, or IS-IS, which is localized to the AS and handles routing the local traffic. Typically, just a few routers in the AS—the routers that connect to other autonomous systems and perhaps some core routers—run BGP in addition to the IGP.

An AOS-Switch supports a single AS, which you define when you configure BGP on the switch.

```
Switch(config)# router bgp <AS>
```

**Note**

In some cases, the ISP might place a company within the ISP's own AS. In this case, however, the company router would use iBGP to communicate with the ISP routers. The company would also need a different AS to connect to another ISP. This study guide does not cover these use cases.

## BGP TCP sessions

As Figure 8-3 shows, BGP neighbors establish a TCP session on port 179. They then open a BGP connection within the session.

This connection carries all messages and routing updates between the neighbors, and the TCP session provides a degree of reliability for the communications. The BGP connection also features keepalives, which helps each router determine its neighbor's reachability.

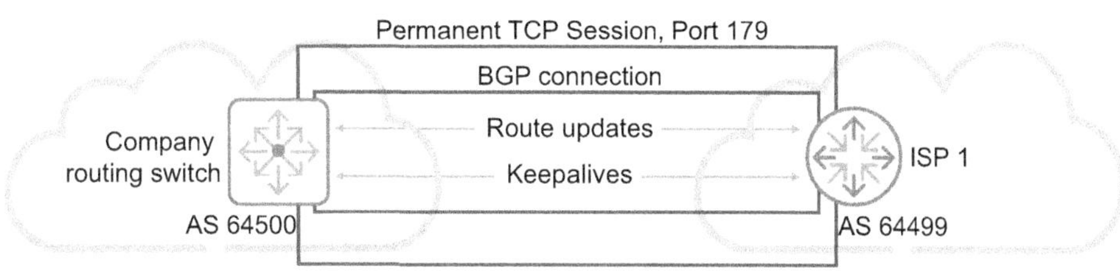


Figure 8-3 BGP TCP sessions

## BGP neighbor addresses

You must manually define each BGP neighbor on your BGP router to enable the router to establish the connection. Use this BGP command to define neighbors on AOS-Switches:

```
Switch(bgp)# neighbor <IP address> remote-as <AS>
```

The remote AS is the AS to which the neighbor belongs. As Figure 8-4 shows, if this AS is different from the AOS-Switch's own AS, the neighbor is automatically defined as an eBGP neighbor. If this AS is the same as the AOS-Switch's AS, the neighbor is automatically defined as an iBGP neighbor.

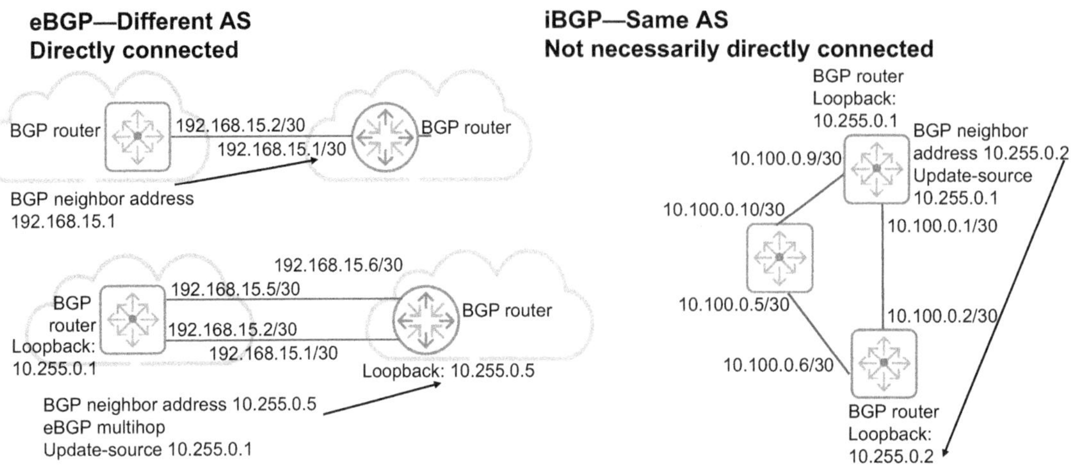


Figure 8-4 BGP neighbor addresses

Guidelines for specifying the neighbor IP address depend on whether the neighbor is an eBGP neighbor or an iBGP neighbor.

## eBGP neighbors

By default, eBGP neighbors must establish the session on a direct Layer 3 connection. In other words, they have IP addresses on the same subnet (a Layer 2 device could intervene without issue). The eBGP protocol enforces this criterion by checking that the neighbor IP address is on a network connected to the local BGP router and also by using messages with a Time to Live (TTL) of 1. In most cases, you should keep this behavior.

However, sometimes you need to configure a session between neighbors on different networks.

For example, your router might have two redundant Layer 3 connections to the same router. Each connection has its own IP address, but you want to establish a single connection to the neighbor with a stable IP address. Therefore, you configure the BGP neighbor's loopback interface IP address as the neighbor IP address on your routing switch. Similarly, the neighbor sets the local router's IP address to its loopback interface. You can then set the neighbor's loopback IP address as the neighbor IP address.

Although the loopback IP addresses are on directly connected routers and are technically only one hop apart, they are not on the same link. You must enable eBGP multihop, which disables the directly connected subnet check and optionally sets the TTL for the BGP messages higher than 1.

```
Switch(bgp)# neighbor <ipv4-addr> ebgp-multihop [2-255]
```

You must also ensure that the routers have routes to each other's loopback interfaces. Create static routes to the neighbor's loopback interface; the next hop for each route is the neighbor's IP address on one of the connected interfaces. Depending on whether you want to load-balance traffic over the redundant links to the ISP router, set the same administrative distance on the routes (load-balance) or different administrative distances (active route has lower distance).

Similarly, ensure that the neighbor creates routes to your router's loopback interface.

Finally, consider one other issue. By default, each switch uses its IP address on the forwarding interface to the neighbor as the source for its BGP messages. The neighbor expects the message from a neighbor IP address configured on it, so it rejects the messages. You can use this command to make the AOS-Switch use its loopback IP address as the source for messages to the BGP neighbor instead:

```
Switch(bgp)# neighbor <ipv4-addr> update-source <local loopback IP address>
```

Another use case for eBGP multihop is when you must reach the ISP router that runs BGP through another router or routers. To set up this solution, you must set the eBGP multihop to the correct number (two if one router intervenes, three if two routers intervene, and so on). Your router also requires a route to the ISP router's IP address, of course. However, it is not recommended to have intervening routers between eBGP neighbors, and you should avoid this setup whenever possible.

### iBGP neighbors

Unlike eBGP neighbors, iBGP neighbors do not have to be directly connected. Your AS might have many routing devices running an IGP such as OSPF, but only two BGP routers, which might be in different locations. Even if the two BGP routers connect directly, you often want them to contact each other's loopback interfaces. The routers can then continue to maintain the BGP session if their direct Layer 3 connection fails and they fail over to an alternative path.

When you plan to connect iBGP neighbors to each other's loopback interfaces, use this command, as in the eBGP scenario:

```
Switch(bgp)# neighbor <ipv4-addr> update-source <local loopback IP address>
```

However, you do not need to enable multihop for iBGP neighbors; iBGP permits multiple hops between neighbors by default.

## MD5 authentication

The ISP might require your router to authenticate. After you define the neighbor, define the password for it.

```
Switch(bgp)# neighbor <IP address> password <password>
```

The BGP neighbors use this password to hash the TCP payload of packets that carry the BGP messages, appending the hash to the packet (see Figure 8-5). If the neighbors' passwords do not match, the TCP session for the BGP connection fails to establish.

Because the neighbors add the MD5 hash to each packet sent on the TCP session, MD5 authentication provides data integrity for all BGP messages and for underlying TCP session. In other words, each neighbor knows that the proper neighbor sent the message and that no one has altered the message. However, MD5 does not provide protection against eavesdropping.

- Hashes IP payload
- Ensures that the peer knows the correct password
- Provides data integrity for all BGP messages

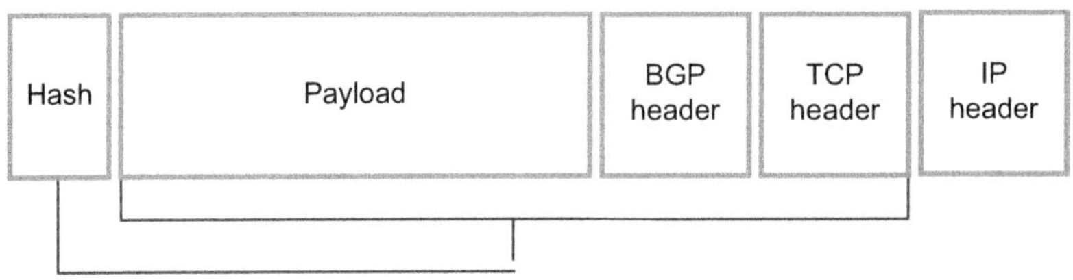


Figure 8-5 MD5 authentication

## Enable BGP

Once you have configured the BGP neighbors, you must enable BGP manually.

```
Switch(bgp)# enable
```

## BGP connection states

Once BGP is enabled on both neighbors, they first establish the TCP session on port 179 (see Figure 8-6). They then send BGP open messages with a list of parameters for the session and, assuming the parameters match, finally send the first keepalive of the session.

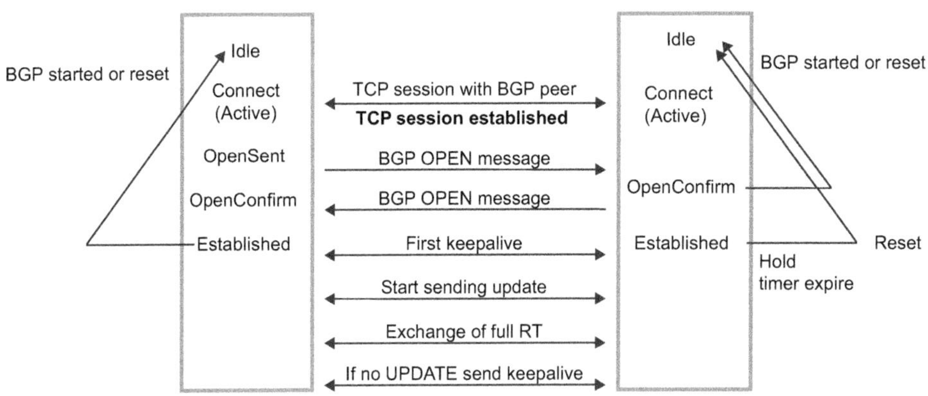


Figure 8-6 BGP connection states

Refer to Figure 8-6 as you trace the states through which a BGP connection might pass.

- The BGP connection begins in the Idle state and returns to this state when the session establishment times out without success or an error occurs.
- The connection typically transitions immediately to the Connect state, in which the router attempts to contact its neighbor at TCP port 179 and waits for a response.

  If the router is set to Passive TCP mode for this neighbor, the session transitions to Active mode, rather than to Connect mode. In this mode, the router waits for the neighbor to initiate the session.

  The connection also moves to the Active state if the router does not receive a response to its TCP session initiation. In this state, the router waits for the neighbor's response and also, after a timer expires, might try to initiate the connection again. The router might wait in Active state for a significant period of time if the TCP session fails to establish. If you see a router in Active mode after several minutes, the neighbor might be unreachable.
- After the BGP neighbors have established the TCP session, the router sends an open message, either immediately or after a configurable delay. The connection also transitions to the OpenSent state or directly to the OpenConfirm state depending on whether the router has already received the neighbor's open message.
- In the OpenSent state, the router waits for the neighbor's open message. Once it receives that message, it verifies that necessary parameters match (for example, the neighbor's AS matches the remote AS configured on your router). Assuming that the parameters match, the router sends a keepalive and transitions to the OpenConfirm state.

  If the parameters do not match, the router sends an error notification and returns to the Idle state. Therefore, if you see a router stuck in the Idle state, you might want to check that you configured the local AS and neighbor AS correctly.
- In the OpenConfirm state, the router waits for neighbor's keepalive message and also sends its own keepalive. It also listens for error notifications such as one indicating that the open message parameters do not match.
- After receiving the neighbor's keepalive, the connection transitions to the Established state.

  The connection remains in this state during normal operation. The neighbors continue to send keepalives. If a BGP router fails to receive a number of keepalives, it ends the connection. Note that the keepalive period is quite long (5 minutes, by default).

New eBGP neighbors exchange their full BGP routing tables. After the eBGP neighbors have exchanged their BGP routing tables, they only exchange updates. For example, a BGP router sends an update if configuration changes affect routing policies or if a topology change has occurred.

Routes remain in the BGP routing table unless an update occurs. A router can also request a route refresh from a neighbor which might be necessary so that the router can apply new policies to routes that it has already received.

## View information about the BGP session

You can view information about the BGP neighbor session by entering:

```
Switch# show ip bgp summary

Peer Information

  Remote Address   Remote-AS Local-AS State         Admin Status
  ---------------- --------- -------- ------------- ------------
  192.168.15.1     46501     46500    Established   Start
```

In this example output, the state is established, which indicates that the switch and its neighbor have opened the BGP session and can exchange routes.

# Receiving routes from BGP neighbors

After BGP neighbors have established a connection, they exchange their entire BGP routing tables. More specifically, they advertise their best route to each network in the BGP routing table to the neighbor. The best route is indicated by the > character, as shown in the Figure 8-7. The asterisk (*) indicates that the route is valid—that is, the next hop is valid.

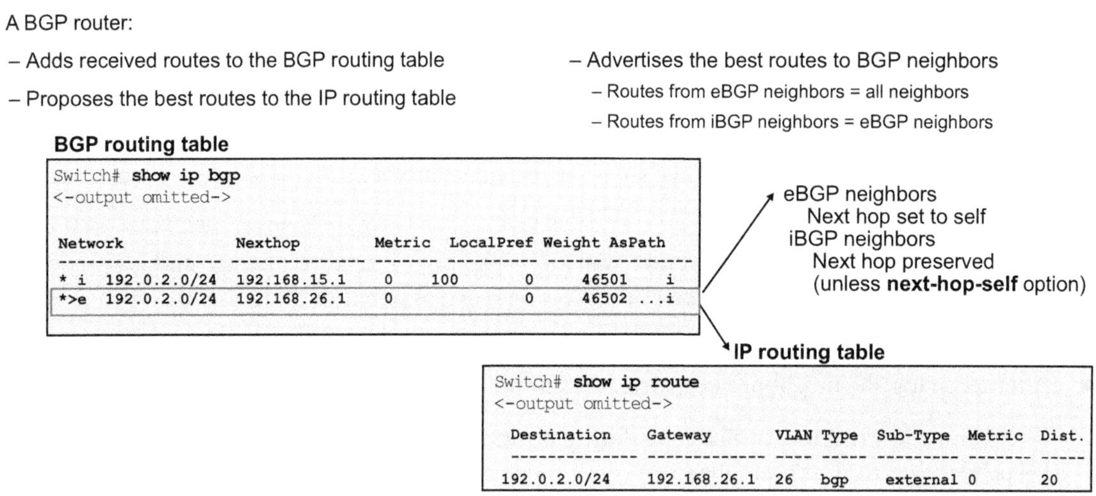


Figure 8-7 Receiving routes from BGP neighbors

In the example shown in Figure 8-7, the company BGP router does not have any routes in its BGP routing table before it establishes a connection with its neighbor. After these connections are established, the neighbors send route advertisements. Figure 8-7 shows just a couple advertisements as an example. Of course, in the real world, BGP routing tables are very large.

Your router follows this process when it receives routes from an *eBGP* neighbor:

- The router adds the routes to its BGP routing table.

  The route specifies the eBGP neighbor as the advertiser. By default, other BGP attributes remain intact.

  If the BGP router has received routes to identical networks from multiple neighbors, it must select the best route. You will look at the specific selection process during the lab.

- The router proposes the best routes to the global IP routing table.
- The router advertises the best routes to other BGP neighbors.

  The routes received from BGP neighbors are already part of the BGP routing table. You do not need to take additional steps to configure the BGP router to announce these routes to other BGP neighbors.

  Of course, a router never advertises a route that it received from a neighbor back to that neighbor. But it does advertise the route to other neighbors even if those neighbors have advertised an identical, but less preferred route to it.

  When a router advertises an eBGP route to another eBGP neighbor, it advertises its IP address on the connection with the neighbor as the next hop. However, when a router advertises an eBGP route to an iBGP neighbor, it retains the advertising eBGP neighbor IP address as the next hop. This means that both of your BGP routers must have a route to both of your ISP routers. Alternatively, you can configure the BGP router to always advertise itself as the next hop with this command:

```
Switch(bgp)# neighbor <IP address> next-hop-self
```

BGP routers handle advertising routes that they have received through iBGP a bit differently. For example, they do not advertise the routes to other iBGP neighbors. And they only advertise the route to eBGP neighbors after they have learned the route in the IGP. However, you do not need to understand these rules in depth because this scenario has only two BGP routers in the local AS. More information and guidelines for more complex networks are covered in advanced Aruba training.

## First criteria in best BGP route selection

To accept a route as a potential best route, the router must first determine whether the next hop is valid. It can only select the route if it has a route to the next hop. You can check the IP routing table to verify that this is true. For example, this output shows how a switch has a route to 192.168.24.0/21, so it can reach BGP routes with a next hop of 192.168.26.1 (which is within that network). The switch does not necessarily select the routes, but it can because they are valid.

```
Switch# show ip route

                          IP Route Entries

  Destination        Gateway        VLAN   Type   Sub-Type  Metric Dist.
  --------------     ------------   -----  ----   --------  ------ -----
<output omitted>
  192.168.24.0/21   10.100.212.2   212    ospf   External2 10      110

Switch# show ip bgp
  Local AS            : 46500 Local Router-id     : 10.255.0.1
  BGP Table Version : 15

  Status codes: * - valid, > - best, i - internal, e - external, s - stale
  Origin codes: i - IGP, e - EGP, ? - incomplete

     Network          Nexthop        Metric LocalPref  Weight  AsPath
     --------------   ------------   ------ ---------  ------  ----------
* i  192.0.2.0/24     192.168.26.1 0        100          0       46502    ...i
*>e  192.0.2.0/24     192.168.15.1 0                     0       46501       i
* i  198.51.100.0/24 192.168.26.1 0         100          0       46502       i
*>e  198.51.100.0/24 192.168.15.1 0                      0       46501    ...i
```

In the multihoming ISP scenarios, your BGP router or routers often receive valid routes to identical networks (same network address *and* prefix length) from multiple neighbors. AOS-Switches use the administrative distance as the first criteria to choose the best route. Because the default eBGP distance is 20 and the default iBGP distance is 200, by default, your BGP router will prefer all routes received from an eBGP neighbor to all routes received from an iBGP neighbor (see the output above and Figure 8-8).

If you keep this behavior, the default routes advertised in OSPF determine to which BGP router various local routing switches send Internet traffic. When the traffic arrives on the BGP router, that router uses its own ISP connection to forward the traffic.

1. Next hop is reachable
2. Administrative distance
   - Default: eBGP routes preferred to iBGP routes
   - Set distance equal to allow standard BGP route selection behavior

**Default administrative distances**
`router bgp <AS> distance bgp 20 200`

Routes from eBGP peer selected

```
Switch# show ip bgp
<-output omitted->
 Network             Nexthop          Metric  LocalPref  Weight AsPath
 ------------------  ---------------  ------- ---------  ------ ---------
 * i  192.0.2.0/24      192.168.26.1  0       100        0      46502 ...i
 *>e  192.0.2.0/24      192.168.15.1  0                  0      46501    i
 * i  198.51.100.0/24   192.168.26.1  0       100        0      46502    i
 *>e  198.51.100.0/24   192.168.15.1  0                  0      46501 ...i
```

**Equal administrative distances**
`router bgp <AS> distance bgp 200 200`

Routes with shorter AS path selected

```
Switch# show ip bgp
<-output omitted->
 Network             Nexthop          Metric  LocalPref  Weight AsPath
 ------------------  ---------------  ------- ---------  ------ ---------
 * i  192.0.2.0/24      192.168.26.1  0       100        0      46502 ...i
 *>e  192.0.2.0/24      192.168.15.1  0                  0      46501    i
 *>i  198.51.100.0/24   192.168.26.1  0       100        0      46502    i
 * e  198.51.100.0/24   192.168.15.1  0                  0      46501 ...i
```

Figure 8-8 First criteria in best BGP route selection

To allow BGP to select the best path for particular traffic, set the administrative distance for eBGP and iBGP to the same value. For example, you can set both to 200 with this command:

```
Switch(config)# router bgp <AS number> distance bgp 200 200
```

Each of your BGP routers then selects the best route to each external destination, based on the criteria discussed in the "More criteria in BGP best route selection" section. Without special manipulation, this is often AS path length, as shown in the Figure 8-8.

In this use case, OSPF routers in your internal network still typically use a default route to decide to which of your BGP routers to send the external traffic. That router then routes the traffic to next hop for the selected best route, which could be an eBGP or iBGP peer.

## More criteria in BGP best route selection

When multiple identical BGP routes are valid and have the same administrative distance, BGP uses the criteria shown in Figure 8-9 to select the best route. For each BGP attribute, Figure 8-9 shows the values that are preferred for each attribute. Attributes are listed in the order by which the router examines them when selecting the best route. That is, the router selects the route with the better weight first. Only if those values are equal does the router move on to examine the next attribute, local preference. (Your router can set the weight for specific routes, and that value has meaning only on the router itself. When it sets the local preference, on the other hand, it communicates that value to iBGP neighbors, but not eBGP neighbors.)

| Attribute or criteria | Attribute type | Preferred values |
|---|---|---|
| Weight | | Highest |
| Local preference | Discretionary | Highest |
| AS path length | Mandatory | Local to this AS (learned by IGP or redistributed)<br>Then shortest path (fewest IDs in list) |
| Origin | Mandatory | i > e > ? |
| MED | Optional non-transitive | Lowest |
| IGP metric to next hop | | Lowest |
| Type of neighbor | | External |
| Age (if enabled) | | Oldest |
| Next hop router ID (if enabled) | Mandatory | Lowest |
| Cluster list (if enabled) | Optional non-transitive | Shortest |
| Neighbor router IP address | | Lowest |

If load sharing is enabled, add multiple with same lowest metric

Figure 8-9 More criteria in BGP best route selection

Without special manipulation of weight and local preference on your part, your router will tend to prefer routes based on the AS path. It will accept the route from the ISP that reaches the networks in question through fewer ISPs. Presumably, the shorter AS path indicates a shorter latency; however, this is not necessarily the case.

If the ISP routers advertise routes with the same number of AS IDs in the AS path, the origin might come into play. Routes that were originally injected into BGP are preferred to routes learned from EGP (deprecated) and redistributed routes. However, often the ISPs will have learned the route from a similar ultimate source, so the origin is identical.

The Multi-Exit Discriminator (MED) would take effect only if the ISP routers have explicitly set this attribute. They might do this if they needed to distinguish between multiple paths into your AS (in a scenario in which the multiple connections are to the same ISP). Generally, a router only compares MED values between routes advertised from the same AS. However, in some cases, you can request different ISPs to send routes with different MED values. You must enter this BGP command to permit the AOS-Switch to compare the MED values between the two ISPs:

```
Switch(bgp)# bgp always-compare-med
```

However, without special manipulation such as that, if the AS path is the same length, your router will probably accept the route from the router to which it has a lower-cost connection. If the metric to both ISPs is the same, the choice becomes nearly arbitrary. If Equal-Cost Multipath (ECMP) is enabled, in fact, the routing AOS-Switch adds multiple routes with the same next hop cost and load balances over them. If ECMP is disabled, the switch selects the route based on age, then router ID, and then the cluster list—but only if these checks are enabled. The final tiebreaker is the advertising router ID.

Similarly, assuming no manipulation of attributes, routers throughout the Internet will tend to route traffic to your company through the ISP to which they are closer.

BGP allows administrators to control several of these attributes, granting both the ISP and you the ability to fine-tune the route selection. Keep in mind that the neighbor router can also manipulate attributes and has ultimate authority over its route selection. Therefore, you can dictate which routes your devices choose, but might not be able to determine the flow for inbound traffic.

Note that the table in Figure 8-9 also indicates the type of attribute. (Rows without an attribute type are not attributes included in the route advertisement, but rather values that the switch determines itself.) It can be helpful to understand the attribute type when you perform more advanced manipulation. Mandatory and discretionary attributes are both well-known attributes that all BGP routers understand; mandatory attributes must be included in every route advertisements, while discretionary attributes are optional. An optional attribute might not be supported by all BGP routers. The "non-transitive" description means that if a BGP router receives this optional attribute and does not support it, it should drop the attribute.

For more details on attributes and route manipulation, attend advanced Aruba training.

## Advertising routes in BGP

You have learned how your BGP router receives and selects routes from its neighbors. If you want the BGP router to advertise routes of its own, such as routes to local networks, you must add those routes to the BGP routing table explicitly (see Figure 8-10). For example, your BGP router needs to advertise the company's IP block to the ISP. You must add a route to that block to the BGP routing table.

You add routes from the BGP router's IP routing table by injecting the routes, by redistributing them from another protocol, such as OSPF, or by redistributing static or connected routes.

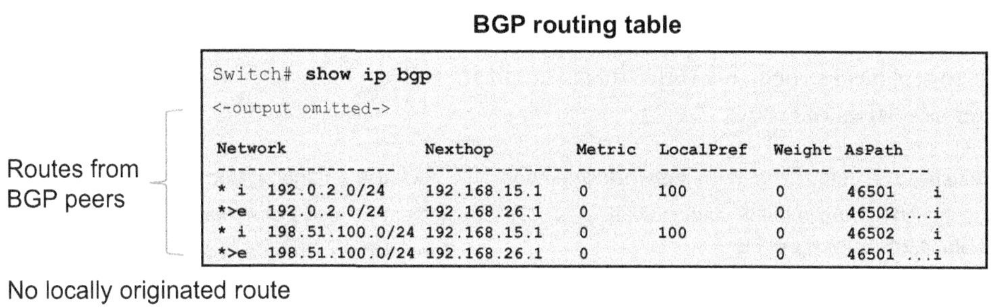


Figure 8-10 Advertising routes in BGP

The next section explains the injection method in more detail, as it is the approach that you should typically take.

Although redistributing routes enables you to import many routes into the BGP routing table with a single command, you do not have the same level of control provided by injecting routes. For example, redistributing OSPF routes into BGP adds all of the OSPF routes indiscriminately, including many private routes that you should not advertise to your ISPs. You can apply a route policy with the redistribute command to filter out undesired routes, but this approach is usually more complicated than you require.

---

**Note**

BGP applies an origin attribute of ? for redistributed routes, indicating an unknown origin. Keep in mind that neighbors prefer routes with an i origin, so the choice to redistribute rather inject the routes might affect whether neighbors choose to route traffic to this router.

---

## Inject routes into the BGP routing table

You can inject any route in the IP routing table into the BGP routing table by entering this command:

```
Switch(bgp)# network <network IP address/prefix length>
```

You must specify a network address and prefix length that matches the route in the routing table exactly. For example, you might want to advertise two ranges to your ISP.

- 203.0.113.0/25
- 203.0.113.128/25

You can enter **network 203.0.113.128/25** on the router with routing table shown in Figure 8-11. The network is added to the BGP routing table because the routing table includes this exact route.

You should always view the BGP routing table to check the routes that your router will advertise to its neighbors. Figure 8-11 shows how the 203.0.113.128/25 route appears in the BGP routing table. When you inject the route into the BGP routing table, the BGP routing process adds a number of BGP-specific attributes, including origin and next hop. The origin of the route is i, indicating that the BGP router has learned this route from one of its IGPs. The next hop is empty, indicating that this router advertises the route.

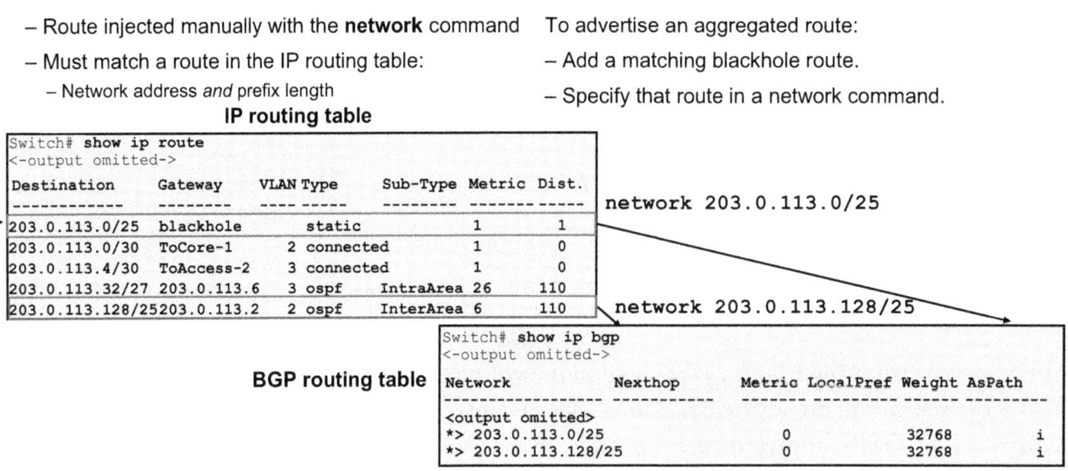


Figure 8-11 Inject routes into the BGP routing table

Sometimes your BGP router has many IP routes within the public IP block that you want to advertise, and you want to inject a single route that aggregates these routes. In this example, you might want to advertise 203.0.113.0/25 to summarize the shorter subnets within that range. When the aggregated route does not exist in the routing table, you must add a static route to the network through the blackhole. Specifying the black hole interface ensures that the route always remains in the routing table. It also allows the router to drop any traffic destined to an IP address within this range, if it does not have a more specific route for that address, as it should.

You can then specify the aggregated network in the BGP process. The network matches the black hole route, so it is added to the BGP table.

Figure 8-11 omits some of the BGP table output to focus on the most important information for the concept. You can see the full output with this command:

```
Switch# show ip bgp

  Local AS             : 46500          Local Router-id  : 10.255.0.1

  BGP Table Version    : 15

  Status codes: * - valid, > - best, i - internal, e - external, s - stale

  Origin codes: i - IGP, e - EGP, ? - incomplete

      Network              Nexthop         Metric  LocalPref  Weight AsPath

      -------              --------        ------  ---------  -----  --------

*>    203.0.113.0/25                       0                  32768         i

*>    203.0.113.128/25                     0                  32768         i

* i   192.0.2.0/24         192.168.26.1    0       100        0      46502 ...i

*>e   192.0.2.0/24         192.168.15.1    0                  0      46501  i

* i   198.51.100.0/24      192.168.26.1    0       100        0      46502  i

*>e   198.51.100.0/24      192.168.15.1    0                  0      46501 ...i
```

## Advertise external routes in OSPF

You need to consider how much of the routing information that your BGP router receives from the ISP routers available to the company IGP, typically OSPF. Although you can redistribute BGP routes into OSPF, it is not typically recommended. The large BGP routing table might overwhelm the OSPF processes on the local router and on other routers throughout the AS.

Often, you can simply have your BGP routers advertise default routes in OSPF. If they are already acting as Area Border Routers (ABRs) for stub areas, they already advertise default routes in those areas. You might need to have the BGP routers advertise default routes in the OSPF backbone, though. A simple approach is to configure a static route through its ISP connection on the BGP router. Then redistribute static routes into OSPF.

**Note**

Your ISP might advertise a default route to your BGP router. In that case, instead of redistributing static routes, you could redistribute just the BGP default route. When you redistribute BGP into OSPF, you apply a route map that permits only that route. However, route maps are covered in other Aruba training.

## Avoid becoming a transit AS

In the multihomed ISP scenario, you only want to advertise *your own* public IP addresses to the ISPs. You do *not* want to announce routes that your BGP routers learn from ISP 1 to ISP 2, nor routes learned from ISP 2 to ISP 1. If your routers do so, it is possible that the ISPs will accept these advertised routes as better than the ones that they are currently using. They could start sending Internet traffic through your AS as a transit AS (see Figure 8-12). Your router will quickly become overburdened by external Internet traffic.

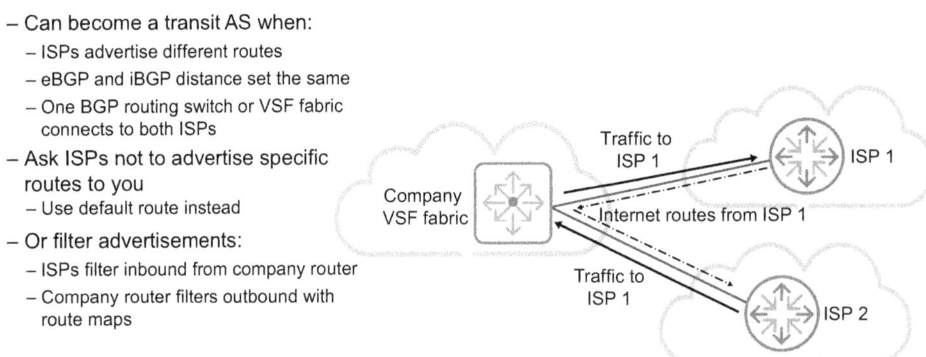


Figure 8-12 Avoid becoming a transit AS

Several scenarios could lead to your AS becoming a transit AS.

- The ISPs advertise Internet routes differently with different aggregation. Any route that your BGP routers receive from only one ISP, they could begin advertising to the other ISP.
- You set the administrative distance for eBGP and iBGP the same so that each BGP router begins to select some routes from its ISP and other routes from its iBGP neighbor. The router then advertises the best routes received from the iBGP neighbor to the ISP.
- You connect a single AOS-Switch or VSF fabric to both ISPs. In this case, the switch has two eBGP neighbors, and it will advertise best routes received from one to the other.

You should communicate with your ISPs to prevent issues in any of these scenarios.

Sometimes you are using BGP primarily to announce your public IP block. For traffic outbound to the Internet, you do not care about finding the best path. You might want to use the connection to one ISP as the primary connection and the other as a standby only if the first fails, or you might want to load balance across both. In cases such as these, you might ask your ISPs not to send any route advertisements to you. You can then create static default routes on the BGP routers, or in some cases, you might want the ISP to send only a default route in BGP.

If you want to receive routing advertisements from the ISPs, you will need to take care that your router does not pass them on to the other ISP. You can ask the ISP router to filter inbound advertisements from you. But it is best practice to filter outbound advertisements yourself. You can learn how to do this in advanced Aruba training.

## Review activity

Based on what you have learned in this chapter, complete Table 8-2 to compare BGP with OSPF.

Table 8-2 BGP and OSPF comparison

| | OSPF | BGP |
|---|---|---|
| Type of routing protocol (IGP or EGP) | | |
| Designed for routing tables of what size | | |
| How neighbor relationships are established | | |
| What neighbors advertise to each other | | |

## Summary

This chapter introduced you to BGP, focusing on how eBGP neighbors use the protocol to exchange routing information between different autonomous systems in a stable, highly manageable manner.

You can establish and monitor eBGP connections between a company router and an ISP router. You can also add routes from your router's global IP routing table to the BGP routing table so that your router advertises the correct networks. Specifically, you have learned how to configure a BGP solution for a company router that connects to two ISP routers.

## Learning check

1. What determines whether your AOS-Switch forms an eBGP relationship versus an iBGP relationship with a neighbor?
   a. whether the "exterior" or "interior" option is appended to the neighbor configuration
   b. whether the neighbor uses a loopback interface for its address or not
   c. whether the neighbor has the same AS number as the AOS-Switch router or not
   d. whether the AOS-Switch is running BGP in exterior or interior mode
2. An administrator enters **network 192.0.2.0/24** in the BGP context on an AOS-Switch. What is required for the switch to add this network to its BGP routing table?
   a. It has a route to any subnet within this range in its IP routing table.
   b. It has this exact route in its IP routing table, learned from any source.
   c. It has learned a route to any subnet within this range using OSPF.
   d. It has learned this exact route using OSPF.
3. What are differences between setting the neighbor IP address for the iBGP neighbor versus the eBGP neighbor?
4. What BGP neighbor state would you see if the connection was failing? What state would you see if it is successful and the BGP connection has opened?
5. An AOS-Switch has routes to these destinations in its routing table:
   - 192.0.2.0/25
   - 192.0.2.128/25

   The network administrator enters this BGP command:

   ```
   Switch(bgp)# network 192.0.2.0/24
   ```

   What else must the administrator do for the switch to advertise the route?

To answer the rest of the questions, refer to the scenario shown in Figure 8-13, as well as the command output below. Assume that Access-1, Core-1, and Core-2 are running OSPF with the area configuration shown and that they have achieved full adjacency as OSPF neighbors. For the purposes of the scenario, 10.1.0.0/16 is the company's "public" IP block. Also, note that Figure 8-13 is simplified to focus on the elements important for answering the questions. Of course, the network actually has more routing switches in area 1 and more OSPF areas, deployed with a similar pattern. Also not pictured is the network's firewall.

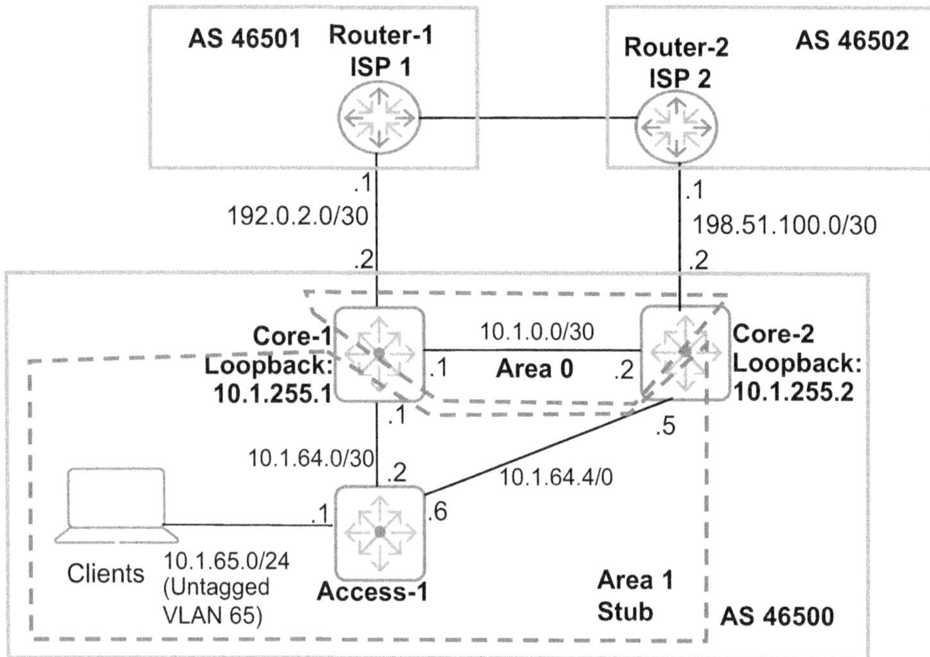


Figure 8-13 Learning check

```
Core-1# show running-config router bgp
Running-config
#
router bgp 46500
   network 10.1.0.0 255.255.0.0
   neighbor 10.1.255.2 remote-as 46500
   neighbor 10.1.255.2 update-source 10.1.255.1
   neighbor 192.0.2.1 remote-as 46501
   exit

Core-1(config)# show ip bgp summary

 Peer Information
```

```
  Remote Address   Remote-AS Local-AS State         Admin Status
  --------------- --------- -------- ------------- ------------
  10.1.255.2       46500     46500    Established   Start
  192.0.2.1        46501     46500    Established   Start

Core-2# show running-config router bgp
Running-config
#
router bgp 46500
   network 10.1.0.0 255.255.0.0
   neighbor 10.1.255.1 remote-as 46500
   neighbor 10.1.255.1 update-source 10.1.255.2
   neighbor 198.51.100.1 remote-as 46502
   exit

Core-2# show ip bgp summary

 Peer Information

  Remote Address   Remote-AS Local-AS State         Admin Status
  --------------- --------- -------- ------------- ------------
  10.1.255.1       46500     46500    Established   Start
  198.51.100.1     46501     46500    Established   Start

Access-1# show ip route ospf
                        IP Route Entries
  Destination    Gateway     VLAN Type   Sub-Type      Metric      Dist.
  -----------    ---------- ---- -----  ---------     -------     -----
  0.0.0.0/0      10.1.64.1   640  ospf   InterArea     2           110
  0.0.0.0/0      10.1.64.5   644  ospf   InterArea     2           110
```

6. Assume that both ISPs advertise a route to 203.0.13.0/24. What criteria will Core-1 and Core-2 use to select the best route? Which route will Core-1 and Core-2 select?
7. Assume that servers connected to Access-1 need to communicate with devices in the 203.0.13.0/24 network. How will traffic outbound to the Internet be load shared on the ISP links? Consider advantages and disadvantages of this flow.
8. If either core switch's link to the ISP fails, the switch should be able to start routing traffic through its link to the other core switch and its ISP. What must you do to ensure that the switch will be able to use the BGP routes advertised through its iBGP neighbor?

# Answers

## Review activity

Table 8-3 BGP and OSPF comparison answers

| | OSPF | BGP |
|---|---|---|
| Type of routing protocol (IGP or EGP) | IGP (a single AS) | EGP (between autonomous systems) |
| Designed for routing tables of what size | Thousands of routes | Hundreds of thousands or even millions of routes<br>*BGP is designed for this number of routes; the number of routes supported by an AOS-Switch depends on its hardware. |
| How neighbor relationships are established | Neighbors automatically discovered on OSPF networks | Connection established in TCP sessions only with manually configured neighbors |
| What neighbors advertise to each other | Link states (within an area)<br>Routes (between areas) | Routes |

## Learning check

1. What determines whether your AOS-Switch forms an eBGP relationship versus an iBGP relationship with a neighbor?
   a. whether the "exterior" or "interior" option is appended to the neighbor configuration
   b. whether the neighbor uses a loopback interface for its address or not
   **c. whether the neighbor has the same AS number as the AOS-Switch router or not**
   d. whether the AOS-Switch is running BGP in exterior or interior mode

2. An administrator enters **network 192.0.2.0/24** in the BGP context on an AOS-Switch. What is required for the switch to add this network to its BGP routing table?

   a. It has a route to any subnet within this range in its IP routing table.

   **b. It has this exact route in its IP routing table, learned from any source.**

   c. It has learned a route to any subnet within this range using OSPF.

   d. It has learned this exact route using OSPF.

3. What are differences between setting the neighbor IP address for the iBGP neighbor versus the eBGP neighbor?

   An eBGP neighbor is indicated by a remote AS number that is different from the local router's. An iBGP neighbor has a remote AS number that is the same as the local routers.

   Typically, eBGP neighbors are directly connected, and you specify the neighbor's IP address on that connection when you add the neighbor in the BGP configuration. On the other hand, iBGP neighbors often are not directly connected. They often communicate using their loopback addresses so that the two devices can maintain the session even if paths change. In this case, you set the neighbor's loopback IP address in the BGP configuration, and you must set the update-source for the iBGP neighbor to the switch's local loopback address.

4. What BGP neighbor state would you see if the connection was failing? What state would you see if it is successful and the BGP connection has opened?

   When the BGP connection fails to establish correctly, you will see that the session remains in the Active state (eventually it will time out and go to the Connect or Idle state). A successful session has the Established state.

5. An AOS-Switch has routes to these destinations in its routing table:

   - 192.0.2.0/25
   - 192.0.2.128/25

   The network administrator enters this BGP command:

   ```
   Switch(bgp)# network 192.0.2.0/24
   ```

   What else must the administrator do for the switch to advertise the route?

   The BGP routing switch must have a route in its IP routing table that exactly matches the network address and prefix length in the **network** command. This switch does not have such a route. Therefore, you must create a static route to 192.0.2.0/45 through the blackhole interface.

6. Assume that both ISPs advertise a route to 203.0.13.0/24. What criteria will Core-1 and Core-2 use to select the best route? Which route will Core-1 and Core-2 select?

   The first criteria AOS-Switches use to choose between routes is administrative distance. The BGP configuration indicates that Core-1 and Core-2 are using the default administrative distance of 20 for eBGP and 200 for iBGP. Therefore, both switches will prefer the route that it receives from its own eBGP neighbor. Core-1 will prefer the route from ISP 1, and Core-2 will prefer the route from ISP 2.

7. Assume that servers connected to Access-1 need to communicate with devices in the 203.0.13.0/24 network. How will traffic outbound to the Internet be load shared on the ISP links? Consider advantages and disadvantages of this flow.

   In this environment, the OSPF configuration ultimately controls how this traffic is load shared on the ISP links. Access-1 represents the default routers for servers communicating on the Internet. As an internal router in a stub area, it uses a default rote for external traffic. The command output shows that the ABRs, Core-1, and Core-2, have advertised default routes with the same cost, so Access-1 is load sharing traffic across them.

   Core-1 and Core-2 each prefers their own local external routes. Traffic that Access-1 happens to send to Core-1, Core-1 forwards on its ISP link. Traffic that happens to be sent to Core-2, on the other hand, continues on Core-2's link.

   This type of behavior might work well for some environments. In other environments, you might want more control over which traffic is forwarded on which link. You could set the administrative distance for external and internal BGP to the same value if you want to use AS path (and other attributes) to select routes.

   Also, keep in mind that this behavior (as well as the behavior that you can achieve through route attribute manipulation) can lead to asymmetric routing: traffic from an Internet host to a local endpoint arrives on a different ISP link from outgoing traffic from that endpoint to that host. If this is a concern to you, you might want to use one ISP link as the primary link and the other just as standby. You can achieve this goal by configuring a lower-cost default OSPF route through one of your BGP routers. You would also need to work with your ISPs so that the standby ISP advertises your routes less favorably than the primary ISP.

8. If either core switch's link to the ISP fails, the switch should be able to start routing traffic through its link to the other core switch and its ISP. What must you do to ensure that the switch will be able to use the BGP routes advertised through its iBGP neighbor?

   You must verify that Core-1 can reach the next hop in the routes that it receives from Core-2 (ISP2 at 198.51.100.1). Similarly, you must verify that Core-2 can reach ISP 1 at 192.0.2.1. You have a couple of options. You can create a static route to the ISP 1 IP address on Core-1 and redistribute that route into OSPF; you can do the same on Core-2. Or, you could redistribute connected routes. Alternatively, you can add the **next-hop-self** option to the Core-2 neighbor configuration on Core-1 and to the Core-1 neighbor configuration on Core-2. Each core switch will then advertise the routes that it receives from its ISP to the other core switch with its own IP address as the next hop (which is reachable for the neighbor), rather than the ISP's address.

# 9 Access Control Lists

EXAM OBJECTIVES

- ✓ Define an access control list (ACL) and identify the criteria by which ACLs select traffic
- ✓ Configure ACLs on AOS-Switches to select given traffic
- ✓ Apply static ACLs to interfaces to meet the needs of a particular scenario
- ✓ Examine an ACL configuration and determine the action taken on specific packets

## Assumed knowledge

Before reading this chapter, you should have a basic understanding of:

- IP addressing
- Open Systems Interconnection (OSI) model
- Multiple Spanning Tree Protocol (MSTP) and Rapid Spanning Tree Protocol (RSTP)
- Link aggregation
- Virtual LANs (VLANs)
- Routing
- Switching

## Introduction

With internal threats so common, you need to secure your network's internal infrastructure and IT resources. In this chapter, you will examine one of the basic mechanisms for controlling traffic: access control lists (ACLs).

The chapter begins with an overview of the services that ACLs perform. You will then learn how the various types of ACLs work, and how to configure them and apply them to interfaces on your AOS-Switches.

## What is an ACL?

An ACL is simply a list of rules against which a network infrastructure device, such as a routing switch, checks packet headers. Each rule consists of specific criteria such as source IP address, destination IP address, and TCP or UDP port number. It also consists of an action:

- permit (select matching packets)
- deny (do not select matching packets)

What the routing switch does with selected packets depends on how you apply the ACL. This chapter focuses on packet filtering ACLs—ACLs that are applied to routing switch interfaces to filter incoming and outgoing traffic. For packet filtering ACLs, the permit action allows packets that match the rule, and the deny action discards packets that match the rule.

**Note**

You might also see rules referred to as access control entries (ACEs).

## Reasons to implement ACLs

This chapter teaches you about applying ACLs to filter traffic. Without such packet filtering ACLs, each routing switch interface accepts all packets and forwards that traffic based on its forwarding tables. ACLs enable you to implement more control, improving network performance and enhancing security. As Figure 9-1 shows, you can apply packet filtering ACLs to filter traffic to or from an endpoint, a group of endpoints, or entire subnets.

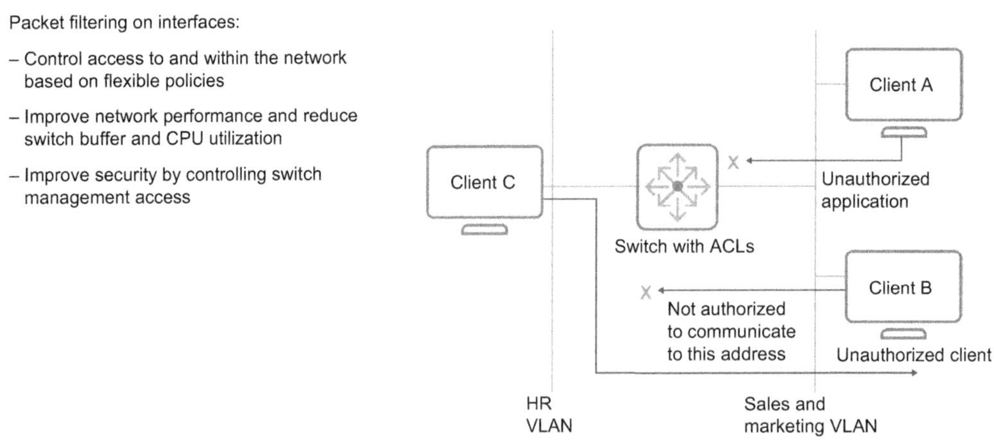


Figure 9-1 Reasons to implement ACLs

You might implement packet-filtering ACLs for reasons such as:

- At the network edge, ACLs can prevent unwanted IP packets from entering the network infrastructure. You can take restrictive approaches in which you permit the required traffic and deny all other traffic. Or you can take a permissive approach in which you deny specific traffic and permit all other traffic. By combining permit and deny rules, you can create highly flexible policies.
- Implementing ACLs at the network edge can also improve network performance and reduce switch buffer and CPU utilization by reducing the volume of packets that upstream switches and routers handle.
- At the network core and distribution layer, ACLs can similarly improve performance and security. For example, you can use ACLs to ensure various collections of clients only have access to selected destinations. These destinations may be specific hosts, entire subnets, or even particular applications. For example, you may want to ensure that all hosts and servers in a given VLAN are only allowed to communicate within that VLAN or with a limited number of other specific VLANs.
- You can also use ACLs to block IP traffic that has the switch as the destination address. For example, ACLs can deny unauthorized clients attempting to access the switch using functions such as Telnet, Secure Shell (SSH), or a web browser.
- In addition to securing the network infrastructure, you can also use ACLs to control a performance problem quickly by limiting IP traffic generated by a specific device, group of devices, or a subnet. This gives you an opportunity to troubleshoot without sacrificing performance for users outside of the problem area.

---

**Note**

Generally, AOS-Switches that support IP routing services also support the use of ACLs. Some switches that provide limited IP routing services support ACLs, but with more limited features. You should check your switch documentation to determine its support for ACLs.

---

## ACL IDs and types

When you create an ACL, you give it a valid ACL identifier (ID) and also determine its type.

### ACL types

Four types of ACLs are covered in this study guide:

- Standard (IPv4 standard)
- Extended (IPv4 extended)
- Standard MAC
- Extended MAC

You can also create IPv6 ACLs; however, this study guide covers only IPv4.

MAC ACLs permit or deny traffic according to the MAC header, and IPv4 ACLs select traffic based on the IP header. Standard ACLs of both types allow you to create rules based solely on the source address, while extended ACLs allow for a wider range of criteria.

## ACL IDs

The ACL ID groups together all the rules in the ACL, allowing you to view the ACL, add rules to the ACL, and otherwise edit the ACL. Each ACL must have a unique ID.

---

**Note**

You can re-use IDs between IPv4 and IPv6 lists. In other words, an ACL's ID must be unique in IPv4, and its ID must be unique in IPv6, but an IPv4 and IPv6 ACL can use the same ID.

---

AOS-Switches use *either* a number or a name to identify an ACL. Assigning a name, as opposed to a number, can make it easier to identify the ACL's intended purpose. The name can be up to 64 case-sensitive alphanumeric characters in length, including spaces. To include spaces in the string you must enclose the string in single or double quotes (" ").

When you create a named IPv4 ACL using this global configuration mode command, you must use the **ip access-list** command and indicate the type:

```
Switch(config)# ip access-list <standard | extended> <acl_name>
```

If you want to use a number for the ID, though, you have two choices. You can use the ip access-list command with a valid ID for that type:

```
Switch(config)# ip access-list standard 1-99
```

```
Switch(config)# ip access-list extended 100-199
```

Or you can use the **access-list** command (no **ip**), in which case you do not need to indicate the type. The ID that you enter determines the type of ACL. When you use this option to create an ACL, you must also configure the first rule, and you cannot specify a sequence ID. Generally using the **ip access-list** commands gives you more freedom.

---

**Note**

Even if you used the access-list command to create a numbered ACL, you can use the ip access-list <standard | extended> command later to edit the list.

---

For MAC ACLs, you must enter the type regardless of whether you are using a name or number for the ID. Enter one of these commands from global configuration mode context:

```
Switch(config)# mac-access-list standard <acl_name | 200-299>
Switch(config)# mac-access-list extended <acl_name | 300-399>
```

Creating the ACL moves you to configuration context for adding rules and editing the list. You will learn more about creating rules in a moment.

You can find which IDs to use for each type in Table 9-1.

Table 9-1 ACL IDs

| ACL type | Standard ACL | Extended ACL | Standard MAC ACL | Extended MAC ACL |
|---|---|---|---|---|
| Valid IDs | Use a number:<br>1–99<br>Or<br>Use an alphanumeric name (< 64 case-sensitive characters, including spaces). | Use a number:<br>100–199<br>Or<br>Use an alphanumeric name (< 64 case-sensitive characters, including spaces). | Use a number:<br>200–299<br>Or<br>Use an alphanumeric name (< 64 case-sensitive characters, including spaces). | Use a number:<br>300–399<br>Or<br>Use an alphanumeric name (< 64 case-sensitive characters, including spaces). |

## ACL rule components

An ACL rule consists of three basic components:

- Sequence ID
- Action
- Matching criteria

### Sequence ID

The sequence ID identifies the rule within the list, enabling you to identify and, if necessary, remove it. The ID also tells the switch when to process this rule in relation to other rules. The ID with the lowest number is processed first. You will look at the implications of processing order in more detail later. Specifying a sequence ID is optional. If you do not specify the sequence ID, the switch assigns an ID automatically, placing the rule at the end of the list.

### Action

A permit action tells the ACL to select any packet that matches the criteria. The deny action tells the ACL not to select any packet that matches the criteria.

When you are using the ACL to filter packets, permitted packets are forwarded and denied packets are dropped.

### Matching criteria

The switch matches traffic against the rule's matching criteria to determine whether the traffic matches that rule.

Standard (IPv4) ACLs and standard MAC ACLs simply select traffic basic on its source IP or MAC address, so the rules are quite simple. Extended and MAC extended ACLs include more matching criteria, giving you more flexibility.

## Example IP ACL rules

You will now learn how to specify rules for IPv4 standard and extended ACLs.

### IPv4 standard ACLs

As Figure 9-2 shows, you can use an IPv4 standard ACL to select traffic based only on its source IP address or range of addresses.

You have three options for specifying the IP addresses:

- You can specify **any**, which matches any address
- You can specify **host** and an address, which matches that single address
- You can specify a range of addresses

To match a range of IP addresses, you must use wildcard bits or prefix lengths. You should be familiar with prefix lengths as a way of indicating a subnet mask. Wildcard bits are reverse logic masks, and you will practice using them to specify a range of IP addresses in the section "Using and interpreting wildcard bits."

The example below rule permits traffic with any source IP address in the 10.101.10.0/24 subnet (the sequence ID is optional):

```
Switch(config-std-nacl)# [10] permit 10.101.10.0/24
```

Table 9-2 shows the syntax for configuring IPv4 standard ACL rules.

Table 9-2 Syntax for IPv4 standard ACL rules

| Rule ID | Action | Source (IP address) |
|---|---|---|
| Optional:<br>1-2147483647 | **permit \| deny** | **any \| host *<IP address>* \| *<network address/ prefix>* \| *<IP address> <wildcard bits>*** |

## IPv4 extended ACLs

An IPv4 extended ACL can select packets based on a variety of packet IP header fields. Figure 9-2 shows some examples of the fields you can use to select packets.

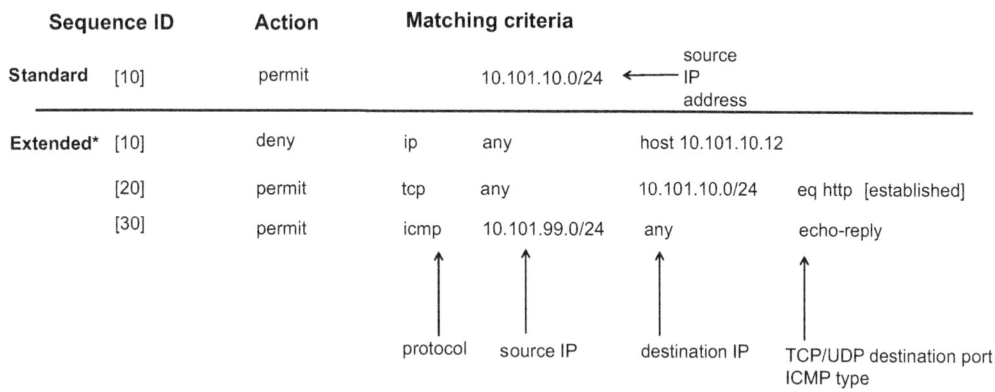


Figure 9-2 Example IP ACL rules

All rules for these types of ACLs include a source and destination IP addresses. You have the same options for specifying the IP addresses as in standard ACLs (any, host <IP address>, or a range specified by prefix length or wildcard bits). If you care about just the source IP address, or just the destination IP address, specify any for the other.

You can further categorize IPv4 extended ACL rules by the IP protocol type, which is the first option that you specify after **permit** or **deny**:

- **ip**—These rules filter traffic based only on its source IP address, destination IP address, or both. The IP protocol and other information in the IP header do not matter. This example rule denies all IP traffic to 10.101.10.12:

  ```
  Switch(config-ext-nacl)# [10] deny ip any host 10.101.10.12
  ```

- **tcp** or **udp**—These rules select particular TCP or UDP applications, typically based on the destination TCP or UDP port or port numbers. You can apply the rule to any IP address or to specific ones. When you specify the port, you must also include a keyword that indicates whether to select that specific port, a range of ports, any port except that port, and other options listed in Table 9-6. Rather than use the port number, you can use the keyword for many well-known ports. For example, if you specify **http**, the switch automatically interprets the port number as 80.

  For TCP only, you can filter traffic based on the TCP flag. For example, you might want to drop TCP RST packets from untrusted IP addresses. You can also include the **established** keyword to indicate that the rule applies only to sessions that are already established. Assume that an ACL is filtering traffic from an untrusted zone to a trusted zone. A rule with the **established** keyword can prevent untrusted endpoints from establishing certain types of TCP sessions, but allow sessions that were established by trusted endpoints to flow.

This example rule permits any HTTP traffic that is destined to subnet 10.101.10.0/24:

```
Switch(config-ext-nacl)# [20] permit tcp any 10.101.10.0/24 eq http
```

- **icmp**—These rules filter ICMP traffic, optionally based on its type. For example, you could permit ICMP replies but prohibit ICMP unreachable packets. Again, you can apply the rule to any IP addresses or specific ones. This example rule permits devices in the 10.101.99.0/24 subnet to send ICMP replies to any destination:

```
Switch(config-ext-nacl)# [30] permit icmp 10.101.99.0/24 any
echo-reply
```

- **igmp**—These rules filter IGMP traffic, optionally based on type and by source and destination address.
- **Other protocols**—These rules let you permit or deny specific IP protocols such as OSPF. The CLI provides keywords for specifying several protocols, as shown in the job aid. If you do not see a keyword for the protocol that you want to control, use the IP protocol number. Unlike with TCP, UDP, ICMP, and IGMP, you can only specify the IP protocol and the source and destination IP addresses, not other options.

The command syntax depends on the type of protocol in the rule. Tables 9-3 through 9-6 provide the complete syntax in the order you should enter the components. The parameters indicated in boldface are required while others are optional.

For any of these types of rules, you can specify a QoS mark so that the rule selects only traffic that meets the other criteria and is also marked for a specific priority. (You will learn more about how QoS priorities affect traffic handling in *Chapter 15: Quality of Service*.) You can specify the traffic's IP precedence value, its Type of Service (ToS) value, or both. Modern networks often use Differentiated Services code points (DSCPs) to mark traffic for priority handling in its IP header. DSCPs use the same IP header fields as IP precedence and ToS, so you can specify a DSCP by specifying both an IP precedence and ToS value.

Table 9-3 Syntax for IPv4 extended ACL rules that use the IP protocol

| Rule ID | Action | Protocol | Source (IP address) | Destination (IP address) | IP precedence | ToS |
|---|---|---|---|---|---|---|
| 1-2147483647 | **permit \| deny** | **ip** | **any \| host <*IP address*> \| <*network address/prefix*> \| <*IP address*> <*wildcard bits*>** | **any \| host <*IP address*> \| <*network address/prefix*> \| <*IP address*> <*wildcard bits*>** | precedence <0-7 \| *name*> | tos <0, 2, 4, 6, 8 \| *name*> |

Table 9-4 Syntax for IPv4 extended ACL rules for TCP and UDP

<table>
<tr><th>Rule ID</th><th>Action</th><th>Prot.</th><th>Src. IP address</th><th>Src. Port</th><th>Dest. IP address</th><th>Dest. port</th><th>TCP flag</th><th>TCP session status</th><th>IP prec.</th><th>ToS</th></tr>
<tr><td>1-2147483647</td><td>permit | deny</td><td>tcp</td><td>any | host <IP address> | <network address/prefix> | <IP address> <wildcard bits></td><td>See syntax in Table 9-6</td><td>any | host <IP address> | <network address/prefix> | <IP address> <wildcard bits></td><td>See syntax in Table 9-6</td><td>rst | syn | fin | ack</td><td>established</td><td>precedence <0-7 | name></td><td>tos <0, 2, 4, 6, 8 | name></td></tr>
<tr><td>1-2147483647</td><td>permit | deny</td><td>udp</td><td>any | host <IP address> | <network address/prefix> | <IP address> <wildcard bits></td><td>See syntax in Table 9-6</td><td>any | host <IP address> | <network address/prefix> | <IP address> <wildcard bits></td><td>See syntax in Table 9-6</td><td></td><td></td><td>precedence <0-7 | name></td><td>tos <0, 2, 4, 6, 8 | name></td></tr>
</table>

Table 9-5 Syntax for IPv4 extended ACL rules for other protocols

<table>
<tr><th>Rule ID</th><th>Action</th><th>Protocol</th><th>Source<br>(IP address)</th><th>Destination<br>(IP address)</th><th>Type</th><th>IP precedence</th><th>ToS</th></tr>
<tr><td>1-2147483647</td><td><b>permit | deny</b></td><td><b>icmp</b></td><td><b>any | host <i><IP address></i> | <i><network address/prefix></i> | <i><IP address> <wildcard bits></i></b></td><td><b>any | host <i><IP address></i> | <i><network address/prefix></i> | <i><IP address> <wildcard bits></i></b></td><td><i><ICMP type name></i> | <0-255></td><td>precedence <0-7 | <i>name</i>></td><td>tos <0, 2, 4, 6, 8 | <i>name</i>></td></tr>
<tr><td>1-2147483647</td><td><b>permit | deny</b></td><td><b>igmp</b></td><td><b>any | host <i><IP address></i> | <i><network address/prefix></i> | <i><IP address> <wildcard bits></i></b></td><td><b>any | host <i><IP address></i> | <i><network address/prefix></i> | <i><IP address> <wildcard bits></i></b></td><td><i><IGMP type name></i></td><td>precedence <0-7 | <i>name</i>></td><td>tos <0, 2, 4, 6, 8 | <i>name</i>></td></tr>
<tr><td>1-2147483647</td><td><b>permit | deny</b></td><td><b>pim<br>ospf<br>esp<br>ah<br>vrrp<br>sctp<br>ip-in-ip<br>ipv6-in-ip<br>gre<br><0-255></b></td><td><b>any | host <i><IP address></i> | <i><network address/prefix></i> | <i><IP address> <wildcard bits></i></b></td><td><b>any | host <i><IP address></i> | <i><network address/prefix></i> | <i><IP address> <wildcard bits></i></b></td><td>N/A</td><td>precedence <0-7 | <i>name</i>></td><td>tos <0, 2, 4, 6, 8 | <i>name</i>></td></tr>
</table>

Table 9-6 Syntax for UDP or TCP port

| Need | Keyword | Example |
|---|---|---|
| Specify one port | eq | eq 80<br>Any traffic with port 80 is selected. |
| Specify a range of ports | range | range 50000–50100<br>Any traffic with port 50000-50100 is selected (including 50000 and 50100). |
| Specify any port with a smaller value than that listed | lt | lt 20<br>Any traffic with port 1-19 (including 1 and 19) is selected. |
| Specify the listed port and any port with a greater value | gt | gt 49999<br>Any traffic with port 50000-65535 (including 50000 and 65535) is selected. |
| Specify all ports except for one (the rule, whether permit or deny, applies to all ports except the listed port) | neq | neq 80<br>Any traffic with port 1-79 and 81-65535 is selected (including 1, 79, 81, and 65535). |

# Example MAC ACL rules

When you want to filter traffic based on MAC address, or when you want to filter various types of non-IP traffic, you should use MAC ACLs.

## Standard MAC ACLs

As Figure 9-3 shows, a standard MAC ACL simply selects traffic based on its source MAC address. A rule can select one MAC address with the **host** option, any MAC address, or a range of MAC addresses, indicated with wildcard bits.

This example rule permits any frame with source MAC address 0050.56AA.AA01:

```
Switch(config-std-macl)# 10 permit host 0050.56AA.AA01
```

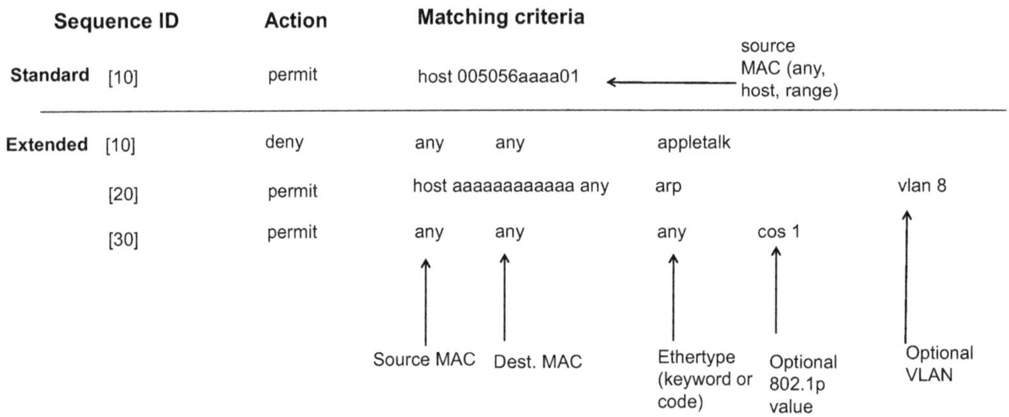


Figure 9-3 Example MAC ACL rules

## Extended MAC ACLs

As Figure 9-3 shows, the match criteria for extended ACLs include:

- Source and/or destination MAC addresses (any, a single address, or a range indicated with wildcard bits)
- Ethertype—You can specify one of several well-known Ethernet protocols such as IP, IPv6, ARP, FCoE, and so on. You can see a list of these protocols by pressing ? in the CLI when you reach the portion of the command for specifying the Ethertype. If the protocol that you want to select does not appear in the list, enter the protocol number. You must specify the Ethertype in all rules. If you want the rule to match all Ethernet traffic, specify **any**.
- Optional VLAN number

---

**Note**

The VLAN value is only applicable when the MAC ACL is applied to a port or link aggregation (trunk) interface.

---

- Optional Class of service (CoS) priority, another name for 802.1p value

This example rule denies all appletalk traffic:

```
Switch(config-ext-macl)# [10] deny any any appletalk
```

This example rule permits ARP traffic from a specific MAC address in a specific VLAN:

```
Switch(config-ext-macl)# [20] permit host AAAA.AAAA.AAAA any arp vlan 8
```

This example rule denies all traffic with CoS value 1:

```
Switch(config-ext-macl)# [30] deny any any any cos 1
```

**Note**

You will learn more about QoS in Chapter 15. Often you do not want to deny traffic with a specific CoS (802.1p) value entirely, but instead remove or change the value.

Table 9-7 lists the syntax for extended MAC ACL rules.

Table 9-7 Syntax for Extended MAC ACL rules

| Rule ID | Action | Source MAC address | Destination MAC address | Ethertype | CoS (802.1p value) | VLAN |
|---|---|---|---|---|---|---|
| 1-2147483647 | permit \| deny | any \| host *<MAC address>* \| *<MAC address> <wildcard bits>* | any \| host *<MAC address>* \| *<MAC address> <wildcard bits>* | any \| *<name>* \| <600-ffff> | cos <0-7> | vlan *<ID>* |

## Determine use cases for ACL types

You will now examine several use cases for how a company wants to filter traffic. You will select the correct type of ACL for the use case. (Answers are included at the end of this chapter.)

1. Attackers can use ICMP to map the network and implement certain exploits and Denial of Service (DoS attacks). For example, in the Smurf attack, the attacker sends an ICMP echo request with a spoofed source address to a broadcast address. Devices then flood the spoofed source with replies.

   The company wants to filter out most ICMP packets that cross from a less-trusted network segment to a trusted subnet. It will allow ICMP reply packets to enter the trusted subnet so that trusted devices can send pings and receive replies.

   Which type of ACL can enforce rules such as these?

2. The company wants to block certain types of non-IP traffic such as appletalk.

   Which type of ACL can enforce rules such as these?

3. The company wants to permit guests to access DHCP services and DNS services from a server in a DMZ. Guests will be allowed to send and receive traffic from the Internet, but should be prohibited from any other access to the company's private subnets.

   Which type of ACL can enforce rules such as these?

4. The company wants to filter traffic between a subnet with servers that hold sensitive information and the rest of the network. Only traffic from certain trusted subnets should be able to enter the server subnet.

   Which type of ACL can enforce rules such as these?

## Processing order and implicit deny

When applying an ACL, the switch compares a packet against each rule's matching criteria in sequence until it finds a match. Figure 9-4 outlines the process the switch uses to process each rule.

By default, AOS-Switches process ACL rules according to each rule's ID (lowest to highest). When the switch finds a match, it takes the action indicated by the matching rule (deny or permit) and stops processing the ACL.

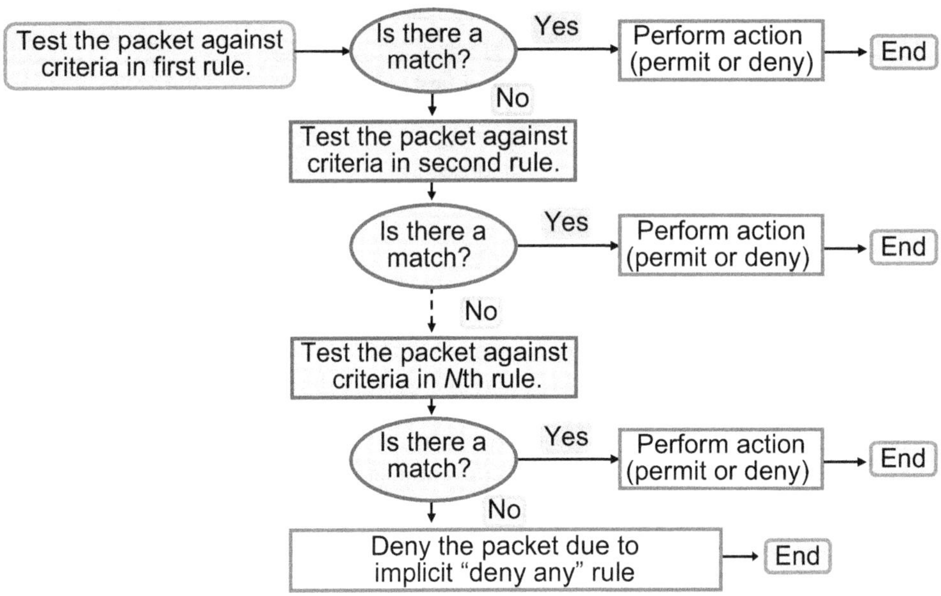


Figure 9-4 Processing order and implicit deny

By combining permit and deny rules, you can create highly flexible policies. For example, you can deny one device within a subnet (such as 10.1.10.10) and permit the complete subnet (10.1.10.0/24). Or with extended ACLs, you can select the traffic associated with a particular application on a particular server; first permit traffic destined to a specific IP address and range of TCP or UDP ports and then deny all other traffic to the IP address.

These scenarios highlight the importance of the order in which the switch processes the rules. For example, in the first scenario, the switch must match packets against the rule that denies a specific device, 10.1.10.10, before the rule that permits the device's subnet, 10.1.10.0/24. If the switch processed the rule that permits the entire subnet first, the switch would permit the packet from 10.1.10.10 and stop processing the ACL. The deny rule would never take effect.

### Implicit action

You also need to understand how your switch treats packets that do not match any of the rules defined in the ACL. You can then avoid blocking or permitting the wrong traffic.

**Important**

AOS-Switches use an implicit deny any for ACLs.

ACLs on AOS-Switches have an implicit "deny any" at the end. If you apply the ACL to an interface and the switch finds no matches between an inbound packet and the configured criteria in an applicable ACL, the switch drops the packet.

The implicit final rule is not displayed when viewing an ACL. Some administrators like to explicitly define the implicit rule at the end of an ACL to clarify the behavior. If you do so, make sure to assign the rule a very high ID so that you can add as many rules as you want.

If you need to override the implicit deny so that a packet that does not have a match is permitted, then you should create a rule that permits all traffic as the last rule in the ACL. Again assign this rule a high ID. Table 9-8 shows the syntax for a "permit any" rule for each ACL type. It suggests the highest valid sequence number.

Table 9-8 Permit any rule based on ACL type

| Standard ACL | Extended ACL | Standard MAC ACL | Extended MAC ACL |
|---|---|---|---|
| [2147483647] permit any | [2147483647] permit ip any any | [2147483647] permit any | [2147483647] permit any any any |

## Applying ACLs to interfaces

After you create an ACL, you can apply it to one or more interfaces. Until you actually assign an ACL to a VLAN or physical interface, it is present in the configuration but not used to filter traffic. When you apply an ACL to an interface using a configuration command, the ACL is called a static ACL. Once you apply the static ACL, it remains on the interface permanently until you modify or remove it.

**Note**

AOS-Switches can also apply dynamic Port-based ACLs (PACLs) as part of an Authentication, Authorization, and Accounting (AAA) solution. This chapter focuses on static ACLs. You will examine dynamic PACLs in *Chapter 10: 802.1X Authentication.* (Remember that not all AOS-Switches support ACLs. Check your switch documentation to determine its support for ACLs.)

You have two choices as you apply a static ACL. First, you choose the interface to which you apply the ACL. Next, you choose the direction for the ACL, which determines whether the ACL filters traffic that arrives on that interface or that is destined out that interface. As you see in Figure 9-5, you can apply both IP and MAC ACLs to VLAN or physical interfaces.

| ACL type | Applied to this interface | Applied in this direction | Creates this ACL type | |
|---|---|---|---|---|
| IP | VLAN | in or out | RACL | Filter routed traffic |
| | | vlan-in or vlan-out | VACL | Filter switched and routed traffic |
| | Physical | in or out | PACL | |
| MAC | VLAN | in or out | VACL | |
| | Physical | in or out | PACL | |

**IMPORTANT**: Applying an ACL ID for an ACL that does not exist or has no entries permits all traffic.

Figure 9-5 Applying ACLs to interfaces

How you apply the ACL determines which type of ACL the ACL becomes in implementation:

- Routed ACL (RACL)
- VLAN ACL (VACL)
- Port-based ACL (PACL)

Whether the switch applies the ACL as a RACL, VACL, or PACL, in turn, determines which packets and frames the switch processes against the ACL:

- RACLs are IP ACLs applied to VLAN interfaces in either the outbound or inbound direction. Inbound RACLs filter traffic that arrives on a VLAN and is routed out another subnet while outbound RACLs filter traffic that is routed out of a VLAN. You use the following commands:

  ```
  Switch(config)# vlan <ID> ip access-group <ACL name> in
  Switch(config)# vlan <ID> ip access-group <ACL name> out
  ```

- VACLs are MAC ACLs applied to VLAN. Or they are IP ACLs applied to VLAN using **vlan-in** or **vlan-out** as the direction rather than in or out. Inbound VACLs filter all traffic that arrives on a VLAN, whether switched or routed. Outbound VACLs filter all traffic that is forwarded out a VLAN, whether the source is within the same subnet (switched) or another subnet (routed). Because both inbound and outbound VACLs filter traffic that arrives on a VLAN and is switched out that VLAN, some of the traffic that they filter overlaps.

  Use these commands to apply IP ACLs as VACLs:

  ```
  Switch(config)# vlan <ID> ip access-group <ACL name> vlan-in
  Switch(config)# vlan <ID> ip access-group <ACL name> vlan-out
  ```

  Use these commands to apply MAC ACLs as VACLs:

  ```
  Switch(config)# vlan <ID> mac-access-group <ACL name> in
  Switch(config)# vlan <ID> mac-access-group <ACL name> out
  ```

- Port-based ACLs (PACLs) are any ACLs applied to physical interfaces. Inbound PACLs filter all traffic that arrives on the interface, whether switched or routed. Outbound PACLs filter all traffic forwarded on the interface, whether switched or routed.

  Use these commands to apply IP or MAC ACLs to a physical interface:

  ```
  Switch(config)# interface <ID> ip access-group <ACL name> <in | out>
  Switch(config)# interface <ID> mac-access-group <ACL name> <in | out>
  ```

You will explore the different ways these ACLs filter traffic in more detail throughout this chapter.

You should also keep in mind that you can apply an ACL to multiple different interfaces, but each interface supports a maximum of one ACL in each direction. On VLAN interfaces, you are allowed to use the same ACL for both the inbound and outbound directions, but often you should not do so because, of course, the source and destination addresses for your rules might not be valid in both directions.

---

**Note**

The extent of ACL support varies among the AOS-Switch families. For example, some switches may support RACLs, VACLs, and both static and dynamic PACLs, whereas other switches may support static PACLs only. In addition, many switches support inbound and outbound RACLs, but only inbound VACLs and PACLs. Refer to your switch documentation for more information.

---

## Tips

Keep the following points in mind when applying ACLs:

- AOS-Switches allow you to assign a nonexistent ACL name or number to an interface; they might provide a warning that the ACL has no rules. When you apply a nonexistent or empty ACL to an interface, the interface permits all traffic until you create an ACL that uses that name or number *and* add a rule to the ACL. The implicit "deny any" does not take effect until at least one rule is defined. In short, you should be careful to specify the correct ID.
- On AOS-Switches, if you delete an assigned ACL from the switch without subsequently removing the ACL from an interface to which it is assigned, the ACL assignment remains on the interface. The empty ACL does not affect traffic (all traffic is permitted). However, the switch will automatically begin applying any new ACL you create with the same identifier (name or number). You should clean up your configurations to ensure that ACLs are applied when and where you expect.

## Example ACL

Figure 9-6 provides a simple example of how you can combine rules into an ACL and apply the ACL to an interface. In this example, you want to strictly control traffic from a device connected on an interface. You configure an IPv4 extended ACL with the two rules shown in Figure 9-6 and apply it inbound on the interface.

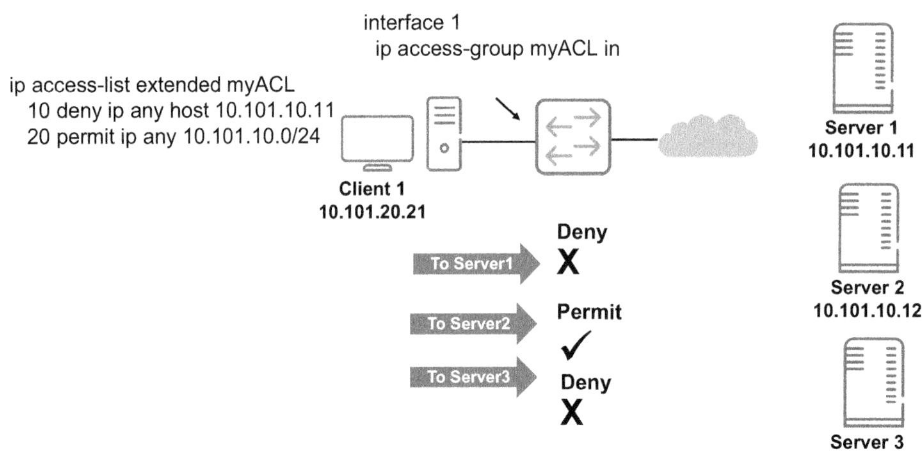


Figure 9-6 Example ACL

When Client 1 tries to send IP traffic to Server 1 shown in Figure 9-6, the switch processes the traffic against the ACL. This traffic matches the first rule, which selects all IP traffic destined to Server 1 at 10.101.10.11. The traffic is dropped.

Next Client 1 tries to send IP traffic to Server 2 at 10.101.10.12. Again the switch processes the traffic against the first rule, but the traffic does not match this rule. The switch then processes the traffic against the second rule, which it does match because 10.101.10.12/30 is within 10.101.10.0/24. The second rule is a permit rule, so the switch forwards the traffic.

Finally, Client 1 tries to send IP traffic to Server 3 at 10.101.30.13. This traffic matches neither rule. Therefore, it is processed by the implicit deny any, and the switch drops it.

## Activity: Plan ACLs

You will now consider two scenarios for implementing an ACL in the network illustrated in Figure 9-7. The answers for this activity are at the end of the chapter; the next section also provides an example configuration based on these plans.

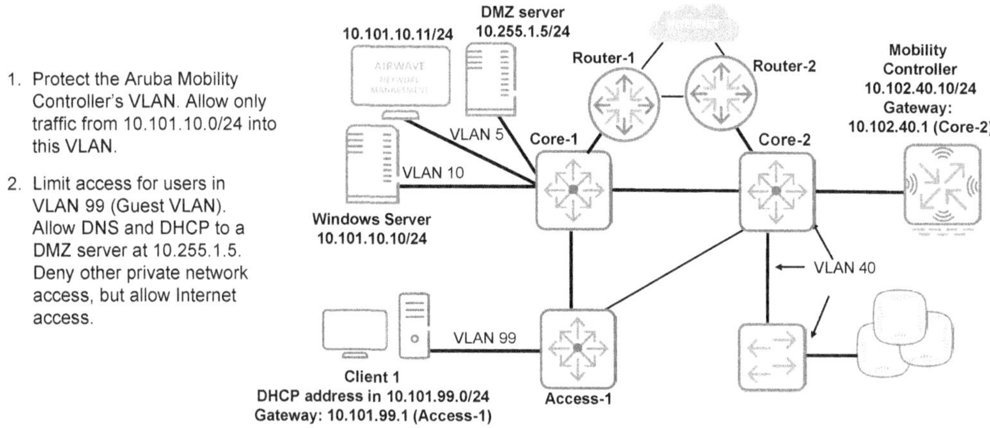


Figure 9-7 Activity: Plan ACLs

## Scenario 1: Protect the mobility infrastructure

Core-2 connects to an Aruba Mobility Controller (MC) in VLAN 40, subnet 10.102.40.0/24. The company wants to prevent users from accessing this network, which should be used only for managing the Aruba MC and communications between the MC and Aruba devices. You have decided to permit only the server subnet (10.101.10.0/24), which contains AirWave and a management station, to access the MC and AP management VLAN. (Note that in this scenario, the APs are in the same VLAN as the MC and a different VLAN from users, which might not be the case in many deployments.)

Answer the questions below to help you plan an ACL that will control traffic in this way. As you answer the questions, keep in mind that you want to fulfill the requirements of the scenario with a single ACL. (The answers to these questions are at the end of the chapter.)

1. Can you use a standard IP ACL for this scenario or is an extended IP ACL required?
2. On which switch and which interface should you apply the ACL? Should you apply the ACL as an inbound or outbound ACL?
3. Begin to plan rules for the ACL. You do not need to specify the precise syntax, but you should plan the rule order, the action for each rule, and the general match criteria for each rule.

## Scenario 2: Control access for less trusted users

In this scenario, VLAN 99 is assigned to less trusted users such as guests. You want to permit the guests' access to the Internet, but deny access to the complete private network with the exception of DHCP and DNS services offered by a DMZ server at 10.255.1.5.

Answer the questions below to help you plan an ACL that will control traffic in this way. As you answer the questions, keep in mind that you want to fulfill the requirements of the scenario with a single ACL.

1. Can you use a standard IP ACL for this scenario or is an extended IP ACL required?
2. On which switch and which interface should you apply the ACL? Should you apply the ACL as an inbound or outbound ACL?
3. Begin to plan rules for the ACL. You do not need to specify the precise syntax, but you should plan the rule order, the action for each rule, and the general match criteria for each rule.

## Configuring the ACL for Scenario 1

The steps below outline how to create an ACL called ToMC that meets the requirements for scenario 1. For this scenario, you would create the ACL on the Core-2 switch.

1. Create a standard IP ACL named "ToMC."

   ```
   Core-2(config)# ip access-list standard ToMC
   ```

2. Configure the permit rule to allow traffic from the server VLAN.

   ```
   Core-2(config-std-nacl)# permit 10.101.10.0/24
   Core-2(config-std-nacl)# exit
   ```

   AOS-switches have an implicit deny by default.

3. Assign the ACL as an outbound ACL on VLAN 40.

   ```
   Core-2(config)# vlan 40 ip access-group ToMC out
   ```

---

**Important**

Be careful to specify the ACL name exactly. The name is case-sensitive. If you make an error, the CLI will accept the command. The switch will create an empty ACL with the indicated name, and your ACL will not take effect.

---

4. After you create the ACL, you can view its rules with the following command. Note how the subnet prefix that you specified has become a mask. What is the mask? You will discuss how this mask, also called "wildcard bits," is used in the section "Detailed look at source and destination IP addresses in ACLs."

   ```
   Core-2(config)# show access-list ToMC
   ```

```
Access Control Lists
  Name: ToMC
  Type: Standard
  Applied: Yes

SEQ  Entry
-------------------------------------------------------------------------------
10   Action: permit
     IP    : 10.101.10.0       Mask: 0.0.0.255
```

5. After you apply the ACL, verify that the ACL is assigned to VLAN 40 interface.

```
Core-2(config)# show access-list vlan 40

Access Lists for VLAN 40

IPv4 Router Inbound            : (None)
IPv4 Router Outbound           : ToMC    Type: Standard
IPv4 VLAN Inbound              : (None)
IPv4 VLAN Outbound             : (None)
IPv4 Connection Rate Filter    : (None)
IPv6 Router Inbound            : (None)
IPv6 Router Outbound           : (None)
IPv6 VLAN Inbound              : (None)
IPv6 VLAN Outbound             : (None)
MAC VLAN Inbound               : (None)
MAC VLAN Outbound              : (None)
```

## Configuring the ACL for Scenario 2

This section provides the configuration for the ACL that you planned for scenario 2.

1. Configure an extended ACL called FromGuests.

```
Access-1(config)# ip access-list extended FromGuests
```

2. Configure the rules that permit DHCP traffic, DNS requests, and ICMP replies to the DMZ server (10.255.1.5).

```
Access-1(config-ext-nacl)# permit udp any host 10.255.1.5 eq bootps
Access-1(config-ext-nacl)# permit udp any host 10.255.1.5 eq dns
Access-1(config-ext-nacl)# permit icmp any host 10.255.1.5 echo-reply
```

**Note**

You can specify 10.101.99.0 0.0.0.255 as the source instead of permitting any source. However, because you plan to assign the ACL to VLAN 99 as an inbound routed ACL, this is not necessary. This approach also gives administrators the freedom to change the IP addressing for the Guest VLAN in the future without changing the ACL. However, if the ACL is applied in a different way, you might need to specify the guest subnet as the source.

3. Configure a rule that denies all access to private network addresses.

```
Access-1(config-ext-nacl)# deny ip any 10.0.0.0/8
```

4. Configure a rule that permits all traffic.

```
Access-1(config-ext-nacl)# permit ip any any
Access-1(config-ext-nacl)# exit
```

5. Apply the ACL as an inbound ACL on VLAN 99.

```
Access-1(config)# vlan 99 ip access-group FromGuests in
```

**Note**

Be careful to specify the ACL name exactly. The name is case-sensitive. If you make an error, the CLI will accept the command. The switch will create an empty ACL with the indicated name, and your ACL will not take effect.

6. You can view the ACL and verify that it has been applied correctly. Note the sequence number (SEQ) applied to the each rule; these IDs are important because they determine the processing order for the ACL rules.

```
Access-1(config)# show access-list FromGuests
  Name: FromGuests
  Type: Extended
  Applied: Yes
```

```
SEQ  Entry
-------------------------------------------------------------------------------
10   Action: permit
     Src IP: 0.0.0.0         Mask: 255.255.255.255   Port(s):
     Dst IP: 10.255.1.5      Mask: 0.0.0.0           Port(s): eq 67
     Proto : UDP
     TOS   : -               Precedence: -

20   Action: permit
     Src IP: 0.0.0.0         Mask: 255.255.255.255   Port(s):
     Dst IP: 10.255.1.5      Mask: 0.0.0.0           Port(s): eq 53
     Proto : UDP
     TOS   : -               Precedence: -

30   Action: permit
     Src IP: 0.0.0.0         Mask: 255.255.255.255   Port(s):
     Dst IP: 10.255.1.5      Mask: 0.0.0.0           Port(s):
     Proto : ICMP (Msg: echo-reply)
     TOS   : -               Precedence: -

40   Action: deny
     Src IP: 0.0.0.0         Mask: 255.255.255.255   Port(s):
     Dst IP: 10.0.0.0        Mask: 0.255.255.255     Port(s):
     Proto : IP
     TOS   : -               Precedence: -

50   Action: permit
     Src IP: 0.0.0.0         Mask: 255.255.255.255   Port(s):
     Dst IP: 0.0.0.0         Mask: 255.255.255.255   Port(s):
     Proto : IP
     TOS   : -               Precedence: -
```

## Detailed look at source and destination IP addresses in ACLs

Now that you have had some practice creating an ACL, you will dive down deeper into the specifics of creating flexible rules. You will begin by learning strategies for specifying the correct range of addresses. Then you will learn about how to use rule IDs to manage your ACLs and to ensure that traffic is processed in the correct order.

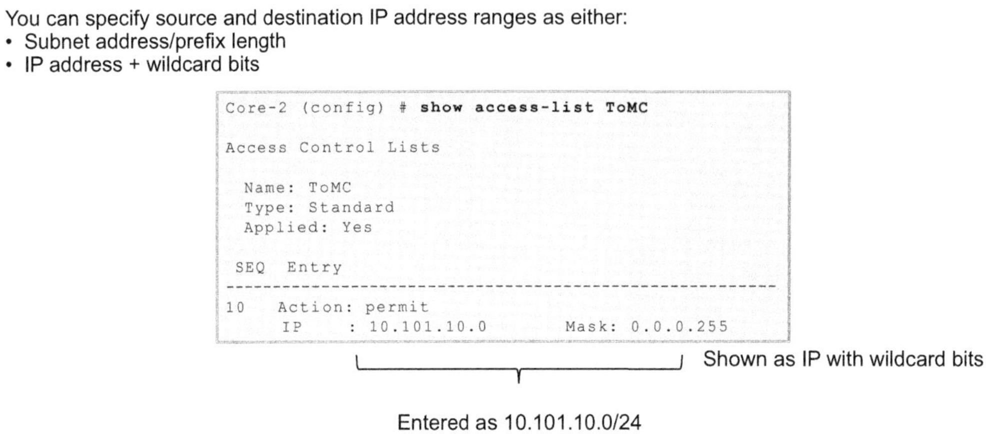


Figure 9-8 Detailed look at source and destination IP addresses in ACLs

You can use a network address and prefix length to define a range of IP addresses in an ACL rule. This option works well when you want to permit or deny an entire subnet.

When you look at an ACL, however, you will see that the range was denoted as shown in Figure 9-8. Instead of 10.101.10.0/24, you see IP: 10.101.10.0 and Mask: 0.0.0.255. This mask is actually wildcard bits, which use reverse logic from subnet masks. If you prefer, you can actually specify the IP address and wildcard bits when you create the rule.

To master both creating and interpreting rules, you need to explore prefix lengths, wildcard bits, and the relationships between them in more depth.

## Specifying IP address ranges with prefix length

When you specify a subnet such as 10.101.10.0/24 in an ACL rule, the rule matches all IP addresses in the subnet from 10.101.10.0 to 10.101.10.255, as shown in Figure 9-9. (Of course, 10.101.10.0 is the subnet address and 10.101.10.255 is the broadcast address, so typical traffic will not use the addresses at either end of the range for the source.)

Subnets with the /24 prefix length are familiar and easy to use. However, you might want to conserve the number of rules within an ACL by specifying larger ranges of IP addresses. Or you might want to specify a subset of a /24 network in one rule rather than several identical rules with different host addresses.

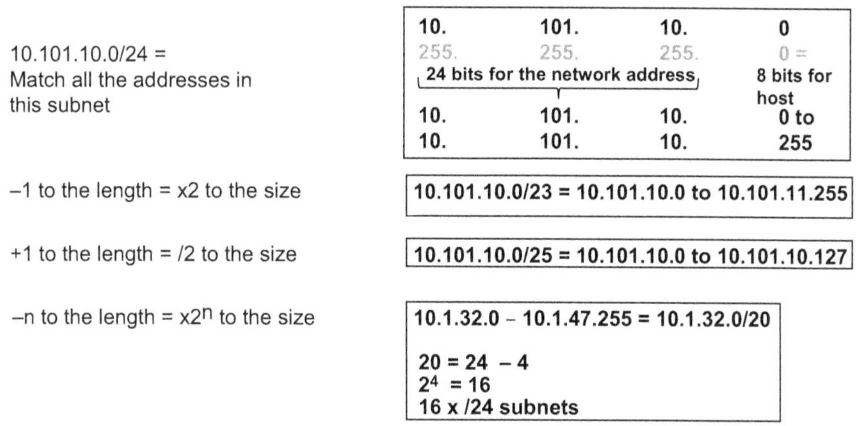


Figure 9-9 Specifying IP address ranges with prefix length

To understand how to specify the desired range of IP addresses, briefly review prefix lengths and their relationship with subnet masks.

## Subnet masks

In common IP addressing, a network (or subnet) mask defines which part of the IP address to use for the network (or subnet) address and which part to use for the hosts on the network:

- The bits set to 1 define the part of the IP address to use for the network address.
- The bits set to 0 define the part of the IP address to use for the host address.

In the example shown in Figure 9-9, the subnet mask is 255.255.255.0, or all 1s within the first three octets. Therefore, 10.1.10.0 is the network address. Valid host numbers in the fourth octet are between 1 and 254. Therefore, valid IP addresses that could be assigned to devices are from 10.1.10.1 through 10.1.10.254. The IP addresses 10.1.10.0 and 10.1.10.255 are reserved for identifying the subnet and broadcast addresses, respectively.

## Prefix lengths

Classless Inter-Domain Routing (CIDR) notation represents a subnet mask by the prefix length. In other words, the prefix length specifies the number of bits set to 1 in the subnet mask. For example, the subnet mask in Figure 9-9 has 24 1s and defines a /24 subnet.

## Rules of thumb for specifying ranges with prefix lengths

You are probably familiar with /8, /16, and /24 subnets. These subnets have their boundaries at the octet border in decimal format, so it is easy to understand the range of addresses included in these subnets.

Sometimes, though, you want to specify ranges of IP addresses of different lengths than these.

As a rule of thumb, you double the size of a subnet when you subtract one from the prefix length. You halve the size when you add one.

For example, 10.101.10.0/23 includes IP addresses in two /24 subnets—IP addresses from 10.101.10.0 to 10.101.11.255. 10.101.10.0/25 includes IP addresses from 10.101.10.0 to 10.101.10.127.

If you want to multiply or divide by more than 2, choose a factor that is a power of 2 such as 4, 8, 16, and so on, and use the related exponent as the number that you add or subtract from the length. For example, you want a rule to select traffic with IP addresses between 10.1.32.0 and 10.1.47.255. This range has 16 /24 subnets, so you subtract 4 from 24 ($2^4 = 16$). You would specify 10.1.32.0/20.

As another example, you want a permit rule to select traffic with source IP addresses between 192.168.4.32 and 192.168.4.39. This range is eight times the size of 192.168.4.32/32, so you would specify 192.168.4.32/29 ($2^3 = 8$).

When you are specifying ranges in this way, you must remember that you are specifying the network address for a subnet. For example, you could not specify 192.168.4.30/29 to select the eight addresses from 192.168.4.30 to 192.168.4.37. This range includes addresses in two different /29 subnets, and 192.168.4.30 is not a valid network address for a /29 subnet. An easy way to check if an IP address is a valid network address for a subnet with a length between /24 and /32 is to determine the subnet's size and make sure that the final octet is divisible by that size. For example, a /29 subnet has 8 IP addresses. 32 is divisible by 8, but 30 is not. You also need to make sure that your range includes a number of addresses that is a power of two (such as 8, 16, 32, and so on).

If you want a range of a different size, you must enter multiple rules. Sometimes it is easier to specify a broader range than you need in the rule and create rules with lower sequence numbers that define exceptions.

You can apply similar logic to larger subnets, paying attention to the most significant octet for that subnet. For example, a /20 subnet includes 16/24 subnets, so the third octet of the network address must be divisible by 16, and the last octet should be zero.

You can find prefix length calculators on the Internet to help you check your addresses.

## Using and interpreting wildcard bits

As you observed in Figure 9-8, when you enter a subnet and prefix length, the **show** commands for examining the ACL will show you wildcard bits. You need to understand how to interpret those bits to determine the range of IP addresses selected by the rule.

### Wildcard bits

Wildcard bits define which bits in a packet's IP address must match the corresponding bits in the rule's IP address and which bits can be wildcards (any value).

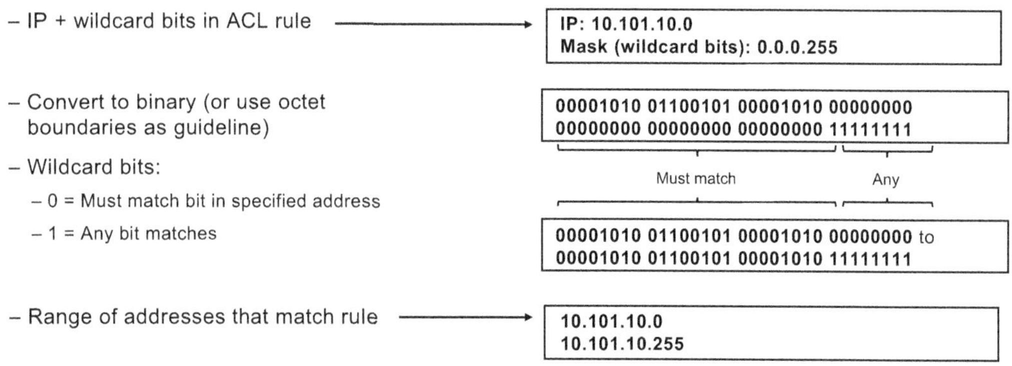


Figure 9-10 Using and interpreting wildcard bits

As Figure 9-10 shows, wildcard bits use a reverse logic from subnet masks:

- A mask-bit setting of 0 ("off") requires a match between the corresponding bits in the packet's address and in the rule's address. Thus, if a bit in the rule's address is set to 1, the rule only selects packets that have the same bit set to 1. Similarly, if the bit in the rule's address is set to 0, the bit in the packet's address must be 0.
- A mask-bit setting of 1 ("on") means the corresponding bits in the packet's address and in the rule's address do not have to be the same. As a matter of standard format, the rule specifies 0 bits for the segment of the IP address that corresponds to 1s in the wildcard mask. The corresponding bits in a matching packet can be either 1 or 0.

**Note**

Although most of the time wildcard bits are continuous zeroes followed by continuous ones, it is possible to have any combination of ones and zeroes. Managing such masks, however, is difficult, and they are not recommended.

## Examples

You will now apply this knowledge to interpret the following command output.

```
Core-2(config)# show access-list ToMC

Access Control Lists

  Name: ToMC

  Type: Standard

  Applied: Yes
```

```
SEQ  Entry
----------------------------------------------------------
10   Action: permit
       IP    : 10.101.10.0        Mask: 0.0.0.255
```

You could convert 10.101.10.0 to binary as shown in Figure 9-10. However, in the example shown in Figure 9-10, the wildcard bits are uniform in each octet, so you do not need to. The wildcard bits for the first three octets are zeros, so only IP addresses that begin with 10.101.10 are selected. The last octet does not matter; the wildcard bits for that octet are 1. In other words, the rule selects IP addresses from 10.101.10.0 to 10.101.10.255.

Suppose that you see a rule with less intuitive wildcard bits. The example in Figure 9-11 shows source IP 192.168.4.32 and Mask: 0.0.0.7. (In this case, mask means wildcard bits.) Which range of source IP addresses matches this rule?

To find out, simply add the wildcard bits to each octet of the IP address. In the example shown in Figure 9-11, the range of source IP addresses that matches the rule is 192.168.4.32 through 192.168.4.39.

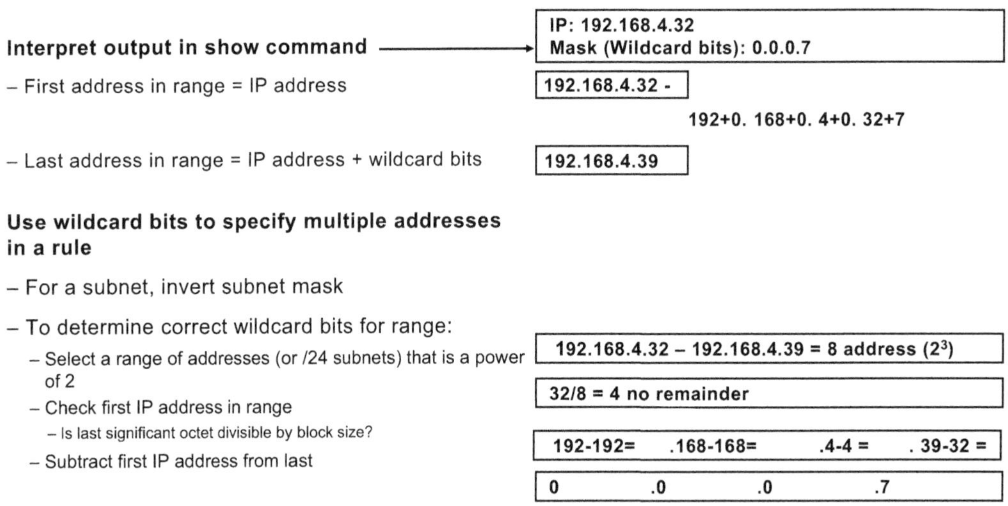


Figure 9-11 Wildcard bit example

Next consider ways to use wildcard bits to specify multiple IP addresses as you create an ACL rule. As you might have guess, a wildcard mask is the inverse of a subnet mask. So if you want to select a subnet with an ACL rule, follow these guidelines:

- Determine the subnet mask.
- Invert the mask. Inverting the mask is simple when you have a mask such as 255.255.255.0. It becomes 0.0.0.255. But you might not find inverting other subnet masks quite as intuitive.

When you are not sure of the subnet mask of the range that you want to specify, you might want to take a different approach. If you choose a proper range, you can simply subtract the first IP address in the range from the last in order to obtain the wildcard bits.

Watch how this works in an example. Suppose you want to create a rule to permit traffic with source IP addresses between 192.168.4.32 and 192.168.4.39. First, you make sure that this is a valid range to specify with wildcard bits. The range has eight IP addresses, and eight is a power of two. So the number of IP addresses is valid. Next you make sure that the first IP address is valid. The final significant octet must be divisible by your block size. In this example, 32 is divisible by eight, so you can start at this IP address.

Now you subtract the first IP address from the last. All octets, except for the last one, cancel out, so you would get wildcard bits of 0.0.0.7. Now you know to specify 192.168.4.32.0.0.0.7 as the rule.

In another example, you might want to specify subnets 10.101.20.0/24 and 10.101.21.0/24 in a single rule. This range has two /24 subnets, and two is a power of two. The last significant octet, 20, is divisible by two. So your range is valid. The range of IP addresses is 10.101.20.0 to 10.101.21.255. To specify this range, specify 10.101.20.0 0.0.1.255.

## Add a rule using the correct wildcard bits

Rather than using the subnet mask when you enter a rule in an ACL, you can specify the correct wildcard bits. For example, you could access the example ToMC ACL provided earlier in this chapter. The ACL name is case-sensitive.

```
Core-2(config)# ip access-list standard ToMC
```

You might want to add a rule to permit all traffic with source IP addresses between 10.101.128.0 and 10.101.255.255 (the 10.101.128.0/17 subnet). To specify a rule with correct wildcard bits, you would enter:

```
Core-2(config-std-nacl)# permit 10.101.128.0 0.0.127.255
Core-2(config-std-nacl)# exit
```

To view the ACL and see that the rule has been added to the end, enter:

```
Core-2(config)# show access-list ToMC
Access Control Lists
  Name: ToMC
  Type: Standard
  Applied: Yes
```

```
SEQ  Entry
----------------------------------------------------------------------
 10   Action: permit
      IP    : 10.101.10.0        Mask: 0.0.0.255

 20   Action: permit
      IP    : 10.101.128.0       Mask: 0.0.127.255
```

## Specifying MAC addresses ranges

When you want to specify a range of MAC addresses in a MAC ACL rule, you must use wildcard bits. However, these bits use hexadecimal format. As Figure 9-12 shows, each 0 indicates that a frame's source or destination MAC address must match the corresponding hexadecimal character in the address in the rule. An f, on the other hand, tells the switch to ignore the corresponding character in frames' addresses.

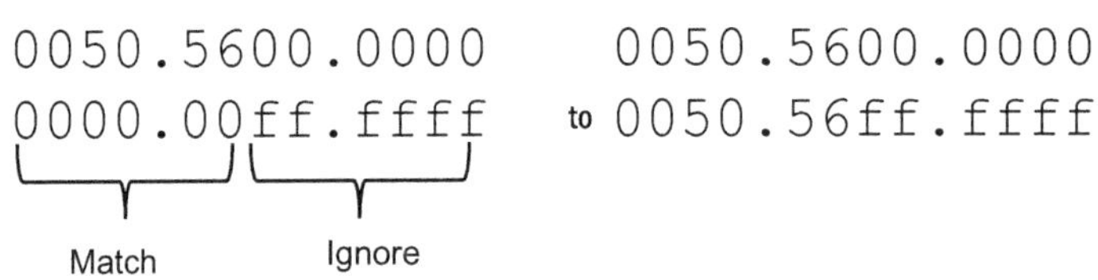


Figure 9-12 Specifying MAC addresses ranges

For example, to match 0050.5600.0000 0000.00ff.ffff, a frame can have any source MAC address that begins with 0050.56.

You can create more complicated rules using different hexadecimal characters in the mask. Determine the exact bits with source or destination MAC addresses that you want the switch to check or ignore. Set checked bits to 0s and ignored bits to 1; then convert to hexadecimal. For example, you enter **0050.5600.0000 0000.0000.0003**. This mask tells the switch to check all bits for all hexadecimal characters until the last character. At that point, the switch checks the first two bits but ignores the last two bits (0011 = hexadecimal 3). This rule selects packets with destination MAC addresses 0050.5600.0000 through 0050-5600-0003. As you see, you can use the guideline of subtracting the first address from the last address to obtain the wildcard bits.

However, complicated rules such as these are usually unnecessary.

## Managing ACL rule sequence

If you do not specify a sequence number when you create a rule, the AOS-Switch assigns an automatic sequence numbers to that ACL rule. You need to ensure that you assign the correct rule IDs so that the ACL selects packets as you expect.

You will now examine these issues in more detail. You can specify the rule ID manually, or you can enter the rules in the order in which you want them processed.

In any case, you must plan the ACL carefully and configure rules for processing in the correct order, generally entering more specific rules with a lower ID than the ID for less specific rules.

## Automatic numbering

If you do not enter a manual ID, the switch automatically adds rule IDs in order, leaving spaces. New rules are added to the *end* of the list, even if spaces exist earlier in the list.

For example as Figure 9-13 shows, if the first rule that you enter does not have a manual ID, an AOS-Switch numbers the rule as 10. Subsequent rules without rule numbers are numbered in increments of 10: 10, 20, 30, and so on. The switch always adds a rule without a manual ID after the *final* explicit rule. If this rule has an ID that is not divisible by 10, such as 45, the switch adds the new rule with the next ID that is divisible by 10, such as 50 (see Figure 9-13).

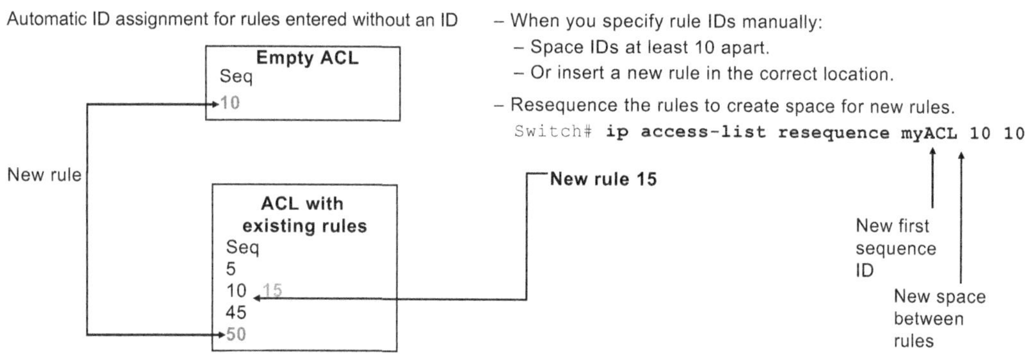


Figure 9-13 Managing ACL rule sequence

## Manual numbering

When you enter rules manually, it is best practice for you to space rule IDs, preferably by 10s, so that you can insert additional rules at a later point, if necessary. Then, when you do not want to add a rule to the end of the list, you can choose a rule ID between existing rules to insert the rule in the correct location.

## Sequence renumbering

Sometimes, despite your best planning, you need to change rule IDs to place rules in the correct order.

From the Named Access Control List (NACL) context, you can also easily remove a rule using the **no <sequence-number>** command. In addition, you can redefine the sequence numbers of all rules in a given ACL using one of these commands:

```
Switch(config)# ip access-list resequence <name> <start-sequence>
<increment>
```

```
Switch(config)# mac-access-list resequence <name> <start-sequence>
<increment>
```

In these commands, **<start-sequence>** is the sequence number you want to assign to the first rule, and **<increment>** is the incrementing value by which subsequent rules will be numbered. This command leaves the rules in the same relative order. However, with more spaces between the rules, you can remove rules and add them in the appropriate location as necessary.

## Logging ACL matches

You now have a good sense of how to create rules. In addition to the other options, an ACL rule on an AOS-Switch can include the **log** option at the end. As Figure 9-14 shows, this option signals the switch to generate an Event Log message when a packet matches a packet. The log is created if the action is "deny" *or* "permit," if there is a match, and if you have enabled ACL logging.

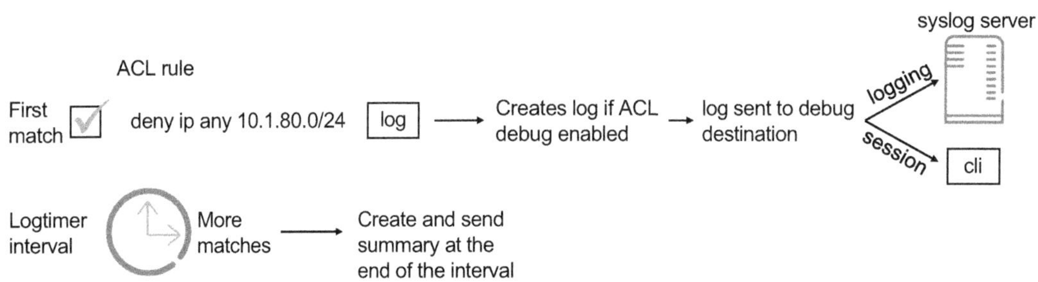


Figure 9-14 Logging ACL matches

To enable ACL logging to a syslog server, you must:

1. Specify the syslog server IP address:

```
Switch(config)# logging <IP address>
```

2. Configure the switch to send log messages to the syslog server.

```
Switch(config)# logging facility syslog
```

3. Set the debug destination to logging.

```
Switch(config)# debug destination logging
```

4. If you also want to see the messages in the CLI, also set the debug destination to session.

   ```
   Switch (config)# debug destination session
   ```

5. Enable ACL debug messages.

   ```
   Switch(config)# debug acl
   ```

The first time that a packet matches the rule with the log option, the switch sends a log to the syslog server. It then tracks the activity over the logtimer interval and sends the syslog server a summary at the end of this interval, which you set with this command (timer set in seconds):

```
Switch (config)# access-list logtimer <30-300>
```

## Activity: Analyzing an ACL

You will now review what you have learned about ACLs. For this activity, assume that an ACL with the rules shown in Table 9-9 has been applied outbound to a VLAN interface, and a switch is now comparing packets being routed out that VLAN against the ACL.

Table 9-9 Standard ACL

| ACL Rule IDs | ACL Rules |
|---|---|
| Rule ID 1 | deny host 10.1.1.31 |
| Rule ID 2 | deny 10.1.1.32 0.0.0.31 |
| Rule ID 3 | permit 10.1.1.0 0.0.0.63 |
| Rule ID 4 | permit 10.1.1.40 0.0.0.7 |
| Rule ID 5 | permit 10.1.1.48 0.0.0.7 |

You want the switch to permit only packets with these source IP addresses:

- 10.1.1.1-10.1.1.30

  10.1.1.0 is the network address in this case, so it is okay if the rule permits packets from the address. The switch will not route packets from it in any case.

- 10.1.1.40-10.1.1.55

  1. What is the current behavior?
  2. How can you reorder the ACL to use the correct sequence?

  (The answers to these questions are provided at the end of the chapter.)

## Inbound RACLs

You should configure a RACL to control traffic at VLAN boundaries and to filter *routed* traffic between subnets. RACLs apply to Layer 3 VLAN interfaces, and you should typically apply them on a routing switch that handles routing for that VLAN.

For example, in Figure 9-15, Core-1 is the core routing switch and the default gateway for VLAN 20. VLAN 20 is also configured on several access layer switches. If you want to apply a RACL to control traffic routed to or from VLAN 20, apply the ACL to VLAN 20 on the core routing switch.

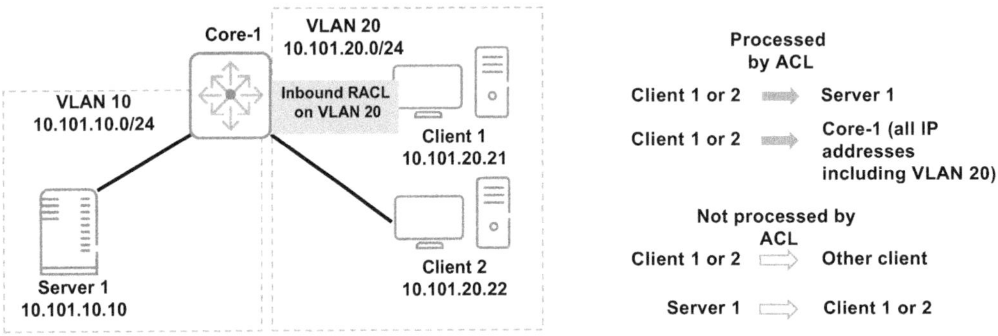


Figure 9-15 Inbound RACLs

RACLs can be either inbound or outbound, and you can apply one RACL per-direction per-VLAN. On AOS-Switches, you apply the ACL to the VLAN and specify the direction (**ip access-group <*name*> <in | out>**).

An inbound RACL processes the following traffic:

- **Traffic received on this VLAN interface and routed out another subnet**—For example, you have applied the RACL inbound to VLAN 20, which uses the 10.101.20.0/24 subnet. The ACL filters packets that arrive in VLAN 20 and are routed to destinations in other subnets. In the example shown in Figure 9-15, this includes traffic from Client 1 or 2 to Server 1. (Note that "arrives in VLAN 20" means that the packet arrives on a port that is untagged for VLAN 20 or with a VLAN tag of 20 on a port that permits such a tag.) Because the ACL applies to traffic that *this* network infrastructure device routes out of this interface, the device must be routing the traffic.
- **Traffic received on this VLAN interface and destined to this network infrastructure device**—An RACL does not filter switched IP traffic unless the switch's own IP address on the interface is the destination. For example, as shown in Figure 9-15, the ACL processes traffic from Client 1 or 2 to all IP addresses on Core-1, including the VLAN 20 IP address. This helps you to protect access to the switch itself. You do not need to enable routing on the switch for the ACL to perform this final service. (Of course, a RACL is typically applied to a switch that routes traffic.)

**Note**

The RACL does *not* filter traffic generated on the interface by the network infrastructure device itself.

In addition, an inbound RACL does not process the following traffic:

- Traffic received on the VLAN and switched on the same subnet (except to the switch itself)

  The inbound ACL does not process traffic between Client 1 and Client 2.

- Traffic received on other VLANs and routed out this VLAN

  The inbound ACL also does not process traffic from Server 1 to either of the clients.

## Outbound RACLs

An outbound RACL filters traffic received from any subnet and routed to a subnet on this VLAN interface. For example, in Figure 9-16 assume you have applied a RACL outbound to a switch's VLAN 20 interface, which uses the 10.101.20.0/24 subnet. The switch receives a packet from Server 1 on VLAN interface 10, and the packet is destined to Client 1 at 10.101.20.21. This ACL processes that packet because the switch routes the packet to VLAN 20.

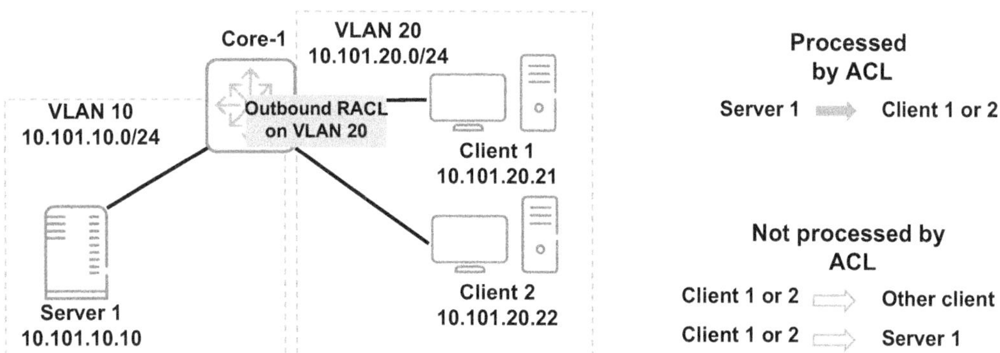


Figure 9-16 Outbound RACLs

An outbound RACL does not process the following traffic:

- Traffic generated by the switch and routed out this VLAN interface
- Traffic received on this VLAN and switched out the same subnet

  For example, if the switch receives a packet destined to 10.101.20.22 from 10.101.20.21, it switches, not routes the packet, so it does not apply the ACL.

- Traffic received on this VLAN and routed out another subnet

  For example, the ACL shown in the figure does not filter traffic from the clients to the server. In other words, the ACL does not process any traffic from the clients.

### Supplemental information: Inbound and outbound RACLs on multinetted VLANs

Typically, RACLs apply to traffic that arrives in one VLAN and is routed out another VLAN. However, they actually apply to any routed traffic. Multinetting allows a VLAN to support multiple subnets. An inbound RACL on a multinetted VLAN controls any traffic that arrives on the VLAN and is routed out another subnet, including a subnet on the *same* VLAN. An outbound RACL controls any traffic that is routed out the VLAN, including when the source subnet is on the same VLAN.

You can apply only one RACL per-interface to inbound traffic and one RACL per-interface to outbound traffic. In the case of a multinetted VLAN, this rule implies the following:

- IP traffic received on different subnets in the same VLAN is screened by the same inbound RACL.
- IP traffic routed out different subnets is screened by the same outbound RACL.

Plan the ACL rules accordingly.

## Inbound VACLs

When you want to control traffic switched within a subnet, you must apply a different type of ACL.

A PACL filters both routed and switched traffic and meets this need. However, when you want to control all devices in a VLAN in the same way, a VACL is the most efficient mechanism. One VACL applies to all ports that are members of the VLAN. The VACL filters all IP traffic entering a switch on the specific VLAN interface. On a multinetted VLAN, this includes inbound IP traffic from any subnet.

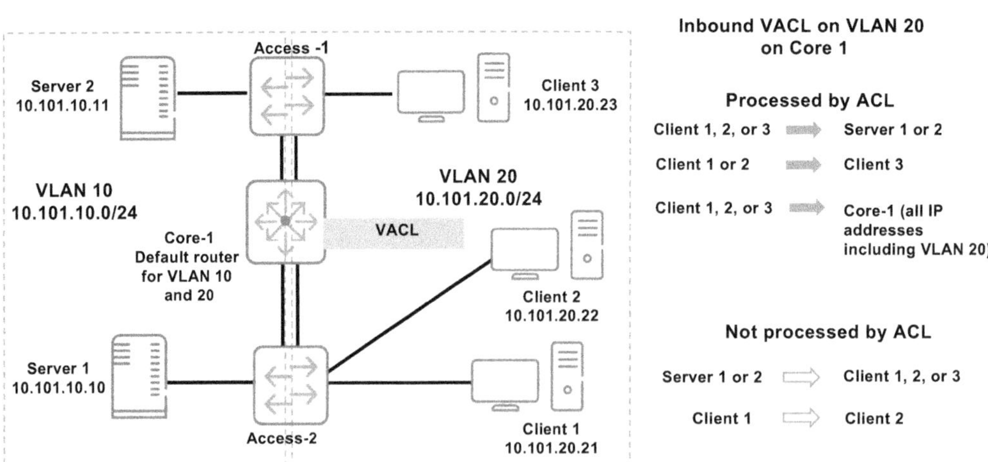


Figure 9-17 Inbound VACLs

As you learned, RACLs applied to VLAN interfaces do not filter traffic that flows within the *same* subnet.

As you learned earlier, a MAC ACL applied to a VLAN in the inbound direction is always an inbound VACL. For an IP ACL applied to a VLAN, you must use the **vlan-in** option.

The inbound VACL processes routed traffic like an inbound RACL. The inbound VACL, however, also filters switched traffic. In specific, the VACL processes this traffic:

- Traffic received on this VLAN interface and routed out another subnet

  In the example shown in Figure 9-17, this is traffic from the clients to the servers.

- Traffic received on this VLAN interface and forwarded in the same subnet

  This is traffic between the clients. However, the VACL placement affects which precise traffic is filtered, as discussed below.

- Traffic received on this VLAN interface and destined to this network infrastructure device (on any interface)

The VACL does *not* process:

- Traffic received on another interface and routed to this VLAN interface. (However, the return traffic from a device in this VLAN would be filtered.)

  In the example shown in Figure 9-17, traffic from the servers to the clients is not processed by the ACL.

- Traffic generated by the switch itself using its IP address on this VLAN and routed out another VLAN

Note that the switch does not require an ACL rule to permit DHCP traffic that it relays itself. However, if the ACL were applied to a switch operating at Layer 2 and not implementing DHCP, you would need to permit DHCP (ports 67 and 68) to and from any address.

You can assign the same ACL to multiple VLANs. AOS-Switches, however, allow you to configure just one inbound VACL per VLAN. (This is in addition to any other ACLs of different types you assign to the VLAN or to ports in the VLAN.)

You also need to consider the correct locations to apply VACLs.

RACLs affect routed traffic, so you naturally apply them at the point at which the traffic that you want to control is routed. But VACLs, both inbound and outbound, control switched traffic, which does not necessary flow through a single point. For example, suppose that you convert the inbound RACL on VLAN 20 to a VACL. The VACL filters all the routed traffic that an inbound RACL would, and it also filters some switched traffic, such as that between Client 1 and Client 3. But traffic between Client 1 and Client 2 does not reach Core-1, so it is not filtered.

## Outbound VACLs

In a moment, you will see how VACLs work when applied closer to the edge. First, examine an outbound VACL. Again, MAC ACLs applied to VLAN interfaces in the outbound direction are always outbound VACLs. IP ACLs must be applied to VLAN interfaces with the **vlan-out** option. (Remember that some switches do not support this option, at the publication of this study guide.)

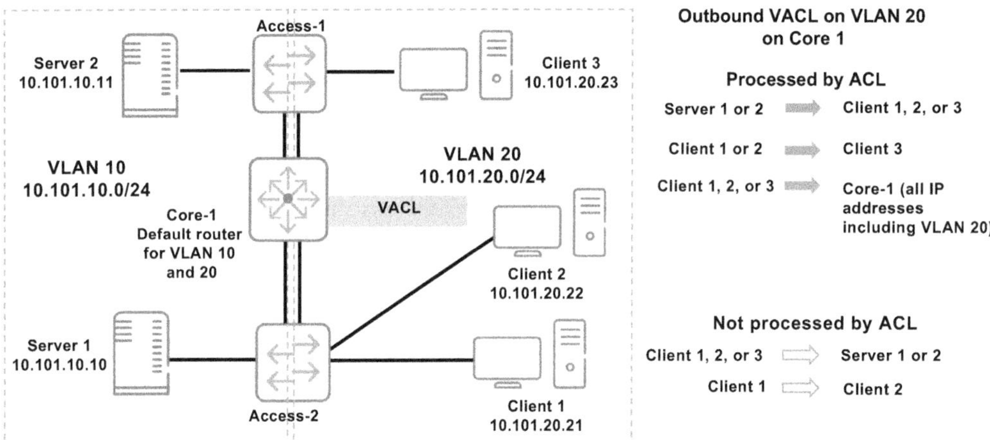


Figure 9-18 Outbound VACLs

As you see in Figure 9-18, an outbound VACL filters traffic much like an outbound RACL, but it also filters traffic switched out the VLAN. Because, by definition, switched traffic arrives on and is forwarded in the same VLAN, this means that an outbound VACL also filters some traffic that arrives on the VLAN.

In specific, the outbound VACL processes this traffic:

- Traffic received on another VLAN interface and routed out this VLAN

  In the example shown in Figure 9-18, this is traffic from the servers to the clients.

- Traffic received on this VLAN interface and switched out this VLAN

  This is traffic between the clients although, again, traffic between clients connected to the same access switch does not reach the ACL. The ACL also processes traffic from the clients to Core-1's own IP address on VLAN 20.

- If multinetting applies, traffic received on one subnet in this VLAN and routed out another subnet on this VLAN

The VACL does *not* process traffic received on this VLAN interface and routed out another VLAN. Here, this includes traffic from the clients to the servers.

The same considerations for applying inbound VACLs apply to outbound VACLs; each VLAN interface supports just one outbound VACL.

Also note that, again, the outbound VACL applied to the Core-1 VLAN 20 interface does not filter traffic between Client 1 and Client 2 because their traffic does not pass through Core-1 (see Figure 9-18).

## VACLs at the edge

You should typically apply VACLs at the access layer where devices connect to the VLAN in question, as shown in Figure 9-19. You can then be certain to filter all switched traffic, as well as the routed traffic. Note that an Aruba switch can filter routed traffic whether or not it is acting as the default router for the VLAN to which the VACL is applied. It simply processes all of the traffic that arrives in this VLAN.

> **Note**
>
> Remember that not all AOS-Switches support ACLs. Check your switch documentation to determine its support for ACLs.

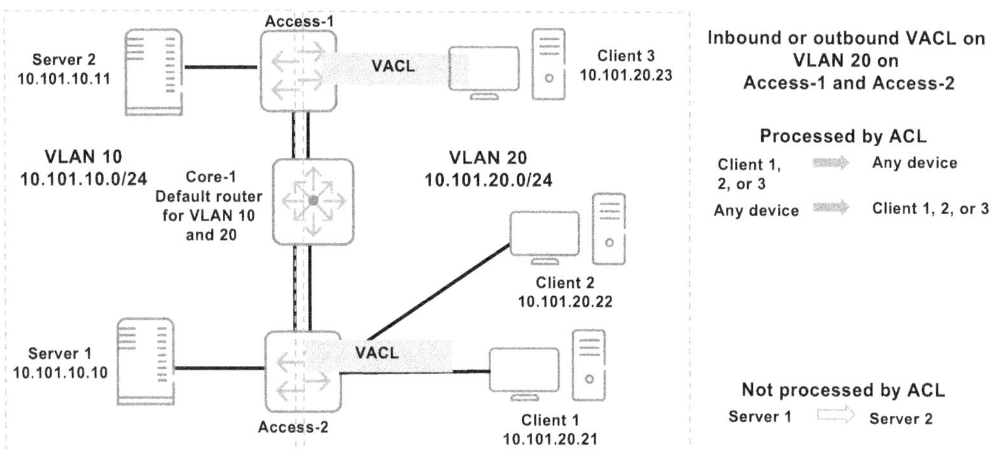


Figure 9-19 VACLs at the edge

You do need to be careful, though, to consider what it means for traffic to arrive in the VLAN. In the "Outbound VACLs" section, you saw that the VACL did not process traffic from the servers to the clients because a VACL applies to traffic that arrives on the VLAN. The traffic from servers arrives on Core-1 in VLAN 10.

However, in the scenario shown in Figure 9-19, Core-1 routes the traffic to VLAN 20, and the traffic from servers to clients arrives on Access-1 and Access-2 *in VLAN 20*. That means that the VACLs applied on the access layer switches now process traffic routed by Core-1 into VLAN 20, as well as traffic that arrives on VLAN 20 on the access layer switches. In the example shown in Figure 9-19, the VACL processes traffic from Server 1 to Client 1 and even traffic from Server 2 to Client 1. Even though both Server 2 and Client 1 are connected to Access-2, the traffic from Server 2 passes to Core-1 for routing and then returns to Access-2 in VLAN 20.

Because, in the example shown in Figure 9-19, the access layer switches are not routing VLAN 20 traffic and do not have IP addresses on VLAN 20, applying the ACL as outbound VACL has the same effect as applying it as an inbound VACL. All traffic that arrives in the VLAN is also forwarded in that VLAN.

If you are planning to apply a VACL to a VLAN on a switch that does not route traffic for that VLAN, be very careful to plan the rules to permit *return traffic* to devices in that VLAN as well as the traffic from the devices.

For example, suppose the FromGuests ACL is applied to Access-1 in the simplified topology shown in Figure 9-20.

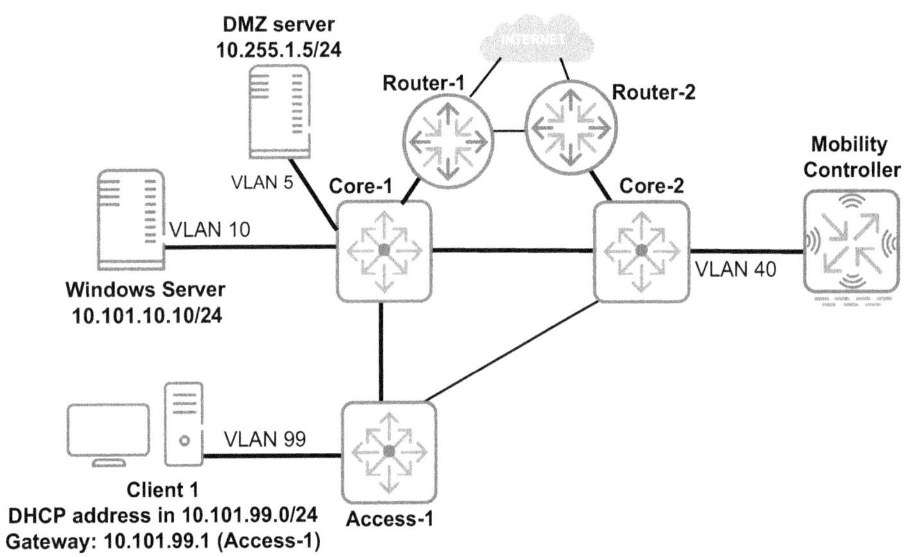


Figure 9-20 Simplified scenario network (Access-1 routing)

The FromGuests ACL, applied inbound on VLAN 99 on Access-1, includes these rules:

```
10 permit udp 0.0.0.0 255.255.255.255 10.255.1.5 0.0.0.0 eq 67
20 permit udp 0.0.0.0 255.255.255.255 10.255.1.5 0.0.0.0 eq 53
30 permit icmp 0.0.0.0 255.255.255.255 10.255.1.5 0.0.0.0 0
40 deny ip 0.0.0.0 255.255.255.255 10.0.0.0 0.255.255.255
50 permit ip 0.0.0.0 255.255.255.255 0.0.0.0 255.255.255.255
```

Think about what happens if you apply the ACL as an inbound VACL on VLAN 99, rather than an inbound RACL. Note that rule 40 uses any as the source IP address; it denies all traffic from any source IP address to any address in the private network. This rule matches return traffic from the Internet to guest devices. However, in this scenario, Access-1 is routing the traffic, so it only filters traffic that arrives on VLAN 99. Therefore, the ACL has the intended effect regardless of whether you specify 10.101.99.0/24 or any as the source. It prevents guests from accessing any device in the private network, including other guest devices, but it prevents certain DHCP, DNS, and ICMP traffic. It also permits guests to reach the Internet.

However, the ACL behavior changes if you are using a topology more like the one shown in Figure 9-21, in which Core-1 routes the VLAN 99 traffic. Access-1 still implements the ACL as a VACL on VLAN 99.

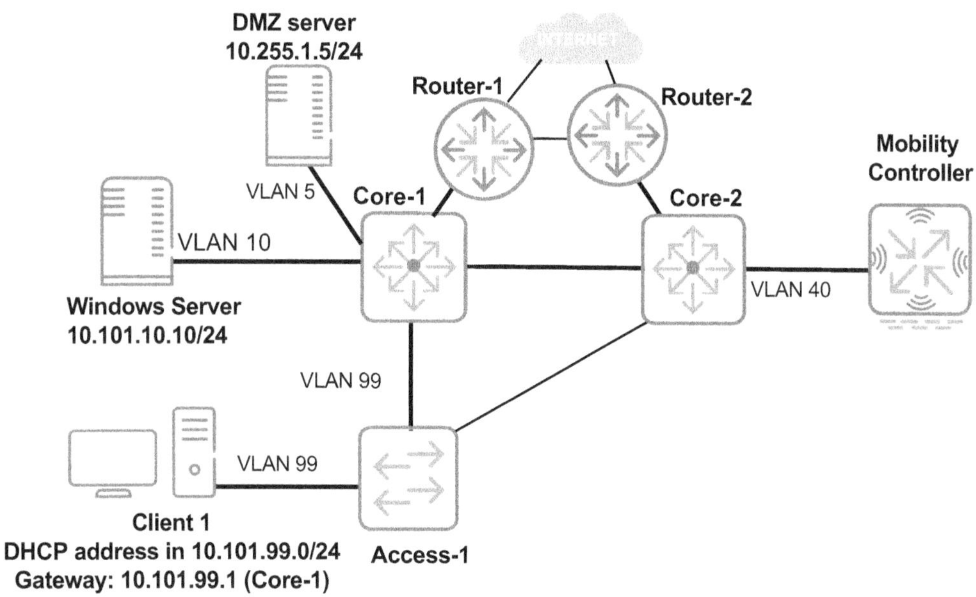


Figure 9-21 Simplified scenario network (Core-1 routing)

You would then need to adjust your approach to ensure that the ACL properly filters return traffic. For example, rule 40 above would now deny return traffic from the Internet to guests in 10.101.99.0/24 because this traffic arrives on VLAN 99 from the viewpoint of Access-1. You might want to change this rule to **40 deny ip 10.101.99.0 0.0.0.255 10.0.0.0 0.255.255.255**. Then return traffic from the Internet to guests would match rule 50 instead and be permitted. Another way that you should adjust to the ACL would be to permit DHCP traffic (UDP ports 67 and 68) to and from all IP addresses.

## Port-based ACLs (PACLs)

On an AOS-Switch, you can apply an IPv4 or MAC ACL to a port or link aggregation to filter traffic inbound or outbound on that physical interface. (Some switches support only inbound PACLs).

An inbound PACL filters *all* inbound traffic regardless of whether it is routed or switched. The PACL also applies to traffic inbound on the interface with a destination on the switch itself. An outbound PACL filters *all* outbound traffic on the port regardless of whether it is routed or switched. Figure 9-22 shows how a PACL applied to a port on Access-2 filters all traffic to or from the connected client.

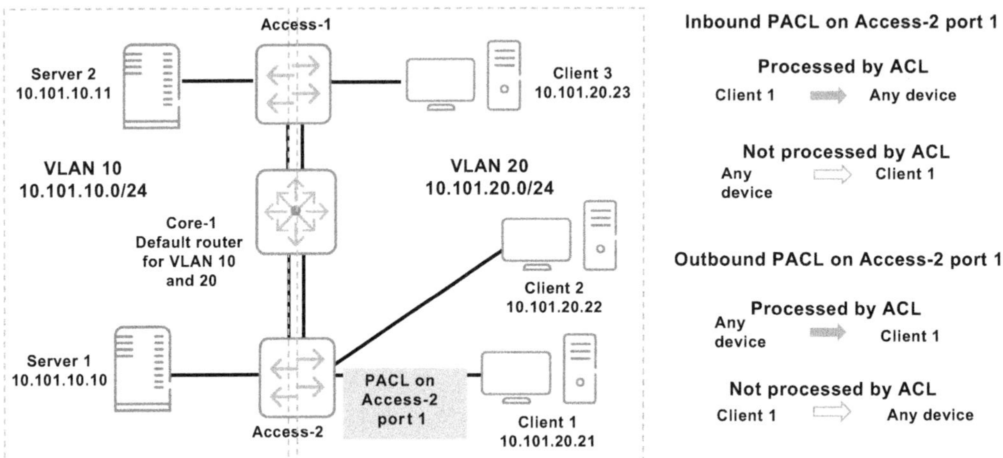


Figure 9-22 Port-based ACLs (PACLs)

You apply the PACL with the same command as a RACL, but you enter the command from the physical interface context rather than the VLAN interface.

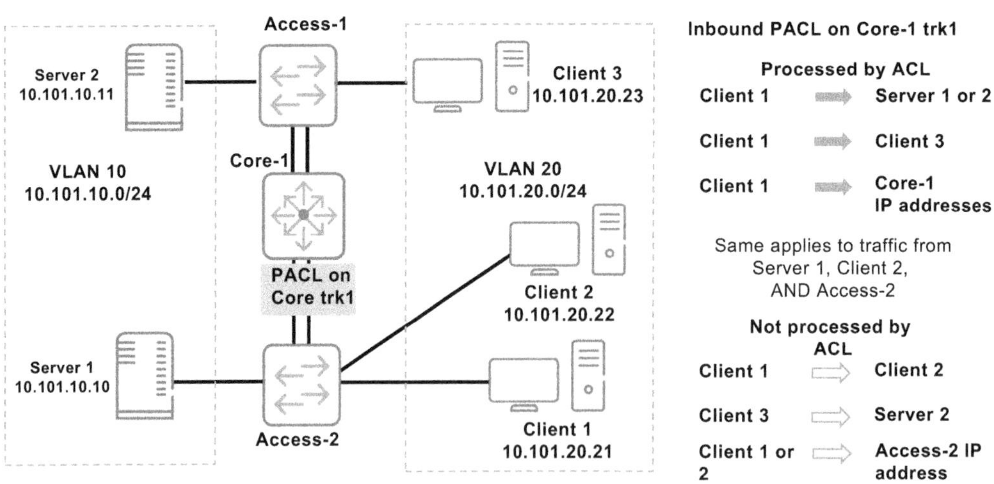


Figure 9-23 Port-based ACls (PACLs)

As always, you need to carefully consider where you apply the ACL. For example, if you apply an ACL to a switch-to-switch link, the ACL affects all incoming traffic from that link. Here you see how an ACL applied inbound on the link aggregation between Access-2 and Core-1 filters all traffic from Client 1, Client 2, and Server 1 that passes through Core-1. The filtering even extends to any traffic that Access-2 sends itself—an important implication for you to keep in mind. However, the ACL, of course, cannot filter any communications that do not pass through it. As long as Core 1 is routing the traffic, traffic between Client 1 and Server 1 is filtered, but traffic between Client 1 and Client 2 is not.

In many cases, when you want to control both routed and switched traffic, you should apply the ACL as close to the edge as possible. You can then ensure that all appropriate traffic is filtered. If you only want to control routed traffic, of course, you should apply the ACL as a RACL on the VLAN interface on the VLAN's default router.

The example in Figure 9-23 also illustrates that you can apply PACLs to link aggregations. Keep a few guidelines in mind. You must apply the PACLs to the link aggregation (trunk) rather than to individual ports within the link aggregation. It then automatically applies to the member ports. (Similarly, removing the PACL from the link aggregation, removes it from member ports.) Removing a port from the link aggregation removes the PACL from that port.

You should also remove any ACLs from a port before adding it to a link aggregation.

## ACL grouping

When you apply an ACL to an interface, the rules on the ACL take up space in the switch's ternary content-addressable memory (TCAM). The TCAM is a type of hardware memory. By processing traffic in the hardware, the switch can apply ACLs without slowing the traffic down. The TCAM has a limited size, so it can be beneficial to limit the space consumed by ACL rules in the TCAM.

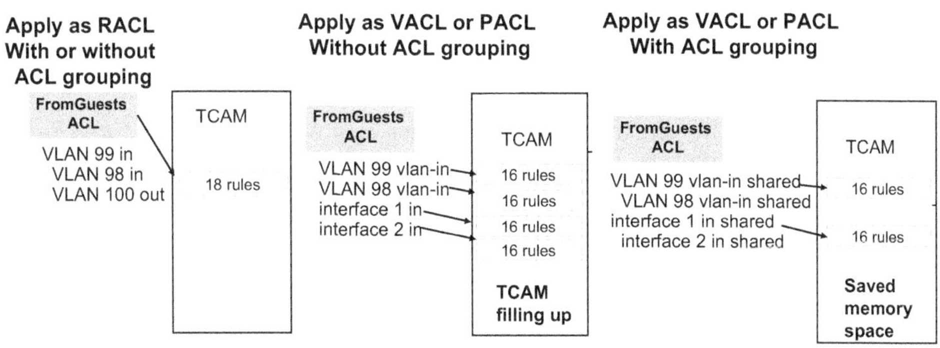


Figure 9-24 ACL grouping

The number of ACL rules supported in the switch memory depends on the switch model. And the number of rules used by an ACL might not correspond precisely with the number of entries that are configured in the ACL. The number also depends on how you apply the ACL (as a RACL, VACL, or

PACL.) The best way to see how many ACL rules your switch is currently using and the number left available is to use the following command:

```
Switch# show access-list resources
```

Sometimes you want to apply the same ACL to multiple interfaces. When you apply an ACL as a RACL on multiple VLAN interfaces, the switch is able to store the rules in that ACL in the memory just once. For example, an ACL named FromGuests might use up 18 rules when you apply it as an inbound RACL on VLAN 99. If you also applied this same ACL as an inbound RACL on VLAN 98, the ACL would continue to consume 18 rules. In fact, you could even apply the same ACL as an outbound RACL on a VLAN interface, and the ACL would continue to use only 18 rules.

However, AOS-Switches, by default, must store the rules for each VACL and PACL applied to an interface separately. For example, you apply the FromGuests ACL as a VACL to VLAN 99, and the ACL takes up the space for 16 rules. You then apply the FromGuests ACL as a VACL to VLAN 98, and the ACL takes up another 16 spaces. If you apply the same ACL to physical interfaces, the ACL continues to consume 16 spaces for each interface to which you apply it.

You can use the ACL grouping feature on an AOS-Switch to enable the switch to store the VACL and PACL rules more efficiently. This feature is disabled by default. Enable it with this command:

```
Switch(config)# access-list grouping
```

Enabling the feature requires the switch to reboot. After the switch reboots, you can begin using the ACL grouping feature. Simply add **shared** at the end of the typical command that you use to apply the ACL to an interface. The ACL in question can be any type of ACL, including IP standard, IP extended, MAC standard, and MAC extended. However, you cannot use the shared option for an IP ACL applied as a RACL (**in** or **out** option on a VLAN interface); as you learned, the switch already stores the rules for RACLs in a shared manner. You can use the **shared** option for MAC ACLs applied to VLAN interfaces with the **in** and **out** options because these are VACLs.

The **shared** option tells the switch to group the ACL with any ACL of the same name when these conditions are met:

- The other ACL is applied in the same way (either as a VACL or PACL) *and* in the same direction.
- The other ACL is also applied with the **shared** option.

For example, you could enter these commands:

```
Switch(config)# vlan 20 ip access-group FromGuests vlan-in shared
Switch(config)# vlan 99 ip access-group FromGuests vlan-in shared
Switch(config)# interface 1 ip access-group FromGuests in shared
Switch(config)# interface 2 ip access-group FromGuests in shared
```

The switch would create two ACL groups, one for the FromGuests ACL applied as a VACL to two VLAN interfaces, and one for the FromGuests ACL applied as a PACL to two physical interfaces. Because the ACL has 16 rules associated with it, the switch would add 32 rules in its memory rather than 64 without ACL grouping. (Note that applying an ACL to both a VLAN and an interface is not necessarily a typical design. This example is simply meant to illustrate how the ACL grouping feature works.)

When you view the ACL statistics for one interface to which a shared ACL is applied, the output shows the hit count for *all* interfaces using the shared ACL. This might make troubleshooting simpler because you do not need to check the statistics for multiple interfaces, but you should keep in mind that you might be seeing hits related to a different interface than you expect.

**Note**

ACL grouping is a feature in the KA/KB/WB16.01 software and higher. It is only supported in some AOS-Switch models. For more information on a specific product or product family, consult the product documentation.

## Activity: Predict filtering behavior

A switch is routing traffic between three VLANs:

- VLAN 1, subnet 10.1.1.0/24
- VLAN 2, subnet 10.1.2.0/24
- VLAN 10, subnet 10.1.10.0/24

The switch also has a route to 10.1.5.0/24 through 10.1.10.2 in VLAN 10.

The ACL shown in the table is applied as an outbound RACL to VLAN 10.

Table 9-10 Extended ACL

| Sequence IDs | AOS-Switch |
|---|---|
| 10 | deny icmp 10.1.2.0 0.0.0.255 any |
| 20 | permit udp 10.1.1.0 0.0.0.255 host 10.1.10.5 eq 53 |
| 30 | permit udp 10.1.2.0 0.0.0.255 host 10.1.10.6 eq 53 |
| 40 | permit tcp 10.1.1.0 0.0.0.255 10.1.10.16 0.0.0.15 eq 80 |
| 50 | permit tcp 10.1.1.0 0.0.0.255 10.1.10.16 0.0.0.15 eq 443 |
| 60 | deny ip any 10.1.10.0 0.0.0.255 |
| 70 | permit ip any any |

Predict whether the switch permits or denies each of these packets. Remember to first consider whether the ACL filters the packet based on how the ACL is applied. Then consider which rule the packet matches:

1. An HTTPS request (TCP port 443) that arrives in VLAN 2 from 10.1.2.20 to 10.1.10.25
2. An HTTPS request (TCP port 443) that arrives in VLAN 1 from 10.1.1.10 to 10.1.10.25
3. A ping that arrives in VLAN 2 from 10.1.2.20 to 10.1.1.100
4. A ping that arrives in VLAN 2 from 10.1.2.10 to 10.1.5.100
5. An HTTP request (TCP port 80) that arrives in VLAN 2 from 10.1.2.30 to 10.1.5.100
6. Now the ACL is removed from VLAN 10 and applied as an inbound RACL on VLAN 1 and on VLAN 2. Consider the five packets listed above. Which packets does the switch handle in a different way (permitting a packet that it once denied or denying a packet that it once permitted)?

## Summary

This chapter provided an overview of the key concepts you need to understand to implement ACLs:

- ACLs are composed of one or more entries called rules and identified by a common ACL ID (a number, a name, or in some cases both).
- Rules specify the matching criteria the switch applies to determine whether the ACL selects a particular packet.
- You can configure two major types of ACLs:
  - You would use a standard ACL when the source address is sufficient to filter the traffic of interest.
  - An extended ACL is useful for more complex filtering requirements.
- Once you create an ACL, you can assign it to a switch interface or to another function. Until you assign the ACL, it has no effect on traffic the switch processes.
- When you assign an ACL to a switch interface, it functions as a packet filter, permitting selected packets and dropping other packets.
- Depending on the switch model, you can assign an ACL to a VLAN interface as an inbound or outbound RACL, to a VLAN interface (inbound) as a VACL, or to a physical port as an inbound or outbound PACL. The type of ACL determines which packets are matched against the ACL.

## Learning check

1. What are the three general components of an ACL rule?
    a. Prefix length, IP or MAC address, and rule action
    b. ACL type, ACL application, and rule
    c. ACL type, subnet mask, and prefix length
    d. Sequence number, action, and matching criteria
2. Choose a type of ACL and list the types of options that you can configure in a rule for that ACL.
3. An administrator wants to configure an IPv4 standard ACL to deny one device within a subnet (10.1.10.10) but permit every other device in the complete subnet (10.1.10.0/24). Which set of ACL entries meets these requirements?
    a. 10 permit 10.1.10.0 0.0.0.255 20 deny host 10.1.10.10
    b. 10 deny host 10.1.10.10 20 permit 10.1.10.0 0.0.0.255
    c. 10 permit host 10.1.10.0 20 deny 10.1.10.10
    d. 10 deny host 10.1.10.10 20 permit host 10.1.10.0
4. You want to control all traffic that a switch receives as tagged or untagged for VLAN 3. The traffic should be controlled regardless of whether it is switched or routed.
    a. On a switch-to-switch interface that carries VLAN 3 with the **out** option
    b. On VLAN 3 with the **in** option
    c. On VLAN 3 with the **out** option
    d. On VLAN 3 with the **vlan-in** option
5. What happens if you do not specify a sequence ID when you create entries for your ACLs? How does the switch assign the automatic sequence numbers? Why is the sequence important?
6. Suppose you create an ACL called ToMC and enter this rule: **permit 10.101.10.0/24**. When you enter **show access-list ToMC,** what would you see for this address in the list of entries?
7. Suppose that you create this ACL on an access layer switch called Access-1:

```
10 permit udp 0.0.0.0 255.255.255.255 10.255.1.5 0.0.0.0 eq 67

20 permit udp 0.0.0.0 255.255.255.255 10.255.1.5 0.0.0.0 eq 53

30 permit icmp 0.0.0.0 255.255.255.255 10.255.1.5 0.0.0.0 0

40 deny ip 0.0.0.0 255.255.255.255 10.0.0.0 0.255.255.255

50 permit ip 0.0.0.0 255.255.255.255 0.0.0.0 255.255.255.255
```

Access-1 is routing traffic for VLAN 99, subnet 10.101.99.0/24. What is the difference between applying the ACL as an inbound RACL and an inbound VACL?

Next consider how the ACL would function if Access-1 did *not* route traffic in VLAN 99, and you applied the ACL as an inbound VACL on this VLAN.

8. A switch is operating at its default settings for ACL grouping. You have applied an IP ACL as an inbound VACL on VLAN 20, and it uses 16 rules in the switch's ACL resource space. You then apply the same ACL as an inbound VACL on VLAN 21. Does the ACL continue to use the same space, or does it require more space?

# Answers

## Determine use cases for ACL types

You will now examine several use cases for how a company wants to filter traffic. You will select the correct type of ACL for the use case.

1. Attackers can use ICMP to map the network and implement certain exploits and Denial of Service (DoS attacks). For example, in the Smurf attack, the attacker sends an ICMP echo request with a spoofed source address to a broadcast address. Devices then flood the spoofed source with replies.

   The company wants to filter out most ICMP packets that cross from a less trusted network segment to a trusted subnet. It will allow ICMP reply packets to enter the trusted subnet so that trusted devices can send pings and receive replies.

   Which type of ACL can enforce rules such as these?

   IP extended ACL

   You can filter by ICMP type in an IP extended ACL.

2. The company wants to block certain types of non-IP traffic such as appletalk.

   Which type of ACL can enforce rules such as these?

   Extended MAC ACL

   Extended MAC ACLs allow you to select Ethertype, which indicates the Layer 3 protocol encapsulated by the MAC header. Appletalk is an example of a non-IP Layer 3 protocol.

3. The company wants to permit guests to access DHCP services and DNS services from a server in a DMZ. Guests will be allowed to send and receive traffic from the Internet, but should be prohibited from any other access to the company's private subnets.

   Which type of ACL can enforce rules such as these?

   IP extended ACL

   To enforce these rules, you will need to specify an authorized destination IP address as well as the correct UDP ports for DHCP and DNS traffic. You must use an IP extended ACL for these options.

4. The company wants to filter traffic between a subnet with servers that hold sensitive information and the rest of the network. Only traffic from certain trusted subnets should be able to enter the server subnet.

   Which type of ACL can enforce rules such as these?

   IP standard ACL

   You can meet the criteria for this situation by selecting traffic by source IP address and filtering out traffic with unauthorized sources as it enters the sensitive server subnet. An IP extended ACL could also meet the needs because it allows you to select traffic by source IP address, as well. (If you applied the ACL to the untrusted subnets, you would have to use an IP extended ACL to deny access to the server subnet as the destination. However, the question implies that you are applying the ACL in this scenario to traffic as it enters the server subnet. You will learn more about applying ACLs in a moment.)

## Activity: Plan ACLs

You considered two scenarios for implementing an ACL in the network illustrated in Figure 9-7 and also in Figure 9-25 below.

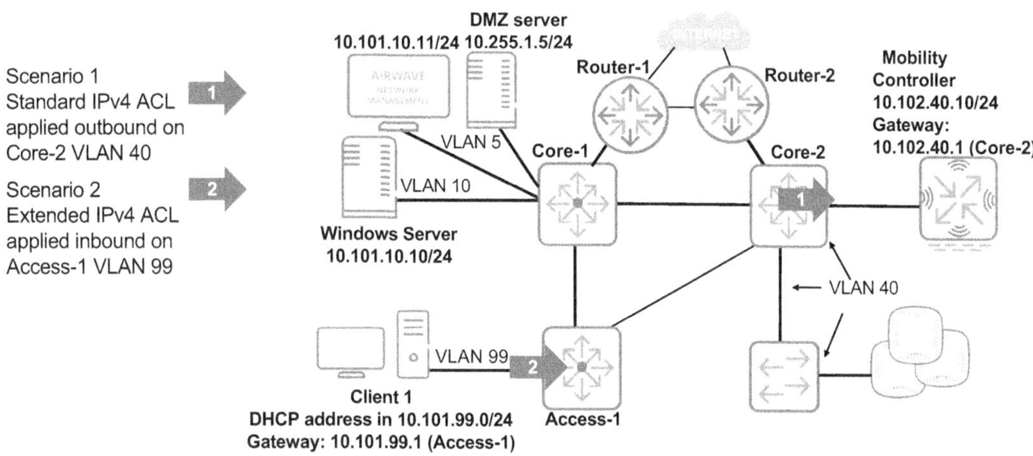


Figure 9-25 Activity: Plan ACLs

### Scenario 1: Protect the mobility infrastructure

Core-2 connects to an Aruba Mobility Controller (MC) in VLAN 40, subnet 10.102.40.0/24. The company wants to prevent users from accessing this network, which should be used only for managing the Aruba MC and communications between the MC and Aruba devices. You have decided to permit only the server subnet (10.101.10.0/24), which contains AirWave and a management station, to access the MC and AP management VLAN.

Answer the questions below to help you plan an ACL that will control traffic in this way. As you answer the questions, keep in mind that you want to fulfill the requirements of the scenario with a single ACL. (The answers to these questions are at the end of the chapter.)

1. Can you use a standard IP ACL for this scenario or is an extended IP ACL required?

   You can use a standard IP ACL. Because you want to apply a single ACL, the ACL should permit authorized source subnets and deny all others. A standard IP ACL can specify authorized sources.

2. On which switch and which interface should you apply the ACL? Should you apply the ACL as an inbound or outbound ACL?

   You want to apply a single ACL, so you should apply the ACL directly to the subnet that you want to protect. You want to control traffic as it enters the subnet from other subnets. You should apply the ACL to VLAN interface 40 on Core-2 as an outbound RACL.

3. Begin to plan rules for the ACL. You do not need to specify the precise syntax, but you should plan the rule order, the action for each rule, and the general match criteria for each rule.

   This ACL requires one rule, which permits traffic from 10.101.10.0/24. The ACL implicitly denies all other traffic.

## Scenario 2: Control access for less trusted users

In this scenario, VLAN 99 is assigned to less trusted users such as guests. You want to permit the guests' access to the Internet, but deny access to the complete private network with the exception of DHCP and DNS services offered by a DMZ server at 10.255.1.5. Begin to plan the ACL. As you answer the questions, keep in mind that you want to fulfill the requirements of the scenario with a single ACL.

1. Can you use a standard IP ACL for this scenario or is an extended IP ACL required?

   An extended IP ACL is required for this scenario for several reasons. One reason is that you want to distinguish between DNS traffic and other IP traffic. Because you want to apply a single ACL, you will also need to select traffic by destination.

2. On which switch and which interface should you apply the ACL? Should you apply the ACL as an inbound or outbound ACL?

   You want to apply a single ACL, so you should apply the ACL directly to the subnet that you want to control. You want to control traffic from the Guest VLAN as it routed out of that VLAN to other subnets. You should therefore apply the ACL to VLAN 99 on Access-1 as an inbound RACL. Applying the ACL to VLAN 99 as a VACL could also fit the needs, but the scenario gave no indication that you should control the traffic between guests.

3. Begin to plan rules for the ACL. You do not need to specify the precise syntax, but you should plan the rule order, the action for each rule, and the general match criteria for each rule.

   This ACL requires several rules.

   The ACL actually does not strictly require a rule to permit DHCP traffic to the server. This is because the users send DHCP discovery and request packets as broadcasts. As nonrouted traffic, an inbound RACL does not apply to them. The inbound RACL also does not apply to traffic from Access-1's own IP address on this VLAN, which it uses to relay the DHCP traffic. If you want to allow the clients to send DHCP release and request messages, you will need to permit DHCP traffic to the server because clients direct these to the DHCP server itself. You might also suggest allowing ICMP replies to the server since some DHCP servers use pings to check whether an address is in use.

   Another rule must permit DNS traffic (selected by UDP port) to the server.

   Another rule, higher in sequence, must deny all private network traffic. You could take a few different approaches to specifying this traffic. The easiest way is just to deny traffic to 10.0.0.0/8. You could also deny traffic to 10.100.0.0/16, 10.101.0.0/16, and 10.102.0.0/16.

   Finally, you need a rule highest in sequence that permits all traffic.

## Activity: Analyzing an ACL

1. What is the current behavior?

   The switch permits packets between 10.1.1.1 and 10.1.1.30 as it should. However, it denies packets between 10.1.1.40 and 10.1.1.55, which it should permit. (It also denies IP addresses 10.1.1.31 through 10.1.1.39 and other IP addresses beyond 10.1.1.55, as it should.)

2. How can you reorder the ACL to use the correct sequence?

   You can create more space in the rule with a command such as this:

   ```
   Switch(config)# ip access-list resequence <name> 10 10
   ```

   You can then delete the rules originally numbered 4 and 5 and insert them before the rule originally numbered 2. For example, the new rule order might be:

   ```
   10 deny host 10.1.1.31

   13 permit 10.1.1.40  0.0.0.7

   16 permit 10.1.1.48  0.0.0.7

   20 deny 10.1.1.32  0.0.0.31

   30 permit 10.1.1.0  0.0.0.63
   ```

## Activity: Predict filtering behavior

1. An HTTPS request (TCP port 443) that arrives in VLAN 2 from 10.1.2.20 to 10.1.10.25

   The switch drops this packet. The ACL processes the traffic because it is routed out VLAN 10. The first rule that the packet matches is rule 60, a deny rule.

2. An HTTPS request (TCP port 443) that arrives in VLAN 1 from 10.1.1.10 to 10.1.10.25

   The switch permits this packet. The ACL processes the traffic because it is routed out VLAN 10. The first rule that the packet matches is rule 50, a permit rule.

3. A ping that arrives in VLAN 2 from 10.1.2.20 to 10.1.1.100

   The switch permits this packet. The ACL does not process the traffic because it is not routed out VLAN 10.

4. A ping that arrives in VLAN 2 from 10.1.2.10 to 10.1.5.100

   The switch denies this packet. The ACL processes the traffic because it is routed out VLAN 10 (to the next hop in the route to 10.1.5.0/24). The first rule that the packet matches is rule 10, a deny rule.

5. An HTTP request (TCP port 80) that arrives in VLAN 2 from 10.1.2.30 to 10.1.5.100

   The switch permits this packet. The ACL processes the traffic because it is routed out VLAN 10 (to the next hop in the route to 10.1.5.0/24). The first rule that it matches is rule 70, a permit rule.

6. Now the ACL is removed from VLAN 10 and applied as an inbound RACL on VLAN 1 and on VLAN 2. Consider the five packets listed above. Which packets does the switch handle in a different way (permitting a packet that it once denied or denying a packet that it once permitted)?

   The ACLs handle all of the traffic in the same way with the exception of the ping that arrives in VLAN 2 from 10.1.2.20 to 10.1.1.100. This traffic is now processed by the ACL, and the switch denies this traffic based on rule 10.

## Learning check

1. What are the three general components of an ACL rule?
   a. Prefix length, IP or MAC address, and rule action
   b. ACL type, ACL application, and rule
   c. ACL type, subnet mask, and prefix length
   **d. Sequence number, action, and matching criteria**

2. Choose a type of ACL and list the types of options that you can configure in a rule for that ACL.

   Depending on the type that you selected, you should have listed options such as these:

   - MAC standard: source MAC address
   - MAC extended: source and destination MAC address, EtherType (encapsulated protocol), VLAN ID, and 802.1p (CoS) value
   - IP standard: source IP address
   - IP extended: source and destination IP address, IP protocol, TCP or UDP source or destination port, ICMP or IGMP type, TCP flags and session status, ToS and IP precedence values

3. An administrator wants to configure an IPv4 standard ACL to deny one device within a subnet (10.1.10.10) but permit every other device in the complete subnet (10.1.10.0/24). Which set of ACL entries meets these requirements?

   a. 10 permit 10.1.10.0 0.0.0.255 20 deny host 10.1.10.10

   **b. 10 deny host 10.1.10.10 20 permit 10.1.10.0 0.0.0.255**

   c. 10 permit host 10.1.10.0 20 deny 10.1.10.10

   d. 10 deny host 10.1.10.10 20 permit host 10.1.10.0

4. You want to control all traffic that a switch receives as tagged or untagged for VLAN 3. The traffic should be controlled regardless of whether it is switched or routed.

   a. On a switch-to-switch interface that carries VLAN 3 with the **out** option

   b. On VLAN 3 with the **in** option

   c. On VLAN 3 with the **out** option

   **d. On VLAN 3 with the vlan-in option**

5. What happens if you do not specify a sequence ID when you create entries for your ACLs? How does the switch assign the automatic sequence numbers? Why is the sequence important?

   The switch automatically assigns sequence number 10 to the first entry that you create, 20 to the next entry, and so on. Every entry must have a sequence number so that the switch knows the order in which to process the ACL. The sequence is particularly important when traffic might match multiple rules. For example, if you have a rule that permits all traffic, that rule must come after rules that deny specific traffic.

6. Suppose you create an ACL called ToMC and enter this rule: **permit 10.101.10.0/24**. When you enter **show access-list ToMC,** what would you see for this address in the list of entries?

   You would see 10.101.10.0 0.0.0.255. 0.0.0.255, which looks a bit like a subnet mask in reverse. These are called wildcard bits, and the AOS-switch software actually always stores addresses in ACL entries with wildcard bits.

7. Suppose that you create this ACL on an access layer switch called Access-1:

```
10 permit udp 0.0.0.0 255.255.255.255 10.255.1.5 0.0.0.0 eq 67

20 permit udp 0.0.0.0 255.255.255.255 10.255.1.5 0.0.0.0 eq 53

30 permit icmp 0.0.0.0 255.255.255.255 10.255.1.5 0.0.0.0 0

40 deny ip 0.0.0.0 255.255.255.255 10.0.0.0 0.255.255.255

50 permit ip 0.0.0.0 255.255.255.255 0.0.0.0 255.255.255.255
```

   Access-1 is routing traffic for VLAN 99, subnet 10.101.99.0/24. What is the difference between applying the ACL as an inbound RACL and an inbound VACL?

   Next consider how the ACL would function if Access-1 did *not* route traffic in VLAN 99, and you applied the ACL as an inbound VACL on this VLAN.

   Similarities and differences between applying the ACL as an inbound RACL and inbound VACL include:

   - When the ACL is applied as a RACL, clients within VLAN 99 can access each other. As a VACL, the ACL filters traffic between clients within VLAN 99. Because all traffic to devices in 10.0.0.0/8 is denied (with the exception of limited services on 10.255.1.5) and because clients have IP addresses in 10.101.99.0/24, clients cannot access each other.
   - When applied both ways, the ACL still allows Access-1 to relay DHCP traffic for the client, which continued to be able to receive an IP address.

   If Access-1 does not route traffic in VLAN 99 and the ACL is applied as an inbound VACL on VLAN 99, this ACL would deny DHCP broadcast traffic. It would also deny return traffic from the Internet, which Access-1 would consider as arriving on VLAN 99 (in which it is routed by the VLAN 99 default router). Therefore, you would need to change the ACL to have the intended effects.

8. A switch is operating at its default settings for ACL grouping. You have applied an IP ACL as an inbound VACL on VLAN 20, and it uses 16 rules in the switch's ACL resource space. You then apply the same ACL as an inbound VACL on VLAN 21. Does the ACL continue to use the same space, or does it require more space?

   The ACL requires more space, using up the space for another 16 rules. If you want this ACL to use the same number of rules no matter how many VLANs you apply it to, you must enable ACL grouping and apply the ACL to the VLANs as a shared ACL.

# 10 802.1X Authentication

## EXAM OBJECTIVES

✓ Implement 802.1X on AOS-Switch ports

✓ Integrate AOS-Switches with an Aruba ClearPass solution, which might apply dynamic Virtual LAN (VLAN) assignments, Access Control Lists (ACLs), quality of service (QoS) priorities, and rate limits

## Assumed knowledge

Before reading this chapter, you should have a basic understanding of:

- IP addressing
- Open Systems Interconnection (OSI) model
- Multiple Spanning Tree Protocol (MSTP) and Rapid Spanning Tree Protocol (RSTP)
- Link aggregation
- Virtual LANs (VLANs)
- Routing
- Switching

## Introduction

This chapter introduces you to port-based authentication and teaches you how to implement 802.1X authentication technology on AOS-Switches.

## Port-based authentication use models

Port-based authentication works within the Authentication, Authorization, and Accounting (AAA) model. AAA provides a framework for implementing centralized policies to control access to particular services. For port-based authentication, network access is the service in question, and the AAA server is usually a RADIUS server. In detail, AAA defines:

- Authentication—A user must prove his or her identity in some way to the authentication server. As you will see, for port-based authentication, the user usually submits a username and password. The user might alternatively submit a digital certificate that includes a valid username and is signed by a trusted certificate authority (CA).
- Authorization—The authenticated user is authorized by a RADIUS server policy to obtain network access. The policy might authorize the user for particular port settings (such as VLAN and rate limit), which the switch port applies dynamically.
- Accounting—The switch submits information about the user's connection to the RADIUS accounting server, supporting user tracking and auditing functions.

Companies typically implement port-based authentication for one or more of these reasons:

- They need to prevent unauthorized users from connecting to open ports. This security may be required to comply with their own security policies, which may include compliance with government regulations.
- They want to provide guest access, ensuring that guests are placed in the proper guest VLAN and also forcing guests to log in for legal and tracking purposes.
- They have user groups with different access rights and want to ensure the correct port settings for each group. Users might connect to any port, so the IT staff would struggle to keep up. In addition, companies may want to ensure users are given consistent access no matter how they login—from a wired or a mobile connection. The authorization component of port-based authentication enables the port to adjust to the user dynamically.

  For example, a school district might have a faculty/administrators VLAN and a student VLAN. Port-based authentication enables any user to connect to any port. Users submit their identity to the centralized authentication server, which directs the switch port to grant the user access in the correct VLAN.

  As you will learn, port-based authentication can also dynamically provision ports with ACLs, rate limits, and other settings.

This chapter focuses on employee authentication use cases.

# 802.1X overview

You will first examine 802.1X, an open-standard technology for controlling users' network access based on their identity.

## 802.1X logical ports

As Figure 10-1 shows, 802.1X forces users to authenticate as soon as the connection between the switch port and the client comes up. To restrict an unauthenticated user so that client can send only authentication messages, 802.1X divides the port into two logical ports.

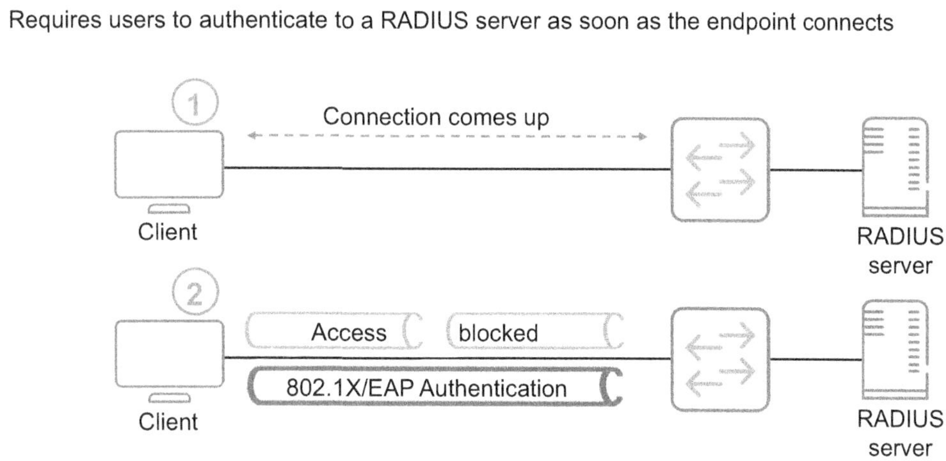


Figure 10-1 802.1X logical ports

### Controlled port

The controlled port allows all types of traffic, but it can be disabled and, by default, is. Both sides of the connection control the port, based on their assessment of the authentication state. In other words, no unauthorized traffic flows across the link.

### Uncontrolled port

The uncontrolled port is always active, but it can carry only the Extensible Authentication Protocol (EAP) packets used for authentication.

Without the uncontrolled port, this high-level of security would shut out all traffic from users, preventing even authorized users from proving that they are authorized.

Note, however, that the uncontrolled port does not carry Dynamic Host Configuration Protocol (DHCP) messages, Domain Name System (DNS) messages, and so on. You will see how 802.1X allows the client to authenticate without an IP address.

## 802.1X roles

To understand 802.1X authentication, you must understand the devices involved in the process and the role each device plays.

- What does the device expect from the process?
- What responsibilities does the device assume?
- What protocols does the device use to communicate?

Keep these questions in mind as you learn about the three devices involved in the 802.1X authentication process.

- Supplicant
- Authenticator
- Authentication server

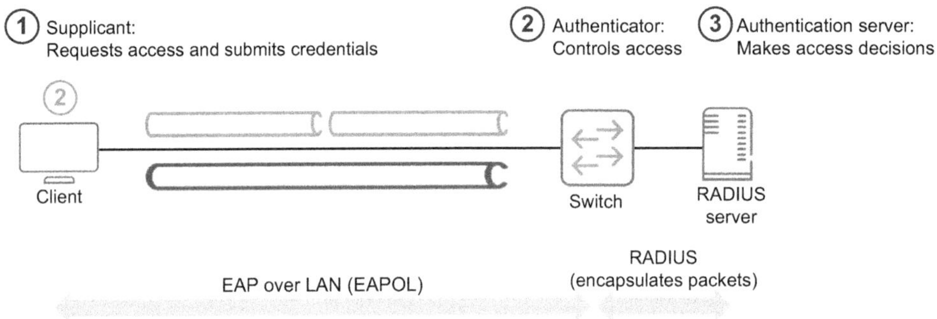


Figure 10-2 802.1X roles

## Supplicant

As Figure 10-2 shows, the supplicant is the 802.1X component that runs on the endpoint attempting to connect to the network.

The supplicant requests access to the network and proves that it deserves this access by authenticating—typically in response to a challenge from the far end of the connection (for example, the switch port).

In addition to responding to a challenge, the supplicant may also initiate the authentication process on its own behalf by transmitting an EAP-Start packet. This mechanism protects supplicants that receive the challenge before the station has entirely booted, causing authentication to timeout before the user can submit his or her credentials.

## Authenticator

The authenticator, which is also shown in Figure 10-2, is the 802.1X component on the other side of the supplicant's connection. In this study guide, the authenticator is the AOS-Switch. The authenticator controls network access, forcing a supplicant to authenticate before it can send any non-EAP traffic over the connection. The authenticator initiates the authentication process but then relays authentication messages between the supplicant and the authentication server.

After the authentication is completed, the authenticator decides how to control the connection. If the authentication server has accepted the user's request, the authenticator opens the controlled port, allowing traffic to flow. In other words, the station is now completely connected to the network. If the authentication server rejects the user's request, the authenticator enforces this denial and keeps the port closed.

### Authentication server

As Figure 10-2 shows, the authentication server makes decisions about whether or not users can access the network. These decisions are based on criteria such as whether the user:

- Can prove his or her identity (the users' credentials are correct)
- Is connecting at the proper time and location

For example, even legitimate guests might be prohibited from accessing the network after regular work hours.

The server also submits its own credentials to the supplicant. In essence, the supplicant and the server authenticate each other, although the authenticator always acts as a proxy in this process.

The authentication server is a RADIUS server, and the authenticator and authentication server use RADIUS messages to communicate. The authenticator encapsulates the supplicant's EAP messages in this protocol.

## 802.1X requirements

Figure 10-3 shows that 802.1X requires particular capabilities on clients, network servers, and switches.

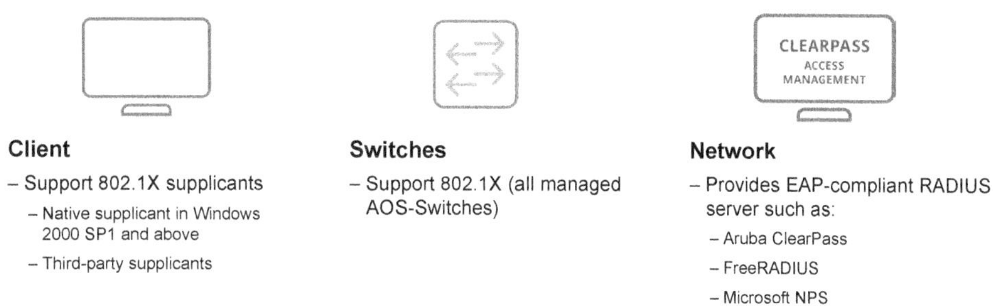


Figure 10-3 802.1X requirements

Any device that needs an Ethernet connection must include an 802.1X supplicant. Windows and Mac operating systems provide native supplicants, which you can use. You can also choose from a number of third-party supplicants, including freely available ones.

The switch must support the authentication standard, which managed AOS-Switches do.

---

**Note**

If your environment includes older switches, they may not support 802.1X. Check your switch documentation to ensure that it is supported.

---

The network also requires a RADIUS server.

- Aruba ClearPass provides a RADIUS server, as well as other capabilities for monitoring and managing user access.
- You can alternatively use a third-party RADIUS server such as Microsoft Network Policy Server (NPS) or an open source server such as FreeRADIUS.

## EAP framework

You will now examine how the supplicant (client), authenticator (switch), and authentication server (RADIUS server) work together to authenticate a client. Understanding this process can help you to pinpoint and troubleshoot issues.

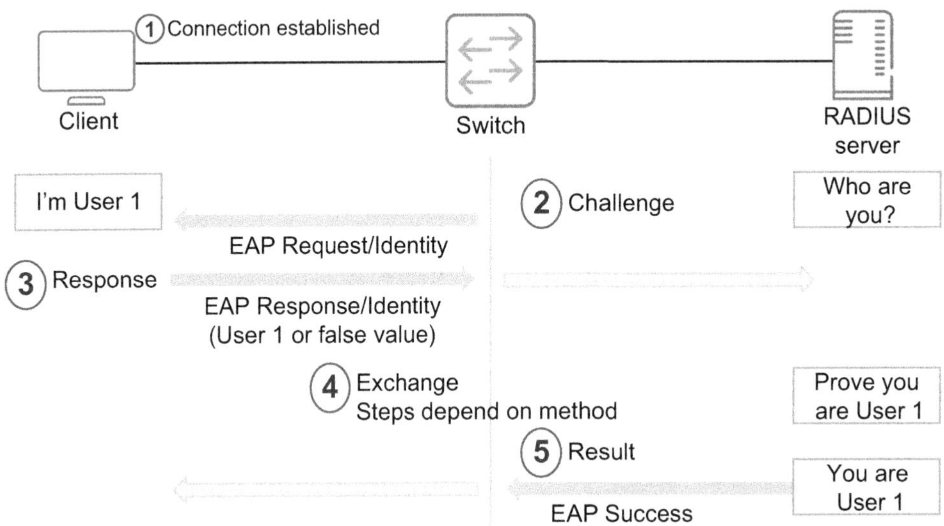


Figure 10-4 EAP framework

EAP, the protocol 802.1X uses for authentication, defines a flexible framework into which you can fit authentication methods that meet the needs of your environment and security policies. Figure 10-4 shows this general framework. As you follow the process, remember that the authenticator (switch) relays all messages from the client to the RADIUS server, encapsulating them with RADIUS as necessary. The vertical line underneath the switch shows the point at which the authenticator encapsulates the messages.

1. The client and switch port establish an Ethernet connection.
2. The switch keeps the controlled port shut, blocking all traffic except EAP, and issues a challenge. The challenge is an EAP Request/Identity packet. Basically, this frame initiates the authentication process and asks the client to identify itself but not to send any other information.

3. The client responds with an EAP Response/Identity packet, which typically includes a username.

   The authenticator includes the user's identity in all future frames so that the server can keep track of which EAP messages belong to which user. The user's identity also marks any accounting frames for the connection—which are important for companies with rigorous auditing requirements. Depending on the EAP method, though, the username submitted at this point might not be the actual username. Some methods have the supplicant submit a false name at this point and the true name later in the process after a secure and encrypted session has been established. This protects the username from hackers.

4. The RADIUS server receives the EAP Response/Identity (forwarded in RADIUS by the switch). The server initiates an EAP method for exchanging credentials. The particular messages and type of authentication credentials exchanged by the client and server depend on the EAP method.

5. Based on information received in step 4, the authentication server determines whether or not the client has authenticated successfully and informs the switch. The switch then either activates the connection and transmits an EAP-Success or leaves the connection deactivated and transmits an EAP-Failure.

## EAP and RADIUS together

You will now take a closer look at how the authenticator (switch) actually relays the messages between the client supplicant and the RADIUS server.

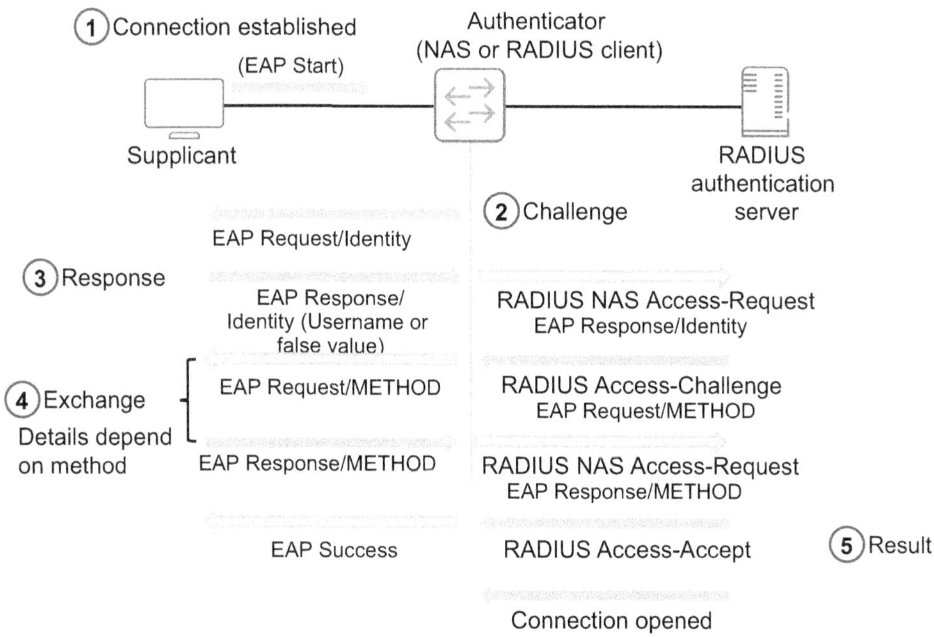


Figure 10-5 EAP and RADIUS together

As Figure 10-5 shows, the authenticator encapsulates a supplicant's EAP message in a RADIUS Access-Request packet. It also hashes the packet with MD5, using the RADIUS shared secret as the key. It adds the hash to a message authenticator field. The authenticator then transmits the packet to the RADIUS server. Because the switch handles the actual delivery of the frames, the client does not need an IP address or any network access.

The RADIUS server checks that the message has arrived from a valid network device (sometimes called a Network Access Server [NAS] or RADIUS client); that is, the switch IP address must match a network device address configured on the server. The RADIUS server also checks the message authenticator field by hashing the packet with its shared secret. If the hashes match, it knows that the valid client truly sent the Access-Request and that the packet was not altered in transit. If the request is not from a known network device with a correct shared secret, the RADIUS server does not respond to the message.

If the switch is known and uses a correct secret, however, the server decapsulates the EAP messages and formulates the appropriate responses, which it encapsulates in RADIUS Challenge messages. These messages are also authenticated with the message authenticator field.

At the end of the process, the RADIUS server sends either:

- An Access-Accept message—Two requirements are met:
  - The client has successfully authenticated.
  - The policy that applies to this Access-Request allows access.
- An Access-Reject message—One of these situations occurred:
  - The client could not complete authentication, whether because the RADIUS server does not trust the authenticator, because the client and server do not support compatible EAP methods, or some other problem.
  - The client does not trust the RADIUS server's certificate, so the server failed authentication.
  - The client failed authentication.
  - The policy that applies to this Access-Request does not allow access.
  - No policy applies to this Access-Request.

To ensure that the switch can participate in this process, you must set the correct RADIUS server address or addresses and the correct RADIUS secret. You need to make sure that the switch uses the same RADIUS authentication port as the RADIUS server. You also need to ensure that the switch sends the RADIUS messages with the source IP address specified as a valid NAS or RADIUS client on the server.

## EAP methods

As mentioned earlier, step 4 in the EAP/RADIUS process depends on the EAP method, which dictates the user must prove his or her identity.

As Figures 10-6 and 10-7 show, the first step in the exchange—the server's EAP Request/METHOD packet—starts the process and indicates the method that the server requires. (Depending on your RADIUS server, you can program it to select methods according to conditions such as user identity and location.)

If the station supports the requested method, it continues the exchange. Otherwise, the station sends an EAP NAK packet, which can suggest a different method. The server, if it supports the alternative method, may then initiate the exchange with the new method. The station and the RADIUS server must agree upon the method for the process to continue.

The sections that follow describe several common methods. Note that Figures 10-6 and 10-7 show the messages passing through the switch. The supplicant and RADIUS server are communicating together, but, as shown in Figure 10-5, the switch is actually encapsulating the supplicant EAP Request messages in RADIUS Access-Request messages to send to the server.

## EAP-Transport Layer Security

Considered one of the most secure EAP methods, EAP-Transport Layer Security (EAP-TLS) uses a TLS handshake to generate encryption keys that secure the rest of the authentication process and to exchange digital certificates.

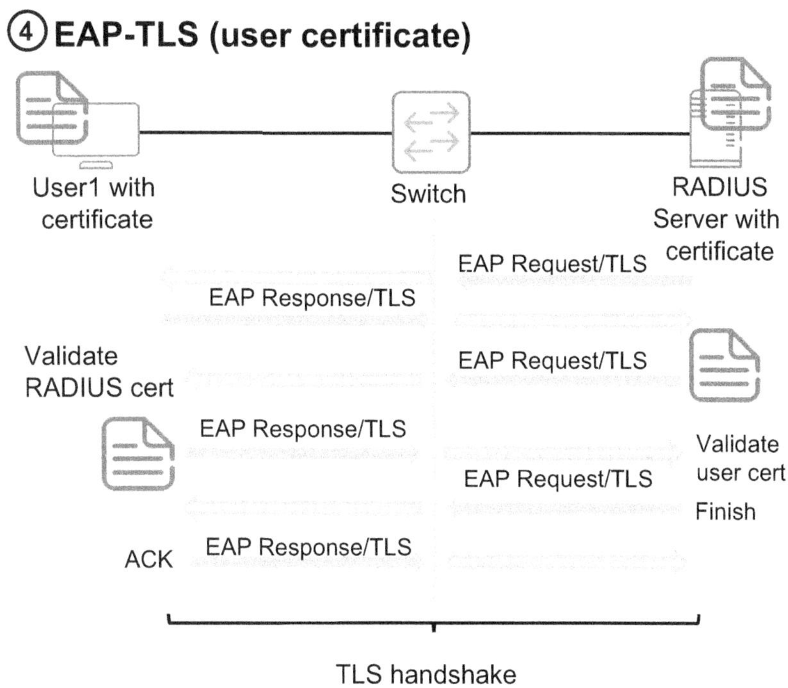


Figure 10-6 EAP-TLS

The EAP Request/TLS and EAP Response/TLS packets include information such as:

- Digital certificates and certificate verifications
- Supported encryption suites
- Values for generating encryption keys (not the keys themselves)

The digital certificate includes the device's identity, and it is signed by a Certificate Authority (CA). The RADIUS server validates the certificate submitted by the user, and the supplicant validates the RADIUS server's certificate. (Validation occurs through asymmetric encryption with public and private keys, but a discussion of such encryption is beyond the scope of this study guide.) The validation process also includes checking the CA signature, so the certificate must be signed by a CA that the device is configured to trust.

After the server validates the user certificate, it sends a message to indicate a successful finish, and the client responds.

Remember that Figure 10-6 shows just the EAP/TLS part of the complete 802.1X authentication process. After these messages, step 5 occurs—the RADIUS server sends a RADIUS Access-Accept.

## Advantages

EAP-TLS is one of the most secure EAP methods because it provides mutual authentication with Public Key Infrastructure (PKI) digital certificates. Digital certificates rely on extremely strong asymmetric keys and are validated by trusted CAs. The digital certificate is typically stored on a laptop or on a smart card, providing stronger security. Although you can set up requirements to force users to create "stronger," and, therefore, more secure passwords, you cannot prevent users from telling people their password or writing it on a paper displayed in plain sight. Generally, it is harder for users to leak certificates inappropriately; systems administrators might, for example, implement security measures to prevent users from copying certificates.

Hackers often run dictionary attacks on passwords, phish for passwords, or use other social engineering techniques to get users to leak their passwords. Although no credentials can be totally secure—malware might be able to steal certificates, for example—digital certificates are more resistant to many common attacks.

Someone who steals a laptop or smart card might be able to gain access to the certificates within, but they are usually protected by an additional layer of security such as a password, which the user must enter before the supplicant can use the certificate. In addition, the user can immediately report the theft, allowing you to revoke the compromised certificate.

## Disadvantages

EAP-TLS is not vulnerable to eavesdropping and replay attacks that affect less secure EAP methods such as EAP-MD5, but security comes at the cost of purchasing and managing the digital certificates—substantially more expensive than managing passwords. Maintaining a large number of certificates requires specialized software and trained IT staff.

In addition, in environments that have multiple operating systems, installing certificates on all clients can be difficult. Bring Your Own Device (BYOD) environments can make managing certificates even more difficult. However, Aruba ClearPass BYOD onboarding capabilities can help companies surmount these challenges. ClearPass Onboard can provide new user devices with limited access and helps users easily download the correct certificates to them.

## PEAP and EAP-Tunneled TLS

Protected EAP (PEAP) was developed to provide much of the security of EAP-TLS without forcing stations to have digital certificates—drastically reducing implementation costs. For this reason, it is among the most commonly used EAP methods.

Tunneled Transport Layer Security (TTLS) is a similar, but less commonly used, method. (TTLS was developed by Funk Software and Certicom; PEAP was developed by Microsoft, Cisco Systems, and RSA Security.)

TTLS and PEAP function in very similar ways. Both methods involve a two-step authentication process; in the first step, the outer method creates a secure tunnel in which the second step takes place.

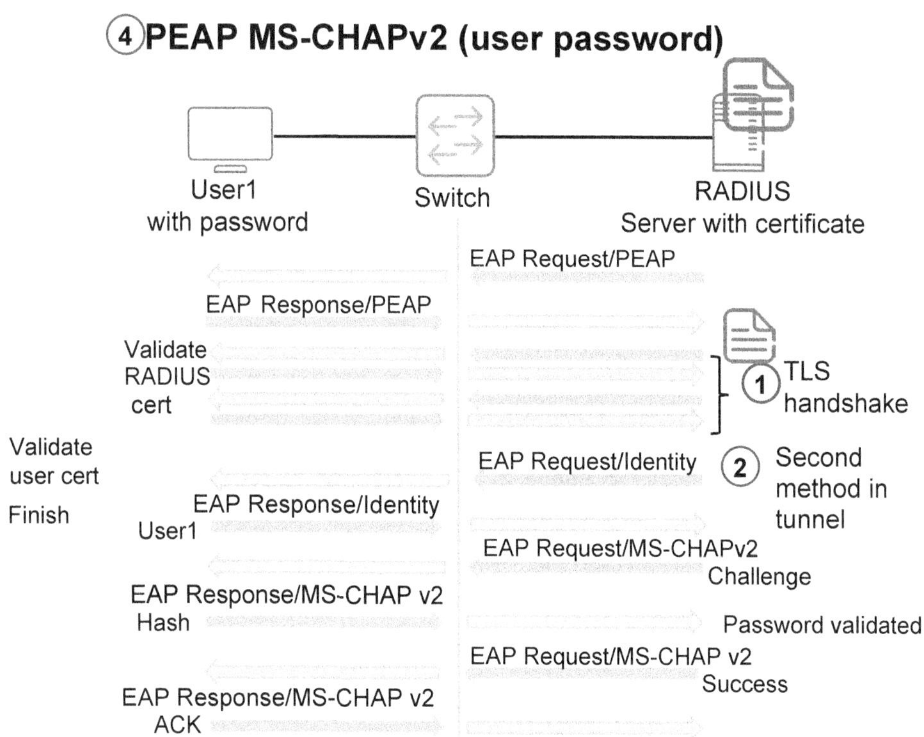


Figure 10-7 PEAP

### Step 1—outer method

Like EAP-TLS, TTLS and PEAP use a TLS handshake to generate encryption keys and negotiate a tunnel secured by those keys. Only the server authenticates itself with a digital certificate during this exchange, but you must ensure that the clients trust the CA that signed the server certificate. The encryption keys for the tunnel are derived from the public key in this certificate.

### Step 2—inner method

The client authenticates itself in the second step; it uses a weaker—and so more easily implemented—authentication method, protected by the secure tunnel in which it takes place.

The RADIUS server sends a new EAP Request/Identity packet and the supplicant responds with their true identity. The server then begins the inner authentication method.

For the inner authentication method, TTLS can use a weaker EAP method, such as EAP-GTC, or a legacy RADIUS method, such as Challenge Handshake Authentication Protocol (CHAP), Password Authentication Protocol (PAP), or Microsoft CHAP variants (MS-CHAP v1 or MS-CHAP v2). PEAP supports methods such as MS-CHAP v2, EAP-Generic Token Card (EAP-GTC), and TLS. Because Windows native supplicants support PEAPv0 with MS-CHAP v2, this is by far the most prevalent EAP method.

Figure 10-7 shows the MS-CHAP v2 method. The RADIUS server sends a challenge. The supplicant responds with a hash of the password. The server validates that the hash is correct, and, if so, it sends a message indicating the success. The supplicant responds.

Again, remember that Figure 10-7 shows just the PEAP part of the complete 802.1X authentication process. After these messages, the tunnel is taken down, and the RADIUS server sends a RADIUS Access-Accept to the switch.

---

**Note**

For 802.1X on wireless connections, whether implemented through EAP-TLS, EAP-TTLS, or PEAP, the authentication server sends the authenticator the encryption material. The wireless client and authenticator continue to use encryption to secure the connection. On Ethernet connections, however, the client and switch port to do not encrypt traffic in this way.

---

### Advantages

Like EAP-TLS, EAP-TTLS and PEAP provide strong, mutual authentication. Because TTLS and PEAP use encrypted tunnels to secure usernames and passwords (rather than require digital certificates on stations), you can implement these methods more easily than you can TLS.

TTLS has one unique benefit—it always protects the username. Depending on how PEAP is implemented, the username might be transmitted in plain text in the initial EAP/Response Identity packet, allowing a hacker to detect the user's identity and possibly lock the user out of his or her account.

### Disadvantages

As compared to EAP-TLS, EAP-TTLS and PEAP have the disadvantage of a weaker authentication method.

## Choosing an EAP method

When choosing an EAP method, you must always consider if both the supplicant and the server support the method (see Figure 10-8). EAP-TTLS tends to be less widely supported. For example, Microsoft Windows does not support TTLS natively; you must install additional software to provide this support.

- Consider:
  - Supported methods on client and RADIUS server
  - Security needs
  - Ease of implementation

| EAP method | RADIUS server certificate | Supplicant certificate |
|---|---|---|
| EAP-TLS | Yes | Yes |
| EAP-TTLS | Yes | No |
| PEAP MS -CHAPv2 | Yes | No |

Figure 10-8 Choosing an EAP method

The AOS-Switch, as the authenticator, simply encapsulates and decapsulates the EAP messages, which it can do for any valid method.

---

**Note**

AOS-Switches can act as 802.1X supplicants and authenticate to an upstream switch. You can also configure local authentication for 802.1X and have the switch act as the authentication server. In these two cases, you would need to consider the EAP methods that the switch supports. However, this study guide does not cover these use cases. Check the documentation for more details.

---

You should also keep in mind the level of security that you require. EAP-TLS tends to be the most secure choice because users authenticate with secure digital certificates. On the other hand, many enterprises prefer PEAP or EAP-TTLS because usernames and passwords provide enough security for their purposes. They value the easier of implementation of PEAP or EAP-TTLS with an inner method such as MS-CHAP v2.

Note that, although some EAP methods do not require client certificates, EAP-TLS, EAP-TTLS, and PEAP all require a certificate on the RADIUS server.

The server uses this certificate to authenticate to the clients and generate key material for the secure TLS tunnel. System administrators should make sure to install a valid certificate, signed by a trusted CA, on the RADIUS server. If they choose to use a self-signed certificate on the RADIUS server, they should install that certificate as trusted on client. Or they could configure the clients to prompt users to validate an untrusted certificate on the first connection.

---

**Note**

EAP-TTLS and PEAP could use TLS as an inner method, which would require a supplicant certificate. However, this is not a typical implementation.

---

## 802.1X configuration

Next, you will look at configuring 802.1X on an AOS-Switch.

### Specifying the RADIUS server

Before you enable 802.1X on a switch, you must set up the authentication server that the switch will use. You can define the RADIUS server with this command:

```
Switch(config)# radius-server host <IP address> [key <secret>]
```

As Figure 10-9 shows, the switch will then send a RADIUS Access-Request to this IP address whenever it needs to complete any form of authentication that uses RADIUS as its type. By default, the switch uses the RADIUS standard UDP port 1812 for the authentication messages. After the RADIUS server has authorized a user for access, the switch can continue to communicate information about the user session in accounting packets sent to port 1813.

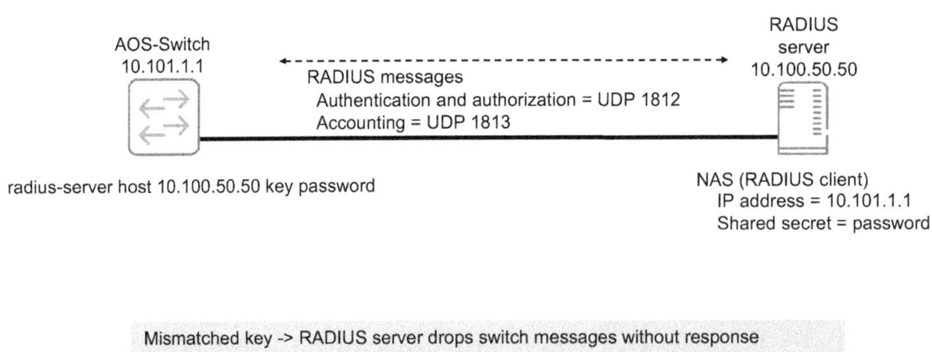


Figure 10-9 Specifying the RADIUS server

You will learn how to configure the switch to use RADIUS for authenticating and accounting 802.1X users in a moment.

**Note**

You can also include the option **auth-port** and **acct-port** options in the **radius-server host** command to change the authentication and accounting ports. You can add a number of other options, which are documented in the switch *Access Security* guide.

### Key or shared secret

The key option in the **radius-server host** command sets an individual shared secret for communicating with the RADIUS server. The RADIUS server has the switch IP address configured on it as a RADIUS client (sometimes called NAS or, on ClearPass, a network device). The shared secret configured for the switch on the RADIUS server must match the key configured for the RADIUS server on the switch. Otherwise, the RADIUS server will not respond to the switch's messages.

Setting the key for the individual server is optional if you set a global key. An individual key configured for a host overrides the global key, but if you do not set an individual key, the RADIUS server uses the global key. You might choose to use the global key if you have multiple RADIUS servers that use the same shared secret. The command for setting a global key is:

```
Switch(config)# radius-server key <secret>
```

## Managing multiple RADIUS servers and RADIUS groups

You can specify up to 15 RADIUS servers with the **radius-server host** command. Companies deploy multiple RADIUS servers to provide redundancy (see Figure 10-10).

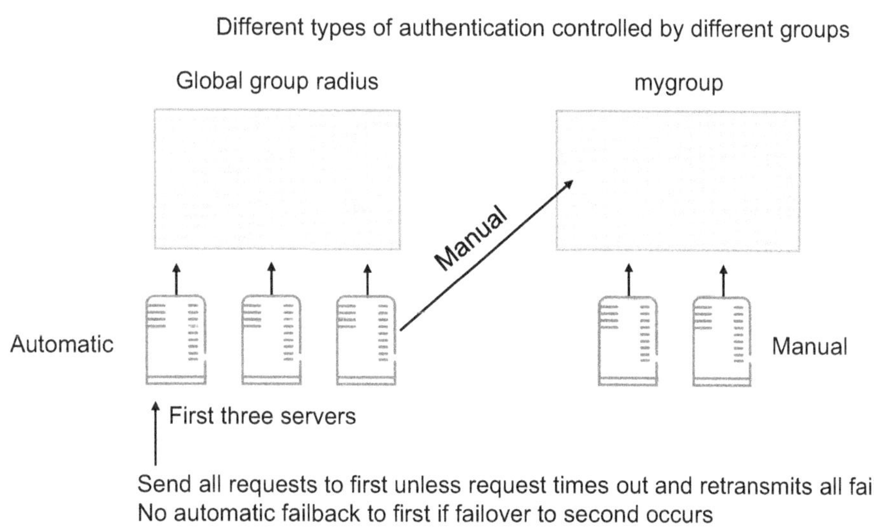


Figure 10-10 Managing multiple RADIUS servers and RADIUS groups

## Global RADIUS server group

The first three servers that you add are automatically added to the global RADIUS server group, which is called **radius**. The switch uses this group, by default, for all types of authentication for which you have enabled RADIUS.

For example, you enter this command to enable RADIUS authentication for 802.1X:

```
Switch(config)# aaa authentication port-access eap-radius
```

Now the switch uses the global **radius** group to authenticate users who connect to ports with 802.1X enabled on them.

Although you can add up to 15 RADIUS servers, only the first three are added to the **radius** group. Other RADIUS servers are only available for use if you create a new RADIUS server group and add them to it. You can see which RADIUS servers are part of the **radius** group with these commands:

```
Switch(config)# show radius
Switch(config)# show server-group radius
```

You cannot edit the **radius** server group. If you want different servers to be part of this group, you must delete the servers that are currently part of the group. For example, you have entered four RADIUS servers, 10.1.10.11, 10.1.10.12, 10.1.10.13, and 10.1.10.14. The first three are in the **radius** group, but you want 10.1.10.14 to be in the group instead of 10.1.10.13. You must delete 10.1.10.13. You can then re-add 10.1.10.13 and use it in different server groups.

## Other RADIUS server groups

This chapter focuses on 802.1X authentication. However, AOS-Switches can use RADIUS with other types of authentication such as captive portal and the authentication of Telnet, SSH, or web UI managers.

When you want to use different RADIUS servers for different types of authentication, you need to place those servers in different RADIUS server groups.

You must first define the RADIUS server. You can then add it to a group. There is no command for creating a group. Instead, the first time that you add a server to a group with a new name, the switch creates the group and adds the specified server to it.

The command for adding a RADIUS server to a new or existing server group is:

```
Switch(config)# aaa server-group radius <group name> host <IP address>
```

Use the **no** form of the command to delete the server from the group. Each group can have up to three RADIUS servers.

A RADIUS server can be part of more than one group. If, for example, you add a server that is part of the **radius** server group to a new group, the server remains part of the **radius** group, as well.

Therefore, you should define the servers that you want to use for the global group *before* adding the servers for the other groups. Otherwise, the servers that you intend for other groups will take up the slots in the global **radius** group.

To use the new RADIUS server group, you must choose the type of authentication to which it applies. Use this command to specify a server group for 802.1X authentication:

```
Switch(config)# aaa authentication port-access eap-radius server-group
<group name>
```

## How the switch handles requests to groups with multiple servers

When a RADIUS server group has multiple servers, the switch does *not* load balance requests to different servers. Instead, it sends all requests to the first server in the group that it successfully accesses. It uses the other servers as backups in case it cannot reach the first server.

For this reason, you should prepare before adding RADIUS servers to your switch and enable 802.1X. Ensure that the switch has connectivity to the RADIUS servers, and the RADIUS servers are configured to accept messages from it. You should then add the RADIUS servers in the order in which you want the switch to use them.

You can see the order in which the switch will attempt to access RADIUS servers in a particular group by entering the **show server-group radius** <*name*> command. The order is generally based on the order in which you specify the servers; you can specify different servers first on different switches for rudimentary load sharing of requests on a switch-wide basis. The switch first attempts to access the server at the top of the list. If the first server does not respond after a certain timeout and number of retransmit attempts, the switch will try to contact the next RADIUS server.

For example, the default timeout is 5 seconds and the default retransmit setting is 3. After 20 seconds, the switch determines that the RADIUS server is not available. The switch then tries to reach the next RADIUS server in the list. If the switch cannot reach that RADIUS server either, after 20 seconds, it tries the next server on the list. If the switch cannot reach any of the servers, it tries the first server in the list again.

However, you can configure the switch to wait a set period after the last failed retransmit to a particular server before attempting to communicate with that server again. You might do this to prevent a switch from endlessly attempting to send RADIUS packets during a network outage. This period is called the dead time.

These are global settings that apply to all RADIUS servers and groups. You can adjust the timeout (in seconds), the number of retransmits, and the dead time (in minutes) with these commands:

```
Switch(config)# radius-server timeout <1-15>

Switch(config)# radius-server retransmit <1-5>

Switch(config)# radius-server dead-time <1-1440>
```

If you want to return the switch to not imposing a dead-time, use this command:

```
Switch(config)# no radius-server dead-time
```

## Ensuring compatibility with ClearPass

When you use Aruba ClearPass as the RADIUS server, it is recommended that you add a few settings to ensure that the AOS-Switch interoperates with the ClearPass RADIUS server correctly (see Figure 10-11).

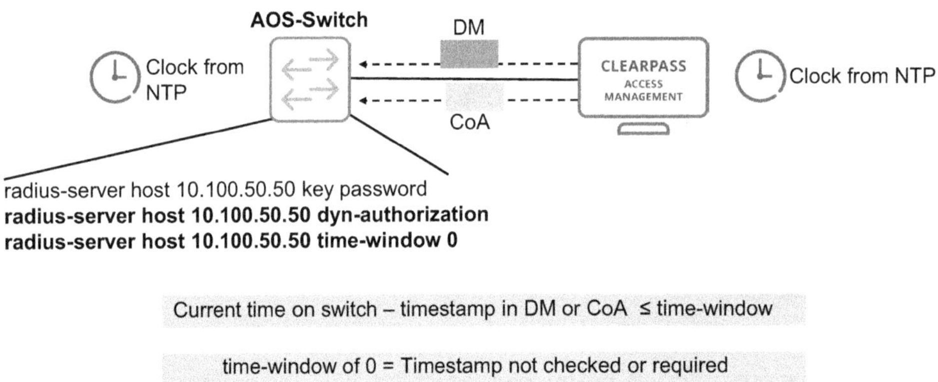


Figure 10-11 Ensuring compatibility with ClearPass

### Enabling acceptance of change of authorization messages

Aruba ClearPass can assess endpoints on an ongoing basis and change an endpoint's authentication status or settings. To make these changes, ClearPass sends disconnect messages (DMs) and change of authorization (CoA) messages. For the switch to accept these messages, you must enable dynamic authorization for the RADIUS server:

```
Switch(config)# radius-server host <IP address> dyn-authorization
```

If you do not include this option, some components of the solution might work, but others will fail.

If dyn-authorization is enabled, the switch accepts these messages on the default UDP port 3799, which is also the default port on ClearPass. You can change that setting, if necessary, in your environment:

```
Switch(config)# radius-server dyn-autz-port <number>
```

If you are using a different RADIUS server from ClearPass, you should check whether the server needs to send DMs and CoA messages.

### Setting the time window

Even when an AOS-Switch is configured to allow CoA and DM messages, it checks these messages to determine if they are current. The message should include a time stamp for the event that caused the RADIUS server to change the user status. The switch only accepts the message if the time between the time stamp and the current time on the switch falls within its RADIUS time window.

The default time window is 300 seconds. You can adjust the time window with this command:

```
Switch(config)# radius-server host <IP address> time-window <0-65535>
```

To ensure that the switch can accept the CoA and DM messages, make sure that the switch has the correct time. It is best practice to configure Network Time Protocol (NTP) on the switch and the RADIUS server and have them take their time from the same clock.

You must also determine whether the RADIUS server always includes a time stamp with its DM and CoA messages. ClearPass does not. Therefore, you must disable the time window check by setting the window to 0:

```
Switch(config)# radius-server host <IP address> time-window 0
```

## Viewing the RADIUS settings on AOS-Switches

To view the RADIUS settings on AOS-Switches, enter this command; example output is provided below:

```
Switch# show radius

 Status and Counters - General RADIUS Information

  Deadtime (minutes)              : 0
  Timeout (seconds)               : 5
  Retransmit Attempts             : 3
  Global Encryption Key           :

  Dynamic Authorization UDP Port  : 3799
  Source IP Selection             : 10.101.1.2
  Source IPv6 Selection           : Outgoing Interface
  Tracking                        : Disabled

                  Auth  Acct  DM/ Time    |
 Server IP Addr   Port  Port  CoA Window  | + Encryption Key       OOBM
 --------------   ----  ----  --- ------ - ---------------------- ----
 10.100.50.50     1812  1813  Yes 300     | password               No
```

Notice the Acct Port in this output. You will learn how to enable RADIUS accounting in the "Enable RADIUS accounting for 802.1X section."

To view the RADIUS statistics for the RADIUS server, enter the following command:

```
Access-1(config)# show radius host 10.100.50.50

 Status and Counters - RADIUS Server Information

  Server IP Addr : 10.100.50.50

  Authentication UDP Port : 1812          Accounting UDP Port   : 1813
  Round Trip Time         : 0             Round Trip Time       : 0
  Pending Requests        : 0             Pending Requests      : 0
  Retransmissions         : 0             Retransmissions       : 0
  Timeouts                : 0             Timeouts              : 0
  Malformed Responses     : 0             Malformed Responses   : 0
  Bad Authenticators      : 0             Bad Authenticators    : 0
  Unknown Types           : 0             Unknown Types         : 0
  Packets Dropped         : 1             Packets Dropped       : 0
  Access Requests         : 35            Accounting Requests   : 11
  Access Challenges       : 31            Accounting Responses  : 11
  Access Accepts          : 3
  Access Rejects          : 0
```

If you see an Access-Reject, you can monitor the session in the RADIUS server to why it is rejecting the authentication. If you see neither Rejects nor Accepts, the RADIUS server is dropping the switch's RADIUS messages, most likely because the secret is incorrect. In this case, you may want to try reconfiguring the password.

## Enabling 802.1X

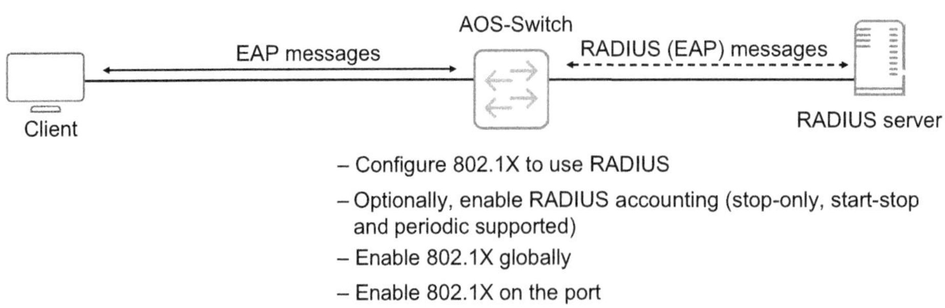


Figure 10-12 Enabling 802.1X

After you have specified the RADIUS server, you can configure 802.1X. Figure 10-12 outlines the process of configuring 802.1X on AOS-Switches.

## Enable RADIUS for 802.1X

First, specify that you want to use RADIUS authentication with 802.1X using this command:

```
Switch(config)# aaa authentication port-access eap-radius
```

This command tells the switch to use the first RADIUS server defined with the **radius-server host** command to authenticate 802.1X users.

## Enable RADIUS accounting for 802.1X

If you want to enable RADIUS accounting for 802.1X, enter this command:

```
Switch(config)# aaa accounting network <stop-only | start-stop> radius
```

RADIUS accounting takes effect after a user successfully authenticates. The switch then creates a session for the user, defining the network access that the user is provided. If you selected start–stop, the switch sends a start accounting message to the RADIUS server when the session begins. With either stop-only or start–stop, the switch sends a message when the session ends (because the user disconnects or the session times out, for example). These messages include a number of standard RADIUS attributes that describe the user's identity (User-Name), location (NAS-IP-Address and NAS-Port), and bandwidth consumption (Acct-Output-Packets and Acct-Input-Packets), as well as other information.

For more detailed session tracking, you can configure the switch to send periodic accounting messages during the session:

```
Switch(config)# aaa accounting update periodic <minutes>
```

Refer to your AOS-Switch manual's list of network accounting attributes for a complete list of the RADIUS accounting attributes that it supports for 802.1X.

## Enable 802.1X

You enable 802.1X on a per-interface basis with this command:

```
Switch(config)# aaa port-access authenticator <port ID list>
```

However, the switch does not actually enforce 802.1X on the specified interfaces until you also enable 802.1X globally.

```
Switch(config)# aaa port-access authenticator active
```

Now the switch will act as described earlier. It will keep the port closed to all non-EAP traffic and send EAP messages to trigger an 802.1X supplicant on the connected device to authenticate. If the user succeeds in authenticating to the RADIUS server, the switch opens the port for normal traffic. If the user fails, the port remains closed.

To view the 802.1X status, enter the following command. In this example, the untagged VLAN is currently unassigned because no client has authenticated yet.

```
Switch# show port-access authenticator
 Port Access Authenticator Status

  Port-access authenticator activated [No] : Yes
  Allow RADIUS-assigned dynamic (GVRP) VLANs [No] : No
  Use LLDP data to authenticate [No] : No
        Auths/  Unauth  Untagged Tagged             % In  RADIUS Cntrl
  Port  Guests  Clients VLAN     VLANs  Port COS    Limit ACL    Dir   Port Mode
  ----- ------- ------- -------- ------ ---------   ----- ------ ----- ---------
  1/1   0/0     1       None     No     No          No    No     both  1000FDx
```

## Customizing authenticated users' access

Beyond the security benefits, port-based authentication such as 802.1X helps network administrators to provision the network edge more quickly. Traditionally, administrators had to configure each port with the appropriate settings for the user who connected to that port. If a user moved, the user might not receive the correct settings without a great deal of effort on the administrator's part.

With 802.1X, the RADIUS server, together with the switch acting as the NAS, have already determined the user's identity as well as other characteristics of the connection, such as the time and location. A RADIUS server policy can use this information to choose the appropriate settings for the connection. The network edge as a whole becomes more flexible and adaptable.

Examples of customized settings include:

- VLAN
- ACL
- Class of Service (CoS), or 802.1p, priority value
- Rate limits (inbound and outbound)

A CoS value tells the switch to give packets from the user a specific priority in forwarding. Generally, the higher the priority value, the higher the priority. However, 802.1p values 1 and 2 have a lower priority than 0, which is used for normal traffic. Rate limits restrict the amount of bandwidth that the user is allowed to send (inbound) or receive (outbound). You will examine the Quality of Service (QoS) priority and rate limits in more detail in *Chapter 15: Quality of Service.*

Because the switch applies these settings to a user session automatically, as dictated by the RADIUS server, these settings are sometimes called RADIUS settings or dynamic settings. For example, a dynamic VLAN assignment is the VLAN assigned to a user session by the RADIUS server when the user authenticates to the network. A dynamic ACL is the (port-based) ACL applied to a user session by the RADIUS server when the user authenticates, and so on.

## How the RADIUS server sends dynamic settings

A RADIUS server such as ClearPass has policies that define the dynamic settings that apply to certain users based on those users' identities and other conditions. As Figure 10-13 shows, the server communicates the dynamic settings to the switch acting as the NAS in Attribute Value Pairs (AVPs) within the RADIUS-Accept message. The switch then applies the AVPs as settings to control the user's traffic.

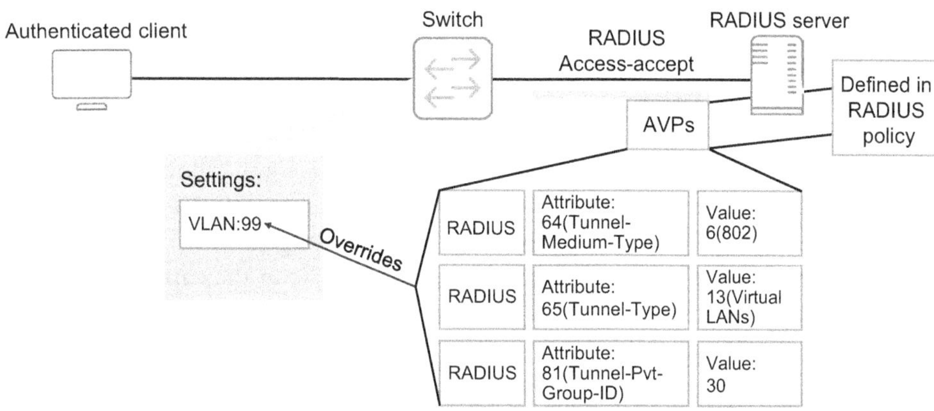


Figure 10-13 How the RADIUS server sends dynamic settings

**Note**

Figure 10-13 shows the dynamic VLAN overriding the static untagged VLAN on the port, which is a good approximation of the behavior when a single device connects to the port. You will learn about exactly how the switch applies the VLAN in more detail later.

Even if you are not in charge of setting up the RADIUS server, it can be useful for you to understand the AVPs behind the settings so that you can coordinate with those who are.

1. Refer to Table 10-1 to find the attribute name or code for the parameter that you want to set. (Table 10-1 presents the AVPs supported by AOS-Switches as of the publication of this study guide; however, you should double-check the guide for your own switches.)

   AVPs fall in several general categories—standard RADIUS, extended RADIUS, and vendor specific. When possible, you should use standard RADIUS attributes because they are supported by many vendors. Depending on the software version, AOS-Switches might support multiple attributes for some settings. Generally, earlier software used vendor-specific attributes while the more up-to-date software added standard RADIUS attributes for applying the same setting. Aruba recommends that you typically use the standard RADIUS setting, and only use the vendor-specific one if you need to accommodate a legacy solution.

   As you see, RADIUS defines two ways to specify a dynamic VLAN. Typically, RADIUS servers send the dynamic untagged VLAN assignment with the Tunnel-Type, Tunnel-Medium-Type, and Tunnel-Private-Group-ID AVPs. Egress-VLANID and Egress-VLAN-Name AVPs are usually used for tagged traffic.

2. Determine the appropriate value for the AVP to set the parameter as required in your environment. The final column provides guidelines. For example, this column for the ACL parameter indicates the proper syntax for an ACL.

   Keep a few guidelines in mind when coordinating the value for a dynamic VLAN with ClearPass administrators. The Tunnel-Private-Group-ID can be a VLAN ID or a name. You might use the name option to simplify policies in a large or multisite network. For example, switches in one building might name VLAN 10 "Students" while switches in another building name VLAN 11 "Students." The RADIUS server could use a single policy to assign students to the "Students" VLAN with the Egress-VLAN-Name AVP. The switch through which the individual student authenticated would then assign the student's untagged traffic to the correct VLAN ID associated with the "Students" name on that switch.

   Be very careful, though, that the name in the attribute matches the name of a VLAN on the switch; names are case sensitive. Similarly, a VLAN ID must match a VLAN on the switch. If the RADIUS server sends a VLAN name or ID that does not exist on the switch, the switch does *not* apply the port's static VLAN to the user session. Instead, the authentication fails—much as it would if the user entered an incorrect password.

   The switch should also have the dynamic VLAN set up, either already statically tagged on its uplinks or configured with IP settings. Otherwise, the switch cannot forward the user traffic to the rest of the network.

3. Provide the AVPs to the RADIUS administrator. For each AVP, include the attribute name (or code) and value.

   Make sure that the RADIUS server supports these AVPs. Also make sure that the administrators know to define the vendor-specific AVPs, when required.

Table 10-1 RADIUS attributes

<table>
<tr><th>Setting</th><th>AVP type</th><th>Attribute name and code</th><th>Value</th></tr>
<tr><td rowspan="3">VLAN (untagged)</td><td rowspan="3">Standard RADIUS</td><td>Tunnel-Medium-Type (64)</td><td>802 (6)</td></tr>
<tr><td>Tunnel-Type (65)</td><td>Virtual LANs (13)</td></tr>
<tr><td>Tunnel-Private-Group-ID (81)</td><td>VLAN ID or name string</td></tr>
<tr><td>VLAN (untagged or tagged)</td><td>Standard RADIUS</td><td>Egress-VLANID (56)</td><td>VLAN ID string</td></tr>
<tr><td>VLAN (untagged or tagged)</td><td>Standard RADIUS</td><td>Egress-VLAN-Name (58)</td><td>VLAN name string</td></tr>
<tr><td>Inbound PACL (IPv4 and IPv6)</td><td>Standard RADIUS</td><td>NAS-Filter-Rule (92)</td><td><permit | deny> in <ip | protocol_number> from <any / IP_address / IP_address/ PrefixLength> to <any / IP_address / IP_address/ PrefixLength> [TCP/UDP port list / ICMPtype] [cnt]<br>cnt tells the switch to count the number of packets that match the rule.</td></tr>
<tr><td>Inbound PACL<br>(IPv4 only or IPv4 and IPv6)<br>Legacy attribute not typically recommended</td><td>Vendor specific<br>HP = 11</td><td>NAS-Filter-Rule (61)</td><td><permit | deny> in <ip | protocol_number> from <any / IP_address / IP_address/ PrefixLength> to <any / IP_address / IP_address/ PrefixLength> [TCP/UDP port list / ICMPtype] [cnt]</td></tr>
<tr><td>Setting for the type of ACL defined with HP VSA 61<br>Legacy attribute not typically recommended</td><td>Vendor specific<br>HP = 11</td><td>HP-NAS-Rules-IPv6 (63)</td><td>1 | 2<br>1 = ACL defined with AVP 61 applies to IPv4 and IPv6 traffic<br>2 = ACL defined with AVP 61 applies only to IPv4 traffic</td></tr>
</table>

(Continued)

Table 10-1 RADIUS attributes—cont'd

| Setting | AVP type | Attribute name and code | Value |
|---|---|---|---|
| Class of service (CoS) priority (802.1p) | Standard RADIUS | User-Priority-Table (59) | X0X1X2X3X4X5X6X7, in which Xn = priority to which traffic with n priority is mapped.<br>For example, this setting configures the switch to apply priority 5 to all user traffic:<br>55555555<br>Enter the same value for every space |
| CoS priority (802.1p)<br>Legacy attribute not typically recommended | Vendor specific<br>HP = 11 | 40 | X0X1X2X3X4X5X6X7, in which Xn = priority to which traffic with n priority is mapped. |
| Ingress rate limit | Vendor-specific<br>HP = 11 | 46 | HP-Bandwidth-Max-<br>Egress = <Kbps> |
| Egress rate limit (most recent assignment applies to the port as a whole) | Vendor-specific<br>HP = 11 | 48 | HP-RATE-LIMIT = <Kbps> |

## How dynamic port ACLs are applied

Figure 10-13 showed the dynamic settings overriding the static ones. However, the behavior is a bit different for dynamic port ACLs.

As Figure 10-14 shows, dynamic port ACL consists of a series of AVPs sent by the RADIUS server. When the server authenticates the client, the ACL is assigned as an *inbound* ACL on the port. Like any PACL, the ACL filters both switched and router traffic. However, the dynamic ACL only applies to traffic with that user's source MAC address. When the client session ends, the ACL is removed from the port. (The switch allows as many dynamic port ACLs on a port as it allows authenticated clients.)

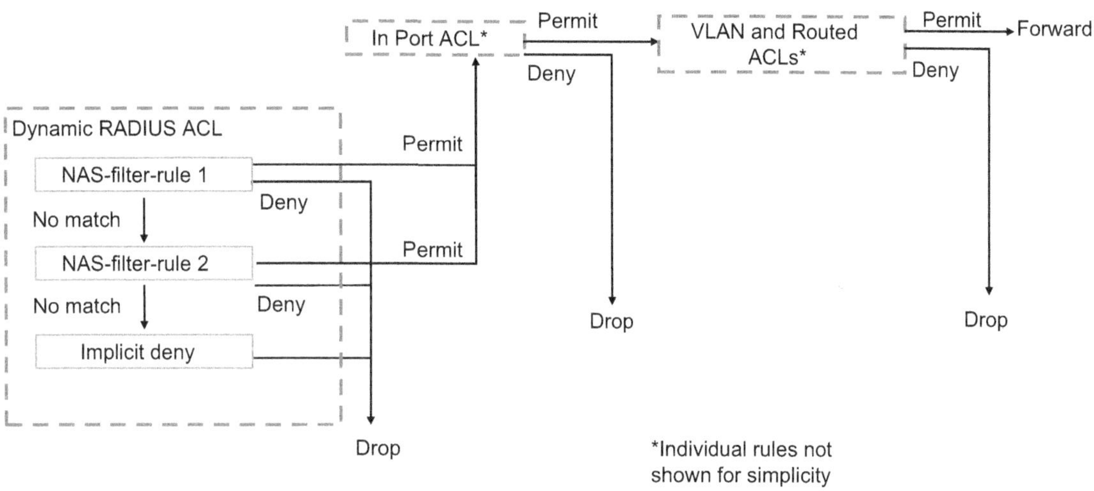


Figure 10-14 How dynamic port ACLs are applied

The dynamic port ACL is essentially an IP extended ACL. The dynamic rules can select traffic by source IP address and destination IP address. It can select all IP traffic or IP traffic of a certain protocol such as TCP or UDP. And it can also select traffic based on its TCP or UDP port or Internet Control Message Protocol (ICMP) type.

You should understand that the dynamic ACL does not replace a static ACL applied to the port, but instead adds to it.

When the switch receives traffic from the user device, it matches the traffic to the first NAS-Filter-Rule (AVP 92) in the list sent by the RADIUS server. If the packet matches the rule, the switch applies the action. If it does not match the rule, the switch checks the packet against the next rule, and so on. If a rule denied the packet, the switch drops it. If a rule permitted the packet, the User ACL permits it to be forwarded. However, if the port also has a static port ACL, the switch then filters the permitted packet again with the static port ACL.

Note that NAS-Filter-Rules have an implicit deny at the end, so if the packet does not match any rules, the switch drops the packet. If you want to change this behavior, remember to tell RADIUS administrators to add a **permit in ip from any to any** rule at the end.

AOS-Switches have hardware resources for applying dynamic ACLs. However, if the RADIUS server applies many long ACLs to many users, a switch's TCAM might begin to fill up. In this case, you might want to apply most rules as an inbound Routed Access Control List (RACL) or a VLAN ACL (VACL). Then you can apply particular rules with a dynamic port ACL.

Remember, though, that the switch will process traffic against every ACL in the packet's path. If any of those rules denies the packet—even if an earlier rule explicitly permitted the packet—the switch drops the packet. For this reason, you should make the inbound RACLs or VACLs as permissive as required for any user group to which they might apply. Then use deny rules in dynamic ACLs to restrict users' rights, as necessary, remembering to add a **permit in ip from any to any** rule at the end.

---

**Note**

This study guide focuses on IPv4; however, dynamic port ACLs can also filter IPv6 traffic. When you use the standard RADIUS attribute (92), rules that specify IPv4 addresses filter IPv4 traffic, and rules that specify IPv6 traffic filter IPv6 traffic. If a rule specifies **any** for an address, it filters both IPv4 and IPv6 traffic. If you want to match only any IPv4 traffic, specify **0.0.0.0/0** instead of **any**. (Similarly, **::/0** specifies any IPv6 address.)

If you use the legacy HP vendor-specific attribute (VSA) (61) on its own, the dynamic port ACL filters only IPv4 traffic, and it drops all IPv6 traffic. You can use HP VSA 63 to change this behavior, though. When HP VSA 63 is set to 1, the rules specified with HP VSA 61 apply to both IPv4 and IPv6 traffic, as described for standard RADIUS ACL rules. When HP VSA 63 is set to 2, the rules specified with HP VSA 61 apply only to IPv4 traffic and IPv6 traffic is dropped.

---

## Applying dynamic settings with Aruba ClearPass

Although you do not need to understand how to set up ClearPass to assign dynamic settings, it can be useful for you to understand how it works at a high-level so that you can better coordinate with ClearPass administrators.

ClearPass uses services to define how to authenticate users. The service can use the local ClearPass database, but ClearPass can also authenticate users to Lightweight Directory Access Protocol (LDAP) servers such as Microsoft Active Directory (AD).

The service also authorizes users. ClearPass uses roles and profiles to enforce the authorization. Every local user has a role such as "Employee" or "Guest," and ClearPass can also map users authenticated to other sources to roles. The profiles define how you want to control authenticated users. A profile states whether ClearPass Accepts or Rejects the user's Access-Request. It also defines the AVPs, such as those for a dynamic VLAN or ACL, that apply to accepted users' sessions.

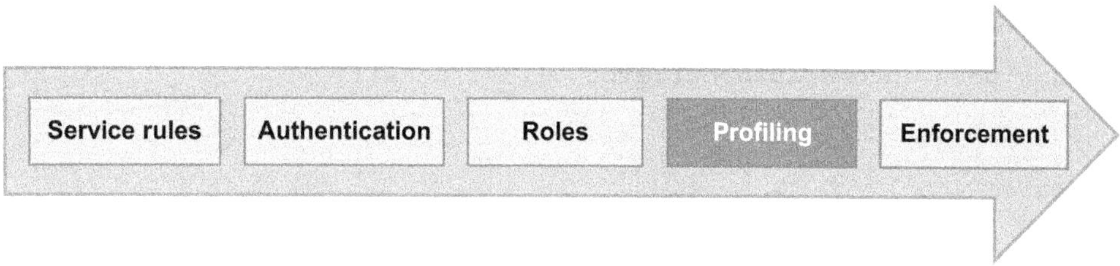


Figure 10-15 Applying dynamic settings with Aruba ClearPass

As Figure 10-15 shows, the service uses a policy to map user roles to profiles. The service also defines a default profile that applies to any user to which none of the rules apply.

ClearPass has a service wizard that helps administrators put together all of the pieces of a policy easily, including configuring the correct AVPs for a dynamic VLAN assignment based on the type of switches acting as authenticators.

## Viewing dynamic settings

You can see the dynamic settings applied to a session with this command:

```
Switch# show port-access authenticator 1/1
Port Access Authenticator Status

  Port-access authenticator activated [No] : Yes
  Allow RADIUS-assigned dynamic (GVRP) VLANs [No] : No
  Use LLDP data to authenticate [No] : No

        Auths/  Unauth  Untagged Tagged              % In  RADIUS Cntrl
  Port  Guests  Clients VLAN     VLANs  Port COS     Limit ACL    Dir   Port Mode
  ----- ------- ------- -------- ------ ---------    ----- ------ ----- ----------
  1/1   1/0     0       30       No     44444444     No    Yes    both  1000FDx
```

You can see more details about the settings for a client with this command:

```
Switch# show port-access authenticator client detail

Port Access Client Status Detail

  Client Base Details :

   Port             : 1/1                Authentication Type : 802.1X
   Client Status    : authenticated      Session Time        : 131 seconds
   Client Name      : 005056973668       Session Timeout     : 0 seconds
   MAC Address      : 005056-973668
   IP               : n/a

  Access Policy Details :

   COS Map          : Not Defined       In Limit Kbps       : Not Set
   Untagged VLAN    : 30                Out Limit Kbps      : Not Set
   Tagged VLANs     : No Tagged VLANs
   Port Mode        : 1000FDx
   RADIUS ACL List :
      deny in ip from any to 10.100.30.0/24 cnt
      permit in ip from any to any

  Captive Portal Details :

   URL              :
```

Also note that, if you enter the **show vlan ports** command for the port enforcing 802.1X, the untagged VLAN dynamically assigned to the port is displayed, rather than the static VLAN.

You can see the dynamic ACLs that are currently applied on the switch with this command:

```
Switch# show access-list radius 1/1


Radius-configured Port-based ACL for
Port 1/1, Client -- 005056-973668


IPv6 ACLs enabled (HP-Nas-Rules-Ipv6): FALSE
deny in ip from any to 10.100.30.0/24 cnt
  Packet Hit Counter 0
permit in ip from any to any
```

## Port-based mode

How an AOS-Switch establishes 802.1X sessions and applies settings to them depends on whether the port is operating in 802.1X port-based or user-based mode. By default, the port uses port-based mode. This mode is set by an undefined client limit (**no aaa port-access authenticator *<port ID list>* client-limit**).

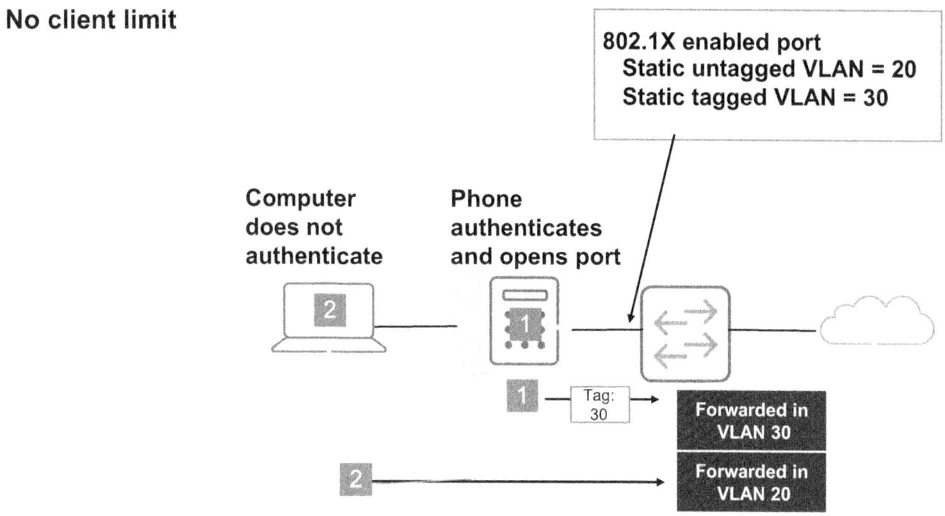


Figure 10-16 Port-based mode

With port-based control as shown in Figure 10-16, the switch establishes a *single* session for all traffic sent and received on the port. As long as any one user passes authentication, the switch permits *all* traffic without referring to the source or destination MAC address. Untagged traffic, regardless of source MAC, is forwarded in the untagged VLAN assigned to the port (either statically or through RADIUS, as you have learned). Any connected device is also allowed to send tagged traffic for any tagged VLAN on the port.

Often, only a single device connects to the switch port, so all traffic does originate from a single source MAC address. However, Figure 10-16 shows an example in which two devices connect on one port—an 802.1X-enabled VoIP phone and a computer. In this example, the phone has authenticated, but the user on the computer has not. However, the computer is still allowed to send its untagged traffic, which the switch assigns to the port's untagged VLAN.

## Additional examples of how port-based mode operates

An 802.1X-enabled interface might also connect to multiple devices if it connects to a hub or perhaps to a switch that does not know how to process EAPOL frames and simply floods them. Figure 10-17 shows how the port-based mode interface handles the traffic.

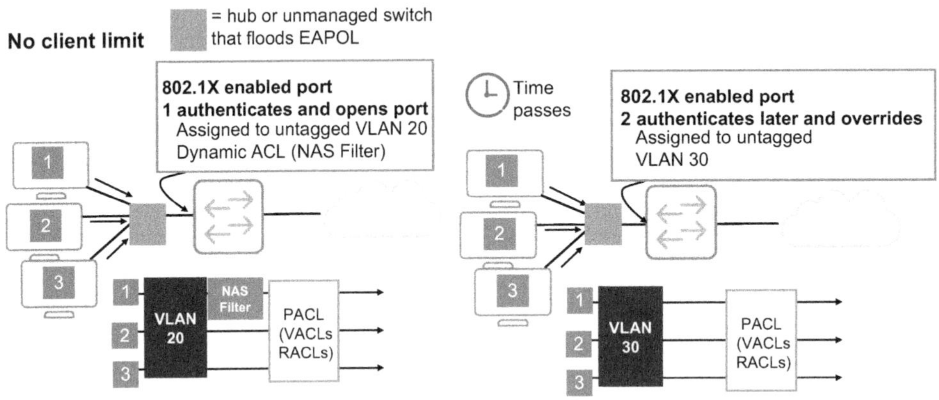

Figure 10-17 Additional examples of how port-based mode operates

The interface has a single untagged VLAN assignment, which is the static VLAN or the dynamic VLAN sent by the RADIUS server when the most recently authorized user authenticated. As you see in the example shown in Figure 10-17, user 1 has authenticated and been assigned to VLAN 20. User 2 and 3 have not authenticated, but they can also send traffic in VLAN 20.

On the other hand, AOS-Switches automatically bind a dynamic ACL to a user's MAC address, even when 802.1X operates in port-based mode on the interface. Therefore, unauthenticated devices can receive access, and their traffic is not filtered by the dynamic ACL. Any static port ACL (PACL) on the port applies to both the authenticated client and the unauthenticated ones—as do in VACLs or RACLs that would normally filter the devices' traffic.

Also keep in mind that if one of the unauthenticated devices authenticates, and the RADIUS server sends new dynamic settings, those new settings override the ones from the first device. This can cause connectivity issues, as the devices are moved to a new VLAN.

If only one device connects to the port at once, port-based mode can work well. But sometimes multiple devices connect to the same port. In these cases, port-based control introduces these potential issues:

- Unauthorized users gaining access to the network by "piggybacking" on the same connection as an authorized device
- Inconsistent dynamic settings
- Dynamic ACLs not controlling all incoming traffic

## User-based mode

User-based mode is recommended for scenarios in which you want the switch port itself to authenticate and control multiple clients. In particular, it is recommended for cases in which the RADIUS server might implement different dynamic settings for different clients. But you should also often enable user-based control even when the port should only connect to a single device to prevent unauthorized devices from "piggybacking" on the port.

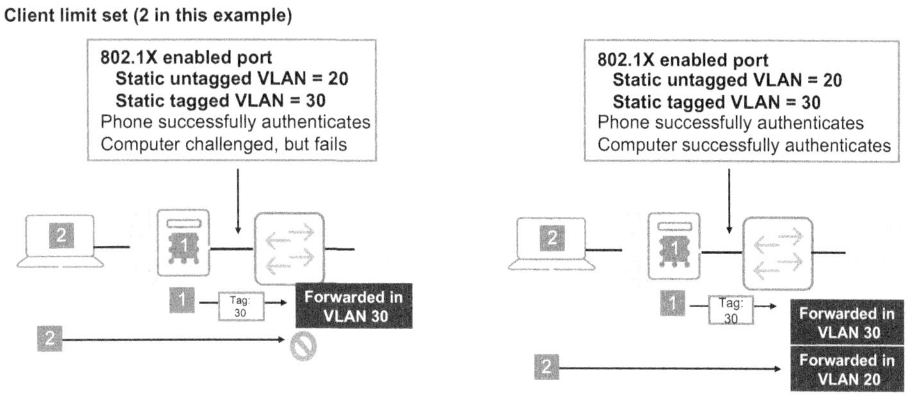


Figure 10-18 User-based mode

As Figure 10-18 shows, in user-based mode, the port authenticates *each* downstream device, as identified by source MAC address. You enable this mode when you set the client limit on the port to any value *including 1*.

```
Switch(config)# aaa port-access authenticator <port ID list> client-
limit <1-32>
```

The port now creates a separate session for each device, and each session has its own authorized status. In other words, the switch permits ingress traffic with a particular source MAC address only if that MAC address's session is authorized. Conversely, it permits egress traffic based on the destination MAC address's authorization status. The limit value indicates how many devices can be authorized.

After you set the limit, the port begins tracking MAC addresses and defines the authorization status and settings for each separately. For example, in the scenario with the computer and the VoIP phone, the switch port sends an EAP Request/Identity to each separate MAC address detected on the port. If the VoIP phone authenticates successfully, but the computer fails, the computer traffic is blocked.

## Additional examples of how user-based mode operates

In Figure 10-19, you see how user-based mode works in the second scenario, which has a client limit of two also for the sake of illustration. Initially, only user 1 has authenticated, so the switch drops user 2's and user 3's traffic. Then user 2 authenticates successfully, so the switch forwards that user's traffic. Now the limit is reached, so user 3 cannot authenticate until another user disconnects.

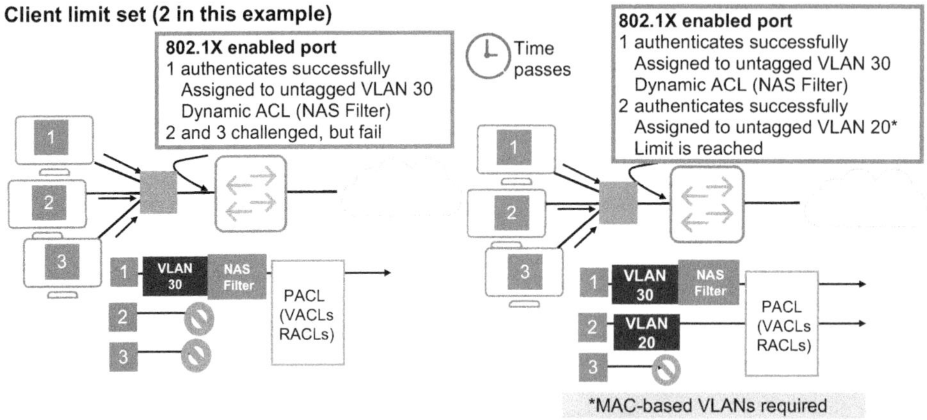


Figure 10-19 Additional examples of how user-based mode operates

The examples in Figure 10-19 also show how port-based mode allows each session to have its own dynamic attributes, such as VLAN and ACL.

In user-based mode, the dynamic VLAN applies to the user's device only. The switch forwards any untagged traffic sent by the user device in the dynamic VLAN. And when it needs to forward traffic to the device, it forwards the traffic without a tag. If the port supports multiple users, the users can have different untagged VLAN assignments. If any users do not receive a dynamic assignment, the static untagged VLAN applies to their traffic.

In the example shown in Figure 10-19, both user 1 and user 2 have authenticated and been assigned to different VLANs. The switch recognizes which user is sending traffic based on source MAC address and forwards the traffic in the correct VLAN.

Note that the switch must flood untagged traffic in all VLANs out of the port. This means that devices will receive broadcasts and multicasts for all untagged VLANs applied to the port. Keep this in mind when you plan multiclient scenarios.

---

**Important**

The switch port hardware must support MAC-based VLANs in order to assign different untagged VLANs to multiple clients connected concurrently. Support for MAC-based VLANs depends on the switch hardware. Newer AOS-Switches such as the 3800, 3810, and 2930 support this feature. The v2 and v3 modules on 5400R switches also support MAC-based VLANs.

If your switch does not support MAC-based VLANs, refer to its *Access Security* guide for more information on how it applies dynamic VLANs in user-based mode when multiple clients authenticate to the port.

---

By default, switches that support MAC-based VLANs automatically apply this feature to all ports, permitting multiple clients to authenticate and be assigned to different untagged VLANs. If you do not want to use this feature—perhaps because you do not want to allow the flooding of traffic in multiple VLANs on the port—enter this command:

```
Switch(config)# aaa port-access <interface ID list> mbv disable
```

If MAC-based VLANs are disabled on a port, the VLAN assigned to the port when the first client connects becomes the port's single untagged VLAN. If another client authenticates and is assigned to another VLAN, the new client's authentication fails.

To re-enable MAC-based authentication on ports, enter this command:

```
Switch(config)# aaa port-access <interface ID list> mbv enable
```

Here, you see an example of how the AOS-Switch tracks each device on the port separately when it operates in user-based mode. In this example, the "employee" user has authenticated on one device, but two other devices on the port have not authenticated.

```
Switch# show port-access client 1/1

 Port Access Client Status

  Port  Client Name   MAC Address       IP Address      User Role         Type  VLAN
  ----- ------------- ----------------- --------------- ----------------- ----- ----
  1/1   employee      005056-000114     n/a                               8021X 20
  1/1                 3822d6-069afb     n/a                               8021X
  1/1                 3822d6-069b2d     n/a                               8021X
```

Here, you see an example in which two users on different devices have authenticated on the same port. Each user has been assigned to a different VLAN, which works because MBVs are enabled.

```
Switch# show port-access client 1/1

 Port Access Client Status

  Port  Client Name   MAC Address       IP Address      User Role         Type  VLAN
  ----- ------------- ----------------- --------------- ----------------- ----- ----
  1/1   employee      005056-000114     n/a                               8021X 20
  1/1   accountant    005056-97362e     n/a                               8021X 30
  1/1                 3822d6-069afb     n/a                               8021X
  1/1                 3822d6-069b2d     n/a                               8021X
```

## User role-based authorization

You have learned how AOS-Switches can accept RADIUS VSAs to customize access for authenticated devices.

Some companies prefer to take a different approach. As Figure 10-20 shows, some companies might be using ClearPass to apply user roles to authenticated users based on their identities and other criteria. Aruba MCs, acting as RADIUS clients, use these roles to decide how to filter user traffic. Rather than create new profiles with the RADIUS VSAs for dynamic VLANs and ACLs, administrators might prefer to have ClearPass simply send a role to AOS-Switches too.

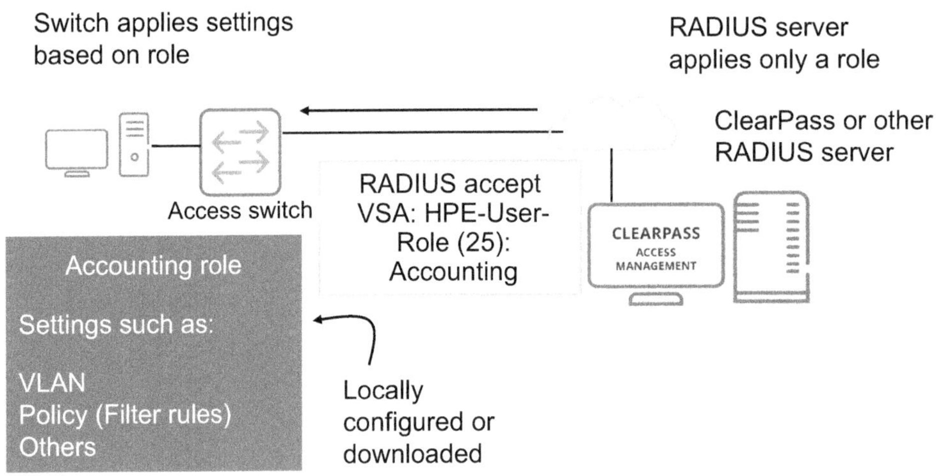


Figure 10-20 User role-based authorization

The VSA that AOS-Switches accept from RADIUS servers like ClearPass has these properties:

- Type: RADIUS vendor-specific for Hewlett Packard Enterprise
- Name: HPE-User-Role
- ID: 25
- Value: *<role name>*

For the switch to accept the user role, you must enable user role authorization globally with this command:

```
Switch(config)# aaa authorization user-role enable
```

When the switch applies the user role to a session, it looks up the settings defined for that role. There are two ways for the switch to receive the user role definitions.

You can define the user role locally. This approach moves the control over customizing settings from RADIUS server administrators to infrastructure administrators, which some companies might prefer.

Or, if the company uses ClearPass, administrators can define user roles centrally on ClearPass, and the switch then downloads those roles. This latter approach leaves the settings centralized at ClearPass, as does the VSA-based approach discussed earlier. However, some ClearPass administrators prefer configuring settings with the user roles as opposed to the RADIUS VSAs. To enable downloading the roles, you must enter this command on the switch:

```
Switch(config)# aaa authorization user-role enable download
```

Downloading the user roles from ClearPass further requires you to define ClearPass as a RADIUS server, set the ClearPass username and password (with the **radius-server cppm identity** command), and install the ClearPass HTTPS root certificate. Refer to the switch *Management and Configuration Guide* for more details on this option.

Whether you configure roles locally, download roles, or both, the name for the roles must match the names sent in User-Role VSA exactly, including case.

Settings that can be defined for the role include the following:

- Untagged VLAN
- Tagged VLANs
- Policy, which is much like a dynamic ACL but can also apply QoS priorities
- Reauthentication period
- Captive portal URL, which is discussed in *Chapter 12: Captive Portal and Other Guest Options*
- Tunneled node redirect, which is discussed in *Chapter 13: Integrating with an Aruba Mobility Solution*

If a setting is undefined in the policy, the switch behaves as it does if a RADIUS server does not send a setting. For example, if you do not define an untagged VLAN, the switch assigns the user to the static VLAN on the port.

The switch *must* be able to apply a user role to every client that connects to a port enforcing port-based authentication. The initial user role applies to any client that fails authentication or any client that passes authentication but is not assigned a profile by the RADIUS server (or, as you will learn in *Chapter 11: MAC Authentication*, local MAC authentication [LMA]). By default, the initial user role is "deny any," a predefined user role that denies all access. However, you can set a different initial user role, if you want, with this command:

```
Switch(config)# aaa authorization user-role initial-role <rolename>
```

You should then configure appropriate settings for that user role.

It is important for you to understand that you can have the RADIUS server send a role *or* have it send dynamic VLANs, ACLs, and other such settings. You cannot combine the approaches on the same switch. If the RADIUS server sends an Access-Accept with both a user role and another authorization VSA, the switch will fail to apply the profile. Instead, it will apply the initial profile to the user, which could deny the user all access.

## Summary

In this chapter, you learned how to enforce 802.1X on an AOS-Switch, using an external RADIUS server such as Aruba ClearPass. You know how to set up the basic solution, and you can also integrate your switches with more advanced solutions that customize user access dynamically.

## Learning check

1. A company plans to use ClearPass to authenticate employees with 802.1X. Which role do AOS-Switches at the access layer play in 802.1X authentication?
    a. supplicants
    b. authenticators
    c. authentication servers
    d. authentication aggregators
2. A network administrator is specifying ClearPass as a RADIUS server on an AOS-Switch. What is one setting that the administrator should configure to prevent issues?
    a. dynamic authorization disabled
    b. dynamic authorization port set to 1812
    c. time window set to 0
    d. time window set below 5 seconds
3. What steps must you complete to enable 802.1X on a switch? What commands would you use?
4. Enabling 802.1X can, of course, interfere with user connections if their clients are not properly set up to complete authentication. What are some steps that you should take as part of the planning and implementing process for an 802.1X solution?
5. A user has authenticated with 802.1X, and the RADIUS server has sent dynamic settings for the switch to apply to the session. How can you view the dynamic settings?
6. An AOS-Switch port connects to an unmanaged switch that floods EAPOL messages and connects to multiple devices. The network administrator has enabled 802.1X globally and on the port. The port has the default setting of no client limit. One device connects and authenticates. What happens if a second device connects?
7. In the scenario for the previous question, how does the switch behavior change if you change the 802.1X client limit on the port to 1? What would happen if you changed the client limit to 5?
8. List some use cases for dynamic VLANs, ACLs, QoS priorities, and rate limits.

# Answers

## Learning check

1. A company plans to use ClearPass to authenticate employees with 802.1X. Which role do AOS-Switches at the access layer play in 802.1X authentication?

   a. supplicants

   **b. authenticators**

   c. authentication servers

   d. authentication aggregators

2. A network administrator is specifying ClearPass as a RADIUS server on an AOS-Switch. What is one setting that the administrator should configure to prevent issues?

   a. dynamic authorization disabled

   b. dynamic authorization port set to 1812

   **c. time window set to 0**

   d. time window set below 5 seconds

3. What steps must you complete to enable 802.1X on a switch? What commands would you use?

   You must enable 802.1X on the port and globally using these commands:

   ```
   Switch(config)# aaa port-access authenticator <interface ID list>
   Switch(config)# aaa port-access authenticator active
   ```

   You might have also listed some of the prerequisite steps before you enable 802.1X. These steps include defining the RADIUS server and configuring setting for it with **radius-server host** commands, as well as setting EAP as the 802.1X authentication method.

4. Enabling 802.1X can, of course, interfere with user connections if their clients are not properly set up to complete authentication. What are some steps that you should take as part of the planning and implementing process for an 802.1X solution?

   You need to make sure that clients are ready to authenticate. For example, they might need to be set up to trust ClearPass's certificate. Users might also need training in how to authenticate and how to avoid common problems.

   Before implementing any form of port-based authentication, you should go through the proper change management processes for planning the solution, ensuring all components are in place, educating users and so on.

   A testing period can help you to avoid issues. ClearPass administrators could initially set up policies that permit access even if users fail authentication. They can, then, find any users failing authentication and resolve the problem. After resolving all problems, they can change the policies to reject users who fail authentication.

ClearPass also provides capabilities for onboarding BYOD devices, allowing them to connect to the network, receive limited access, and obtain the certificates and settings they need for 802.1X authentication. You will learn more about setting up AOS-Switches to work with a BYOD or guest solution in *Chapter 12: Captive Portal and Other Guest Options*.

5. A user has authenticated with 802.1X, and the RADIUS server has sent dynamic settings for the switch to apply to the session. How can you view the dynamic settings?

   You can see these settings in several ways. Examples include the following:

   - The **show port-access <interface ID> authenticator** command shows how many clients are authenticated and unauthenticated on the port and a short view of settings applied to the port
   - The **show port-access <interface ID> clients [detail]** command provides more details about each client authenticated on a port and the dynamic settings applied to that client.

   When a dynamic VLAN has been applied to a port, you can also see the VLAN with commands that you traditionally use to view VLANs such as **show vlan** and **show vlan port <interface ID>**. You can use the **show access-list radius <interface ID>** command to view dynamic ACLs.

6. An AOS-Switch port connects to an unmanaged switch that floods EAPOL messages and connects to multiple devices. The network administrator has enabled 802.1X globally and on the port. The port has the default setting of no client limit. One device connects and authenticates. What happens if a second device connects?

   The second device will be able to send and receive traffic without authenticating.

7. In the scenario for the previous question, how does the switch behavior change if you change the 802.1X client limit on the port to 1? What would happen if you changed the client limit to 5?

   If you change the client limit to 1, the behavior changes. The second device does not receive access. Even if you changed the client limit to 5, the second device continues to receive no access until it authenticates. This is because the client limit changes how the switch port behaves. The port looks at the source MAC addresses for incoming traffic and authenticates devices separately up to the client limit. So two devices could connect on a port with a client limit of 5, but the switch will not accept traffic from any device until that device authenticates.

   After multiple devices connect, the AOS-Switch will list both devices as connected and authorized, and each device can have its own dynamic settings.

8. List some use cases for dynamic VLANs, ACLs, QoS priorities, and rate limits.

   Many different use cases exist, including the following:

   - Placing normal employees and contractors in different VLANs
   - Placing different departments in different VLANs
   - Assigning specialized devices (capable of 802.1X authentication) such as Point of Sales (PoS) devices to special VLANs
   - Placing various user groups in the same VLAN but assigning different groups different ACL rules to further customize their rights
   - Assigning a QoS priority to specialized devices such as VoIP phones or PoS devices
   - Applying different rate limits to users and to other types of devices
   - Applying special rate limits to a user group that requires more bandwidth (such as graphical designers)

   Dynamic port ACLs enable you to apply different access rights to users in the same VLAN based on their identity rather than port alone.

   You can enhance network and switch management access security and traffic control by permitting or denying authenticated clients access to specific network resources—individual servers, entire subnets, and even the switch management interfaces. This includes preventing clients from using applications, such as Telnet, Secure Shell Protocol (SSH), web browsers, and Simple Network Management Protocol (SNMP), if you do not want their access privileges to include these capabilities.

# 11 MAC Authentication

EXAM OBJECTIVES

✓ Implement RADIUS-based MAC Authentication (MAC-Auth) on AOS-Switch ports

✓ Implement local MAC Authentication (LMA) on AOS-Switch ports

## Assumed knowledge

Before reading this chapter, you should have a basic understanding of:

- IP addressing
- Open Systems Interconnection (OSI) model
- Multiple Spanning Tree Protocol (MSTP) and Rapid Spanning Tree Protocol (RSTP)
- Link aggregation
- Virtual LANs (VLANs)
- Routing
- Switching
- 802.1X

## Introduction

This chapter teaches you how to implement MAC Authentication (MAC-Auth) technology on AOS-Switches.

## MAC-Auth use cases

MAC-Auth allows companies to impose network access control for devices with limited capabilities.

Essentially, the switch uses a client's MAC address to authenticate the client. Because Ethernet clients always include their MAC address as the source of their Ethernet frames, the client does not need to be configured to submit credentials. Therefore, this authentication method provides an option for devices that do not have a user interface or support for 802.1X.

When you need rigorous security, it is recommended that you use 802.1X whenever possible. Often it is trivial for a hacker to discover MAC addresses used in your system, whether by eavesdropping or accessing a legitimate device. The hacker can then easily spoof an authorized MAC address. MAC authentication might also be more difficult to manage than other forms of authentication, requiring directory or domain administrators to create accounts for each MAC address on each device, whereas 802.1X can use the user accounts already in the directory or domain.

Rather than a security measure, MAC-Auth is perhaps most useful for simplifying the provisioning for devices such as printers, Internet of Things (IoT) devices, IP phones, and security cameras. In addition to permitting a device network access based on its group, the authentication server can assign the dynamic settings, such as a VLAN ID and QoS priority, to device's session.

Two types of MAC-Auth are available.

- RADIUS MAC-Auth—RADIUS MAC-Auth relies on a RADIUS server to approve or reject the authentication request.
- Local MAC Authentication (LMA)—With LMA, the switch checks the MAC address against a local list. (Check your switch documentation to determine whether the switch supports this option.)

## RADIUS-based MAC-Auth

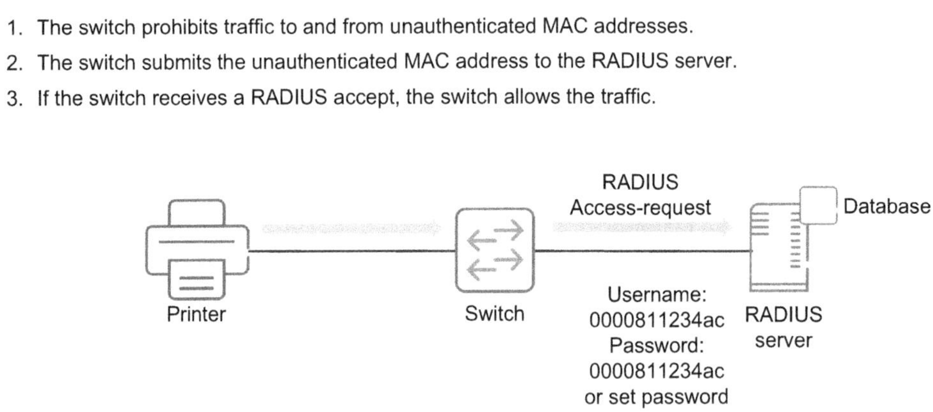


Figure 11-1 RADIUS-based MAC-Auth

You can enable RADIUS-based MAC-Auth on individual switch ports. Figure 11-1 shows the basic process that occurs when a client connects to an AOS-Switch port that enforces RADIUS MAC-Auth. Additional explanation is provided below:

1. The client is initially unauthenticated. The switch does not transmit traffic on the line. Authentication is not triggered until the client begins to send traffic on its own. This traffic is initially dropped while the switch completes the next steps.
2. The switch submits credentials to a RADIUS server on the client's behalf.

   Often these credentials consist of the client's MAC address as the username and password. However, the password can be different from the MAC address.
3. The RADIUS server authenticates the MAC address against a user account. Only the switch and the server are involved in the exchange of authentication messages, unlike other port-based authentication methods. The RADIUS server uses its user database—which should have an account for the client's MAC address—and policies to determine whether to grant access. It communicates its decision to the switch in a RADIUS Accept-Access or Reject-Access message.
4. The switch handles the client according to the RADIUS server's decision.
   - If the server accepted access, the switch allows all traffic to and from the client with that MAC address.
   - If the server rejected access, the client remains in the unauthenticated state, and the switch handles its traffic as indicated in step 1.

     The switch continues to examine incoming frames. If a new client connects, the switch will authenticate that client. The switch also attempts to authenticate the client for which authentication failed again. By default, the switch suppresses authentication requests for such clients over the quiet period—by default, 60 seconds. It then sends another authentication request.

## RADIUS-based MAC-Auth options

You need to make several choices related to RADIUS MAC-Auth. The sections that follow describe each of these choices.

### Authentication protocol

You have two choices for the protocol that the switch uses to send the credentials to the RADIUS server.

- PEAPv0/MS-CHAPv2
- Challenge Handshake Authentication Protocol (CHAP)

You learned about how RADIUS works with EAP in *Chapter 10: 802.1X Authentication*. AOS-Switches can use PEAPv0/MS-CHAPv2 for MAC-Auth. In this case, the switch acts as the authentication client rather than the client itself, generating the EAP request messages. PEAP often offers the best option because it secures the credentials within a tunnel between the switch and the RADIUS server. It requires the RADIUS server to have a certificate; however, most RADIUS servers already require a certificate for various functions. The ability to use relatively secure PEAP is a key advantage of AOS-Switches.

Alternatively, on the AOS-Switches, you can choose CHAP for the authentication protocol. RADIUS has specific messages for CHAP authentication and most RADIUS servers support this option. You should be aware that the mechanisms of CHAP require passwords to be stored with reversible encryption, which poses a potential security hazard and is not typical for most directories and domains. This limitation would mean, for example, that the directory, domain, or RADIUS administrator who creates the accounts for the clients would have to take special measures to store the passwords with reversible encryption. (For a Microsoft Windows domain, the administrators can edit the group policy object (GPO) and enable reversal encryption in the computer policies for account settings.)

The command for setting the protocol is:

```
Switch(config)# aaa authentication mac-based <chap-radius | peap-mschapv2>
```

## Credentials

You need to decide the precise credentials that switches will send so that the RADIUS, directory, or domain administrator can set up the accounts accordingly.

By default, AOS-Switches send the MAC address for both the username and password. You can set up a global password, which the switch uses for the password instead of the device's MAC address. The switch itself places the password in the authentication request. No configuration is required on the client. The switch continues to use the client's MAC address for the username, so every client requires a user account on the RADIUS server (or background directory).

The password option is intended to add a bit of security to the solution. However, keep in mind that hackers can still spoof an authorized MAC address, connect to the switch, and gain access to the network because the switch adds the password on its end. Remember that MAC-Auth provides basic security; you should use 802.1X when you require more rigorous security.

## MAC address format

When you are using MAC addresses for the username, password, or both, you must ensure that the switch sends the credentials with the same format used in the user accounts. Table 11-1 presents the options and the syntax for configuring a specific format for AOS-Switches.

---

**Note**

Accounts in Microsoft Active Directory (AD) domains cannot use colons, so choose a format that does not include colons if you use AD.

---

Table 11-1 MAC address formats

| Format | AOS-Switch syntax |
|---|---|
| Beginning of the command for specifying one of these formats: | aaa port-access mac-based addr-format |
| aabbccddeeff | no-delimiter |
| aabbcc-ddeeff | single-dash |
| aa-bb-cc-dd-ee-ff | multi-dash |
| aa:bb:cc:dd:ee:ff | multi-colon |
| AABBCCDDEEFF | no-delimiter-uppercase |
| AABBCC-DDEEFF | single-dash-uppercase |
| AA-BB-CC-DD-EE-FF | multi-dash-uppercase |
| AA:BB:CC:DD:EE:FF | multi-colon-uppercase |

## MAC-Auth and provisioning with ClearPass

Aruba ClearPass can fulfill the role of RADIUS server for MAC-Auth as well as for 802.1X.

ClearPass provides MAC-Auth specific service templates that make it easy for administrators to set up ClearPass to act as the RADIUS server for your MAC-Auth solution. As Figure 11-2 shows, the service can specify profiles to apply to clients based on their MAC addresses and other capabilities. In this way, ClearPass can communicate the correct settings for the connected device, which the switch applies to the port in much the same way as it applies settings with 802.1X. For example, if you are using MAC-Auth to authenticate IP phones, ClearPass policies could assign the correct voice VLAN and QoS priority for the phones' traffic.

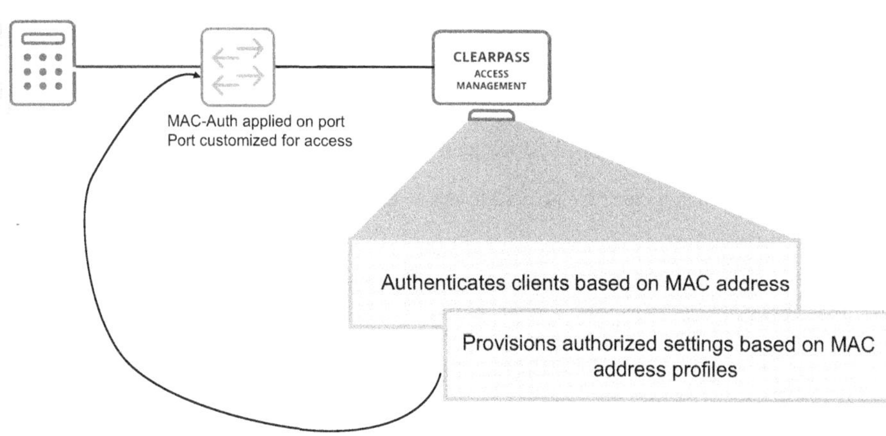


Figure 11-2 MAC-Auth and provisioning with ClearPass

## RADIUS-based MAC-Auth configuration process

The steps for implementing RADIUS MAC-Auth are provided below for your reference:

1. Specify your RADIUS server. In the following example, you are using only the global group. These commands specify the server and set the proper options for ClearPass. Remember to set the key to match the secret configured for this switch on ClearPass.

   ```
   Switch(config)# radius-server host <IP address> key <secret>
   ```

   ```
   Switch(config)# radius-server host <IP address> dyn-authorization
   ```

   ```
   Switch(config)# radius-server host <IP address> time-window 0
   ```

2. Configure the format for the MAC-Auth credentials so that they match the credentials configured on the RADIUS server (or its backend directory). See Table 11-1 for formats. (ClearPass often uses the no-delimiter option, which is also the default option on AOS-Switches.)

   ```
   Switch(config)# aaa port-access mac-based addr-format <format>
   ```

3. If you want the switch to send a password, rather than MAC address in the password field, specify the global (fixed) password.

   ```
   Switch(config)# aaa port-access mac-based password <password>
   ```

4. Choose between PEAP and CHAP for the authentication protocol. (Remember that CHAP requires passwords to be stored with reversible encryption, which is not the default for many directories.)

   ```
   Switch(config)# aaa authentication mac-based <chap-radius
   | peap-mschapv2>
   ```

5. Optionally, you can adjust other settings such as the timers for the quiet period, logging out inactive clients, and re-authenticating clients. (If you set the reauth period to 0, the switch does not enforce reauthentication.) All of these timers are set in seconds. You can refer to your switch's *Access Security Guide* to learn about more MAC-Auth-related options.

   ```
   Switch(config)# aaa port-access mac-based <port_ID_list> quiet-period
   <1-65535>
   ```

   ```
   Switch(config)# aaa port-access mac-based <port_ID_list> logoff-period
   <60-9999999>
   ```

   ```
   Switch(config)# aaa port-access mac-based <port_ID_list> reauth-period
   <0-9999999>
   ```

6. Enable MAC-Auth on the individual ports that you want to enforce this type of authentication.

   ```
   Switch(config)# aaa port-access mac-based <port_ID_list>
   ```

## Local MAC-Auth

LMA proceeds in a similar manner to RADIUS MAC-Auth. As Figure 11-3 shows, however, the switch checks the client MAC address against local lists of MAC addresses, rather than accounts on a RADIUS server. These lists are called MAC groups.

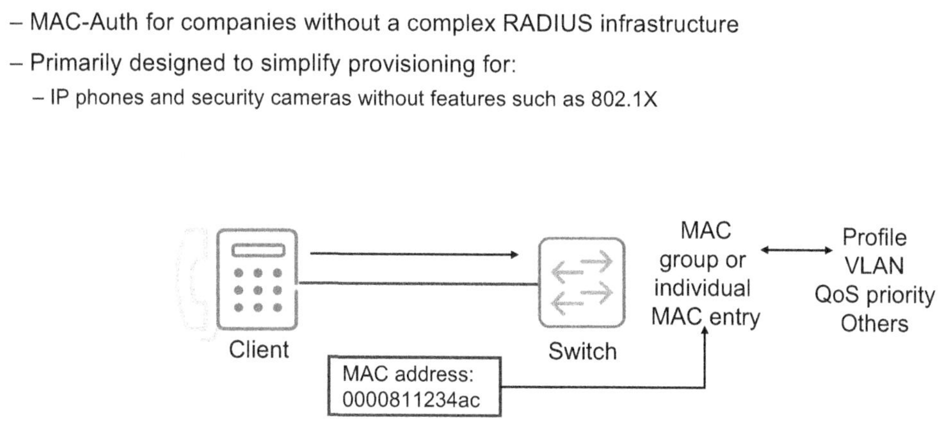


Figure 11-3 Local MAC-Auth

Because you must set up the MAC groups on every switch that enforces LMA, LMA might be less scalable than RADIUS MAC-Auth. However, MAC masks and a default group help to simplify the MAC group setup. LMA gives benefits of MAC-Auth without having to create a RADIUS infrastructure.

Although in some cases LMA can provide rudimentary access security, it is primarily designed to simplify provisioning for devices such as IP phones and security cameras. When the switch matches a client's source address to the MAC group, it not only permits the client network access, it also applies dynamic settings such as VLAN ID and QoS priority, based on the profile that is bound to that MAC group.

In this way, LMA simplifies deployment for devices such as IP phones and security cameras, working for devices that do not support 802.1X.

LMA is enabled with this command:

```
Switch(config)# aaa port-access local-mac <port_ID_list>
```

You can check that LMA is applied to the correct ports with the **show port-access [local-mac] config** command.

## MAC groups

You will now learn more about defining the MAC groups against which LMA checks clients' MAC addresses.

### Ways to create MAC groups

AOS-Switches support several default (factory-shipped) groups that are already configured to match specific types of IP phones such as HPE, Aastra Avaya, 3Com, and Cisco phones. However, LMA cannot actively use these groups. You must create a configured group from the default group with this command:

```
Switch(config)# aaa port-access local-mac mac-group default
<default group name> <group name>
```

After you create the new group based on the default group, the switch can authenticate devices to it, and you can associate profiles with it. You can also add entries to the group, if you want.

You can also create your own empty MAC group by using this command:

```
Switch (config)# aaa port-access local-mac mac-group <group name>
```

In this case, you *must* add entries to the group.

The switch can support multiple MAC groups. When a switch port enforces LMA, the switch authenticates a connected device's MAC address to all of the groups.

### Entries for MAC groups

To add entries to a MAC group, access the configuration context for that group with this command:

```
Switch(config)# aaa port-access local-mac mac-group <group name>
```

MAC groups can include three types of entries.

- A single MAC address

  Use this command to add a single MAC address to a MAC group.

  ```
  Switch(Mac-Group-<group name>)# mac-addr <MAC address>
  ```

  You can also add a string of single MAC addresses by specifying multiple addresses in the command. For example, enter:

  ```
  Switch(Mac-Group-<group name>)# mac-addr 005056000001 005056001324
  ```

- A MAC Organizationally Unique Identifier (OUI)

  A MAC OUI is the first 24-bits, or six characters, of the MAC address. It identifies the device vendor. Use this command to add an OUI to a MAC group.

  ```
  Switch(Mac-Group-<group name>)# mac-oui <MAC OUI>
  ```

  Again, you can enter a string of OUIs with a single command.

- A range of MAC addresses, specified with a mask

  Sometimes a vendor OUI applies to multiple types of devices, and you want to specify the type of device more precisely. You can specify as much of the MAC address as you want, and then use a bit mask to indicate that the MAC address can have any characters after that point.

  ```
  Switch(Mac-Group-<group name>)# mac-mask <MAC address/mask>
  ```

  Each character in a MAC address is four bits, so the correct mask is the number of characters that you enter multiplied by four. For example, this command adds an entry to the "myphones" group and matches MAC addresses between 002622bb0000 and 002622bbffff.

  ```
  Switch(Mac-Group-<group name>)# mac-mask 002622bb/32
  ```

  Again, you can specify a string of MAC addresses with masks in a single command.

---

**Note**

As with other commands in the Aruba CLI, you can enter a complete command from the global configuration context rather than enter the MAC group context.

---

## View MAC groups

To view the default MAC groups, enter **show port-access local-mac mac-group default**. You will see a list of group names and the MAC-OUI or MAC-OUIs associated with that group.

To view MAC groups you create, enter:

```
Switch# show port-access local-mac mac-group
```

You will see output similar to the following:

```
List of Local-MAC MAC Group :

MAC Group Name                     MAC Type  MAC
---------------------------------  --------- --------------

myphones                           mac-oui   005056

myphones                           mac-oui   2c4138
```

## Profiles

The switch *must* be able to apply a profile to a device in order for the device to succeed LMA. In other words, a device's MAC address might match a MAC group; however, the device will not pass LMA until you associate that MAC group with a profile.

A profile contains the settings that you want to apply to particular types of devices. Settings include a tagged VLAN assignment, untagged VLAN assignment, and Class of Service (CoS) setting (see Figure 11-4).

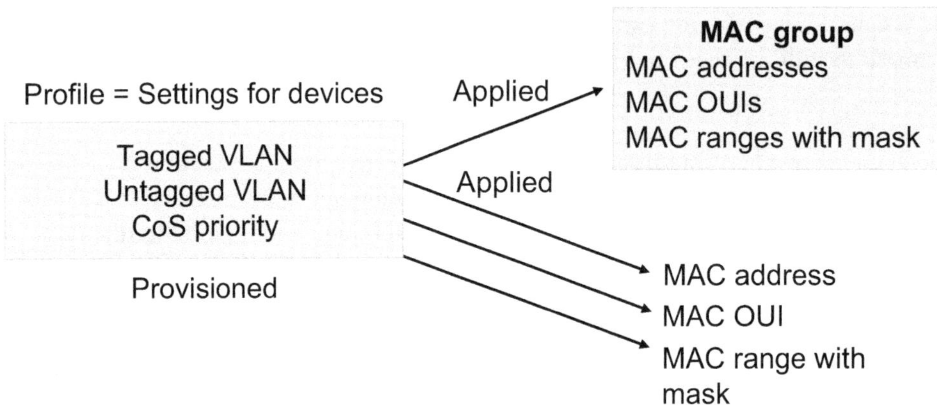


Figure 11-4 Profiles

Use this command to create the profile and configure its settings.

```
Switch(config)# aaa port-access local-mac profile <profile name>
```

You will then enter a configuration context in which you can configure various settings. You do not have to specify all of the settings in a profile. If the profile has a setting undefined, the switch will retain the port setting for that parameter when it applies the profile.

```
Switch(Profile-<profile name>)# vlan tagged <ID>
Switch(Profile-<profile name>)# vlan untagged <ID>
Switch(Profile-<profile name>)# cos <0-7>
```

Note that you can enter all of the settings in a single command with a command such as this:

```
Switch(config)# aaa port-access local-mac profile <profile name> vlan
tagged <ID> untagged <ID> cos <0-7>
```

Make sure that the VLANs that you create in the profiles exist on the switch. If a profile includes *any* tagged or untagged VLAN assignment for a VLAN that does not exist on the switch, LMA denies access to clients assigned to that profile. You do not need to configure the VLAN on the edge ports because the switch assigns them to the ports dynamically. However, typically you do need to assign the VLAN as a tagged VLAN on uplinks so that the switch can forward traffic across the network.

### Binding profiles to MAC groups

You must apply a MAC group in order for it to take effect and for the switch to authenticate devices' MAC addresses to it. When you map a profile to a group, it is called an "applied" profile. Use this command:

```
Switch(config)# aaa port-access local-mac apply profile <profile name> mac-group <group name>
```

When the switch matches a MAC address to a MAC group, it assigns the settings in the applied profile to the device's session (any traffic to or from the device MAC address).

### Applying profiles to individual MAC entries

Usually, it is easiest to manage profiles by applying them to a group with multiple entries. However, if you choose, you can apply a profile directly to a MAC address, MAC OUI, or range of MAC addresses specified with a MAC mask. Use the following commands:

```
Switch(config)# aaa port-access local-mac apply profile <profile name> mac-addr <MAC address>
```

```
Switch(config)# aaa port-access local-mac apply profile <profile name> mac-oui <MAC OUI>
```

```
Switch(config)# aaa port-access local-mac apply profile <profile name> mac-mask <MAC address/mask>
```

---

**Note**

If you have enabled user role-based authorization, discussed in *Chapter 10: 802.1X Authentication,* you can apply user roles to MAC addresses, MAC OUIs, or ranges of MAC addresses instead of applying profiles.

---

### View profile settings

To verify that your profile is correct and applied correctly, enter:

```
Switch# show port-access local-mac profile

List of Local-MAC Profiles :

Profile-Name     : myphones

Tagged VLANs     :

Untagged VLANs : 30

CoS              : 5

Applied          : Yes
```

You can use the **show port-access local-mac association** command to view the MAC addresses associated with the profile.

## LMA Unauthorized-client VLAN

As you have seen, LMA simplifies provisioning. Rather than having to determine which switch ports will connect to IP phones and then manually provision the voice VLAN and correct priority settings on those ports, you can use MAC groups and profiles to dynamically apply the correct settings when an IP phone connects.

However, this use case implies that user devices such as desktop computers might sometimes connect to ports that enforce LMA. Because the computers' MAC addresses are not listed in a MAC group, the switch will deny access to them (see Figure 11-5).

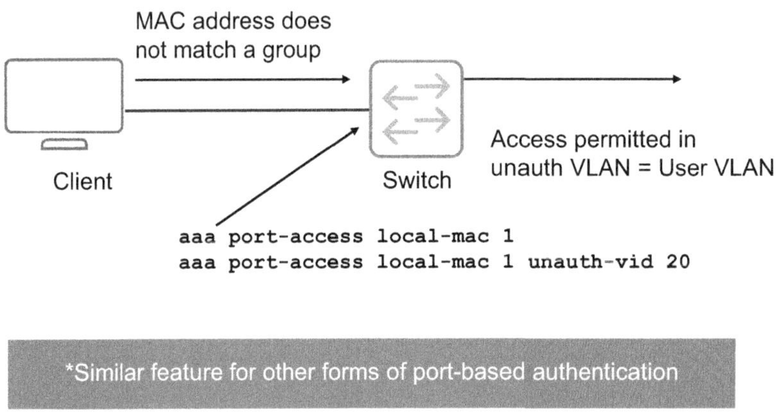


Figure 11-5 LMA Unauthorized-client VLAN

You could create another MAC group that specifies the range of MAC addresses for valid clients in your environment. However, if you are using LMA to simplify provisioning and do not care about security, you can take a much simpler approach. As Figure 11-5 shows, you can set the Unauthorized-client VLAN for each port enforcing LMA to the correct user VLAN on that switch.

```
Switch(config)# aaa port-access local-mac <port_ID_list> unauth-vid <ID>
```

The switch will then assign any devices that fail LMA to this VLAN. If you want, you can make the Unauthorized VLAN ID the same as the static VLAN assigned to the port. Failing LMA means that the device's MAC address does not match a MAC group, OUI, range, or address applied to a profile. A device might fail to receive access because it matches a profile, but the profile has an invalid VLAN ID. In that case, the device is not considered to have failed authentication, and it is *not* assigned to the Unauthorized-client VLAN.

Similar considerations apply when you are using RADIUS-based MAC-Auth for provisioning devices such as IP phones rather than for security. To set an Unauthorized-client VLAN for RADIUS MAC-Auth, enter this command:

```
Switch(config)# aaa port-access mac-based <port_ID_list> unauth-vid <ID>
```

## Implementing MAC-Auth on ports connected to multiple clients

You have assumed until now that you are implementing authentication on edge ports that support one endpoint at a time, which is true in many environments. However, you often apply LMA and RADIUS MAC-Auth to IP phones. In addition, a computer often connects to the IP phone, and the IP phone then connects to the switch port on a second port. In another scenario, a company might have a hub, an unmanaged switch or an unmanaged AP to which multiple devices connect.

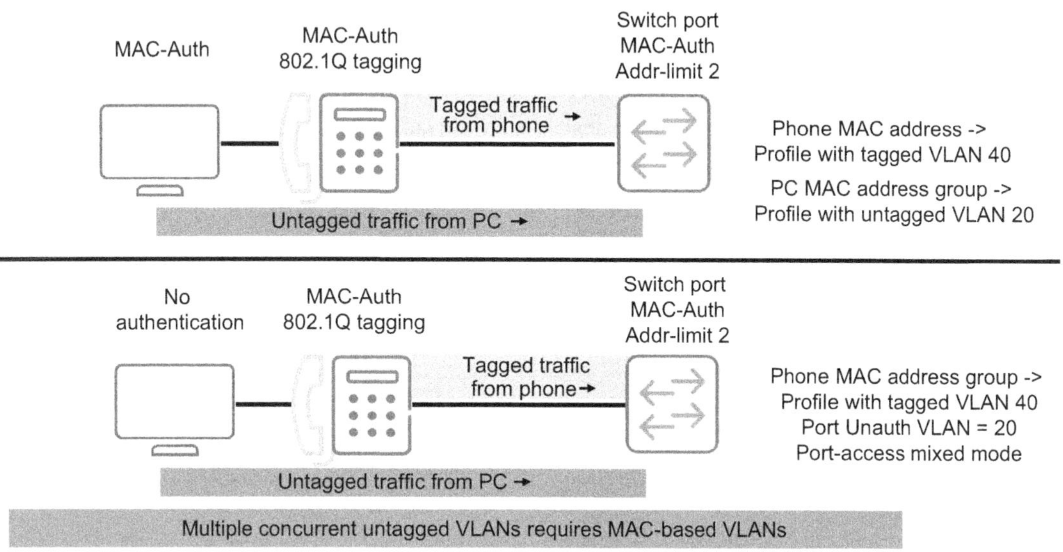


Figure 11-6 Implementing MAC-Auth on ports connected to multiple clients

For these scenarios, set up LMA or RADIUS MAC-Auth as you learned how to do earlier. By default, the switch allows only one MAC address to authenticate on the port at the same time. After a connected client passes authentication, the switch drops traffic received from any other MAC address even if that address would otherwise pass authentication. As Figure 11-6 shows, you need to raise the MAC address limit with this command, using the appropriate option for RADIUS MAC-Auth or LMA.

```
Switch(config)# aaa port-access <mac-based | local-mac> <port-list>
addr-limit <1-256>
```

You typically assign tagged VLANs to IP phones and untagged VLANs to computers. If you want to enforce authentication for the computers, you can assign the untagged VLAN through the RADIUS or LMA profile, or you can have computers use the port's static VLAN.

Or if you do not want to authenticate computers, you can set an Unauthorized-client VLAN for LMA or RADIUS MAC-Auth. By default, the switch *will* not place a client in the Unauthorized-client VLAN if an authorized client is connected to the same port at the same time. For this scenario, you must enter this command to enable authorized and unauthorized clients to connect concurrently.

```
Switch(config)# aaa port-access <port ID list> mixed
```

---

**Note**

LMA, like 802.1X, can use MAC-based VLANs to assigned different clients to different untagged VLANs at the same time. The same guidelines and restrictions discussed in *Chapter 10: 802.1X Authentication* apply.

---

## Combining MAC-Auth and 802.1X

A port can support multiple authentication methods, enabling it to authenticate different types of devices and users. For example, you have devices that are capable of completing 802.1X authentication but also some devices (such as IP phones and printers) that are not.

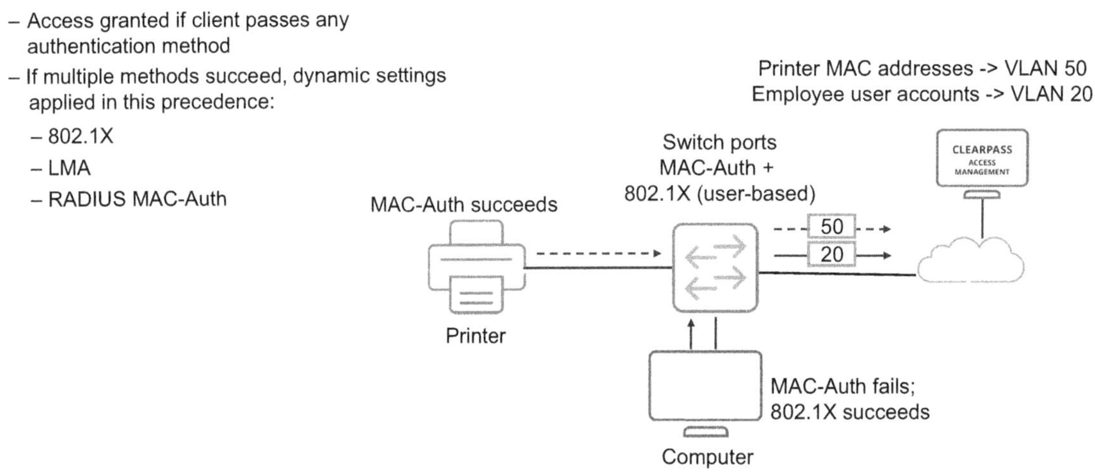


Figure 11-7 Combining MAC-Auth and 802.1X

First, you will look at a scenario in which a port supports one device at a time, but you are not sure which type of device will connect to a specific port (see Figure 11-7). You want to make sure that any type of device can pass authentication and receive the correct customized access.

You want to make sure that each port supports either:

- RADIUS MAC-Auth and 802.1X authentication
- LMA and 802.1X authentication

Because the use of 802.1X implies that you have a RADIUS infrastructure, you might choose to combine RADIUS MAC-Auth and 802.1X. However, sometimes this RADIUS infrastructure is not set up to authenticate devices by MAC address, and you find it simpler to use LMA.

A port that implements RADIUS MAC-Auth or LMA with 802.1X immediately uses the device's MAC address to submit an access request, just as it would if MAC-Auth were the only authentication method.

- If RADIUS MAC-Auth or LMA succeeds, the device is authorized for network access with the settings returned by the RADIUS server or LMA profile.
- If RADIUS MAC-Auth or LMA fails, the user still has the option to pass 802.1X authentication. If the user succeeds, the device is authorized for network access with the settings returned by the RADIUS server.
- If both types of authentication fail, the device is prohibited access.
- Even if RADIUS MAC-Auth or LMA succeeds, the user device might initiate 802.1X. (However, the switch itself will not.) If the user then authenticates successfully with 802.1X, the settings returned at the end of the 802.1X process take precedence over any settings applied by RADIUS MAC-Auth or LMA.

Keep in mind the following guidelines when enabling MAC-Auth or LMA and 802.1X on the same port:

- Ensure that the port operates in user-based mode for 802.1X. Set a client limit with this command, even if that client limit is 1.

  ```
  Switch(config)# aaa port-access authenticator <port ID list> client-limit <1-32>
  ```

- Ensure that each type of device and user receives the correct VLAN assignment. For example, you might have the RADIUS server or LMA profile assign MAC-Auth clients to different VLANs from 802.1X users.
- MAC-Auth and LMA remain vulnerable to spoofing. If you are concerned about untrusted users accessing the port, you should take appropriate measures to filter traffic in the VLANs assigned to MAC-Auth clients.
- If you are using MAC-Auth, make sure that the RADIUS server has the correct policies and accounts for providing MAC-Auth only for the headless devices that require it. Similarly, if you are using LMA, only set up MAC groups and profiles for the headless devices. MAC-Auth is the weakest link in the security system, so you want clients capable of 802.1X to fail initial authentication and perform 802.1X authentication instead. Also note that, although 802.1X settings take precedence, it can interfere with a client's connection to first be placed in a VLAN by MAC-Auth and then be placed in another VLAN after 802.1X authentication. Also, a client that has successfully received access with MAC-Auth or LMA sometimes might not initiate 802.1X.

> **Note**
>
> Although not a typical use case, you can enable LMA and RADIUS-based MAC-Auth on the same port. In this case, the switch first checks the client MAC address locally using LMA. If LMA fails to find a match, the switch submits the client MAC address as an authentication request to the RADIUS server. If the client passes either form of MAC-Auth, it is allowed access.
>
> Because the switch applies LMA first, the LMA profile settings take precedence. (Even if the RADIUS server has an account for the client, if LMA also has an account, the switch never sends the access request to the RADIUS server.)

## Combining MAC-Auth and 802.1X in multiple client scenarios

Figure 11-8 shows multiple client scenarios that are similar to the ones that you examined earlier. Now, however, the switch enforces 802.1X authentication for some devices such as computers, rather than MAC authentication or no authentication.

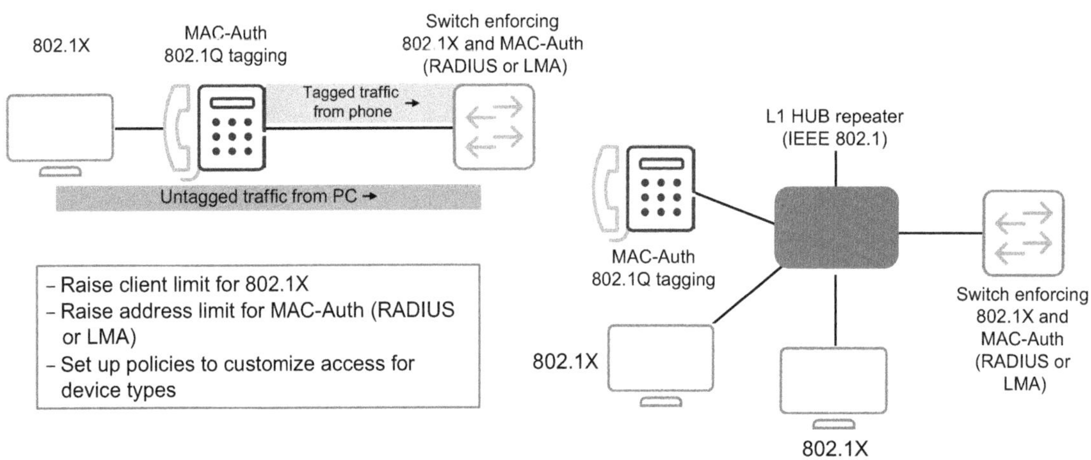


Figure 11-8 Combining MAC-Auth and 802.1X in multiple client scenarios

To support this scenario, you should enable both 802.1X and RADIUS MAC-Auth or LMA. Then make sure that you raise *both* the client limit for 802.1X and the address limit for RADIUS MAC-Auth or LMA to accommodate the number of devices that the port should support. The switch counts the 802.1X limit separately from the RADIUS MAC-Auth or LMA limit, but clients might be able to succeed multiple forms of authentication, or you might not know which forms of authentication clients will use.

Set up policies to customize access for the different types of devices, as you have learned how to do in *Chapter 10: 802.1X Authentication* and throughout this chapter.

## Using Authorized-client VLANs

You have one more option for customizing the VLANs to which different types of devices are assigned.

As Figure 11-9 shows, you can set an Authorized-client VLAN individually for each authentication method. This VLAN overrides the port's static untagged VLAN for any device that successfully authenticates with that method. However, it is overridden by any VLAN assignment sent by the RADIUS server.

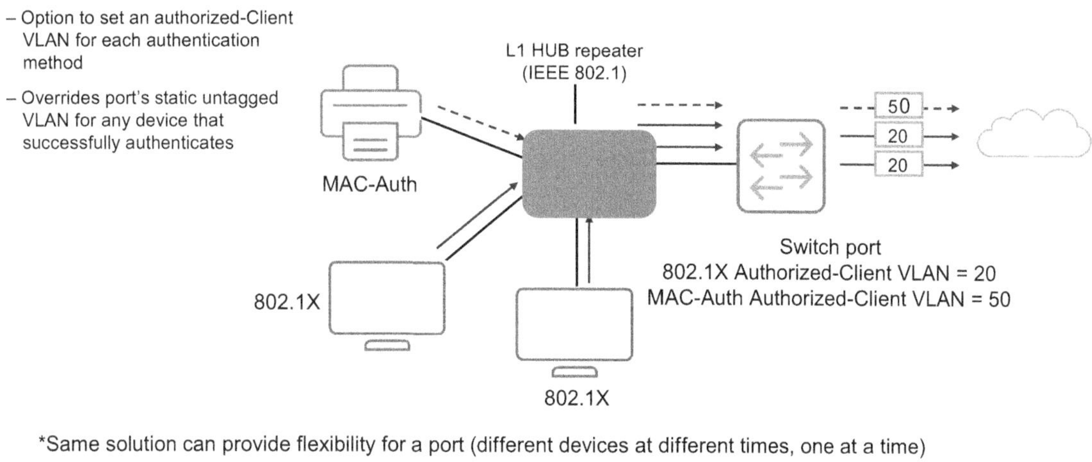


Figure 11-9 Using Authorized-client VLANs

The Authorized-client VLAN can be a simple way to separate different types of devices if your RADIUS server does not send VLAN assignments. (When you are using LMA, it is usually best to set the VLAN with a profile.) For example, you could set one Authorized-client VLAN for 802.1X and a different Authorized-client VLAN for RADIUS MAC-Auth. Because MAC-Auth is less secure, this VLAN might be more tightly controlled within the network.

Note that the Authorized-client is an untagged VLAN. As for RADIUS untagged VLAN assignments, the Authorized-client VLAN does not affect static tagged VLAN assignments on the port. Any authenticated client can send or receive tagged traffic for any tagged VLAN statically configured on the port. If you want to assign a tagged VLAN to a device dynamically, use RADIUS or LMA profiles.

## Summary

In this chapter, you explored appropriate situations for implementing MAC-Auth solutions. You now know when and how to set up the basic solutions, and you can also create solutions that combine 802.1X and MAC-Auth.

## Learning check

1. A network administrator sets up both 802.1X and RADIUS-based MAC-Auth on a port. For which clients does the RADIUS server need accounts with their MAC addresses?
   a. All clients
   b. Clients that do not support 802.1X
   c. Clients that support 802.1X
   d. Clients that support CHAP
2. Why might an administrator use LMA rather than RADIUS MAC-Auth?
   a. LMA is more scalable.
   b. LMA allows the use of user accounts already in the directory or domain.
   c. LMA is a more secure authentication method.
   d. LMA does not require the creation of a RADIUS infrastructure.
3. What checks should you make to verify that LMA is ready to provision clients with the correct settings?
4. A network administrator has created a profile and applied it to a MAC group. The administrator accidentally specified a VLAN that does not exist on the switch as the untagged VLAN for the profile. What happens when a client connects and has a MAC address that matches this profile?

## Answers

### Learning check

1. A network administrator sets up both 802.1X and RADIUS-based MAC-Auth on a port. For which clients does the RADIUS server need accounts with their MAC addresses?
   a. All clients
   **b. Clients that do not support 802.1X**
   c. Clients that support 802.1X
   d. Clients that support CHAP
2. Why might an administrator use LMA rather than RADIUS MAC-Auth?
   a. LMA is more scalable.
   b. LMA allows the use of user accounts already in the directory or domain.
   c. LMA is a more secure authentication method.
   **d. LMA does not require the creation of a RADIUS infrastructure.**

3. What checks should you make to verify that LMA is ready to provision clients with the correct settings?

   You should check that the profile is not only provisioned but also applied with the **show port-access local-mac profile** command. You might also want to make sure that the profile is applied to the correct MAC addresses or OUIs (or group with these addresses). You can use the **show port-access local-mac association** command for this purpose. You should also check that LMA is applied to the correct ports. You can use the **show port-access config** command for this purpose.

4. A network administrator has created a profile and applied it to a MAC group. The administrator accidentally specified a VLAN that does not exist on the switch as the untagged VLAN for the profile. What happens when a client connects and has a MAC address that matches this profile?

   When the client connects, the authentication fails because LMA cannot able to apply a valid VLAN ID to the client.

# 12 Captive Portal and Other Guest Options

EXAM OBJECTIVES

- ✓ Configure captive portal authentication on AOS-Switches to integrate them with an Aruba ClearPass solution
- ✓ Implement Web Authentication (Web-Auth) on AOS-Switch ports
- ✓ Combine multiple forms of authentication on a switch port that supports one or more simultaneous users
- ✓ Use the Unauthenticated VLAN on AOS-Switches to provide guest access

## Assumed knowledge

Before reading this chapter, you should have a basic understanding of:

- IP addressing
- Open Systems Interconnection (OSI) model
- Multiple Spanning Tree Protocol (MSTP) and Rapid Spanning Tree Protocol (RSTP)
- Link aggregation
- Virtual LANs (VLANs)
- Routing
- Switching
- 802.1X
- MAC-Auth

## Introduction

Today, network services, such as access to email and the Internet, are expected to be readily available and always on. If companies do not provide these network services to them, their competition will.

This chapter teaches you how to configure AOS-Switches to provide that access in several different ways. You will begin by considering the types of solutions at a high level.

# Guest access

Different companies have different expectations and needs for their guest access solution. Some companies might allow guests limited access without any authentication. However, most companies want guests to log in through a Web portal of some kind. Even if they do not care whether the guests authenticate, they want the guests to accept an agreement for legal purposes.

The company's expectations will dictate whether you need to configure AOS-Switches at the access layer to enforce or participate in a Web-based authentication solution, or whether you can simply place guests in a guest VLAN. You will focus on the Web-based authentication—also called portal authentication—solutions for most of this chapter. At the end, however, you will learn how you can enforce authentication for employees, but allow limited access to guests without forcing the guests to log in.

# Web-based authentication

Web-based authentication was developed to provide an easier way for users to log in to a network without special requirements on the part of their devices, nor expertise on the part of the users. Users simply open a Web browser and are directed to a login page, in which they can enter credentials or sometimes simply accept an agreement to log in.

Due to the simplicity from the user standpoint, but also the relatively lower security, companies often use Web-based authentication to provide guest access. However, some SMBs also use Web-based authentication for employees.

## Advantages of Web-Auth

Security solutions such as 802.1X require specific capabilities, but any client can authenticate to a switch that uses Web-Auth as long as the user has a legitimate username and password and a web browser.

Web-Auth also lets companies control what users see before they receive network access. The company can present a customizable webpage that shows the guest information about the company providing the complimentary access. The company can also force the user to consent to terms and conditions, which can be a legal requirement in many regions.

Environments with external users who may benefit from Web-Auth include the following:

- Hospitals
- Universities
- Libraries, hotels, and other businesses that provide courtesy Ethernet access

## Disadvantages of Web-Auth

Web-Auth does not provide as rigorous security as 802.1X. Users have a degree of network access before they authenticate. The credentials and authentication protocol might not be as secure as with 802.1X; however, you can improve the security by using HTTPS rather than HTTP.

Because Web-Auth requires interaction with the user, you cannot use it to authenticate devices without a user interface.

You should also note that the local Web-Auth features are quite limited. However, the switches can integrate with Aruba ClearPass, which is a sophisticated guest and Bring Your Own Device (BYOD) solution.

## Types of Web-based authentication

In the past, Web-based authentication was as simple as a login page and perhaps a backend authentication server.

However, these solutions have evolved. As Figure 12-1 shows, solution such as ClearPass provides a Web portal as part of its complete user access management solution. Such a solution helps users to log in more easily with features such as self-registration. It also helps companies track and monitor users, and it controls their access in sophisticated ways.

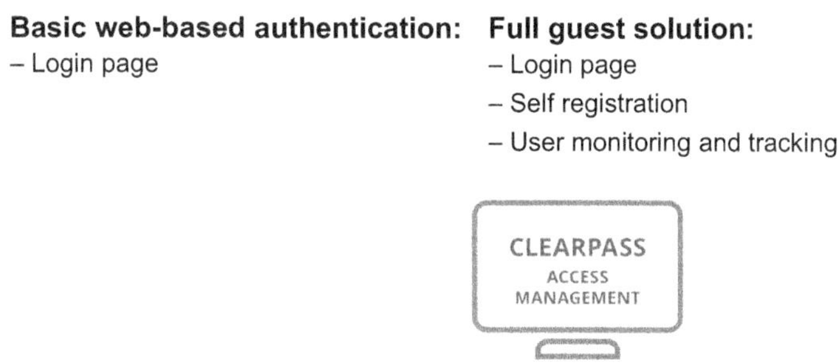


Figure 12-1 Types of Web-based authentication

## Additional capabilities of a solution such as Aruba ClearPass

To meet the needs of a modern workforce, companies have found that they need some of the capabilities traditionally associated with guest access solutions for their employees (see Figure 12-2).

For example, if they have a BYOD environment, in which employees connect their own devices to the network. IT staff often struggle to implement the proper security controls for such an environment. If the network enforces authentication, users find it difficult to configure their devices to connect, but the IT staff cannot easily keep up with the help requests either. If the network does not enforce authentication, on the other hand, the company risks opening its network to unauthorized or insecure devices, as well as exposing sensitive data on devices to unauthorized access.

Figure 12-2 Additional capabilities of a solution such as Aruba ClearPass

ClearPass Onboard provides BYOD onboarding to help companies surmount these challenges. Employees can use the Web portal to register and onboard their own devices to prepare them for more rigorous authentication.

Some solutions, including ClearPass's OnGuard component, also provide endpoint integrity features. Endpoint integrity checks devices for compliance with specific security policies, helps to remediate devices that fail the compliance checks, and appropriately controls devices that cannot come into compliance (for example, by placing them in a quarantine VLAN with limited access).

## AOS-Switches' support for Web-based authentication

As illustrated in Figure 12-3, AOS-Switches support a variety of Web-based authentication options to meet the needs of any company.

- Local Web-Auth—For companies with very simple needs, you can enable Web-Auth. The switch provides a local portal in which users can log in. It authenticates user credentials to a RADIUS server.
- Enhanced Web-Auth (EWA)—If the company wants to use Web-Auth model, but prefers to customize the web page, you can set up Web-Auth with an EWA server. The switch still hosts the local portal, but instead of using the default pages, it fetches pages from the EWA server and presents those to users. The switch continues to handle the user authentication.
- Captive portal—For companies who want the benefits of a full guest and BYOD access management solution, AOS-Switches can use captive portal authentication to integrate with Aruba ClearPass. Aruba ClearPass provides the RADIUS server and portal server; the Policy Manager and Guest components are required for this solution. ClearPass OnGuard is required if companies want the endpoint integrity features.

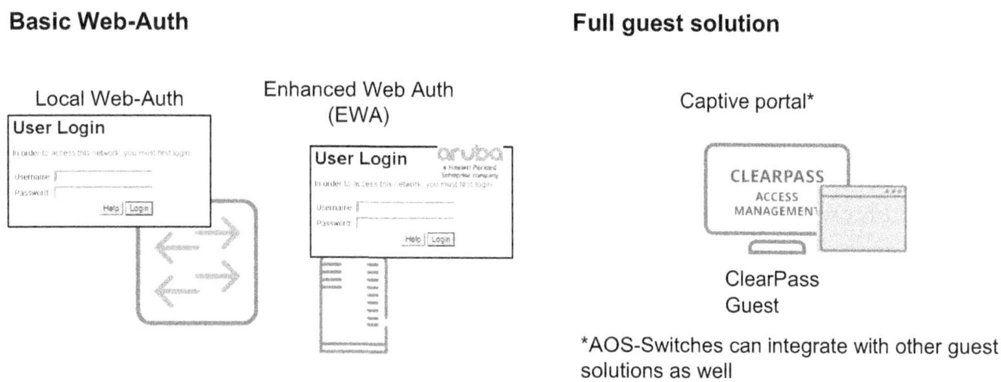


Figure 12-3 AOS-Switches' support for Web-based authentication

Each of these solutions is mutually exclusive. If you want to enable captive portal authentication and integrate the AOS-Switch in a ClearPass Guest solution, you cannot enable Web-Auth on any of the switch ports.

**Note**

AOS-Switches can also integrate with HPE Intelligent Management Center's (IMC's) BYOD solution using the BYOD redirect feature. Or, it can use MAC-Auth with Failure Redirect (MAFR) to redirect users who fail MAC authentication to register with a server that then adds their MAC address to the authorized list. These features are intended for similar use cases as the captive portal feature, and the use of each feature is mutually exclusive. BYOD redirect and MAFR are not covered in this study guide.

## Captive portal authentication

You will now learn how to implement the captive portal authentication solution, which is the solution preferred by most companies seeking a full guest or BYOD access solution.

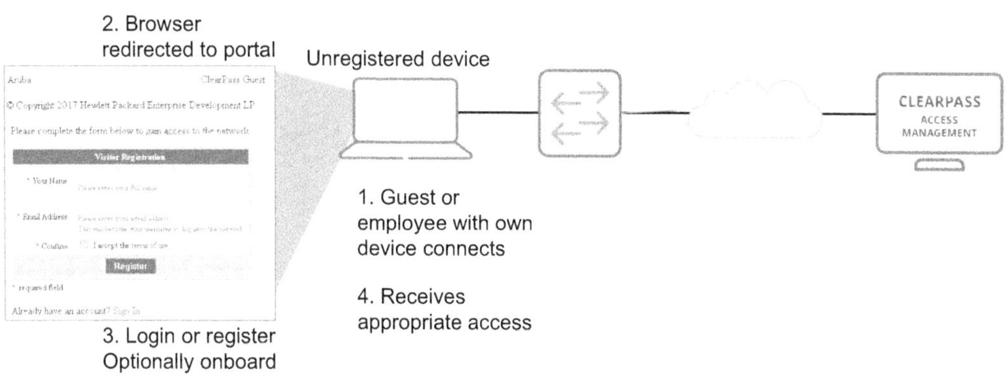


Figure 12-4 Captive portal authentication

The captive portal authentication feature requires close teamwork between the AOS-Switch and Aruba ClearPass. You can better understand how to set up the feature and how the feature works if you first look at the user experience that the feature is intended to deliver.

As Figure 12-4 shows, a user connects a new device to a free Ethernet jack, which is connected to an AOS-Switch port, or associates with an Aruba access point (AP). The user powers on the device and opens the Web browser. The user sees a portal page, which provides options for logging in as an employee or a guest. At this point, the user device is locked down, so the user cannot browse to other pages or receive access to other network services.

For an employee login, the user would need to enter valid employee credentials such as those stored in on Windows Active Directory. Guests would sign in with credentials created for guests, or they might be allowed to create their own account and log in with that. The options are controlled by the ClearPass Guest solution.

After logging in or registering for an account, the user is permitted network access, customized based on their identity and possibly other factors such as the health of their device. For example, an employee might receive different access rights than a guest. And a device that complies with security policies will receive fuller access than a potentially insecure device.

If the user connects with the same device later or in a different location, the device is provided the same access rights transparently.

## Authentication enforced on the AOS-Switch

You will now look at how the captive portal solution delivers this experience. As Figure 12-5 shows, you must implement RADIUS-based MAC-Auth on any switch port to which users might connect their devices. The switch can then submit access requests for all devices to Aruba ClearPass so that ClearPass can decide how to control the devices' access.

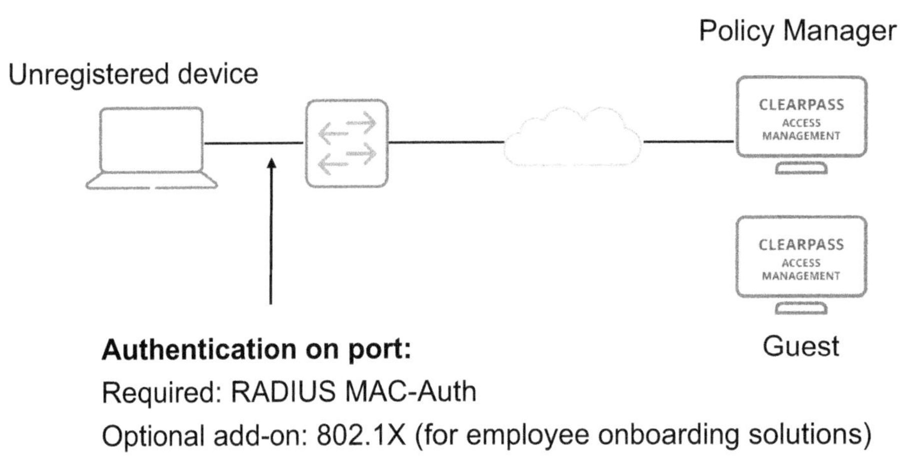


Figure 12-5 Authentication enforced on the AOS-Switch

You can optionally add 802.1X if you want registered devices to eventually authenticate with 802.1X. In this case, ClearPass Onboard would deploy the correct configuration settings and certificates for supporting 802.1X to devices connected to the captive portal. Companies usually use this option for employee BYOD devices, which require more security than guest devices. This chapter focuses more on the guest access option, though.

Remember that captive portal is *not* compatible with any form of Web-Auth on the port. If you enable captive portal globally, you cannot enable Web-Auth on any port. Similarly, you must disable Web-Auth on all ports before you can enable captive portal.

## High-level authentication process

Figure 12-6 provides a high-level overview of what occurs when an unregistered guest device connects. As soon as the device sends any traffic, the switch sends a MAC-Auth Access-Request with the device's MAC address.

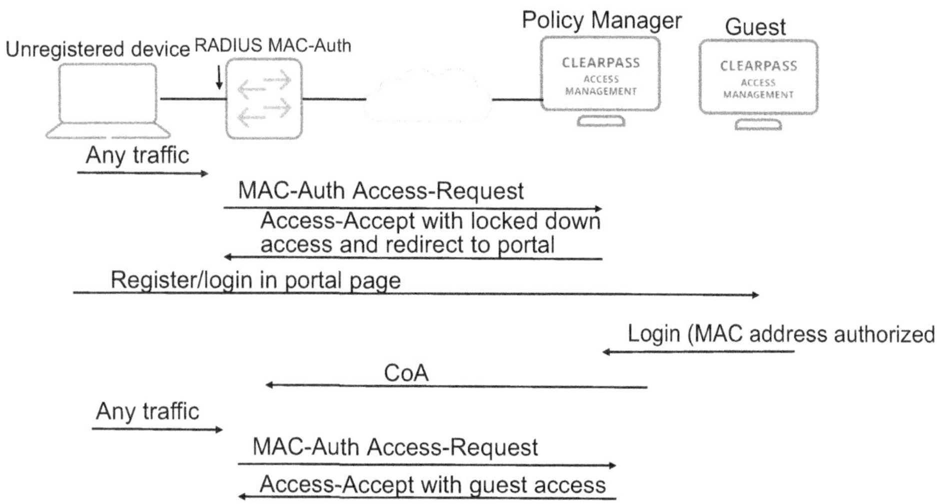


Figure 12-6 High-level authentication process

Because the device is unknown, ClearPass sends an Access-Accept with various dynamic settings to limit the device's access and redirect the device to the portal page on ClearPass Guest. The guest uses this page to login or to register and then log in. At the end of this process, ClearPass Guest logs the user into ClearPass Policy Manager. Policy Manager sends a Change of Authorization (CoA) to the switch. Now when the device sends any traffic again, the switch sends a new MAC-Auth Access-Request to ClearPass Policy Manager. Policy Manager now knows the guest device MAC address and sends an Access-Accept with the proper settings for this guest. The guest user can now receive appropriate access such as access to the Internet.

## More detailed look at the redirection to the captive portal

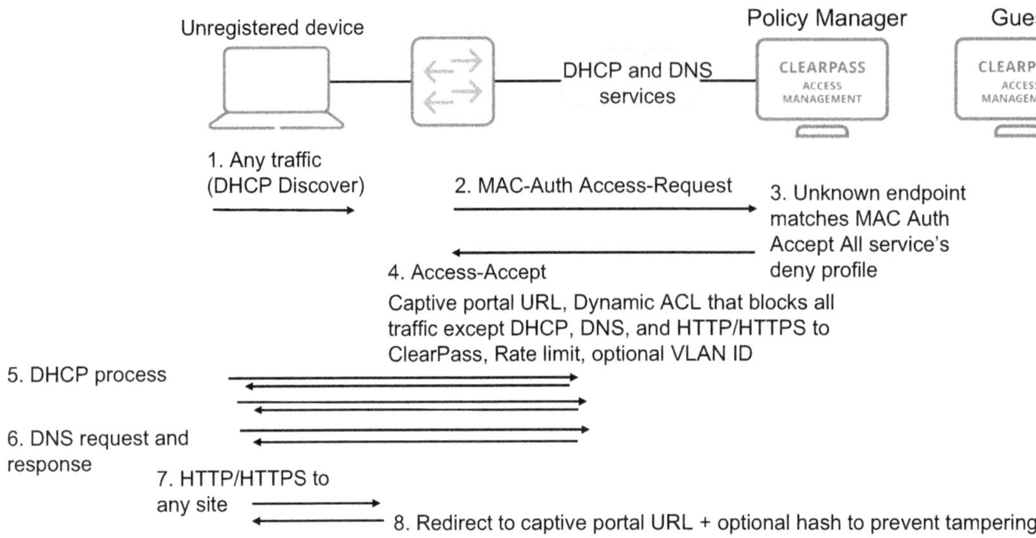


Figure 12-7 More detailed look at the redirection to the captive portal

You will now look at this process in more detail so that you can better understand what is required on the switch and what you should expect to occur during a successful process. Refer to Figure 12-7 as you read about the process.

1. The process begins when the unregistered guest device sends any traffic, typically a Dynamic Host Configuration Protocol (DHCP) discover.
2. The switch port enforces RADIUS MAC-Auth, so it sends an Access-Request to ClearPass Policy Manager, which must be defined as its RADIUS server.
3. At this point, ClearPass Policy Manager does not know the guest device MAC address. Typically, when a device cannot authenticate, the RADIUS server sends a RADIUS Reject message, and the switch port denies access. However, for a captive portal solution, ClearPass, as the RADIUS server, behaves differently. It uses a service with a special type of MAC-Auth (called Allow All MAC-Auth). When a device fails authentication, this service matches the device to a "deny any" profile rather than simply rejects the access. The profile defines various RADIUS attributes and VSAs to apply to the device's session.
4. ClearPass sends a RADIUS Access-Accept with these attributes to apply to the device's session. These attributes include the following:
    - A captive portal URL, which indicates the URL of the ClearPass portal in which users will log in or register.

    The URL must use a standard format such as https://clearpass.example.com. If administrators plan to redirect clients to an HTTPS URL, they must ensure that ClearPass has a certificate that is signed by a well-known trusted certificate authority.

- A dynamic ACL with IP filter rules to:
  - Permit only DHCP traffic, Domain Name System (DNS) traffic, and HTTP or HTTPS traffic to ClearPass
  - Redirect other HTTP and HTTPS to the redirect URL
- A rate limit to reduce the risk of untrusted users or devices launching a Denial of Service (DoS) attack (this VSA is not required, but it is recommended).

  The command output below shows example dynamic settings that are applied to a guest device at this point in the process:

```
Switch# show port-access client detail

Port Access Client Status Detail

Client Base Details :

Port            : 1/1                  Authentication Type : mac-based
Client Status   : authenticated        Session Time        : 131 seconds
Client Name     : 005056973668         Session Timeout     : 0 seconds
MAC Address     : 005056-973668
IP              : n/a

Access Policy Details :

COS Map         : Not Defined          In Limit Kbps       : 10000
Untagged VLAN   : 199                  Out Limit Kbps      : Not Set
Tagged VLANs    : No Tagged VLANs
Port Mode       : 1000FDx
RADIUS ACL List :
  permit in tcp from any to 10.100.50.50 80
  permit in tcp from any to 10.100.50.50 443
  deny in tcp from any to any 80 cpy
  deny in tcp from any to any 443 cpy
  permit in udp from any to any 67
  permit in udp from any to any 53

Captive Portal Details :

URL             : https://10.100.50.50/guest/guest_register.php/
```

5. Although the device is blocked from most network access, it can send DHCP messages and receive an IP address.
6. And when the user opens a browser and attempts to browse to a site, the device can use DNS to resolve the hostname.
7. The device then sends an HTTP or HTTPS request to the IP address.
8. The AOS-Switch intercepts that request and sends a response, posing as that address and redirecting the browser to the captive portal URL.

   The switch actually appends some information to the URL in a query string. This information includes the device's MAC address and IP address, a timestamp, and the originally requested URL. Hackers could try to obtain inappropriate access by altering the ACL. To prevent this from occurring, the ClearPass portal can require a hash appended to any requests, created by hashing the URL with a secret key. It only responds to requests that have the correct hash and drops other requests. If this security feature is enabled on ClearPass, you must configure a key on your AOS-Switches that matches the key on ClearPass.

## More detailed look at the login process

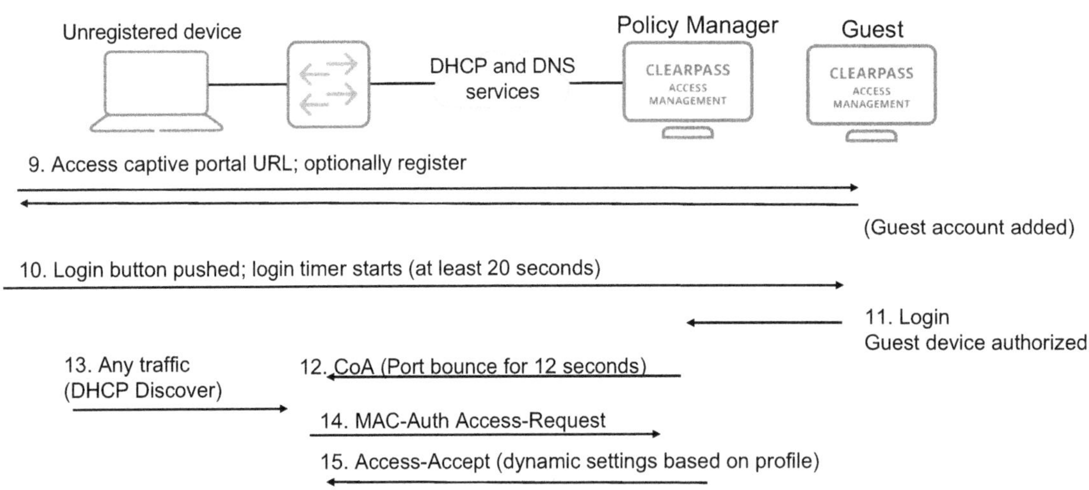


Figure 12-8 More detailed look at the login process

Figure 12-8 outlines the login process explained in detail below:

9. The unregistered device now accesses the ClearPass guest portal page. As you see, traffic flows between the client and the ClearPass Guest portal without any proxying by the switch.
10. The guest might be able to register for an account based on how the portal page is set up.

    The ClearPass portal's appearance and functionality is highly customizable. Depending on how administrators have set up and customized the portal, guests might log in with an account that has been provided to them or self-register for an account through the portal. The portal might grant all self-registering users immediate access, force them to activate the account through a text message or force them to receive sponsor approval. ClearPass transparently adds a newly registered account to the guest repository.

11. When the user clicks a login button, ClearPass Guest transparently logs the guest into the Policy Manager. Because the wired solution will use MAC-Auth to authenticate the registered devices, ClearPass Guest also makes sure that the guest device's MAC address (submitted in the URL) becomes authorized. The portal page begins a login countdown—recommended at about 20 seconds for a solution that uses AOS-Switches.

    How the MAC address is authorized depends on the solution. ClearPass might add the guest device to special guest endpoint repository and pair the device with the guest account, or ClearPass Guest might tell ClearPass Policy Manager to change the guest device, automatically discovered in ClearPass's global Endpoint Repository, to a known device. In any case, ClearPass Policy Manager will now be able to recognize the device MAC address as a known address associated with the known guest.

12. The successful guest login also triggers ClearPass to send a "port bounce" CoA message to the switch. This message causes the switch to de-authenticate the device and holds the port closed for a certain period of time—12 seconds is recommended. Note that ClearPass can be configured to use either a Disconnect Message (DM) or CoA for this purpose, but you should tell ClearPass administrators to use a port bounce CoA for AOS-Switches.

    It is important that the switch is set up to accept this message. You must enable dynamic authorization when you specify ClearPass as the RADIUS server, and you must make sure that the port is correct. The default dynamic authorization port on both AOS-Switches and ClearPass is 3799. (If the switch does not accept the CoA message, the client will not reauthenticate, as explained in steps 13 and 14, and the client will continue to be redirected to the portal.)

13. When the port opens again, the device starts to send traffic (probably a DHCP Discover).

14. The switch port enforces MAC-Auth for the device again.

15. Now ClearPass finds the MAC address as a known endpoint, so it authorizes the device for access, assigning it to a profile based on policy settings. For example, it might apply a guest profile that assigns the device to a guest VLAN using the same RADIUS VSAs that you learned about in the chapter on 802.1X.

    Because the login counter on the portal page is several seconds longer than the port bounce time, the authentication process is complete before the countdown ends. The guest is now connected to the network and can receive the appropriate services, based on the settings applied by ClearPass.

The command output below shows how new dynamic settings are applied to the guest device:

```
Switch# show port-access client detail

Port Access Client Status Detail

  Client Base Details :

   Port            : 1/1             Authentication Type : mac-based
   Client Status   : authenticated   Session Time        : 118 seconds
   Client Name     : 005056973668    Session Timeout     : 300 seconds
   MAC Address     : 005056-973668
   IP              : n/a

Access Policy Details :

   COS Map         : Not Defined      In Limit Kbps       : Not Set
   Untagged VLAN   : 99               Out Limit Kbps      : Not Set
   Tagged VLANs    : No Tagged VLANs
   Port Mode       : 1000FDx
   RADIUS ACL List :
      permit in tcp from any to any 80
      permit in tcp from any to any 443
      permit in udp from any to any 67
      permit in udp from any to any 53

   Captive Portal Details :
   URL              :
```

The next time that the guest connects the device, the MAC-Auth process occurs in the background, and the guest once again receives guest-level access without having to pass through the portal. (ClearPass administrators can also choose to set up the solution such that ClearPass forces the guest to log in through the portal again after a certain period of time.)

## BYOD onboard

If the company is using the captive portal for BYOD, ClearPass administrators will have set up the portal a bit differently. Employees typically log in to a device provisioning page on the portal with their existing domain or LDAP credentials. They then click a few buttons to accept a configuration that prepares their devices for 802.1X by configuring Extensible Authentication Protocol (EAP) settings and deploying certificates.

After this process, ClearPass sends a port bounce message to the AOS-Switch port, forcing the port to close for several seconds. The device then automatically authenticates through 802.1X using the settings deployed during the provisioning process. ClearPass uses the 802.1X service to authenticate the user. The port is now open to the user with optional customization based on the ClearPass policies and profiles.

Because the switch port still enforces MAC-Auth, the switch might also submit a MAC-Auth request for the device, and the device could fail that check. However, the 802.1X authentication settings take precedence, so the device will receive the correct access and will not be redirected to the portal.

Companies could also choose to combine guest and BYOD solutions by adding a link to the device provisioning page on the guest login or registration page.

## Optional VLAN for unregistered devices

When ClearPass sends the settings to redirect unknown devices to the captive portal, it can also send a dynamic VLAN assignment. This VLAN isolates unregistered devices in their own VLAN. Such isolation is not strictly required for security because the dynamic ACL locks down the unregistered devices' network access. However, you might prefer to place unauthenticated devices in their own VLAN for several reasons.

- So unauthenticated users cannot gain information about your IP addressing scheme.
- When examining traffic, you can distinguish between unauthenticated and authenticated clients.
- Unauthenticated devices cannot use up IP addresses that authenticated clients require. Otherwise, hackers could attempt to obtain a lot of IP addresses to lock out legitimate users.
- You can direct unauthenticated devices to different DHCP and DNS servers than authenticated users. This can help to prevent hackers from launching DoS attacks on these services.

If ClearPass sends a VLAN assignment for unregistered devices, remember that you must add this VLAN to your network.

– Provides a different address range for unregistered devices

– Allows direction to different DHCP and DNS servers

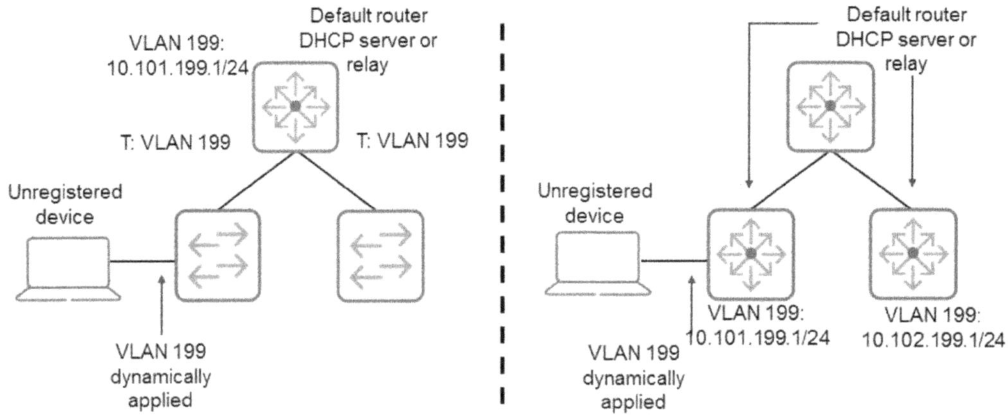


Figure 12-9 Optional VLAN for unregistered devices

When routing occurs at the core layer, tag the VLAN on the access switch uplinks and configure the VLAN and default router IP address on the core switch (or VSF fabric) (as shown in Figure 12-9). When routing occurs at the access layer, each access layer switch is the default router for the unregistered VLAN. Every switch uses the same VLAN ID but must associate that ID with a different subnet. The same principle applies if you are routing at the distribution layer in a three-tier topology.

Remember to configure DHCP services on the switch or switches acting as a default router. The switch can either act as the DHCP server or implement DHCP relay to a network DHCP server.

Also, set up routing as appropriate to allow communication between the unregistered VLAN and the ClearPass guest server. For example, you might need to enable Open Shortest Path First (OSPF), preferably in passive mode, on the VLAN.

## Configuring an AOS-Switch to integrate with the Aruba ClearPass captive portal

You now understand how the captive portal solution works. Configuring an AOS-Switch to participate in the solution is simple because ClearPass handles most of the functionality. You simply need to complete the steps outlined in the sections below.

### Install a CA-signed certificate

Although the user device communicates directly with the ClearPass portal during most of the login process, the switch does handle the original redirection. The switch can only redirect HTTPS traffic if it has a certificate set for the captive portal usage. You should make sure to set up a certificate for this purpose. Otherwise, users who browse to HTTPS pages will have trouble being redirected to the portal.

Although the switch can use a self-signed certificate for this purpose, it is recommended you that you install one signed by a trusted CA so that users do not receive an error.

You must first create a Trusted Anchor (TA) profile for the CA that will sign the certificate.

```
Switch(config)# crypto pki ta-profile <name>
```

You can add more options to the command above to retrieve a Certificate Revocation List (CRL), set a different profile for checking the CRL, and so on.

Optionally, create an identify profile, which specifies the certificate's subject name. For example, you could enter the following command to set the subject name to the IP address that the switch uses on the VLAN assigned to unregistered devices.

```
Switch(config)# crypto pki identity-profile access1 subject common-name
<IP address>
```

Next use this command to create a certificate signing request (CSR):

```
Switch(config)# crypto pki create-csr certificate-name <name> ta-profile
    <name> usage <all | captive-portal> [subject common-name <common
    name> [other options]] [key-type <ecdsa | rsa>] [valid-start
    <MMDDYY>]
```

The subject option is required if you have not created a separate identity profile.

The command line interface (CLI) outputs a request, which you must copy into a file, and submit to the CA. After the CA signs the request, you can load the certificate with this command:

```
Switch(config)# crypto pki install-signed-certificate
```

You will be prompted to paste the certificate.

After you paste in the certificate, you can verify that you have installed the certificate. Enter:

```
Switch(config)# show crypto pki local-certificate

   Name                 Usage         Expiration     Parent / Profile

   ----------------     -----------   ------------   --------------------

   Portal               CaptivePortal 2018/07/03     default
```

### Create a self-signed certificate (alternative)

Use this command if you choose to create a self-signed certificate:

```
Switch(config)# crypto pki enroll-self-signed certificate-name <name>
    usage <all | captive-portal> [subject common-name <common name>
    [other options]] [key-type <ecdsa | rsa>] [valid-start <MMDDYY>]
```

Again, the subject option is required if you have not created a separate identity profile.

## Configure the switch to support captive portal

You can then enable captive portal with this command:

```
Switch(config)# aaa authentication captive-portal enable
```

If ClearPass requires URL validation, make sure to enable hashing with a shared secret that matches the one on ClearPass.

```
Switch(config)# aaa authentication captive-portal url-hash-key
    <plaintext | encrypted> <KEY>
```

The encrypted option is only available if the switch has **encrypt-credentials** enabled globally. When encrypt-credentials is enabled and you enter a key with the **plaintext** option, the key is automatically encrypted and stored in the configuration with the **encrypted** option and that encrypted key. You can then backup that configuration and restore it without exposing the key to unauthorized viewers.

You can check the captive portal settings by entering:

```
Switch(config)# show captive-portal

 Captive Portal Configuration

  Redirection Enabled     : Yes
  URL Hash Key Configured  : Yes
```

You can also view the captive portal profile. In the example below, the profile indicates that the switch is expecting to receive the captive portal URL for each device from the RADIUS server, which is the default profile.

```
Access-1(config)# show captive-portal profile

 Captive Portal Profile Configuration

  Name : use-radius-vsa
  Type : predefined
  URL  :
```

## Set up authentication

As part of the authentication setup, make sure to specify ClearPass Policy Manager as the RADIUS server. Configure the correct shared secret and enable dynamic authorization. Also, set the time window to 0 as you learned how to do in previous chapters.

```
Switch(config)# radius-server host <IP address> key <secret>
Switch(config)# radius-server host <IP address> dyn-authorization
Switch(config)# radius-server host <IP address> time-window 0
```

Also, make sure that you understand whether ClearPass is deployed as a high-availability cluster. The cluster provides shared configuration and databases, but not a virtual IP address. Therefore, you must make sure to specify all ClearPass servers as RADIUS servers on the switch. As you learned in a previous chapter, AOS-Switches do not load balance requests between RADIUS servers. Instead, they send all requests to the first defined server unless the request to that server times out and all retries expire. If you want, you can configure one RADIUS server IP address first on half of the switches, and a different server IP address first on the other half of the switches. (You cannot define a hostname for the RADIUS server, so a DNS-based load balancer will not work.)

You are now ready to enable RADIUS MAC-Auth (or both 802.1X and RADIUS MAC-Auth are enabled) on the edge ports.

```
Switch(config)# aaa port-access mac-based <port_ID_list>
```

Refer to the *Chapter 10: 802.1X Authentication* and *Chapter 11: MAC Authentication* for more detailed discussions of these authentication methods.

## Web-Auth and EWA

If the company just needs a simple portal page for guests to log in through, you can use the AOS-Switches' built-in Web-Auth capabilities instead of the ClearPass captive portal.

| Web-Auth | EWA |
|---|---|
| – Host login pages locally | – Host login pages locally |
| – Authenticate users to RADIUS server | – Authenticate users to RADIUS server |
| – Provide no customization for login pages | – Load login pages from an external location with some customization permitted |

Figure 12-10 Web-Auth and EWA

As Figure 12-10 shows, the switch supports two basic forms of built-in Web-Auth.

- Web-Auth
- EWA

Both forms of authentication rely on the AOS-Switch to host basic login pages. With both forms, the AOS-Switch also authenticates guests to a RADIUS server. However, basic Web-Auth provides no customization for login pages. EWA allows companies to obtain some basic customization for these pages. The switch still hosts the pages. It simply retrieves the customized pages from the external location and then serves them to the guests.

## Local Web-Auth to a RADIUS server

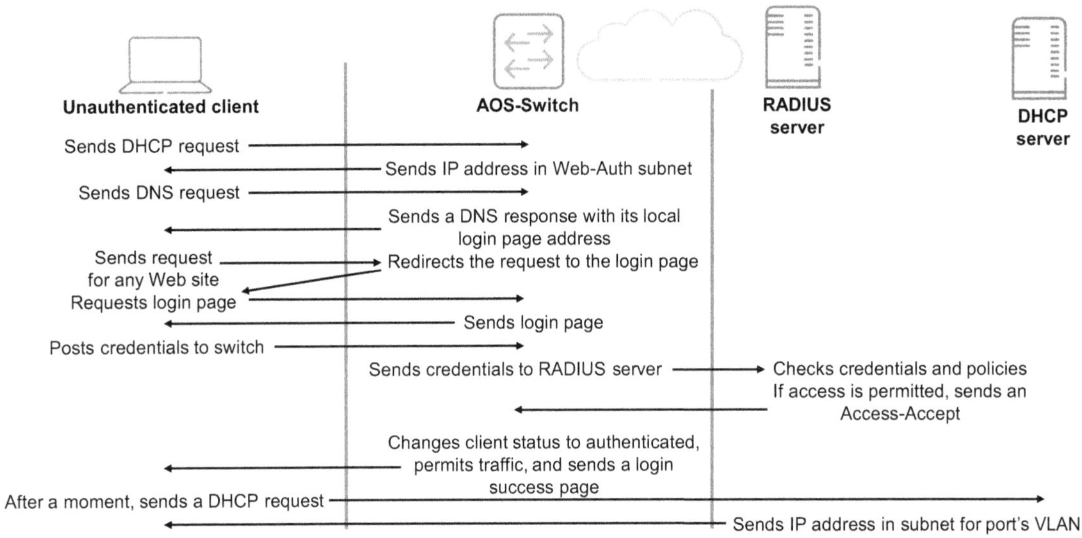


Figure 12-11 Local Web-Auth to a RADIUS server

You can enforce Web-Auth on an AOS-Switch physical interface. The switch will then redirect guests to a login page hosted on the switch itself. It authenticates the guests to a backend RADIUS server, though. Figure 12-11 outlines this solution, which is described below:

1. The user's client establishes a connection with the switch port that enforces Web-Auth.

   The switch drops all traffic from the unauthenticated client except DHCP and DNS traffic. The switch itself automatically offers these services when you enable Web-Auth, protecting network servers from unauthenticated clients.

2. The client sends a DHCP request.

3. The switch responds with IP settings, including an IP address in the Web-Auth subnet (default 192.168.0.0/24). The lease for this address is very short, 10 seconds, by default. (If the lease runs out before the user finishes authenticating, the switch allows the client to renew its same IP address.)

4. The user opens a browser and attempts to reach a webpage. First, the client sends a DNS request for the hostname in the URL.

5. The switch sends a DNS response mapping its own IP address to the requested hostname. This IP address is the default gateway for the Web-Auth subnet, which the switch uses to host the login page, rather than an IP address manually configured on the switch.

6. The device attempts to open an HTTP or HTTPS session with the switch.

7. The switch recognizes the TCP port and redirects the client to the login webpage hosted on itself (index.html). Because the switch uses the Web-Auth IP address to host the webpage, the client only has access to this page; it cannot, for example, reach the switch's web browser management interface.

8. The user submits credentials to the login webpage (index.html).
9. The switch extracts the credentials and submits them to the RADIUS server.

   At the same time, it directs the guest device to an authenticating page (authen.hmtl).
10. The RADIUS server both authenticates the credentials and uses a policy to determine the level of access that the user is allowed.
11. The switch enforces the decision, either continuing to block the client's traffic (Access-Reject) or giving the client authenticated status (Access-Accept). The switch port permits all traffic to and from the authenticated client, as limited by dynamic settings in the Access-Accept.

    The switch also directs the device browser to the proper page, either a failure one (retry_login.html, reject_unauthvlan.html, or reject_novlan.html) or a success one (accept.html). The success page has a timer.
12. The client's DHCP lease for the temporary IP address rapidly expires. Now when the client sends a renew request, the switch ignores it.
13. The client then sends a DHCP discovery, which the switch forwards on the client's VLAN. The client receives a valid IP address for the network. By now the timer has timed out, and the device is redirected to a welcome page (redirect-URL) or the page to which it originally browsed.

The switch also has other login pages that are used in special cases, not covered in the steps above. For example, it shows a timeout page if the request to the RADIUS server times out. If you are interested in learning more about the pages, refer to your switch's *Access Security Guide.*

## Basic Web-Auth setup

You specify the RADIUS server settings as you have already learned in other chapters. Then enabling Web-Auth can be as simple as entering a command to enable it on the port.

However, it is recommended that you consider a few other settings to ensure a good user experience. (You also have several more options that you can configure for Web-Auth, besides the ones described here, which you can read about in your switch's *Access Security Guide.*)

### Redirect URL

You should configure a redirect URL. After a user successfully authenticates, the switch redirects the user's browser to this URL; you can choose any welcome webpage that you like. If you do not specify this URL, depending on their browsers, users might not see the success page and fail to understand that they have successfully logged in.

```
Switch(config)# aaa port-access web-based <port ID list> redirect-url <URL>
```

Use standard URL format such as **http://server.example.com/welcome.**

## Unauthenticated client DHCP subnet

If you want, you can also change the subnet for unauthenticated Web-Auth clients. You might want to do this if the switch is already using the default subnet (default 192.168.0.0/24). Use this command:

```
Switch(config)# aaa port-access web-based dhcp-addr <network address>/<prefix length>
```

The command for changing the Web-Auth subnet requires a valid IP address within the subnet and a prefix length of 24 or less (in other words, a subnet of /24 size or larger). Whatever IP address you configure, the switch will use the lowest valid IP address in the subnet as its own during the Web-Auth process. It will assign other IP addresses in the subnet to unauthenticated devices. For clarity, you should configure the lowest valid IP address in the subnet. For example, configure 192.168.1.1/24.

You should choose a unique, unused subnet for the Web-Auth subnet. Although the CLI allows you to specify an IP address on a subnet already configured on a switch VLAN, doing so can cause confusion.

## Certificate

It is recommended that you install a certificate on the switch. Otherwise, the switch cannot redirect HTTPS requests to the login page. Refer to the previous instructions for installing a certificate. However, set the usage to web or all. A CA-signed certificate is recommended to prevent errors.

Installing the certificate on its own does not make the switch use HTTPS for the login page. It simply allows the switch to redirect clients that attempt to browse to an HTTPS site to its HTTP page. However, after you have installed the web certificate, you can configure the switch to use HTTPS for the login page with this command:

```
Switch(config)# aaa port-access web-based <port ID list> ssl-login
```

The switch then redirects both HTTP and HTTPS requests to its HTTPS page.

## Support for multiple clients

You should consider whether more than one client will connect on the port. For example, the AOS-Switch might connect to an unmanaged switch or hub in a conference room. In the latest software as of the publication of this study guide, AOS-Switches authenticate Web-Auth clients based on their MAC address. By default, only one MAC address is permitted on the port. You can raise the client limit with this command:

```
Switch(config)# aaa port-access web-based <port ID list> client-limit <limit>
```

The switch can assign different clients on the port to different VLANs, as instructed by the RADIUS server—as long as the port supports MAC-based VLANs.

### Web-Auth enabled

After specifying the options, enable Web-Auth on the ports:

```
Switch(config)# aaa port-access web-based <port ID list>
```

Enabling Web-Auth automatically enables the switch to act as a DHCP server in the Web-Auth subnet, as well as to respond to unauthenticated clients DNS requests, without further configuration.

## EWA

Many companies want to customize the login pages with their own logos and branding. You cannot alter the login pages on the AOS-Switch itself. Instead, you can configure EWA, which enables the switch to use customized login pages stored on an external web server.

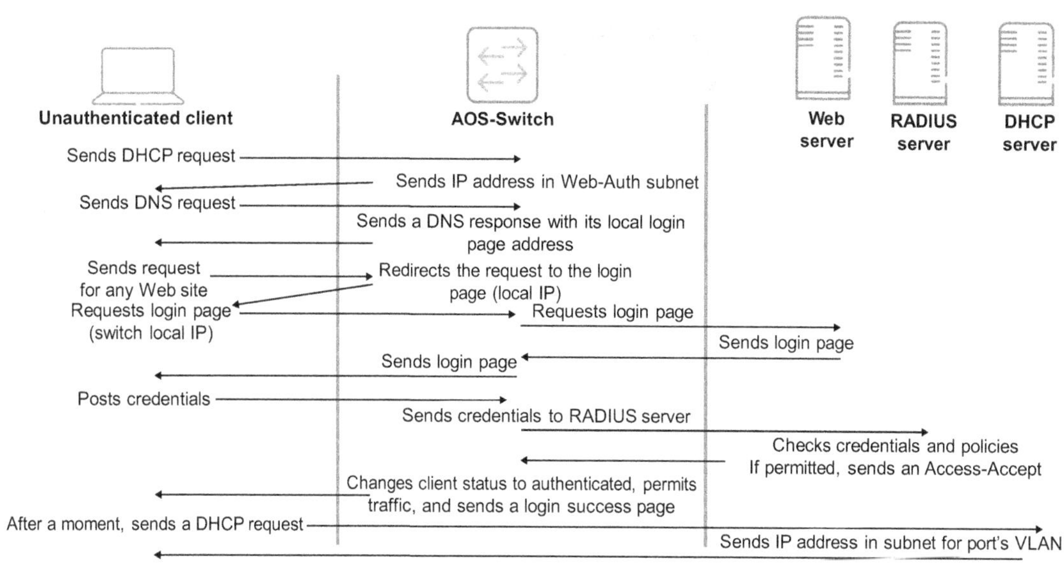


Figure 12-12 EWA

As Figure 12-12 shows, the process for EWA does not differ from basic Web-Auth until the step at which the unauthenticated user attempts to browse to a webpage. Once again, the switch redirects the user to its local address on the Web-Auth subnet. However, instead of returning a local webpage, the switch initiates contact with the external web server URL, which you have configured in the switch's Web-Auth settings. The switch receives the webpage from this server, and it then sends the page to the client.

The login page includes code that posts the credentials to the switch, and authentication proceeds as before.

At each point in the process, the switch requests a different webpage from the external web server. For example, the switch initially requests a page called index.html. While authenticating the user, the switch requests (and sends on to the client) a page called authen.html. The next page discusses requirements for setting up the pages on the external server.

Note a couple of implementation considerations. Guest clients only communicate with the AOS-Switch and do not actually access the external web server. Therefore, you do not need to worry about extending the temporary subnet into the actual network. You can also use the same unauthorized subnet address on all switches.

## Guidelines for EWA

You set up this solution the same as the previous one. However, you must also specify the external web server's IP address or hostname, as well as the path to the login pages if the path is not the server's default one.

If you want to specify a hostname, you must first ensure that the switch has a DNS server for resolving the hostname. If the switch receives a DHCP IP address, it might already have a DNS server address. The command for specifying the DNS server statically is:

```
Switch(config)# ip dns server-address priority 1 <IP address>
```

Use this CLI command to specify the EWA server:

```
Switch(config)# aaa port-access web-based ewa-server <IP address
|hostname> [<page-path>]
```

Because the AOS-Switch requests specific pages at specific points in the process, the web server must have a precise set of pages that use these exact names:

- accept.html
- authen.html
- index.html
- reject_novlan.html
- reject_unauthvlan.html (if you are using an unauthenticated client VLAN)
- retry_login.html
- sslredirect.html
- timeout.html

These web pages must also include specific code such as the form in which users submit their credentials with the fieldnames that the switch expects. It is recommended that you download template login pages provided on the download page for your switch's software. A company's web designers can customize these pages as much as they like as long as they do not change a few pieces of code, which are documented in your switches' *Access Security Guide*.

## Limited access with no authentication

In this scenario, the guests do not have to authenticate to the AOS-Switch or ClearPass. Instead, the switch places unauthenticated devices in a VLAN with limited access.

As a prerequisite for this scenario, you or another administrator must establish this VLAN. The default router for this VLAN often enforces ACLs that restrict the guests from accessing the Internet. The default router might be a third-party guest solution that provides proxy web services, content filtering, and other such services—or it might redirect guest traffic to such a solution. If the access layer is not routing, remember to tag the appropriate switch-to-switch links with the VLAN.

### 802.1X Unauthorized-client VLAN

When you know that guests will connect in certain areas only, you can simply configure the switch ports that serve in that area as untagged members of the guest VLAN. Often, though, companies want flexible edge ports that can adapt to the device, providing employee devices with full access and placing guest devices in their isolated VLAN.

In this case, you must implement an authentication method such as 802.1X on the edge ports to ensure that only authorized employees are given employee-level access. (Web-Auth or MAC-Auth can also work, but are less recommended for employee authentication.)

You can then define an 802.1X Unauthorized-client VLAN. The switch places devices that do not pass 802.1X authentication in this VLAN, rather than blocking their traffic.

The switch port assigns a device's traffic to the Unauthorized-client VLAN in all of these cases:

- Device never participates in the 802.1X process (no EAP messages)
- Device attempts to complete 802.1X authentication, but authentication fails for any reason, including:
  - Invalid credentials
  - RADIUS policy does not permit access
  - RADIUS server timeout and no secondary authentication method
  - Device supplicant rejects RADIUS server certificate

**Note**

The switch assigns the unauthenticated devices' *untagged* traffic to the Unauthorized-client VLAN. The switch drops any tagged traffic from these devices, even if the switch port has tagged memberships. Authenticated devices, on the other hand, can send tagged and untagged traffic.

To set up an Unauthorized-client VLAN for one or more interfaces that implement 802.1X, use this command:

```
Switch(config)# aaa port-access authenticator <port ID list> unauth-vid
<ID>
```

**Important**

If you have combined 802.1X with MAC-Auth, Local MAC Authentication (LMA), or Web-Auth, you must set the Unauthorized-client VLAN for MAC-Auth, LMA, or Web-Auth rather than for 802.1X.

## Guidelines for using the 802.1X Unauthorized-client VLAN

On AOS-Switches, a switch port with a static VLAN ID and an Unauthorized-client VLAN ID is automatically part of the Unauthorized-client VLAN as soon as a device connects and the EAP request times out. This behavior helps guest devices and other devices without 802.1X supplicants to connect more quickly.

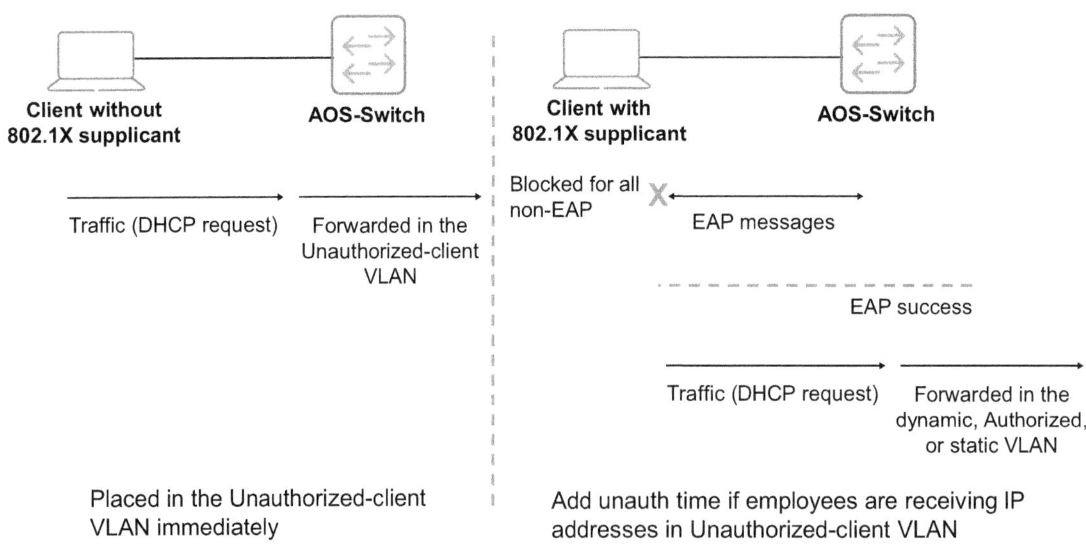


Figure 12-13 Guidelines for using the 802.1X Unauthorized-client VLAN

As Figure 12-13 shows, however, it might cause issues for users who *do* use 802.1X to log in. After a device passes authentication, the port becomes an untagged member of the VLAN assigned to the authorized user. This VLAN is determined in this order:

- The dynamic VLAN, if sent by the RADIUS server
- The authorized VLAN, if set
- The static VLAN

If the user's device allows non-EAP traffic before authentication, it might receive a DHCP address in the Unauthorized-client VLAN, causing it to lose connectivity after the port moves to the VLAN for the authenticated user. Depending on its OS, the device usually drops the IP address after some delay and obtains a valid one.

You can use the unauth-period to prevent these connectivity delays for 802.1X devices.

```
Switch(config)# aaa port-access authenticator <port ID list> unauth-period
<seconds>
```

When you set this period, the switch port delays placing a connected device in the Unauthorized-client VLAN until the client has failed to authenticate during that period. During this time, all traffic except EAP messages is blocked, giving the 802.1X device time to log in. Fine-tune the unauth period to balance delays for guest devices with delays for 802.1X devices.

## Supporting multiple employees and guests with the Unauthorized-client VLAN

As you know, an AOS-Switch port can enforce authentication on a port that connects to multiple endpoints. For example, a company might have a hub in a conference room, which then connects to the AOS-Switch.

The AOS-Switch can support a mix of employee and guest devices on this port. Remember to configure 802.1X in user-based mode by raising the client limit to an appropriate value, based on the number of devices expected on the port.

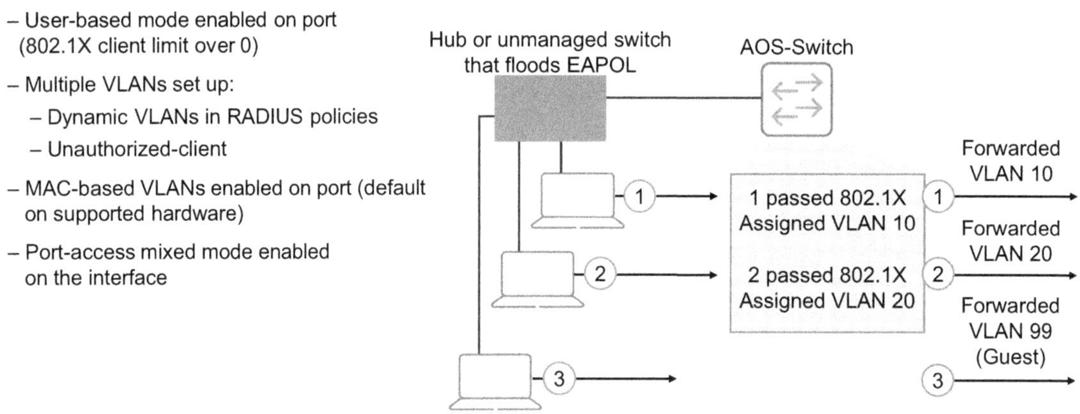


Figure 12-14 Supporting multiple employees and guests with the Unauthorized-client VLAN

As Figure 12-14 shows, you can have employees use the static VLAN on the port or create an 802.1X Authorized-client VLAN for them. Or, you can have the RADIUS server assign them to dynamic VLANs. Guest devices, which fail 802.1X, are placed in the Unauthorized-client VLAN. Because different clients are placed in different VLANs concurrently, the switch hardware must support MAC-based VLANs (MBVs), and MBV must be enabled on the port. You must also enable mixed mode; otherwise, the unauthorized clients are blocked when a client passes authentication.

Use this command to enable mixed mode on interfaces:

```
Switch(config)# aaa port-access <port ID list> mixed
```

You might have a similar scenario—a mix of concurrent employee and guest devices on a single port—with a captive portal solution as well. In that case, you would combine 802.1X in user-mode with MAC-Auth and enable captive portal. Remember to raise the client limit for 802.1X and the address limit for MAC-Auth.

## Summary

In this chapter, you explored appropriate situations for implementing various guest and BYOD solutions. You can implement captive portal authentication to integrate AOS-Switches with an Aruba ClearPass Guest or Onboard solution.

For companies with more basic needs, you can set up Web-Auth on the switch itself. Or you can establish an Unauthorized-client VLAN to provide limited access to devices that fail authentication.

## Learning check

1. Which correctly describes the relationship between captive portal authentication and Web-Auth on an AOS-Switch?
   a. Web-Auth must be enabled on individual switch ports when captive portal is enabled globally.
   b. Web-Auth cannot be enabled on any switch ports when captive portal is enabled globally.
   c. Web-Auth and captive portal can be enabled on different switch ports on the same switch.
   d. Web-Auth and captive portal must both be enabled on a switch port for the captive portal solution to work.
2. What is one benefit of an Aruba ClearPass Guest solution?
   a. It automatically activates the proper authentication settings on AOS-Switch ports.
   b. It enables companies to develop mobile engagement services for their guests.
   c. It provides self-registration through a captive portal for guests.
   d. It provides load balancing through a virtual IP address.
3. A company wants to implement a ClearPass Guest captive portal solution. The ClearPass policy places unauthenticated guest devices in a different VLAN from the guest VLAN. What setup do you need to complete within the network infrastructure to prepare for the solution?
4. What RADIUS messages and client status should you expect for unregistered devices if captive portal is working correctly? What commands can you use to check these settings?
5. An AOS-Switch is configured to support captive portal. It enforces MAC-Auth to the ClearPass Policy Manager, which is defined as a RADIUS server on the switch. What issue would occur if the switch does not have dynamic authorization enabled for the ClearPass RADIUS server? How could you troubleshoot this issue?

# Answers

## Learning check

1. Which correctly describes the relationship between captive portal authentication and Web-Auth on an AOS-Switch?

    a. Web-Auth must be enabled on individual switch ports when captive portal is enabled globally.

    **b. Web-Auth cannot be enabled on any switch ports when captive portal is enabled globally.**

    c. Web-Auth and captive portal can be enabled on different switch ports on the same switch.

    d. Web-Auth and captive portal must both be enabled on a switch port for the captive portal solution to work.

2. What is one benefit of an Aruba ClearPass Guest solution?

    a. It automatically activates the proper authentication settings on AOS-Switch ports.

    b. It enables companies to develop mobile engagement services for their guests.

    **c. It provides self-registration through a captive portal for guests.**

    d. It provides load balancing through a virtual IP address.

3. A company wants to implement a ClearPass Guest captive portal solution. The ClearPass policy places unauthenticated guest devices in a different VLAN from the guest VLAN. What setup do you need to complete within the network infrastructure to prepare for the solution?

    You need to set up the VLANs for unregistered and guest devices if they are not already deployed in the network. You should make sure that each VLAN is extended from the access layer to the routing switch that acts as the default router. You need to configure the correct IP address on the default router, make the VLAN routable (for example, advertise it in OSPF), and specify the correct helper IP address. You should verify that server administrators set up DHCP services for the VLANs, and you should ensure that a DNS server is reachable for devices in the VLAN.

    You then need to set up the access layer switches to integrate with the solution, which includes configuring ClearPass Policy Manager as the RADIUS server; enabling captive portal; setting a captive portal URL hash key, if required; installing a captive portal certificate; and enabling MAC-Auth of interfaces.

4. What RADIUS messages and client status should you expect for unregistered devices if captive portal is working correctly? What commands can you use to check these settings?

    You should expect the switch and ClearPass to exchange RADIUS request and challenge messages related to MAC-Auth. ClearPass should send an Access-Accept, and you should see that the device becomes authorized. When you check the detailed client status, you should see that it is being controlled with several NAS filter rules, including ones that permit DNS and DHCP and ones that redirect HTTP and HTTPS traffic to the captive portal URL. You should also see the captive portal URL setting.

You can use commands such as the **show port-access client *<interface ID list>* detail** command.

5. An AOS-Switch is configured to support captive portal. It enforces MAC-Auth to the ClearPass Policy Manager, which is defined as a RADIUS server on the switch. What issue would occur if the switch does not have dynamic authorization enabled for the ClearPass RADIUS server? How could you troubleshoot this issue?

   Unregistered guest clients can reach the captive portal and seem to log in successfully. However, when the login timer expires, the user does not receive network access. Instead, the user will be redirected to the login page. This happens because the switch did not accept the CoA message, so the user device remained controlled with the unregistered device VSAs. If your guests experience similar issues, you can check the RADIUS server configuration on your AOS-Switch and make sure that dynamic authorization is enabled, dynamic authorization is using the correct right port, and the time window is set to 0.

# 13 Integrating with an Aruba Mobility Solution

EXAM OBJECTIVES

✓ Configure tunneled-node on AOS-Switches

✓ Describe when and how to configure Provisioning API (PAPI) enhanced security, high availability, and fallback switching for tunneled-node

## Assumed knowledge

- Switching
- Routing
- Familiarity with Aruba Access Points (APs) and Aruba Mobility Controllers (MCs)

## Introduction

This study guide focuses on AOS-Switches, but switches will likely only be part of your solution in an Aruba Mobile First Network. In addition to Aruba AirWave, for network management, and Aruba ClearPass, for user access management, you may also have Aruba APs connected to Aruba MCs. You might want to leverage the access control, firewall, and packet inspection capabilities of the MCs to secure wired endpoints as well. In this chapter, you will learn how to use the tunneled-node feature for this purpose.

## Use cases

You should use the tunneled-node feature whenever you want to apply the same traffic control capabilities that an Aruba controller-based solution traditionally provides for wireless traffic to wired traffic as well (see Figure 13-1). The tunneled-node feature can also play a role in unifying access control for users so that the same policies apply regardless of whether they have a wired or wireless connection.

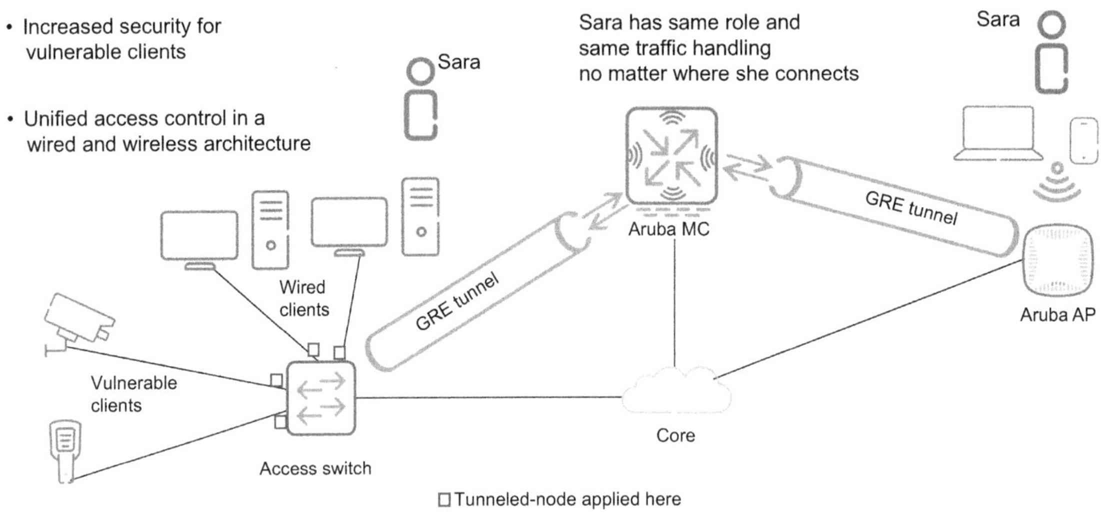


Figure 13-1 Use cases

> **Note**
> The tunneled-node feature is supported with MC appliances, not with virtual mobility controllers (VMCs).

Tunneled-node offers many benefits. For example, a company might have vulnerable devices that require extra filtering for their traffic. Surveillance cameras, payment card readers, and some Internet of Things (IoT) devices can be easily hacked or blocked by Denial of Service (DoS) attacks because they do not have an internal firewall. By having the switch tunnel all the client's traffic to the MC—just like an AP tunnels all traffic to the MC using Generic Routing Encapsulation (GRE)—you can take advantage of the controller's security features to protect both the vulnerable device and the network. These security features include a stateful firewall, deep packet inspection (DPI), and fingerprinting.

Aruba ClearPass and port-based authentication implemented on switches provide one method for unifying access policies. Both the MCs and AOS-Switches can enforce 802.1X authentication to users and apply the policies returned by ClearPass. However, ClearPass cannot simply send the same settings to both MCs and switches. For example, ClearPass often simply sends the role assigned to a user to an MC, and the MC has firewall rules associated with that role configured on it. On the other hand, ClearPass would need to send a policy with dynamic access control lists (ACLs) to apply similar controls to an AOS-Switch.

Tunneled-node provides tighter and simpler unification of wired and wireless access. Switches simply tunnel traffic to the MC, which handles the traffic much as it would handle traffic tunneled from an AP. An employee can connect through their desktop, log in, be assigned a role, and receive customized access. Later the employee can connect wirelessly using a laptop in a meeting room, log in, be assigned the same role, and receive the same access.

Keep in mind that tunneling the wired devices' traffic to the MC, of course, increases the demands on that device. Network architects will need to plan the Aruba solution's capacity and licensing accordingly. A list of general guidelines is provided later in this chapter.

## Tunneling traffic to an MC

As Figure 13-2 shows, the tunneled-node feature creates a GRE tunnel between the AOS-Switch and an Aruba MC using the same technology that encapsulates packets between Aruba APs and MCs.

The switch and MC also establish a control channel that uses PAPI, the same Aruba protocol that MCs use to send configs and other important messages to APs. PAPI traffic is always carried outside of the GRE tunnels in a separate PAPI control channel.

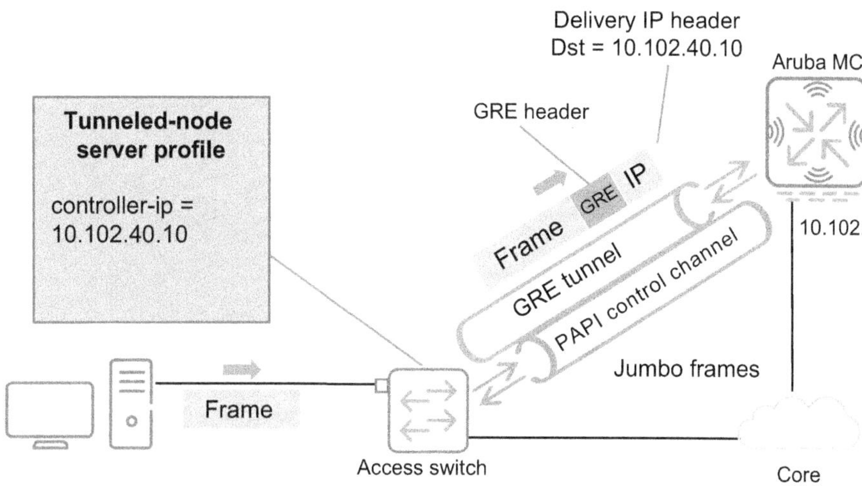


Figure 13-2 Tunneling traffic to an MC

You enable the AOS-Switch to create the tunnel and channel by defining a tunnel server profile on the AOS-Switch.

```
Switch(config)# tunneled-node-server
```

You can create a maximum of one profile. Define the IP address of an MC with this command:

```
Switch(tunneled-node-server)# controller-ip <IP_address>
```

After you enable the profile, the switch establishes the tunnel, encapsulates all tunneled-node traffic, and sends the traffic over this tunnel. You enable the profile with this command:

```
Switch(tunneled-node-server)# enable
```

You can see the profile configuration with this command:

```
Switch# show tunneled-node-server

   Tunneled Node Server Information

    State : Enabled

    Primary Controller : 10.102.40.10

    Backup Controller :

    Keepalive Interval (seconds) : 8

    Mode : Port-based
```

You can check the state of the tunnel to the MC with this command:

```
Switch# show tunneled-node-server state

  Tunneled Node Port State

    Active Controller IP Address : 10.102.40.10

    Port   State

    ------ -------------------------

    1/1    Complete
```

## Using PAPI enhanced security

As Figure 13-3 shows, switches use PAPI to communicate with the MC.

This communication creates a potential security risk. Rogue devices could start sending PAPI messages to the APs and switches and disrupt functionality. They could also try to insert spoofed PAPI messages on the controller to disrupt communications or obtain information about the network. PAPI enhanced security minimizes this risk by using an MD5 and user-configurable key to hash the message. If a rogue device tries to spoof or tamper with a message, the hash will not check out because the rogue does not know the correct key to create the hash.

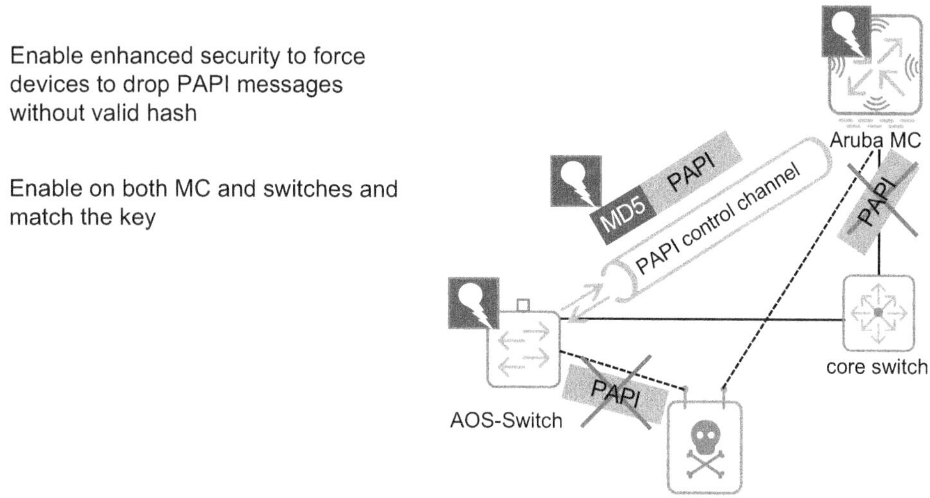


Figure 13-3 Using PAPI enhanced security

If administrators have enabled PAPI enhanced security on the MC, you must set a matching PAPI key on the switch. The key must be between 10 and 64 characters. The switch then no longer accepts PAPI messages unless they have a valid hash created with this key. It is also able to send its PAPI messages with the correct key. Enhanced security mode is disabled by default. Enable PAPI enhanced security with this command:

```
Switch(config)# papi-security key-value <key_value>
```

You can use the **no** form of the command to remove PAPI enhanced security.

## Modes

How the switch selects tunneled-node traffic depends on the mode. You can configure tunneled-node in port-based mode or role-based mode (see Figure 13-4).

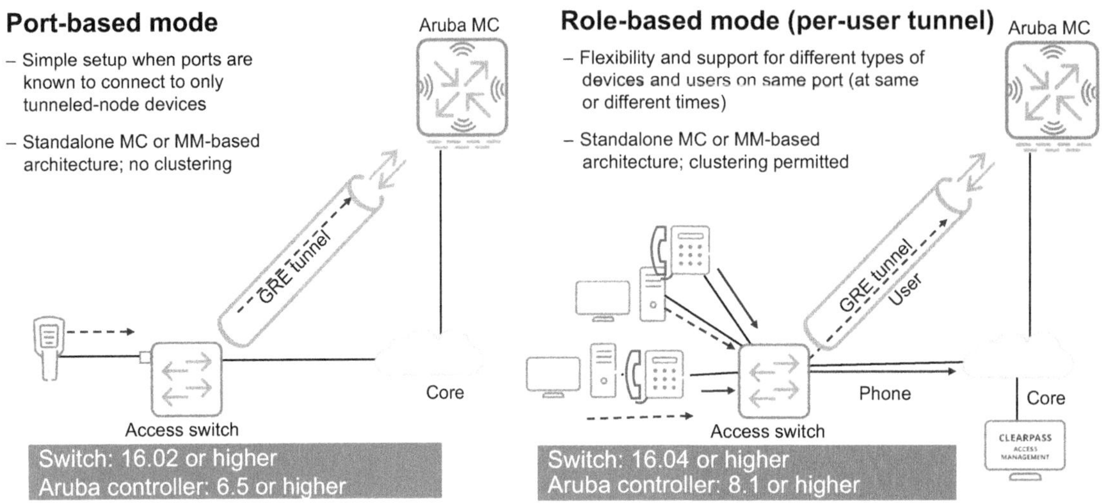


Figure 13-4 Modes

The mode applies to the feature globally on the switch and is defined in the profile, using the following command:

```
Switch(tunneled-node-server)# mode <port-based | role-based>
```

Port-based mode is available on Aruba 2920, 2930F, 2930M, 3800, 3810, and 5400R Series switches with software XX16.02 and above. As of software KA/KB/WC16.04, Aruba 2930F, 2930M, 3810, and 5400R zl2 Series switches support role-based mode.

In port-based mode, the switch forwards all traffic that is received on a port to the controller. This mode works well when you know that you want to tunnel all traffic from any device that might connect to the port.

Role-based mode gives you more flexibility. The switch authenticates devices on the port. Based on the profile applied during authentication, the switch decides whether to tunnel the device's traffic or switch it locally. If the device connected to the port changes, the switch can make a new decision for the new device connected to the port. If multiple devices connect to the port, the switch can tunnel some devices' traffic and switch other devices' traffic. Use this mode when you need flexibility. Perhaps you want to tunnel IoT devices' traffic but forward employee traffic locally, and you cannot be sure to which port each device will connect. Or, perhaps you want to tunnel employee traffic, but you want to forward IP phone traffic locally for lower latency. Role-based mode also has the advantage of not consuming licenses on the MC. You might also hear role-based mode referred to as per-user tunnel mode (PUTM).

Both modes work with a standalone MC or with an MC that is part of a multicontroller architecture managed by a Mobility Master (MM). However, role-based mode works with clustering, which enhances resiliency and provides better load-balancing. Aruba MCs require software 8.1 or above to support role-based mode. MCs with this software level negotiate the mode being used when they establish the PAPI control channel and GRE tunnel with the switch.

# Port-based tunneled-node

You will examine port-based tunneled node first.

## Enabling tunneled-node on ports

When the switch uses port-based tunneled node, you must determine which ports connect to devices for which you want to tunnel the traffic. You then apply the tunneled-node server profile to those ports.

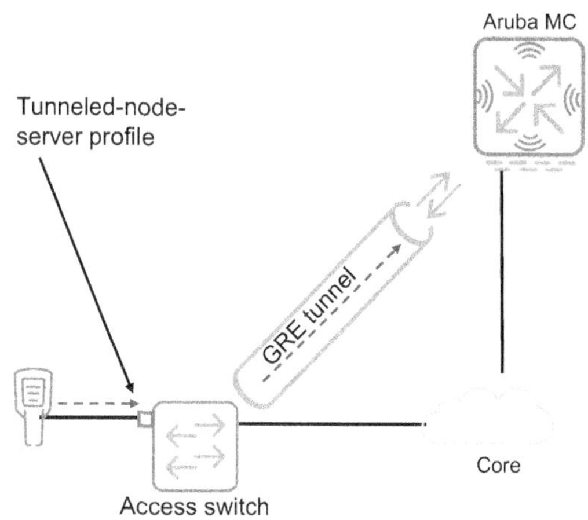


Figure 13-5 Enabling tunneled-node on ports

For example, if a port connects to a vulnerable payment card reader, you apply the profile to that port (see Figure 13-5). Use this command:

```
Switch(config)# interface <port ID list> tunneled-node-server
```

**Note**
Certain features are prohibited on tunneled-node ports, as well as on VLANs configured on tunneled-node ports. You will learn more about these restrictions later in the chapter.

Applying the profile makes the port function like a controlled Aruba AP. The switch no longer forwards traffic that arrives on the ports locally as it normally would. Instead, it uses the GRE tunnel to send all the traffic to the IP address that you configured in the tunnel server profile.

The tunnel acts at Layer 2. It encapsulates not just the IP payload but also the MAC header, and it forwards all traffic including broadcasts and multicasts.

The main difference between the tunneled-node and AP-based tunnels is that tunneled-node encapsulates 802.3 instead of 802.11 frames. Note also that often wireless traffic is encrypted; however, wired traffic is not encrypted, and GRE does not provide encryption either. However, the wired network infrastructure is typically trusted, so encryption is not required.

Note that the switch continues to function as normal for all traffic that arrives on the non-tunneled-node ports.

---

**Important**

Tunneled-node ports are intended for wired endpoints. You should avoid plugging controlled Aruba APs into wired tunneled ports because these APs are already fulfilling similar functions on their own. You would be causing the network to encapsulate wireless clients' traffic twice. Lab tests show that the tunneled-node will still operate properly, but the double encapsulation can create performance and resource issues.

---

## How the MC handles tunneled-node traffic

From its side, the MC divides the arriving tunneled traffic into one tunnel per tunneled-node port. It decapsulates the traffic and applies various controls to it. While learning how to configure the MC to control tunneled-node traffic is beyond the scope of this study guide, you should understand how the configuration on the switch plays into the MC's decisions.

As Figure 13-6 shows, the switch communicates the untagged VLAN configured on a tunneled-node port to the MC. The MC must have this VLAN configured on it. It then handles the tunneled traffic based on the settings in the wired Authentication, Authorization, and Accounting (AAA) profile assigned to that VLAN. For example, the MC might apply MAC Auth or 802.1X—or some combination. After the successful authentication, the controller applies a role to the traffic. Then based on that role, it controls the traffic with firewall policies or performs other policy actions. Finally, it forwards the packet towards its destination.

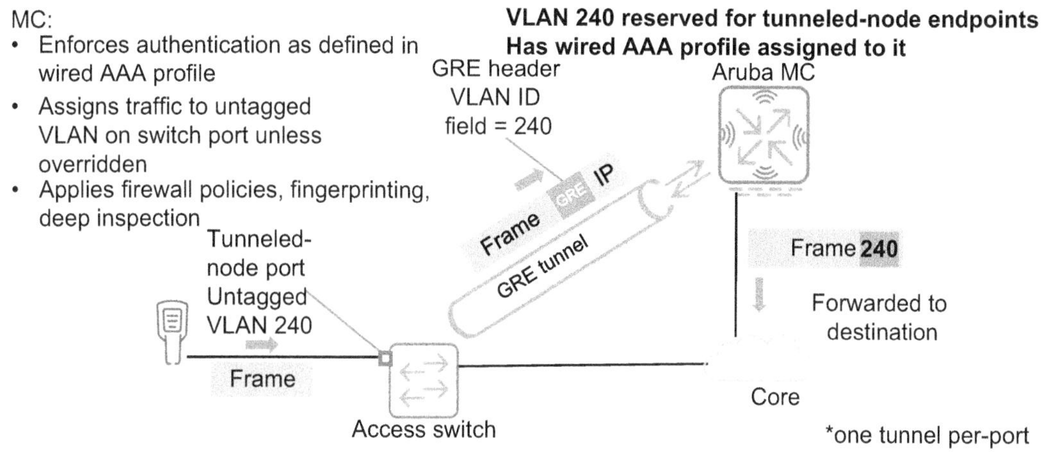


Figure 13-6 How the MC handles tunneled-node traffic

The MC must also be set up to forward the traffic in the tunneled-node ports' untagged VLAN at Layer 2 or Layer 3, as desired. In the figure, the MC is using Layer 2 forwarding. It forwards the frame tagged for VLAN 240. If the MC were using Layer 3 forwarding, it would have an IP address on VLAN 240 and route traffic out of this VLAN.

You can configure different VLANs on different tunneled-node ports to inform the controller to assign those nodes to different VLANs. However, the MC is also capable of applying different firewall rules to different devices in the same VLAN, again based on dynamic settings applied during authentication. For example, the MC could enforce MAC-Auth and use the devices' MAC addresses to assign different roles to different devices. You should coordinate with the MC administrators and make sure to match the switch configuration with their desired configuration.

Keep in mind that the switch is simply using the untagged VLAN on the tunneled-node port to communicate the desired default VLAN to the controller. It is *not* switching the tunneled-nodes' traffic in this VLAN, so you don't need to tag it on the switches' uplinks as you normally would. (The use of fallback switching mode makes an exception as you will learn later.) Instead, the VLAN exists on the MC at the distribution or core. In keeping with this design, the switch is restricted from implementing many normal features—such as an IP address—on any untagged VLAN on a tunneled-node port. Aruba recommends reserving the tunneled-node VLANs for tunneled-node ports only.

You should also understand that the MC can override the default VLAN assignment after it authenticates the device. For example, it might apply 802.1X authentication to tunneled-nodes and receive a dynamic VLAN assignment from Aruba ClearPass. The MC would then forward the tunneled-node device traffic in this VLAN, rather than the untagged VLAN configured on the switch port. Even if you plan to apply dynamic VLANs for some devices, though, the MC must support the untagged VLAN on tunneled-node ports; the VLAN defines the wired AAA profile.

Finally, note that Figure 13-6 shows a single tunneled-node port on the AOS-Switch for simplicity. When tunneled-node is applied to multiple ports, the MC sees one tunnel *per port*.

# Role-based tunneled node

You will now examine role-based tunneled-node.

## User role-based authorization

Role-based tunneled-node requires the AOS-Switch to use user role-based authorization. Figure 13-7 shows what you learned about this feature in previous chapters. The RADIUS server sends a vendor specific attribute (VSA) with a user-role name. The switch has a corresponding user role configured on it with settings to apply to the user. The user role tells the switch whether to tunnel a user's traffic or not and also applies other settings.

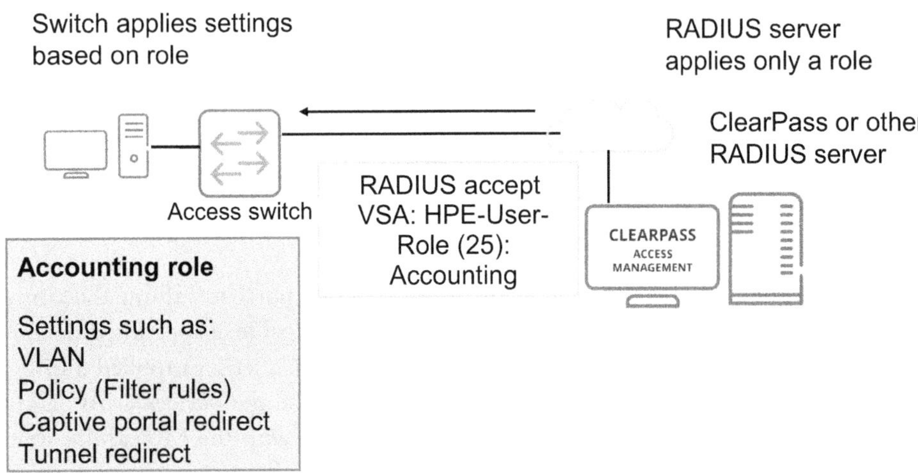


Figure 13-7 User role-based authorization

You can configure the user roles locally, as explained in this chapter, or download the roles from ClearPass.

## Roles for role-based tunnel-node

With this brief background in user-role based authorization, you can understand how to set up role-based tunneled-node.

First, you set up the tunnel node server profile, as you learned how to do for port-based tunneled-node. However, you set the mode to role-based.

In addition, you do *not* apply the tunneled node server profile to the ports that might need to tunnel traffic. Instead, apply 802.1X, RADIUS MAC-Auth, LMA, or some combination to them. Devices and users authenticate and are assigned to a role, which determines how the switch handles their traffic.

Typically, you set up the switch to authenticate users and devices to Aruba ClearPass. However, if the company does not have Aruba ClearPass, you can set up the solution to work using LMA.

You must coordinate the RADIUS VSA- or LMA-assigned roles with roles that you create on the switch. Create a role on the switch for each of these roles. (Check your switch documentation for the current maximum number of user roles with your current software.)

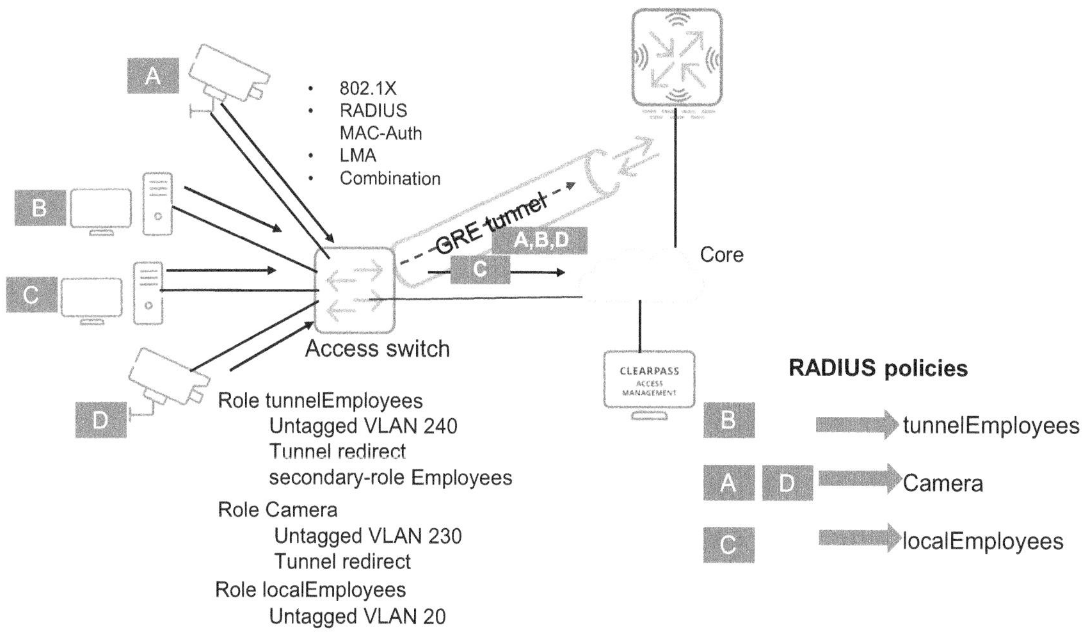


Figure 13-8 Roles for role-based tunnel-node

Figure 13-8 shows examples of roles assigned by ClearPass and the settings for those roles on the AOS-Switch. For each role that applies to devices that need their traffic tunneled, define two settings:

- Untagged VLAN

  The untagged VLAN ID is required and determines the VLAN to which the MC assigns the device's traffic. While the VLAN is applied to the port dynamically (you do not need to assign the VLAN to ports statically), the VLAN *must* exist on the switch.

- Tunneled node redirect

  With the tunneled node redirect setting, you can optionally define a secondary role. The MC applies the secondary role to the tunneled user traffic. If you do not define this role, the MC applies the initial role defined in its tunneled user AAA policy.

This command output shows example settings for the tunnelEmployees role:

```
Switch# show user-role tunnelEmployees
  User Role Information
    Name : tunnelEmployees
    Type : local
    Reauthentication Period (seconds) : 0
    Untagged VLAN : 240
    Tagged VLAN :
    Captive Portal Profile :
    Policy :
    Tunnelednode Server Redirect : Enabled
    Secondary Role Name : Employees
```

Remember to also define roles for users and devices that do *not* need their traffic tunneled. Then configure the appropriate settings for them. It is best practice to assign a role to all authenticated users and devices. Otherwise, the authenticated users and devices are treated the same way as unauthenticated ones and assigned to the initial role.

In Figure 13-8, you see an example in which the switch enforces 802.1X and RADIUS-based MAC-Auth on the port. ClearPass assigns most employees who authenticate with 802.1X the "localEmployees" role. This role is associated with untagged VLAN 20 on the AOS-Switch. The switch dynamically assigns the employee's untagged traffic to this VLAN and forwards the traffic as normal.

ClearPass assigns finance users, who need access to sensitive centralized databases, to a special "tunnelEmployees" role. The switch associates this role with untagged VLAN 240 and enables tunneled node tunneling. ClearPass authenticates security cameras based on MAC address and assigns them to the "Camera" role. The switch associates this role with untagged VLAN 230 and tunneled node redirect. The switch encapsulates the finance user's traffic and the cameras' traffic and tunnels it to the MC, indicating a different VLAN for each.

In another scenario, the switch could enforce LMA on the port. Administrators create a MAC group with IoT device OUIs. They associate this MAC group with the "iot" role. This role assigns the traffic to untagged VLAN 230 and enables tunneled node redirect. Any device that fails MAC authentication is assigned to the initial role, which they define as "employees." The "employees" role has no settings. It permits all access, and the switch forwards the traffic locally in the port's untagged VLAN.

You can see a list of devices that have been assigned to roles that enable tunneling with this command:

```
Switch# show tunneled-node-users all

 PORT     MAC-ADDRESS        TUNNEL-STATUS      SECONDARY-USERROLEFAILURE-REASON
 1/1      005056-97768e      UP                 Employees
```

## How the MC handles role-based tunneled-node traffic

When the MC and switch first establish the PAPI channel between them, the switch indicates that it is using role-based tunneled node. This tells the MC to create a per-user tunnel for each device's traffic that an AOS-Switch tunnels to it.

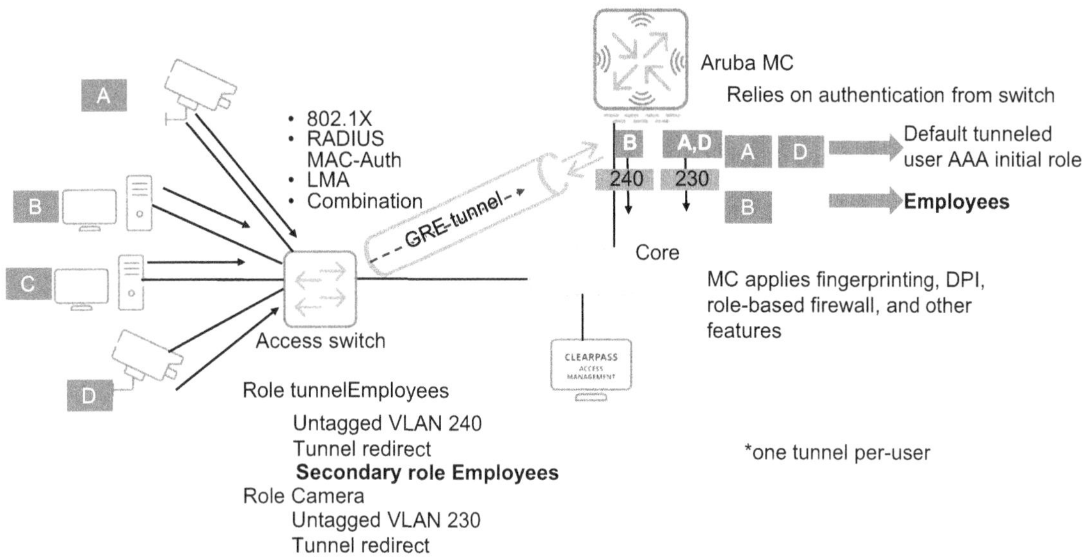


Figure 13-9 How the MC handles role-based tunneled-node traffic

The MC maps this traffic to the tunneled-user AAA profile, rather than the wired AAA profile. It either applies the initial role in this profile to the user tunnel, or, if the switch sent a secondary role, this role overrides the initial role. For example, in Figure 13-9, the MC assigns tunnelEmployees to the Employees role because the switch specifies this role as the secondary role. In either case, the MC does not apply authentication to the tunneled traffic—the switch has already done that. The MC does apply the firewall rules and policies for the role, fingerprints the traffic, applies DPI, and enforces any other security measures configure on the MC.

The MC then forwards the traffic in the VLAN indicated by the switch in the tunnel header. Because the MC did not enforce authentication for the device, it cannot override this VLAN assignment. This is why you must configure an untagged VLAN ID for any role that uses tunneled node redirect on the switch.

Note that Figure 13-9 shows one tunnel icon for simplicity. The controller actually maintains one tunnel per-user.

# High availability

You now know how to set up tunneled-node. Next, you will learn how to enhance the solution with high availability. To ensure uninterrupted connectivity for tunneled-nodes, you should work with the MC administrators to design the solution such that the AOS-Switch can tunnel traffic to at least two MCs.

When the primary and backup MCs are in the same subnet, MC administrators should set up Virtual Router Redundancy Protocol (VRRP) between the MCs. Preferably, the MCs should also form a cluster. As you will see in more detail in a moment, clustering provides better load balancing and more seamless failover. (It also provides better roaming, but this is more a concern for wireless traffic than tunneled-node traffic.)

However, only role-based tunneled-node, not port-based tunneled-node, is supported in cluster environments. You must also ensure that the Aruba MC software supports the feature for tunneled-node switches; your MCs must use software 8.1 or higher.

In either mode, you can configure a backup controller on the switch either instead of, or in addition to, the VRRP or cluster-based redundancy.

You will now look at each of these options in more detail.

## Supporting high availability with VRRP

Figure 13-10 shows the VRRP approach when the redundant MCs are not part of a cluster.

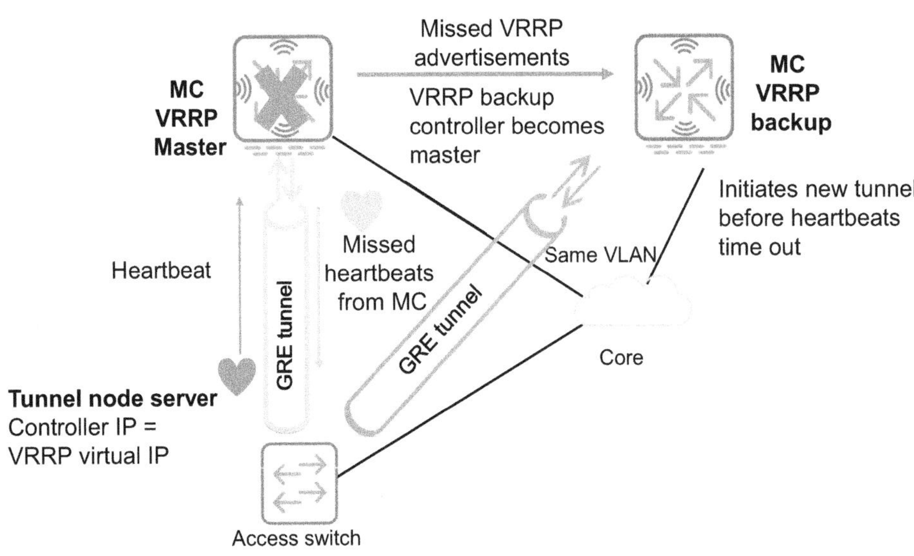


Figure 13-10 Supporting high availability with VRRP

You do not need to complete any extra configuration on the AOS-Switch. You simply specify the VRRP virtual IP address as the tunnel node server. The switch establishes the GRE and PAPI tunnels with the VRRP Master. If that controller fails, the backup controller becomes Master and takes control of the virtual IP address after missing, by default, three VRRP advertisements.

As the GRE traffic begins to arrive on the new Master, that Master can re-establish the GRE tunnel with the AOS-Switch. The AOS-Switch itself is maintaining the status of its tunnel with heartbeats, called keepalives in the switch command line interface (CLI). The switch and the controller send keepalives every second. (Note that the controller maintains one tunnel per tunneled node port or user on the switch; however, the switch and controller exchange heartbeats over a single tunnel.) If the switch fails to receive keepalives from the controller over the keepalive timeout period—by default, eight seconds—it tears down the GRE and PAPI tunnels and attempts to re-establish them. Because VRRP fails over more quickly, the VRRP advertisement interval determines the failover time more than the keepalives timeout in this case.

If you want, though, you can adjust the keepalive period with this command (set in seconds).

```
Switch(config)# tunneled-node-server keepalive interval <1-8>
```

Note that MC administrators might choose either an active-active or active-standby configuration. If they have chosen the active-active configuration, the MCs use two VRRP virtual router identifier (VRIDs), with different virtual IP addresses and each controller acting as the master for a different VRID. You will need to specify one VRID's IP address in the tunnel server profile for half of your switches and the other VRID's IP address in the tunnel server profile for the other half of the switches.

## Supporting high availability with clustering

When the switch uses role-based tunneled-node, it can tunnel traffic to clustered MCs. These MCs typically also use VRRP, although not always. However, the cluster enables load balancing and failover capabilities beyond the VRRP mechanisms.

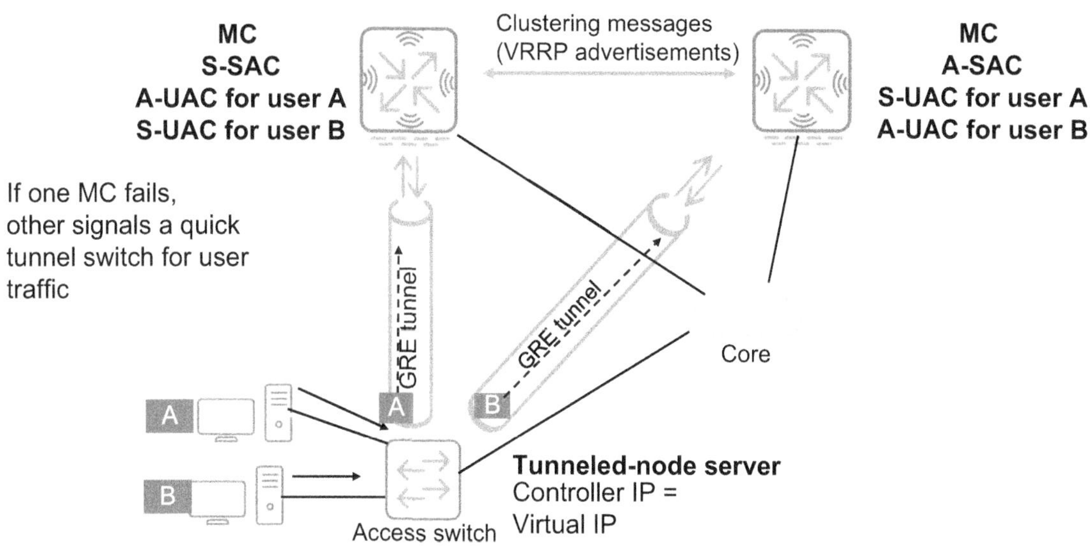


Figure 13-11 Supporting high availability with clustering

With this method, again, you only need to set a single tunnel node server (controller) IP address on the AOS-Switch. Use the virtual IP address for the cluster, as shown in Figure 13-11. When the switch contacts this IP address, it receives assignments with the actual IP addresses of two MCs. One is the switch's active Switch Anchor Controller (A-SAC) and the other is the switch's standby SAC (S-SAC). The switch establishes tunnels with both controllers.

In addition, the switch receives a bucket-map. When the switch starts tunneling a new device's traffic, the switch hashes information about the session. It looks up the hash in the bucket map to determine the correct active User Anchor Controller (A-UAC) and standby UAC (S-UAC) for that device. The switch tunnels the device's traffic to the A-UAC, but the state for the session is synchronized between the A-UAC and the S-UAC, enabling more seamless failover. (The degree of synchronized information depends on the device's needs.) In addition, because the cluster dictates where the switch tunnels each user's traffic, load balancing is improved.

If the switch's A-SAC or any of its A-UACs fail, the cluster can detect that failure very quickly and signal to the switch to failover to the appropriate standby tunnel, rather than the switch having to wait for its heartbeats to time out.

You can see information about the SACs, UACs, and bucket list with this command:

```
Switch# show tunneled-node-server state

Local Master Server (LMS) State

  LMS Type  IP Address       State       Capability    Role
  Primary   : 10.102.40.10   Complete    Per User      Operational Primary

Switch Anchor Controller (SAC) State

            IP Address       Mac Address               State
  SAC       : 10.102.40.11   204c03-1207a0             Registered

User Anchor Controller (UAC) : 10.102.40.12

 User            Port   VLAN   State          Bucket ID
 005056-973668   1      240    Registered     201
```

## Supporting high availability with a backup controller

As you have seen, the AOS-Switch can participate in high availability solutions with a *single* controller IP address specified in its tunneled node server profile. This profile can also include a backup controller, though, specified with this command:

```
Switch(config)# tunneled-node-server backup-controller-ip <IP_address>
```

The backup controller allows the switch to failover to an MC (or VRRP group or cluster) in a different subnet from its primary MC (or VRRP group or cluster), as shown in Figure 13-12.

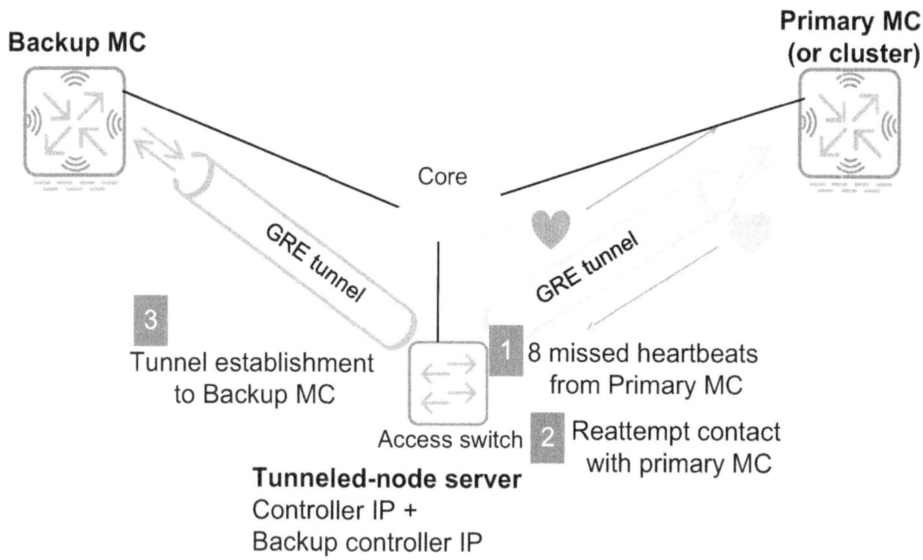


Figure 13-12 Supporting high availability with a backup controller

As discussed earlier, the switch and its MC—or any of its SACs and UACs when clustering is used—send each other keepalives over the GRE tunnel every second to assess the tunnel's health. If the switch fails to hear keepalives over the keepalive timeout period, it attempts to re-establish communications with the *primary* controller twice. That could succeed when the failed MC is part of a VRRP group. In this scenario, though, the company has a standalone MC at the site, so this attempt fails. After the second failure, the switch establishes a tunnel with the backup controller.

After switching over to the backup controller, the switch continues to check whether the primary controller is back up every 30 seconds. If it re-establishes communication with the primary controller, it moves its tunnel back to that controller.

Again, MC administrators might choose an active-standby or active-active deployment. Communicate with them to determine whether all switches will use the same primary controller IP and backup controller IP (active-standby) or whether you should alternate these roles on different switches (active-active). Often, the MCs are deployed in different locations, and each switch uses the local MC as its primary MC and the remote MC as its backup.

**Note**

Once you have applied a tunnel node profile to a port, you cannot change the primary or backup controller IP, so plan for high availability in advance.

### Combining approaches

You can also combine a backup controller with the redundancy mechanisms described in previous sections. For example, you can have four controllers, two in one subnet and two in another subnet (perhaps in another location). One VRRP group with optional cluster provides the first level of redundancy for local AOS-Switches, and other VRRP group with optional cluster acts as the backup controller, adding a second level of redundancy.

## Controlling failure behavior

An AOS-Switch's tunneled-node tunnel is "up" when both of these conditions are met:

- The switch can reach any of its potential MCs.
- The switch has received a bootstrap message response from an MC, enabling the switch to start establishing the GRE tunnel.

A tunnel is down when either of those conditions is not met. Perhaps the switch has lost its link to the network's only MC, or perhaps it has lost its link to all of them. Although properly planning high availability should prevent the tunnel from going down, you must understand what the switch does if it does.

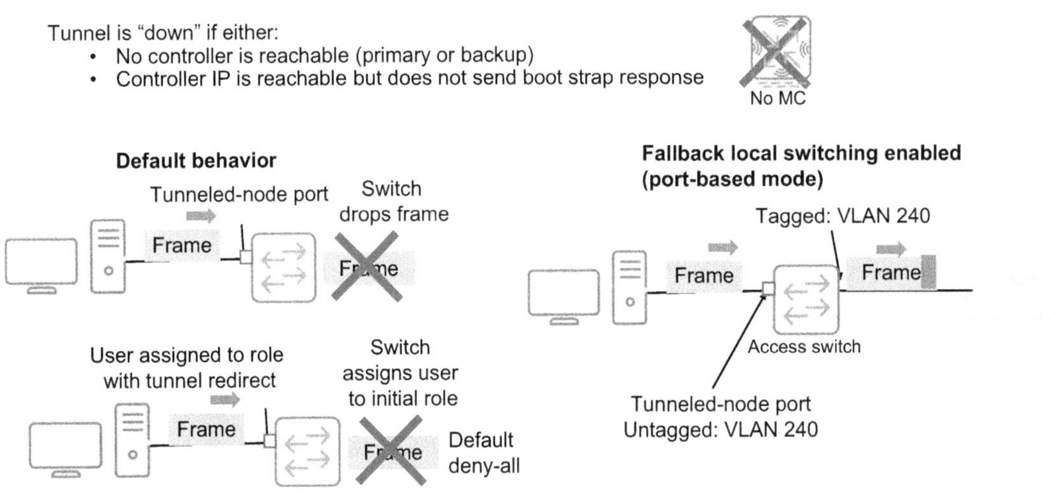


Figure 13-13 Controlling failure behavior

In port-based mode, you have a choice. By default, the switch drops traffic on tunneled-node ports if the tunnel fails, as shown in Figure 13-13. If you are using the tunnel to protect the network from vulnerable clients, you may choose to keep this behavior.

If you want the switch to switch the traffic locally in the case of a failure, enter this command:

```
Switch(config)# interface <port ID list> tunneled-node-server
fallback-local-switching
```

If you choose this option, make sure that the untagged VLAN on the tunneled-node ports provides the devices with the proper connectivity. Typically, you will tag the VLAN on switch-to-switch ports. The distribution or core switches should be configured to control the traffic appropriately. Remember that you cannot configure IP settings on a VLAN assigned to tunneled-node ports, so the switch must switch, not route, the traffic.

You must configure the **tunneled-node-server fallback-local-switching** command before the failure occurs. If you enter the command *after* a failure, the switch will continue to drop the traffic until its connection with the MC is restored. If another failure occurs, though, the switch will apply the new behavior.

In role-based mode, if the switch cannot establish a tunnel with an MC, it places any user or device assigned to a role that uses tunneling to the initial role instead. Remember that this is the same role for devices that fail authentication. If this role denies all access, the tunneled-node devices' traffic is dropped. But if you have set up a different role for this initial role, the devices will receive access with its settings.

## Implementation restrictions

You will now focus on some guidelines for ensuring that your tunneled-node solution proceeds smoothly.

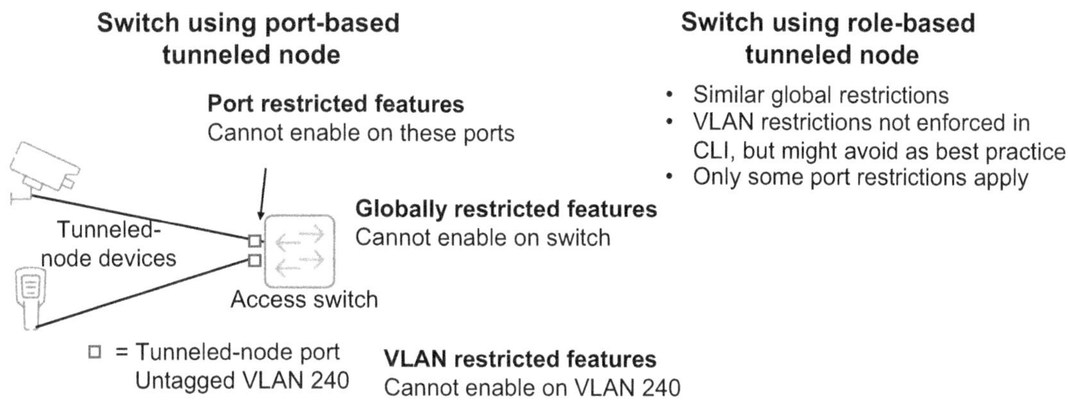


Figure 13-14 Implementation restrictions

Figure 13-14 shows how the restrictions associated with the tunneled-node feature come in three types:

- Global restrictions—You cannot use globally restricted features on a switch that uses tunneled-node. Role-based tunneled-node requires user-roles to be enabled, which adds restrictions of its own.
- VLAN restrictions—Some features are restricted only on tunneled-node VLANs. A tunneled-node VLAN is defined as a VLAN on a port to which a tunneled node server profile is applied. You can apply the VLAN-restricted features to any other VLAN on the switch, but not one of

the tunneled-node VLANs. If a port is assigned to a VLAN that already uses one of the restricted features, you cannot apply a tunneled-node profile to that port until you remove the restricted features.

If you are using role-based mode, tunneled-node endpoints are assigned to VLANs in their user role. You are not restricted by the CLI from applying the VLAN-restricted features to a VLAN in a user role that enables tunneling; however, you should often avoid using these features because they might not behave as you expect. For example, you could set up DHCP relay on the VLAN assigned to tunneled node endpoints. However, the endpoints have their traffic tunneled to the controller, and the switch's DHCP relay settings do not apply. You should not mix tunneled and non-tunneled endpoints in the same VLAN, so there is no reason to set up DHCP relay.

- Port restrictions—When you use port-based mode, some features are restricted on tunneled-node ports specifically. You can still implement the features on other ports. Again, the restriction is enforced both before you apply a tunneled-node profile to the port and after. Many of these restrictions do not apply to role-based mode; however, the features often will not apply to any endpoints that connect to the port and are assigned to a tunneled-node profile. In addition, role-based mode requires some form of port-based authentication, which comes with restrictions of its own.

Table 13-1 shows the restricted features and classifies them by type.

Table 13-1 Restricted features

| Feature | Type of restriction (port-based) | Type of restriction (role-based) |
|---|---|---|
| Meshing | Global | Global |
| QinQ | Global | Global |
| Distributed trunking | Global | Global |
| IPv4 multicast routing | Global | Global |
| Virtual Extensible LAN (VxLAN) | Global | Global |
| Bring Your Own Device (BYOD) redirect | Global | Global |
| IP address (manual or Dynamic Host Configuration Protocol [DHCP]) | VLAN | No restriction |
| DHCP client/server/relay | VLAN | VLAN<br>Can be applied to VLAN, but does not apply to tunneled-node endpoints assigned to that VLAN |
| Policy-based routing (PBR) policies | VLAN | VLAN<br>Can be applied to VLAN, but does not apply to tunneled-node endpoints assigned to that VLAN |

Table 13-1 Restricted features—cont'd

| Feature | Type of restriction (port-based) | Type of restriction (role-based) |
|---|---|---|
| DHCP snooping (IPv4 or IPv6) | VLAN<br>Can be enabled on VLAN, but does not apply to tunneled-node ports assigned to that VLAN | VLAN<br>Can be applied to VLAN, but does not apply to tunneled-node endpoints assigned to that VLAN |
| Address Resolution Protocol (ARP) protect | VLAN<br>Can be enabled on VLAN, but does not apply to tunneled-node ports assigned to that VLAN | VLAN<br>Can be applied to VLAN, but does not apply to tunneled-node endpoints assigned to that VLAN |
| 802.1X | Port | No restriction |
| MAC-Auth | Port | No restriction |
| Web-Auth | Port | Global for EWA (due to user-roles being enabled)<br>Port for all Web-Auth |
| Local MAC-Auth (LMA) | Port | No restriction |
| Port security | Port | No restriction<br>But port-access mode required if using 802.1X |
| RA guard | Port | Port<br>Can be applied to the port, but does not apply to tunneled-node endpoints on that port |
| Virtual Switching Framework (VSF) link | Port | Port<br>Not supported with port-based authentication |
| Source port/Multicast filters | Port | Port<br>Can be applied to the port, but does not apply to tunneled-node endpoints on that port |
| Port trunking (manual or Link Aggregation Control Protocol [LACP] link aggregation) | Port | Port<br>Not supported with port-based authentication |
| Dynamic IP lockdown (DIPL) and DIPLv6 | Port | Port<br>Can be applied to the port, but does not apply to tunneled-node endpoints on that port |
| Connection rate filtering | Port | Port<br>Can be applied to the port, but does not apply to tunneled-node endpoints on that port |

## Guidelines for the path between tunneled-node switch and MCs

You should check the network infrastructure between the AOS-Switches that implement tunneled-node and the MCs. Make sure that the infrastructure will not interfere with communications in any way.

If any firewalls or network infrastructure devices with ACLs are in the path, as shown in Figure 13-15, they must allow GRE and PAPI traffic. Enable GRE on IP protocol 47 and PAPI on UDP port 8211. You must also understand that NAT cannot be applied in the path between the switch and the controller. It is best if you can direct the tunneled-node switch to a local MC.

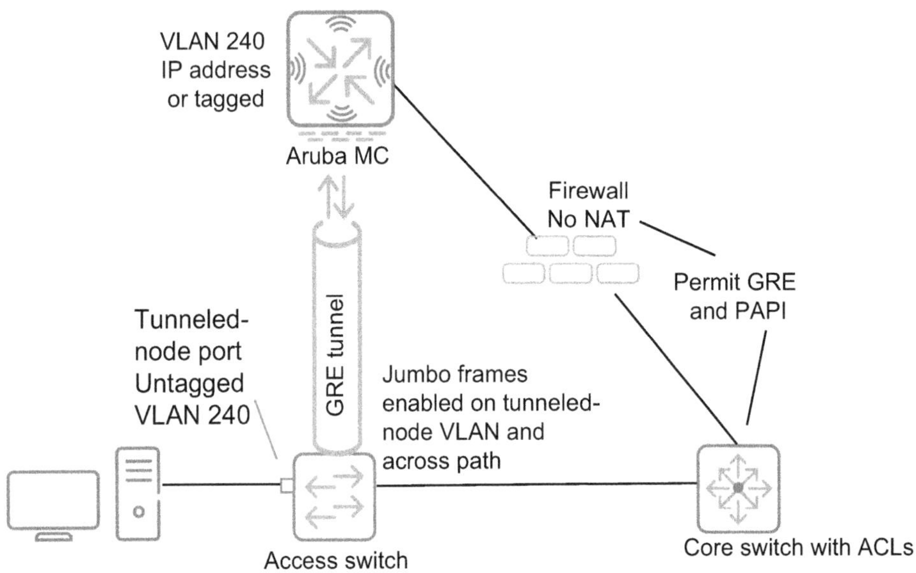


Figure 13-15 Guidelines for the path between tunneled-node switch and MCs

Also, keep in mind that encapsulating frames can cause them to exceed the maximum transmission unit (MTU). However, tunneled-node ports do not support the features typically used to prevent MTU violations, including fragmentation, PMTU detection, or reassembly. Aruba recommends that you enable jumbo frames across the path from the switch to the MC. On AOS-Switches, you enable jumbo frames on a VLAN basis. Make sure that every VLAN that carries traffic between the switch and the MC supports jumbo frames.

Make sure that you know the IP address that your AOS-Switches will use to establish the tunnel with the MC. Typically, the switch acts at Layer 2 and has a single IP address and a default gateway for reaching all other subnets. But if your switch has multiple IP addresses, it uses the IP address on the forwarding VLAN for its route to the MC. Make sure that the MC can also reach this IP address (through its own route or its default gateway).

## MC licensing and capacity considerations

The MC requires no special set up to create tunnels with AOS-Switches running tunneled-node (an exception is that before software 8.0, an MC working with port-based tunneled node might need the wired access concentrator server enabled). The MC automatically accepts the switches' PAPI messages and requests to establish tunnels—as long as these conditions are fulfilled:

- The switch has the correct PAPI key if PAPI security is enabled
- The MC has the necessary licenses for a port-based tunneled-node switch

Figure 13-16 shows the licensing and capacity considerations.

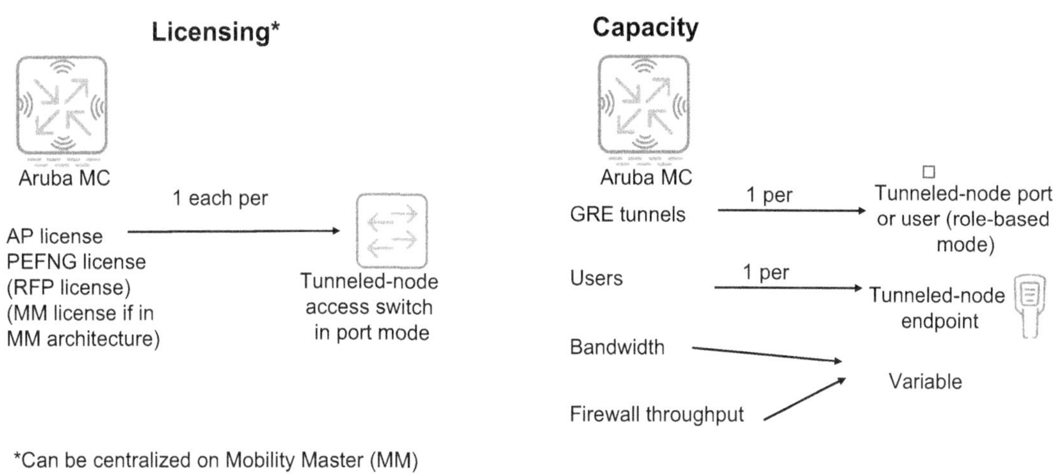


Figure 13-16 MC licensing and capacity considerations

A standalone MC (or centralized MM-based solution) needs one AP license for each switch that is running tunneled-node in port-based node. If the solution is using firewall functionality, it also needs one Next Generation Policy Enforcement Firewall (PEFNG) license for each port-based tunneled-node switch.

If the MC is using the RF Protect features, it should have one RFP license for each port-based tunneled-node switch. The RFP license is not strictly required. However, licensing works such that, when RF Protect is enabled, the MC should have the same number of AP, PEFNG, and RFP licenses; if it has fewer RFP licenses, it disables the excess AP and PEFNG licenses until it has the same count. The company might choose to deploy Aruba MCs dedicated to supporting the wired tunneled nodes. In this case, the MC would not use RF Protect, and the RFP licenses would not be required.

If the MC is part of an MM-based solution, an MM license is also required for the port-based tunneled-node switch, just as it would be for an AP.

To conserve licenses, you may choose to consolidate the tunneled-node ports to one or just a few switches.

When a switch uses role-based mode, the Aruba MC does not require licenses to support it.

As mentioned earlier, architects should consider the tunneled-node feature as they plan. In addition to the licensing requirements, they should keep in mind tunneling requirements. In port-based mode, the MC treats each tunneled-node port as a separate tunnel for enhanced visibility. This means that architects must count every tunneled-node port, not switch, when determining if the controller can support enough tunnels. They should also remember that a single tunneled-node port could connect to multiple devices (if, for example, the port connects to an unmanaged switch), which could raise the user count.

In role-based mode, the MC treats each user as a separate tunnel. Again, architects should ensure that MCs can support enough tunnels and users.

Finally, for either mode, architects should consider the effects of the wired traffic on the firewall throughput and whether the controller can support the bandwidth.

Of course, administrators will also need to implement the policies for controlling wired traffic. However, configuring the MC to control and forward the traffic is beyond the scope of this guide and should be handled by an experienced Aruba controller administrator.

---

**Note**

Also, make sure that your MCs are running up-to-date software. ArubaOS 8.1 is required for role-based mode.

---

## Summary

In this chapter, you learned how tunneled-node provides an option for integrating Aruba switches with an Aruba Mobility Solution. You can use tunneled-node to increase security for vulnerable devices or to unify policy enforcement in a wired and wireless architecture.

You can now configure tunneled-node with PAPI enhanced security, high availability, and failover options. You now know how to implement tunneled-node on the switch and controller, including which settings and licenses you need.

## Learning check

1. How does the MC assign a VLAN to traffic received on a GRE tunnel with an AOS-Switch that operates in port-based mode?
    a. The MC has a pool of VLANs configured on it, and it assigns traffic from each tunneled-node endpoint to a VLAN in a round-robin fashion.
    b. It assigns all traffic from tunneled-node endpoints to the same VLAN, which is configured on the MC statically.

   c. It assigns the traffic to the VLAN communicated by the AOS-Switch even if it receives a different VLAN assignment from a RADIUS server.
   d. It assigns the traffic to the VLAN communicated by the AOS-Switch unless a dynamic setting overrides it.

2. Why is it important for administrators to understand which VLAN a tunneled-node switch uses to reach the MC? (Select two.)
   a. They must enable jumbo frames on the VLAN in case encapsulated frames exceed the MTU.
   b. They must enable GRE and PAPI on this VLAN.
   c. Certain features, such as IP settings, are restricted on this VLAN.
   d. The IP address on this VLAN is the default GRE source, and the MC must be able to reach it.
   e. They must associate the tunneled-node license with this VLAN.
3. What are ways AOS-Switches and MCs can provide continued connectivity for tunneled-node endpoints if an MC fails? What considerations should administrators make as they plan for high availability?
4. Consider a scenario in which you have configured port-based tunneled-node on an AOS-Switch. You connect a device, but the device cannot undergo authentication or receive an IP address. How would you go about troubleshooting this issue? What commands would you enter and for what information would you look?
5. An AOS-Switch is using port-based tunneled-node. VLAN 240 is the untagged VLAN on a tunneled-node port. What is different about this VLAN as opposed to an untagged VLAN assigned to an edge port without tunneled-node? Where else should VLAN 240 be configured in the network?
6. Compare port-based and role-based tunneled-node. Consider factors such as:
   - How you set up the feature
   - How devices are authenticated and controlled
   - Where you configure VLANs
   - How the functionality appears to the user or device

# Answers

## Learning check

1. How does the MC assign a VLAN to traffic received on a GRE tunnel with an AOS-Switch that operates in port-based mode?
   a. The MC has a pool of VLANs configured on it, and it assigns traffic from each tunneled-node endpoint to a VLAN in a round-robin fashion.
   b. It assigns all traffic from tunneled-node endpoints to the same VLAN, which is configured on the MC statically.
   c. It assigns the traffic to the VLAN communicated by the AOS-Switch even if it receives a different VLAN assignment from a RADIUS server.
   **d. It assigns the traffic to the VLAN communicated by the AOS-Switch unless a dynamic setting overrides it.**
2. Why is it important for administrators to understand which VLAN a tunneled-node switch uses to reach the MC? (Select two.)
   **a. They must enable jumbo frames on the VLAN in case encapsulated frames exceed the MTU.**
   b. They must enable GRE and PAPI on this VLAN.
   c. Certain features, such as IP settings, are restricted on this VLAN.
   **d. The IP address on this VLAN is the default GRE source, and the MC must be able to reach it.**
   e. They must associate the tunneled-node license with this VLAN.
3. What are ways AOS-Switches and MCs can provide continued connectivity for tunneled-node endpoints if an MC fails? What considerations should administrators make as they plan for high availability?

   You have many different options based on how the MCs are set up and the tunneled-node mode used by the AOS-Switch. You can configure a backup controller IP address in the switch's tunneled-node server profile, which the switch contacts if it loses connectivity with its primary controller. However, if MCs are using VRRP or VRRP and clustering, the switch can failover to a standby MC even without a backup controller IP address. You need to coordinate with the MC administrators and understand how they plan to set up the MCs. You also need to be aware of restrictions such as the inability of port-based mode to work with clustering and the proper ArubaOS controller software version.

4. Consider a scenario in which you have configured port-based tunneled-node on an AOS-Switch. You connect a device, but the device cannot undergo authentication or receive an IP address. How would you go about troubleshooting this issue? What commands would you enter and for what information would you look?

You should first verify that the switch has established a tunnel with the MC. Use the **show tunneled-node-server state** command. If the tunnel is down, you could check the IP address and PAPI key, if the MC enforces PAPI security. You could also ask the MC administrators to check the licenses on the MC.

If the tunnel is up, you can check with the MC administrators about what type of authentication they are implementing. You can also check the untagged VLAN on the tunneled node port and make sure that one matches on the MC.

5. An AOS-Switch is using port-based tunneled-node. VLAN 240 is the untagged VLAN on a tunneled-node port. What is different about this VLAN as opposed to an untagged VLAN assigned to an edge port without tunneled-node? Where else should VLAN 240 be configured in the network?

   Typically, you would tag on uplinks any VLANs that are configured on an access switch's edge ports. (Or if the access layer switch is routing, would set up an IP address and routing for the VLANs.) However, the switch does not actually handle traffic in the untagged VLAN on tunneled-node ports. Instead, the VLAN exists on the MC, which is set up to forward traffic in this VLAN at Layer 2 or Layer 3. If the MC handles the traffic at Layer 2, the link between the MC and a core or distribution layer switch carries the VLAN. And the core or distribution layer switch acts as the default router for the VLAN.

6. Compare port-based and role-based tunneled-node. Consider factors such as:

   - How you set up the feature
   - How devices are authenticated and controlled
   - Where you configure VLANs
   - How the functionality appears to the user or device

   You set up the tunneled-node-server profile in much the same way for both modes; however, you select a different mode in the profile. Activating tunneling, though, is different. With port-based mode, you apply the profile to a port. With role-based mode, you need to perform more additional setup, creating the proper user roles. You also need to set up authentication on ports. Then, though, the tunneling occurs dynamically.

   With port-based mode, the MC enforces authentication, and with role-based mode, the AOS-Switch enforces authentication. However, with both modes, the MC can apply other security features.

   With port-based mode, you set the untagged VLAN for the tunneled-node port on the port itself. For role-based mode, you must set the untagged VLAN in the user role. Both modes have the MC forward traffic in this VLAN (although the VLAN could be overridden during authentication with port-based mode).

   The experience for the tunneled-node user or device could be very much the same for both modes. It does not really matter whether the switch or MC enforces authentication from this perspective. With role-based mode, users have more flexibility over which devices connect to which ports.

# 14 Secure Device Management

EXAM OBJECTIVES

- ✓ Set up RADIUS authentication and authorization for managers
- ✓ Describe the differences between Simple Network Management Protocol (SNMP) v2c and v3 and configure SNMPv3 settings on AOS-Switches
- ✓ Explain how technologies such as Remote Monitoring (RMON), sFlow, and traffic mirroring allow you to monitor network traffic
- ✓ Explain best practices for managing configurations and monitoring network traffic using a solution such as Aruba AirWave

## Assumed knowledge

Before reading this chapter, you should have a basic understanding of:

- Role-based access control (RBAC) on AOS-Switches
- SNMPv2c

## Introduction

In this chapter, you will learn about technologies that enable you to manage your network infrastructure devices more securely. You will also look at network management, exploring ways to troubleshoot problems, and examine network traffic patterns or network data more closely.

## Management user authentication options

You will first learn how to use a RADIUS server such as Aruba ClearPass to authenticate management users who need to gain access to an AOS-Switch.

AOS-Switches give you granular control over how management users are authenticated. As Figure 14-1 shows, you can specify the authentication method—whether authentication to local user accounts, a RADIUS server, or a TACACS+ server—individually for each combination of access type and access level. (In fact, you can specify a primary authentication method and a secondary authentication method for both. You will learn more about when the switch applies the secondary method a bit later.)

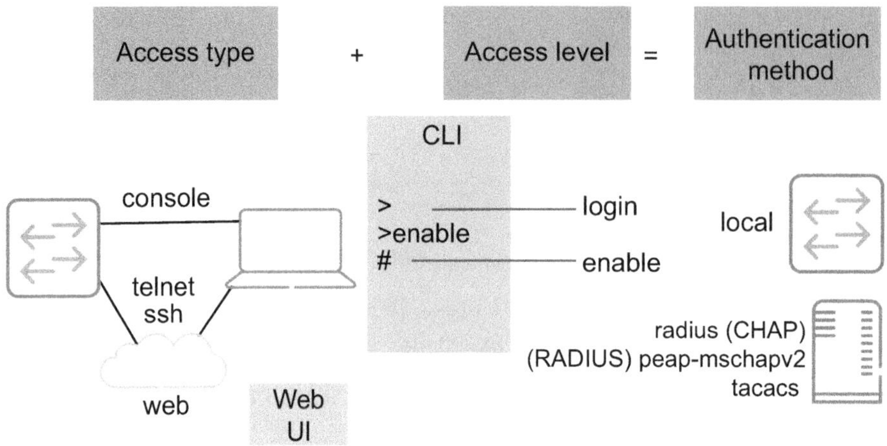


Figure 14-1 Management user authentication options

## Access types

Access types include three ways to access the command line interface (CLI).

- Through the console port
- Telnet (through the production network or through an out of band management [OOBM] network)
- Secure Shell (SSH) (through the production network or through an OOBM network)

The fourth access type is access to the web user interface (UI), either through HTTP or HTTPS.

## Access level

Each of these types of access also has two access levels, for which you can specify the authentication methods separately. The access level determines at what point authentication is applied and the rights given to the user.

- Login—The user is prompted to authenticate at login and, after successful authentication, receives operator rights.
- Enable—The user is prompted to authenticate when moving from basic mode to enable mode and, after successful authentication, receives manager rights.

If an authentication method is set for both access levels, the switch enforces both. The user must log in when initially accessing the CLI, and the user must authenticate again when moving to enable mode. An exception applies when the switch is authenticating users locally. Then the user can log in with manager credentials when initially accessing the switch and is immediately placed in enable mode. (Later on, you will learn about another exception to this rule when the switch has login privilege mode enabled.)

The login versus enable distinction is most useful for the CLI. You can set authentication methods separately for login and enable access levels for the Web UI; however, typically, you should set the same method for both. The switch enforces the login method when a user first browses to a switch IP address. After users log in, they typically do not have the opportunity to log in again, so the enable mode method never applies. There is one exception: if you set the login method to local and do not configure local operator or manager passwords, the switch does not enforce authentication when the user first browses to the Web UI. Users receive immediate access to a dashboard and monitoring information. If you have applied RADIUS for the web enable authentication method, users can then click the User icon in the UI's top bar and choose to log in. At that point, the switch authenticates the user to the RADIUS server, and if the authentication succeeds, the user receives access to the full Web UI with control over management and configuration

## Review of default authentication methods

By default, AOS-Switches enforce local authentication for login and enable level access for all types of access. Local authentication authenticates management users to the manager and operator accounts configured on the switch. However, because the switch has no passwords for the default manager and operator accounts, the switch does not actually enforce authentication until you create a password for either or both accounts (see Figure 14-2).

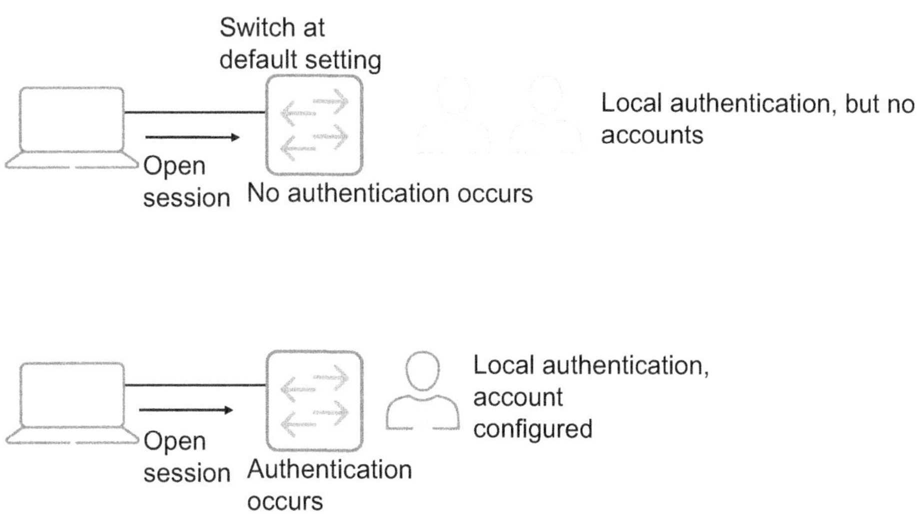


Figure 14-2 Review of default authentication methods

## RADIUS servers for authenticating management users

Consider the following question: Why would you use centralized RADIUS servers to authenticate managers rather than local accounts? (See the "Answers" section at the end of the chapter.)

> **Note**
> AOS-Switches also support authentication of manager users to a TACACS+ server for console, Telnet, and SSH access (but not for web UI access). This study guide does not cover this option. For more information, refer to your switch's *Access Security Guide*.

To set up RADIUS authentication for managers, begin by defining RADIUS servers on the switch just as you do for 802.1X or other forms of authentication. If you are already using RADIUS with port-based authentication, but you want to authenticate management users to different RADIUS servers, simply add the different RADIUS servers to different groups (see Figure 14-3). You can then specify the correct group when you configure RADIUS as the authentication method.

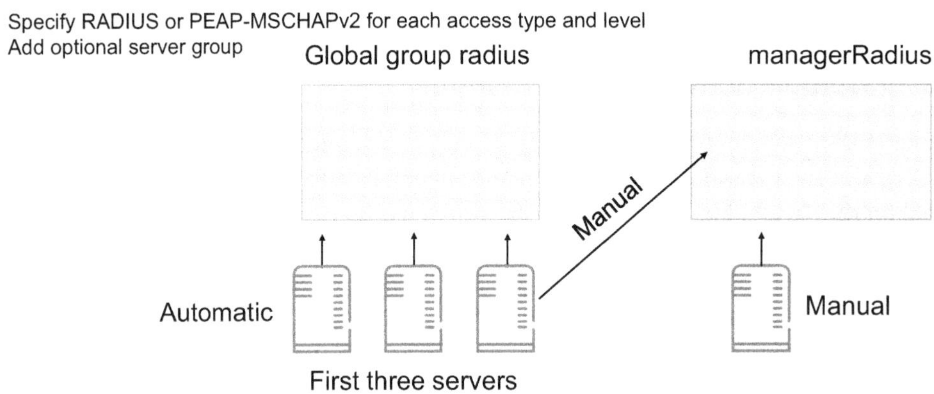


Figure 14-3 RADIUS servers for authenticating management users

Refer to *Chapter 10: 802.1X Authentication* for a review on configuring RADIUS servers and groups.

After you have set up the RADIUS servers, you can use the following command to configure the switch to apply RADIUS authentication to the desired access types and levels:

```
Switch(config)# aaa authentication <console | telnet | ssh | web>
   <enable | login> <radius| peap-mschapv2> [server-group <group name>]
```

Specify the server group if you want to use different RADIUS servers from the global group.

For example, if you wanted to change the authentication source for SSH login and enable mode access to RADIUS, you would enter:

```
Switch(config)# aaa authentication ssh login radius local
Switch(config)# aaa authentication ssh enable radius local
```

To verify the change, you would enter:

```
Switch# show authentication
<-output omitted->
                | Login       Login        Login
  Access Task   | Primary     Server Group Secondary
  ------------- + ----------- ------------ ----------
<-output omitted->
  SSH           | Radius      radius       Local
  <-output omitted->
                | Enable      Enable       Enable
  Access Task   | Primary     Server Group Secondary
  ------------- + ----------- ------------ ----------
<-output omitted->
  SSH           | Radius      radius       Local
```

In this output, you can see that local is the secondary authentication method. You will learn more about this in the "Secondary authentication method" section.

## RADIUS authorization of operator or manager access

RADIUS authenticates a manager and authorizes the manager for the correct access level in a single step. You can take several different approaches to setting up the authorization, depending on how much you want to distinguish different levels of access.

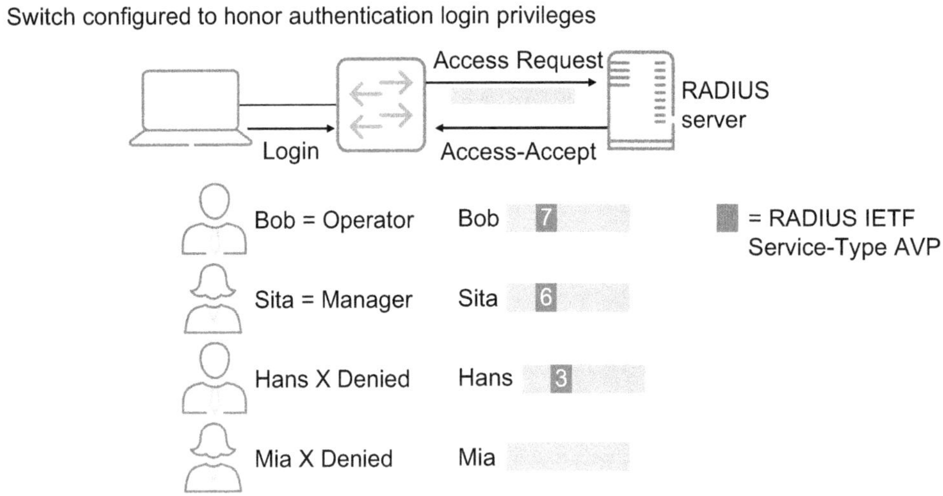


Figure 14-4 RADIUS authorization of operator or manager access

By default, the AOS-Switch provides the requested level of access to any user as long as the RADIUS server sends an Access-Accept (see Figure 14-4). The RADIUS server might be set up so that it only authenticates admin users, as opposed to any company user, when the switch requests authentication for a login or enable request. However, depending on the RADIUS server setup, this behavior could open the possibility of any user receiving management access.

If you want the switch to only provide management access to users for whom the RADIUS server sends a specific attribute authorizing that access, you must enable login privilege-mode.

```
Switch(config)# aaa authentication login privilege-mode
```

Enabling this mode also allows you to divide your management users into operators and managers.

When you use this mode, the RADIUS server must be configured to send an Attribute Value Pair (AVP) that authorizes users for the correct access level. The switch checks for the standard RADIUS Service-Type AVP in the RADIUS server's Access-Accept packet. It takes action accordingly.

- 7 = Access permitted at operator level (NAS-Prompt-User)
- 6 = Access permitted at manager level (Administrative-User)
- Null or other value = Access denied

The switch applies the access level immediately, no matter when the authentication occurs. For example, you have enabled RADIUS authentication for both login and enable SSH access. The user initiates an SSH session and authenticates. The RADIUS server returns an Access-Accept with 6 for the Service-Type. The switch places the user in enable mode rather than basic mode, and the user does not need to log in again.

For web UI authentication, manager access corresponds to full access to the Web UI. Operator access corresponds to a more limited version of the UI, which enables the user to view status and settings, but not change them.

## RADIUS-based command authorization

Some environments call for more granular control over management users than operator versus manager. Perhaps the company has administrators who should be able to configure the switch but should not have control over other administrators' credentials. Perhaps an administrator should be able to control VLANs and routing, but should not control port-based authentication. Or maybe different VLANs are used by different departments, and some administrators should be able to configure some VLANs but not others.

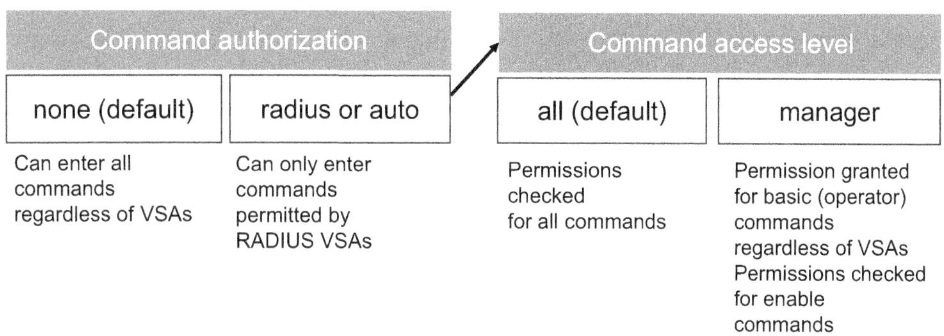


Figure 14-5 RADIUS-based command authorization

Understanding RBAC is a prerequisite for this chapter so you should know how AOS-Switches support RBAC for local users.

Figure 14-5 shows another option: you can use command authorization to assign different rights to different management users at a granular level. You will now learn how to incorporate command authorization with RADIUS authentication.

The first step is to enable command authorization, which configures the switch to restrict users to entering the commands assigned to their group. Because you are using RADIUS authentication, you should specify either **radius** or **auto** for command authorization mode with this command:

```
Switch(config)# aaa authorization commands <radius | auto | local |
    tacacs>
```

The best choice is usually **auto**, which allows the switch to use the same method that it used for authenticating the user to authorize the user. The auto option will allow you, for example, to enforce local authentication and authorization for console access, but RADIUS authentication and authorization for Telnet and SSH access.

To enforce RADIUS command authorization, the switch requires vendor-specific attributes (VSAs) from the RADIUS server, which tell the switch which commands the user is allowed to enter. You will learn more about these VSAs in a moment.

You can also configure for which commands the switch checks the privileges.

```
Switch(config)# aaa authorization command access-level <all | manager>
```

By default, the switch checks the privileges for all commands. The **manager** option tells the switch to only check privileges for enable mode commands. Users can then enter basic mode commands even if the RADIUS VSAs would otherwise not permit these commands.

## VSAs for defining command authorization

When the switch is configured to use RADIUS command authorization, the RADIUS server must be configured to send two VSAs within the Access-Accept for the user. These VSAs control which commands the user can enter. Both VSAs use a vendor type of 11. The names of the two different VSAs are "HPE-Command-Exception" and "HPE-Command-String" (see Figure 14-6).

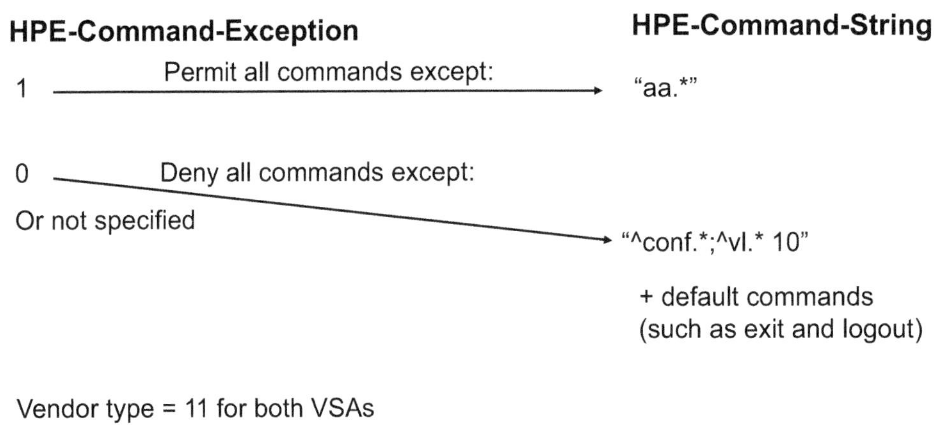


Figure 14-6 VSAs for defining command authorization

The "HPE-Command-Exception" VSA can have a value of 1 or 0. The value determines how the switch treats the commands listed in the "HPE-Command-String" VSA.

- 1—Permissive approach in which the user is authorized for all commands except commands that are explicitly denied. The "HPE-Command-String" VSA will act as a deny list.
- 0—Restrictive approach in which the user is denied all commands except commands that are explicitly permitted and several default commands. The "HPE-Command-String" VSA will act as a deny list.

The default commands are ones such as **exit** and **logoff**, which are always permitted to prevent a misconfiguration of the VSAs from leaving the switch in an unmanageable state.

The "HPE-Command-String" VSA provides the list of commands, either the commands that are denied or permitted, depending on the value of the "HPE-Command-Exception" VSA. The commands use regular expressions.

If you do not define this VSA or if you define it but leave the list empty, the switch follows this behavior, depending on how the "HPE-Command-Exception" VSA defined the list:

- Deny list (1)—The user can enter all commands.
- Permit list (0)—The user can enter only the default commands.

It is best practice to always configure the RADIUS server to send the "HPE-Command-Exception" VSA to define the type of list. If the server does not, the switch takes a restrictive approach and interprets the command list as a permit list. If the server sends neither VSA, though, the switch does not allow the user to log in.

Table 14-1 summarizes this behavior.

**Note**

You can use RADIUS command authorization with or without enabling authentication login privilege mode. If you choose to combine these two features, then operators are restricted to basic mode and then controlled by the command list after that. For example, an operator could be assigned a permit list that permits the enable command and configure commands; however, the operator would still be restricted to basic mode and could not enter those commands.

Table 14-1 HPE command string and exception

| HPE-command-exception | HPE-command-string | Description |
|---|---|---|
| Not present | Not present | If command authorization is enabled and the RADIUS server does not provide any authorization attributes in an Access-Accept packet, the user is denied access to the server. This message appears: "Access denied: no user's authorization info supplied by the RADIUS server." |
| DenyList-PermitOthers(1) | Not present | Authenticated user is allowed to execute all commands available on the switch. |
| PermitList-DenyOthers(0) | Not present | Authenticated user can only execute a minimal set of commands (those that are available by default to any user). |
| DenyList-PermitOthers(1) | Commands List | Authenticated user may execute all commands except those in the Commands list. |

(Continued)

Table 14-1 HPE command string and exception—cont'd

| HPE-command-exception | HPE-command-string | Description |
|---|---|---|
| PermitList-DenyOthers(0) | Commands List | Authenticated user can execute only those commands provided in the Commands List, plus the default commands. |
| Not present | Commands List | Authenticated user can only execute commands from the Commands List, plus the default commands. |
| Not present | Empty Commands List | Authenticate user can only execute a minimal set of commands (those that are available by default to any user). |
| DenyList-PermitOthers(1) | Empty Commands List | Authenticated user is allowed to execute all commands available on the switch. |
| PermitList-DenyOthers(0) | Empty Commands List | Authenticate user can only execute a minimal set of commands (those that are available by default to any user). |

## Secondary authentication method

When you configure RADIUS as the primary authentication method for a combination of access type and access level, you must choose a secondary method as well. The switch enforces the secondary method only when it cannot reach a RADIUS server associated with this access type. For example, suppose you have specified RADIUS server group "managerRadius" as the primary authentication method for login and enabled SSH access. This group has two RADIUS servers. The switch considers the primary method to have failed when its maximum number of retries have timed out for both servers (see Figure 14-7).

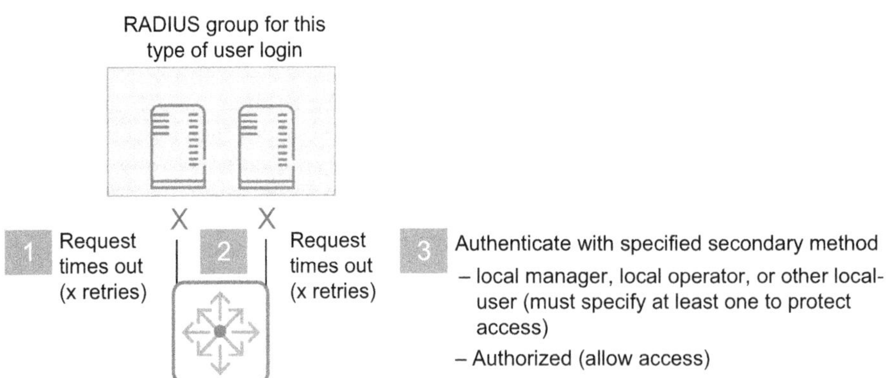


Figure 14-7 Secondary authentication method

At that point, the switch enforces the secondary authentication method. Valid options are:

- local—The switch still forces users to log in, but they can use the manager, operator, or local user accounts configured on the switch. (If command authorization is set to RADIUS, the switch also falls back to local command authorization). If none of these accounts are configured, users are not forced to log in. Configuring any of these accounts—including a local user one—protects the switch in a failover situation.
- authorized—The switch does not force users to log in. Any user can access the switch as long as the connectivity issue continues, and the user receives unrestricted manager level access.
- none—The switch does not allow users to log in. You should avoid using this option to prevent connectivity issues from locking managers out of the switch.

For the best security and the best resiliency, you should select **local** as the secondary method for all types of access that you are using. Also remember to configure at least one manager account, operator account, or local-user account. You are required to select **local** as the secondary method for console access when the primary method is **radius**.

## SNMP

SNMP is an industry-standard protocol that allows you to manage and monitor a variety of network devices from a central location (see Figure 14-8). Using an SNMP application, you can configure network devices and apply consistent security and management policies to all the devices on your network. You can also monitor SNMP-compliant devices for conditions requiring administrative attention—for example, a server has gone down, a LAN or WAN link is no longer available, or a link has become congested. You can track device uptime, link states, and many other device information variables. When a problem occurs, SNMP-compliant devices send an alert message to one or more designated SNMP servers, and you can then take steps to resolve the problem. In this section, you will learn how to use a RADIUS server such as Aruba ClearPass to authenticate management users who need to gain access to an AOS-Switch.

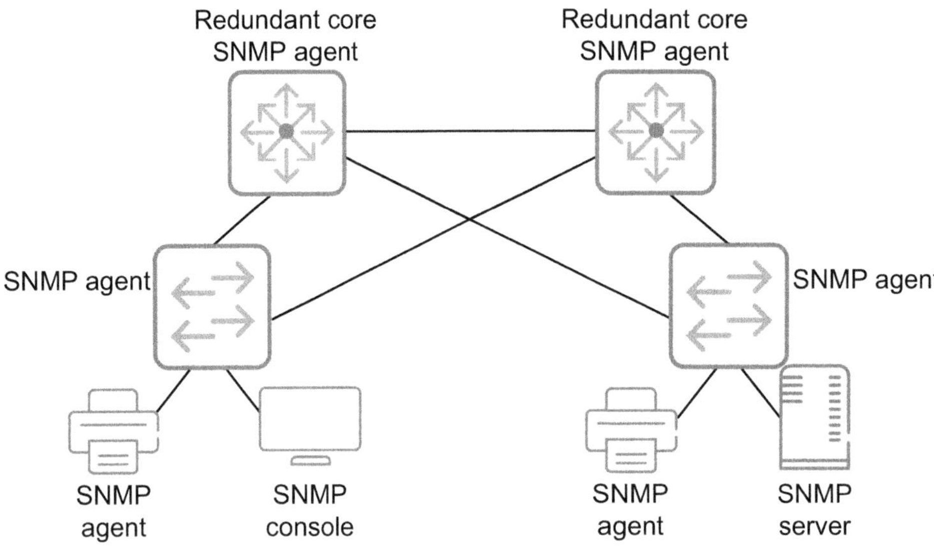


Figure 14-8 SNMP

## SNMP review

SNMPv2 is listed as a prerequisite for this chapter. You will now review your knowledge of basic SNMP concepts, SNMP operations, and SNMP communities by answering the following questions.

1. Briefly, describe the relationship between SNMP clients or agents and servers. What are examples of SNMP clients? What are examples of SNMP servers?

2. Match each SNMP operation to its description.

    ____ Get, GetNext, GetBulk

    ____ Set

    ____ Trap and Inform

    a. The SNMP server uses this operation or these operations to define the value of object instances on an agent.

    b. Agents use this operation or these operations to notify the SNMP server of a significant event.

    c. The SNMP server uses this operation or these operations to request information about one or more object instances from an agent.

3. SNMP versions 1 and 2c use community strings to restrict SNMP access. Briefly, describe how an SNMP agent uses each community.
   - Read only
   - Read write
   - Trap
4. When you enable SNMP on devices, why is it important to change the default settings?
5. What are some of the security weaknesses in SNMPv1 and 2c? What are some of the attacks to which these versions are vulnerable?

## SNMP objects, OIDs, and MIBs

Before diving into more details about SNMPv3, you will review SNMP objects in a bit more depth.

An SNMP object is simply the basic unit on which SNMP operates. Objects vary widely. An object can be a switch's system ID, data in its IP routing table, or the counter value for traffic sent and received on a port. Every object is uniquely defined by an object identifier (OID). For example, if an SNMP solution wants to check the counters for traffic sent on a switch interface, the solution sends a GET request with the precise OID for that counter on that specific interface.

For the solution to work, of course, the server and the agent need to agree on the OID for every piece of information that the server might want to use or every setting that it might want to configure. A message information base (MIB) defines the meaning of each OID.

The SNMP MIB is a large hierarchical tree with MIBs that are managed by different entities. Some MIBs are defined by industry standards bodies, such as the Institute of Electrical and Electronics Engineers (IEEE) or the Internet Engineering Task Force (IETF). Other MIBs are defined by individual vendors, such as Aruba, to expose objects specific to their devices. You can download all of the MIBs supported by your AOS-Switch from the same location that you download its software. Many SNMP solutions allow you to extend their capabilities by loading vendor-specific MIBs on them.

## SNMPv3 benefits

SNMPv3 addresses the major security flaws in SNMP versions 1 and 2c. It provides true authentication, as well as the options for data privacy and authentication. As Figure 14-9 shows, SNMPv3 defines a User-based Security Model (USM), allowing you to enforce both privacy and integrity for communications between SNMP agents and the SNMP server.

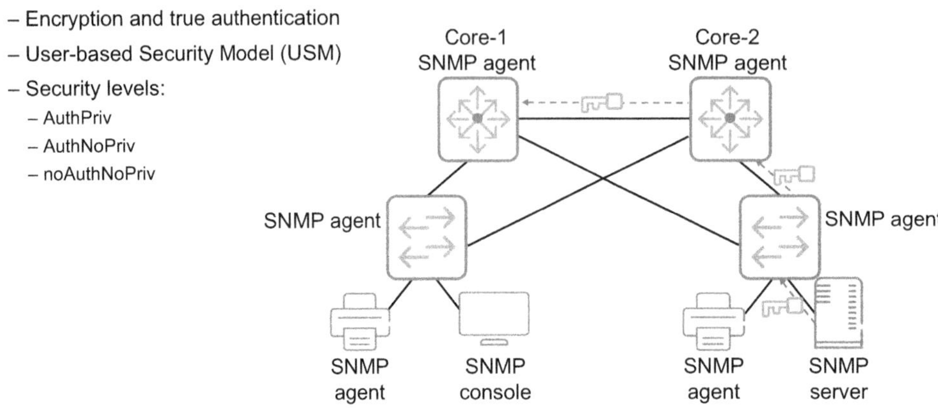


Figure 14-9 SNMPv3 benefits

To enforce authentication and privacy, SNMPv3 uses usernames and passwords. A user's authentication password is converted into a localized key. This key, along with the SNMP engine timestamp and the actual message, is compressed into a message digest using either the MD5 or SHA algorithm. This message digest is then forwarded with the packet. If a hacker attempts to alter the packet, the packet will no longer match the message digest, so the agent will drop it.

A user's privacy password can encrypt the message packet. SNMPv3 uses one of two encryption algorithms, AES and 3DES, to encrypt the localized key and the SNMP packet. This ensures that intercepted SNMP messages cannot be read.

You can choose the level of security to require for each user's messages.

- AuthPriv—This security level provides authentication and privacy, enforcing the strongest security for SNMP.
- AuthNoPriv—This level provides authentication but no privacy.
- noAuthNoPriv—This level does not provide authentication or privacy.

---

**Note**

For more information about SNMPv3 and USM, see RFC 3414 at http://www.ietf.org/rfc/rfc3414.txt.

---

## SNMPv3 users

When you create an SNMPv3 user, you set the username and the privacy and authentication passwords for that user (see Figure 14-10). For each password that you set, you must also specify the algorithm used with that password. For authentication, SHA is more secure than MD5; and for privacy, AES is more secure than DES.

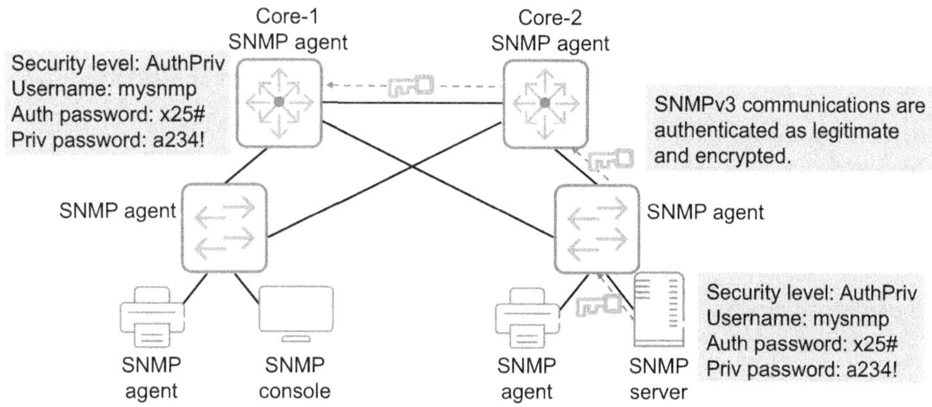


Figure 14-10 SNMPv3 users

A user account does not require an authentication password and encryption password. However, the account must have the passwords that correspond to the access type for their group, as you will see in a moment.

The command for creating an SNMPv3 user is:

```
Switch(config)# snmpv3 user <USER_NAME> [auth <md5|sha> <AUTH_PASS>]
   [priv <des|aes> <PRIV_PASS>]
```

The username, algorithms, and passwords that you set on the switch must match exactly those set on the SNMP solution.

## SNMPv3 groups

As Figure 14-11 shows, you must assign the SNMPv3 user to an SNMPv3 group in order for the user to receive access to the switch.

SNMPv3 groups set the security level required for users. The user must have the proper passwords for implementing that level of security. For example, you can only assign a user to the managerpriv group if that user has both an authentication password and a privacy password. The SNMPv3 group also controls the level of read and write access that users in that group receive.

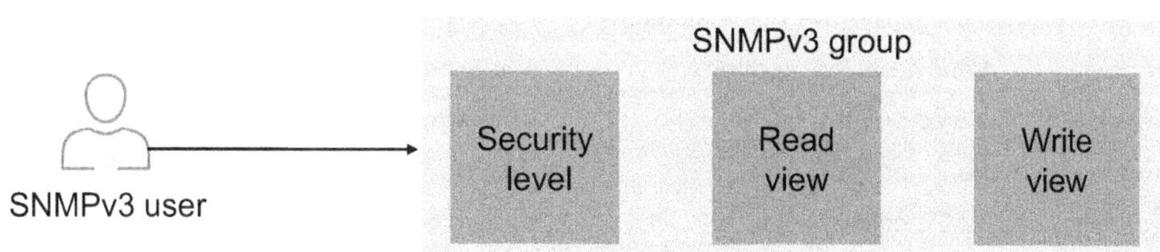


Figure 14-11 SNMPv3 groups

## SNMPv3 predefined groups and associated rights

You now understand how AOS-Switches control access to SNMP objects and MIBs.

AOS-Switches have eight predefined SNMPv3 groups, which are listed in Table 14-2. Four groups are used by SNMPv3 users. The other four control access for SNMPv2c or SNMPv1 management applications when you permit both SNMPv3 and SNMPv1/v2c, as described in more detail later in this section.

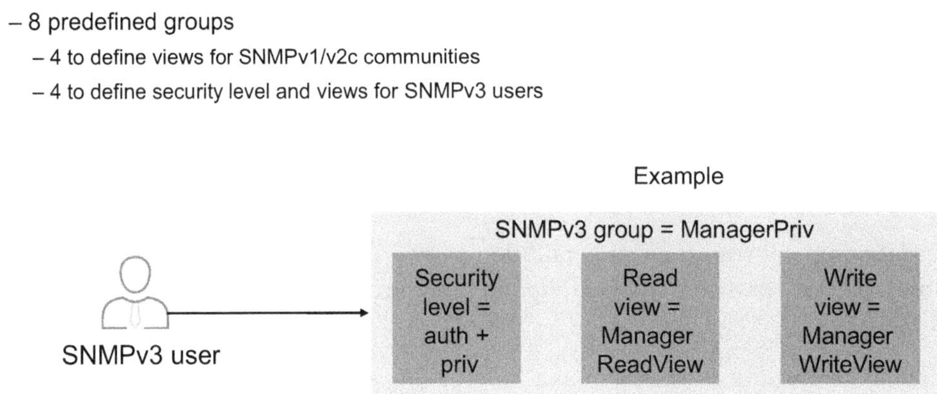


Figure 14-12 SNMPv3 predefined groups and associated rights

The command for assigning a user to one of these groups is:

```
Switch(config)# snmpv3 group <groupname> user <name> sec-model <ver1 |
   ver2c | ver3>
```

Figure 14-12 shows an SNMPv3 user that is assigned to the ManagerPriv group.

Table 14-2 Group-level access

| Group Name | Group Security Level | Group Read View | Group Write View |
|---|---|---|---|
| managerpriv | Ver3 must have authentication and privacy | ManagerReadView | ManagerWriteView |
| managerauth | Ver3 must have authentication | ManagerReadView | ManagerWriteView |
| operatorauth | Ver3 must have authentication | OperatorReadView | DiscoveryView |
| operatornoauth | Ver3 no authentication | OperatorReadView | DiscoveryView |
| commanagerrw | Ver2c or ver1 | ManagerReadView | ManagerWriteView |
| commanagerr | Ver2c or ver1 | ManagerReadView | DiscoveryView |
| comoperatorrw | Ver2c or ver1 | OperatorReadView | OperatorReadView |
| comoperatorr | Ver2c or ver1 | OperatorReadView | DiscoveryView |

The read view defines which objects a user can get, and the write view defines which objects users can set.

- ManagerReadView includes all managed objects.
- ManagerWriteView includes all managed objects except vacmContextTable, vacmAccessTable, and vacmViewTreeFamilyTable. These are related to defining view-based access control to objects.
- OperatorReadView includes all objects except vacmContextTable, vacmAccessTable, vacmViewTreeFamily-Table, as well as icfSecurityMIB, hpSwitchIpTftp-Mode, usmUserTable, and snmpCommunityTable. These additional objects are related to controlling SNMP and other management access; exposing them to operators could allow the operators to gain unauthorized access.
- The Discovery View includes only a samplingProbe MIB.

To view the exact MIBs associated with each view, enter this command:

```
Switch(config)# show snmpv3 view
```

**Note**
All SNMPv3 groups and views are predefined on the switch. There is no method to modify or add groups or views to those that are predefined on the switch.

## SNMPv1/2c versus SNMPv3 operation

By default, an AOS-Switch uses SNMPv1/v2c. You must enable SNMPv3 with this command:

```
Switch(config)# snmpv3 enable
```

When you enable SNMPv3, you are prompted to create a user, which uses the username "initial," MD5 authentication, DES privacy, and the passwords of your choice. You can also optionally create a user that uses SHA authentication and DES privacy. For security best practices, you should create your own user accounts after enabling SNMPv3 and then delete the "initial" user.

When you enable SNMPv3, you will also be asked whether you want to restrict SNMPv1/v2c to read-only access. Answering "yes" to this prompt is equivalent to later entering this command:

```
Switch(config)# snmpv3 restricted-access
```

After you enable SNMPv3, you can also prevent the switch from accepting any SNMPv1/v2c messages, including read-only ones. To do so, use the following command:

```
Switch(config)# snmpv3 only
```

| SNMPv1 /v2c enabled | SNMPv3 enabled | SNMPv3 restricted access | SNMPv3 only | Read messages accepted | Write messages accepted | SNMP traps and informs sent |
|---|---|---|---|---|---|---|
| X | | N/A(enabled or not) | N/A(enabled or not) | SNMPv1/v2c | SNMPv1/v2c | SNMPv1/v2c |
| X | X | | | SNMPv1/v2c SNMPv3 | SNMPv2/v2c SNMPv3 | SNMPv1/v2c SNMPv3 |
| X | X | X | | SNMPv1/v2c SNMPv3 | SNMPv3 | SNMPv1/v2c SNMPv3 |
| X | X | N/A (enabled or not) | X | SNMPv3 | SNMPv3 | SNMPv1/v2c SNMPv3 |
| | X | N/A (enabled or not) | N/A (enabled or not) | SNMPv3 | SNMPv3 | SNMPv3 |

Figure 14-13 SNMPv1/2c versus SNMPv3 operation

Based on which of these options you select, the switch will either use SNMPv3 exclusively or allow the use of both SNMPv3 and SNMPv1/v2c (see Figure 14-13). The following describes the ways in which SNMPv3 and SNMPv1/v2c can coexist on an AOS-Switch.

- SNMPv3 not enabled—This is the default operation. The switch accepts only SNMPv1/2c messages and uses v1/2c communities to control read and write access. Each v1/2c community has two parameters.
  - The MIB view (manager or operator) controls whether the community has access to all objects or to all objects except those in the CONFIG MIB.
  - The Write Access (restricted or unrestricted) controls whether the community has read-only or read-write access.
- SNMPv3 enabled and no other restrictions are configured—The switch accepts SNMPv1/2c and SNMPv3 messages. It uses SNMPv3 users and groups to control SNMPv3 read and write access. It maps SNMPv1/v2 communities to SNMPv3 groups to control access for SNMPv2 messages.

  Refer to Table 14-2 to see the mappings. For example, the group commanagerrw corresponds to any community with the "manager unrestricted" settings, and so forth. You can also create custom mappings. See your *Management and Configuration Guide* for more information.
- SNMPv3 enabled and SNMPv3 restricted-access only enabled—The switch accepts SNMPv1/2c messages and SNMPv3 messages. Again, it maps SNMPv1/v2 communities to SNMPv3 groups to control access for SNMPv2 messages. However, all SNMPv1/2c communities are mapped to either commanagerro or comoperatorro.
- SNMPv3 enabled and SNMPv3 only enabled (restrict only access enabled or disabled)—The switch only accepts SNMPv3 messages.

Note that whatever the SNMPv3 restrictions, the switch will still send SNMPv1/v2c traps if you have configured an SNMP host that uses an SNMPv1/v2c community and if SNMPv1/v2 is enabled.

You can end the traps by disabling SNMPv1/v2c entirely by entering this command:

```
Switch(config)# no snmp-server enable
```

## Ensure SNMPv3 settings match on AOS-Switches and AirWave

You will now review how to set up SNMPv3 settings on an AOS-Switch and then ensure that the AirWave settings match.

### Configure SNMPv3 settings on the AOS-Switch

1. Set the SNMP contact information.

   ```
   Switch(config)# snmp-server contact <contact> location <lab>
   ```

2. If your switches have multiple IP addresses, you might want to set which IP address it uses to respond to SNMP messages. Use this command:

   ```
   Switch(config)# snmp-server response-source <IP address>
   ```

3. Enable SNMPv3.

   ```
   Switch(config)# snmpv3 enable
   ```

4. The CLI will prompt for additional input. First, it will prompt you for an authentication password for the "initial" user. You will later delete this user, so you can set any password.

   ```
   password
   ```

5. Then the CLI asks whether to add a SHA user. Choose no. You will add a user on your own in a moment.

   ```
   n
   ```

6. Then the CLI asks whether to restrict SNMPv1/v2c communities to read-only access. In this example, you can choose either yes or no because you will disable SNMPv1/v2c entirely in a moment.

   ```
   y
   ```

7. Create an SNMPv3 user. In this example, you are using the name, **airwave**. In a production environment, you would set a secure password, but for this example, you will simply use "password."

   ```
   Switch(config)# snmpv3 user airwave auth sha password priv aes
   password
   ```

8. Add the SNMPv3 user to the ManagerPriv SNMPv3 group, which has unrestricted read-write access to the switch.

   ```
   Switch(config)# snmpv3 group managerpriv user airwave sec-model ver3
   ```

9. Remove the initial user, which you are not using for this example.

```
Switch(config)# no snmpv3 user initial
```

10. Restrict SNMP to SNMPv3 only.

```
Switch(config)# snmpv3 only
```

11. Verify the SNMP settings.

```
Switch(config)# show snmpv3 user
 Status and Counters - SNMP v3 Global Configuration Information

  User Name                        Auth. Protocol   Privacy Protocol
  -------------------------------- ---------------- ----------------
  airwave                           SHA              CFB AES-12

Core-2(config)# show snmpv3 group
 Status and Counters - SNMP v3 Global Configuration Information

  Security Name                 Security Model Group Name
  ---------------------------   -------------- --------------------
  CommunityManagerReadOnly      ver1           ComManagerR
  CommunityManagerReadWrite     ver1           ComManagerRW
  CommunityOperatorReadOnly     ver1           ComOperatorR
  CommunityOperatorReadWrite    ver1           ComOperatorRW
  CommunityManagerReadOnly      ver2c          ComManagerR
  CommunityManagerReadWrite     ver2c          ComManagerRW
  CommunityOperatorReadOnly     ver2c          ComOperatorR
  CommunityOperatorReadWrite    ver2c          ComOperatorRW
  airwave                       ver3           ManagerPriv

Switch(config)# show snmpv3 enable
 Status and Counters - SNMP v3 Global Configuration Information

  SNMP v3 enabled : Yes
```

## Configure the management settings in Aruba AirWave

You will now see how AirWave uses the proper settings to communicate with the switches. You can configure the SNMPv3 settings when you add a switch initially. The steps below explain how to configure SNMPv3 settings on switches that have already been discovered and added to AirWave with SNMPv2. In this example, the switches are in a group called Site 2 switches.

1. Access the AirWave Management Platform window in your web browser. Enter the login credentials to log in.

First, you must configure AirWave to use the proper SNMP version to manage the switches. In this example, the Site 2 switches group contains the switches on which you configured SNMPv3.

2. Move to the **Groups** > **List** page.
3. Click **Site 2 switches** (see Figure 14-14).

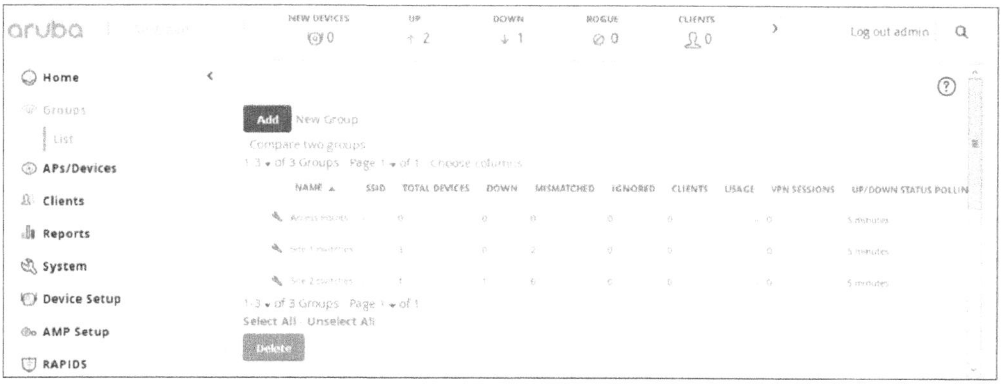


Figure 14-14 Configure management settings in Aruba AirWave

4. Click **Basic** (see Figure 14-15).

Figure 14-15 Configure management settings in Aruba AirWave

5. Find the **Universal Devices, Routers, and Switches** section. (If you set the group to refer to specific switch models, you might need to find the Aruba switches section instead.)
6. Set **3** for **SNMP version**.
7. Click **Save and Apply** (see Figure 14-16).

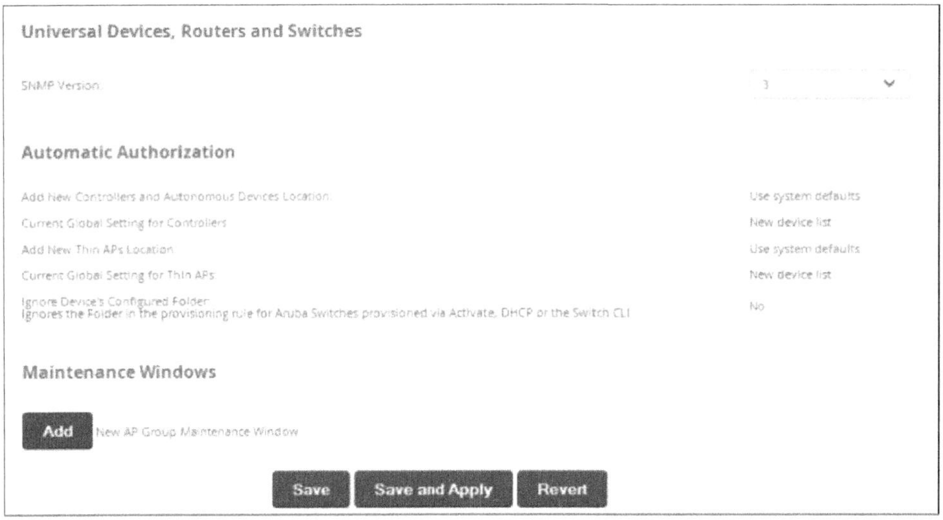


Figure 14-16 Configure management settings in Aruba AirWave

8. Click **Apply Changes Now** (see Figure 14-17).

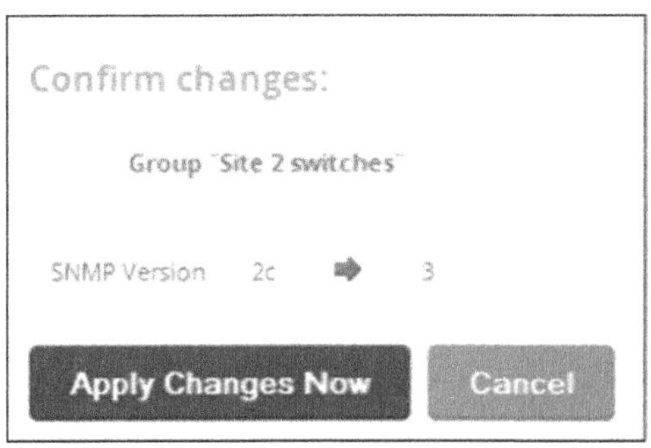


Figure 14-17 Configure management settings in Aruba AirWave

Next, you must update the management settings that the switch uses for the switch and specify the credentials for the SNMPv3 users.

9. Move to the **APs/Devices** > **List** page (see Figure 14-18).

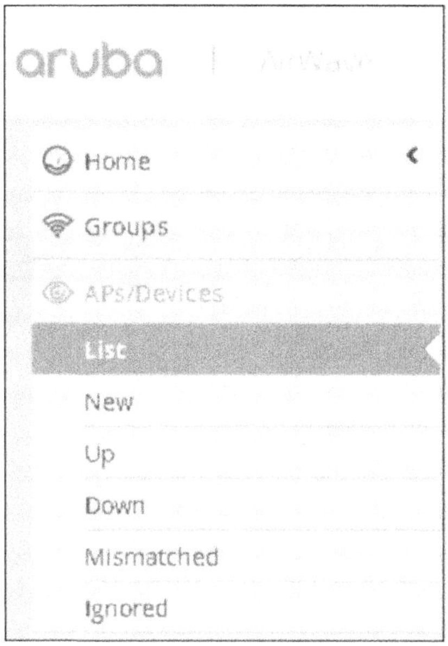


Figure 14-18 Configure management settings in Aruba AirWave

10. Scroll to the Devices List.
11. Click the pencil icon next to the list.
12. You can now apply a variety of actions to the devices. Select the checkboxes for the switches for which you want to update the settings. You can select the checkbox at the top of the list to select all devices.
13. For Device Actions, select **Update the credentials used to communicate with these devices**.
14. Click **Update** (see Figure 14-19).

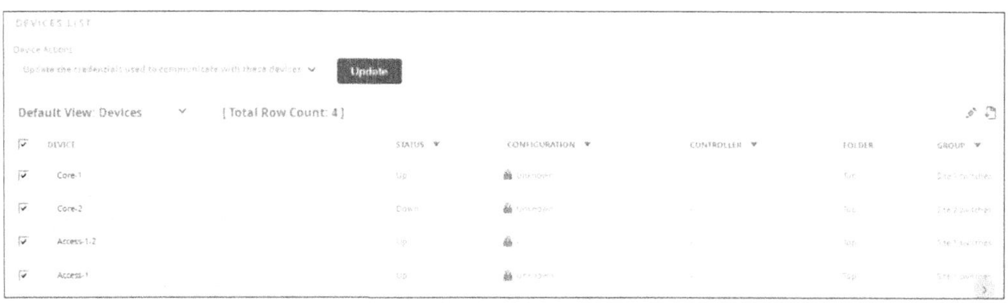


Figure 14-19 Configure management settings in Aruba AirWave

15. Fill in the SNMPv3 settings to match those on the switches, as shown in Figure 14-20. Fill in the **SNMPv3 username**, **Auth Password**, **Confirm Auth Password**, **Privacy Password**, and **Confirm Privacy Password**. The passwords are all **password** in this example. Also, set the **SNMPv3 Auth Protocol** to **SHA-1** and the **SNMPv3 Privacy Protocol** to **AES**.
16. Click **Update**.

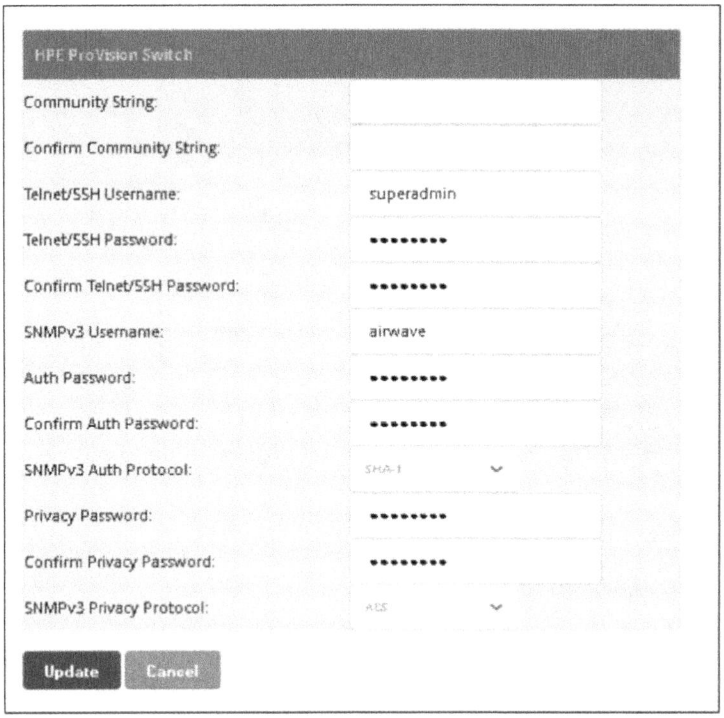


Figure 14-20 Configure management settings in Aruba AirWave

17. Apply the changes (see Figure 14-21).

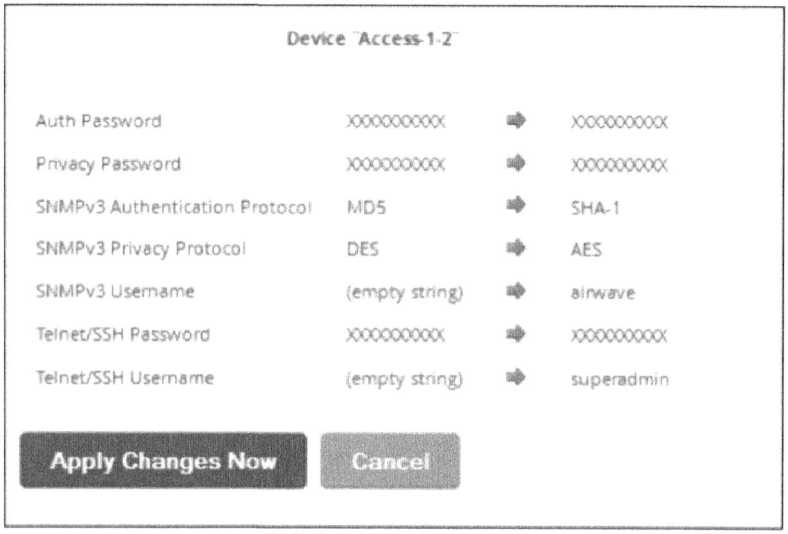


Figure 14-21 Configure management settings in Aruba AirWave

AirWave is now using SNMPv3 to manage the devices.

## SNMPv3 notifications

As you reviewed earlier, SNMP agents use traps to notify an SNMP server of significant events. As Figure 14-22 shows, setting up SNMPv3 notifications consists of:

- Defining globally what events can generate a trap

  This step applies to setting up traps sent to SNMPv2c servers as well.

- Defining SNMPv3 notification targets to which generated traps are sent

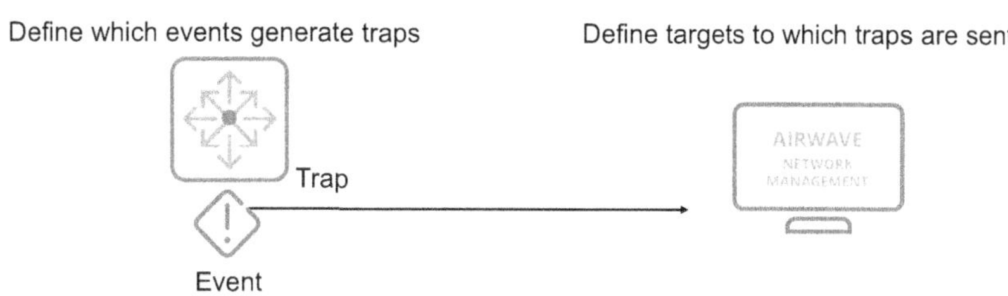


Figure 14-22 SNMPv3 notifications

## Defining traps

| Trap types | Configuration | Command for CLI config |
|---|---|---|
| Well-known or fixed | Always enabled for "public" community only | |
| Event log traps | Always enabled, but can be filtered when target set up | |
| RMON threshold traps | | rmon alarm (covered later) |
| Security and config event traps | CLI, Web, or SNMP | snmp-server enable traps<br>mac-count-notify and mac-notify options also require enabling on interface |
| Hardware event traps | | set-mib |

Figure 14-23 Defining traps

Figure 14-23 summaries the types of traps AOS-Switches generate. These are described in more depth below:

- Fixed or well-known traps—These are traps such as "coldStart," "warmStart," "linkDown," and "linkUp." You do not need to enable these traps. The switch automatically sends these traps to trap receivers using the public community name. These traps cannot be redirected to other communities. If you change or delete the default public community name, these traps are not sent.

  However, you can enable traps for some of these events—such as link changes—using the **snmp-server enable trap** command. Then you can use the SNMPv2c community or SNMPv3 user account of your choice.

- Traps associated with RMON thresholds
- Event log traps

  Whenever the switch logs an event to its local log, it can also generate an SNMP trap. However, many of these events are filtered. You will learn over the next sections how you control whether the switch sends event log traps to specific notification destinations or not.

- Specifically enabled security and configuration event traps

  You can set specific events that you want to create SNMP traps. The switch always sends these traps to the SNMP trap destinations even if you are filtering event log traps. These traps give you more control over choosing the relevant information for your environment. You can filter out all or most event log traps, but still, have the switch send traps for the events that you choose.

Use this command to enable and disable traps for security and configuration management related events:

Switch(config)# **[no] snmp-server enable traps <event type>**

Event types include Address Resolution Protocol (ARP) protection detecting a spoofed ARP message, a manager login failure, and many others indicated in Table 14-3.

The **mac-notify** and **mac-count-notify** options enable the switch to send traps when a MAC address is learned or when an interface exceeds the maximum number of allowed MAC addresses. However, in order for the switch to generate a trap, the notification also has to be enabled on the interface that learned the MAC address. By default, these notifications are disabled on all interfaces. The commands for enabling these options on interfaces are:

```
Switch(config)# interface <port ID list> mac-count-notify traps [1-128]
Switch(config)# interface <port ID list> mac-notify traps [aged |
   learned | removed]
```

Table 14-3 Event traps

| Event type | When event occurs |
|---|---|
| arp-protect | ARP packets are received with an invalid source or destination MAC address, an invalid IP address, or an invalid IP-to-MAC binding. |
| auth-server-fail | If the connection with a RADIUS or TACACS+ authentication server fails. |
| dhcp-server | Events related to the switches' Dynamic Host Configuration Protocol (DHCP) server functionality occurs. |
| dhcp-snooping \| dhcpv6-snooping | DHCP packets are received from an untrusted source, or DHCP packets contain an invalid IP-to-MAC or IPv6-to-MAC binding. |
| dyn-ip-lockdown \| dyn-ipv6-lockdown | The switch is out of hardware resources needed to program a dynamic IP or IPv6 lockdown rule. |
| link-change <PORT-LIST> | Link state on a port changes from up to down, or the reverse. |
| login-failure-mgr | A user attempts to log in with the manager account but fails. |
| password-change-mgr | A manager password is reset. |
| mac-count-notify | The number of MAC addresses learned on a specified port exceeds the threshold. |
| mac-notify | Globally enables the generation of SNMP trap notifications upon MAC address table changes. |
| port-security | A failed authentication attempt occurs through a web, MAC, or 801.X authentication session. |
| running-config-change | Changes to the running configuration file are made. |

*(Continued)*

Table 14-3 Event traps—cont'd

| Event type | When event occurs |
|---|---|
| snmp-authentication [extended \| standard] | A failed authentication attempt via SNMP occurs. Defaults to extended. |
| startup-config-change | Changes to the startup configuration file are made. (Defaults to disabled.) |
| macsec | A MACsec event occurs. |
| macsec failures | A MACsec Connectivity Association (CA) fails to establish or a MACsec CA terminates due to MACsec Key Agreement (MKA) keep-alive timeout. |

Events related to changes to the hardware can also generate traps. Table 14-4 presents the ID for these events and Table 14-5 presents the meaning of the number after -i. To control whether the hardware event triggers a log, a trap, neither, or both, use this command:

```
Switch(config)# setMib eventType.<event_Id> -i <1-4>
```

Table 14-4 Event IDs

| Event ID | Severity | Action | Message |
|---|---|---|---|
| 68 | Info | Slot Insertion | I 06/20/16 09:18:43 00068 chassis: AM1: Slot C Inserted |
| 67 | Info | Slot Removal | I 06/20/16 09:18:50 00067 chassis: AM1: Slot C Removed |
| 405 | Info | Transceiver Insertion | I 06/20/16 09:18:56 00405 ports: AM1: port A23 xcvr hotswap insert |
| 406 | Info | Transceiver Removal | I 06/20/16 09:19:04 00406 ports: AM1: port A23 xcvr hotswap remove |
| 552 | Warning | Stacking module Insertion | W 04/20/16 09:20:43 00552 chassis: ST1-CMDR: Stacking Module insertion detected: Reboot required |
| 552 | Warning | Stacking module Removal | W 06/20/16 09:19:43 00552 chassis: ST1-CMDR: Stacking Module removal detected: Reboot required |

Table 14-5 Enabling and disabling traps

| Event type | When event occurs |
|---|---|
| Disable both the log and trap | 1 |
| Enable log only | 2 |
| Enable trap only | 3 |
| Enable both the log and trap (Default) | 4 |

## SNMPv3 notification targets

Next, you will learn how to define a notification targets.

When possible, you should prefer using SNMPv3 notification targets to SNMPv2 trap hosts because the SNMPv3 notification process allows messages to be authenticated and encrypted. Although defining an SNMPv3 target is a bit more complex, you have more control and security with this option.

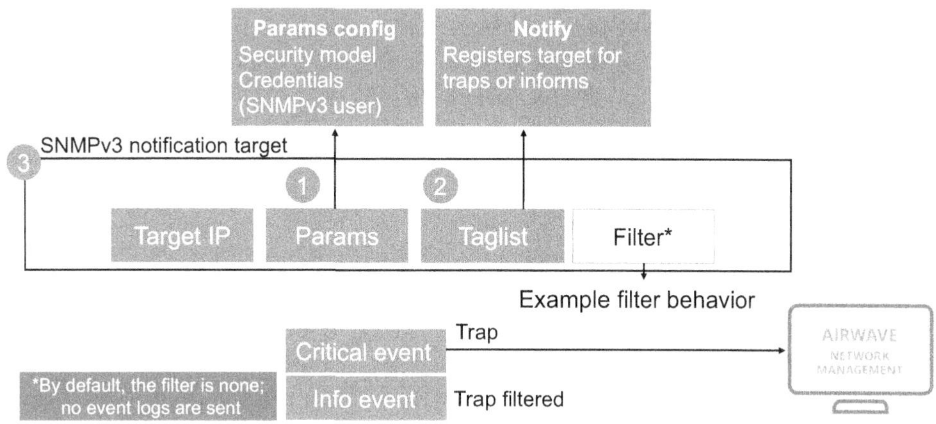


Figure 14-24 SNMPv3 notification targets

As shown in Figure 14-24, you need to define two configurations, a params configuration and a notify entry, before you configure notification targets.

Enter this command to define a params configuration that uses SNMPv3 security:

```
Switch(config)# snmpv3 params <params name> user <SNMPv3 username>
   sec-model ver3 message-processing ver3 <noauth | auth | priv>
```

Enter this command to configure the notify entry and associate it with a taglist:

```
Switch(config)# snmpv3 notify <notify name> tagvalue <taglist name>
```

The switch checks the notify table when it is identifying targets for traps; the taglist associates the notify entry with a target IP address. You can choose any intuitive value for the notify name and for the taglist name. However, you are prohibited from using numbers one to ten as names because the switch uses these names for notify entries that it creates on its own (such as when you specify **inform** for the SNMPv2 host configuration and the switch maps the SNMPv2 host configuration to an SNMPv3 target.)

You can then reference those configurations when you set up a notification target. This target has three required components for the switch to send traps to the host.

- Target IP address—Defines the IP address to which the notification is sent.
- Params name—Associates the receiver with a params configuration, which you must create before configuring the target. The params configuration specifies whether you send the notifications as

SNMPv2 messages or SNMPv3 messages, as well as the related security parameters. You should specify a configured SNMPv3 user when you use the SNMPv3 security model.

- Taglist—Associates the receiver with an SNMPv3 notification configuration, which you must create before configuring the target. You must specify this setting; otherwise, the switch will not find the target.

Optionally, you can limit the traps sent with a filter.

- Filter—Defines the level of events for which the switch forwards traps. If you do not configure this setting, it is at the default value, which is none; the switch does not send any event log traps to the notification target. You can alternatively set the filter option to one of the following:
  - all—Sends all event log messages.
  - not info—Sends all event log messages that are not for information only.
  - critical—Sends only event log messages for critical error conditions.
  - debug—Sends event log messages at the debug level.

  The filter only affects traps automatically generated from event log messages. The filter does not affect whether the switch sends traps associated with RMON thresholds; it also has no effect on traps that you specifically enable with the **snmp-server enable trap** commands.

For example, enter this command to configure a trap notification target that sends all event log messages more critical than info:

```
Switch(config)# snmpv3 targetaddress <target name> params <params name>
   <IP address> filter not-info
```

When the switch generates a trap, it sends the trap to all SNMPv3 notification targets that you have configured. Two exceptions apply:

- You can filter the events sent to a specific target based on the event severity level.
- A switch automatically sends all messages created when a system threshold is reached to the network management station that configured the threshold, regardless of the trap receiver configuration.

## SNMPv2 trap hosts

If you need to define an SNMPv2c trap target, you can use this command:

```
Switch(config)# snmp-server host <IP address> community <community
   name> [trap-level all | critical | not-info | debug | none]
   [informs]
```

The switch sends these traps with an SNMPv2c community name, which should match the trap community on the SNMP server. The trap level tells the switch which level of event logs to send as traps, much like the filter. Use the optional **inform** option to tell the switch to send informs to this target rather than traps.

You can view SNMP trap configuration by entering the **show snmp-server trap** command. The output shows which traps are enabled and disabled. You can also verify which server is configured as a trap host.

```
Switch# show snmp-server trap
 Trap Receivers

  Link-Change Traps Enabled on Ports [All] : All

  Traps Category                            Current Status

  _____________________________________     _________________

  SNMP Authentication                     : Extended
  Password change                         : Enabled
  Login failures                          : Enabled
  Port-Security                           : Enabled
  Authorization Server Contact            : Enabled
  DHCP-Snooping                           : Enabled
  DHCPv6-Snooping Out of Resource         : Enabled
  DHCPv6-Snooping Errant Replies          : Enabled
  Dynamic ARP Protection                  : Enabled
  Dynamic IP Lockdown                     : Enabled
  Dynamic IPv6 Lockdown Out of Resource   : Enabled
  Dynamic IPv6 Lockdown Violations        : Enabled
  Startup Config change                   : Disabled
  Running Config Change                   : Disabled
  MAC address table changes               : Disabled
  MAC Address Count                       : Disabled
  DHCP-Server                             : Enabled
  NTP-Client                              : Disabled
  MACsec Failures                         : Enabled
  ND Snooping Out of Resources Traps      : Enabled
```

```
Address            Community        Events     Type     Retry     Timeout
-----------------  ---------------  ---------  -------  --------  --------
10.101.10.11       public           Critical   trap     3         15
```

## Configuration auditing

In this section, you will explore best practices for network maintenance and monitoring tasks. Aruba AirWave helps you to follow best practices for managing and auditing configurations so that you can avoid and resolve issues.

First, when AirWave discovers a network infrastructure device, it retrieves the device configuration. You can also set up schedules for backing up devices' configurations or set up on-demand retrieval, ensuring that you always have an up-to-date archive.

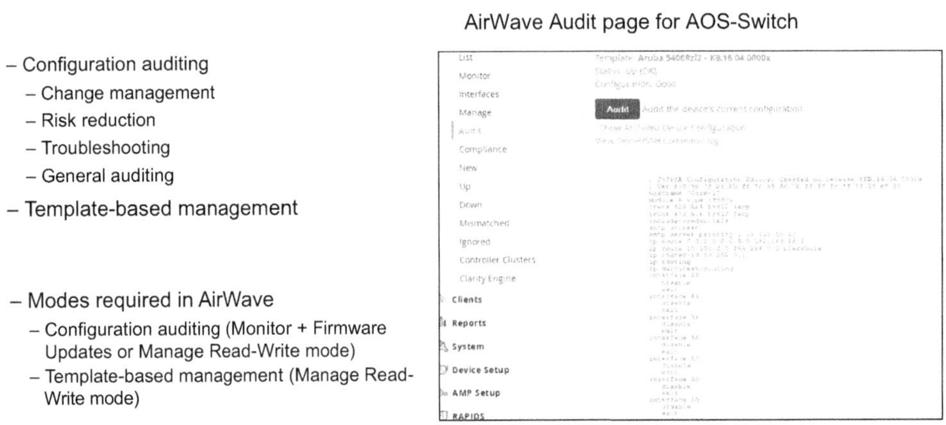


Figure 14-25 Configuration auditing

These configurations can help you in change management. As you know, changes to the network can cause unforeseen repercussions. You need to follow careful change management processes before making any change to the network such as installing new software, implementing a new protocol, or extending the access layer to a new building. Having an archive with the current configuration file on each network infrastructure device can help you understand your environment. You can analyze how your proposed changes will affect the infrastructure and whether you will need to make other changes. For example, you can plan new VLANs and IP addresses for extending the network, avoiding overlap, and ensuring that new IP addresses fall within ABR summary ranges. AirWave's network mapping and monitoring features also help in these efforts.

Before you make any change, it is also crucial that you have a known good configuration for each device. You can then more easily and more quickly roll back the network to a healthy state if changes do not proceed as planned.

Some companies also must collect and archive configurations as part of their IT auditing processes.

As Figure 14-25 shows, AirWave further helps administrators to follow good change management practices through its template-based management approach. When you add a device to AirWave, you assign it to a group. AirWave then compares the device's configuration to the configuration template associated with that device's group. A group can even have multiple templates, specific to the device model and, optionally, software version. AirWave tracks differences between a device's actual configuration and the template associated with it, which can help you to troubleshoot issues such as a change that has not undergone the proper planning and change management processes.

You can use these configuration auditing features for any AOS-Switch discovered in AirWave. If you raise the device management level to Manage Read&Write, you can further use the template to manage the device. Template-based management, in which you make changes to the device template, rather than to individual switch configurations, helps you to follow best practices as well. Not only can you make the changes much more quickly, you can ensure that they apply consistently across the network.

## Monitoring network traffic and events

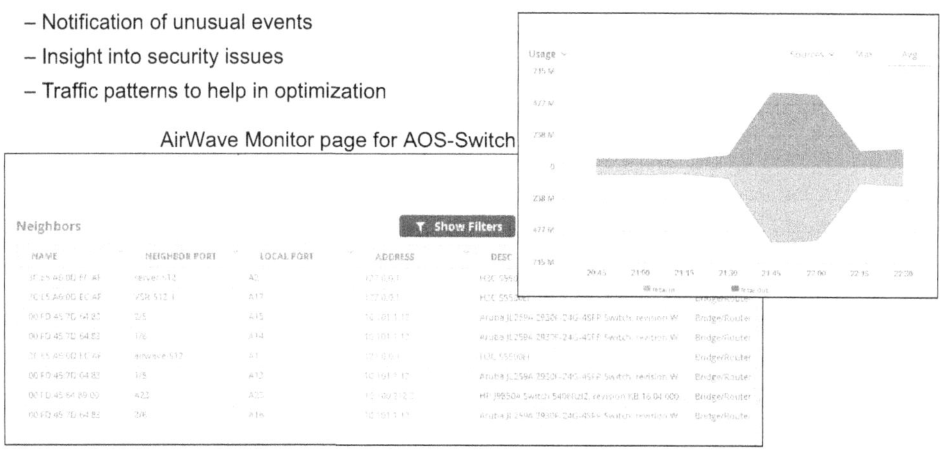


Figure 14-26 Monitoring network traffic and events

You have just explored the value of having visibility into and control over network infrastructure devices' configurations. As Figure 14-26 shows, other types of visibility can be equally useful. Some examples are listed below:

- Notifications of unusual events—When you check on the network, you need to see at a glance what has changed and what has happened of significance. Switches can register events and send alerts and alarms for significant events. For example, you need to know when a switch uplink goes down. Even if you have the proper redundancy protocols in place for the switch to failover to another link, you need to replace the link to restore the best functionality and prevent future issues.

Other events might be security related. You will learn about a variety of security features such as DHCP snooping and ARP protection later in *Chapter 16: Additional Security Features*. These features can generate alerts and traps to notify administrators of potential security breaches.

- Insight into errors and early indications of issues—Administrators should be aware when a link, while still functional, is showing signs of potential issues. Dropped packets, for example, could indicate network congestion that needs to be addressed. A high percentage of Cyclic Redundancy Check (CRC) errors could indicate physical media that is beginning to give out.
- Traffic patterns—It can also be useful to monitor normal traffic patterns. When and where do you normally see peak usage? Who are your top talkers (top sources of traffic)? With this information, you can optimize performance and plan for the future—such as the best place to add bandwidth to prevent congestion in the future. If uplinks have uneven typical bandwidth usage, you might reconsider the type of load balancing used by link aggregation or investigate your routing protocol's costs and selected routes.

  When you use AirWave to monitor your switches, you can find information about traffic patterns in several places, including the Network Deviations page and the Monitor page for a switch.

  Insight into normal traffic patterns can also help you to more easily pinpoint anomalies. An endpoint that suddenly starts sending much more traffic than it ever has before could be hijacked by malware. (If you are interested in gaining more insight into anomalies and more power in stopping potential attacks, investigate Aruba Niara.)

The rest of this chapter introduces technologies that help you monitor the network in all of these ways. These technologies often work in conjunction with a centralized management solution such as AirWave. For example, RMON helps the switch to determine when it should generate an SNMP trap with information about the system, and AirWave receives the traps and helps to present them to administrators in an intuitive and useful way.

## RMON—collect information on a port

RMON can run on a network infrastructure device and monitor traffic sent and received on that device's ports. This sampling protocol profiles the sessions and applications in use in a network and also provides information about port statistics such as link utilization. RMON focuses on collecting port statistics but also alerts network management solutions when particular thresholds are crossed.

RMON works in conjunction with SNMP. RMON was designed to inform SNMP solutions such as AirWave about traffic-related information in a more efficient manner. For example, administrators might need to monitor when ports' utilization exceeds a specific percentage. Because SNMP traps do not provide this information, the SNMP solution would need to send many periodic get messages, querying network devices. The solution might also need to compare and otherwise analyze information collected at different times, adding to its processing burdens.

RMON removes these burdens. As Figure 14-27 shows, each local device monitors its own ports' statistics, consolidating and storing the information to be queried as required. The local device also automatically sends alarms when various thresholds are exceeded.

Many AOS-Switches can act as RMON agents, which support four RMON groups. (An RMON group is a defined object that implements a specific RMON function.) To configure RMON on the switch, you define alarms as well as the actions taken when alarms are triggered (events). (Some SNMP solutions can also use SNMP to configure their own RMON alarms on the switch.)

## Using RMON to collect information

The RMON monitoring function is automatically enabled on all interfaces. It creates a table to store various statistics for that interface. AOS-Switches support two types of monitoring functions (defined in RMON groups).

- Ethernet statistics group—The ethernetStatsTable stores statistics such as network collisions, CRC alignment errors, undersize/oversize packets, broadcasts, multicasts, bytes received, packets received, and so on. Every time that RMON checks the interface, it overwrites its table with a cumulative sum of statistics.
- Ethernet History group—The ethernetHistoryTable stores statistics such as bandwidth utilization, number of errors, and number of packets. For history group entries, every time that RMON checks the interface, it creates a new bucket with statistics for just the latest period.

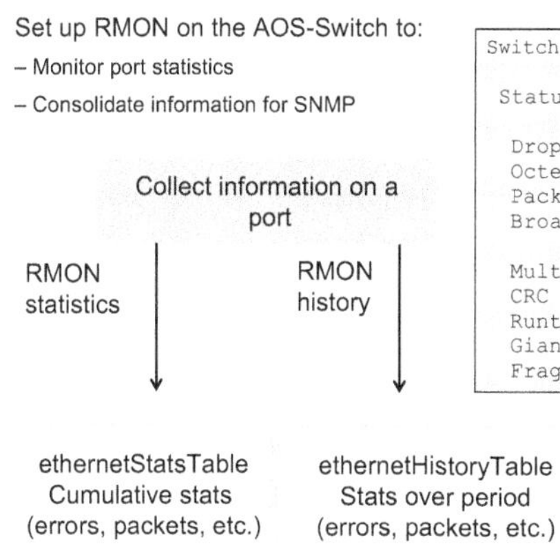


```
Switch# show rmon statistics 1/5

 Status and Counters - Port Counters for port 1/5

  Drop events     : 0            Jabbers              : 0
  Octets          : 1,182,628    Collisions           : 0
  Packets         : 8627         64 oct pkts          : 0
  Broadcast pkts  : 4            65-127 oct pkts      : 5435

  Multicast pkts  : 6090         128-255 oct pkts     : 1837
  CRC errors      : 0            256-511 oct pkts     : 1218
  Runts           : 0            512-1023 oct pkts    : 135
  Giants          : 0            1024-1518 oct pkts   : 2
  Fragments       : 0
```

Figure 14-27 RMON—collect information on a port

Network management solutions can use SNMP get messages to collect the information in these tables as required. You can also view the tables in the CLI with one of these commands:

```
Switch# show rmon
```

```
Switch# show rmon statistics <port ID list>
```

Figure 14-27 shows the output from the **show rmon statistics** command.

You might also want to set up alarms that automatically inform the network management solution of relevant information. The next section explains how.

## RMON—generate alarms

You can define an alarm that triggers when the statistics collected for an entry pass a specific threshold. For example, you might want to monitor an interface that you have noticed is congested. You can create an RMON alarm to send a trap when an excessive number of packets are dropped. Or, you might have noticed in the **show interface <ID>** output that an interface has some errors on it, but you do not know when or why the errors occurred. You could set up an RMON alarm to trigger a trap when such an error occurs again (see Figure 14-28).

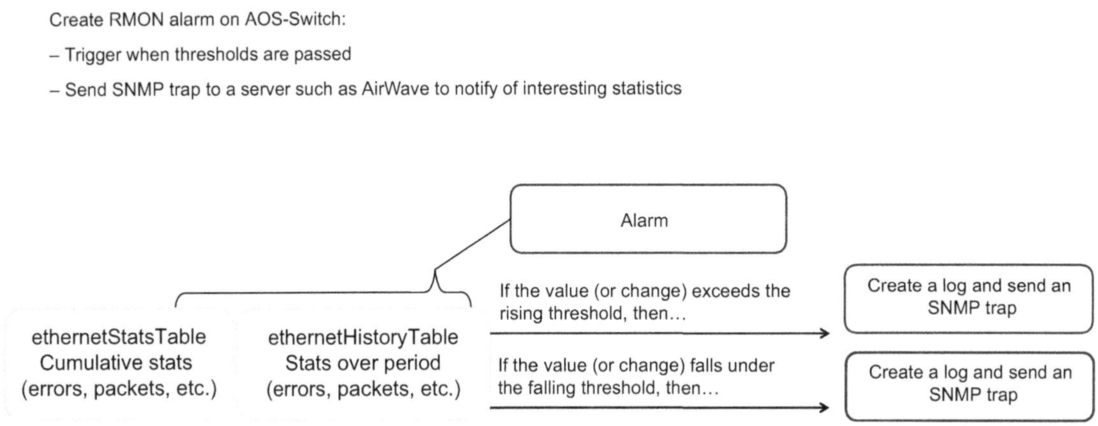


Figure 14-28 RMON—generate alarms

You create an RMON alarm, which specifies:

- The alarm variable associated with the specific statistic in the table that you want to monitor

  You can specify this variable by OID such as 1.3.6.1.2.1.16.1.1.1.4 or name such as etherStatsOctets. To monitor a specific interface, end the variable with the interface ID that you want to monitor. For example, specify etherStatsOctets.1 to monitor the bytes sent and received on interface 1 or a1 (on a modular switch).

  You can download the MIBs supported by your switch from the same location that you download the software. Table 14-6 presents the names for common object names defined in RFC 2819.

- A sampling interval
- The rising threshold value
- The event that defines the action that RMON should take when the rising threshold value is exceeded

- The falling threshold value
- The event that defines the action that RMON should take when the statistic falls below the falling threshold value (can be the same or different as the rising threshold event)
- Whether the threshold values refer to the actual value in the table (absolute) or to a change from the value in the previous sample (delta)

**Note**

The alarm triggers when the value first crosses a threshold but not again—unless it has subsequently crossed the other threshold. Therefore, a rising alarm is always succeeded by a falling alarm and vice versa. In other words, when the value first exceeds the rising threshold value, the alarm triggers, but for as long as the value continues to exceed the rising threshold value, no more alarms occur. A new alarm only triggers when the value falls below the falling threshold value.

The command syntax for creating an alarm is:

```
Switch(config)# rmon alarm <entry number> <alarm-variable> <sampling-
interval> <absolute | delta> rising-threshold <thresholdvalue1>
falling-threshold <threshold-value> [owner string]
```

**Note**

Refer to your AOS-Switch's *Management and Configuration Guide* for information about how many RMON entries, events, and alarms it supports.

When the alarm triggers, the switch sends an SNMP trap to the trap receivers configured on it. Figure 14-29 shows an example of SNMP traps on AirWave. The trap at the top of the list was triggered by an RMON alarm monitoring oversize (giant) packets.

Figure 14-29 Example SNMP traps received by AirWave

Table 14-6 Names of common RMON objects for the alarm variable

| EtherStatsEntry | EtherHistoryEntry |
|---|---|
| etherStatsDropEvents | etherHistoryDropEvents |
| etherStatsOctets | etherHistoryOctets |
| etherStatsPkts | etherHistoryPkts |
| etherStatsBroadcastPkts | etherHistoryBroadcastPkts |
| etherStatsMulticastPkts | etherHistoryMulticastPkts |
| etherStatsCRCAlignErrors | etherHistoryCRCAlignErrors |
| etherStatsUndersizePkts | etherHistoryUndersizePkts |
| etherStatsOversizePkts | etherHistoryOversizePkts |
| etherStatsFragments | etherHistoryFragments |
| etherStatsJabbers | etherHistoryJabbers |
| etherStatsCollisions | etherHistoryCollisions |
| etherStatsPkts64Octets | etherHistoryUtilization |
| etherStatsPkts65to127Octets | |
| etherStatsPkts128to255Octets | |
| etherStatsPkts256to511Octets | |
| etherStatsPkts512to1023Octets | |
| etherStatsPkts1024to1518Octets | |

## Other monitoring features

You will now learn about a few more ways to monitor traffic on AOS-Switches, unrelated to Aruba AirWave.

- sFlow
- Local traffic mirroring
- Remote traffic mirroring

### sFlow

AOS-Switches support sFlow, an industry-standard technology that uses statistical sampling to enable network monitoring. As Figure 14-30 shows, sFlow relies on two components.

- sFlow agents
- sFlow collector (which is also sometimes called a receiver)

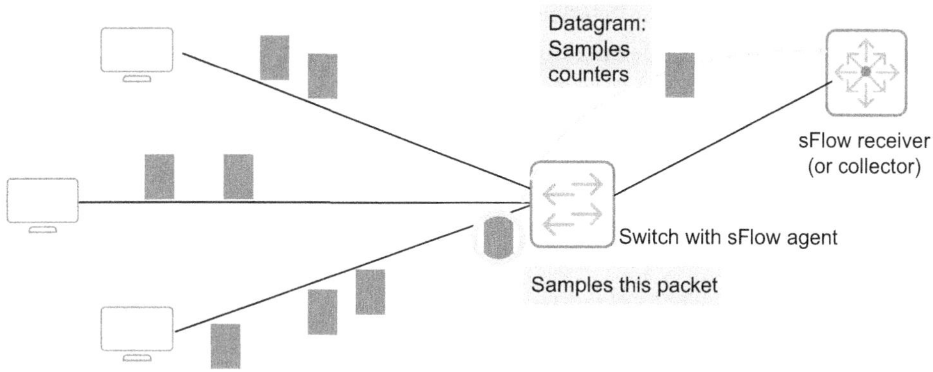


Figure 14-30 sFlow

sFlow agents run on network devices—such as switches, routers, and access points—gathering information about the packets transmitted on these devices and sending that information to the sFlow collector for analysis. Specifically, agents can send traffic samples and polling counters.

For traffic samples, the sFlow standard defines all the packets that a network device receives on one interface and are forwarded to another interface as a "flow." Using a statistically accurate algorithm, the sFlow agent examines on average one of every *n*th packet, where *n* is the number of packets. The samples are taken "on average" because sFlow employs some randomness to avoid sampling packets at precise intervals that might coincide with certain traffic patterns.

An sFlow agent packages sampled information into small datagrams, which include Layer 2 through 7 information, such as:

- Source and destination interface
- Sampled packet header
- Length of sampled packet
- Forwarding decision the switch made for this packet

An sFlow agent can also use counter polling to gather traffic statistics. It polls data sources at specified intervals, adds this information to the sFlow datagrams, and sends them to a specified sFlow collector. On the AOS-Switches, the data sources are ports (Ethernet interfaces).

The agents can include information from several packets into a single datagram. Because traffic samples are compact and agents sample only a small percentage of traffic, sFlow does not require a large amount of network bandwidth or processing power on network devices.

To forward the datagram to the sFlow collector, the sFlow agent appends a UDP header and an IP header to the datagram and encapsulates the packet in an Ethernet frame.

AOS-Switches implement sFlow in hardware—which is typically how sFlow is implemented. This allows the switch to deliver the information quickly and efficiently.

The sFlow collector analyzes the packaged information from each sFlow agent on a wireless and wired network. From this information, the sFlow collector can create a statistical model of network traffic that can be used for a variety of purposes, including network traffic management, security auditing, or troubleshooting.

---

**Note**

For more information about sFlow, visit http://sflow.org.

---

## Configuring sFlow on AOS-Switches

To configure sFlow on AOS-Switches, you configure the IP address of the sFlow receiver.

```
Switch(config)# sflow <receiver-instance> destination <IP address>
    [udp-port-num]
```

Replace ***<receiver-instance>*** with the number 1, 2, or 3. The AOS-Switches support three sFlow instances.

Replace ***<udp-port-num>*** with a UDP port. If you do not include this option in the command, the AOS-Switch will use the default UDP destination port, 6343.

You can also specify which ports should be sampled and the sampling rate, using the following command:

```
Switch(config)# sflow <receiver-instance> sampling <port-list> <sampling
    rate>
```

Again, replace ***<receiver-instance>*** with the number 1, 2, or 3.

Replace ***<port-list>*** with the ports that you want to have sFlow sample.

Replace ***<sampling rate>*** with the rate you want to use for sampling. If you set the value to 100, for example, the switch samples about 1 out of every 100 packets. The lower the value, the higher the percentage of packets that are sampled. Set 0 to disable sampling.

Finally, you can specify the polling interval:

```
Switch(config)# sflow <receiver-instance> polling <port-list> <polling
    interval>
```

Replace ***<receiver-instance>*** with the number 1, 2, or 3.

Replace ***<port-list>*** with the ports that you want to have sFlow poll.

Replace ***<polling interval>*** with a value that determines how frequently (in seconds) sFlow polls the interfaces. Set 0 to disable polling.

## Local traffic mirroring

Traffic mirroring allows a switch to copy frames that arrive or are sent from a particular port or VLAN and forward them to another port (see Figure 14-31). You can use port mirroring to monitor network traffic to detect threats, troubleshoot problems, or manage the network. For example, you might want to send certain traffic to a security appliance such as an Intrusion Detection System (IDS) device, which can examine the traffic and detect possible threats, or, you may want to send traffic to a network protocol analyzer, which you can use to examine the traffic and troubleshoot a network problem.

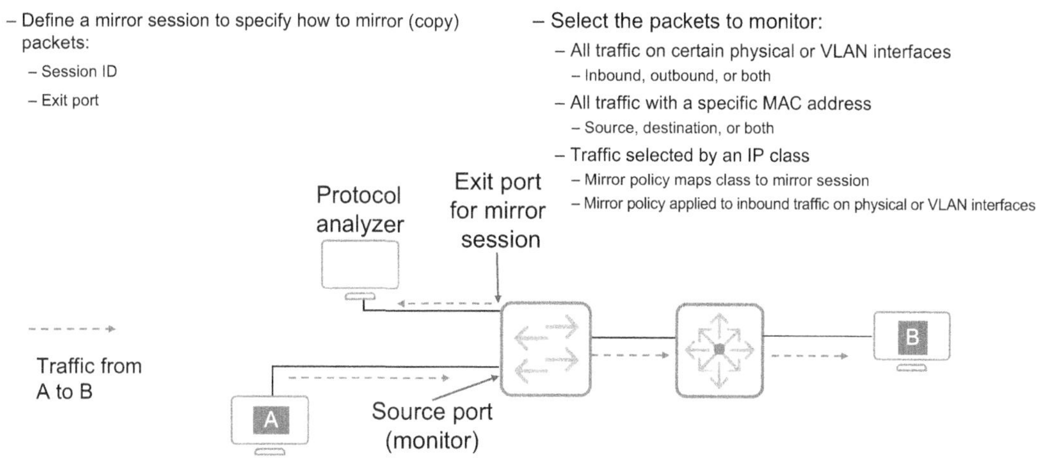


Figure 14-31 Local traffic mirroring

The simplest form of traffic mirroring is local mirroring, in which the switch mirroring the packets sends the copies out a local port.

To configure local traffic mirroring on AOS-Switches, you first enter the mirror command, followed by the session number—1 to 4—and then specify the exit port. You can give the mirror session an optional name. The exit port must be a single physical interface and cannot be a link aggregation.

```
Switch(config)# mirror <1-4> [name <session name>] port <port_ID>
```

You can configure one or more mirror sessions to use the same exit port, or you can specify different exit ports in different sessions to send mirrored traffic to different destination device or on different links to the same destination device. In the latter case, you would want to make sure to set up different sources for each mirroring session. You can create up to four mirror sessions.

Next, you configure the source, which defines which traffic the switch copies and transmits out the exit port.

You can define the source for the mirror in several ways.

- By interface—Mirror all inbound, all outbound, or all inbound and outbound traffic that arrives on specific interfaces. The interfaces can be:
  - One or more physical interfaces
  - One or more link aggregations (trk interfaces)
  - One or more VLANs

  Enter one of these commands to specify the interfaces on which you want to apply mirroring.

  ```
  Switch(config)# interface <port ID list> monitor all <in | out |
     both> mirror <session_ID>
  ```

  ```
  Switch(config)# vlan <ID> monitor all [in | out | both] mirror
     <session_ID>
  ```

  If you want to select traffic that is entering the source switch on the selected interface, include the **in** option. If you want to select traffic that is leaving the interface, use the **out** option, and if you want all traffic being transmitted on that interface, use the **both** option.

  The mirror session ID tells the switch the destination (for local mirroring, the exit port) to which to mirror the traffic.

- Globally by MAC address—Mirror all traffic with a specific source or destination MAC address.

  ```
  Switch(config)# monitor mac <mac-address> <src | dest | both>
     mirror <session_ID>
  ```

  Use **src** or **dest** to indicate whether you want to mirror traffic with the specified MAC address as its source or destination. If you want to mirror the traffic, in either case, use **both**.

- By mirror policy applied to an interface—Mirror only some of the traffic that arrives on a physical interface, link aggregation, or VLAN. For this option, you create one or more IP traffic classes to select the traffic. You then create a mirror policy with statements that map each traffic class to a mirror action. The mirror action indicates the ID for the mirror session out which the traffic is mirrored. You can send different classes of traffic out different mirror sessions. Finally, you apply the mirror policy to a physical interface, link aggregation, or VLAN. The policy applies to inbound traffic only.

  Note that you cannot apply a mirror policy to an interface that is already specified as a source interface for a mirror session (with the **interface <*ID*> monitor** command).

  For more information on configuring mirror policies refer to the *Management and Configuration Guide* for your AOS-Switch.

---

**Note**

Earlier versions of AOS-Switch software used ACLs to select inbound traffic that you wanted to mirror. Check the guide for the software that you are using to determine the functionality of your switch.

---

## Remote traffic mirroring

AOS-Switches also support remote port mirroring, in which the switch forwards the mirrored packets to a destination connected to a different switch (see Figure 14-32).

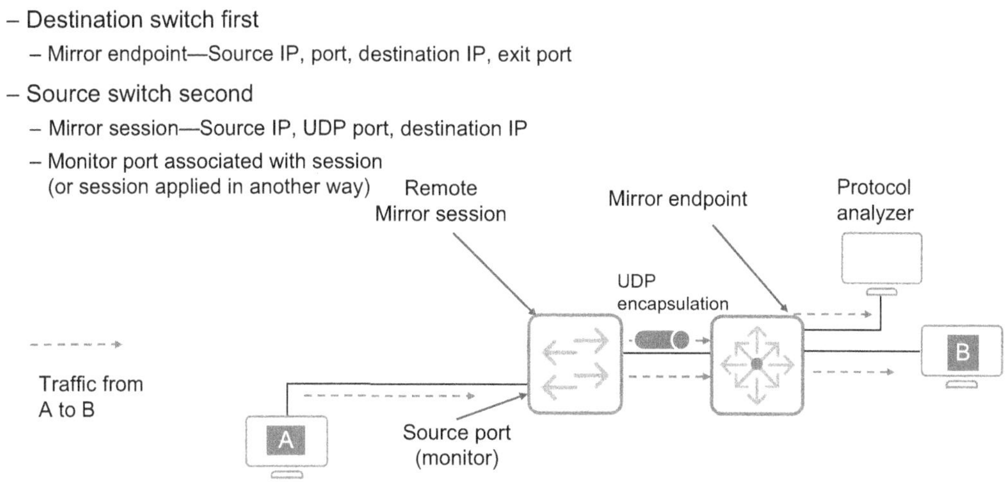


Figure 14-32 Remote traffic mirroring

The switch achieves this by encapsulating the mirrored packets in a UDP header that uses the remote switch's IP address as the destination and a specific UDP source port. The remote, or destination, switch is configured to decapsulate traffic from this UDP port and to forward the traffic out an exit port.

### Destination switch

To set up remote mirroring on AOS-Switches, configure the destination switch before the source switch. If the destination switch is not ready to handle the mirrored traffic forwarded by another switch, performance may be adversely affected.

On the destination switch, you use define the source and destination switch IP addresses, the UDP port for the mirror session, and the exit port that connects to the mirror destination.

```
DestinationSwitch(config)# mirror endpoint ip <src-ip> <src-udp-port>
   <dst-ip> <exit-port>
```

When you configure the ***<src-ip-add>***, ***<src-udp-port>***, and ***<dst-ip-add>*** options, you must match exactly the settings that you will configure for the mirror session on the source switch. If the settings do not match, the destination switch will not recognize the mirror session and will not know how to handle the mirrored data stream.

You replace ***<src-ip>*** with the IP address on the VLAN that the source switch uses to reach the destination switch.

You replace *<src-udp-port>* with a unique UDP port number to use for the mirror session. This unique port number helps the destination switch identify the session from the source switch.

You replace *<dst-ip>* with an IP address on this—the destination—switch.

You replace *<exit-port>* with the exit port on the destination switch.

## Source switch

You are then ready to set up the source switch. First, create the mirror session. However, instead of specifying an exit port, specify a remote IP.

```
LocalSwitch(config)# mirror <session> remote ip <src-ip> <src-udp-port>
    <dst-ip> [truncation]
```

Include **remote ip** to identify the destination as a remote switch.

- Replace *<src-ip>* with an IP address on this—the source—switch. This must be the same source IP address that you configured on the destination switch.
- Replace *<src-udp-port>* with the unique UDP port number to use for the session.
- Replace *<dst-ip>* with an IP address on the destination switch. Again, this must be the same destination IP address that you configured on the destination switch.

When you enter this **mirror** command, the CLI displays a reminder message, telling you that you must first configure the destination switch for the remote mirror session. You must confirm that you have already configured the destination switch to apply the command.

You then define the source for the mirror session, just as you would for local mirroring.

**Note**

Because there is no industry standard for port mirroring, you cannot implement remote mirroring between AOS-Switches and other vendors' switches. However, while the source and destination switches must both be AOS-Switches, the devices in between the switches can be any type of switch.

## Enabling jumbo frames or using the truncation option

When the source switch sends the mirrored data stream to the destination switch, it adds a 54-byte proprietary header to the information field, increasing the total size of the frame. On a typical network using the default maximum transmission unit (MTU) of 1500 bytes, the switch can mirror untagged frames with information fields that are smaller than or equal to 1446 bytes. This is because the 54-byte proprietary header (which is inserted into the Ethernet frame of the data field) when coupled with the header and footer of the MAC frame, may exceed the limits of the hardware—either 1518 bytes (normal untagged Ethernet frame) or 1522 bytes (802.1Q tagged).

Consequently, a switch could receive a frame larger than what it is configured to handle. If the switch receives frames that have data fields larger than 1446 bytes, in normal operation, it will drop the frames because the new header makes these packets exceed the maximum frame size for legacy Ethernet, either 1518 or 1522. (If this happens, the switch may log that it has received "giants.") The switch will forward the frames to their regular destination—as long as the received frames do not exceed the default MTU, which is typically set by sending devices at 1500 bytes for legacy Ethernet.

You can handle large frames in one of two ways:

- Enable jumbo frames—If you want to capture all interesting traffic, you should enable jumbo frames. The switch can then transmit a frame that is a total of 9220 bytes, which must include the 54-byte header and the 4-byte 802.1Q tag (if applicable). Remember that jumbo frames are supported only on ports operating at 1 Gbps or greater.

  To allow these larger frames to be transmitted across your network, you must enable all the switches that might carry the mirrored traffic to support jumbo frames. These switches include both the source and destination switches and any switches in between. If you have redundant paths between the switches (if Spanning Tree is running in your environment, for example), you must enable jumbo frames on those switches as well.

  On each switch, enable jumbo frames on the VLAN that carries the mirrored traffic with this global configuration mode context command:

  ```
  Switch(config)# vlan <vlan_id> jumbo
  ```

- Enable truncation of oversized frames—You can include the **truncation** option in your **mirror** ***<session ID>*** command on the source switch. In this case, the switch will truncate the part of the frame that is larger than the MTU size you specify. When the switch truncates the frame, it will make the frame size a multiple of 18 bytes. For example, suppose you specify that the MTU is 1000 bytes and the switch receives a frame that is larger than 1000 bytes. The switch would truncate the frame to 990 bytes (55 x 18 bytes).

## Summary

In this chapter, you learned about best practices for network management. You learned how to set up AOS-Switches to enforce secure, centralized authentication of managers. You also learned how to configure SNMPv3, which is a more secure option for SNMP management.

You then turned your attention to strategies and technologies for monitoring network traffic using tools such as Aruba AirWave.

## Learning check

1. An AOS-Switch authenticates SSH managers to a RADIUS server. The switch has authentication login privileges enabled and is at the default setting for command authorization. Which customized settings can the RADIUS server apply to the manager session?
   a. A command permit list
   b. A command deny list
   c. A service type for manager or operator level
   d. A management level from 1 to 15
2. What is the process for configuring local mirroring on an AOS-Switch?
3. Which statement best describes RMON?
   a. It collects port statistics and alerts network management solutions, such as SNMP, when particular thresholds are crossed.
   b. It relies on agents that run on network devices to gather information about transmitted packets and send the data to the collector component for analysis.
   c. It includes an exporter that identifies flows, a collector that receives and saves records, and an analyzer that compiles the records and presents them in a meaningful way.
   d. It can identify and gather data about a flow and then export the information either through traditional data export methods or through aggregation data export.
4. An AOS-Switch is authenticating Telnet and SSH users to a RADIUS server for both initial logins and for accessing enable mode. A user who is only supposed to receive operator access logs in. The user moves to enable mode and is prompted to log in again.

   The RADIUS server sends an Access-Accept with this RADIUS standard AVP:

   Service-Type = 7 (NAS-Prompt-User)

   What might be the issue? What must you do to ensure that this user receives operator access only, as desired?
5. You have set up an AOS-Switch to authenticate Telnet and SSH users to a RADIUS server. How do you ensure the proper security for logins even if the switch loses connectivity to this server?
6. What SNMP settings does an AOS-Switch have by default?
7. How can you increase the security for SNMP on an AOS-Switch?
8. How can you use AirWave to make network monitoring and management tasks easier?
9. What are some examples of ways that you can use RMON alarms?

# Answers

## RADIUS servers for authenticating management users

Consider the following question: Why would you use centralized RADIUS servers to authenticate managers rather than local accounts?

After the initial setup, the RADIUS approach can be easier to manage and maintain. Rather than configure consistent credentials on every switch, administrators can manage credentials on a central database.

RADIUS authentication also provides better security. Instead of sharing credentials, all managers can have their own accounts, making it less likely for credentials to leak to an unauthorized user. If a manager leaves the organization, the company can revoke just that manager's account rather than change the credentials on every network device.

Regularly changing passwords is a critical security best practice. Many enterprise RADIUS servers connect into a backend database (such as Active Directory) that enforces password best practices such as complexity requirements and periodic password changes.

## SNMP review

1. Briefly, describe the relationship between SNMP clients or agents and servers. What are examples of SNMP clients? What are examples of SNMP servers?

   SNMP agents (which function as clients) run on managed devices such as switches, routers, servers, and printers. They can submit information to an SNMP server, as well as be managed by the server. The SNMP server is a management application that requests, handles, and analyzes the information from the managed devices. Aruba AirWave is one example of an SNMP server. Other centralized management platforms also support SNMP.

2. Match each SNMP operation to its description.

   __c__ Get, GetNext, GetBulk

   __a__ Set

   __b__ Trap and Inform

   a. The SNMP server uses this operation or these operations to define the value of object instances on an agent.

   b. Agents use this operation or these operations to notify the SNMP server of a significant event.

   c. The SNMP server uses this operation or these operations to request information about one or more object instances from an agent.

3. SNMP versions 1 and 2c use community strings to restrict SNMP access. Briefly, describe how an SNMP agent uses each community.

   – Read only

   The agent accepts Get, GetNext, and GetBulk messages that have the correct read-only community. It does not accept Set messages with this community. In other words, the community is limited to reading SNMP information only.

   – Read write

   The agent accepts Get, GetNext, GetBulk, and Set messages that have the correct read-write community. In other words, this community provides full access to SNMP functions, including the ability to make changes on managed devices.

   – Trap

   The agent includes the trap community when it sends trap messages. A trap message is a spontaneous update to a trap receiver, usually in response to an alarm. The receiver can use the community to validate that the traps come from a valid source.

4. When you enable SNMP on devices, why is it important to change the default settings?

   SNMP-compliant devices typically use "public" as the default read-only community and either "public" or "private" as the default read-write community. Many organizations do not change these default settings, leaving their managed devices and SNMP servers vulnerable to hackers.

5. What are some of the security weaknesses in SNMPv1 and 2c? What are some of the attacks to which these versions are vulnerable?

Possible answers:

- SNMP communities do not provide strong access control for SNMP agents and servers.
- SNMP versions 1 and 2c do not include any security features to protect the data exchanged between the devices and the SNMP server.
- The packets and the community strings are not encrypted, so a hacker could intercept and read them.
- These versions do not provide message integrity measures, so a hacker could intercept messages, tamper with the data, and then send it to the SNMP server.

Possible attacks include:

- Man-in-the-middle—An attacker can alter SNMP messages generated on behalf of an authorized user in such a way as to affect management operations. An attacker with read-write access can infiltrate any SNMP-managed device.

- Impersonation—By assuming the identity of a user who has the appropriate authorizations, an attacker can gain read-write access to management operations.
- Reconnaissance—Because early implementations do not encrypt the community string or SNMP packet information, an attacker can eavesdrop on the exchanges between SNMP agents and an SNMP server. The attacker can then collect information about the network or discover the read-write community string.
- Unauthorized access—Early versions of SNMP are vulnerable to replay attacks. During natural operation, most networks will experience packets that are reordered, delayed, or replayed. Knowing this, an attacker can maliciously reorder, delay, or resend packets to gain unauthorized access to management operations.
- Brute force—An attacker can use a brute-force attack to discover network community strings.

## Learning check

1. An AOS-Switch authenticates SSH managers to a RADIUS server. The switch has authentication login privileges enabled and is at the default setting for command authorization. Which customized settings can the RADIUS server apply to the manager session?

    a. A command permit list

    b. A command deny list

    **c. A service type for manager or operator level**

    d. A management level from 1 to 15

2. What is the process for configuring local mirroring on an AOS-Switch?

    Configure the mirror session and specify an exit port, which is the port on which the mirrored traffic is forwarded. Apply monitoring in one of several ways based on how you want to select traffic for mirroring. You can configure an interface with the **monitor** command and the mirror session. Or you can apply the mirror session to MAC addresses. Or you can use a traffic class to select traffic and reference that class in a mirroring policy.

3. Which statement best describes RMON?

    **a. It collects port statistics and alerts network management solutions, such as SNMP, when particular thresholds are crossed.**

    b. It relies on agents that run on network devices to gather information about transmitted packets and send the data to the collector component for analysis.

c. It includes an exporter that identifies flows, a collector that receives and saves records, and an analyzer that compiles the records and presents them in a meaningful way.

d. It can identify and gather data about a flow and then export the information either through traditional data export methods or through aggregation data export.

4. An AOS-Switch is authenticating Telnet and SSH users to a RADIUS server for both initial logins and for accessing enable mode. A user who is only supposed to receive operator access logs in. The user moves to enable mode and is prompted to log in again.

   The RADIUS server sends an Access-Accept with this RADIUS standard AVP:

   Service-Type = 7 (NAS-Prompt-User)

   What might be the issue? What must you do to ensure that this user receives operator access only, as desired?

   The RADIUS server is set up correctly; the Service-Type VSA 7 grants operator level access. However, the switch does not honor the VSA by default. Instead, it simply allows the requested access (in this case, access to enable mode) if the RADIUS server sends an Access-Accept. Based on the description of the behavior, the switch is operating at this default setting. You must specifically enable the switch to honor the VSA by entering **aaa authentication login privilege-mode**. After you do so, if the user attempts to access enable mode, and the RADIUS server sends Service-Type 7, the switch will deny the access.

5. You have set up an AOS-Switch to authenticate Telnet and SSH users to a RADIUS server. How do you ensure the proper security for logins even if the switch loses connectivity to this server?

   You set the secondary authentication mode to local, *and* you create a local user account. This will ensure that the switch continues to authenticate users if it cannot reach the RADIUS server.

6. What SNMP settings does an AOS-Switch have by default?

   SNMPv1/v2c is enabled, but SNMPv3 is disabled. The switch has a default community, **public**, which permits read and write access.

7. How can you increase the security for SNMP on an AOS-Switch?

   You can configure SNMPv3 on the switches. You can define a user that uses encryption and authentication and assigned the user to the ManagerPriv community. You can also set SNMPv3 to SNMPv3 only mode or SNMPv3 restricted access, depending on whether you want the switch to accept no SNMPv1/v2c messages or to accept read, but not write, messages. You must also configure the SNMP server with corresponding SNMPv3 settings.

8. How can you use AirWave to make network monitoring and management tasks easier?

   These are just some examples of AirWave capabilities:

   AirWave helps managers audit switches' configurations and find changes. You can automate and schedule backups. You can audit firmware versions and update out-of-date firmware.

   You can set up AirWave as a trap host on your switches and enable the switch to send various traps and event logs to it. You can check traps and event logs to find significant events that might indicate network problems or security issues. For example, you can see that an interface has failed.

   You can use the Clarity and other dashboards to see changes in traffic patterns.

9. What are some examples of ways that you can use RMON alarms?

   RMON alarms can alert an SNMP server—and through the SNMP server, administrators—to significant changes in Ethernet statistics. The statistics can tip administrators off to congestion or other issues. For example, jabber could indicate hardware errors, and oversized packets could indicate that the MTU is wrong on a device.

# 15 Quality of Service

EXAM OBJECTIVES

- ✓ Describe how AOS-Switches prioritize traffic based on its queue
- ✓ Configure AOS-Switches to honor the appropriate Quality of Service (QoS) marks applied by other devices
- ✓ Configure AOS-Switches to select traffic, apply the appropriate QoS marks, and place the traffic in the proper priority queues
- ✓ Implement rate limiting
- ✓ Configure a voice virtual LAN (VLAN) and Link Layer Discovery Protocol-Media Endpoint Devices (LLDP-MED)

## Assumed knowledge

Before reading this chapter, you should have a basic understanding of:

- IP addressing
- Open Systems Interconnection (OSI) model
- Link aggregation
- Virtual LANs (VLANs)
- Routing
- Switching

## Introduction

In the contemporary enterprise network, from the branch office to the campus LAN through the network core, a complex mixture of network applications share links. AOS-Switches, as key components of Aruba Mobile First Networks, can respond to the needs of heterogeneous traffic flows.

In this chapter, you will learn how to implement QoS mechanisms that improve the experience of users running a variety of network applications from traditional ones to voice and video applications.

## Dealing with congestion

The chapter teaches you how to implement the many sophisticated QoS features on AOS-Switches. To implement these features successfully, however, you must first understand their goal. This section briefly introduces you to some of the problems that these QoS features attempt to solve.

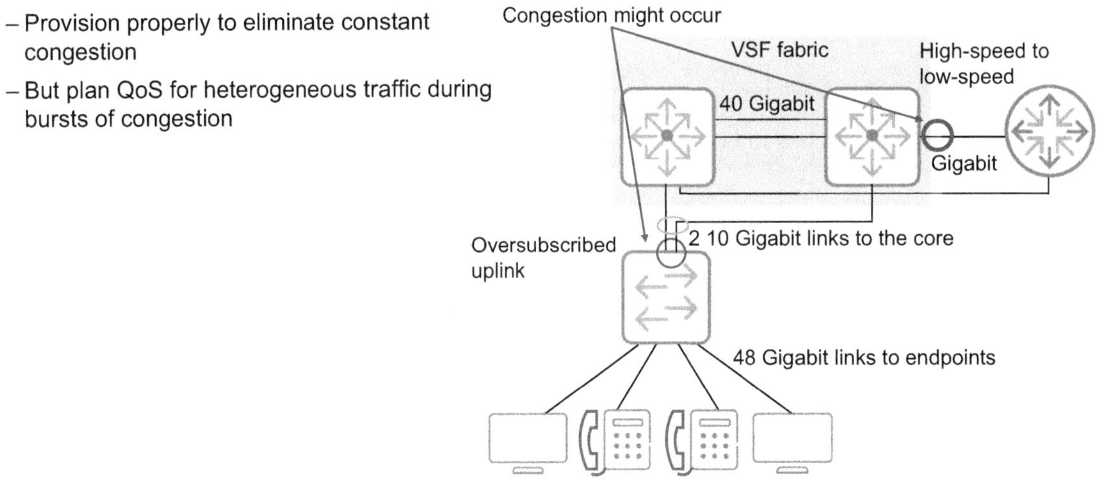


Figure 15-1 Dealing with congestion

In many environments, switch-to-switch links are oversubscribed; that is, they provide less bandwidth for outgoing traffic than the total amount of traffic that could be incoming from other devices—often many times less. Usually, endpoints need to send and receive only a small fraction of their bandwidth, so oversubscription makes sense. However, on a moment-to-moment basis, fluctuating traffic patterns and bursts of traffic can cause congestion, as shown in Figure 15-1. The lower-bandwidth link acts as a bottleneck, and if traffic continues to arrive more quickly than the port can forward it, the port's buffers fill, and it drops traffic.

A properly designed network architecture can help to eliminate common sources of congestion. For example, a flattened architecture, when appropriate, can reduce latency by eliminating the distribution layer. Architects should properly provision uplinks based on user and device needs. Nonetheless, even a well-designed network features oversubscription and the possibility of momentary bursts of congestion, which can cause great damage for time-sensitive solutions. Network infrastructure devices must implement QoS mechanisms to protect this sensitive traffic and ensure that users have a positive experience running all necessary applications.

QoS mechanisms also help companies to enforce business policies that prioritize certain applications or segments of the network.

## TCP and UDP response to congestion

In general, "best-effort" delivery is satisfactory for data traffic. TCP applications are not usually disrupted by packet loss because TCP provides acknowledgment and flow-control mechanisms that ensure dropped packets will be retransmitted. Each segment of a TCP/IP message includes sequence numbers that inform receivers of the proper order and number of packets in the transmission. The receiver in a TCP transmission acknowledges packets by returning messages that include the highest sequence number it has received. TCP applications include a "window" parameter that determines how many bytes can be outstanding and unacknowledged by the receiver at any given moment. This parameter limits the number of packets that can be acknowledged by a single control packet. Delay in delivery of packets or excessive packet loss prompts the sender and receiver to establish a smaller window size. Furthermore, TCP applications back off when network congestion is detected, enabling applications to share bandwidth.

UDP, on the other hand, does not provide acknowledgments or flow control, which enables UDP applications to generate less overhead than TCP applications. Some UDP applications include their own error-checking procedures. However, in most cases, UDP applications are designed to minimize the need for retransmission and use UDP as a transport mechanism precisely because of its lower overhead and network efficiency. UDP also does not provide any back-off procedures.

Because UDP applications do not respond to congestion in any way, they can continue to contribute to congestion, which can also have drastic effects on time-sensitive real-time traffic such as voice and video.

## Impact of congestion on real-time traffic

Voice traffic is sensitive to delay, sometimes called latency, which is the amount of time that passes between the sending of a transmission and its arrival at the receiving station.

In Figure 15-2, the rectangles represent packets traveling from sender to receiver. In both examples, the packets are sent at a consistent rate.

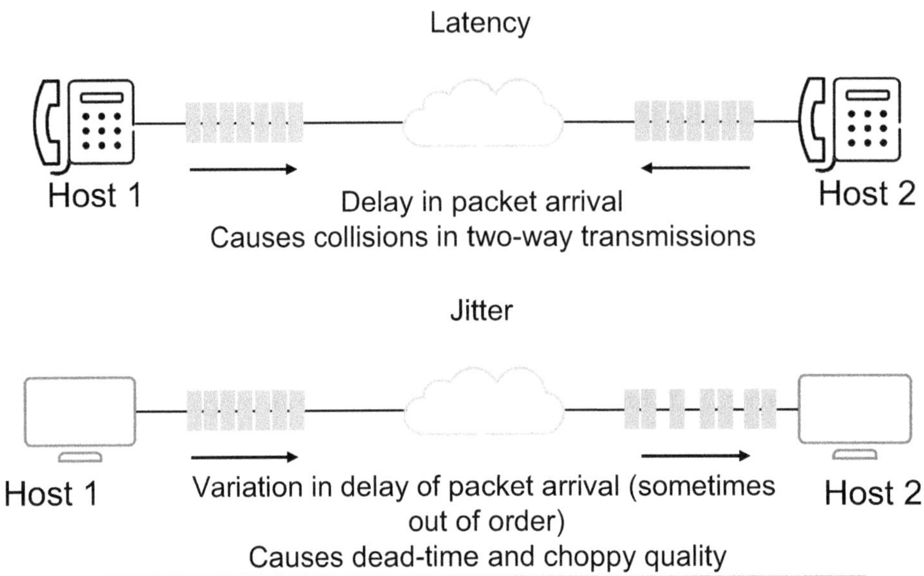


| Type of traffic | Needs |
|---|---|
| Voice (two-way) | Low jitter, Low latency |
| Video (one-way) | Low jitter |

Figure 15-2 Impact of congestion on real-time traffic

In the delay example, latency within the network cloud inevitably causes some elapsed time between transmission and reception. In the case of unidirectional traffic (as video traffic often is), this predictable, measurable period of time is usually tolerable, regardless of its length. However, because multidirectional voice traffic is nearly always interactive, excessive delay can result in conversation collisions. For example, in Figure 15-2, Host 1 begins transmitting in the belief that Host 2 is not transmitting. However, because Host 2 is still transmitting, bits from Host 2 begin arriving before Host 1 concludes its transmission. The conversations overlap.

Voice traffic is also sensitive to jitter, which is the variation in intervals between the arrivals of packets or, in other words, the difference between when a packet is expected and when it actually arrives. Video is also sensitive to jitter.

Figure 15-2 shows how Host 1 sends data at a constant rate to Host 2. However, devices within the cloud that represents the network experience varying levels of congestion that result in some packets being delayed. The outcome is a variation in the interval between packet arrival, which results in a choppy voice or video stream.

Jitter can have significant effect on real-time applications even if they require very small data streams. For instance, an IP telephone sends a very small packet every 20–30 milliseconds (ms). In order for the receiver to properly interpret the stream, the packets must arrive at the same rate. If the interval between packets grows to 50 ms, for instance, the transmission will be unsatisfactory for many users.

### Delay over various media

Delay is the interval between the time that a message leaves the sender's mouth and the time that it reaches the receiver's ear. Some delay is inevitable, especially in transmissions over significant distances. While the speed of light in a vacuum is 186,000 miles per second (267,000 km per second), signals move through fiber or copper cable at approximately 125,000 miles per second (200,000 km per second). Consequently, a fiber network stretching halfway around the Earth introduces a delay of approximately 70 ms under the best of circumstances with additional delay introduced by the physical transport medium. During periods of congestion, the delay can be much longer.

The effects of delay upon application performance depend heavily upon the expectations of users. The International Telecommunications Union (ITU) recommends no more than 150 ms end-to-end delay for voice traffic. Greater delay can cause conversation collisions when each party begins to speak because the line appears quiet. Most users will find this situation to be unacceptable.

## The challenges in providing QoS

Consider the following questions:

- Which types of applications are most sensitive to congestion, and what is the effect of congestion on the experience of using those applications?
- What could network infrastructure devices do to improve these applications' performance?

You could read entire books on the subject of the challenges posed in delivering the best QoS for a heterogeneous mix of network applications; probing all the design principles is beyond the scope of this study guide. However, you can understand some basic implications of what you have learned in the previous sections.

- All traffic does not require the same handling to receive an appropriate level of service. For example, many TCP applications can tolerate a degree of degradation of service because TCP provides for retransmission of packets and otherwise handles congestion well. In particular, applications such as file transfer applications can experience momentary periods of poor service because the user cares only about the end result.
- Time-sensitive traffic requires prioritization over other traffic so that it is transmitted immediately. This prioritization ensures that traffic transmitted at a constant rate by an endpoint such as an IP phone continues to be transmitted at a constant rate throughout the network, minimizing jitter.
- Less important UDP traffic must be prevented from monopolizing a link because the application will not back off on its own.
- In general, an enterprise might wish to enforce rate limits that ensure certain classes of traffic use only their fair share of bandwidth.
- Congestion can cause widespread degradation of service as all packets are suddenly dropped. Both TCP and UDP traffic is subject to being dropped, but TCP traffic can often tolerate packet

loss better because it has built-in recovery mechanisms. UDP applications such as those for streaming voice and video cannot recover lost packets. In any case, the lost packets would have little value if recovered due to the real-time nature of the application. Instead, the application must attempt to move on without the packet. However, if too many packets are lost at once, user experience suffers. Users have a better experience when the network infrastructure responds to congestion gracefully by dropping less important or sensitive traffic.

### QoS use case

QoS can help to provide sensitive applications such as voice and video the handling that they need.

As you will learn throughout the rest of this chapter, AOS-Switches provide high QoS by recognizing traffic that requires special handling at the edge. They can then give that traffic the high priority that it requires as they forward it across the network (see Figure 15-3).

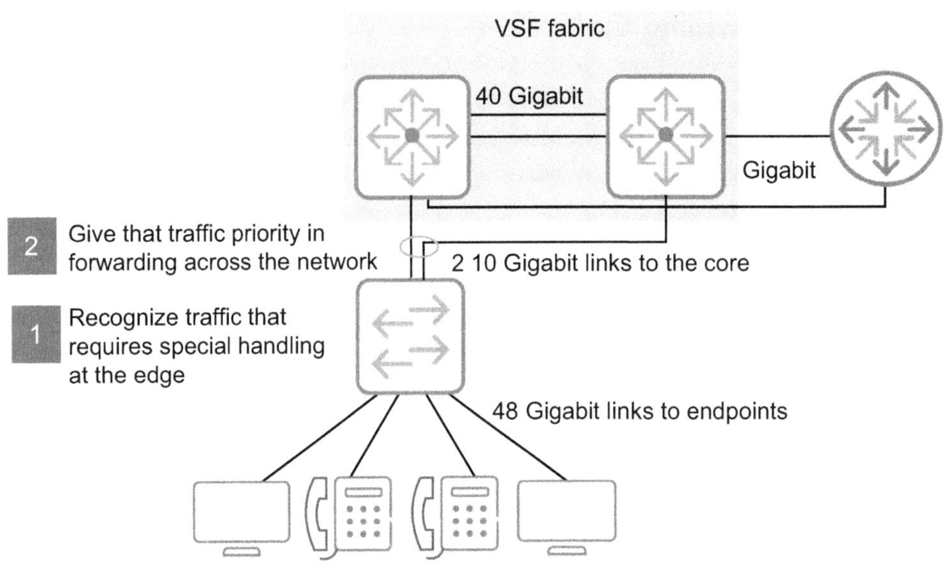


Figure 15-3 QoS use case

## Queuing and scheduling

You will now learn about how AOS-Switches can prioritize traffic into various groups for transmission, or queues. Queue scheduling enables switches to provide high-priority traffic—particularly, voice and video traffic—the priority forwarding that it requires.

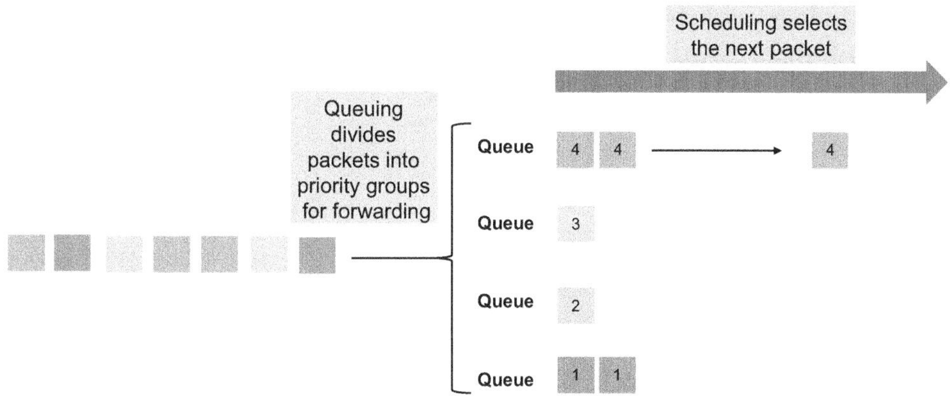

Figure 15-4 Queuing and scheduling

As a switch prepares to transmit traffic, it places the traffic in an egress queue for the egress port. (The buffer size determines how much traffic the switch can buffer, and you can find the specifications for your switch in its documentation.) This is called queuing.

A switch port that does not implement QoS places all packets in the same egress queue in the order in which they arrive. It follows a simple mechanism, called First In First Out (FIFO), to schedule the packets for transmission. It forwards the first packet that arrived, then the next, and so forth.

As you learned, however, some packets need priority service. For example, voice packets, transmitted at a constant rate by the endpoint, must be delivered as soon as they arrive to maintain that constant rate (avoiding jitter). To prioritize particular traffic, the switch implements priority queuing, in which it sorts various packets into multiple queues. AOS-Switches support up to eight egress queues per-port.

Once a switch has queued traffic in multiple, priority-based queues, the port's scheduling mechanism selects the next packet for forwarding (see Figure 15-4). Scheduling works in tandem with queuing, ensuring that packets in high-priority queues are transmitted more promptly than packets in other queues. AOS-Switches use strict priority (SP) queuing together with guaranteed minimum bandwidth (GMB).

## SP scheduling

AOS-Switches use SP scheduling.

SP scheduling always forwards the highest priority traffic first. That is, the port forwards all packets in queue 7. When that queue empties, the port forwards all packets in queue 6. If that queue does not include any packets, the port forwards all packets in queue 5, and so forth.

– Always serves packets in the highest priority queue with packets to forward

– Can starve low priority queues entirely

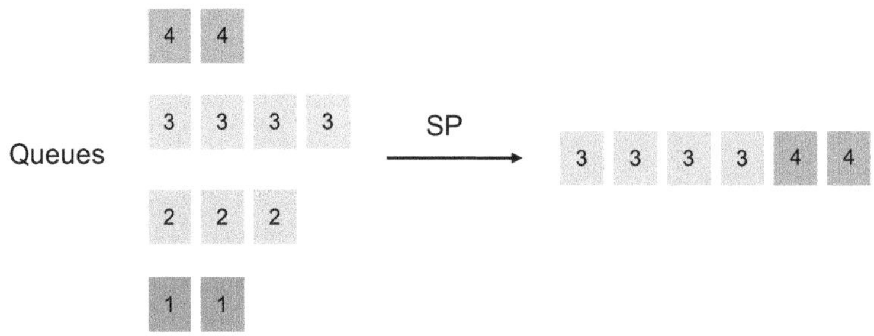


Figure 15-5 SP scheduling

Under SP, the port will never forward a packet in a priority queue as long as a higher priority queue includes even one packet. For example, in Figure 15-5, queue 4, queue 3, queue 2, and queue 1, each includes several packets. The port schedules the two packets in queue 4 for transmission and then the four packets in queue 3. Next, the port would forward a packet in queue 2—unless another packet arrives for transmission and is assigned to queue 3 or 4. In that case, the higher priority packet is forwarded first. If higher priority traffic continues to arrive, traffic in the lower priority never receives a chance to be forwarded, and traffic in those queues is starved out entirely.

SP works best when the network assigns only a few applications, which take a relatively low amount of bandwidth, to the higher priority queues (network control traffic and VoIP, for example). The switch then forwards this traffic immediately when it arrives, but still has bandwidth left over for the majority of traffic in the best effort queue.

```
Switch# show policy voice
Statements for policy "voice"

policy qos "voice"
     10 class ipv4 "voice" action dscp ef
     exit
```

## GMB

AOS-Switches use SP scheduling, but add GMB to ensure that high priority queues do not starve out lower priority queues.

GMB allocates the specified percentage of the port's service cycle to each queue. In other words, that queue is guaranteed the specified percentage of the port's bandwidth. If, at any moment, the queue does not need the full guaranteed percentage, the unused bandwidth is allocated to other queues according to SP scheduling. If the queue needs more bandwidth than the guaranteed level, it *might* receive the required bandwidth depending on whether any bandwidth remains and whether higher priority queues require it.

- Prevents higher priority traffic from starving out lower priority traffic
- Each priority queue guaranteed up to the specified percentage
- Unused bandwidth allocated according to SP
- Individual settings per port

```
Switch# show bandwidth output 1/1-1/4
 Outbound Guaranteed Minimum Bandwidth Percentage

  Port  Q1     Q2     Q3     Q4     Q5      Q6     Q7     Q8
  ----- ------ ------ ------ ------ ------  ------ ------ ------
  1/1   2      3      30     10     10      10     15     20
  1/2   2      3      30     10     10      10     15     20
  1/3   2      3      30     10     10      10     15     20
  1/4   2      3      30     10     10      10     15     20
```

Figure 15-6 GMB

The switch maintains individual GMB percentages for each physical interface. Figure 15-6 shows examples for a switch that has four queues per port (depending on the switch hardware, you can adjust the number of queues up to eight, as you will learn in more detail later). The total bandwidth guarantees must add to 100 percent or less.

You can check the GMB percentages assigned with this command:

```
Switch# show bandwidth output [port_ID_list]
```

In many cases, you can begin with the default settings and either keep them or make minor adjustments. At default settings, the AOS-Switches allocate most bandwidth to normal traffic. However, you might want to adjust the GMB for your high priority queues if you expect that they will require more bandwidth. Remember that unallocated and unused bandwidth is assigned based on SP, so you should allocate the lower priority queues the minimum amount of bandwidth that you want them to receive in the worst-case scenario.

You can set the GMB for any queue on an interface to 0 if you do not want to guarantee any bandwidth for that queue. For example, your QoS solution does not assign any traffic to that queue, so you want to be able to allocate a higher GMB to the queues that you are actually using. (Note that setting the GMB to zero does not necessarily mean that the switch will not forward traffic in that queue. It simply means that the switch will forward queues with GMBs first and then serve the queues with no GMB in order of priority if any bandwidth is leftover.)

Use this command to set the GMB percentages for one or more interfaces. The first percentage that you specify applies to queue 1, the second to queue 2, and so on to queue 8 (the highest priority queue). You must specify a percentage for every queue on the interface. The command below is the command for a switch using eight queues per port. If the switch were only using four or two queues, you would use the same command, but only need to enter four or two percentages.

```
Switch(config)# interface <port_ID_list> bandwidth-min output <0-100>
   <0-100> <0-100> <0-100> <0-100> <0-100> <0-100> <0-100>
```

For example, you could enter:

```
Switch(config)# interface 1-8 bandwidth-min output 0 0 25 10 15 15 15 20
```

## GMB example

Figure 15-7 shows an example of GMB in action. Consider a switch that supports four queues on each port and is using these GBM settings for that port:

- 30 percent for queue 4
- 20 percent for queue 3
- 40 percent for queue 2
- 10 percent for queue 1

At the moment, the port would need to use:

- 20 percent of the cycle to fully serve traffic in queue 4 (the highest priority queue)
- 25 percent of the cycle to fully serve traffic in queue 3
- 50 percent of the cycle to fully serve traffic in queue 2 (the normal priority queue)
- 40 percent of the cycle to fully serve traffic in queue 1

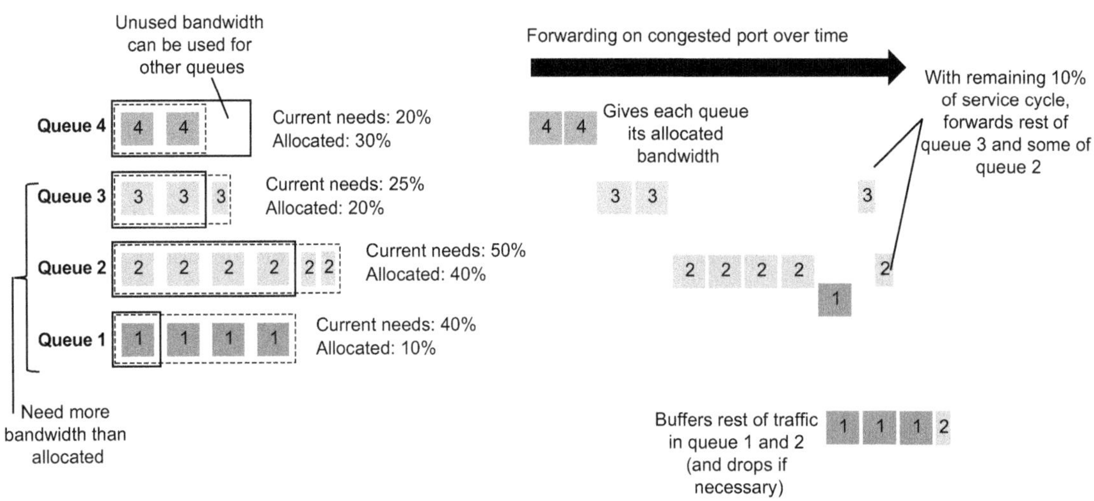


Figure 15-7 GMB example

As you see, the percentages add up to more than 100 percent. The port is congested. The port behaves as follows:

- It forwards all of the traffic in queue 4, which requires 20 percent of the service cycle, less than the guaranteed 30 percent.
- It forwards most of the traffic in queue 3, up to the guaranteed 20 percent. Queue 3 still needs 5 percent of the service cycle.
- It forwards most of the traffic in queue 2, up to the guaranteed 40 percent. Queue 2 still needs 10 percent of the service cycle.
- It forwards some of the traffic in queue 1, up to the guaranteed 10 percent. Queue 1 still needs 30 percent of the service cycle.

The port has 10 percent of the service cycle remaining. It now serves the traffic based on SP.

- It forwards all of the remaining traffic in queue 3, which is the highest priority queue with remaining traffic.
- It uses the rest of the service cycle to forward some of the remaining traffic in queue 2.
- It buffers the rest of the traffic in queue 2 and queue 1 (and, if necessary, eventually drops it).

Without GMB, queue 1 would have been almost entirely starved out, but with GMB queue 1 did receive some bandwidth. In this example, the behavior for queue 2 was the same as it would have been without GMB. However, if queue 3 started to consume more bandwidth—for example, 50 percent rather than 25 percent—queue 2 would be protected up to 40 percent.

## Viewing how traffic is forwarded in egress queues

The GMB example showed you a snapshot of how the AOS-Switch port behaves if it needs to forward traffic during a period of congestion. The default GMB values work for many networks. But you can check how well they are working in your network with this command:

```
Switch# show interface queues <port ID>
```

As shown in Figure 15-8, this command outputs the number of packets and bytes forwarded in each queue on the interface, as well as how many packets and bytes have been dropped. (In this example, the switch has eight egress queues per port rather than the four queues of the previous example.) If you see an excessive number of dropped packets for a particular queue, you might need to rethink the bandwidth guaranteed to that queue—or alternatively which traffic is assigned to that queue.

```
Switch# show interface queues a1

 Status and Counters - Port Counters for port A1

  Name    :
  MAC Address       : 00fd45-64fcff
  Link Status       : Up
  Port Enabled      : Yes
  Port Totals (Since boot or last clear) :
   Rx Packets       : 6,399                Tx Packets         : 9,424
   Rx Bytes         : 588,933              Tx Bytes           : 1,903,949
   Rx Drop Packets  : 0                    Tx Drop Packets    : 0
   Rx Drop Bytes    : 0                    Tx Drop Bytes      : 0

  Egress Queue Totals (Since boot or last clear) :
     Tx Packets          Dropped Packets    Tx Bytes           Dropped Bytes
 Q1  436                 0                  186,620            0
 Q2  0                   0                  0                  0
 Q3  3,111               0                  202,834            0
 Q4  0                   0                  0                  0
 Q5  2,126               0                  1,142,722          0
 Q6  3,236               0                  236,129            0
 Q7  0                   0                  0                  0
 Q8  516                 0                  135,708            0
```

Figure 15-8 Viewing how traffic is forwarded in egress queues

Much of the rest of this chapter concentrates on helping you understand how an AOS-Switch determines the correct queue for various types of traffic. The interaction of settings can sometimes be complex, so this command can also be very helpful in showing you in which queues the switch actually is forwarding traffic.

## Controlling the number of queues

The number of egress queues per port depends on the switch hardware. Many AOS-Switches support up to eight egress queues, identified as 1-8, per port.

If you really do need the granularity of eight queues in an AOS-Switch that supports them, you can keep the number of queues at the default setting. However, you can also reduce the number of queues, as shown in Figure 15-9. For example, many companies do not actually classify traffic into eight classes and do not need eight queues. You might reduce the number of queues to four if you only need to differentiate between high, normal, and lower than normal traffic. Reducing the number of queues increases the amount of buffering space available to each queue, which might be important for switches with less overall memory for buffering. By buffering traffic in a queue rather than dropping it, the switch might be able to forward the traffic during the next service cycle. In this way, a good sized buffer for each queue helps to improve the overall experience.

- Number of egress queues per port depends on switch hardware and configured setting
- Set queue number based on the level of granularity that you need
- Fewer queues = More buffering space per-queue

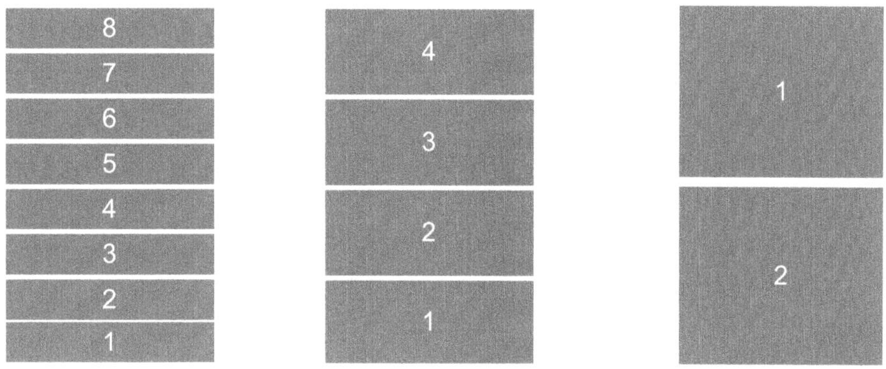


Figure 15-9 Controlling the number of queues

The number of queues per port is a global setting. If you change the number to four, every interface then has four egress queues. Use this command to set the number of queues:

```
Switch(config)# qos queue-config <2-queues | 4-queues | 8-queues>
```

The command requires a reboot to take effect. You will be prompted to save your configuration and reboot.

## Introduction to QoS marks

Now that you understand how AOS-Switches can queue traffic and deliver service to different queues based on their priority, you need to learn how the switch decides which traffic belongs to which queue.

To communicate the desired priority for traffic between network infrastructure devices, the devices use Class of Service (CoS) marks. These mechanisms define specific values, which request specific priorities for traffic marked with that value. As you will see, AOS-Switches can take these values into account when determining how to queue traffic.

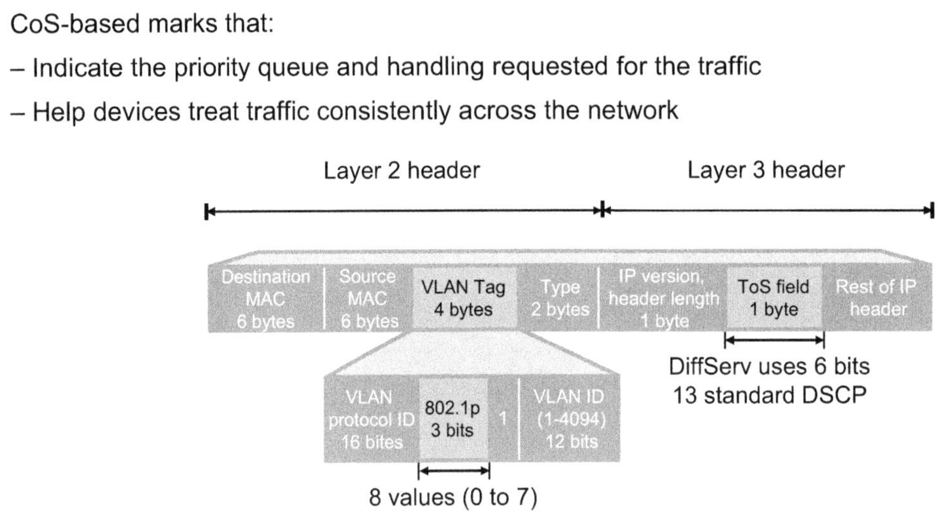


Figure 15-10 Introduction to QoS marks

As Figure 15-10 shows, the values reside within frame or packet headers and can be passed on with the traffic from device to device. Ethernet LANs carrying IP traffic typically support two types of QoS marks: 802.1p, which defines values carried in the Layer 2 802.1Q VLAN tag, and Differentiated Services Code Point (DSCP), which defines values carried in the Type of Service (ToS) field of an IP header. The sections below provide more details about these marks.

## Layer 2: 802.1p

The 802.1p standard uses a three-bit field in the 802.1Q VLAN tag to indicate priority (see Figure 15-10). It defines eight values between 0 and 7. Note that because the VLAN tag carries the priority value, untagged traffic cannot use 802.1p to request a specific priority level. Although Figure 15-10 shows an Ethernet frame that encapsulates an IP packet, an Ethernet frame with an 802.1p field can encapsulate any Layer 3 protocol supported by Ethernet.

## Layer 3 protocols

This section covers QoS marks that apply at Layer 3 (see Figure 15-10).

### ToS and IP precedence bits (no longer used)

ToS is not often used currently, but it can helpful to understand what ToS is if you hear it referenced.

As Figure 15-10 shows, every IP packet includes an eight-bit field called the ToS field. As originally defined, the ToS field contained two subfields—a three-bit IP precedence field used for relative prioritization and a four-bit subfield for the specific ToS desired by an individual packet. The remaining bit, bit 7, is called the must be zero (MBZ) bit and is unused.

The three IP precedence bits in the most significant position were to be used to provide eight levels of precedence or priority. The levels are labeled 0 to 7, with 7 being the highest priority and 0 the lowest. The values 6 and 7 are reserved for "Internet" and "network" uses, respectively. This enables routing updates and other critical traffic to have a higher priority than user-generated traffic. The highest user-defined value is 5, which represents "critical" priority.

The four ToS bits were designed to allow applications to instruct routers to choose routing paths with one of the following four characteristics: minimized delay, maximized throughput, maximized reliability, and minimized cost. Only one of the four bits could be "turned on," that is, set to 1.

## Differentiated Services (current)

Seeking to improve IP ToS, in 1998 an Internet Engineering Task Force (IETF) working group redefined the use of the ToS header in Request for Comments (RFC) 2474. Under the new definition, the first six bits define 64 Differentiated Services (DiffServ) "codepoints" (DSCPs). Instead of defining priority relative to each other, the 64 DSCPs are intended to define distinct forwarding behaviors or Per Hop Behaviors. Any one of 64 values may appear in a six-bit field; however, RFC 2597 defined 12 Assured Forwarding (AF) DSCPs. These 12 DSCPs break down into four classes indicated by the first three bits (class 1 has the lowest priority and class 4 the highest). Each class includes three DSCPs, indicated by the second three bits, which request a drop precedence.

RFC 2598 defines an Expedited Forwarding (EF) DSCP that is intended to produce the lowest levels of jitter and delay. Table 15-1 presents the 13 defined DSCPs. You will see later in the chapter how AOS-Switches map these DSCPs to priority queues.

The DSCPs that are divisible by eight are called Class Selector (CS) and correlate to legacy IP precedence values. For example, DSCP 8 is called CS1.

Table 15-1 AF and EF DSCPs

| PHB | AF Class | AF drop precedence | Decimal DSCP |
|---|---|---|---|
| AF11 | 1001 | Drop last 010 | 10 |
| AF12 | 1001 | Drop second 100 | 12 |
| AF13 | 1001 | Drop first 110 | 14 |
| AF21 | 2010 | Drop last 010 | 18 |
| AF22 | 2010 | Drop second 100 | 20 |
| AF23 | 2010 | Drop first 110 | 22 |
| AF31 | 3011 | Drop last 010 | 26 |
| AF32 | 3011 | Drop second 100 | 28 |
| AF33 | 3011 | Drop first 110 | 30 |
| AF41 | 4100 | Drop last 010 | 34 |
| AF42 | 4100 | Drop second 100 | 36 |
| AF43 | 4100 | Drop first 110 | 38 |
| EF | Requests highest priority for lowest jitter and latency | | 46(101110) |

Network administrators are free to use the remaining 51 DSCPs in any way they choose.

Under the original DiffServ definition, two bits of the eight-bit ToS field were initially allocated as "unused." In 2001, however, RFC 3168 redefined the two unused bits as Congestion Experienced (CE) bits, meaning that routers can use them to signal other devices when they experience congestion. If the CE bits are not in use, a router that experiences significant congestion that causes buffer overflows will drop newer packets rather than place them in its queues. This signals to end stations that they should use a smaller TCP window.

### DSCP compatibility with IP precedence

DSCP and IP precedence can exist in parallel because DiffServ intentionally preserves the three high order bits for traffic class.

If some applications look for only the three high order bits, they will recognize the IP Precedence value. An application or device that is using the DiffServ interpretation will interpret those same three bits from its own perspective. Applications and devices will arrive at the same relative priority, although the actual values are different.

# Methods for prioritizing and queuing traffic

You can follow two strategies for configuring your AOS-Switches device to divide traffic into priority queues for transmission.

## Honoring QoS marks

As you learned, devices can mark traffic with QoS values, which request a specific-priority level for that traffic. AOS-Switches can recognize these marks and honor them by assigning the traffic to the corresponding queue.

You should implement this strategy on switch ports that connect to trusted devices—such as servers—which run applications that are capable of selecting and marking their own priority. You should also implement this strategy on switch-to-switch ports (or router-to-switch ports) when the connecting device provides the intelligence, classifying traffic, and inserting the correct QoS mark.

## Classifying traffic

AOS-Switches can also classify traffic according to a variety of criteria on multiple OSI layers. Then, based on those criteria, they can map the traffic to the desired outbound queue. As you will learn later, they can also mark the traffic with a QoS value, requesting that other devices in the traffic path implement a similar prioritization strategy.

Classify traffic locally when you want this local switch to control precisely how it queues traffic.

Generally, you should configure QoS classification as close to the edge of a domain as possible, enabling the domain to implement consistent controls for traffic across its entire journey through the domain. Ideally, you should deploy intelligent switches, capable of making these decisions, at the access layer. The switches can then classify the traffic correctly from the beginning of its journey. Switches at the edge of a service provider network might also use this strategy to control and classify incoming customer traffic.

Of course, as part of your QoS configuration, you must examine other network infrastructure devices in traffic's path, ensuring that these devices are prepared to honor the QoS marks.

### Mix of strategies

Although for clarity this section will describe how to implement each strategy separately, you can implement both strategies on the same switch. For example, you could configure ports that connect to servers to honor QoS marks set by some applications and also create policies that classify traffic from other applications—or override the honored priorities according to more important business priorities as interpreted by QoS policies.

## Honoring QoS marks

You will now examine how to configure AOS-Switches to honor QoS marks in more detail.

### Honoring 802.1p

By default, AOS-Switches honor incoming 802.1p values in frames' headers. In the absence of other classification policies, the switches use these values to assign the frame to a priority queue on the egress port. If the traffic is forwarded with a tag, the outgoing traffic also maintains the incoming 802.1p value.

A switch with eight outbound queues per-port creates a one-to-one correspondence between each priority value and a queue. The 802.1p value 7 maps to the highest priority queue, which is numbered 8 in the command line interface (CLI). But normal priority traffic (value 0) is not mapped to the lowest numbered queue. Instead, it is mapped to queue 3, and there are two priority levels lower than normal: values 1 and 2. In the absence of other prioritization policies, untagged traffic, which has no 802.1p field, is assigned a value of "0" and forwarded with normal priority in queue 3.

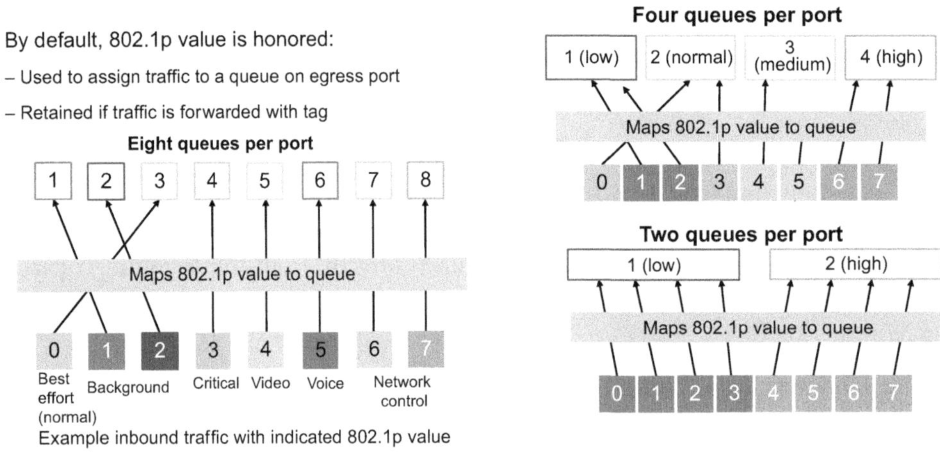


Figure 15-11 Honoring 802.1p

As you learned earlier, some switches might maintain only four or two egress queues per port, depending on the hardware capabilities and the configured setting. Table 15-2 presents how the 802.1p values map to eight, four, and two queues.

Figure 15-11 also gives examples of the types of traffic that might be assigned various 802.1p values. The two highest values, 6 and 7, are reserved for network control traffic (for example, AOS-Switches automatically forward packets such as spanning tree Bridge Protocol Data Units (BPDUs) and Open Shortest Path First (OSPF) hellos with high priority). Voice, 5, and video, 4, are given the next highest priority. Then mission-critical applications receive the next highest priority, 802.1p value 3. Next, the switch gives its best effort to traffic with the default priority. Finally, 802.1p values 1 and 2 are assigned to background traffic, which is less important or can tolerate delay.

These examples are mostly in line with the recommendations in the IEEE802.1Q-2014 standard. The exception is that this standard recommends 802.1p value 2 for traffic that requires an excellent effort—in other words, better than default. However, the AOS-Switches were designed to comply with the original 802.1D recommendations, which designated a *less* than normal priority for 802.1p 2 as well as 1, so you would not want to follow the 802.1Q-2014 standard recommendations for value 2 unless your switch supports the custom mapping described below.

Some QoS implementations might still use the 802.1D recommendations for all the classes. With these recommendations, voice traffic is assigned 802.1p value 6 and video, value 5.

Table 15-2 Mapping 802.1p values to configured queues

| 802.1p value | 8 configured queues | 4 configured queues | 2 configured queues |
|---|---|---|---|
| 1 | 1 | 1 | 1 |
| 2 | 2 | 1 | 1 |
| 0 | 3 | 2 | 1 |
| 3 | 4 | 2 | 1 |
| 4 | 5 | 3 | 2 |
| 5 | 6 | 3 | 2 |
| 6 | 7 | 4 | 2 |
| 7 | 8 | 4 | 2 |

## Supplemental note on mappings

Figure 15-11 and Table 15-2 show the default 802.1p value-to-queue mappings. On some AOS-Switches only, you can change the behavior by using traffic templates. (Refer to your switch documentation.) These switches have a default-tcgt traffic template, which applies the mappings shown in Table 15-15-2hey also have a dot1q-tcgt traffic template, which you can apply to change the mappings. The dot1q-tcgt template is the same as the default one except that it reverses the priority for 802.1p 2 and 802.1p 0. In other words, 802.1p 1 is the lowest priority, then 802.1p 0, and then 802.1p 2. This brings the mappings in sync with the 802.1Q-2014 recommendations. You should apply the dot1q-tcgt template if other network infrastructure devices in your network use those mappings.

Use this command to apply a different traffic template:

```
Switch(config)# qos queue-config [2-queues | 4-queues | 8-queues] traffic-
   template <name>
```

The command requires a reboot.

You can also create your own traffic template with this command:

```
Switch(config)# qos traffic-template <name>
```

You can then create or remove the mappings between an 802.1p value and a queue with this command:

```
Switch(cfg-tcgt-<name>)# [no] map-traffic-group <queue> priority <802.1p
   value>
```

After defining the desired mappings, apply the template.

View the names of configured traffic templates and which template is active with this command:

```
Switch# show qos traffic-template
```

Add the name of the template to view the mappings:

```
Switch# show qos traffic-template <name>
```

## Honoring DSCP

On AOS-Switches, the QoS type of service setting determines whether the switch honors incoming Layer 3 values. When type of service is disabled, the switch does not refer to a packet's DSCP, in the ToS field, to determine the packet's priority. It only examines the frame's 802.1p value and uses the rules that you examined in the previous frame. If the frame does not have an 802.1p value, the switch assigns the frame to the normal priority queue (queue 3, when numbered from 1-8). The incoming DSCP is preserved in outgoing traffic, but it does not affect how the switch itself queues and prioritizes the traffic. Generally, type of service is disabled by default, but you should check your switch's documentation. If you need to disable type of service, enter this command:

```
Switch(config)# no qos type-of-service
```

Sometimes you want the switch to honor incoming DSCP, rather than 802.1p values. For example, applications might be configured to set a DSCP on endpoints that are not 802.1Q enabled. To allow the switch to honor incoming DSCP globally, set the type of service to Diff-Serv with this command:

```
Switch(config)# qos type-of-service diff-services
```

---

**Note**

You can also set the type of service to IP precedence, which maps incoming packets' IP precedence—the first three bits in the ToS field—to an 802.1p value and queue. However, IP precedence is deprecated.

---

With type of service set to DiffServ, the switch checks each incoming packet's DSCP. If a DSCP map exists for that DSCP, the switch assigns the packet to the 802.1p priority value—and corresponding queue—specified in that map. For example, Figure 15-12 shows that a frame with no 802.1p value (no tag) and DSCP 34. The DSCP map for this value specifies 802.1p 4, so the frame receives that priority, and the switch forwards it in queue 5 on the egress port.

The 802.1p value determined by the DSCP map overrides any incoming 802.1p value, as shown for the frame with 802.1p value 5 and DSCP 34 in Figure 15-12. This frame now receives a new 802.1p value and egress queue, based on the DSCP map.

You must be aware that some AOS-Switches, depending on the software version, might not automatically map all DSCPs to a queue. Therefore, you must be careful to check that your switch has DSCP maps for the values that your network uses. For traffic with a DSCP that has no map, the switch uses the 802.1p value, if any. If the traffic has no 802.1p value because the traffic is untagged, the switch forwards the traffic at normal priority.

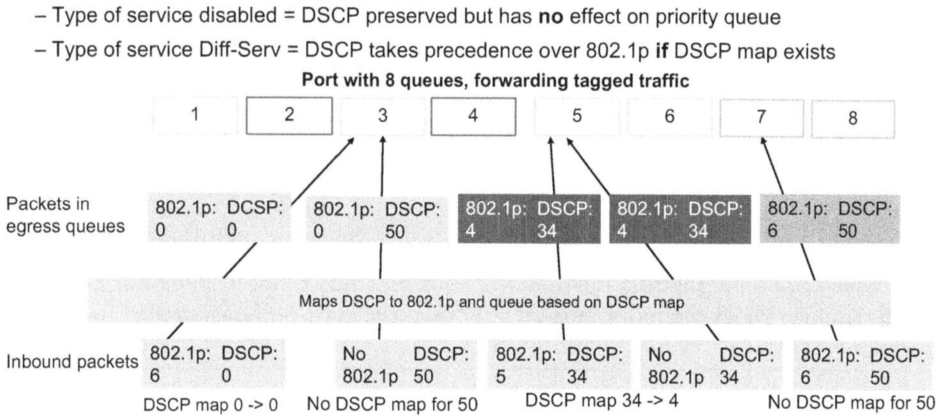


Figure 15-12 Honoring DSCP

For example, as shown in Figure 15-12, traffic might arrive with DSCP 50, which has no DSCP map. If the traffic has an 802.1p value such as 6, the switch uses that to prioritize the traffic. But if the traffic has no 802.1p value, the switch forwards it as the normal. Although the switch does not actually prioritize the packet, the packet maintains DSCP 50 as it is forwarded, which can make it difficult for you to troubleshoot the issue.

Finally, it is important that you understand that AOS-Switches generally have a DSCP map for DSCP 0, which maps to 802.1p value 0. All IP traffic has a DSCP; if nothing has set the DSCP, then the value is 0. This means that you should be careful when you set the type of service to DiffServ. You might think that traffic "does not have a DSCP value," so an 802.1p value will take effect. However, the traffic "without a value" actually has DSCP value 0, which overrides the 802.1p value and sets it to 0, as you see for the packet at the left in Figure 15-12. This behavior might be desirable or not in your system, depending on whether you want to switch to clear unauthorized 802.1p values or whether you wanted to use those values together with DSCP. If you are planning to use DiffServ as the type of service, you must plan your solution accordingly. Either make sure that all traffic that needs to be prioritized has a non-0 DSCP, or, if you want to use 802.1p to classify some traffic, remove the DSCP mapping for DSCP 0.

You can view the maps with this command:

```
Switch# show qos dscp-map
```

DSCP without mappings is listed as **no-override** for the 802.1p value.

You can change the default mappings and also add mappings for other DSCPs. For example, AF21 is mapped to 802.1p value 2, but you might want to assign AF21 a higher priority than 0. You might remap this DSCP to 802.1p value 3. You can enter the <dscp> as a binary value, decimal value, or one of the pre-defined names:

```
Switch(config)# qos dscp-map <dscp> priority <802.1p value>
```

You can view the mappings configured on the switch by entering:

```
Switch(config)# show qos dscp-map
```

If No-Override is shown instead of an 802.1p value, no map exists for that DSCP.

**Note**

Table 15-3 and Table 15-4 present the default mappings in the AOS-Switch XX.16.04 code, which are different from previous versions and may differ from model to model. You should carefully check the mappings on your own switches and ensure that they align with your plans.

Table 15-3 Named DSCP mappings

| Policy name | DSCP CodePoint (binary) | DSCP value (decimal) | 802.1p value | Mapped queue (with default template) |
|---|---|---|---|---|
| CS 0 | 000000 | 0 | 0 | 3 |
| CS 1 | 001000 | 8 | 1 | 1 |
| AF 11 | 001010 | 10 | 1 | 1 |
| AF 12 | 001100 | 12 | 1 | 1 |
| AF 13 | 001110 | 14 | 1 | 1 |
| CS 2 | 010000 | 16 | 2 | 2 |
| AF 21 | 010010 | 18 | 2 | 2 |
| AF 22 | 010100 | 20 | 2 | 2 |
| AF 23 | 010110 | 22 | 2 | 2 |
| CS 3 | 011000 | 24 | 3 | 4 |
| AF 31 | 011010 | 26 | 3 | 4 |
| AF 32 | 011100 | 28 | 3 | 4 |
| AF 33 | 011110 | 30 | 3 | 4 |
| CS 4 | 100000 | 32 | 4 | 5 |
| AF 41 | 100010 | 34 | 4 | 5 |
| AF 42 | 100100 | 36 | 4 | 5 |
| AF 43 | 100110 | 38 | 4 | 5 |
| CS 5 | 101000 | 40 | 5 | 6 |
| EF | 101110 | 46 | 7 | 8 |
| CS 6 | 110000 | 48 | 6 | 7 |
| CS 7 | 111000 | 56 | 7 | 8 |

Table 15-4 Unnamed DSCP mappings

| DSCP value (decimal) | 802.1p value | Mapped queue (with default template) |
|---|---|---|
| 1-7 | 0 | 3 |
| 9,11,13,15 | 1 | 1 |
| 17,19,21,23 | 2 | 2 |
| 25,27,29,31 | 3 | 4 |
| 33,35,37,39 | 4 | 5 |
| 41-45,47 | 5 | 6 |
| 49-55 | 6 | 7 |
| 57-63 | 7 | 8 |

## Controlling trusted value at a port level

Instead of setting type of service to DiffServ globally, you can manipulate the QoS trust setting on individual ports with this command:

```
Switch(config)# interface <port ID list> qos trust <default | dot1p |
    none | dscp | ip-prec | device aruba-ap>
```

You will now learn some use cases for the various settings. Refer to Figure 15-13 as you review these use cases.

Setting the global type of service to DiffServ configures the switch to use DSCP to prioritize *all* incoming traffic. Sometimes, though, you only want the switch to trust the DSCP received on some ports. You might want to use the 802.1p value to prioritize traffic on switch-to-switch ports, but the DSCP on ports connected to trusted servers, for example. If this is the case for your network, you should keep type of service disabled globally. Instead, set the QoS trust setting to **dscp** on the interfaces connected to the trusted servers.

The switch then acts much as if the type of service setting is DiffServ, but only for traffic received on that interface.

- It uses the traffic's DSCP to prioritize the traffic if a DSCP map exists for that DSCP. The switch also changes the 802.1p value to match the one in the DSCP map.
- If no DSCP map exists for the traffic's DSCP, the switch sets the 802.1p value to 0 and forwards the traffic in the default queue. This behavior is different from that when the global type of service is DiffServ and the port uses the default trust setting. (In that case, the switch uses the 802.1p value, if any, to prioritize the traffic.)

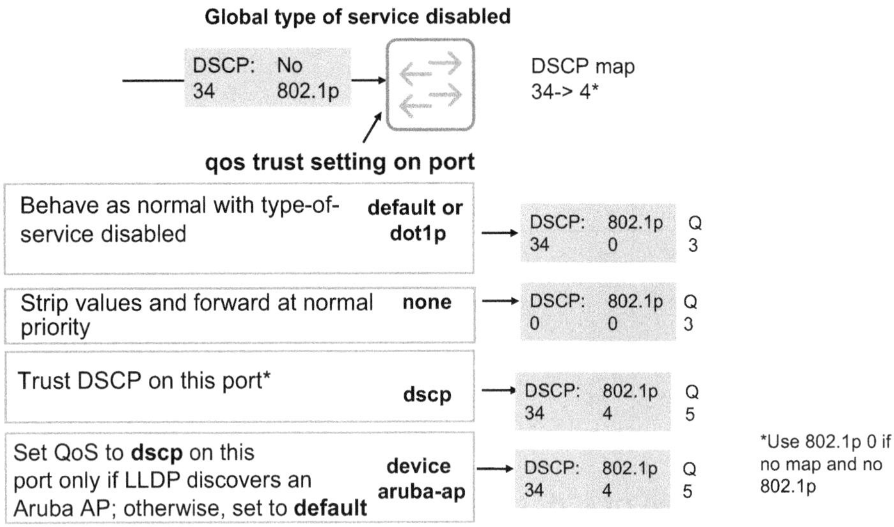


Figure 15-13 Controlling trusted value at a port level (Global type of service disabled)

You can also configure the switch to trust DSCP on a specific port, but only if the port is connected to a specific device type. As of the publication of this study guide, the supported device type is Aruba AP (**qos trust device aruba-ap**). This setting can help you integrate your wired and wireless infrastructure more seamlessly. You want the switch to honor any DSCP added by the Aruba APs as the switch forwards wireless users' traffic through the Ethernet backend. However, you do want to trust DSCP added by user devices. You do not have to track to which ports APs connect and set them up to trust DSCP in advance. Instead, you can set all edge ports to trust DSCP based on the device type. Then the switch honors DSCP if it detects an Aruba AP on the port. Otherwise, the switch behaves as if in the default QoS mode.

Other interfaces, which have the default setting—called **default**—for QoS trust, continue to act as normal when type of service is disabled globally. The switch uses the 802.1p value, if any, to prioritize the traffic. If the traffic has no 802.1p value, it forwards the traffic with normal priority. In either case, the switch leaves any DSCP intact, but the DSCP has no effect on the traffic's egress priority queue. Setting the QoS trust to 802.1p (**dot1p**) has the same effect as setting it to default.

When an interface connects to less trusted user devices, you might want to disable QoS trust on the port entirely by setting QoS trust to **none**. The switch then ignores any incoming 802.1p or DSCP value and forwards the traffic as normal. It also remarks the DSCP and 802.1p value, if any, as 0. (You could create a QoS policy that has much the same effect, but disabling trust on the port is much simpler.)

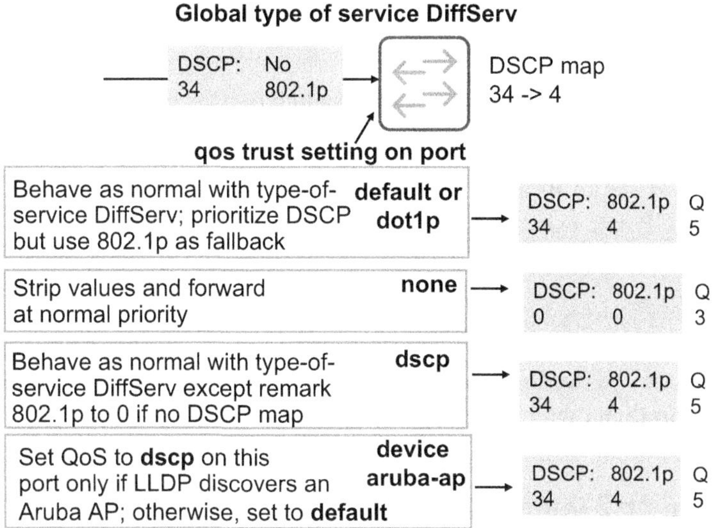


Figure 15-14 Controlling trusted value at a port level (Global type of service DiffServ)

You should understand that, when the type of service is set to DiffServ globally, the switch always prioritizes traffic based on the DSCP in preference to the 802.1p value regardless of the interface's QoS trust setting. The one exception is the **none** setting for QoS trust. Regardless of the global type of service setting, when an interface has QoS trust set to **none**, the switch remarks the 802.1p and DSCP values to 0 and forwards the traffic at normal priority (see Figure 15-14).

The QoS trust setting does have one other effect when the global type of service is DiffServ: how traffic is prioritized when no DSCP map exists for incoming traffic's DSCP. If you want the switch to use an 802.1p value, if any, to prioritize this traffic, set the interface's QoS trust to default or 802.1p. If you want the switch to mark this traffic with 802.1p value 0 and forward the traffic in the default queue, set the interface QoS setting to DSCP. (When the global type of service is DiffServ, setting the QoS trust to device type has the same effect as setting it to DSCP. The switch still uses the DSCP to prioritize traffic from *any* device on that port due to the global setting. The device type setting is primarily meant to be used when type of service is disabled.)

In summary, keep these tips in mind:

- If you do not want to switch to honor 802.1p or DSCP on certain ports, set the QoS trust to **none** on those ports.
- If you want to use 802.1p in preference to DSCP on any ports, leave the global type of service setting disabled. You can then set QoS trust to **dscp** or **device aruba-ap** on individual ports if you want.

- If you set the global type of service to DiffServ, the switch will use DSCP in preference to 802.1p to prioritize traffic received on all ports.
  - Leave the setting at **default** if you want the switch to use the 802.1p value to prioritize traffic when no DSCP map exists for the DSCP.
  - Change the setting to **dscp** if you want the switch to forward traffic in the default queue when no DSCP map exists for the DSCP.

# Classifying traffic for QoS

You will now move on to the classification strategy. You will learn how AOS-Switches can select traffic and apply a priority on their own based on a variety of features.

## Classifying at Layer 2 versus Layer 3

Before you look at the specific methods for classifying traffic, you should understand the two types of priority values that you can apply to traffic: 802.1p priority and DSCP.

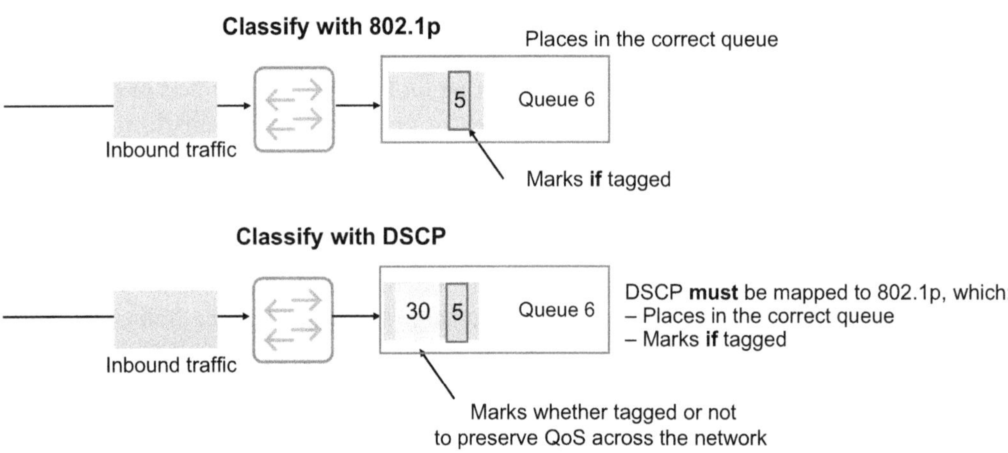


Figure 15-15 Classifying at Layer 2 versus Layer 3

Remember that when you classify traffic, you typically have two goals: configuring the switch in which priority queue to place the traffic and communicating the desired priority to other network infrastructure devices in the traffic's path.

As Figure 15-15 shows, the switch can only transmit an 802.1p value in tagged traffic. In addition, the priority field in the 802.1Q tag is discarded whenever a switch or router replaces the Layer 2 header. For instance, if a Layer 2 prioritized frame is forwarded through an untagged port, the entire tag, including the 802.1p prioritization value, will be discarded. A WAN router that forwards the packet over a different media also removes the Ethernet header.

---

**Note**

Although the tag will be destroyed whenever the frame is forwarded at Layer 3 because the forwarding process requires the routing switch or router to create a new Layer 2 header, Q-compliant routers such as the AOS-Switches can preserve the tag. They copy the priority value from the tag of the inbound frame into the tag of the outbound frame before forwarding it. However, the copying only works if the traffic is forwarded as tagged.

---

For these reasons, when you classify traffic, you might need to assign the traffic a DSCP in addition to an 802.1p value. The DSCP is not modified by the Layer 2 or Layer 3 forwarding processes (unless an infrastructure device is explicitly configured to change the DSCP), allowing the traffic to maintain its priority across the LAN and WAN links.

When you actually configure the priority, you will find that you often must choose between setting an 802.1p value or a DSCP in the command. You can set an 802.1p value if you know that the switch will send all classified traffic with a tag.

If the switch might send untagged traffic, set a DSCP value when you create the classification. Although you seem to be setting only a DSCP, the DSCP must be mapped to an 802.1p value. This is because AOS-Switches use a frame's 802.1p value as the ultimate determinant of the frame's priority queue. The switch also adds this 802.1p value to the traffic, if it forwards the traffic as tagged. You will receive an error message in the CLI (or Web UI) if you configure a traffic classification that uses a DSCP that does not have a mapping. You must create the map first, and then you can re-attempt the configuration.

## Classifying based on interface

AOS-Switches can classify traffic in several different ways. First, you will look at classifying traffic based on the interface on which it arrives. Typically, you would use this strategy when you want to prioritize all traffic from a particular endpoint in the same way. For example, you could prioritize an IP phone's traffic.

You can assign the priority to a physical interface or a VLAN interface (see Figure 15-16).

- Apply 802.1p value or DSCP directly to physical or VLAN interface
- Typically used to prioritize **all** traffic from a device or devices
- Priority overridden by incoming DSCP if type of service is DiffServ and DSCP map exists
  - Set QoS trust to none or remove unwanted DSCP maps
  - Or, for VoIP phones, use LLDP-MED (discussed later) to ensure phone sends correct incoming DSCP

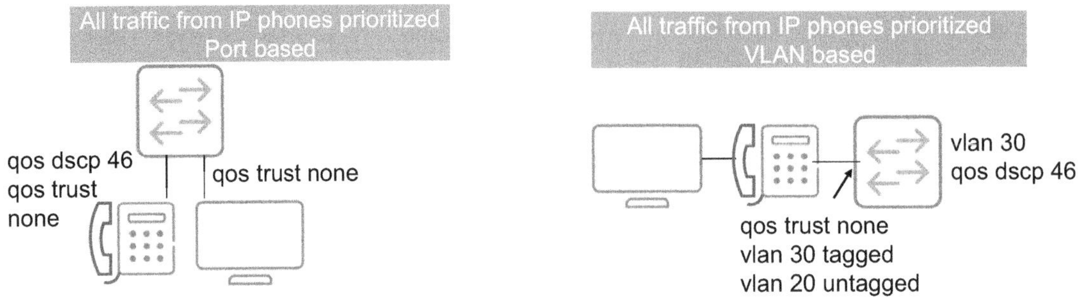


Figure 15-16 Classifying based on interface

## Physical interface

To assign all traffic incoming on a port to the same queue, you simply specify the priority that you want to assign to the port by accessing the interface. Enter this command if you want to use 802.1p:

```
Switch(config)# interface <port_ID_list> qos priority <0-7>
```

Enter this command if you want to use DSCP:

```
Switch(config)# interface <port_ID_list> qos dscp <codepoint>
```

You can specify the codepoint as a binary value (000000-111111), digital value (0-63), or named AF, EF, or CS class such as af11.

As you learned, you should apply a DSCP when you want to help downstream devices maintain the priority across the complete traffic path. Remember to check that the switch has the proper DSCP maps before entering the **qos dscp** command on the interface. The switch will also mark the traffic with the 802.1p value associated with this map if it forwards the traffic with a tag.

## VLAN

Often the devices for which you want to prioritize the traffic all belong to the same VLAN. For example, it is best practice to assign VoIP phones to their own VLAN. By doing so, you protect the phones to a degree from excessive broadcasts and other congestion. You can then configure the desired 802.1p value or DSCP value for that VLAN rather than on each individual port.

The VLAN configuration also enables you to prioritize VoIP traffic over computer traffic when the two devices share the same port. The switch receives the VoIP traffic with a tag for the voice VLAN and applies the configured 802.1p value or DSCP and 802.1p value. The computer traffic arrives in a different VLAN with no special priority specific.

To configure a VLAN priority, enter one of these commands:

```
Switch(config)# vlan <ID> qos priority <0-7>

Switch(config)# vlan <ID> qos dscp <codepoint>
```

### Interaction with incoming DSCP

On AOS-Switches, incoming DSCP takes precedence over the 802.1p value or DSCP set on the port or VLAN *if* a DSCP map exists and if type of service is set to DiffServ globally. This could cause an issue because DSCP 0 is mapped to 802.1p value 0, by default. Therefore, all IP traffic, which has the default DSCP of 0, is forwarded at normal priority rather than the priority that you chose.

To ensure that the port or VLAN QoS value overrides incoming DSCP, you can take a few approaches. You can leave the type of service setting disabled globally, or, if you need to honor DSCP on other ports, you can set the QoS trust to none on ports receiving the traffic that you are classifying yourself. (Default and none are the only valid QoS trust settings when you set a port priority.) Alternatively, you could remove just the unwanted DSCP map such as the map for DSCP 0. Then the switch will assign the port or VLAN QoS value to traffic with DSCP 0.

Finally, note that you can use LLDP-MED to ensure that VoIP phones send traffic with the same DSCP that you configure for the phone's VLAN.

## Classifying with global QoS policies

AOS-Switches can classify traffic based on a variety of Layer 2 to Layer 4 settings using flexible QoS policies. You would use QoS policies to classify traffic whenever you need to select traffic on a more granular basis. You can use global or classifier-based policies for this purpose. This section focuses on the global policies. You will look at classified-based policies a bit later.

Figure 15-17 shows a few examples of global QoS policies. Each statement that specifies the criterion and the priority that you want to associate with that criterion.

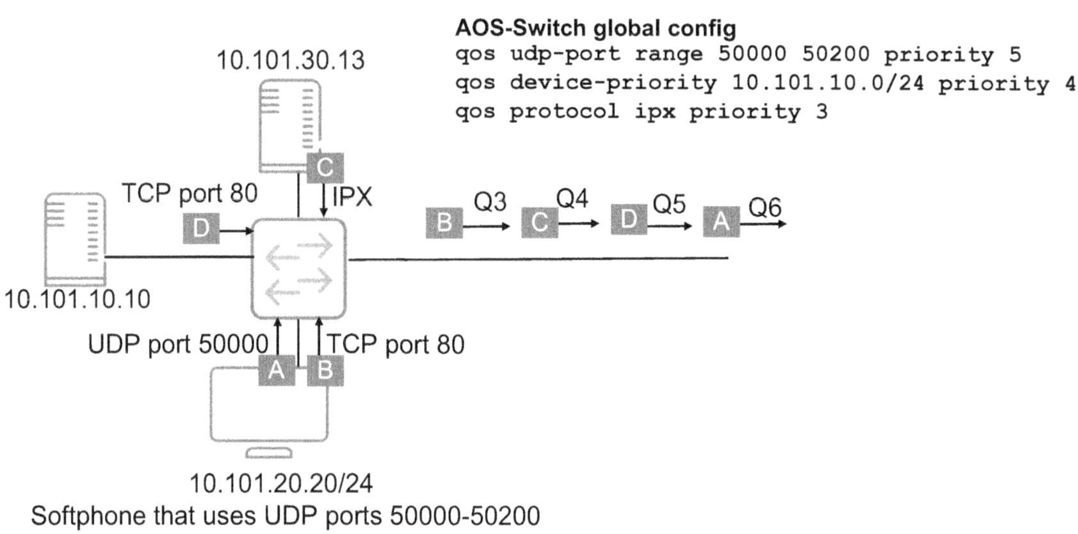


Figure 15-17 Classifying with global QoS policies

For example, suppose that your network has computers with softphones that use UDP ports 50000 through 50200 for VoIP traffic. You can specify 802.1p value 5 for this range of ports, as shown in the Figure 15-17. Now, the AOS-Switch assigns all traffic that is destined to these UDP ports this value and places the traffic in egress queue 6 for forwarding (on a switch using eight queues, numbered 1 to 8). The command for specifying the QoS mark for a range of TCP or UDP ports is:

```
Switch(config)# qos <tcp-port | udp-port> range <first port> <last port>
    {priority <0-7> | dscp <codepoint>}
```

The command for specifying the QoS mark for a single TCP or UDP port is:

```
Switch(config)# qos <tcp-port | udp-port> <port> <priority <0-7> | dscp
   <codepoint>>
```

You can also classify traffic by source or destination IP address. You do not specify source or destination IP address separately. Rather you designate a priority for devices with specific IP addresses, and the priority applies to all traffic both to and from the device. In the example shown in Figure 15-17, all traffic to or from devices in the 10.101.10.0/24 network is assigned priority value 4 and forwarded in queue 5. The command is:

```
Switch(config)# qos device-priority <IP address  | network address/
  prefix length> {priority <0-7> | dscp <codepoint>}
```

You can also classify traffic based on the Ethernet protocol:

```
Switch(config)# qos protocol <protocol> priority <0-7>
```

In the example in Figure 15-17, Internetwork Packet Exchange (IPX) traffic is assigned 802.1p value 3 (queue 4). Other examples of protocols that you can prioritize include Address Resolution Protocol (ARP), AppleTalk, IP, Systems Network Architecture (SNA), and Netbeui.

You can set the priority for these criteria to an 802.1p value or DSCP. Remember that if you attempt to set a DSCP, that DSCP must be mapped to an 802.1p value already. One exception applies: you can only set an 802.1p value for Ethernet protocols. Most of these protocols are non-IP protocols, and a DSCP requires an IP header.

## Interaction of QoS classifications and incoming values

As you set up multiple ways classify traffic, the criteria might overlap. For example, you might specify 802.1p value 2 for ingress switch port 1, value 3 for traffic to and from 10.1.2.10, and priority 4 for TCP port 5060. When traffic matches multiple criteria, the switch applies the QoS value applied by the criteria type with the highest precedence. In this example, traffic that arrives on switch port 1 from 10.1.2.10 destined for TCP port 5060 is assigned to 802.1p value 4; the TCP port takes precedence. Traffic that arrives on switch port 1 from 10.1.2.10 destined for TCP port 80 (no configured priority) is assigned 802.1p value 3; the IP address takes precedence over the ingress port.

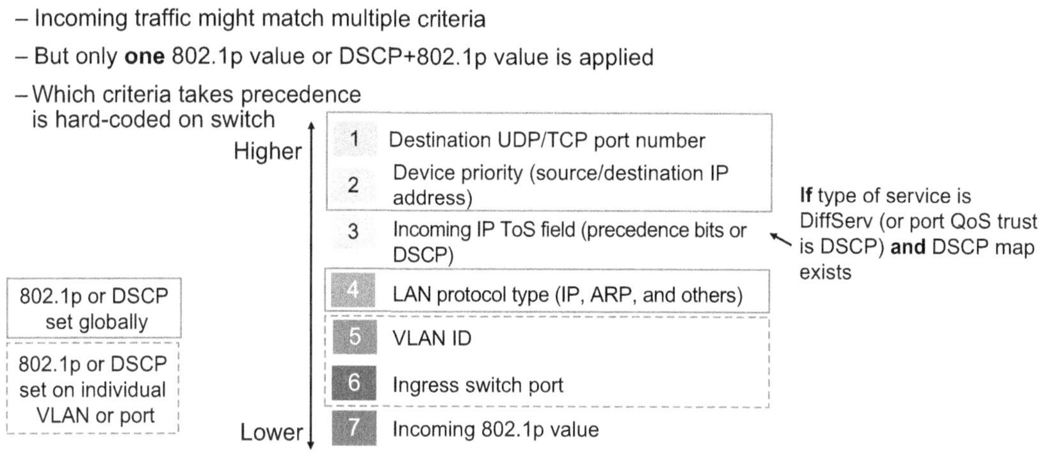


Figure 15-18 Interaction of QoS classifications and incoming values

As Figure 15-18 shows, a globally defined QoS value for UDP port, TCP port, or source/destination IP address takes precedence over all incoming values. However, incoming DSCP takes precedence over other configured classifications if DSCP is trusted on the incoming port and a DSCP map exists. DSCP trust could be set on an individual port basis, or the type of service could be set to Diff-Serv globally and the port has any trust setting except none.

An incoming 802.1p value, on the other hand, is overridden by any other setting.

## Classifying traffic with classifier-based QoS policies

Rather than use the global settings to classify traffic on AOS-Switches, you might want to use the classifier-based QoS model, which has been available since software release K14.01. This model gives you more flexibility in selecting traffic and power in defining how the switch treats that traffic.

**Note**

This feature is only supported in some AOS-Switch models. For information on a specific product or product family, consult the product documentation.

To implement classifier-based QoS, you first create one or more traffic classes (see Figure 15-19). A class selects traffic according to a variety of granular criteria in either the MAC or IP header. You then create a QoS policy, which maps each class to an action such as assigning DSCP priority 30 and 802.1p value 5. Finally, you apply the QoS policy to a specific port or VLAN.

Classifier-based QoS is designed to work with existing globally configured, switch-wide QoS settings. You can classify most traffic with global statements and then configure QoS policies that override the global policies for a subset of traffic based on the port or VLAN on which the traffic arrives.

- Prioritize traffic based on more granular criteria
  - Example: Different priorities for the same destination TCP port but different destination subnets
- Prioritize based on MAC header criteria
- Group multiple selection criteria together
- Apply different QoS policies to traffic arriving on different ports or VLANs
- Apply more types of actions:
  - Prioritization
  - Rate limiting

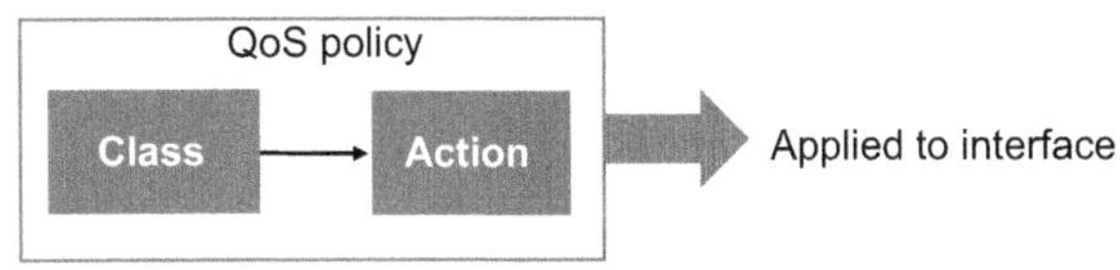


Figure 15-19 Classifying traffic with classifier-based QoS policies

Or, you can use QoS policies alone to finely select and define the classes of traffic that you want to manage. For example, when you use the global settings, you must place all traffic destined to TCP port 21 in the same priority queue. With a classifier-based QoS policy, on the other hand, you can create a class that selects traffic destined to TCP port 21 and subnet 10.1.2.0/24. You can then handle that traffic differently from traffic destined to TCP port 21 and a subnet 10.1.3.0/24. You can also use criteria such as source or destination MAC address, which are not available with the global policies.

A classifier-based QoS policy is also useful when you need to define multiple criteria to match all traffic that you want to prioritize in a specific way. For example, you can create a voice class that selects traffic destined to various UDP ports.

Classifier-based QoS also gives you more options for actions. You will focus on the prioritization actions for now and look at the rate limiting options later.

---

**Important**

Classifier-based policies take precedence over and override globally configured, switch-wide QoS settings, as well as settings applied directly to a VLAN or port. Carefully plan your QoS strategies in advance, identifying the network traffic that you can globally configure and the traffic on which you want to execute customized, classifier-based QoS actions.

Global policies will still affect traffic that is not selected by a classifier-based policy. And, as you learned before, if no policy of any type selects the traffic, the switch can honor the inbound 802.1p or DSCP value, based on the type-of-service setting.

---

## Creating traffic classes

You will now learn how to select traffic for your QoS policy by creating traffic classes.

- IP traffic classes, which select traffic based on criteria in the IP header
- MAC traffic classes, which select traffic based on criteria in the MAC header (consult the product documentation to determine if your switch supports MAC traffic classes)

You should plan to use just one type of class for each policy.

To define a traffic class, use this command:

```
Switch(config)# [no] class <ipv4|mac> <classname>
```

The **no** form of the command removes the existing class.

---

**Note**

You can also create IPv6 traffic classes. However, this study guide does not cover IPv6.

---

After you enter this command, you enter the class configuration context to specify match criteria. You can think of a traffic class a bit like an extended Access Control List (ACL) that is selecting traffic for the action specified in the QoS policy, rather than telling the switch whether or not to forward the traffic. As Figure 15-20 shows, a **match** statement selects traffic for the action specified in the QoS. An **ignore** statement tells the switch to not select that traffic and stop processing the traffic class. Traffic that does not match any of the **match** or **ignore** statements is not selected by the class.

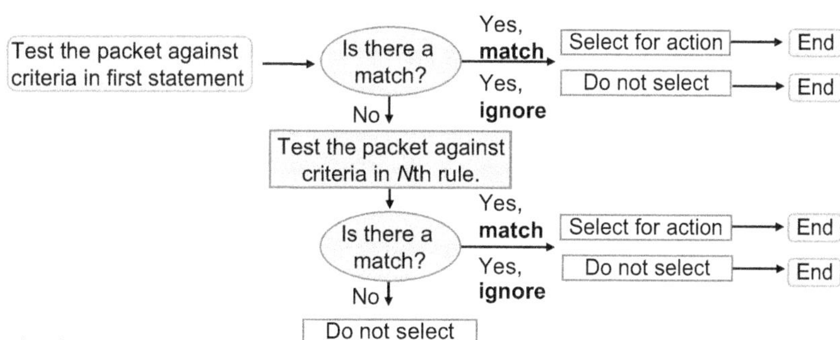


Example classes

| Class type | Class name | Statements |
|---|---|---|
| **IPv4**<br>Select based on IP header and optional VLAN ID | SSH_Critical | match tcp any 10.1.2.0/24 eq 22 |
| **IPv4**<br>Select based on IP header and optional VLAN ID | SSH | ignore tcp any 10.1.99.0/24 eq 22<br>match tcp any any eq 22 |
| **MAC**<br>Select based on MAC header | FCoE | match any any fcoe |

Figure 15-20 Creating traffic classes

Just as with ACLs, the order of entries is important because the switch checks traffic against the statements in numerical order (lowest to highest). Enter the statements in the order in which you want the switch to process them; the switch automatically assigns a sequence number in ascending order, spaced ten apart. You can also specify the sequence number in the command to order the statements yourself.

By using multiple **match** and **ignore** commands that search multiple fields in packet headers you can select the exact traffic you want to prioritize on a port or VLAN interface.

Match criteria for IPv4 classes are similar to criteria for extended IPv4 ACLs and include:

- IP source address or range
- IP destination address or range
- IP protocol (such as Internet Control Message Protocol [ICMP], TCP, UDP, and so on)
- IP precedence bits
- ToS bits
- DSCP
- UDP or TCP source or destination port (use the same keywords as with ACL rules)
- TCP flags
- ICMP type
- Internet Group Management Protocol (IGMP) type
- VLAN ID (the VLAN ID selects all incoming traffic that is assigned to this VLAN, whether through a VLAN tag or an untagged assignment)

Match criteria for MAC classes include:

- Source MAC address or range
- Destination MAC address or range
- EtherType
- CoS (802.1p value)
- VLAN (the VLAN ID selects all incoming traffic that is assigned to this VLAN, whether through a VLAN tag or an untagged assignment)

You can look up the precise syntax and options for these match statements in your AOS-Switch's *Advanced Traffic Management Guide*.

## Configuring and applying classifier-based QoS policies

A QoS policy consists of one or more actions that are configured for each class of traffic. To create a QoS service policy that classifies and prioritizes traffic, follow these steps:

1. Enter this command to create the QoS policy and enter the policy context:

   ```
   Switch(config)# policy qos <policy-name>
   ```

2. Enter a **class** command from the policy configuration context. This command specifies the actions that you want to execute on packets that match the match criteria in the specified class. When you want to prioritize traffic, use this command:

   ```
   Switch(policy-qos)# [seq-number] class <ipv4|mac> <classname>
      [action priority <0-7>] [action dscp <codepoint>]
   ```

   You must set at least one action. For MAC classes, you can set an 802.1p value, but not a DSCP. For IPv4 classes, you can specify an 802.1p value, DSCP, or both. When you specify a DSCP alone, the DSCP must have a DSCP map defined. However, you can also specify both an 802.1p priority value and a DSCP value. Then, rather than apply the 802.1p value mapped to the DSCP, to the selected traffic, the switch applies the 802.1p value specified in the command.

   Optionally, enter a value for the sequence number at the beginning of the command. If you do not specify a sequence number, the switch automatically numbers the statement in increments of ten, using the same process that it uses for ACLs. Like ACLs and traffic classes, the switch processes class statements in order from the lowest to the highest sequence number. (Figure 15-21 shows some examples.)

**Note**

You can also configure IP precedence settings; however, this study guide does not focus on IP precedence, which is deprecated.

3. You can configure multiple classes in a policy, specifying the desired action for each class.

**Important**

A policy **cannot** include both MAC classes and IPv4 or IPv6 classes. However, a policy can have both IPv4 and IPv6 classes.

4. When you are finished configuring the policy, apply it to a physical or VLAN interface. You can only apply policies that remark priority in the inbound direction. The policy classifies traffic that *arrives* on this interface for prioritization; the prioritization occurs when the traffic is forwarded out any interface. All traffic that arrives on the physical or VLAN interface is matched against the policy, whether the traffic is switched or routed. Note that you cannot apply a policy to a VLAN if the policy includes classes that match traffic based on VLAN ID.

   Use this command to apply the policy to a physical interface. Note that the physical interface could be a manual or static Link Aggregation Control Protocol (LACP) link with an ID such as trk1.

   ```
   Switch(config)# interface <ID> service-policy <policy-name> in
   ```

   Use this command to apply the policy to a VLAN:

   ```
   Switch(config)# vlan <ID> service-policy <policy-name> in
   ```

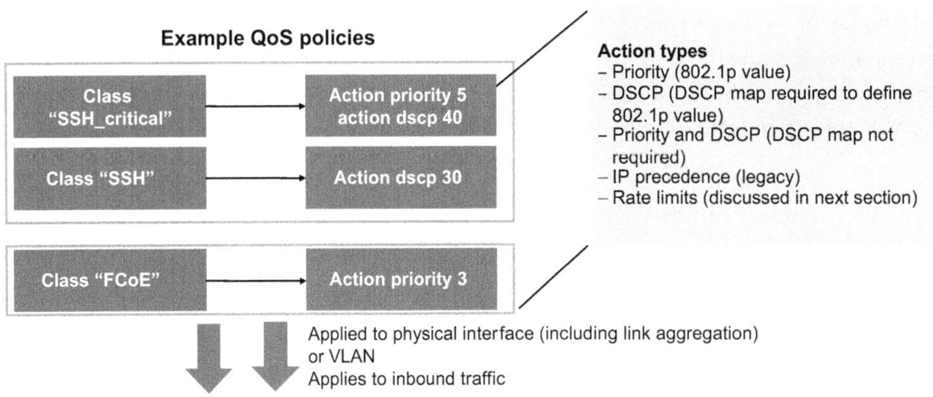


Figure 15-21 Configuring and applying classifier-based QoS policies

## Verifying classifier-based QoS policies

Use this command to check the configuration for a QoS policy ("voice" in this example):

```
Switch# show policy voice

Statements for policy "voice"

policy qos "voice"

     10 class ipv4 "voice" action dscp ef

     exit
```

You can use this command to check which QoS policy, if any, is applied to a list of ports or VLANs:

```
Switch# show policy <ports | vlan> <ID list>
```

You can use this command to verify that a QoS policy applied to an interface or VLAN is selecting packets:

```
Switch# show statistics policy <name> <port | vlan> <ID>
```

For example, you check the policy named "voice" applied to interface 1.

```
Switch# show statistics policy <name> <port | vlan> <ID>
 Hit Counts for Policy voice in the last 148 seconds
  Total
      10 class ipv4 "voice" action dscp ef
(   496 )     10 match udp 0.0.0.0 255.255.255.255 0.0.0.0 255.255.255.255
 eq 5001
```

## QoS policy example

Figure 15-22 shows an example of a QoS policy and how it affects traffic. This QoS policy is applied to VLAN 30, which is the untagged VLAN on the port that connects to the computer. The computer sends a Secure Shell (SSH) packet destined to 10.1.2.100. The switch checks the packet against the first class in the QoS policy. This packet matches that policy, so the switch applies the 802.1p value indicated in the action and places the packet in the corresponding egress queue on the outbound port.

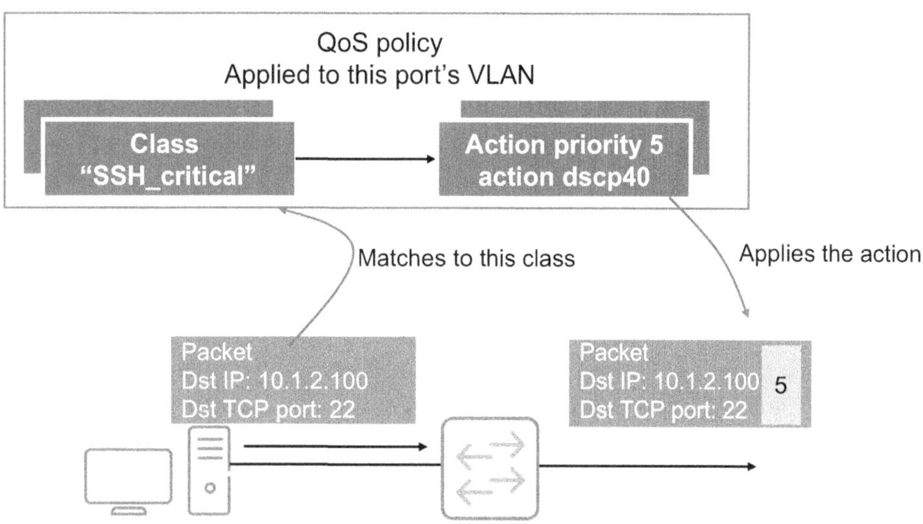


Figure 15-22 QoS policy example

If the computer sends another packet, which does not match the class, the switch will check it against the next class in the policy and so on until it reaches the end of the policy. If a packet does not match any of the classes in the policy, the switch forwards it without altering the priority.

## Summary of how traffic is marked and prioritized

Traffic might match multiple QoS policies, and it might arrive with its own QoS marks. As you learned before, the switch determines traffic's egress QoS marks and queue based on only *one* criterion, and the switch values specific criteria types over other types. Classifier-based QoS policies override all other ways of classifying traffic, as shown in Figure 15-23.

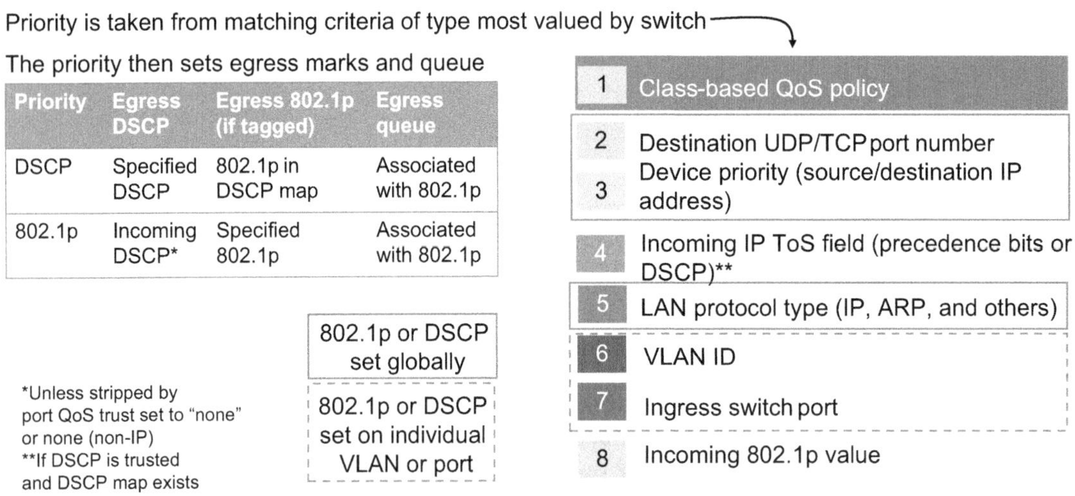


Figure 15-23 Summary of how traffic is marked and prioritized

Any of the classification methods can specify a DSCP or an 802.1p value (**priority**). If the criteria specify a DSCP, the switch forwards the traffic in the queue associated with the 802.1p value mapped to the DSCP. If the criteria specify an 802.1p value, the switch forwards the traffic in the queue associated with that value.

If none of the criteria apply—and incoming traffic is untagged so it has no 802.1p value—the traffic is assigned 802.1p value 0 and forwarded at normal priority.

The egress marks are closely tied to the traffic's egress priority queue; however, traffic in the same queue could have different DSCP. The rules briefly summarized are:

- DSCP—IP traffic (tagged or untagged) always includes a DSCP, which might be 0. If the policy or interface setting used to classify the traffic specified a DSCP, the traffic uses that DSCP. If that policy or interface setting specified an 802.1p value, the switch maintains the incoming DSCP. The exception is that an ingress port set to QoS trust none can strip incoming marks.

- 802.1p value—As long as the traffic is tagged, the switch includes an 802.1p value in the outgoing frame. This value corresponds to the egress priority queue, which the switch has determined based on the applied 802.1p value or the 802.1p value mapped to the applied DSCP. Table 15-5 lists the default mappings. Untagged traffic, of course, cannot carry an 802.1p value.Review

Table 15-5 Mapping 802.1p values to configured queues with default traffic template

| 802.1p value | 8 configured queues | 4 configured queues | 2 configured queues |
|---|---|---|---|
| 1 | 1 | 1 | 1 |
| 2 | 2 | 1 | 1 |
| 0 | 3 | 2 | 1 |
| 3 | 4 | 2 | 1 |
| 4 | 5 | 3 | 2 |
| 5 | 6 | 3 | 2 |
| 6 | 7 | 4 | 2 |
| 7 | 8 | 4 | 2 |

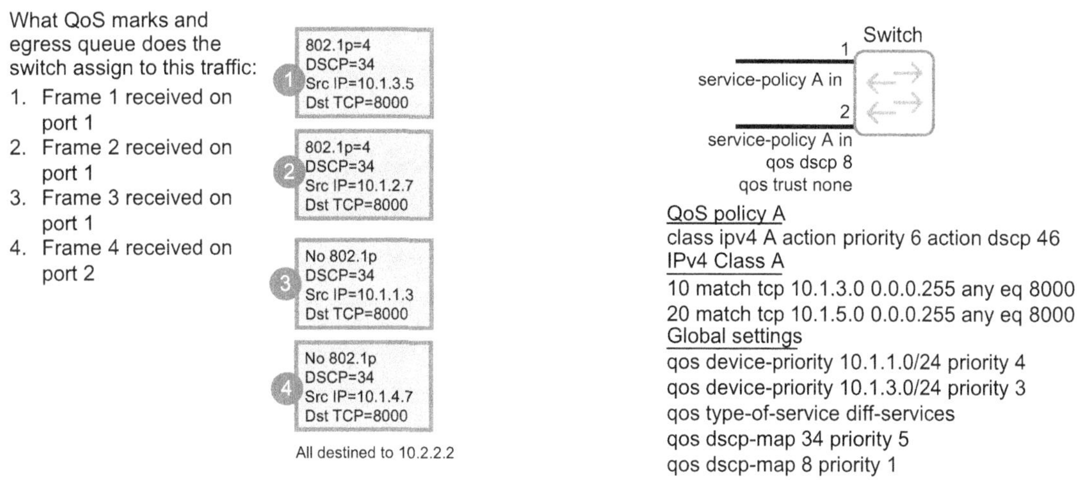


Figure 15-24 Review

You will now review how class-based QoS policies, global QoS policies, and incoming QoS values interact. Refer to Figure 15-24 as you consider a simple scenario.

An AOS-Switch has the following settings:

```
interface 1
 service-policy A in
 exit
interface 2
 service-policy A in
 qos dscp 8
 qos trust none
 exit
class ipv4 A
 10 match tcp 10.1.3.0 0.0.0.255 0.0.0.0 255.255.255.255 eq 8000
 20 match tcp 10.1.5.0 0.0.0.255 0.0.0.0 255.255.255.255 eq 8000
 exit
policy qos A
 10 class ipv4 A action priority 6 action dscp 46
 exit
qos device-priority 10.1.1.0/24 priority 4
qos device-priority 10.1.3.0/24 priority 3
qos type-of-service diff-services
qos dscp-map 34 priority 5
qos dscp-map 8 priority 1
vlan 1
 name DEFAULT VLAN
 no untagged 2
 untagged 1
 exit
```

```
vlan 2
 name VLAN2
 tagged 1
 exit
vlan 3
 name VLAN3
 tagged 1
 exit
vlan 4
 name VLAN4
 untagged 2
 exit
```

Consider four frames:

- Frame 1:
  - Includes 802.1Q tag (VLAN 3)
  - 802.1p = 4
  - DSCP = 34
  - Source IP address = 10.1.3.5
  - Destination TCP port = 8000
- Frame 2:
  - Includes 802.1Q tag (VLAN 2)
  - 802.1p = 4
  - DSCP = 34
  - Source IP address = 10.1.2.7
  - Destination TCP port = 8000
- Frame 3:
  - Does not include a 802.1Q tag
  - DSCP = 34
  - Source IP address = 10.1.1.3
  - Destination TCP port = 8000

- Frame 4:
  - Does not include a 802.1Q tag
  - DSCP = 34
  - Source IP address = 10.1.4.7
  - Destination TCP port = 8000

---

**Note**

This configuration and the QoS values in the incoming frames are not necessarily typical for a production QoS configuration. Instead, they are designed to ensure that you understand all of the principles covered in this chapter.

---

Based on this information, answer the following questions (assume that the frame is in the correct VLAN and is accepted):

1. Frame 1 arrives on port 1. To which priority queue does the switch assign it? What QoS marks does the outgoing traffic include (assume that the traffic is transmitted with a tag)?
2. Frame 2 arrives on port 1. To which priority queue does the switch assign it? What QoS marks does the outgoing traffic include (assume that the traffic is transmitted with a tag)?
3. Frame 3 arrives on port 1. To which priority queue does the switch assign it? What QoS marks does the outgoing traffic include (assume that the traffic is transmitted with a tag)?
4. Frame 4 arrives on port 2. To which priority queue does the switch assign it? What QoS marks does the outgoing traffic include (assume that the traffic is transmitted with a tag)?

## Rate limiting

Classifying and prioritizing critical and time-sensitive traffic helps to ensure a better experience for your users. Another important aspect of improving the network's performance is reducing congestion. You can reduce congestion by rate limiting less important traffic, which you will now learn how to do.

- Prevent monopolizing of bandwidth by:
  - Less important or less trusted devices
  - Less important applications
- Mitigate effects of viruses, worms, or broadcasts storms
- Examples:
  - Limit guest traffic
  - Limit gaming traffic

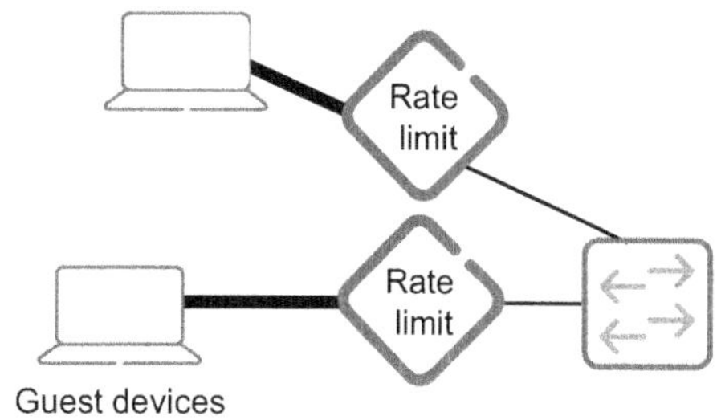


Figure 15-25 Rate limiting

Rate limiting allows the switch to control maximum rate for traffic sent or received on a port (see Figure 15-25). Rate limits can apply to all packets through a port (port-based) or to packets in a specified traffic class (class-based).

You can implement rate limiting to prevent less important users and applications from monopolizing bandwidth. Guest devices are a prime example of devices that you might want to rate limit, both because guest traffic is often less mission-critical and because guest users are less trusted. Rate limits can also help you to mitigate the effects of viruses, worms, or broadcast storms. (You will look at connection-rate throttling, an AOS-Switch technology for dynamically throttling down suspicious traffic in *Chapter 16: Additional Security Features.*)

Sometimes you might identify applications that the company tolerates enough not to filter with ACLs, but does not want to monopolize bandwidth. For example, universities might want to rate limit gaming traffic in the library computer lab.

## Port-based rate limiting

Port-based rate limiting allows network administrators to apply rate limits to traffic inbound or outbound on a port. Aruba typically recommends configuring rate limiting only on edge ports so that you do not interfere with switches' ability to forward important network traffic.

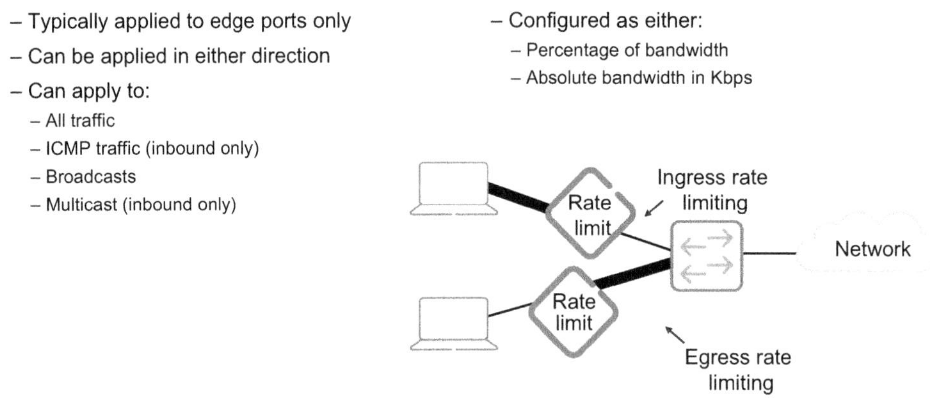


Figure 15-26 Port-based rate limiting

As Figure 15-26 shows, an ingress rate limit drops traffic incoming on the port that exceeds the specified limit. An egress rate limit causes the port to drop traffic destined to the connected device if forwarding that traffic would cause the port to exceed the configured limit. Often, traffic flows more heavily from server-to-client. Therefore, creating an egress rate limit on an endpoint's port can prevent that endpoint from demanding too much traffic and indirectly from consuming too much of the bandwidth on its switch's uplink.

You can set either limit as a percentage of the total bandwidth on the port or as an absolute value in Kbps.

## Rate limit all traffic

When you configure the rate limit, you can choose to apply the traffic to all packets sent or received on the port. Enter this command:

```
Switch(config)# interface <port_ID_list> rate-limit all <in|out> {kbps
  <kbps> | percent <0-100>}
```

It is not recommended that you set a rate limit of zero or under 13 Kbps. If you want to block traffic entirely, use an ACL.

## Rate limit ICMP traffic

The AOS-Switches allow you to apply limits specifically for ICMP traffic. Malware such as viruses and worms might start sending a large amount of ICMP traffic. However, users often have legitimate reasons to occasionally send a ping. Network administrators might need to use ICMP for troubleshooting. An ICMP rate limit on an edge port can allow the legitimate use while also protecting the network from the malware. A typical ICMP limit for a 1GbE (or even 10GbE) edge port is between

100 and 10,000 Kbps (10 Mbps), depending on how aggressively you want to limit. If the port is operating at 10 or 100 Mbps, set the limit between 1 and 5 percent.

Use this command to configure the limit, which applies to inbound traffic:

```
Switch(config)# interface <port_ID_list> rate-limit icmp [ip-all | ipv4
  | ipv6] {kbps <kbps> | percent <0-100>}
```

Enter **ipv4** or **ipv6** to apply the ICMP rate just to ICMP messages of that version; enter **ip**-all to apply the rate limit to both versions. If you do not specify one of these options, the rate limit automatically applies just to IPv4. You can only specify one type of ICMP rate limit on an interface; if you enter a second command to limit a different type, that rate limit writes over the previous one.

## Rate limit broadcast and multicast traffic

You might not care about limiting a device's traffic, but do want to mitigate the effects of a broadcast or multicast storm. You can enter this command to limit broadcast or multicast traffic incoming on a port:

```
Switch(config)# interface <port_ID_list> rate-limit <bcast | mcast> in
    {kbps <kbps> | percent <0-100>}
```

You can also apply an egress broadcast rate limit, which is set as a percentage of traffic on the port:

```
Switch(config)# interface <port_ID_list> broadcast-limit <0-99>
```

Setting 0 disables egress broadcast limiting.

As always, you should scope your network's requirements before applying multicast and broadcast limits. Some desired applications rely heavily on multicast and broadcasts. Determine the typical percentage of bandwidth multicast and broadcast typically requires and set the limit above that. Again, generally avoid applying rate limits to ports that connect to other infrastructure devices. A multicast rate limit, for example, could interfere with important routing protocols.

## Combining rate limits

You can apply multiple types of rate limits to a port. For example, you can apply both an ingress and an egress rate limit on all traffic. You could also apply an inbound limit on ICMP. You should understand, though, that combining a rate limit that applies to all traffic with a rate limit on specific type of traffic might lead to the switch dropping the specific type of traffic before it reaches its configured limit. For example, a port has an ingress rate limit of 100 Mbps and an ICMP rate limit of 10 Mbps. The device is sending only 8 Mbps of ICMP traffic, but 100 Mbps of other traffic. Some ICMP packets could be dropped.

You can apply both an inbound broadcast and a multicast rate limit together. However, you cannot apply either of these types of rate limits at the same time as an inbound rate limit on all traffic.

You should check the documentation for your switch's precise capabilities.

**Note**

You cannot set any of these rate limits on a link aggregation (trunk interface). If you must apply a rate limit to a link aggregation, instead apply the individual rate limits to each interface in the trunk.

## Egress per-queue rate limiting

Sometimes you need more flexibility in applying rate limiting to a port. For example, a port connects to a client that receives traffic with normal priority and also critical traffic assigned to queue 6. You want to rate limit the egress traffic, but rate limiting does not take priority into account when it drops traffic. The port is just as likely to drop the high priority traffic as the normal traffic, interfering with the critical application.

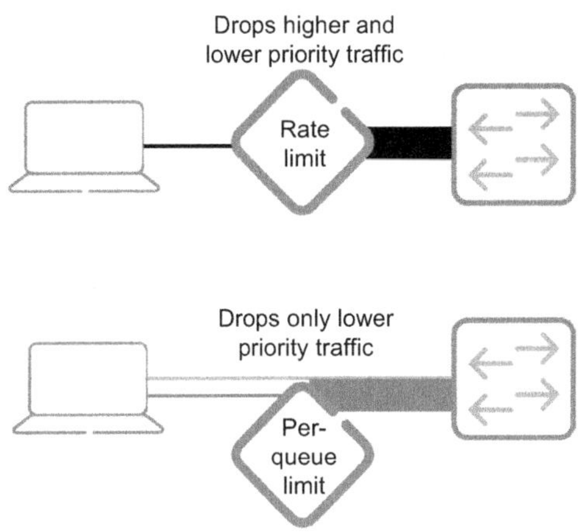


Figure 15-27 Egress per-queue rate limiting

Some AOS-Switches support egress queue-based rate limiting. As Figure 15-27 shows, you can then apply the desired rate limit to traffic in lower priority queues while allowing the higher priority traffic to flow without restriction. (The more basic Layer 2 switches do not support this feature; check your switch documentation.)

Enter this command to configure the egress rate limit on a queue:

```
Switch(config)# interface <port_ID_list> rate-limit queues out percent
  <0-100> <0-100> <0-100> <0-100> <0-100> <0-100> <0-100> <0-100>
```

In this command, you must specify the rate limit for each priority queue as a percentage. The first percentage that you enter applies to queue 1, the second to queue 2, and so on to queue 8 (the highest priority queue). If you do not want to rate limit a specific priority queue, set the percentage to 100. The total percentage for all of the queue's rate limits can exceed 100 percent because these are limits—not guarantees. (Without a limit, every priority queue has a "limit" of 100 percent.) Of course, if all priority queues are trying to use 100 percent of the bandwidth, the switch will drop some of the traffic due to congestion. The rate limit that you set for each queue must equal or exceed the GMB for that queue on that interface.

You are allowed to combine an egress per-queue rate limit with an egress rate limit that applies to all traffic. However, you should understand that one rate limit might drop traffic while the other rate limit would otherwise allow the traffic to keep flowing. For example, you apply a 50,000 Kbps egress limit on all traffic and a 30,000 Kbps egress limit on queue 3. The switch will drop traffic in queue 3 that exceeds 30,000 Kbps even if the port has not exceeded the 50,000 Kbps limit. Similarly, if the port exceeds the global limit, but not the per-queue limit, the port might randomly select traffic in that queue for dropping.

**Note**

Unlink other rate limits, you must apply egress per-queue rate limits to a link aggregation (trunk interface) rather than the individual interfaces within the link aggregation. However, the limit applies separately to each interface within the link aggregation.

## Class-based rate limiting

When you want to limit certain undesired types of traffic more granularly, you should use class-based rate limiting. For example, you might want to limit traffic destined to TCP and UDP ports 1119, which is associated with gaming, while leaving other traffic to flow without restriction.

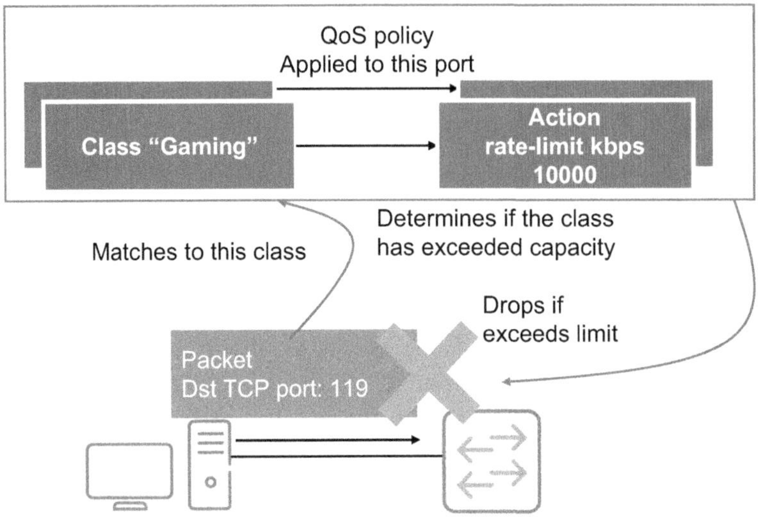


Figure 15-28 Class-based rate limiting

Follow these steps to create a QoS policy that functions like the one shown in Figure 15-28:

1. Create one or more traffic classes that select the traffic to which you want to apply the rate limit.
   a. Create the traffic class.

   ```
   Switch(config)# class <ipv4| ipv6 | mac> <classname>
   ```

   b. Use **match** and **ignore** commands to select traffic for the class. You can match (or ignore) traffic based on a variety of IP or MAC header fields. Refer back to the earlier section on traffic classes.
2. Create a QoS policy. Enter:

   ```
   Switch(config)# policy qos <policy-name>
   ```

3. Enter one or more class action commands from the policy configuration context. For the action select rate limit. Note that for classifier-based rate limiting, you always set the limit in Kbps, rather than as a percentage. It is recommended that you set the limit at least over 13 Kbps. If you want, you can combine the rate limit with setting a priority for the traffic.

```
Switch(policy-qos)# [seq-number] class <ipv4| ipv6 | mac>
<classname> action rate-limit kbps <kbps> [action priority <0-7>]
[action dscp <codepoint>]
```

4. Apply the QoS policy to a physical interface, including a trunk interface (link aggregation), or to a VLAN. If the policy only includes rate limit actions, you can apply the policy inbound or outbound, creating an ingress or egress rate limit. However, if any of the actions set a QoS mark, you can only apply the policy inbound.

```
Switch(config)# interface <port_ID_list> service-policy <policy-
   name> <in | out>
```

```
Switch(config)# vlan <VLAN ID> service-policy <policy-name> <in | out>
```

If an interface is part of a link aggregation, you must apply the QoS policy to the link aggregation and not the individual interface. The switch controls the bandwidth on individual ports such that the total bandwidth used on the link aggregation does not exceed the configured limit. If the link aggregation spans multiple modules or port banks controlled by different ASICs, keep in mind that the rate limit might not apply exactly as you expect. The switch calculates a rate limit on a per-module or per-port bank basis.

When you apply the policy to a VLAN, the rate limit restricts the total amount of traffic that is received untagged or tagged in that VLAN (inbound limit) or forwarded out that VLAN (outbound limit). Again, the switch calculates the rate limit on a per-module or per-port bank basis. The switch uses the configured limit to determine the correct limit to apply to interfaces that carry that VLAN, again applying the limits on a per-ASIC basis. If the VLAN spans multiple modules or port banks controlled by different ASICs, the rate limit might not apply exactly as you expect.

You have learned about many types of rate limits. Table 15-6 presents which rate limits can be applied to a port at the same time. An X indicates that the limits can be applied together; no X means that only one of the limits can be applied. If you attempt to assign a QoS policy with a rate limit action to a VLAN with any ports that have an incompatible rate limit, the policy will fail to apply.

Table 15-6 Rate limit interoperation

| | All out | Broadcast out | Queue out | Class-based out | All in | ICMP (in) | Broadcast in | Multicast in | Class-based in |
|---|---|---|---|---|---|---|---|---|---|
| **All out** | N/A | X | X | X | X | X | X | X | X |
| **Broadcast out** | X | N/A | X | X | X | X | X | X | X |
| **Queue out** | X | X | N/A | X | X | X | X | X | X |
| **Class-based out** | X | X | X | N/A | X | | X | X | X |
| **All in** | X | X | X | X | N/A | X | | | X |
| **ICMP (in)** | X | X | X | | X | N/A | X | X | |
| **Broadcast in** | X | X | X | X | | X | N/A | X | X |
| **Multicast in** | X | X | | | | X | X | N/A | X |
| **Class-based in** | X | X | X | X | X | | X | X | N/A |

## User-based rate limits

As you learned earlier in this study guide, the switch can receive dynamic settings from a RADIUS server. These HPE vendor-specific attributes (vendor ID 11) can set the ingress or egress rate limit for users:

- HPE-Bandwidth-Max-Egress(46) = ingress rate limit
- HPE-RATE-LIMIT(48) = egress rate limit

The RADIUS server must send the rate limit in Kbps; percentage is not allowed. The rate limit should be set in even increments. If the limit is more specific, the switch rounds the rate limit to the nearest increment. Valid increments depend on the total value for the rate limit. Lower rate limits are more granular.

The switch applies ingress rate limits on a per-user basis. If a port supports multiple users, each user has their own rate limit. Keep in mind that the rate limit is not a guaranteed and is limited by the total bandwidth on the port. For example, if five users on a 1 GbE port each have an ingress rate limit of 300,000 Kbps, the users will not all be able to reach their maximum at the same time. The maximum available bandwidth can be further limited by static rate limits. If you do not want this behavior, avoid setting static rate limits on ports that might receive dynamic limits.

The switch applies egress rate limits on a per-port basis. If a port supports multiple users, the limit applied during the last authentication overrides earlier settings, including dynamic and static ones.

Table 15-7 presents the increments for user-based rate limits.

Table 15-7 Increments for user-based rate limits

| Limit | Increment | Example |
|---|---|---|
| 1-10,999,999 bps<br>1-10,999 Kbps<br>up to 10.999 Mbps | 100 Kbps | 5,250 Kbps = 5,200 Kbps |
| 11,000,000-100,999,999 bps<br>11,000-100,999 Kbps<br>11-100.999 Mbps | 1 Mbps | 50,250 Kbps = 50,000 Kbps |
| 101,000,000-999,999,999 bps<br>101,000-999,999 Kbps<br>101 Mbps to 999.999 Mbps | 10 Mbps | 234,000 = 230,000 Kbps |
| 1,000,000,000-10,000,000,000 bps<br>1,000,000-10,000,000 Kbps<br>(1 Gbps to 10 Gbps) | 100 Mbps | 1,250,000 Kbps = 1,200,000 Kbps |

## LLDP-MED

You have learned how to set up a switch port to connect to a VoIP phone or a VoIP phone and computer. You have learned that you should typically place VoIP phones in their own VLAN and configure a high priority for that VLAN. You have also learned how to set up the port to support the voice VLAN as a tagged VLAN and the user or data VLAN as an untagged VLAN.

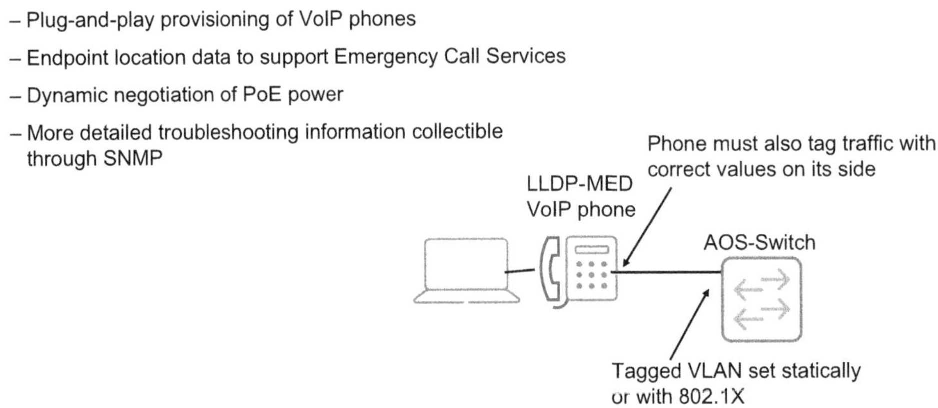


Figure 15-29 LLDP-MED

However, setting up the switch port to receive the tagged traffic is not enough. As Figure 15-29 shows, the phone also needs to know the VLAN ID that it is supposed to include in the tag. Administrators can program this individually on each phone, but doing so takes time. LLDP-MED enables the switch to dynamically inform a connecting phone of the correct VLAN ID, as well as the correct 802.1p and DSCP settings. In this way, LLDP-MED provides automatic, plug-and-play provisioning for LLDP-MED capable VoIP phones.

The switch can also communicate other information to the phone, including its physical location. This information can help to support Emergency Call Services (ECS).

When phones receive Power over Ethernet (PoE) from the switch, LLDP-MED can help the switch to allocate and deliver exactly the power that the phone needs.

LLDP-MED can also help in tracking and troubleshooting VoIP phones through a central management platform. SNMP servers can read detailed VoIP endpoint data inventory, PoE status, and information to help troubleshoot the IP telephony network and call quality issues.

### Review interoperation with authentication

You have learned that you can use authentication to dynamically set the VLAN assignment for a VoIP phone when the phone connects. This sets the VLAN automatically on the *switch* side. LLDP-MED is still required to make the configuration automatic on the *VoIP phone's* side.

You can certainly use 802.1X with LLDP-MED, though. Simply set up 802.1X on the port as you learned how to do in *Chapter 10: 802.1X Authentication*. Make sure that IP phones support 802.1X and that the RADIUS server has policies and accounts for authenticating them. If you want the server to send the tagged VLAN assignment dynamically, make sure that it has the proper policies for doing so (again see *Chapter 10: 802.1X Authentication*).

For this scenario, you probably want the computer and IP phone to authenticate separately so that an unauthorized user cannot piggyback on the IP phone's session. Make sure to set the 802.1X client-limit to two so that the port operates in user-mode and authenticates each device separately.

If you want to enforce 802.1X but the IP phones do not support it, combine 802.1X for users and MAC-Auth for IP phones as you learned how to do in *Chapter11: MAC Authentication*.

## Enabling LLDP-MED

To support LLDP-MED, an AOS-Switch must have LLDP enabled globally, which it is by default. If you need to re-enable LLDP, enter this command:

```
Switch(config)# lldp run
```

The switch port that connects to the VoIP phone must also be enabled to send and receive LLDP messages. Again, this support is enabled by default. If necessary, you can re-enable it with this command:

```
Switch(config)# lldp admin-status <port ID list> tx_rx
```

You should check whether the switch port is transmitting the LLDP-MED TLVs with this command:

```
Switch# show lldp config <interface ID list>
```

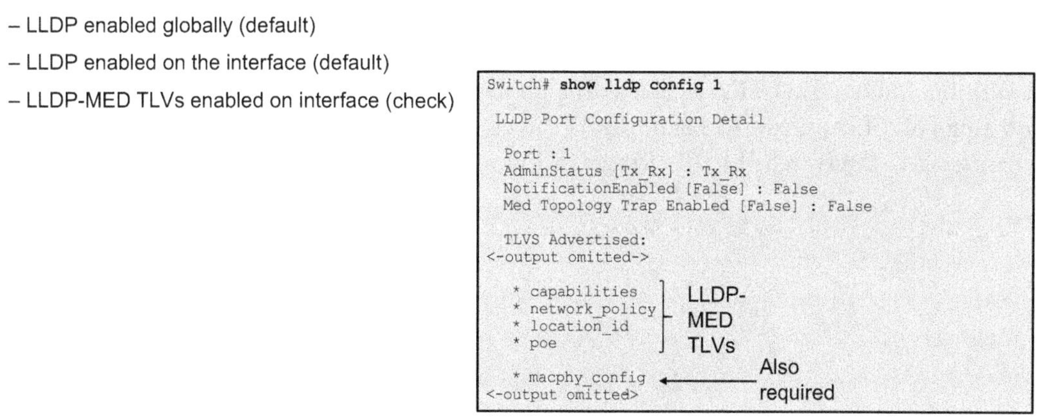


Figure 15-30 Enabling LLDP-MED

Figure 15-30 shows the four LLDP-MED TLVs that you should look for:

- capabilities

  The capabilities TLV enable the switch to detect LLDP-MED capable endpoints, their class, and their capabilities.

- network_policy

  The switch communicates the proper VLAN ID and QoS settings in this TLV.

- location_ID

  The switch communicates the physical location in this TLV.

- poe

  The switch advertises its capabilities as a power sourcing equipment (PSE). The VoIP phone can also use this TLV to request a specific amount of power after it first powers up or dynamically throughout the connection. Note that PoE+ defines its own LLDP TLV for negotiating the power (a dot3 TLV called poeplus_config), and the phone might use this TLV instead. In either case, the switch will allocate the requested amount of power and reserve it for this port even if the phone is not drawing the full power at the moment.

In addition to the four LLDP-MED TLVs, LLDP-MED also requires the macphy_config TLV to be enabled.

If you need to enable any of these TLVs, use these commands:

```
Switch(config)# lldp config <port ID list> medTlvEnable <capabilities |
   network_policy | location_id | poe>
Switch(config)# lldp config <port ID list> dot3TlvEnable macphy_config
```

## Configuring information advertised in the LLDP-MED TLVs

Now assume that a phone that also supports LLDP-MED boots up and connects to an AOS-Switch port with the LLDP-MED TLVs enabled. The phone completes a handshake with the switch port, negotiating PoE (if required). As Figure 15-31 shows, the AOS-Switch and the phone also exchange LLDP messages. The switch's LLDP message includes many TLVs.

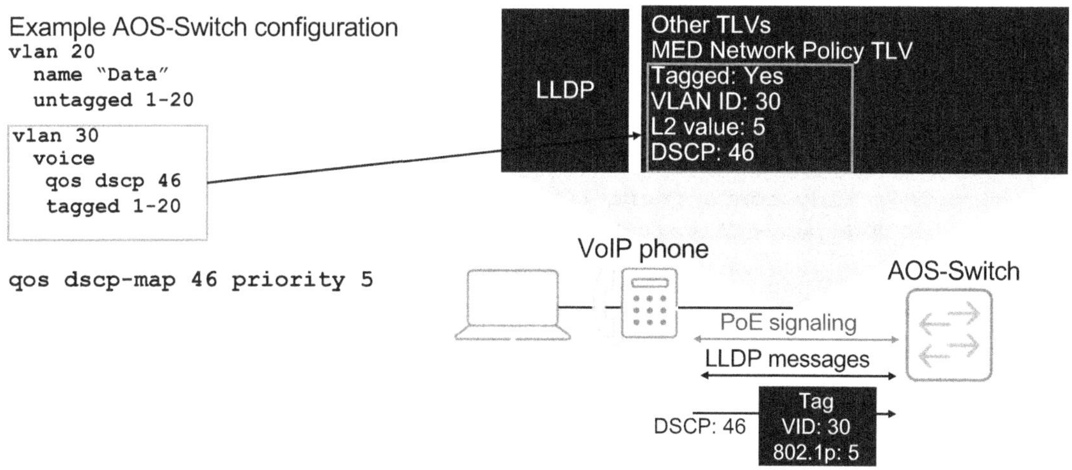


Figure 15-31 Configuring information advertised in the LLDP-MED TLVs

The network_policy TLV and the location_id TLV require preconfiguration to ensure that the switch advertises the correct information.

## network_policy TLV

The switch automatically takes the information for the network_policy TLV from the VLAN on the port that is defined as the voice VLAN. For example, VoIP phones belong in VLAN 30.

This VLAN has this configuration on the switch:

```
vlan 30
   voice
   qos dscp 46
   tagged 1-20
```

The "voice" setting tells the switch to advertise the settings associated with this VLAN in the network_policy TLV. In the example shown in Figure 15-31, the TLV tells the phone to send tagged traffic in VLAN 30, to set the DSCP to 46, and to set the 802.1p value to 5.

The RFC-defined DSCP typical for voice is EF or 46. Depending on the switch software, the default DSCP map for 46 might be 802.1p value 7 or 802.1p value 5. It is not recommended to set the priority lower than 5. You could alternatively set an 802.1p value on the VLAN (**qos priority** command), in which case the network_policy TLV would not specify a DSCP.

In the example shown in Figure 15-31, the phone ports are tagged for the voice VLAN, which is typical for today's IP phones. However, you could assign the voice VLAN as the untagged port if you have legacy phones that send untagged traffic. Remember that if a computer connects through the phone, you should set the port's untagged VLAN to the appropriate user or data VLAN.

### location_id TLV

It is best practice to populate the location_id TLV for each switch port that might connect to a VoIP phone with the correct location information. For example, the command for specifying the civic address of a media endpoint such as a phone is:

```
Switch(config)# lldp config <port ID> medPortLocation civic-addr <country
   code> 2 <CA type> <CA value> [<CA type> <CA value>]
```

A CA type specifies the type of location being indicated, such as three for a city. You can specify many CA types and values in order to program the city, street, address, and building, for example. For a list of CA types, see your switch *Management and Configuration Guide*.

You can alternatively specify an Emergency Line Identification Number (ELIN), which is used in North America, if such numbers have been assigned to your phones:

```
Switch(config)# lldp config <port ID> medPortLocation elin-addr <octet>
```

## Summary

This chapter has presented the need for switches to handle each traffic flow appropriately, depending on the network application, the traffic's business importance, and other, minutely adjustable, criteria. You can now configure AOS-Switches to prioritize incoming traffic and assign it to the appropriate queue for transmission. And you can mark outgoing traffic with the appropriate QoS value in order to implement a consistent QoS strategy throughout the network.

You can also implement rate limiting.

Finally, you can use the voice VLAN and LLDP-MED to provision the VoIP phone with the correct priority settings.

## Learning check

1. A switch port is tagged for several VLANs. How can an administrator force the switch to forward all traffic that arrives on the port in the normal queue regardless of incoming 802.1p and DSCP values?
   a. Disable type of service.
   b. Delete all DSCP maps.
   c. Set the port priority to 0.
   d. Set the QoS trust on the port to none.

2. Assume that all interfaces use the default setting for QoS trust. What are the two circumstances in which the switch uses traffic's 802.1p value to prioritize the traffic rather than its DSCP? (Select two.)
   a. When the 802.1p value is 7
   b. When no DCSP map exists for that DSCP
   c. When type of service is disabled
   d. When GMB is enabled
   e. When the traffic is sent by an LLDP-MED capable VoIP phone
3. How can class-based rate limiting reduce congestion?
   a. It limits the traffic on ports based on the type of device that LLDP discovers on the port.
   b. It lowers the priority of certain types of traffic inbound or outbound on a port.
   c. It allocates the specified percentage of the port's service cycle to each queue.
   d. It limits the bandwidth for specific types of traffic inbound or outbound on a port.
4. An AOS-Switch connects to an LLDP-MED capable VoIP phone that supports 802.1Q. The switch has LLDP-MED enabled on the port. How can administrators configure the switch to tell the phones to send traffic marked with 802.1p value 5?
   a. Configure the phones' VLAN as a voice VLAN and set the priority on that VLAN.
   b. Configure the phones' VLAN as a voice VLAN and set the priority in the LLDP settings.
   c. Create a traffic class that selects LLDP-MED traffic and use a QoS policy to assign the priority to that class.
   d. Create a traffic class that selects traffic to the TCP port used by the phones and use a QoS policy to assign the priority to that class.

For the next questions in this learning check, refer to Figure 15-32.

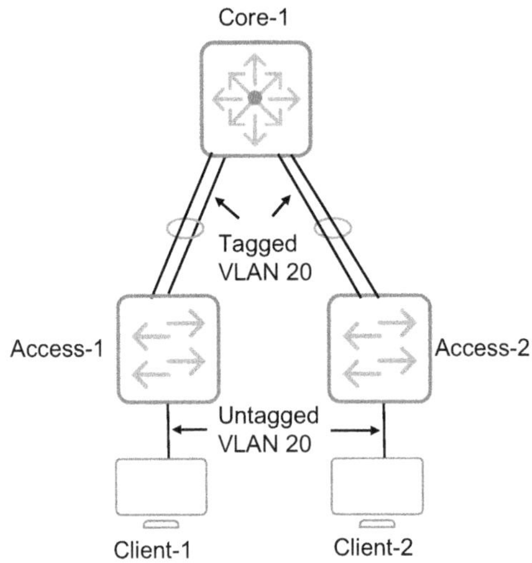


Figure 15-32 Exhibit for learning checks

5. The AOS-Switches shown in Figure 15-32 are operating at default settings for QoS. A voice application on Client-1 is sending traffic to Client-2 with DSCP 46; however, the QoS for the application is poor. Will running a packet capture at the destination and checking for a DSCP verify that the network has granted the traffic high priority? How can you check the priority given to the traffic?
6. In the scenario in the previous question, what should the administrator change to improve the QoS for the application?
7. The network administrator has set the type of service to DiffServ on Access-1 and Access-2 in Figure 15-32, but not on Core-1. Core-1 uses the default QoS trust on all ports. A voice application on Client-1 sends traffic with DSCP 46. Will the core switch grant this traffic high priority or normal priority?
8. An AOS-Switch has the type of service set to DiffServ. The network administrator sets the QoS trust to none on the port connected to a client. A voice application on the client sends traffic with DSCP 46. Will the switch grant this traffic high priority or normal priority?
9. Discuss the differences between setting a port priority on the client interface and applying a QoS policy to the interface.

# Answers

## Review

1. Frame 1 arrives on port 1. To which priority queue does the switch assign it? What QoS marks does the outgoing traffic include (assume that the traffic is transmitted with a tag)?

   The traffic is forwarded in queue 7 (second highest) with 802.1p value 6 and DSCP 46.

   The traffic is selected by the service policy, which takes precedence over other settings. The switch assigns the traffic the DSCP and 802.1p value specified in the matched action within the policy.

2. Frame 2 arrives on port 1. To which priority queue does the switch assign it? What QoS marks does the outgoing traffic include (assume that the traffic is transmitted with a tag)?

   The traffic is forwarded in queue 6 (third highest) with 802.1p value 5 and DSCP 34.

   This traffic does not match the service policy applied to the interface. It also does not match any of the global QoS policies except that it has a DSCP map for its DSCP. The switch is using Diff-Serv for the type of service, and the port is using the default QoS trust setting. Therefore, the switch uses the DSCP map to set the 802.1p value and prioritize the traffic.

3. Frame 3 arrives on port 1. To which priority queue does the switch assign it? What QoS marks does the outgoing traffic include (assume that the traffic is transmitted with a tag)?

   The traffic is forwarded in queue 5 (fourth highest) with 802.1p value 4 and DSCP 34.

   This packet does not match the service policy applied to the interface, but it does match a global policy for device priority, which sets the 802.1p value to 4. This policy overrides the DSCP map, which would set the 802.1p value to 5. However, the switch does retain the DSCP.

4. Frame 4 arrives on port 2. To which priority queue does the switch assign it? What QoS marks does the outgoing traffic include (assume that the traffic is transmitted with a tag)?

   The traffic is forwarded in queue 1 (lowest) with 802.1p value 1 and DSCP 8.

   This traffic does not match the service policy applied to the interface. It also does not match any of the global QoS policies except that it has a DSCP map for its DSCP. However, QoS trust is disabled on the port, so the switch ignores this DSCP and applies the port DSCP of 8. This DSCP maps to priority 1, so the switch forwards the traffic in the lowest priority queue.

## Learning check

1. A switch port is tagged for several VLANs. How can an administrator force the switch to forward all traffic that arrives on the port in the normal queue regardless of incoming 802.1p and DSCP values?
   a. Disable type of service.
   b. Delete all DSCP maps.
   c. Set the port priority to 0.
   **d. Set the QoS trust on the port to none.**
2. Assume that all interfaces use the default setting for QoS trust. What are the two circumstances in which the switch uses traffic's 802.1p value to prioritize the traffic rather than its DSCP? (Select two.)
   a. When the 802.1p value is 7
   **b. When no DCSP map exists for that DSCP**
   **c. When type of service is disabled**
   d. When GMB is enabled
   e. When the traffic is sent by an LLDP-MED capable VoIP phone
3. How can class-based rate limiting reduce congestion?
   a. It limits the traffic on ports based on the type of device that LLDP discovers on the port.
   b. It lowers the priority of certain types of traffic inbound or outbound on a port.
   c. It allocates the specified percentage of the port's service cycle to each queue.
   **d. It limits the bandwidth for specific types of traffic inbound or outbound on a port.**
4. An AOS-Switch connects to an LLDP-MED capable VoIP phone that supports 802.1Q. The switch has LLDP-MED enabled on the port. How can administrators configure the switch to tell the phones to send traffic marked with 802.1p value 5?
   **a. Configure the phones' VLAN as a voice VLAN and set the priority on that VLAN.**
   b. Configure the phones' VLAN as a voice VLAN and set the priority in the LLDP settings.
   c. Create a traffic class that selects LLDP-MED traffic and use a QoS policy to assign the priority to that class.
   d. Create a traffic class that selects traffic to the TCP port used by the phones and use a QoS policy to assign the priority to that class.

5. The AOS-Switches shown in Figure 15-32 are operating at default settings for QoS. A voice application on Client-1 is sending traffic to Client-2 with DSCP 46; however, the QoS for the application is poor. Will running a packet capture at the destination and checking for a DSCP verify that the network has granted the traffic high priority? How can you check the priority given to the traffic?

   Simply checking that the traffic has the proper DSCP at the destination does not always give you the best information about whether the traffic is truly being prioritized. Switches often retain DSCP even when they do not honor them. Checking the actual egress queues that the switch is using gives you the best information. You can check this queue on each switch in the path by clearing statistics, running the applications, and then entering the **show interface queue <*interface port list*>** command. (Remember to check the outbound port, not the port on which the switch is receiving the traffic to be prioritized.)

6. In the scenario in the previous question, what should the administrator change to improve the QoS for the application?

   The switches are acting at their default settings, which means that they do not honor the DSCP sent by the client. You should configure at least the access switches to trust DSCP, either globally (by setting type of service to DiffServ) or on the clients' interfaces (by setting the QoS trust to DSCP). You should also verify that the switches have a DSCP map for DSCP 46 with an appropriate 802.1p value (5, 6, or 7). Then the access switches will use the DSCP 46 to prioritize the traffic between the clients.

7. The network administrator has set the type of service to DiffServ on Access-1 and Access-2 in Figure 15-32, but not on Core-1. Core-1 uses the default QoS trust on all ports. A voice application on Client-1 sends traffic with DSCP 46. Will the core switch grant this traffic high priority or normal priority

   Core-1 *does* grant this traffic high priority. This is because, when the access switches use the DSCP to prioritize the traffic, the switches automatically assign outgoing tagged traffic the 802.1p value in that DSCP's map. The access and core switches use a tagged VLAN to forward traffic to each other. The core switch, by default, trusts 802.1p values received on all ports, so it prioritizes the traffic.

8. An AOS-Switch has the type of service set to DiffServ. The network administrator sets the QoS trust to none on the port connected to a client. A voice application on the client sends traffic with DSCP 46. Will the switch grant this traffic high priority or normal priority?

   The switch will *not* grant this traffic high priority. The none setting for QoS trust causes the switch to set the DSCP value to 0 and not use it to prioritize the traffic.

9. Discuss the differences between setting a port priority on the client interface and applying a QoS policy to the interface.

   A port priority affects all of the traffic on the interface. A QoS policy gives you more control. You can select traffic with specific criteria in the MAC or IP header and prioritize just that traffic. For example, you could select traffic based on its destination, its TCP or UDP destination ports, or a combination of these criteria. A QoS policy also allows you to set rate limits on specific traffic.

# 16 Additional Security Features

EXAM OBJECTIVES

- ✓ Implement Dynamic Host Configuration Protocol (DHCP) snooping and Address Resolution Protocol (ARP) protection to defend networks against DHCP exploits, ARP snooping, and ARP poisoning attacks
- ✓ Implement the proper port security measures for various use cases
- ✓ Explain how MAC lockdown differs from port security and use the proper solution for each use case
- ✓ Implement connection rate filtering (also called Virus Throttling) to provide a first layer of protection against viruses and worms

## Assumed knowledge

Before reading this chapter, you should have a basic understanding of:

- DHCP
- ARP
- IP and MAC address
- Open Systems Interconnection (OSI) model
- Spanning Tree Protocol (STP)
- Multiple Spanning Tree Protocol (MSTP)
- Rapid Tree Spanning Protocol (RSTP)
- Link aggregation
- Virtual LANs (VLANs)
- Switching
- Static and dynamic routing

## Introduction

In this study guide, you have learned about several ways that attackers infiltrate or sabotage your network. This chapter outlines several additional attacks and explains how you can configure your AOS-Switches to protect your network against them. For example, you will learn about vulnerabilities that DHCP and ARP can introduce and the protections against these vulnerabilities that AOS-Switches provide. You will also learn about how AOS-Switch port security features protect against eavesdropping and unauthorized access, how its MAC lockdown feature can help to protect your network against MAC spoofing, and about how connection rate filtering can augment your intrusion detection and intrusion prevention systems to protect against viruses and worms.

## DHCP attacks

You will first learn how to use DHCP snooping to protect your network against DHCP attacks.

Because DHCP was designed to work in the trusted internal network, it does not provide authentication or access controls. A DHCP server has no way of verifying that the client requesting an address is a legitimate client on the network, and the DHCP client has no way of knowing if the DHCP server that offers it an address is a legitimate server. As a result, DHCP is vulnerable to attacks from both rogue clients and servers.

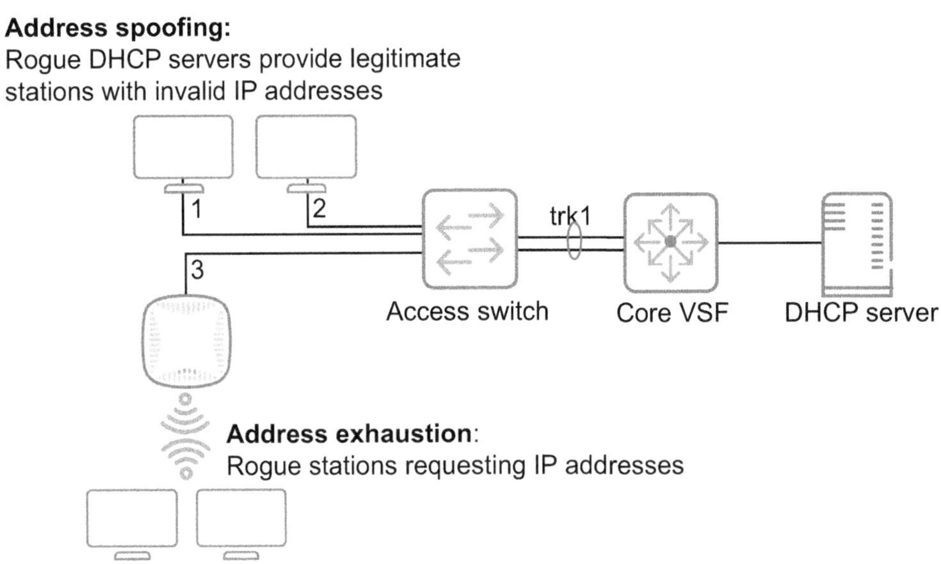


Figure 16-1 DHCP attacks

You need to protect your network from two types of common DHCP attacks (see Figure 16-1).

- Address spoofing—A rogue DHCP server on the network can assign invalid addresses to network devices. Without valid IP addresses and network gateway addresses, these devices are unable to connect to any other IP network devices, which prevents users from reaching the resources they need to do their jobs.
- Address exhaustion—An attacker can access the network and request IP addresses until the DHCP server's supply of available addresses is exhausted. This prevents legitimate hosts from receiving IP addresses and accessing the network.

Both of these attacks can disrupt network service and open the door to security breaches. For example, a rogue DHCP server might respond to a client's DHCP discover request with the rogue server's own IP address as the default gateway, setting up the client for a man-in-the-middle attack.

## Using DHCP snooping to protect against DHCP attacks

You should implement support for DHCP snooping to protect your network against address spoofing and address exhaustion attacks. Because, on its own, the straightforward DHCP process offers no security, your switch takes the role of a security guard, overseeing DHCP exchanges and ensuring that endpoints act as they should.

AOS-Switches support DHCPv4 and DHCPv6 snooping. You should configure both versions to block unintended or rogue DHCP server packets. However, because this study guide focuses on IPv6, this chapter covers DHCPv4 snooping.

---

**Note**

Most AOS-Switches support DHCP snooping. Check your switch documentation for up-to-date information.

---

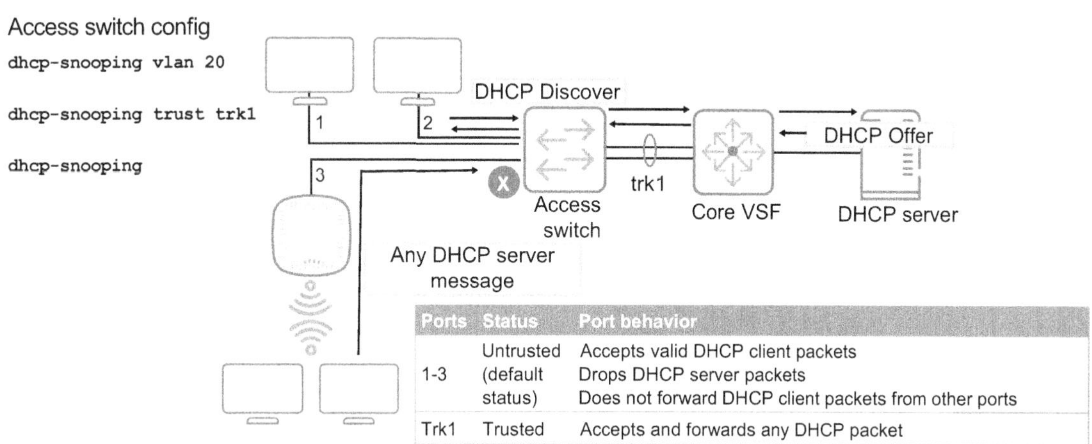


| Ports | Status | Port behavior |
|---|---|---|
| 1-3 | Untrusted (default status) | Accepts valid DHCP client packets<br>Drops DHCP server packets<br>Does not forward DHCP client packets from other ports |
| Trk1 | Trusted | Accepts and forwards any DHCP packet |

Figure 16-2 Using DHCP snooping to protect against DHCP attacks

## How DHCP snooping works

With DHCP snooping, the switch distinguishes between trusted and untrusted ports, as shown in Figure 16-2. Trusted ports connect to the network's own trusted devices, such as a DHCP server or, if the server is centralized, an upstream core or distribution layer switch. The switch allows DHCP packets to flow freely on these ports.

On untrusted ports, on the other hand, the switch filters DHCP packets and determines whether or not they are allowed.

For example, only DHCP servers should send Offer and Acknowledgement packets, so if the switch detects these types of packets on an untrusted port, it immediately discards them. On the untrusted ports, the switch only accepts DHCP client packets.

- Discover
- Request
- Decline
- Inform
- Release

The switch also verifies information in the DHCP clients' Discover and Request packets against the packet headers before allowing the packets onto the network. For example, the switch drops packets in which the source MAC address does not match the DHCP client MAC address—a sign of spoofing. In a few sections, you'll see how the switch treats untrusted packets with option 82—another potential sign of suspicious behavior.

Finally, although the switch accepts DHCP client packets on untrusted ports, it does not *forward* them on these ports. This behavior prevents other clients from hearing each other's DHCP traffic. Instead, the DHCP packets flow only on trusted ports toward the server. You must define a trusted port, not only so that the switch will accept DHCP server packets on that port, but also so that the switch will forward DHCP client packets on it.

Enabling DHCP snooping on a VLAN automatically makes all ports untrusted ports for DHCP packets in that VLAN. The port does *not* necessarily carry traffic in the DHCP snooping VLAN; it is still untrusted. In Figure 16-2, the access switch connects to clients in VLAN 20 and to the core Virtual Switching Framework (VSF) in VLAN 20. However, it is possible that access switch could route traffic and implement DHCP relay itself. In that case, it would relay DHCP client packets toward the server on a link aggregation interface assigned to a different VLAN. However, you would still need to make that link aggregation a trusted DHCP snooping port. Otherwise, the switch will not relay client packets from VLAN 20 out the link aggregation. If you have a redundant link toward the DHCP server, it is important to remember to make that link a trusted port as well.

By filtering DHCP packets, the switch acts like a firewall between untrusted endpoints and DHCP servers. In this way, the switch protects your network from DHCP attacks.

## Configuration

DHCP snooping operates on an individual VLAN level. Generally, you enable this feature on user VLANs, especially untrusted ones such as guest VLANs. To enable DHCP snooping, you must enable the feature both globally and on the desired VLANs.

To enable DHCP globally, enter this command:

```
Switch(config)# dhcp-snooping
```

Use this command to enable DHCP snooping on a VLAN:

```
Switch(config)# dhcp-snooping vlan <VLAN_ID_range>
```

You can specify a range of VLAN IDs in the command. If you need to specify noncontiguous VLANs, enter the command multiple times.

You can alternatively enable DHCP snooping from the VLAN context.

```
Switch(config)# vlan <ID> dhcp-snooping
```

To configure the dhcp-snooping trust *<port_ID_list>* DHCP snooping trusted ports, enter:

```
Switch(config)# dhcp-snooping trust <port_ID_list>
```

You can also configure a port as a trusted port at the interface context.

```
Switch(config)# interface <port_ID_list> dhcp-snooping trust
```

You can verify that DHCP snooping is enabled with the correct settings by entering the **show dhcp-snooping** command.

```
Switch# show dhcp-snooping
 DHCP Snooping Information
  DHCP Snooping               : Yes
  Enabled VLANs               : 20
  Verify MAC address          : Yes
  Option 82 untrusted policy  : drop
  Option 82 insertion         : Yes
  Option 82 remote-id         : mac
  Store lease database        : Not configured
                Max      Current Bindings
   Port  Trust  Bindings  Static   Dynamic
  -----  -----  --------  -------  -------
  Trk1   Yes     -         -        -
  Ports 1-48 are untrusted
```

In addition, you can view the DHCP snooping binding table and observe the information that the switch has collected.

```
Switch# show dhcp-snooping binding
  MacAddress        IP              VLAN Interface Time Left
  ----------------- --------------- ---- --------- ---------
  005056-973668     10.101.20.23    20   1         3524
```

You can also view DHCP snooping statistics.

```
Switch# show dhcp-snooping stats
Packet type  Action   Reason                        Count
 ----------- ------- ---------------------------- ---------
 server      forward  from trusted port              2
 client      forward  to trusted port                0
 server      drop     received on untrusted port     0
 server      drop     unauthorized server            0
 client      drop     destination on untrusted port  1
 client      drop     untrusted option 82 field      0
 client      drop     bad DHCP release request       0
 client      drop     failed verify MAC check        0
 client      drop     failed on max-binding limit    0
```

## Authorized servers

You can increase the level of security that DHCP snooping provides by configuring authorized servers. When you configure authorized server addresses, the switch must receive packets from DHCP servers on a trusted port *and* the packets must have a source address that is on the authorized server list (see Figure 16-3). If the server address is not on the list, even if the port is trusted, the switch considers the packet invalid and drops it.

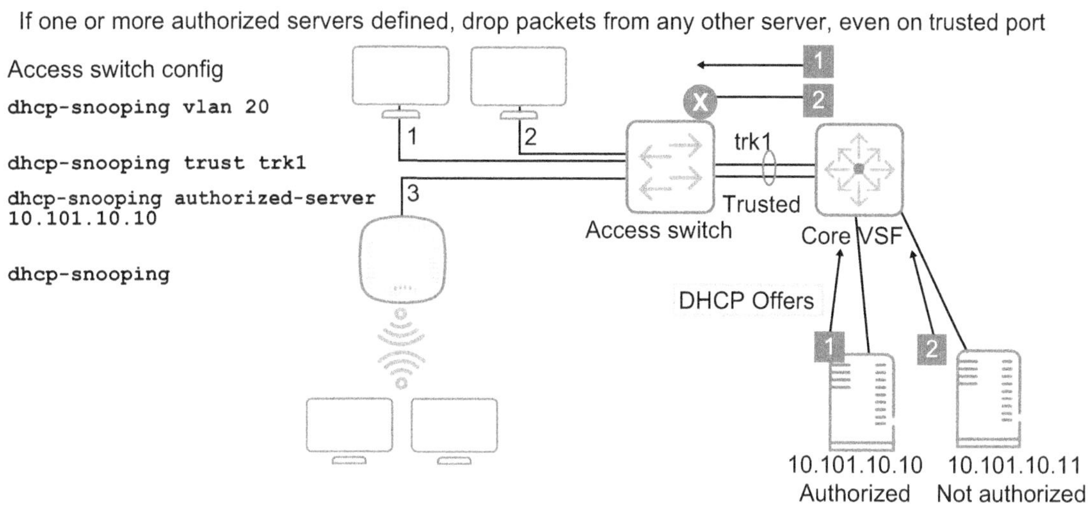


Figure 16-3 Authorized servers

Configuring authorized servers is optional. If you do not configure them, your switch will consider all DHCP server packets that arrive on trusted ports to be valid. To configure authorized servers, enter:

```
Switch(config)# dhcp-snooping authorized-server <IP_address>
```

You can configure multiple authorized DHCP servers.

## Inserting option 82 with DHCP snooping

You have learned how DHCP snooping blocks DHCP attacks by filtering DHCP packets on untrusted ports. DHCP snooping can also facilitate the functions of DHCP itself.

The DHCP option 82 helps your DHCP server to apply specialized policies when assigning endpoints IP addresses and other configuration information. For example, you often want certain ranges of IP addresses to be associated within certain areas. And a service provider's DHCP server might limit a certain switch port to a set number of IP addresses, ensuring that a subscriber network does not consume too many addresses.

To a DHCP server, however, all incoming DHCP packets look the same. With option 82, your intelligent edge switch acts as the DHCP server's eyes, adding the information that the DHCP server needs to select the correct policy. This information includes the switch's IP or MAC address (remote ID) and the physical switch port on which the request arrived (circuit ID).

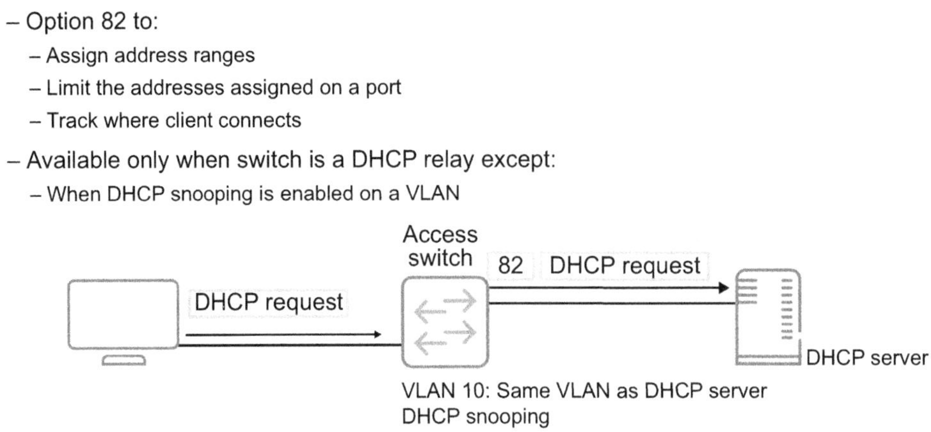


Figure 16-4 Inserting option 82 with DHCP snooping

A limitation of option 82 is that switches can insert option 82 information only when they are acting as relays for DHCP requests. In other words, unless the switch is the relay, it cannot manipulate DHCP requests. Instead, the switch must pass on DHCP requests just as it forwards any other data frame. This limitation comes into effect in two scenarios.

- Another switch acts as the DHCP relay but does not insert the correct option 82.
- The DHCP client is on the same subnet as the DHCP server, so your switch does not need to act as a relay. Figure 16-4 shows this scenario.

With DHCP snooping enabled for a VLAN, however, your AOS-Switch pays attention to *all* DHCP packets on untrusted ports, so the switch can always insert option 82.

## Controlling the insertion of option 82

When you enable DHCP snooping on a VLAN, the AOS-Switch, by default, inserts this information in all DHCP Discover and Request packets received in the VLAN:

- its own remote ID
- the ID of the physical port on which the DHCP request arrived (circuit ID)

You can disable or re-enable this function with this command:

```
Switch(config)# [no] dhcp-snooping option 82
```

To select the remote ID, enter this command:

```
Switch(config)# dhcp-snooping option 82 remote-id <mac | subnet-ip |
mgmt-ip>
```

The remote ID types are:

- its MAC address (mac)
- its IP address on the VLAN that received the request (subnet-ip)
- its management IP address (mgmt-ip)

The default remote ID is **mac**.

The DHCP snooping switch also, by default, filters option 82 in received packets based on the untrusted policy, which you will learn about in the "Filtering option 82 from connected devices" section.

You must use DHCP snooping to insert option 82 when a switch does not act as DHCP relay. When the switch does act as DHCP relay, you have a choice. You can use DHCP snooping to control the insertion, or you can use DHCP relay settings. While a switch acting as a DHCP relay does not, by default, add option 82 to relayed packets, you can enable it to do so. You enable this function by configuring the policy for filtering option 82 in relayed packets—as described in the "Filtering option 82 from connected devices" section.

If you enable option 82 insertion and filtering with both DHCP relay and DHCP snooping, the DHCP snooping settings take precedence. If you enable DHCP snooping, but disable DHCP snooping option 82 insertion, though, the switch uses the DHCP relay settings. In other words, if you want to suppress option 82 insertion, you must both disable option 82 in DHCP snooping and also make sure not to enable it with DHCP relay.

## Filtering option 82 from connected devices

Option 82 is a valuable tool, but one that can be hijacked by endpoints in an untrusted network. For example, a hacker can create an option 82 to manipulate the DHCP server into sending a station the wrong configuration.

Your AOS-Switch can snoop for option 82 inside of DHCP requests from untrusted ports.

- The switch can drop the request entirely (**drop**)
- The switch can forward the request as it is, keeping the option (**keep**)
- The switch can forward the request but replace the unauthorized option 82 with its own option (**replace**)

The untrusted policy is global for all VLANs and interfaces. However, it applies only to untrusted ports. The switch accepts DHCP packets with any options on trusted ports.

By default, DHCP snooping uses the **drop** option. It detects and drops any DHCP request that includes option 82 and is received on an untrusted port. You should preserve this behavior whenever your switch connects directly to untrusted clients, and an improper option 82 indicates a potential attack.

If you want to take a slightly more permissive approach, controlling the policy but still allowing clients to receive DHCP settings if they include option 82, choose the **replace** option.

You should use the **keep** option when your solution requires devices on untrusted ports to set option 82. This might be the case when you implement DHCP snooping on both access layer and distribution or core switches. You want the access layer switches to set option 82 because you are tracking information about the exact location at which clients connect. However, if in this circumstance you wanted the distribution or core switch to control the remote ID, you could use the **replace** option.

If you are using DHCP snooping to control option 82 insertion and filtering, select the desired action with this command:

```
Switch(config)# dhcp-snooping option 82 untrusted-policy <drop | keep |
replace>
```

If you have chosen to use DHCP relay to insert and filter option 82, use this command. At the same time, set the desired remote ID:

```
Switch(config)# dhcp-relay option 82 <drop | keep | replace> <mac | ip
| mgmt-vlan>
```

Remember that the DHCP snooping settings take precedence.

## ARP snooping and poisoning

You will now learn about how malefactors can use the ARP protocol to attack your network. You will then learn how to use ARP protection to secure the network.

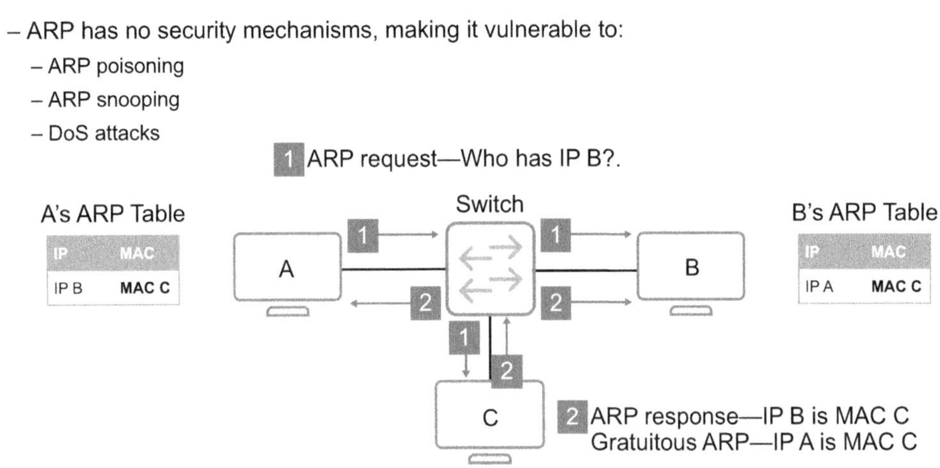


Figure 16-5 ARP snooping and poisoning

As you know, ARP helps devices resolve a device's IP address to its MAC address. Switches and other ARP devices use ARP to create and populate a table of known IP addresses and the MAC addresses that are associated with them. ARP devices request information for unknown MAC addresses. Most ARP devices update their tables every time they receive an ARP packet even if they did not request the information. This makes ARP vulnerable to attacks such as ARP poisoning, ARP snooping, and Denial of Service (DoS).

ARP poisoning occurs when an unauthorized device sends an illegitimate, falsified ARP response, and other devices use the response to change their ARP tables. In the example shown in Figure 16-5:

1. Device A broadcasts an ARP request for device B's MAC address.
2. Device C, the intruder, responds with an ARP response that maps its MAC address to B's IP address.

   At the same time, C sends a gratuitous ARP packet posing as A, so if B, the legitimate owner of the IP address, tries to send its own ARP response, only C receives it.

When A and B update their ARP tables with the spoofed entries, their ARP tables are considered "poisoned." Because B's IP address is matched with C's MAC address, all IP traffic that A wants to send to B is sent to C instead. And the same occurs when B wants to send traffic to A.

Now we should understand how C is not a good network citizen. By positioning itself as the "man-in-the-middle," device C can capture information such as usernames and passwords, email messages, and other confidential company information.

ARP poisoning can also take the form of unsolicited ARP responses and can lead to DoS attacks. For example, device C can poison the ARP table by associating the network gateway's IP address with the MAC address of a station. Because the station does not have access to outside networks, outgoing traffic is prevented from leaving the network. The station may also be overwhelmed by the outgoing traffic.

## ARP protection

AOS-Switches can protect your network against ARP poisoning attacks. You enable the ARP protection feature on VLANs with this command:

```
Switch(config)# arp-protect vlan <VLAN_ID_range>
```

You must also enable the feature globally for it to take effect on the VLANs. (When you set this up in the real world, you should make sure that you have planned and followed the guidelines outlined in this chapter.)

```
Switch(config)# arp-protect
```

You can verify that ARP protection is enabled with the correct settings by entering:

```
Switch# show arp-protect
 ARP Protection Information

  ARP Protection Enabled : Yes
  Protected Vlans   : 20
  Validate          :

  Port  Trust
  Trk1  Yes

  Ports 1-48 are untrusted
```

Like the DHCP snooping feature, the ARP protection feature allows you to designate trusted and untrusted ports. By default, all ports are untrusted in the context of ARP protection. This means that the switch will check the ARP requests and responses received on all ports that are members of the protected VLANs.

If a port is untrusted, the intelligent edge switch:

- intercepts all ARP requests and responses received on that port
- verifies that each of these intercepted packets has a valid IP-to-MAC address binding

If the binding is valid, the switch updates its local ARP cache or forwards the packet to the appropriate destination. If the binding is invalid, the switch simply drops the packet, preventing other devices from receiving it and being tricked by the faulty information.

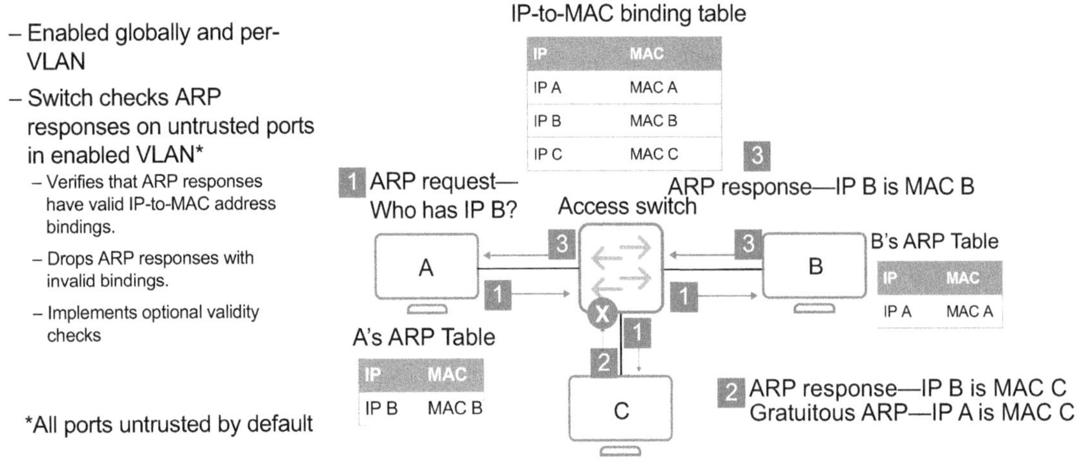


Figure 16-6 ARP protection

You can see how this protects the network in Figure 16-6.

1. Device A broadcasts an ARP request for device B's MAC address.
2. Device C, the intruder, responds with an ARP response that maps its MAC address to B's IP address. It also sends a gratuitous ARP posing as A.

   Now, though, the traffic arrives on an untrusted port in a VLAN on which ARP protection is enabled. Therefore, the switch checks both ARP messages and sees that the IP-to-MAC address binding is incorrect. The switch drops the requests.
3. B sends its legitimate ARP response. This response also arrives on an untrusted port in an ARP protection VLAN. However, its IP-to-MAC address binding is correct, so the switch forwards it as normal. Now A and B can exchange traffic.

## Additional checks

In addition to verifying IP-to-MAC address bindings, you can configure the switch to perform three other checks.

- src-mac—The switch checks ARP request and response packets to ensure that the source MAC address in the Ethernet header matches the sender MAC address in the body of the ARP packet. If the two addresses do not match, the switch discards the packet.
- dest-mac—The switch checks each unicast ARP response packet to ensure that the destination MAC address in the Ethernet header matches the target MAC address in the body of the ARP packet. If the two do not match, the switch drops the packet.
- ip—The switch checks the sender and target IP addresses of ARP packets and drops any ARP packets that have an invalid address. Invalid IP addresses include:
  - 0.0.0.0
  - 255.255.255.255
  - all IP multicast addresses
  - Class E IP addresses

By default, none of these checks are enabled. Use this command to enable one or more of these checks:

```
Switch(config)# arp-protect validate [src-mac] [dest-mac] [ip]
```

## DHCP snooping and ARP protection

In most VLANs, devices receive their IP addresses using DHCP, and these addresses can change. The switch needs a way discover the correct MAC to IP bindings automatically and dynamically.

DHCP snooping fulfills this function.

As Figure 16-7 shows, DHCP snooping builds and maintains a DHCP snooping-binding table, which tracks the MAC address, IP address, lease time, VLAN number, and interface information that corresponds to each DHCP lease. Using this table, the switch can learn which IP addresses should legitimately send traffic on which ports and which MAC address can legitimately use an IP address. Therefore, you must typically enable DHCP snooping as part of configuring ARP protection.

If you are not using DHCP to assign IP addresses in the protected VLAN, you can configure static IP-to-MAC address bindings, and the switch will use this information to verify ARP packets. However, most networks, do, of course, use DHCP.

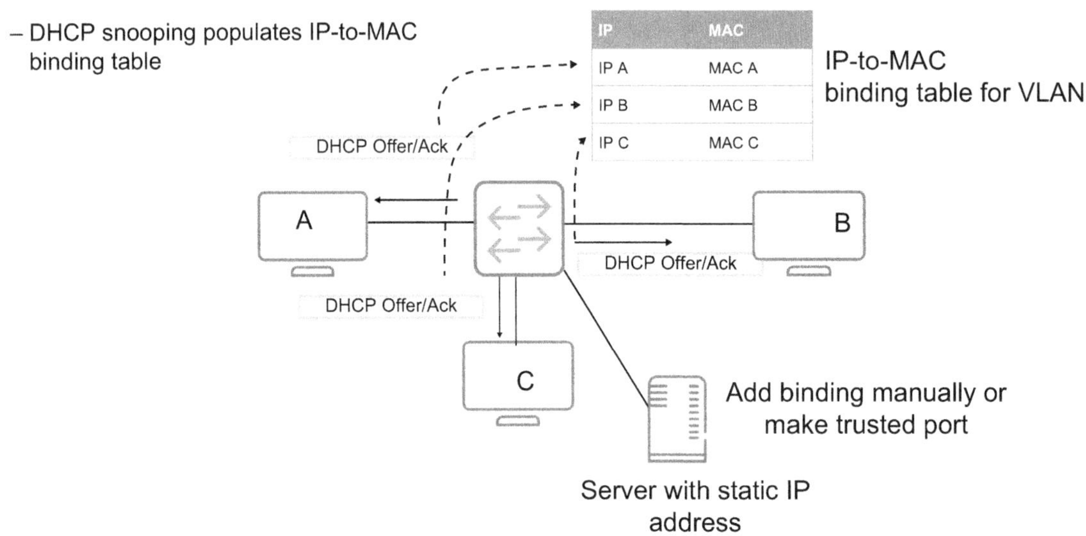


Figure 16-7 DHCP snooping and ARP protection

Even when you are using DHCP and DHCP snooping, you may need to add a couple static IP-to-MAC address bindings to the DHCP snooping table. This allows the switch can verify IP-to-MAC bindings for devices that have been assigned static IP addresses. You must also specify the interface for the static binding.

Use this command to create a static binding:

```
Switch(config)# ip source-binding <VLAN_ID> <IP_address> <MAC_address>
<port_ID>
```

In an active network, you should generally wait at least a week after enabling DHCP snooping to enable ARP. This ensures that the table is properly built up.

**Note**

For increased security and protection against any form of IP spoofing, you can implement dynamic IP lockdown (ip source-lockdown). This feature goes further than ARP protection and enforces the correct source IP address and MAC address for *all* IP traffic on a port. Like ARP protection, dynamic IP lockdown requires DHCP snooping to populate the IP-to-MAC binding table. For more details on implementing dynamic IP lockdown, refer to your switch's *Access Security Guide*.

## Guidelines for using dynamic ARP protection

Generally, you should configure ARP protection as close to the network edge as possible. If all of your access layer switches implement ARP protection, you usually do not need to configure it on distribution and core switches, which are presumably protected physically and connect only to trusted devices. Your environment might have different needs, however.

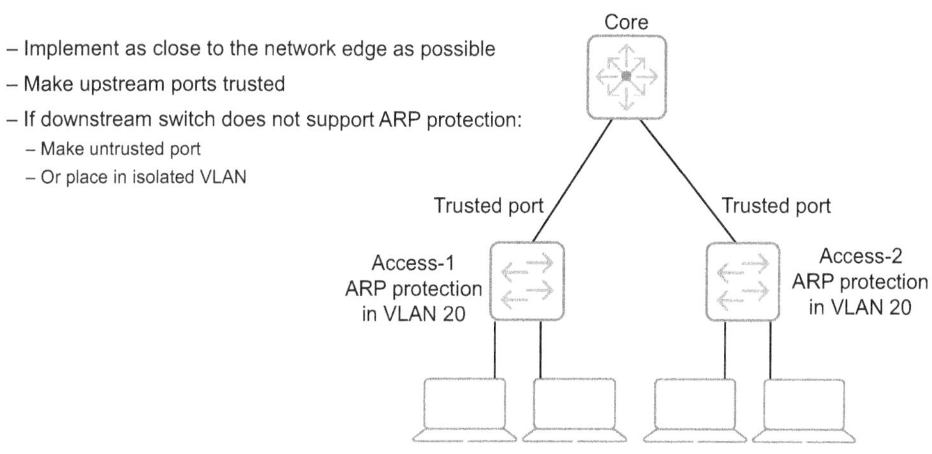


Figure 16-8 Guidelines for using dynamic ARP protection

On switches that enforce ARP protection, make upstream ports, connected to the distribution layer or core, trusted ports (see Figure 16-8). The switch will not check the ARP requests and responses that it receives on the trusted ports. When switches across the access layer implement DHCP snooping and ARP protection, each switch only learns the DHCP bindings for clients connected on its own untrusted ports. Therefore, the switch is only capable of monitoring the ARP traffic for hosts connected on these ports. It must trust the ARP traffic arriving from other parts of the network, or it will find that the traffic has no binding and interfere with legitimate communications. In any case, allowing switches to trust traffic that arrives from other switches eliminates double filtering of traffic and reduces the burden on each switch.

If your AOS-Switch connects to a less intelligent *downstream* switch that does not implement DHCP snooping and ARP protection, you might decide to leave the port connected to that switch as untrusted. You must make sure, though, that all DHCP requests will flow through your AOS-Switch so that it can construct the proper binding table. If you choose to make the port trusted, it is better to place the less intelligent switch in its own VLAN to prevent untrusted ARP packets from passing to the protected network.

All ports are untrusted by default—although, of course, they only filter ARP traffic that arrives in a VLAN on which ARP protection is enabled. To configure a trusted port, enter this command:

```
Switch(config)# arp-protect trust <port_ID_list>
```

## The dangers of eavesdropping and unauthorized access

In this section, you will learn how to configure port security on your AOS-Switches to protect your network against eavesdropping and unauthorized devices.

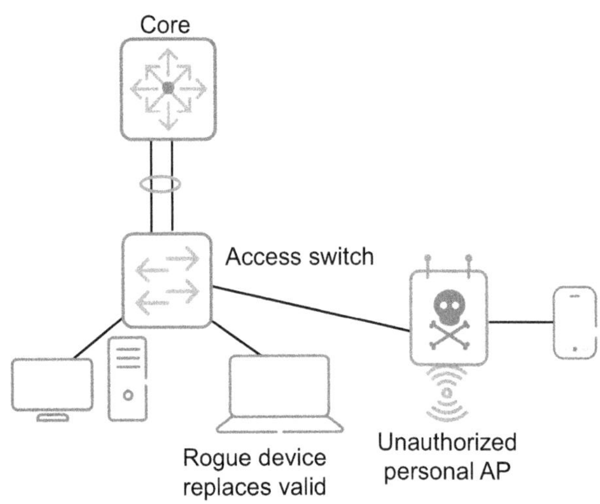


Figure 16-9 The dangers of eavesdropping and unauthorized access

Many organizations provide Ethernet connections that enable employees and visitors to access their networks. While the practice of providing ready access makes things convenient for busy people who have work to do, it also creates vulnerabilities.

For example, an unhappy employee who is leaving the company might easily plug in a hidden packet monitoring device on his last day, enabling him to intercept network traffic and illegally copy the organization's data. Or, a careless employee might use a connection in an empty cubicle to connect an unauthorized device that could jeopardize the network's health—a personal Access Point (AP), for example (see Figure 16-9).

Eavesdropping and unauthorized access are undeniably dangerous. Through them, malicious intruders can gain access to passwords, processes, and other sensitive information. AOS-Switches include a port security feature to help organizations protect themselves against these attacks.

You should be aware that, like MAC authentication, parts of port security can be susceptible to MAC spoofing. For the highest level of security, you should use 802.1X. You can also combine 802.1X and port security, as you will learn.

## Port security

Port security addresses these threats by allowing the switch to track the MAC addresses of devices that attempt to connect through a port, check these addresses against a list of authorized MAC addresses, and take action when a MAC address is not on the authorized list (see Figure 16-10).

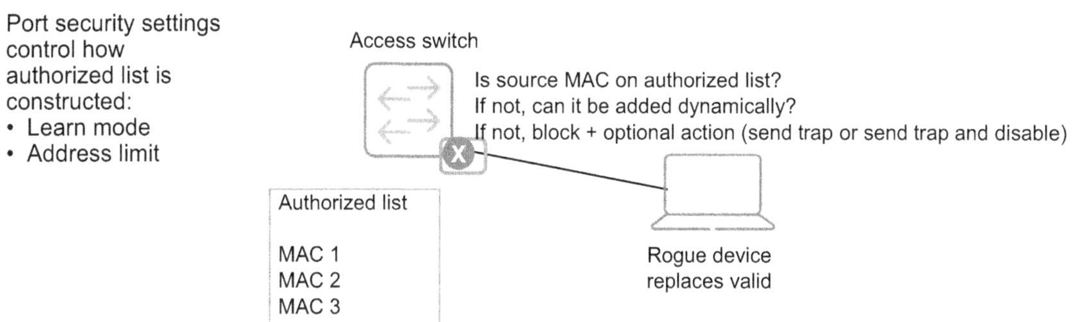


Figure 16-10 Port security

You can control how the port learns the MAC addresses that are on its authorized list, the number of MAC addresses the list contains, and what you want to happen if an unauthorized device attempts to connect through the port.

## Port security learn modes

Port security enables you to specify the learn modes for individual switch ports or for a range of ports. The learn mode controls these factors:

- How MAC addresses are added to the port's authorized list
- How authorized MAC addresses are stored—are they stored permanently or aged out
- Whether the number of MAC addresses authorized on the port is limited

Table 16-1 summarizes the possible learn modes. Note that the switch always defines a port security mode for each port. Continuous mode, the default mode, is simply the mode for a port that is not enforcing port security. In other words, the port acts as expected for an Ethernet interface.

For continuous and limited-continuous mode, addresses age out if they are not regularly used, in which case the port automatically deletes them from the authorized list. To determine "regular use," the port uses the MAC age interval in the switch's System Information configuration. The default MAC age time is five minutes. With these modes, it is possible for unwanted devices to become authorized devices.

As you see in Table 16-1, static mode populates the port's authorized MAC address list in two ways.

- Automatic learning
- Manual configuration

If you enter fewer MAC addresses manually than you specify in the address limit, the switch will automatically learn—and add to its authorized list—MAC addresses of other devices that are connected to it. Only configured mode blocks the port for all devices except those manually configured.

Table 16-1 Port security learn modes

| Learn mode | How MAC addresses are authorized | How authorized MAC addresses are stored | Whether the number of authorized MAC addresses is limited |
|---|---|---|---|
| Continuous | Learned automatically | Temporary—aged out | Not limited |
| Limited-continuous | Learned automatically | Temporary—aged out | Limited (default 1) |
| Static | Learned automatically<br>Entered manually (number cannot exceed limit) | Permanent—stored in configuration after they are learned automatically or specified manually | Limited (default 1) |
| Configured | Entered manually (number cannot exceed limit) | Permanent—stored in the configuration | Limited (default 1) |

## The address limit parameter

The `address-limit` parameter determines the maximum number of authorized MAC addresses that the port can allow as authorized. This parameter is available only for the static, configured, and continuous-limited modes. The number of supported addresses depends on the switch model; check your configuration guide for more details.

## Port security actions

The port security feature automatically blocks traffic from devices whose MAC addresses are not on the port's authorized list. In addition to this action, you can configure how the port should notify you when it detects an unauthorized device. Actions include:

- none—Prevents port security from sending a Simple Network Management Protocol (SNMP) trap. This is the default value, so if you do not use the action parameter to send an alarm or send an alarm and disable the port, the port does nothing more than block traffic from the intruder.
- send-alarm—Causes the switch to send an SNMP trap to a network management station.
- send-disable—Sets an intrusion flag, sends an alarm to a network management station, and disables the port. If you re-enable the port you should also use the clear-intrusion-flag command to remove the intrusion flag. Otherwise, the switch will not disable the port again if it detects the same or a different unauthorized MAC address.

The correct mode depends on how you want to use the port security feature. You will now consider some examples of why and how port security might be implemented.

## Use case 1: Limit devices on an edge port

### Scenario

In the first use case that you will examine, you want to prevent hackers from inserting their device on an authorized device's port. You also want to prevent users from connecting unauthorized hubs, switches, or APs that enable multiple devices to connect through a single edge port. In other words, each access layer edge port should only connect to one endpoint. You want the switch to send a notification message if more than one device attempts to access the network through the port and block the second device.

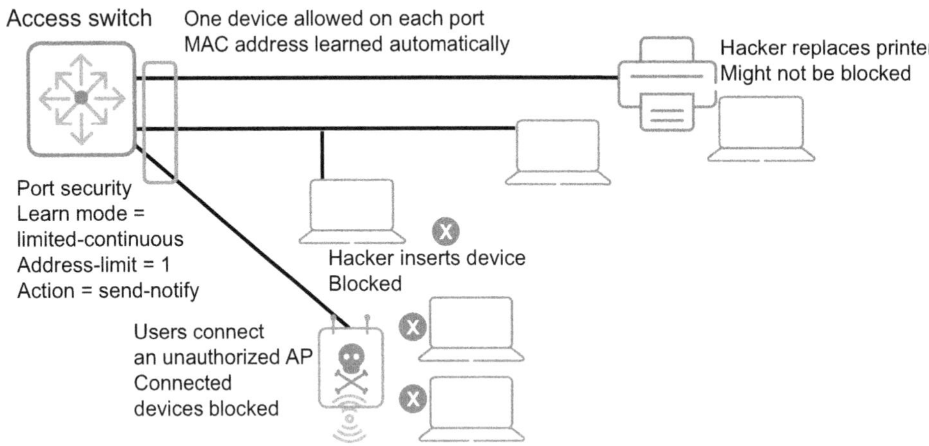


Figure 16-11 Use case 1: Limit devices on an edge port

In the example shown in Figure 16-11, you see that the switch allows each individual client device to connect to the network. However, when users attempt to connect a switch and connect multiple devices through the unauthorized switch, the AOS-Switch blocks the connected devices. An alert can notify administrators of the issue and enable them to remove the unauthorized device.

Similarly, if a hacker attempts to insert their device on a connection, the switch detects and blocks the new device.

However, users can move or replace their devices without causing issues. For example, if IT staff need to install a new computer, they can connect it to the old computer's jack with no issues. They disconnect the old computer, and its MAC address ages out. When they connect the new computer, the port has 0 authorized MAC addresses and is allowed one, so it learns the new device's MAC address.

Note one potential issue with this setup: if hackers disconnect an unattended device such as a printer and connect their own device, this form of port security might not detect the issue. If the printer's address ages out before the hackers connect their device, the port learns the new device's MAC address, and the device is allowed to connect. For this reason, you might want to use the configuration shown for the next use case for, particularly, vulnerable ports.

## Learn mode and address limit

In this scenario, configure the port to use the limited-continuous learn mode. Set the address limit to 1 to ensure that each edge port connects to only one endpoint. Or, if your company connects a computer and IP phone on the same switch port, set the address limit to 2. (Occasionally, you might have a situation in which the port should permit more devices. For example, a port might connect to an unmanaged switch with 12 ports, in which case you should set the limit to 12.)

The switch will automatically learn up MAC addresses up to the limit, so administrators do not have to configure the MAC addresses for devices manually. The addresses will also age out, so if employees need to replace or move devices, they can do so without having to bother IT staff to update the configuration.

### Action

In this scenario, you may simply want to block the new device that attempts a connection, in which case you won't need to specify an action. The action is none by default. (Remember that port security always blocks the unauthorized MAC addresses. None refers to the fact that the switch sends no notification.)

Often, though, you want the switch to send a notification as well as block the unauthorized device so that administrators can determine what has happened and resolve the issue. Set the **action** parameter to **send-alarm**.

And if you want port security to disable the port in addition to sending an alarm, you should set the **action** parameter to **send-disable**. However, be aware that the **send-disable** action will block the port for the authorized device as well as the unauthorized one.

Your configuration for this use case might look like this if you opt to block the unauthorized device and send a notification:

```
Switch(config)# port-security <port-list> learn-mode limited-continuous
address-limit 1 action send-alarm
```

## Use case 2: Preventing changes to the devices connected to ports

### Scenario

This use case is similar to Use case 1. In this use case, however, you want to prevent a situation such as hackers disconnecting a printer and connecting their own device in its place (see Figure 16-12). Although you do not want the hassle of manually configuring the authorized MAC address list for each port, you want the switch to notify you if a device changes and to block the new device.

For this scenario, you should enable port security on switch ports at a time when you know the switch is connected to the authorized devices. The switch will then learn the MAC addresses for the authorized devices automatically. Port security will detect if the device on a port changes later and block the new device.

This configuration provides more security than the previous one because it tracks and blocks changes. However, this security comes at the cost of an increased hassle for IT staff, which must clear the current MAC address to allow a new one to be learned whenever users need to change equipment.

You might choose to use this configuration on more vulnerable ports such as printer ports and IT security camera ports in public areas. Because you set the port security settings for ports individually, you can use the configuration illustrated in Figure 16-11 for more protected ports in users' offices, allowing more flexibility there.

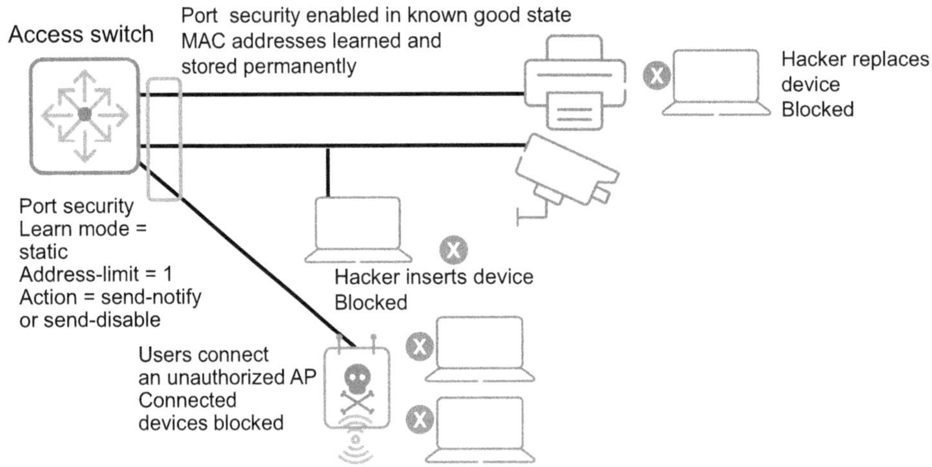


Figure 16-12 Use case 2: Preventing changes to the devices connected to ports

## Learn mode and address limit

For this use case, again set the address limit to 1 in most situations. (You can set the limit to 2 if you connect computers and IP phones to the same port.)

Set the learn mode to **static**. This mode allows the switch to automatically learn MAC addresses up to the address limit that you configure. The learned addresses are added to the switch configuration. They do not age out and they persist across reboots (as long as the switch configuration has been saved). Therefore, port security will detect if someone changes the device.

## Action

The same considerations for setting the action in the previous use case apply to this one. You typically should send an alert, at least, so that you can have a clue as to why a device on a port is being blocked.

Your configuration for this use case might look like this if you opt to block the unauthorized device and send a notification:

```
Switch(config)# port-security <port-list> learn-mode static address-
limit 1 action send-alarm
```

If you want port security to disable the port entirely in the case of an unauthorized connection attempt, your configuration might look like this:

```
Switch(config)# port-security <port-list> learn-mode static address-
limit 1 action send-disable
```

## Use case 3: Exactly controlling devices that can connect to a port

### Scenario

In this use case, you want to manually specify the precise devices that are authorized to connect to particular ports. Perhaps you are setting up a switch remotely, and you cannot guarantee a period of time in which the switch can safely learn the correct MAC addresses on its ports, or perhaps you want some flexibility in which devices connect to which port, so you want to configure multiple authorized MAC addresses on each port. You will authorize the desired MAC addresses on the ports, and the switch will then only allow traffic from those addresses. You can also set an address limit.

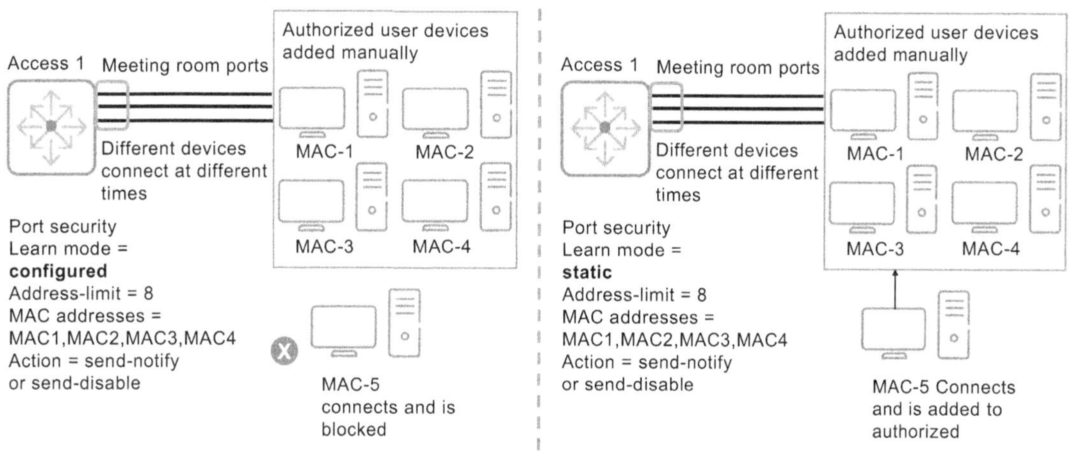


Figure 16-13 Use case 3: Exactly controlling devices that can connect to a port

Figure 16-13 shows a scenario in which a switch has several edge ports connected to jacks in a meeting room. The room is used by several employees, who connect their devices to different jacks at different times. It is not feasible for the administrators to wait for the switch to learn all the authorized MAC addresses that might connect to the ports. Instead, they configure the MAC address for each user's laptop as an authorized MAC address on all of the ports.

If someone tries to connect an unauthorized device to one of the ports, the switch blocks traffic from that MAC address and perhaps sends a warning.

### Settings

To satisfy the requirements of this scenario, you have two options for the learn mode.

The generally preferred option is configured. This learn mode disables learning of authorized MAC addresses on the port entirely. The switch only allows the MAC address or addresses that are manually configured on the port.

You should usually set the address limit to the same number of MAC addresses that you will configure manually. If the address limit is lower, the switch will not allow you to configure addresses past the limit. On the other hand, setting the limit higher does not pose a security risk. The switch will *not* allow more MAC addresses than are configured because, when the learn mode is configured, the switch only allows the manually specified addresses and never learns addresses on its own. You could set the limit higher than the number of MAC addresses that you configure to allow administrators to add more authorized MAC addresses later without having to remember to raise the limit.

For the scenario shown in Figure 16-13, you might use these commands:

```
Switch(config)# port-security B1-B8 learn-mode configured address-limit 8

Switch(config)# port-security B1-B8 mac-address aaaaaa-aaaaaa aaaaaa-aaaaab aaaaaa-aaaaac aaaaaa-aaaaad
```

Even though the limit is eight, the switch will only allow the four MAC addresses listed in the command. Later administrators can add four more MAC addresses.

You could also use static learn mode for this scenario. Static learn mode allows you to use a hybrid approach in which you enter some MAC addresses manually and the switch also learns MAC addresses.

For example, you set the learn mode to static, set the address limit to eight, and specify four MAC addresses manually.

```
Switch(config)# port-security B1-B8 learn-mode static address-limit 8

Switch(config)# port-security B1-B8 mac-address aaaaaa-aaaaaa aaaaaa-aaaaab aaaaaa-aaaaac aaaaaa-aaaaad
```

The switch always permits any of those four MAC addresses on any of these ports, just as it would with configured mode. However, the switch will also learn and authorize the MAC addresses for the next four devices to connect on the port. Note that the devices might not connect to the port at the same time. A user could connect a device, and the switch would learn and store the MAC address permanently after the device disconnects.

This configuration would let the users bring a few new devices without having to alert network administrators. On the other hand, it might also allow people to connect unauthorized devices. If they happen to do so before the address limit is filled, the port would learn these devices' MAC addresses and treat them as if they were authorized devices.

If you do not want the switch to learn more MAC addresses than the ones that you specify, make sure to set the address limit to the same number of manually configured addresses—or better yet, use configured learn mode.

## Use case 4: Combining port security with 802.1X port-based authentication

### Scenario

By default, a port enforcing 802.1X operates in the continuous learn mode. However, even in this mode, 802.1X on its own fulfills many of the roles that port security does. As long as you set a client limit so that the port operates in user-based mode, the port permits only authorized devices to send traffic on the port. 802.1X also allows you to limit how many devices connect to the port.

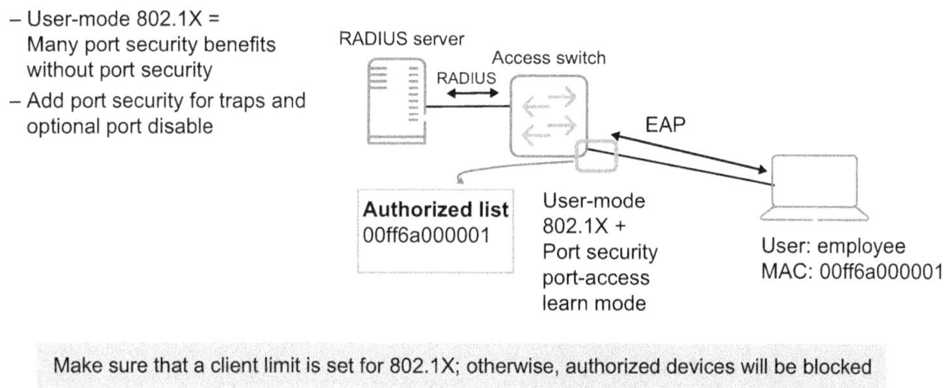


Figure 16-14 Use case 4: Combining port security with 802.1X port-based authentication

Sometimes, though, you might want to add port security to the 802.1X-enabled port (see Figure 16-14). Then the switch can send an alarm if an unauthorized device tries to send traffic on the port. For high-security scenarios, you can even configure the switch to shut down the port entirely if an unauthorized device tries to transmit.

## Settings

To fulfill these functions, enable port-security on the port in **port-access** learn mode, which is the only other mode besides continuous permitted on 802.1X-enabled ports. In this mode, the switch automatically learns MAC addresses that succeed 802.1X authentication. For the learning to work, though, you must make sure that the port is operating in user-based mode; set a client limit of 1 or more. Otherwise, the port cannot add 802.1X authorized client MAC addresses to the port security authorized list, and the authorized clients are blocked.

You cannot configure authorized MAC addresses manually in this learn mode. 802.1X handles this function entirely. You also cannot configure a port security address limit. Instead, control the number of MAC addresses allowed by setting the 802.1X client limit.

These commands provide an example of setting up 802.1X and port security together:

```
Switch(config)# aaa port-access authenticator <port ID list>

Switch(config)# aaa port-access authenticator <port ID list> client-limit <limit>

Switch(config)# port-security <port ID list> learn-mode port-access action <send-alarm | send-disable>

Switch(config)# aaa port-access authenticator active
```

In addition to these commands, you must also select RADIUS authentication and set up the RADIUS server as you learned how to do in *Chapter 10: 802.1X Authentication*. Also, make sure that your RADIUS server is ready to authenticate and authorize users.

## Eavesdropping protection

Port security blocks traffic that arrives on a port from an unauthorized MAC address, but you should also consider traffic destined *out* the port. Switches forward this traffic on a port:

- Broadcasts
- Multicasts (but, if Internet Group Management Protocol [IGMP] is enabled, only multicasts that the connected device has requested)
- Unicasts to MAC addresses learned on that port
- Unicasts to unknown MAC addresses

Unknown unicasts can be present in a network when a device first connects to the network, and switches have not yet learned its MAC address. They can also occur when a device's MAC address ages out of switches' forwarding tables before its address ages out of other devices' ARP tables. Flooding of unicasts can pose a security risk because endpoints receive traffic that is not intended for them. A hacker running a packet sniffer can collect those packets and discover information about the network, as well as other potentially sensitive information.

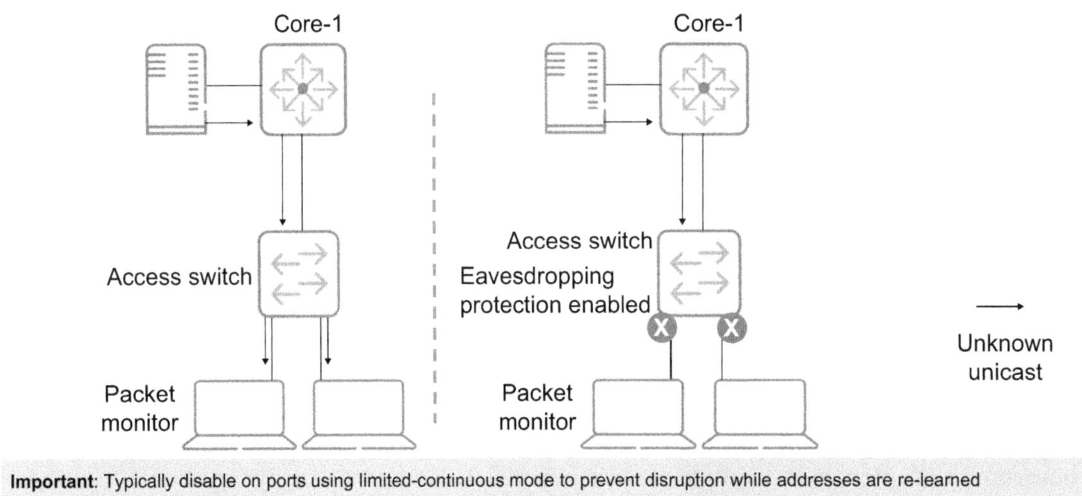


Figure 16-15 Eavesdropping protection

As Figure 16-15 shows, enabling eavesdrop protection on a port closes this vulnerability by blocking the flooding of unicast packets with unknown destinations on that port. Eavesdrop protection does not affect multicast and broadcast traffic.

By default, eavesdrop protecting is enabled on every switch port on port security is enabled in one of these modes:

- Limited-continuous
- Static
- Configured

Eavesdrop protection can appear to be enabled on ports that use continuous or port-access mode; however, the switch does not actually implement eavesdrop protection on these ports.

Keep in mind that Ethernet requires the flooding of unknown unicasts for a reason—so that traffic can flow while switches dynamically learn where endpoints are located. Eavesdropping protection works well when the switch always knows the exact MAC addresses connected to it—in other words, in configured mode and in static mode (after the initial learning period). In limited-continuous mode, on the other hand, MAC addresses learned on the port age out. Eavesdrop protection could periodically interfere with traffic flow as addresses age out, and it could complicate and delay the relearning of addresses. It is recommended that you disable eavesdrop protection in this mode.

To enable or disable eavesdropping protection, enter this command:

```
Switch(config)# [no] port-security 1/1 eavesdrop-prevention
```

## MAC lockdown

In this section, you will learn about a port-based security feature that you can use to help prevent MAC spoofing exploits. MAC lockdown is primarily intended to prevent MAC address spoofing. It enables you to bind a specific MAC address to a single port. If another port receives traffic on that MAC address, presumably a device is spoofing the address. As Figure 16-16 shows, the switch blocks the traffic. It also generates a warning level event.

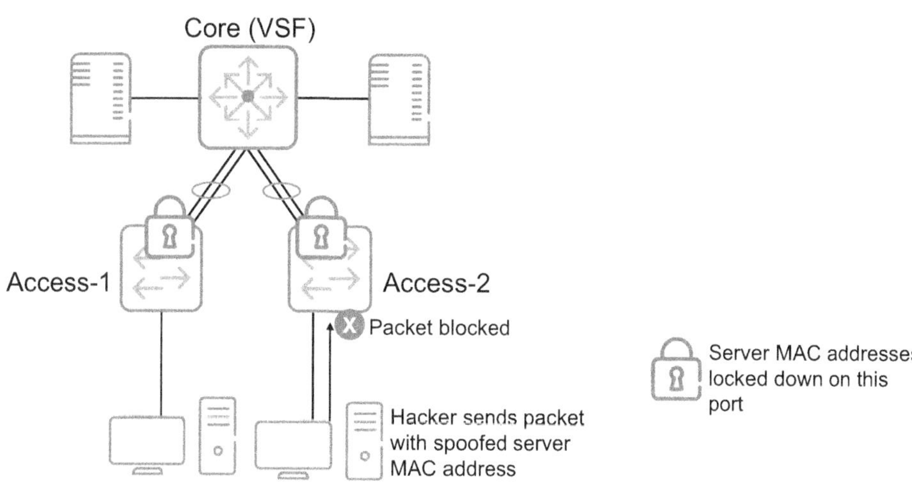


Figure 16-16 MAC lockdown

Also called static MAC addressing, MAC lockdown controls MAC learning. As Figure 16-16 shows, you are essentially creating a static entry in the switch's MAC forwarding table, which binds the specified MAC address with the specified port. Not only does the switch drop any traffic from this MAC address on another port, it never learns the address on another port, and it always forwards traffic to the address on this port.

Because a MAC forwarding table can only associate a MAC address with a single port (or link aggregation), you can only bind a MAC address to a single port with MAC lockdown. Remember, though, that switches maintain a separate MAC forwarding table for each VLAN. You can bind a MAC address to a port in one VLAN and then bind the same address to any port in another VLAN. (Although having the same MAC address in different VLANs is not necessarily typical or desired, it can occur in some circumstances.)

Figure 16-16 shows an example of a network which is using a single VLAN for the user devices and servers shown. Servers connect to the core. Server MAC addresses should not be the source for any traffic sent from user devices. Each access layer switch binds the server MAC addresses to its link aggregation to the core. If traffic with a server MAC address arrives on another port, the switch drops the traffic. Figure 16-16 shows a simple topology at the core, but it could be more complex. You can move servers around within the core network, and yet MAC lockdown will still prevent a user at the edge from hijacking their MAC addresses and stealing data.

Keep in mind that your network topology might separate servers and clients in different subnets. When the network routes traffic between clients and servers, the source MAC address for traffic from servers to clients will not be the server MAC address all the way to the edge. Instead, the clients' default gateway will use its MAC address as the source when routing traffic into their subnet. If most traffic is being routed in and out of the untrusted subnet, you might not need to implement MAC lockdown, or you might choose to lock down just the default gateway MAC address on the access layer switches.

MAC lockdown can also be used to restrict device movement. If you provision ports with settings such as VLANs statically, a user who connects a device to the wrong port can potentially bypass access controls. MAC lockdown ensures that each device connects to the correct port with the correct settings. However, MAC-Auth is usually a more flexible and manageable way to ensure similar controls. Instead of binding a MAC address to a specific port with the correct configuration, the RADIUS server dynamically applies the correct configuration to the port when a MAC address connects to it. Even if you do not have a RADIUS server, you can use local MAC authentication (LMA). If your goal is truly to prevent a device from moving, though, you can use MAC lockdown for that purpose.

To configure MAC lockdown, enter this command:

```
Switch(config)# static-mac <mac-addr> interface <port_ID> [vlan <ID>]
```

The VLAN that you specify in the command above determines to which table you add the binding. You can bind a MAC address to a port in one VLAN, and the switch can still accept traffic from the MAC address in question on any port in other VLANs. So you should be very careful to create the binding in the correct VLAN. If you do not specify a VLAN, the switch places the binding in the MAC forwarding table for VLAN 1.

## Considering redundant links

Before you deploy MAC lockdown, consider how you are handling data link layer redundancy. The typically preferred method, shown in Figure 16-16, relies on VSF at the core (and distribution layer, if you have a three-tier topology). Each access layer switch (or VSF fabric or stack) has a single logical uplink. This means each switch has only one path on which traffic from the core can flow. You can safely lock down the MAC addresses because all traffic from the servers always arrives on a single logical link.

If, however, you are using RSTP or MSTP on links between the access layer and core, MAC lockdown will either not work or it will defeat the purpose of providing redundant network paths. You can only bind a MAC address to one link. If that link fails, and the network fails over to another link, the switch will block traffic from the locked down addresses on the newly active link. Therefore, each access layer switch can truly only have one link to the core. (You can still implement redundancy within the core.)

If you want to use MAC lockdown in a topology such as this, you should rethink your topology and solution. You might want to consider migrating to a VSF based topology, or you might choose to use MAC access lists instead of MAC lockdown. You could apply standard MAC access lists to edge ports, denying traffic with the source MAC addresses that you want to protect from spoofing.

## MAC lockdown versus port security

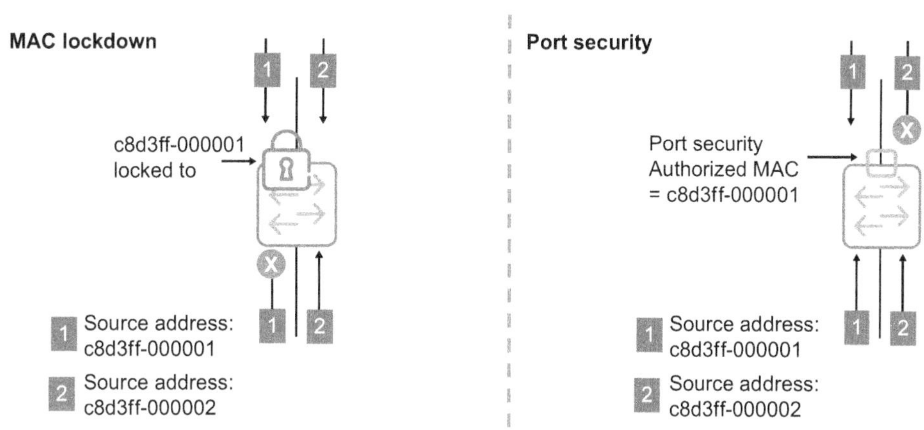


Figure 16-17 MAC lockdown versus port security

Sometimes administrators can confuse MAC lockdown with port security. However, the features act conversely.

As you see in Figure 16-17, associating MAC addresses with a port using MAC lockdown has no effect on the traffic that the port can receive. It can still receive traffic from any MAC address. However, the bound MAC addresses are dropped if received on other ports.

On the other hand, with port security, only MAC addresses authorized for the port are accepted on the port. However, an authorized MAC address on one port can send traffic on another port without restriction.

**Important**
You cannot configure MAC lockdown and port security on the same port.

## Connection rate filtering

You will now learn how to use connection rate filtering (Virus throttling) to help protect your network from virus and worm attacks.

Malware such as viruses and worms are infamous for churning out connection requests at a high rate. AOS-Switches can help augment the intrusion detection and prevention systems (IDSs and IPSs) that already protect your network with connection rate filtering.

Connection rate filtering checks all inbound IPv4 traffic on a port for behavior that might indicate a virus or worm. (Connection rate filtering is currently unavailable for IPv6.) Rather than stop virus attacks based on signature files, as your IDS/IPS systems do, connection rate filtering monitors behavior.

This feature works on the principle that viruses and worms request sessions with a large number of devices on the network as they attempt to spread. Because it does not rely on signature files, connection rate filtering can help mitigate the effects of both known and unknown viruses and worms.

### Operation

Connection rate filtering limits the number of a host's or endpoint device's new outgoing connections based on the parameters you set (see Figure 16-18). When an endpoint makes a connection request, connection rate filtering takes these steps:

- It compares the destination for the packet to a working set (short list) of recently contacted destinations.
- If the destination is listed in the working set, the new connection is allowed and all packets to that destination are processed immediately.
- If the destination endpoint is not listed in the working set, the connection rate filtering feature checks the connection rate threshold for the source. The connection rate threshold determines how many new connections an endpoint is allowed to make in a set time period. You will learn more about connection rate thresholds in an upcoming segment of this section. The connection rate is a good indicator of virus activity. For example, in most circumstances, an endpoint may open one new connection per second while an infected endpoint may attempt to open hundreds.

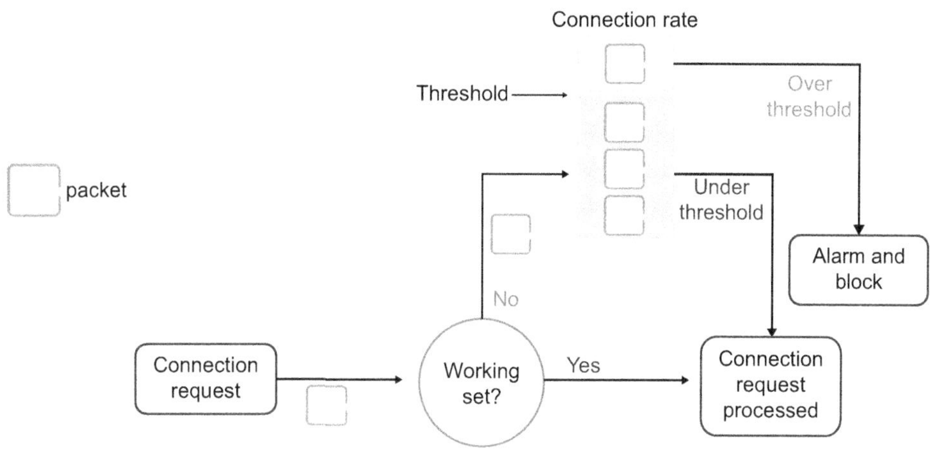


Figure 16-18 Operation

## Action

To enable connection rate filtering on a physical interface, you choose the action the switch should take when a host's connection request rate exceeds the threshold limit (see Figure 16-19). You can choose one of three actions:

- Notify only—When a host or endpoint device's connection request rate exceeds the limit, and while the potential attack is still underway, the switch generates an event log that identifies the suspect device's IP address and (if you have configured a trap receiver on the switch) an SNMP trap notice.
- Throttle—With this action, the switch temporarily blocks inbound IP traffic from the suspect host for a penalty period that is related to the threshold sensitivity you have configured for the port. (The next segment of this section explains sensitivity levels for threshold configurations.) It also generates an event-log notice similar to the notice that the notify-only action generates. When the penalty period expires, connection rate filtering again allows IP traffic from the suspect host as it reevaluates the host's activity. If the host continues to exceed its connection-rate-filter threshold, the switch blocks traffic for another penalty period, and so forth.
- Block—This action blocks all IP traffic from the suspect host. As with the other actions, the switch generates an event log entry and potentially an SNMP trap notice.

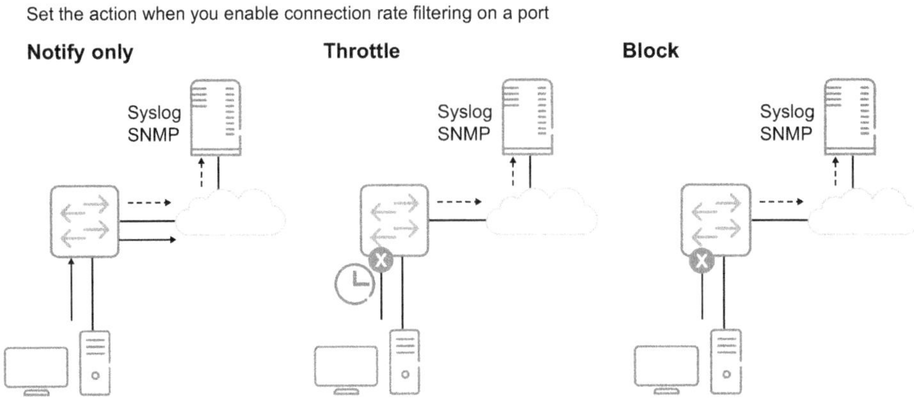


Figure 16-19 Action

Note that the block and throttle actions apply to host IP address, not to the port as a whole.

You should understand the implications of connection rate filtering. First, whether the switch throttles or blocks suspicious traffic, it does so on traffic that is inbound from the host, not on traffic outbound to the host. Next, you cannot cancel a throttle action (so be careful when you set the sensitivity): the penalty period must expire. On the other hand, you must manually cancel a block. Again, carefully tuning the sensitivity is key to saving yourself the effort of unblocking a wrongfully blocked host.

You set the action per-interface when you enable connection rate filtering on that interface.

```
Switch(config)# filter connection rate <port_ID_list> <notify-only |
throttle | block>
```

**Note**

You enable connection rate filtering on the trk interface rather than the interfaces within the link aggregation. If you have already enabled connection rate filtering on interfaces and you want to add those interfaces to a link aggregation, you must first disable connection rate filtering on them.

## Unblocking a blocked host

After connection rate filtering has blocked a host, you must explicitly unblock the host. Typically, you should do so with this command:

```
Switch(config)# connection-rate-filter unblock {all | host <IP address> |
<IP subnet/prefix length>}
```

The **all** option unblocks all blocked IP addresses. You can alternatively unblock a single IP address or all addresses in a subnet.

This command unblocks traffic from the device in question, but connection rate filtering continues to apply to the port. You should take steps to resolve the issue that caused the device to be blocked in the first place (remove the virus before unblocking the device, for example).

If you want to disable connection rate filtering on the port with the blocked port, you can enter this command, which also unblocks the IP address:

```
Switch(config)# no filter connection rate <port_ID_list>
```

These two actions also unblock hosts—although you would not typically want to take them in an active network, just to unblock a host:

- Rebooting the switch
- Deleting the VLAN through which the host is connected

Changing a port's setting, disabling the connection rate filter, or applying a connection rate access control list will not unblock your blocked host.

## Sensitivity

Even after you have enabled connection rate filtering on the port, it does not take effect until you enable the feature globally. You enable connection rate filtering globally by setting the sensitivity level.

Set the sensitivity to enable connection rate filtering globally (activates the feature on enabled ports)

| Throttle mode (sensitivity) | Frequency of IP connection requests from the same source | Mean number of new destination hosts in the frequency period | Penalty period |
|---|---|---|---|
| Low | <0.1 second | 54 | <30 seconds |
| Medium | <1.0 second | 37 | 30 – 60 seconds |
| High | <1.0 second | 22 | 60 – 90 seconds |
| Aggressive | <1.0 second | 15 | 90 – 120 seconds |

Figure 16-20 Sensitivity

You have four options for configuring sensitivity levels. These options are summarized in Figure 16-20 and described in more depth below:

- Low—This is the lowest possible connection rate sensitivity. That is, it allows the highest rate of connection-related IP traffic from the host: up to a mean of 54 destinations in less than 0.1 seconds (or 540 destinations in less than one second). Hosts that exceed this rate and trigger a throttling action will have their traffic blocked for less than 30 seconds.
- Medium—This sensitivity setting allows a lower connection rate, up to a mean of 37 destinations in less than a second. Hosts that exceed this rate and trigger a throttling action will have their traffic blocked for between 30 and 60 seconds.
- High—This setting allows a still lower mean connection rate of up to 22 destinations in a second. Hosts that exceed this rate and trigger throttling will have their traffic blocked for between 60 and 90 seconds.
- Aggressive—This sensitivity setting offers the lowest available connection rate with a mean of only 15 destinations in a second. Hosts that trigger throttling actions will have their traffic blocked for between 90 and 120 seconds.

Enter this command to set the sensitivity and enable connection rate filtering:

```
Switch(config)# connection-rate-filter sensitivity <low | medium | high |
aggressive>
```

## Implementation recommendations

Aruba recommends implementing connection rate filtering as close as possible to the network edge. This approach minimizes the number of IP addresses that this feature must monitor. It also enables switches to mitigate the problem as close to the source as possible, where action is most effective.

It is also best practice to test the deployment before allowing the feature to throttle or block traffic. Choose a sensitivity level that you think will work for your network; you might set the sensitivity a bit high because you will not actually be taking any action yet. Then choose the **notify-only** action and enable connection rate filtering on the desired ports.

Allow the feature to run for several weeks. Analyze any alerts that connection rate filtering triggers. Are the threats genuine, or has legitimate behavior been flagged? While traffic from malware is usually distinct from normal network traffic, some hosts—such as Microsoft Active Directory servers—legitimately generate requests for multiple connections within short timeframes. Connection rate filtering can generate false positives on such hosts.

If many different hosts are operating legitimately and generating false positives, you should lower the sensitivity and run the test again. If just one or two hosts, such as AD servers, are generating false positives, you can keep the sensitivity level. However, you should take action to disable filtering for those hosts, as described in the "Excluding hosts from filtering" section.

When you have finished tuning sensitivity and dealing with false positives, you can change the action to throttle or block, if you desire.

## Excluding hosts from filtering

A trusted host might make a high number of connection requests under normal operation. If the host in question is the only device on the port, you can disable connection rate filtering on the port with this command:

```
Switch(config)# no filter connection rate <port_ID_list>
```

Sometimes, though, the host in question might connect on the same port as other hosts, to which you still want to apply filtering. For example, it might be a Virtual Machine (VM) on a virtualized server. Or it, as well as other hosts, might connect to a switch that does not support connection rate filtering, which then connects to the connection rate filtering switch. You can still selectively disable connection rate filtering for the host. You can apply a connection rate filtering Access Control List (ACL) to tell the switch which traffic to filter and which to ignore.

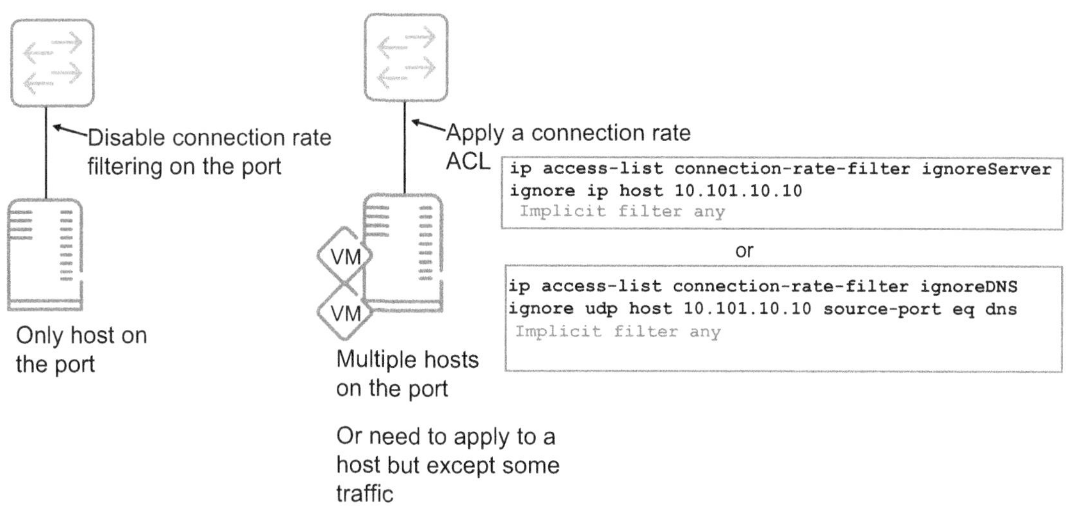


Figure 16-21 Excluding hosts from filtering

As Figure 16-21 shows, connection rate filtering ACL is a special type of ACL. Instead of permit and deny rules, it uses ignore and filter rules. These rules can select traffic based on:

- IP protocol
- IP source address (a single address or a range)
- For UDP or TCP rules, source port, destination port, or both

If a packet matches an ignore rule, the switch does not apply connection rate filtering. If the packet matches a filter rule, or no rule, the switch applies connection rate filtering.

You can create a simple list such as this to exclude a single host from filtering:

```
Switch(config)# ip access-list connection-rate-filter ignoreDNSserver
Switch(config-crf-nacl)# ignore ip host 10.101.10.10
```

You can also use connection rate filter ACLs to exclude only certain types of traffic while still monitoring other types of traffic. The selected traffic does not count toward the host's permitted number of connections. For example, this list tells the switch to ignore a Domain Name System (DNS) server's DNS replies when monitoring the server's connection rate:

```
Switch(config)# ip access-list connection-rate-filter ignoreDNS
Switch(config-crf-nacl)# ignore udp host 10.101.10.10 source-port eq dns
```

However, the switch continues to track other connections and take action if the connection rate exceeds the permitted rate.

You must apply the connection rate filter to a VLAN in order for it to take effect.

```
Switch(config)# vlan <ID> ip access-group <name> connection-rate-filter
```

The ACL takes effect on any traffic that is assigned to this VLAN and that arrives on a port with connection rate filtering enabled on it.

It is important that you understand that connection rate filtering penalties apply to the host as a whole. If you apply the ignoreDNSserver ACL, the switch will not monitor the connection rate for 10.101.10.10 at all. Therefore, it will never apply a penalty to this host. However, if you apply the ignoreDNS ACL, the switch will continue to monitor non-DNS traffic from 10.101.10.10 (and other hosts). If that traffic triggers the switch to block the host's traffic temporarily or permanently, the block will apply to DNS traffic from the blocked host, as well. Keep this in mind when you are deciding whether to ignore all traffic from a host or just some traffic.

## Summary

You have learned how to secure your network with several AOS-Switch features, including DHCP snooping, ARP protection, port security, MAC lockdown, and connection rate filtering. You can now follow best practices as you implement these features.

## Learning check

1. Port security has detected a MAC address on a port. The learn mode is set to static, the address limit to 1, and the action to none. Currently, no MAC addresses are configured as authorized on the port. What does the switch do?
   a. Learns the MAC address as an authorized address and permits the traffic.
   b. Does not learn the MAC address, but permits the traffic.
   c. Does not learn the MAC address and drops the traffic.
   d. Does not learn the MAC address, drops the traffic, and sends an SNMP trap.
2. A network administrator enables DHCP snooping on a VLAN and globally. The administrator has not configured any other DHCP snooping settings. Which correctly describes which ports are trusted or untrusted for DHCP operations in this VLAN?
   a. All ports that support untagged traffic only are untrusted; all ports that support multiple tagged VLANs are trusted.
   b. All ports that connect to endpoints are untrusted; all link aggregations are trusted.
   c. All ports on the switch are untrusted.
   d. All ports on the switch are trusted.
3. What information does the switch track in the DHCP snooping binding table?
4. How does a switch obtain the IP-to-MAC binding table that it uses for ARP protection?
5. You can view alerts from security measures by checking the log in the switch command line interface (CLI). How else might you want the switch to handle the alerts?
6. Describe the switch's behavior when you set the connection rate filter to throttle and the switch detects suspicious behavior, indicating a device may be infected.

# Answers

## Learning check

1. Port security has detected a MAC address on a port. The learn mode is set to static, the address limit to 1, and the action to none. Currently, no MAC addresses are configured as authorized on the port. What does the switch do?
   **a. Learns the MAC address as an authorized address and permits the traffic.**
   b. Does not learn the MAC address, but permits the traffic.
   c. Does not learn the MAC address and drops the traffic.
   d. Does not learn the MAC address, drops the traffic, and sends an SNMP trap.

2. A network administrator enables DHCP snooping on a VLAN and globally. The administrator has not configured any other DHCP snooping settings. Which correctly describes which ports are trusted or untrusted for DHCP in this VLAN?

    a. All ports that support untagged traffic only are untrusted; all ports that support multiple tagged VLANs are trusted.

    b. All ports that connect to endpoints are untrusted; all link aggregations are trusted.

    **c. All ports on the switch are untrusted.**

    d. All ports on the switch are trusted.

3. What information does the switch track in the DHCP snooping binding table?

    The DHCP snooping table tracks the MAC address, IP address, lease time, binding type, VLAN number, and interface information that corresponds to each DHCP lease.

4. How does a switch obtain the IP-to-MAC binding table that it uses for ARP protection?

    You enable DHCP snooping. The switch uses this feature to build the IP-to-MAC binding table.

5. You can view alerts from security measures by checking the log in the switch CLI. How else might you want the switch to handle the alerts?

    You might want the switch to forward the alerts to a centralized management solution such as Aruba AirWave. You could then easily see and act on the alerts. You learned how to set up SNMP trap receivers and enable SNMP traps for security alarms in *Chapter 14: Secure Device Management*. In AirWave you can set up triggers to take action—such as send notifications—when specific events or traps occur, if you want.

6. Describe the switch's behavior when you set the connection-rate filter to throttle and the switch detects suspicious behavior, indicating a device may be infected.

    The switch will temporarily block traffic from the offending device. The switch will periodically stop blocking the traffic, but it could start blocking the traffic again if the device continues to violate the limit.

# 17 Practice Exam

## Introduction

The Implementing Aruba Campus Switching Solutions exam tests your skills with wired configurations of Aruba Mobile First Solutions in complex two-tier and three-tier networks with redundancy. The exam tests your skills to build to a given implementation plan and deploy consistent wired access control technologies to mirror the wireless access control policies. It also tests your ability to configure specialized applications and security requirements for a network.

The intent of this study guide is to set expectations about the context of the exam and to help candidates prepare for it. Recommended training to prepare for this exam can be found at the HPE Certification and Learning website (https://certification-learning.hpe.com). It is important to note that, although training is recommended for exam preparation, successful completion of the training alone does not guarantee that you will pass the exam. In addition to training, exam items are based on knowledge gained from on-the-job experience and application and on other supplemental reference material that may be specified in this guide.

## Minimum qualifications

Typical candidates for this exam are networking IT professionals who have advanced-level implementation experience with Aruba wired switching solutions. This candidate has a minimum of 4–5 years of general networking experience and 2 years of experience focused on interpreting network architectures and customer requirements to install and configure Aruba solutions.

## HPE6-A45 exam details

Below are details about the HPE6-A45 exam.

- Number of items: 60
- Exam time: 1 hour 30 minutes
- Passing score: 67%
- Item types: Multiple choice (single-response) and multiple choice (multiple-response)
- Reference material: No online or hard copy reference material is allowed at the testing site.

## HPE6-A45 testing objectives

This exam validates that you can successfully perform the following objectives. Each main objective is given a weighting, indicating the emphasis this item has in the exam.

- Plan the wired network solution.

  Weighting: **14%**

  - Given a scenario with an architect's design and/or customer requirements, identify gaps between the design and customer requirements.
  - Given a scenario with an architect's design and/or customer requirements, determine an appropriate implementation, monitoring, and management plan.

- Install and configure the wired network solution.

  Weighting: **46%**

  - Given an implementation plan, configure backplane stacking and Virtual Switching Framework (VSF).
  - Given an implementation plan, explain how to configure Layer 2 technologies.
  - Given an implementation plan, explain how to configure and validate Layer 3 interfaces, services, routing protocols, and overlays.
  - Explain multicast features and configuration concepts.
  - Explain AOS-Switch security features and configuration concepts.
  - Explain QoS AOS-Switch features and configuration concepts.
  - Explain mobility integration features and configuration concepts.

- Troubleshoot the wired network solution.

  Weighting: **27%**

  - Given a scenario, identify a failure such as an IP mismatch, VLAN mismatch, hardware failure, or configuration error.
  - Given an action plan to remediate an issue, determine the implications to the network state.
  - Given a scenario, determine the cause of the performance problem such as QoS issue, configuration issue with hardware and software, and end node.
  - Given a scenario, predict the outcome based on the changes to the security configuration.
  - Given a scenario with an identified security issue, determine the remediation actions.

- Manage, maintain, optimize, and monitor the wired network solution.

  Weighting: **13%**

  - Given a scenario, determine a strategy to implement configuration management (maintenance, auditing, backup, and archiving) and to monitor the network.
  - Analyze data that represents the operational state of a network and determine the appropriate action.

## Test preparation questions and answers

The following questions help you to measure your understanding of the material presented in this study guide and determine if you are prepared to take the HPE6-A45 exam. Read all of the choices for each question carefully before selecting the correct answer. Remember to select all correct answers for each question.

### Questions

You can check your responses in the "Answers" section at the end of this chapter.

1. A university does not want students and guests to replace equipment in various public areas with their own devices. The network administrator wants to implement port security on ports in those areas to prevent such changes. The network administrator does not want to have to specify the authorized MAC addresses manually. The administrator will set the port security address limit to 1.

   What is the correct port security learn mode for this scenario?

   a. limited-continuous

   b. port-access

   c. static

   d. configured

2. Refer to the network in Figure 17-1.

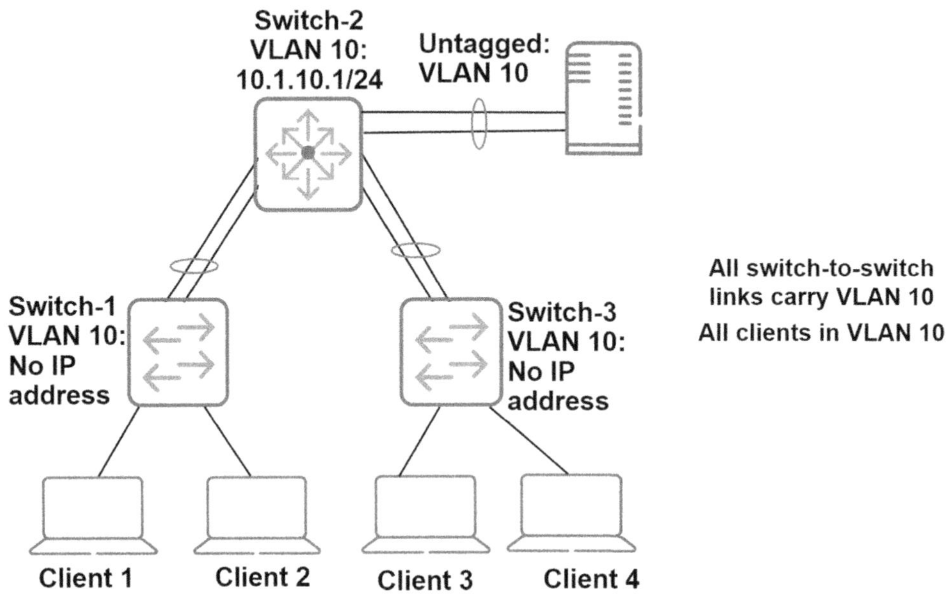


Figure 17-1 Question 2 network topology

What is one reason to enable Internet Group Management Protocol (IGMP) on VLAN 10 on Switch-1 and Switch-3?

a. To provide backup for the IGMP querier role

b. To allow the IGMP reports from clients to reach Switch-2

c. To filter multicasts on all edge ports that do not need them

d. To allow IGMP to interoperate with a multicast routing protocol

3. A customer needs a distribution layer AOS-Switch that supports VSF, dynamic routing, access control lists (ACLs), 10GbE downlinks, and 40GbE uplinks. The customer is considering 2930F Series switches. Which switches better fit the needs?

a. 8400 Series switches

b. 5400R zl2 Series switches

c. 2930M Series switches

d. 2540 Series switches

4. Refer to the network in Figure 17-2 and the command output below.

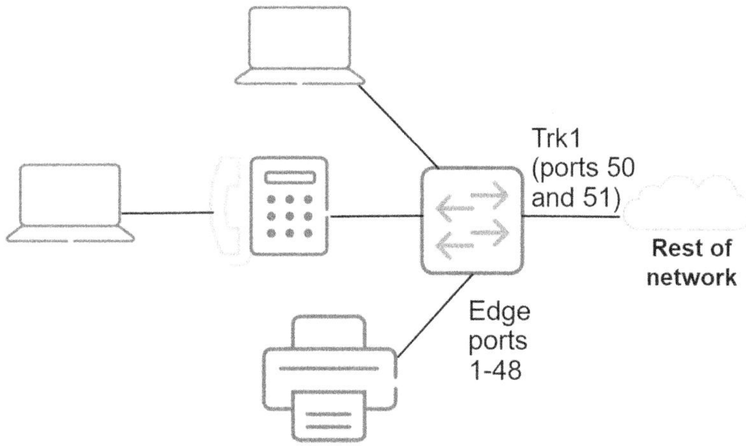


Figure 17-2 Question 4 network topology

```
Switch-1# show port-access config
 Port Access Status Summary

  Port-access authenticator activated [No] : No
  Allow RADIUS-assigned dynamic (GVRP) VLANs [No] : No
  Use LLDP data to authenticate [No] : No

        802.1X  802.1X   Web      Mac      LMA   Cntrl Mixed    Speed
  Port  Supp    Auth     Auth     Auth     Auth  Dir   Mode     VSA   MBV
  ----- ------- -------- -------- -------- ----- ----- -------- ----- ---
  1     No      No       No       No       Yes   both  No       No    Yes
<same settings on ports 1-48>
```

A company has several types of devices that connect to ports, including VoIP phones and computers. The company wants to use local MAC authentication (LMA) groups and profiles to provision settings for phones. The company does not care about authenticating users, so the switch will place all other devices in an unauthenticated VLAN. The command output shows the authentication configuration for edge ports.

Based on the exhibit, which step must the administrator complete for the solution to succeed?

a. Enable port-access mixed-mode on edge pots.

b. Disable MAC-based VLANs (MBVs) on edge ports.

c. Activate the port-access authenticator globally.

d. Allow RADIUS-assigned dynamic (GVRP) VLANs.

5. Refer to the network in Figure 17-3 and the command output below.

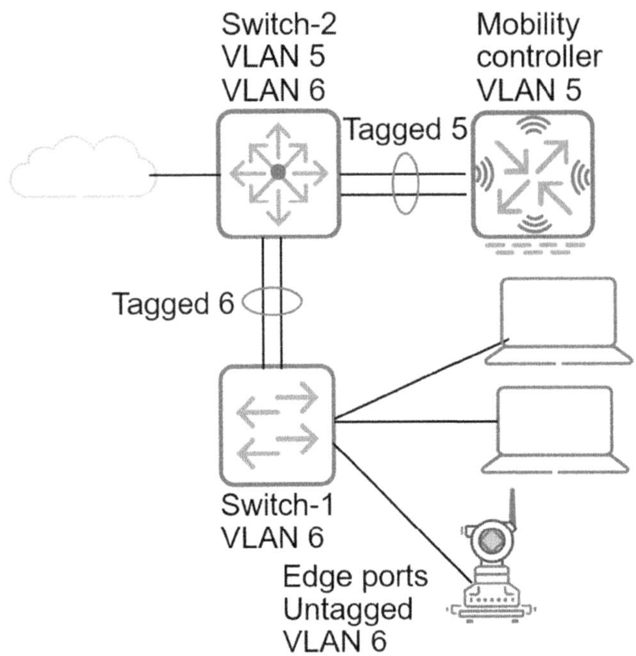


Figure 17-3 Question 5 VLAN 5 and 6 design

```
Switch-1(config)# show user-role iot
 User Role Information

   Name                                  : iot
   Type                                  : local
   Reauthentication Period (seconds)     : 0
   Untagged VLAN                         : 5
   Tagged VLAN                           :
   Captive Portal Profile                :
   Policy                                :
   Tunnelednode Server Redirect          : Enabled
   Secondary Role Name                   : iot
```

```
Switch-1(config)# show user-role employees
 User Role Information

   Name                                  : employees
   Type                                  : local
   Reauthentication Period (seconds)     : 0
   Untagged VLAN                         :
   Tagged VLAN                           :
   Captive Portal Profile                :
   Policy                                :
   Tunnelednode Server Redirect          :
   Secondary Role Name                   :
```

The network administrator needs to set up role-based tunneled-node on an AOS-Switch. The switch should forward employee traffic locally in VLAN 6. The switch should tunnel IoT traffic to the Aruba Mobility Controller (MC). The MC supports VLAN 5 and will forward the traffic in this VLAN at Layer 2.

The command output shows the roles.

Figure 17-3 shows how the network administrator plans to configure VLANs 5 and 6 for this solution. In the figure, a VLAN under a device name indicates that the device is configured with that VLAN. The figure also indicates which VLANs are statically configured on each link.

What change to the plan should the administrator make?

a. Create VLAN 5 on Switch-1, but do not assign any interfaces to it.

b. Configure VLAN 5 as the untagged VLAN on Switch-1 edge ports.

c. On Switch-2, remove VLAN 5 from the link to the MC and add it to the link to Switch-1.

d. On Switch-2, add VLAN 6 to the link to the MC.

6. Refer to the command output below.

```
snmp-server community "myrw" unrestricted

snmp-server contact MyName location Exam

snmp-server host 10.10.10.10 community "myrw"

snmpv3 enable

snmpv3 user "admin" auth sha "password" priv aes "password"

snmpv3 group managerpriv user "admin" sec-model ver3

snmpv3 only

snmpv3 params "myparams" user "admin" sec-model ver3 message-processing
ver3 priv

snmpv3 notify "mynotify" taglist "mytaglist"

snmpv3 target "mytarget" 10.10.10.10 params "myparams" taglist "mytaglist"
```

An AOS-Switch was using SNMPv2c. The company security policy then changed. Switches must now accept only SNMPv3 Get and Set messages, and it must only send SNMPv3 traps.

Administrators added the SNMPv3 settings but did not remove the SNMPv2c ones. The command output above shows the current configuration on the switch.

Which correctly describes how well the switch complies with the new company policy?

a. The switch complies with the policy. It rejects SNMPv2c Get and Set messages and does not send SNMPv2c traps.

b. The switch does not comply with the policy. It rejects SNMPv2c Get and Set messages, but sends SNMPv2c traps.

c. The switch does not comply with the policy. It rejects SNMPv2c Set messages, but it accepts Get messages. It also sends SNMPv2c traps.

d. The switch does not comply with the policy. It accepts SNMPv2c Get and Set messages. And it sends SNMPv2c traps.

7. A network administrator needs to configure four Aruba 2930F switches in a VSF fabric. The administrator wants to set up VSF with a plug-and-play setup. The administrator will configure VSF on the future commander and then connect the other switches at factory default settings.

What is one requirement that the administrator must fulfill on the future commander for this setup to work?

a. Enable fast software update (FSU) so the commander can update members' software.

b. Set up VLAN MAD on the default VLAN and enable VLAN MAD.

c. Use strict provisioning to add other members and assign them unique domain IDs.

d. Provision the other members and set up their VSF links.

8. Refer to the network topology in Figure 17-4.

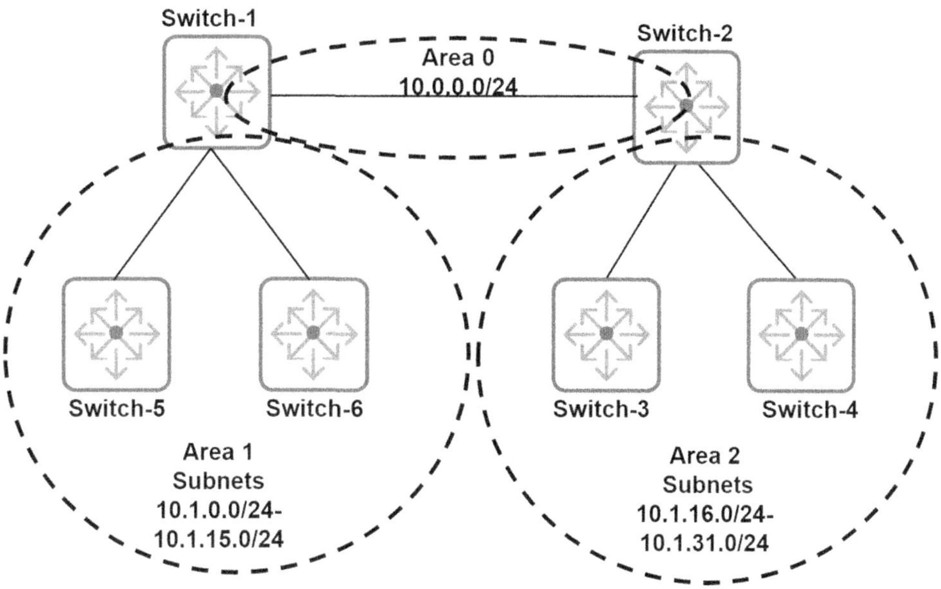


Figure 17-4 Question 8 network topology

Figure 17-4 shows a company network. The company wants to make each site a different area and to aggregate routes between areas into a single route for each area. Which area summary range or ranges should the administrator configure on Switch-1?

a. Area 0 ranges = 10.0.0.0/24 and 10.1.16.0/20

b. Area 0 range = 10.0.0.0/24 and 10.1.0.0/20

c. Area 0 range = 10.0.0.0/24; area 1 range = 10.1.0.0/20

d. Area 0 range = 10.1.0.0/20; area 1 ranges = 10.0.0.0/24 and 10.1.16.0/20

9. Refer to the network topology in Figure 17-5.

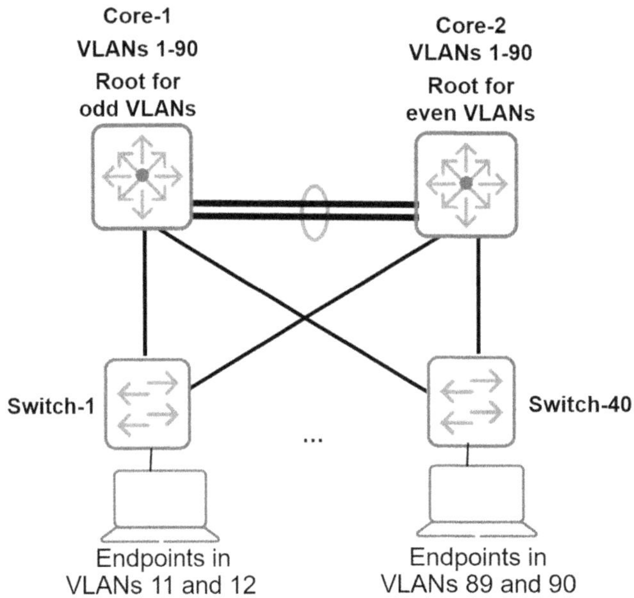


Figure 17-5 Question 9 network topology

The network administrator needs to implement RPVST+ on AOS-Switches at the access layer of a heterogeneous network. What is a best practice for the links between each access layer switch and the core?

a. Add only the VLANs that the access layer switch needs to support.

b. Add all of the VLANs used in the spanning tree domain.

c. Make sure that VLAN 1 is removed from the link.

d. Implement root guard in the VLANs for which the connected switch is root.

10. A network administrator implements Open Shortest Path First (OSPF) with multiple areas. The network administrator wants to redistribute external routes in area 1 and keep those routes local to the area. On which routing devices, must the administrator configure area 1 as a not so stubby area (NSSA)?

a. Only the device that redistributes external routes

b. Only the area border routers (ABRs) for area 1

c. Both the devices that redistributes external routes and the ABRs

d. All OSPF routing devices in the area

11. Refer to the network topology in Figure 17-6 and the command output below.

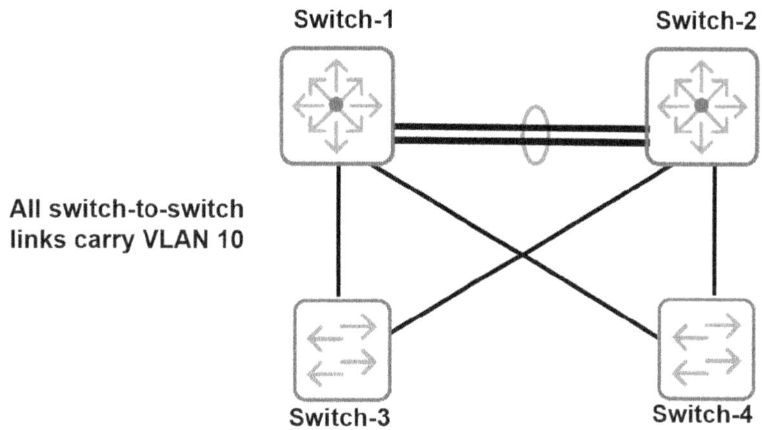


Figure 17-6 Question 11 network topology

```
Switch-1(config)# router vrrp ipv4 enable
Switch-1(config)# vlan 10
Switch-1(vlan-10)# ip address 10.1.10.1/24
Switch-1(vlan-10)# vrrp vrid 10
Switch-1(vlan-10-vrid-10)# virtual-ip 10.1.10.1
Switch-1(vlan-10-vrid-10)# enable

Switch-2(config)# router vrrp ipv4 enable
Switch-2(config)# vlan 10
Switch-2(vlan-10)# ip address 10.1.10.2/24
Switch-2(vlan-10)# vrrp vrid 10
Switch-2(vlan-10-vrid-10)# virtual-ip 10.1.10.1
Switch-2(vlan-10-vrid-10)# priority 254
Switch-2(vlan-10-vrid-10)# enable
```

The second exhibit shows the commands that the network administrator plans to enter on Switch-1 and Switch-2. What does the administrator need to change to make Switch-2 Master for the VLAN 10 VRID during normal operation?

a. Set the VRRP priority value to 1 on Switch-1.

b. Set the VRRP priority value to 1 on Switch-2.

c. Enable preempt mode on Switch-2.

d. Change the VLAN 10 IP address on Switch-1.

12. Refer to the network topology in Figure 17-7 and the command output below.

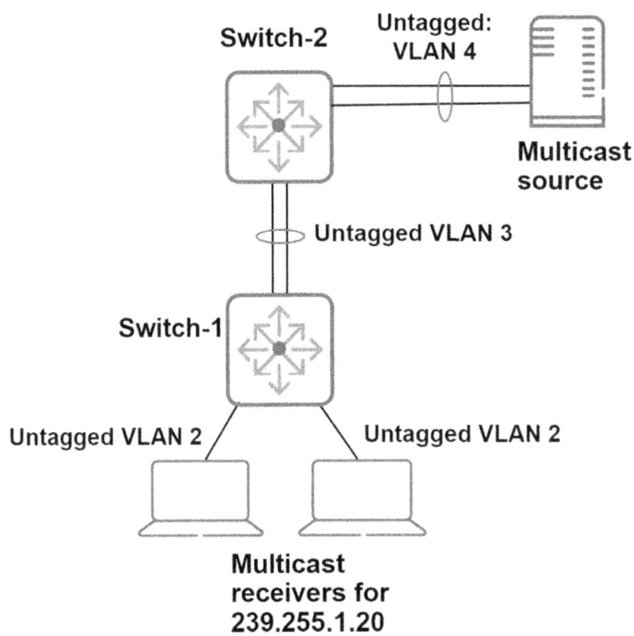


Figure 17-7 Question 12 network topology

```
#Switch-1 partial running-config
ip multicast-routing
router pim
  enable
  exit
router ospf
   area 0.0.0.1
   enable
   exit
vlan 2
   name "Users"
   untagged 1-48
   ip address 10.1.2.1 255.255.255.0
   ip helper-address 10.1.4.10
   ip igmp
   ip ospf 10.1.2.1 area 0.0.0.1
vlan 3
   name "ToSwitch-2"
   untagged trk1
   ip address 10.1.3.1 255.255.255.252
   ip ospf 10.1.3.1 area 0.0.0.1
   ip pim-dense
      ip-addr any
      exit
   exit

#Switch-2 partial running-config
ip multicast-routing
router pim
  enable
  exit
```

```
router ospf
   area 0.0.0.1
   enable
   exit
vlan 3
   name "ToSwitch-1"
   untagged trk1
   ip address 10.1.3.2 255.255.255.252
   ip ospf 10.1.3.2 area 0.0.0.1
   ip pim-dense
      ip-addr any
      exit
   exit
vlan 4
   name "Users"
   untagged 1-48
   ip address 10.1.4.1 255.255.255.0
   ip igmp
   ip ospf 10.1.4.1 area 0.0.0.1
   ip pim-dense
      ip-addr any
      exit
   exit
```

The source begins to send multicasts to 239.255.1.20. However, the endpoints listening for those multicasts do not receive them. What should the administrator do to fix the problem?

a. Enable IGMP on VLAN 3 on Switch-1 and Switch-2.

b. Enable PIM-DM on VLAN 2 on Switch-1.

c. Configure an RP address on VLAN 3 on Switch-1.

d. Configure an RP address on VLAN 3 on Switch-2.

13. View the backplane stack in Figure 17-8.

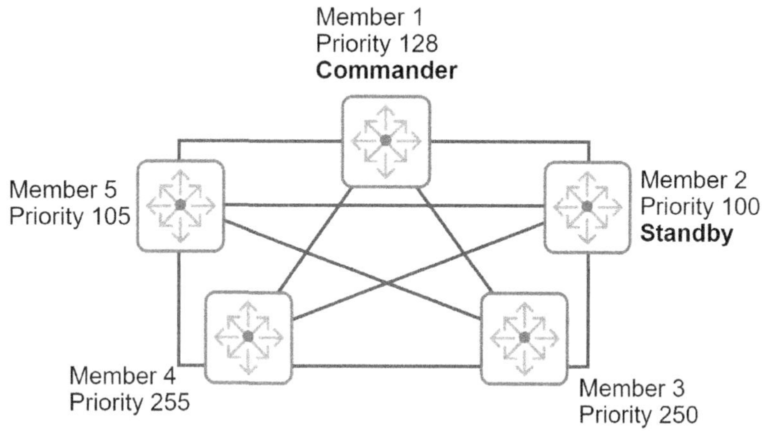


Figure 17-8 Question 13 backplane stack

The switches are configured with backplane stacking and the priorities shown in the exhibit. Member 1 is currently commander, and Member 2 is currently standby. Then a power issue causes all of the switches to power down and then power back up at the same time.

All switches have the same stack ID revision. Which switches become commander and standby after the stack re-establishes?

a. Member 1 is commander, and Member 2 is standby.

b. Member 1 is commander, and Member 4 is standby.

c. Member 2 is commander, and Member 5 is standby.

d. Member 4 is commander, and Member 3 is standby.

14. Refer to the network topology in Figure 17-9 and the command output below.

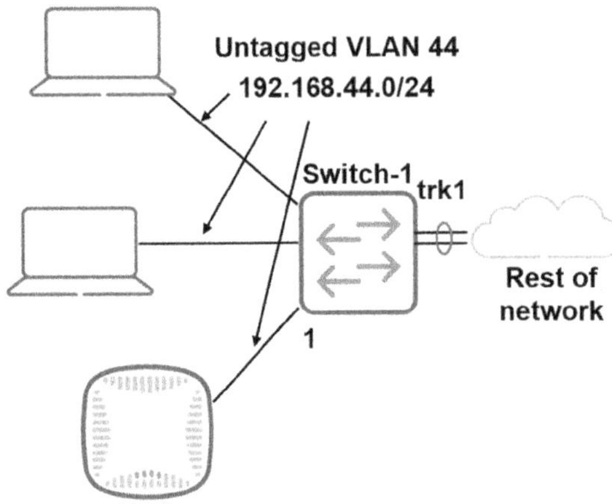


Figure 17-9 Question 14 network topology

```
#Switch-1 global QoS running-config
qos device-priority 192.168.44.0/24 dscp 8
#
Switch-1# show running-config interface 1,trk1
interface 1
  untagged vlan 44
  qos trust device aruba-ap
interface trk1
  tagged vlan 44
  qos trust dscp
```

A company has set a low priority for devices in VLAN 44, 192.168.44.0/24, which is used by guests. An Aruba AP is also deployed on this VLAN, but the company wants to honor the DSCP in traffic to and from the AP. The switch is using the default DSCP maps, which meet the needs for this scenario. Currently, however, the AP traffic does not receive the desired priority. What causes this issue?

a. The global type of service is disabled instead of set to Differentiated Services (DiffServ).

b. The global device-based QoS policy overrides the incoming DSCP.

c. The AP interface does not have 802.1X authentication enabled on it.

d. The AP interface does not have a QoS DSCP value set on it.

15. An AOS-Switch needs to integrate with an Aruba ClearPass Guest captive portal solution. ClearPass is at IP address 10.100.40.10, and the switch has 10.100.40.10 specified as the RADIUS server for MAC-Auth. What is another requirement for the configuration on the AOS-Switch?

    a. It has the ClearPass Guest URL defined as the web-based authentication redirect page.

    b. 10.100.40.10 is specified as the Enhanced Web Auth (EWA) server.

    c. Dynamic authorization is enabled for the 10.100.40.10 RADIUS server.

    d. The captive portal URL hash key matches the RADIUS key for 10.100.40.10.

16. Refer to the network topology in Figure 17-10.

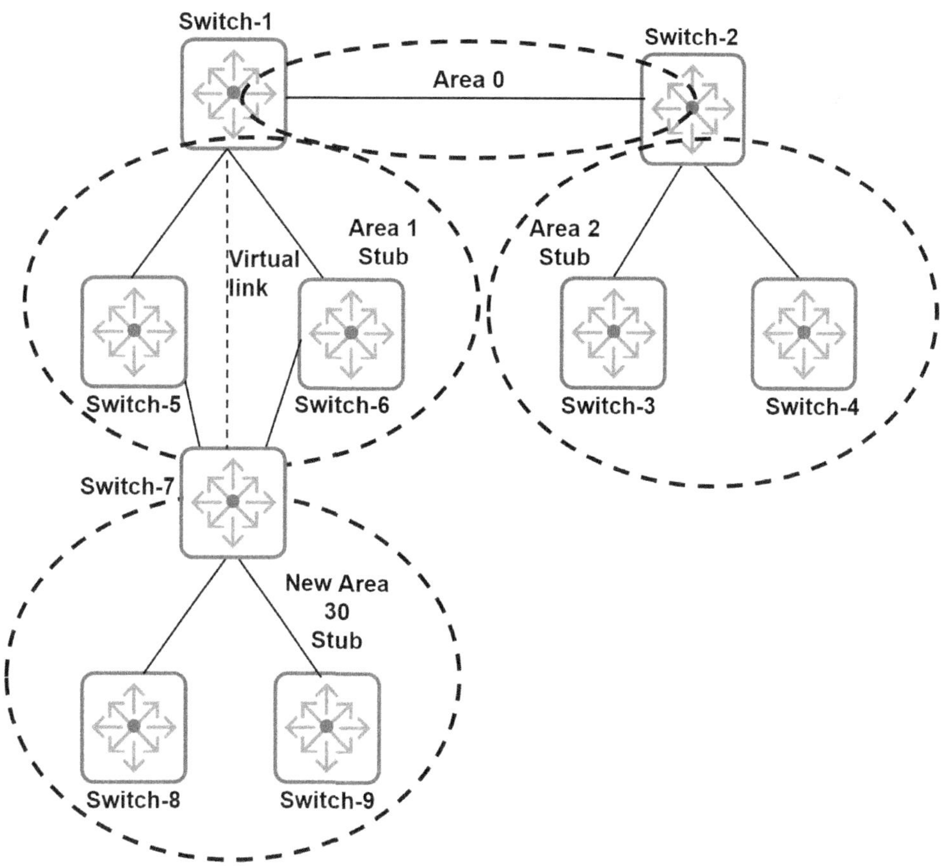


Figure 17-10 Question 16 network topology

A network administrator plans to establish a new OSPF area and a virtual link, as shown in the exhibit. What must the administrator correct to make the plan work?

a. Area 1 must be redefined as a normal area.

b. Area 30 must be redefined as an NSSA.

c. Switch-7 must have an interface in area 0.

d. Switch-1 and Switch-7 must be directly connected.

17. Refer to the network topology in Figure 17-11 and the command output below.

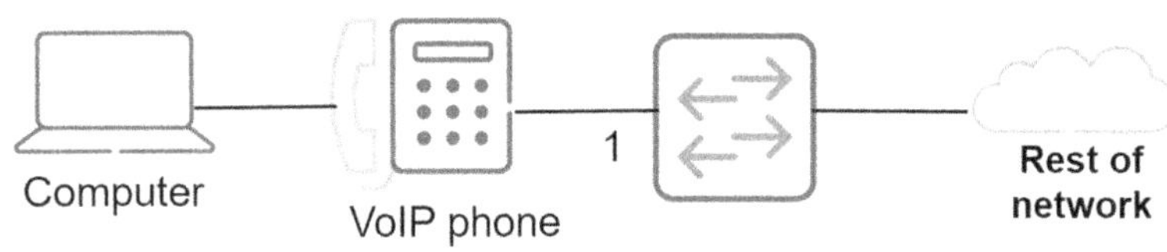


Figure 17-11 Question 17 network topology

```
Switch-1# show running-config interface 1
interface 1
  vlan 20 untagged
  vlan 21 tagged
  aaa port-access authenticator client-limit 2
```

The VoIP phone is configured to forward tagged traffic in VLAN 21. It connects and authenticates successfully. The computer does not authenticate but starts to send untagged traffic to request a DHCP address. How does the switch handle this traffic?

a. It forwards the traffic in VLAN 20.

b. It forwards the traffic in VLAN 21.

c. It drops the traffic.

d. It relays the DHCP traffic to the RADIUS server.

18. A link is performing poorly. What can the network administrator view to look for signs of a hardware malfunction?

a. ACL resource usage

b. RMON tables

c. sFlow port counters

d. SNMPv3 views

19. Refer to the command output below.

```
Switch-1# show access-list myList
Access Control Lists

  Name: myList
  Type: Extended
  Applied: Yes

 SEQ  Entry
-------------------------------------------------------------------------------
  10  Action: permit
      Src IP: 0.0.0.0          Mask: 255.255.255.255   Port(s):
      Dst IP: 0.0.0.0         Mask: 255.255.255.255   Port(s): eq 53
      Proto : UDP
      TOS   : -                Precedence: -

 20   Action: deny
      Src IP: 10.1.3.0         Mask: 0.0.0.255
      Dst IP: 10.1.4.0         Mask: 0.0.0.127         Port(s):
      Proto : IP
      TOS   : -                Precedence: -

 30   Action: permit
      Src IP: 10.1.3.0          Mask: 0.0.0.255        Port(s):
      Dst IP: 0.0.0.0           Mask: 0.0.0.0          Port(s):
      Proto : IP
      TOS   : -                Precedence: -
```

Switch-1 is routing traffic between VLAN 3, 10.1.3.0/24, and VLAN 4, 10.1.4.0/24. The network administrator has applied the ACL shown above with this command:

```
Switch-1(config)# vlan 3 ip access-group myList in
```

VLAN 4 has no ACLs applied to it.

How does the switch handle these packets?

- Packet 1 = DNS traffic from 10.1.3.10 to 10.1.4.5
- Packet 2 = HTTP traffic from 10.1.4.200 to 10.1.3.5
- Packet 3 = HTTP traffic from 10.1.3.11 to 10.1.4.100

  a. It permits Packets 1 and 2 and denies Packet 3.

  b. It permits Packet 1 and denies Packets 2 and 3.

  c. It permits Packet 2 and denies Packets 1 and 3.

  d. It permits Packet 3 and denies Packets 1 and 2.

20. A network administrator sees that the ACL resource space on an AOS-Switch does not have much room left. Currently, the extended IP ACL named myList is applied inbound on 40 physical interfaces, and the administrator wants to reapply the ACL with the **shared** option. However, when the administrator tries to enter the command, the CLI produces an error, and the help key shows that the option is not available. What should the administrator do to enable this option?

    a. Move the ACL to VLAN interfaces and apply with the **in** option.

    b. Recreate the ACL as a standard IP ACL.

    c. Enable ACL grouping and reboot.

    d. Recreate the ACL with the **shared** option after the ACL name.

21. Refer to the network topology in Figure 17-12.

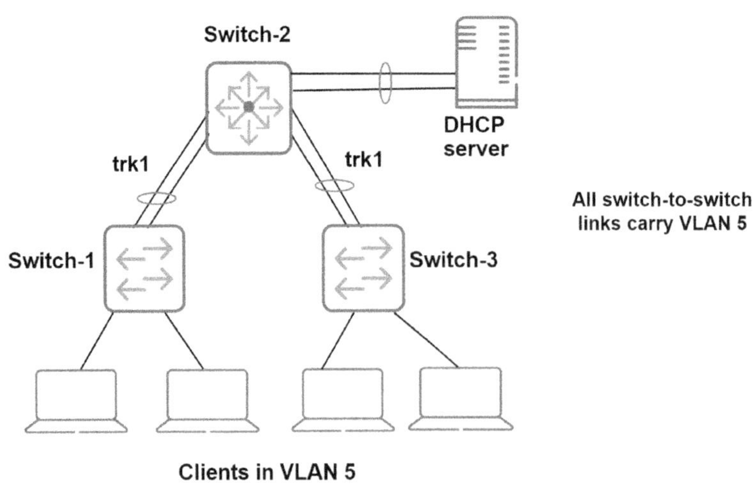


Figure 17-12 Question 21 network topology

```
Switch-X(config)# dhcp-snooping vlan 5
Switch-X(config)# dhcp-snooping trust trk1
Switch-X(config)# arp-protect vlan 5
Switch-X(config)# arp-protect trust trk1
Switch-X(config)# arp-protect
```

AOS-Switches in this network currently have no configurations for DHCP snooping or ARP protection. The network administrator plans to enter the commands shown in the second exhibit on the access layer switches, Switch-1 and Switch-3. What error in these commands will cause a serious issue?

a. No authorized DHCP server is configured.

b. The wrong interfaces are set as trusted interfaces.

c. ARP protection and DHCP snooping are enabled on the same VLAN.

d. DHCP snooping is not enabled globally.

22. Refer to the command output below.

```
Switch-1# show interface queues 49
Status and Counters - Port Counters for port 49
<-output omitted->

 Egress Queue Totals (Since boot or last clear) :
     Tx Packets   Dropped Packets   Tx Bytes      Dropped Bytes
 Q1  34           0                 6,158         0
 Q2  0            0                 0             0
 Q3  1,010        287,815           1,775,467     423,450,834
 Q4  303,012      0                 398,341,341   0
 Q5  403,043      0                 452,341,341   0
 Q6  350,090      0                 300,382,031   0
 Q7  3700         0                 328,654       0
 Q8  1054         0                 199,002       0
```

A network administrator notices that normal priority traffic is being starved out by higher priority traffic on an Aruba 5406R switch. What can the administrator do to address this issue?

a. Set a higher guaranteed minimum bandwidth (GMB) for queue 3.

b. Change the scheduling mechanism to weighted fair queuing (WFQ).

c. Increase the number of per-port queues used by the switch.

d. Enable type of services and set it to DiffServ.

23. Refer to the network topology in Figure 17-13 and command output below.

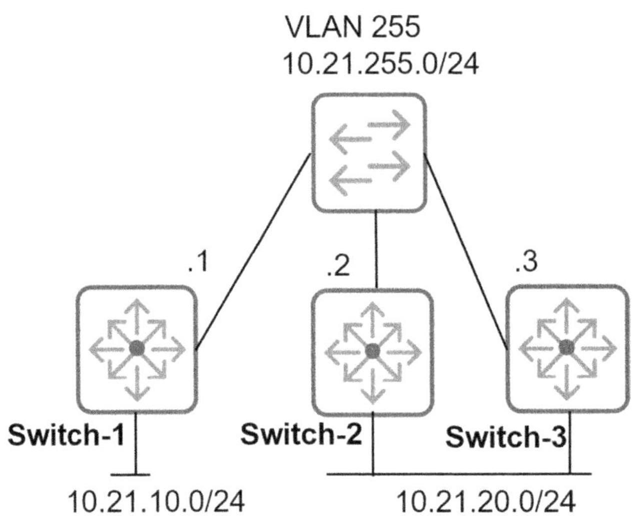


Figure 17-13 Question 23 network topology

```
Switch-1# show bfd
 Bidirectional Forwarding Detection (BFD) Information

  Administrative Status : Enabled
  Echo Source IP        :   10.21.0.1

  Maximum number of sessions supported         : 128
  Number of sessions reserved for internal use : 0
  Total Number of Sessions : 2
  Number of Sessions Up    : 2
  Number of Sessions Down  : 0

  Global Statistics:
  Total Number of Control Packets Transmitted  : 120
  Total Number of Control Packets Received     : 121
  Total Number of Control Packets Dropped      : 0

  Session VLAN  Source IP    Destination IP Echo     State Application
  ------- ----  -----------  -------------- -------  ----- -----------
  1       255   10.21.255.1  10.21.255.2    Enabled  Up    OSPF
  2       255   10.21.255.1  10.21.255.3    Enabled  Up    OSPF
```

All three switches have these settings on VLAN 255:

- OSPF BFD Min transmit interval (Tx timer) = 2 seconds
- OSPF BFD min receive interval (Rx timer) = 1 seconds
- OSPF BFD min echo receive interval = 500 milliseconds
- OSPF BFD detect multiplier = 3
- OSPF dead timer = 40 seconds

If Switch-1 loses IP connectivity with Switch-2, how quickly can Switch-1 detect the issue and take down the OSPF relationship?

a. In 1.5 seconds

b. In 3 seconds

c. In 6 seconds

d. In 40 seconds

24. A company has Aruba wired and wireless infrastructure. What should network administrators do to support centralized monitoring, auditing, and backing up of AOS-Switch configurations?

    a. Deploy Aruba ClearPass Onboard and integrate the switches with it.

    b. Add licenses for the switches on an Aruba MC.

    c. Make sure that the switch TFTP server is enabled in permissive mode.

    d. Deploy Aruba AirWave and discover the AOS-Switches in it.

25. Refer to the network topology in Figure 17-14 and the commands below.

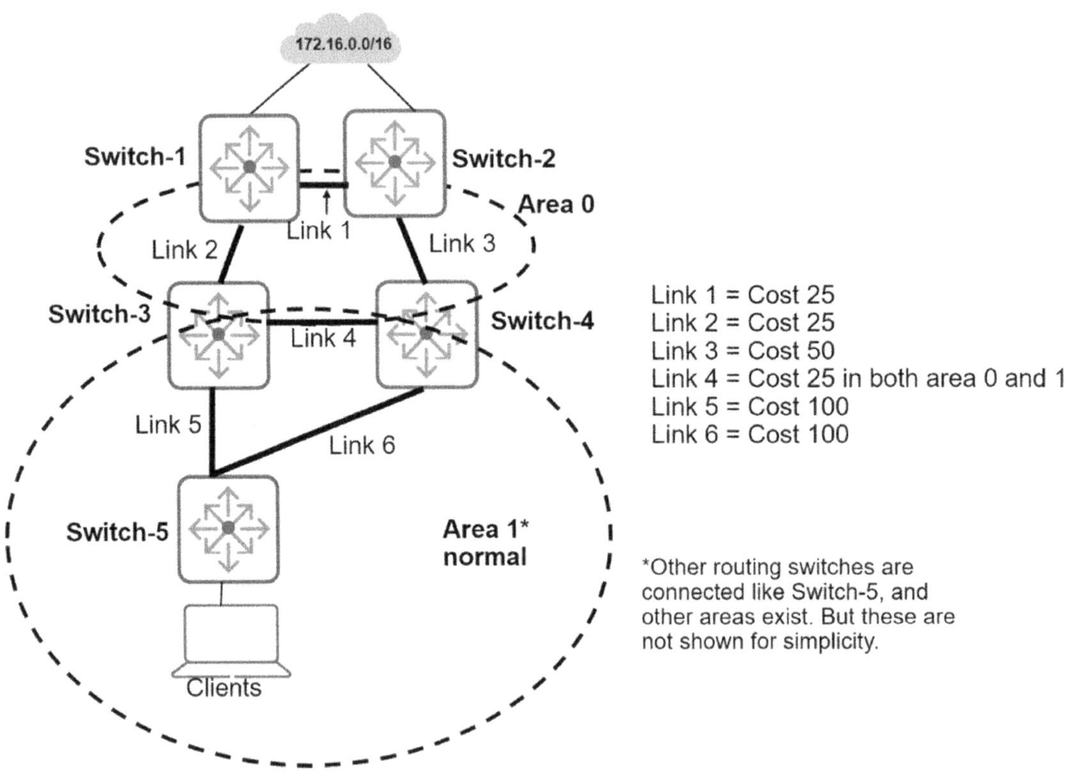


Figure 17-14 Question 25 network topology

```
Switch-1(ospf)# metric-type type2
Switch-1(ospf)# default-metric 70
Switch-1(ospf)# redistribute static

Switch-2(ospf)# metric-type type2
Switch-2(ospf)# default-metric 50
Switch-2(ospf)# redistribute static
```

Initially, all links are up and running OSPF as shown in the first exhibit, and all OSPF routing switches have achieved adjacency. Switch-1 and Switch-2 currently have active static routes to 172.16.0.0/16; however, other switches do not.

Then the network administrator enters the commands shown above. Switch-5 is using the default ECMP setting. How will Switch-5 begin to forward traffic destined to the 172.16.0.0/16 network?

a. It will send all of the traffic on Link 5.

b. It will send all of the traffic on Link 6.

c. It will load-balance the traffic on Link 5 and Link 6.

d. It will drop the trafic.

26. Refer to the network topology in Figure 17-15 and the command output below.

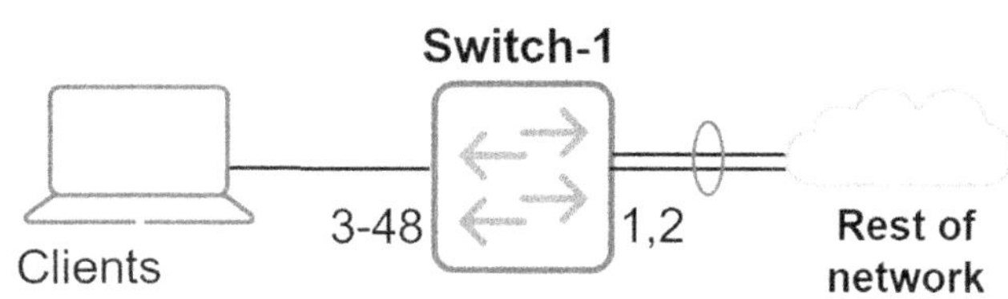


Figure 17-15 Question 26 network topology

```
Switch-1# show interface 1

Status and Counters - Port Counters for port 1

  Name  :
  MAC Address      : 00fd45-7dc65b
  Link Status      : Up
  Totals (Since boot or last clear) :
   Bytes Rx        : 19,391,833,943    Bytes Tx        : 29,087,750,915
   Unicast Rx      : 3,029,974         Unicast Tx      : 4,434,108
   Bcast/Mcast Rx : 63,100             Bcast/Mcast Tx  :  69,966
  Errors (Since boot or last clear) :
   FCS Rx          : 0                 Drops Tx        : 0
   Alignment Rx    : 0                 Collisions Tx   : 0
   Runts Rx        : 0                 Late Colln      : 0
   Giants Rx       : 0                 Excessive Colln : 0
   Total Rx Errors: 0                  Deferred Tx     : 0
  Others (Since boot or last clear) :
   Discard Rx      : 0                 Out Queue Len   : 0
   Unknown Protos : 0
  Rates (5 minute weighted average) :
   Total Rx (bps) : 601,341,923    Total Tx (bps) :   905,203,422
   Unicast Rx (Pkts/sec) : 93,959  Unicast Tx (Pkts/sec) : 137,683
   B/Mcast Rx (Pkts/sec) : 10      B/Mcast Tx (Pkts/sec) : 11
   Utilization Rx   : 60.13 %      Utilization Tx   : 90.52 %
```

Alerted to high usage on a switch by a management solution, network administrators have examined the utilization on the uplink interfaces several times an hour during problem times. The exhibit shows output typical of times of congestion.

What could help allocate bandwidth fairly among the devices connected to this switch, as well as reduce the congestion that occurs on this switch's uplink?

a. a broadcast rate limit on each edge port

b. an inbound rate limit on each edge port

c. an outbound rate limit on interfaces 1 and 2

d. an inbound rate limit on interfaces 1 and 2

27. Refer to the running-config below.

```
#Switch RADIUS and 802.1X running-config
radius-server key password
radius-server host 10.10.10.5 key password1
radius-server host 10.10.10.6
#AAA running-config
aaa server-group radius mygroup host 10.10.10.5
aaa server-group radius mygroup host 10.10.10.6
aaa authentication port-access eap-radius server-group mygroup
aaa port-access authenticator 1-48 client-limit 1
aaa port-access authenticator active
```

The network administrator has configured 802.1X and RADIUS settings on an AOS-Switch as shown above. When devices connect to 802.1X ports, the switch sends RADIUS messages to 10.10.10.5 but not to 10.10.10.6. What explains this behavior?

a. The two RADIUS servers must be in the global RADIUS group in order for the switch to load balance 802.1X requests to them.

b. The administrator has not specified a RADIUS key for the second RADIUS server, so the switch cannot send messages to it.

c. The switch will only contact the second RADIUS server if it loses connectivity with the first.

d. The switch must have dynamic authorization enabled for the RADIUS servers in order to dynamically balance messages to both.

28. Refer to the running-config.

```
Switch-1# show running-config interface 1-48
interface 1
  vlan 2 untagged
  vlan 3 tagged

  aaa port-access authenticator client-limit 2
<same configuration for other interfaces>
```

The exhibit shows the running-config for edge ports on an AOS-Switch. The switch is running MSTP.

A user connected both ports on a VoIP phone to a switch, and this created an issue that interfered with network connectivity. What can the administrator do to prevent such an issue in the future?

a. Raise the 802.1X client limit on the edge ports.
b. Implement root guard on the edge ports.
c. Implement loop protection on the edge ports.
d. Enable LLDP-MED on the edge ports.

29. Refer to the network topology in Figure 17-16 and the command output below. (An active routing switch would typically have more OSPF and Border Gateway Protocol (BGP) routes. The number of routes are reduced for simplicity for the sake of answering the question.)

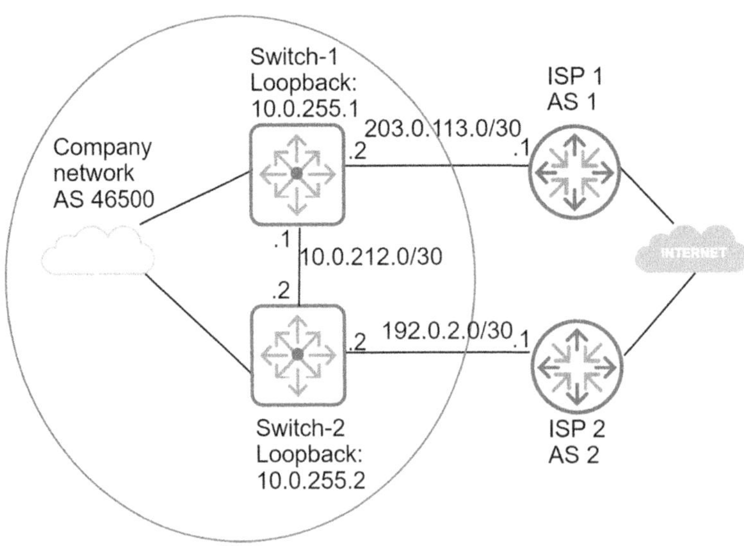


Figure 17-16 Question 29 network topology

```
Switch-1# show ip bgp
Local AS : 46500 Local Router-id : 10.0.255.1
BGP Table Version : 30
Status codes: * - valid, > - best, i - internal, e - external, s - stale
Origin codes: i - IGP, e - EGP, ? - incomplete
Network            Nexthop     Metric  LocalPref  Weight  AsPath
------------------ ----------  ------- ---------  ------  -------
*>  198.51.100.0/24             0                  32768        i
* i 198.51.100.0/24  10.0.255.2  0       100          0         i
* i 1.0.0.0/8        192.0.2.1   0       100          0     2 1 i
*>e 1.0.0.0/8        203.0.113.1 0                    0       1 i
* i 2.0.0.0/8        192.0.2.1   0       100          0       2 i
*>e 2.0.0.0/8        203.0.113.1 0                    0     1 2 i

Switch-1# show ip route
                              IP Route Entries

  Destination        Gateway       VLAN Type      Sub-Type   Metric Dist.
  ----------------   -----------   ------------- ---------   ------ -----
  1.0.0.0/8          203.0.113.1   100 bgp        external   0       20
  2.0.0.0/8          203.0.113.1   100 bgp        external   0       20
  10.0.212.0/30      VLAN212       212 connected             25      0
  10.0.213.0/30      VLAN213       213 connected             25      0
  10.0.255.1/32      lo1           connected                 1       0
  10.0.255.2/32      10.0.212.2    212 ospf       IntraArea  26      110
  10.1.0.0/16        10.0.213.2    213 ospf       InterArea  75      110
  192.0.2.0/30       10.0.212.2    212 ospf       external   10      110
  198.51.100.0/25    VLAN10        10 connected              1       0
  198.51.100.128/25 VLAN128        128 connected             1       0
  198.51.100.0/24    blackhole     static                    1       1
  203.0.113.0/30     VLAN100       100 connected             1       0
  127.0.0.0/8        reject        static                    0       0
  127.0.0.1/32       lo0           connected                 1       0
```

Network administrators want Switch-1 to choose the BGP route to 2.0.0.0/8 through 192.0.2.1. What should the administrators do to achieve this goal?

a. Set next-hop-self for the Switch-1 neighbor in the Switch-2 BGP configuration.

b. Lower the OSPF metric on the link between Switch-1 and Switch-2.

c. Configure the **network 2.0.0.0/8** command in the BGP configuration on Switch-2.

d. Set the BGP administrative distance the same for external and internal BGP.

30. What are two advantages of implementing role-based tunneled node as compared to port-based tunneled node? (Select two.)

a. Role-based tunneled node does not require AP and PEFNG licenses for the switch on the MC while the port-based tunneled node does.

b. Role-based tunneled node supports the configuration of a backup controller in the tunnel-server profile while port-based tunneled-node does not.

c. Role-based tunneled node provides a simpler setup with authentication enforced on the MC while port-based tunneled node required authentication configured on the port.

d. Role-based tunneled-node enables the MC to apply firewall rules and deep packet inspection (DPI) to wired traffic while port-based tunneled-node does not.

e. Role-based tunneled node enables the switch to work with MCs that are deployed in a cluster while port-based tunneled-node does not.

## Answers

1. **C** is correct. In static mode, the switch learns MAC addresses up to the limit and then saves those addresses permanently. The network administrator does not want to configure authorized MAC addresses manually. This mode lets the administrator enable port security when the desired equipment is connected, and the switch then automatically learns each device's MAC address on the port. The address is stored permanently, and if a new device connects, port security detects the issue.

   **A** is incorrect. In limited-continuous mode with an address limit of 1, the switch prevents multiple devices connecting on the port at the same time (which would occur if a rogue switch or AP connected). However, this mode would not prevent students from replacing equipment.

   **B** is incorrect. Port-access mode is the option used with 802.1X, but the scenario did not mention the need for 802.1X.

   **D** is incorrect. The configured mode prevents changes to equipment on the port, but it requires the network administrator to configure authorized addresses in advance.

   For more information, see *Chapter 16: Additional Security Features*.

2. **C** is correct. Enabling IGMP on a VLAN that does not have an IP address enables IGMP snooping. The IGMP snooping switches can listen for endpoints' IGMP reports and build up a multicast forwarding table. They can then forward multicasts on the correct ports and filter them on the other ports.

   **A** is incorrect. Switch-1 and Switch-3 do not have IP addresses on VLAN 10 so they cannot fulfill the IGMP querier role.

   **B** is incorrect. The IGMP reports can flow throughout the VLAN without Switch-1 or Switch-3 implementing IGMP.

   **D** is incorrect. Switch-1 and Switch-3 are operating at Layer 2. If the network required multicast routing, Switch-2 would implement IGMP and PIM. Switch-1 and Switch-3 could implement IGMP or not without affecting the multicast routing solution.

   For more information, see *Chapter 6: Internet Group Management Protocol (IGMP).*

3. **B** is correct. The 5400R Series supports all of these features and is recommended at the distribution layer (as well as the access layer and core).

   **A** is incorrect. The 8400 Series do not run AOS.

   **C** is incorrect. The 2930M Series is more typically recommended at the access layer. It provides primarily 1GbE connectivity with 10GbE uplinks. It also supports backplane stacking rather than VSF.

   **D** is incorrect. The 2540 Series is more typically recommended at the access layer. It does not support all of the required features.

   For more information, refer to *Chapter 1: Introduction to Aruba Solutions.*

4. **A** is correct. The exhibit shows that a VoIP phone (authenticated device) and computer (unauthenticated) might connect on the same port at the same time. Therefore, mixed mode is required.

   **B** is incorrect. MBVs enable a port to support multiple untagged VLANs on a port. In this scenario, MBVs might be required or not, depending on whether VoIP phones are assigned to a tagged or untagged VLAN. However, disabling them will not help to make the solution work.

   **C** is incorrect. The global port-access authenticator option applies only to 802.1X and is not required to activate LMA on a port.

   **D** is incorrect. This setting enables the assignment of users and devices to VLANs that are established with GVRP, but the scenario does not indicate that GVRP is in use.

   For more information, see *Chapter 11: MAC Authentication.*

5. **A** is correct. Switch-1 must support VLAN 5 in order to apply this VLAN to devices assigned to the IoT role. However, Switch-1 does not need to carry this VLAN on any interfaces. It will tunnel traffic to the MC, which will handle the forwarding.

**B** is incorrect. The role for employees does not specify an untagged VLAN ID, so the switch will apply the port's static untagged VLAN to devices assigned to the employee role. Employee traffic should be forwarded in VLAN 6, so you must keep the VLAN 6 untagged assignment. When an IoT device connects, the switch will dynamically apply the untagged VLAN 5 assignment in the role, so you do not need to configure the VLAN on the port manually.

**C** is incorrect. Because the MC is handling VLAN 5 at Layer 2, it must forward the traffic to the core switch in VLAN 5. Therefore, the Switch-2-to-MC link must support this traffic. The Switch-1 to Switch-2 link does not require VLAN 5 because Switch-1 is tunneling the traffic in whatever VLAN it uses to communicate with the MC.

**D** is incorrect. VLAN 6 is used for employee traffic, which Switch-1 forwards locally. This traffic does not need to pass to the MC.

For more information, refer to *Chapter 13: Integrating with an Aruba Mobility Solution.*

6. **B** is correct. The configuration indicates that SNMPv2c (snmp-server) is not disabled. SNMPv3 only is enabled. In these circumstances, the switch rejects all SNMPv2c messages, but it does send SNMPv2 traps if an SNMPv2 trap host is configured, as shown in the command output.

   **A** is incorrect. The switch sends SMNPv2c traps because an SNMPv2c host is configured and SNMPv2c is still enabled.

   **C** is incorrect. This is the behavior when SNMPv3 restricted access is enabled, not SNMPv3 only.

   **D** is incorrect. When SNMPv3 only is enabled, the switch rejects SNMPv2c Get and Set messages even if the messages match an SNMPv2c community that still exists on the switch.

   For more information, see *Chapter 14: Secure Device Management.*

7. **D** is correct. Because you are not setting up the VSF links on the members themselves, you must provision the members on the commander and set up their VSF links. As members receive VSF messages from the commander, they can then join the fabric and set up their own links. They can then send VSF messages on those links to enable the member connected to them (but not to the commander) to join.

   **A** is incorrect. FSU is a feature on Aruba 5400R Series switches, which enables the VSF fabric to update the software on one member at a time after the establishment of the fabric.

   **B** is incorrect. It is best practice to implement a form of MAD (either LLDP MAD or VLAN MAD). However, setting up VLAN MAD does not help in the VSF fabric establishment. Also, you must set up VLAN MAD on a VLAN dedicated to that purpose.

   **C** is incorrect. You can use strict provisioning or loose provisioning to add the other members for a plug-and-play set up. All members must use the same domain ID, which, in a plug-and-play setup, the members receive from the commander.

   For more information, refer to *Chapter 4: Aruba Backplane Stacking and Virtual Switching Framework (VSF).*

8. **C** is correct. The area ranges indicate the range of routes within the area. The ABR then advertises that summarized range rather than the individual routes in other areas. In this network, area 0 uses the 10.0.0.0/24 range. Area 1 has /24 subnets in the 10.1.0.0/20 range.

   **A** is incorrect. Area 0 only needs the range of networks actually within area 0. Switch-1 learns the area 2 aggregated route from Switch-2; it is incorrect to try to specify the range manually. This answer also does not include a range in area 1. With this configuration, Switch-1 would advertise the area 1 routes individually in area 0, which goes against the solution criteria.

   **B** is incorrect. The range of networks in area 1 should be configured as a range for area *1*. The ABR can then advertise that range to other ABRs such as Switch-2 through the backbone.

   **D** is incorrect. The range of networks in each area should be configured as a range for that area.

   For more information, see *Chapter 5: Advanced Open Shortest Path First (OSPF)*.

9. **A** is correct. RPVST+ sends a separate BPDU and establishes a separate spanning tree for each VLAN. Using a high number of VLANs can cause a burden on the switch's processing power. Therefore, it is best practice to carry only the VLANs that a switch needs to support on each link and implement RPVST+ only on those VLANs.

   **B** is incorrect because carrying all of the VLANs can impose burdens on the access layer switch's processing power. This recommendation is different from the best practice for MSTP, in which all switch-to-switch links should carry all VLANs used in the spanning tree domain to prevent issues in which a link is selected to forward traffic for an instance, but the link does not support all VLANs in that instance. With RPVST+, though, if the link between the core switches fails, the topology for each VLAN will be able to fail over to a link that carries that VLAN. This is because the RPVST+ BPDU for the VLAN is only sent on links that carry the VLAN.

   **C** is incorrect. RPVST+ uses VLAN 1 to send RSTP BPDUs for compatibility with standard spanning tree. Even if you do not think you need this compatibility, it is not best practice to remove VLAN 1 from links.

   **D** is incorrect. Root guard prevents the switch from accepting superior BPDUs (BPDUs that would cause the port to become root). It should be implemented on edge ports, not ports that connect to the root.

   For more information, see *Chapter 2: Data Link Layer Redundancy Technologies*.

10. **D** is correct. All OSPF routing devices in the area must define the area in the same way. Otherwise, they cannot achieve adjacency with each other.

    **A**, **B**, and **C** are incorrect because they indicate that some OSPF routing devices define the area as an NSSA and others do not.

    For more information, see *Chapter 5: Advanced Open Shortest Path First (OSPF)*.

11. **D** is correct. Switch-1 has the same IP address as the VRRP virtual IP address. Therefore, it is the VRRP Owner and automatically always has a priority of 255. Changing the IP address makes it so that Switch-1 is no longer the owner and uses the default priority of 100. Switch-2 will then become master.

    **A** and **B** are incorrect. With VRRP, the VRRP router (or routing switch) with the higher priority value becomes Master. However, you cannot set a lower value on Switch-1 because it is Owner and always uses 255.

    **C** is incorrect. Preempt mode would allow Switch-2 to take over the role from Switch-1 if it had higher priority. However, Switch-1 has higher priority because it is owner.

    For more information, see *Chapter 3: Virtual Router Redundancy Protocol (VRRP).*

12. **B** is correct. Both IGMP and PIM-DM must be enabled on the VLAN with multicast receivers. Otherwise, Switch-1 cannot discover the multicast groups for which endpoints are listening and add them to the PIM multicast routes when the source begins to stream.

    **A** is incorrect. IGMP is not required on VLANs without any endpoints. This VLAN needs to run PIM-DM, but this protocol is already enabled on the VLAN.

    **C** and **D** are incorrect. If the network were using PIM-SM, Switch-1 and Switch-2 would need to know an RP address, which can be configured on the switch manually or which the switch can learn from a bootstrap router (BSR). (In the latter case, the **router pim rp-candidate** command is configured on the switches that you want to be RPs.) However, PIM-DM does not use RP addresses.

    For more information, see *Chapter 7: Protocol Independent Multicast (PIM).*

13. **D** is correct. When all of the members reboot at about the same time and need to reform the stack, they hold an election. The first criteria in the election is stack ID revision, which is the same on all switches. The next criteria is priority. Member 4 has the highest priority value, so it becomes commander. It then selects Member 3 as standby because Member 3 has the next highest priority.

    **A**, **B**, and **C** are incorrect; they do not indicate the correct member roles. It is true that the current commander (which used to be Member 1) retains the role even if a new member with higher priority joins the stack. But in this case, all switches boot at the same time, so an election is held.

    For more information, refer to *Chapter 4: Aruba Backplane Stacking and Virtual Switching Framework (VSF).*

14. **B** is correct. A global device-based QoS policy overrides the incoming DSCP. For this use case, administrators could remove the device QoS policy and apply the policy to the VLAN instead. Because type of service is disabled, the switch would not accept incoming DSCP from guest devices, and the VLAN priority would apply. But it will trust the incoming DSCP from the AP, and those will override the VLAN priority.

    **A** is incorrect. Setting the QoS trust to **device aruba-ap** works when the type of service is disabled. The issue is that the global device-based priority is overriding the DSCP.

**C** is incorrect. The device-based QoS trust feature works by detecting the AP type in the LLDP messages. 802.1X is not required.

**D** is incorrect. The interface does not need to have a DSCP value set on it for the switch to honor the incoming values.

For more information, see *Chapter 15: Quality of Service.*

15. **C** is correct. Dynamic authorization is required for the switch to accept ClearPass's Change of Authorization (CoA) message after the guest logs in. This CoA message lets the switch apply the correct settings for the authorized guest and stop redirecting the guest to the portal.

    **A** is incorrect. Authenticated guests are redirected to the web-based authentication redirect page when the switch itself enforces web-based authentication. This page is *not* used when the switch implements captive portal.

    **B** is incorrect. EWA is used with the switch's own Web-Auth features. These features are mutually exclusive with captive portal. (The switch receives the necessary URL for the redirect dynamically from ClearPass when unregistered devices undergo MAC-Auth.)

    **D** is incorrect. The captive portal URL hash key must match the key configured for the URL hashing feature on ClearPass Guest. This key is separate from the RADIUS key defined for the switch on ClearPass Policy Manager.

    For more information, see *Chapter 12: Captive Portal and Other Guest Options.*

16. **A** is correct. The virtual link is established in area 1, which is also called the transit area. This area must be a normal area.

    **B** is incorrect. Area 30 is the area that is connected to area 0 through the virtual link. This area has no special requirements and can be a normal area, stub area, or NSSA, as you choose.

    **C** is incorrect. The virtual link enables Switch-7 to act as an ABR even though it does not have any interfaces in area 0.

    **D** is incorrect. The virtual link can be established over multiple hops.

    For more information, refer to *Chapter 5: Advanced Open Shortest Path First (OSPF).*

17. **C** is correct. The exhibit shows that this interface has a client-limit configured on it, which makes the port operate in user-based mode. In this mode, the switch attempts to authenticate every device that connects to the port. Because the computer did not authenticate, the switch drops its traffic. (It would also send an EAP request to start the 802.1X process, but continues to drop other traffic until the device responds and authenticates successfully.)

    **A** is incorrect. Because the switch port is operating in user-based mode, it does not accept traffic from unauthenticated devices even though the client limit has not yet been reached. If the switch were operating in port-based mode (no client limit), it would forward the traffic in VLAN 20.

    **B** is incorrect. VLAN 21 is the tagged VLAN, and Device 2 is sending untagged traffic. In addition, the switch port does not accept traffic from unauthenticated devices.

**D** is incorrect. The 802.1X process does not involve relaying all types of client traffic to the RADIUS server. Instead, the switch initiates EAP. Then, if the connected device responds with EAP messages, the switch relays those messages to the RADIUS server.

For more information, see *Chapter 10: 802.1X Authentication*.

18. **B** is correct. The RMON tables show cumulative Ethernet interface statistics, as well as statistics over intervals. These statistics include CRC errors, jabber, and other signs of a malfunctioning NIC or transceiver.

    **A** is incorrect. ACL resource usage shows how many rules ACLs are taking up in the switch memory.

    **C** is incorrect. The sFlow port counters help sFlow collectors to build up a picture of traffic patterns and network utilization. The samples collected by sFlow can also provide insight into the types of applications in use. The sFlow information does not give good insight into hardware issues.

    **D** is incorrect. SNMPv3 views are assigned to SNMPv3 groups and control which MIBs users assigned to those groups can read and write.

    For more information, refer to *Chapter 14: Secure Device Management*.

19. **A** is correct. Packet 1 is processed by the ACL because it is received on VLAN 3 and routed to a different subnet. This packet matches rule 10, so it is permitted. Packet 2 is not processed by the ACL because it is not received on VLAN 3. VLAN 4 has no ACLs applied to it, so the packet is permitted. Packet 3 is processed by the ACL because it is received on VLAN 3 and routed to a different subnet. This packet does not match rule 10, but does match rule 20, which denies traffic from 10.1.3.0-10.1.3.255 and to 10.1.4.0-10.1.4.127. Therefore, Packet 3 is denied.

    **B**, **C**, and **D** are incorrect for these reasons outlined above.

    For more information, see *Chapter 9: Access Control Lists*.

20. **C** is correct. The shared option is not available until the ACL grouping feature is enabled. When you enable this feature, the switch reboots. You can then apply the ACL to multiple physical interfaces with the **shared** option and save ACL resource space. (You could also apply the ACL to multiple VLANs with the **vlan-in** or **vlan-out** option; however, this is not how the administrator wants to apply the ACLs in this scenario.)

    **A** is incorrect. The **shared** option is not available for routed ACLs (RACLs), which an IP ACL applied to a VLAN with the **in** option is. Removing the ACL from the physical interfaces and applying the ACL to VLANs with the **in** option could save space, but the ACLs would not have the same effect as they had when applied to the physical interfaces.

    **B** is incorrect. The **shared** option is available for both standard and extended ACLs. In addition, you cannot recreate an extended ACL as a standard ACL and retain the same behavior.

**D** is incorrect. After ACL grouping is enabled, you can use the **shared** option when applying the ACL. You do not use the option when creating the ACL.

For more information, refer to *Chapter 9: Access Control Lists.*

21. **D** is correct. DHCP snooping must be enabled globally as well as on a VLAN. Before implementing ARP protection, you should enable DHCP snooping and give the switch time to build up the IP-to-MAC binding table. Otherwise, the switch will drop legitimate ARP traffic, and endpoints will not be able to communicate.

    **A** is incorrect. DHCP snooping can function without the configuration of an authorized DHCP server. In this case, the switch accepts any DHCP server packets received on a trusted port.

    **B** is incorrect. It is typically best practice to set switch interfaces that connect to the core (or distribution layer) as trusted ports for DHCP snooping and ARP protection.

    **C** is incorrect. ARP protection and DHCP snooping should be enabled on the same VLAN.

    For more information, refer to *Chapter 16: Additional Security Features.*

22. **A** is correct. The GMB for a queue allocates a certain amount of bandwidth to queue. Each queue receives its GMB before queues are served according to strict priority. This prevents lower priority traffic from being starved out. The interface output indicates that many packets are being dropped in queue 3 (for normal priority traffic). If administrators want this queue to be able to forward more traffic, they must raise the GMB.

    **B** is incorrect. The AOS-Switches use GMB plus strict priority scheduling, and you cannot change the method to WFQ.

    **C** is incorrect. The switch is already at the maximum number of queues per-port. In any case, changing the number of queues will only make a difference if you also make sure that you have allocated the correct GMB for the queue associated with normal priority traffic.

    **D** is incorrect. Setting the type of service to DiffServ enables the switch to use incoming DSCP to prioritize traffic. It does not affect the scheduling mechanisms for forwarding traffic placed in different queues.

    For more information, refer to *Chapter 15: Quality of Service.*

23. **A** is correct. The exhibit indicates that the switch is using BFD to check connectivity with OSPF neighbors such as Switch-2 on VLAN 255. It also shows that echo mode is enabled for the BFD session with Switch-2. When echo mode is enabled, the detect time for the BFD session is the detect multiplier times the minimum echo interval for the session. The min echo receive interval matches on all switches and is 500 ms. Multiplying 500 ms by 3 equals 1.5 seconds.

    **B** is incorrect. This is the minimum receive timer multiplied by the detect multiplier. Even if echo mode were disabled, this answer would be incorrect. Each switch compares its min Tx timer with the other side's min Rx timer. It uses the higher timer to set its active Tx timer. Its expected receive interval is the other side's active Tx timer. In this scenario, the active transmit timer on both sides is the same and equals 2.

**C** is incorrect. This would be the time to detect the issue if echo mode were disabled.

**D** is incorrect. This is the OSPF dead timer. However, BFD will detect the issue first and take down the relationship.

For more information, see *Chapter 5: Advanced Open Shortest Path First (OSPF).*

24. **D** is correct. Aruba AirWave provides centralized monitoring and management of a wide variety of infrastructure devices, including AOS-Switches. Features include configuration auditing and backups, as well as many others.

    **A** is incorrect. ClearPass Onboard provides onboarding for client devices.

    **B** is incorrect. You need to license an MC to support an AOS-Switch when the switch implements port-based tunneled-node. However, this feature enables the switches to tunnel device traffic to an MC. It does not enable configuration management.

    **C** is incorrect. AirWave can use the TFTP client capabilities on the switch to copy files to and from the switch. The switch TFTP server is used to upload files to other network devices and is not specifically required for the purposes listed in the question.

    For more information, see *Chapter 14: Secure Device Management.*

25. **C** is correct. Area 1 is a normal area, so Switch-5 receives the external Type 5 LSAs. The type 2 metric means that Switch-5 selects the LSA from Switch-2 as best because it has a lower metric. Switch-5 then chooses the best path to reach Switch-2. Switch-5 has two equally low-cost paths to Switch-2, one through Switch-3 (Link 5 to Link 2 to Link 1 = 100 + 25 + 25 = 150) and through Switch-4 (Link 6 to Link 3 = 100 + 50 = 150). Therefore, Switch-5 load balances the traffic over Link 5 and Link 6.

    **A** is incorrect. A would be correct if Switch-1 and Switch-2 used a type 1 metric. In that case, the total cost through Switch-1 would be 195 (125 for the shortest path to Switch-1 + 70 for the external metric) as opposed to 200 through Switch-2 (150 for the shortest path to Switch-2 + 50 for the external metric). And Switch-3 offers a lower-cost route to Switch-1. However, this network is using type2 metrics.

    **B** is incorrect. Switch-4 does not offer a lower-cost path to Switch-2 than Switch-3. OSPF uses path cost rather than hop count.

    **D** is incorrect. Switch-5 will receive the external route given that all switches have achieved adjacency.

    For more information, see *Chapter 5: Advanced Open Shortest Path First (OSPF).*

26. **B** is correct. The exhibit indicates that congestion is occurring with traffic transmitted on uplink interfaces. This traffic comes from devices connected to edge ports. An inbound rate limit on the edge ports can ensure that each device uses only its fair share of the bandwidth and reduce the congestion for traffic transmitted on the uplink. (The exhibit indicates moderately high usage for received traffic. The administrator could add an outbound rate limit on the edge ports to help prevent future congestion in this direction; however, this was not provided as an option.)

**A** is incorrect. The exhibit does not indicate an excessive number of broadcasts, so a broadcast rate limit on edge ports will not help to reduce congestion.

**C** is incorrect. An outbound rate limit on the uplinks could reduce congestion in other areas of the network, but will only cause more traffic to be dropped on this uplink. Applying the rate limit to the uplinks does not help to allocate bandwidth fairly among the connected devices.

**D** is incorrect. This rate limit would drop traffic received on the uplinks, which will do nothing to relieve congestion for traffic transmitted on these links.

For more information, see *Chapter 15: Quality of Service.*

27. **C** is correct. A RADIUS group used for an authentication method can have multiple RADIUS servers as shown here. However, AOS-Switches do not load balance RADIUS requests across them. Instead, the switch sends all requests to the first server listed. If its requests and retries time out, it then contacts the second server.

    **A** is incorrect. The behavior is the same no matter which group you are using. (In addition, if these are the first two RADIUS servers configured on the switch, they are also in the global RADIUS group.)

    **B** is incorrect. This configuration has a global RADIUS key defined. The switch will use this key when contacting the second RADIUS server, which does not have an individual key defined for it.

    **D** is incorrect. Dynamic authorization permits a switch to accept CoA and disconnect messages (DMs). It has no relation to how the switch chooses to which server to send RADIUS requests.

    For more information, see *Chapter 10: 802.1X Authentication.*

28. **C** is correct. By connecting both VoIP phone ports to the switch, the user created a loop. The switch port enforces 802.1X in user-based mode, so it dropped its BPDUs that looped back to itself as unauthorized traffic. Loop protection is intended to prevent loops in situations such as these.

    **A** is incorrect. Raising the client limit does not change the switch behavior, so the loop would still be created.

    **B** is incorrect. The switch is not processing the BPDU, so root guard will not prevent this issue.

    **D** is incorrect. LLDP-MED helps to provision VoIP phones with the correct VLAN and QoS priority settings. It cannot help to eliminate the loop.

    For more information, see *Chapter 2: Data Link Layer Redundancy Technologies.*

29. **D** is correct. The BGP routing table shows that Switch-1 has two 2.0.0.0/8 routes. You can see in the IP routing table that Switch-1 has IP connectivity to both next hops in these routes, so both routes are valid. Because Switch-1 and Switch-2 are not manipulating the routes' weight or local preferences, the most critical criteria for selecting the best route are, first,

administrative distance, and then AS path length. You can see that the AS path length for the 2.0.0.0/8 route through 192.0.2.1 is shorter than that for the selected route. Therefore, Switch-1 must be using administrative distance to choose between the routes. One route is internal and the other is external. The switch selects the external route, so the external BGP distance must be lower than the internal BGP distance, as it is by default. By setting the administrative distance for external and internal routes the same, you will force Switch-1 to use other criteria to choose between the routes. In this case, the next non-tying criterion is AS path length. Switch-1 will now choose the 2.0.0.0/8 route through 192.0.2.1, which has a shorter path length.

**A** is incorrect. Setting the next-hop-self option for the Switch-1 neighbor on Switch-2 will cause Switch-2 to advertise the externally learned routes, including 2.0.0.0/8, to Switch-1 with next hop 10.0.255.2 instead of 192.0.2.1. This could make a difference in Switch-1 selecting the route if Switch-1 used to be unable to reach the next hop and now can. However, in this case, Switch-1 could reach the next hop before and can still reach the next hop. In both cases, Switch-1 will still prefer the 2.0.0.0/8 route that it learned from its ISP router.

**B** is incorrect. The metric to the next hop can play a role in BGP route selection, but this factor is much lower in the list than administrative distance and AS path length. Because you can see that the two 2.0.0.0/8 routes have different AS path lengths, the metric will not play a role.

**C** is incorrect. The **network** command is required to inject routes learned by other methods into the BGP routing table. It is not used to advertise routes learned from other BGP neighbors. A BGP router automatically advertises routes learned from eBGP neighbors to other BGP neighbors.

For more information, see *Chapter 8: Border Gateway Protocol (BGP)*.

30. **A** is correct. Role-based tunneled node does not require licenses on the MC while port-based tunneled-node does. **E** is also correct. Only role-based tunneled-node can work with MCs that use clustering.

    **B** is incorrect. Both role-based and port-based tunneled-node support the configuration of a backup controller.

    **C** is incorrect. Port-based tunneled node does not permit authenticated to be enabled on the switch port; instead, the MC implements authentication. Role-based tunneled node, on the other hand, requires authentication on the switch port to assign devices to the role with tunnel redirect enabled.

    **D** is incorrect. With both role-based and port-based tunneled-node, the MC can provide these benefits.

    For more information, see *Chapter 13: Integrating with an Aruba Mobility Solution*.

# Index


## A

**Access-Accept message 338**

**Access Control List (ACL) 294, 424, 535, 536**

- analysis 309
- connection rate filtering 599–600
- control access, less trusted users 295–299
- definition 278
- example 294
- filtering behavior, prediction 321–322
- grouping 319–321
- ID groups 280–281
- implementation 278–279
- interfaces 291–293
- IP addresses
  - source and destination 300
  - specifying ranges with prefix lengths 300–302
- IPv4 extended 283–287
- IPv4 standard 282
- logging matches 308–309
- MAC address
  - extended 288–289
  - specifying ranges 306
  - standard 287–288
- mobility infrastructure, protection 295–297
- PACLs 318–319
- processing order and implicit deny 290–291
- RACLs
  - inbound 310–311
  - outbound 311–312
- rule components 281–282
- rule sequence 306–308
- types 279–280
- use cases 289
- VACLs
  - at the edge 315–317
  - inbound 312–313
  - outbound 314–315
- wildcard bits
  - adding rule 305–306
  - definition 302
  - examples 303–305
  - reverse logic from subnet masks 303
  - source and destination IP addresses 300, 303

**access-list command (no ip), 280**

**Access Point (AP) 398, 581**

**Access-Reject message 338**

**ACL identifier (ID) 280–281**

**Active Switch Anchor Controller (A-SAC) 438**

**Active User Anchor Controller (A-UAC) 438**

**Address exhaustion 567**

**Address limit parameter 583**

**Address Resolution Protocol (ARP) 532**

- protection 576–577
  - and DHCP snooping 577–578
  - feature 576
  - guidelines 579–580
  - IP-to-MAC address bindings 577
  - settings 576
  - VLANs 575
- snooping and poisoning 574–575

**Address spoofing 567**

**Advanced Open Shortest Path First (OSPF) systems**

- adjacency 109–111
- authentication 181
  - MD5 configuration 184
  - options 182–183
  - simple configuration 183
- basic setup 106–107
- external routes 136
  - ASBRs 138–143
  - excessive route elimination 143–144, 146
  - inter-area route elimination 146
  - need for redistributing 137–138
  - NSSA 148–149
  - scenario 149–150
  - stub areas 144–148
- failover and convergence
  - area borders 166
  - BFD 168–172
  - factors 165
  - failed neighbor relationships, detecting 166–168
  - graceful restart 172–178
  - routers 166
- LSAs 111–113
- LSUs 114–115
- multi-area overview
  - ABRs 126–129
  - aggregating summaries 131–133
  - inter-area routes, filtering 133–134
  - intra-areas routes *vs.* inter-area routes 126
  - LSDB size 127
  - need for route aggregation 130
  - Segment 1 and 2 127
- neighbors 108–109
- one area topology
  - dedicated VLAN per link 124–125
  - enabling OSPF 117–120
  - example 116
  - LSUs 120–124
  - Router-1 configuration 117
  - VLAN 10, 22, and 32 120–124
- overview 106
- redundant networks
  - ABRs 152–153
  - external route metrics 156
  - inter-area routes 154–155
  - interface cost setting 151–152
  - route selection 163–164
  - type 1 metric 160–161
  - type 2 metric 156–158
- router ID 108
- SPF algorithm 113–114
- virtual links
  - ABR 10.255.0.3 and ABR 10.255.0.2 180
  - configuration process 180–181
  - example situations 179
  - non-backbone and transit area 179–180

**Advanced Traffic Management Guide 536**

**AOS-Switches 504, 508**

- captive portal authentication
  - authentication enforced on 398–399
  - authentication setup 408–409
  - CA-signed certificate 406–407
  - Ethernet jack 397–398
  - full guest/BYOD access solution 397
  - high-level overview 399
  - login process 402–405
  - redirection process 400–402
  - self-signed certificate 407

switch configuration 408
unregistered devices, optional VLAN for 405–406
Windows Active Directory 398
DHCPv4 and DHCPv6 snooping 567
DSCP 522, 531
EAP 343
eavesdropping and unauthorized access 580–581
802.1p values 519, 520
802.1X Unauthorized-client VLAN
device's traffic 415
guidelines 416–417
multiple employees and guests 417–418
EWA
authen.html 414
guidelines 414–415
index.html 414
process for 413
GMB 510–512
guest access 394
ICMP traffic 546–547
LLDP-MED 555
QoS policies 531
RADIUS server 349–350
SP scheduling 509–510
web-based authentication
advantages 394
Aruba ClearPass 395–396
basic login pages 409
certificate 412
disadvantages 395
multiple clients 412–413
RADIUS server 410–411
redirect URL 411
support for 396–397
switch enabling 413
types 395
unauthenticated clients 412
**AppleTalk 532**
**"Applied" profile 383**
**Area border routers (ABRs) 126, 267**
aggregating summaries 131–133
multiple areas 128
need for route aggregation 130
Type 3 LSAs 127, 129
**Aruba access point (AP) 398**
**Aruba AirWave 5–6**
**Aruba backplane stacking**
benefits 72
chain topology 73
deterministic configuration 76–77
election process 78
factors 73
mesh topology 74
plug-and-go installation method 77–78
ring topology 73–74
roles 74–76
stack fragments 80–81
stack operations 79–80
standby member 78
supporting on 72
**Aruba ClearPass 6–7, 348–349, 358–359, 366, 377**
**Aruba 5400R zl2 Switch Series 4**
**Aruba Mobile First Network 2–3**
**Aruba Mobility Controller (MC) 295**
**Aruba Mobility Solution**
high availability 435
backup controller 438–440
clustering 437–438
failure behavior, controlling 440–441
VRRP 436–437

licensing and capacity 445–446
tunneled-node traffic
feature 425
guidelines 444
implementation restrictions 441–443
PAPI enhanced security 426–427
port-based node 427–431
role-based node 427–428, 432–435
server profile 425–426
use cases 423–425
**Aruba Switch solutions**
Aruba 2930F Switch Series 5
Aruba 3810 Switch Series 5
Aruba 5400R zl2 Switch Series 4
wired and wireless architecture 3
**Aruba 2930F Switch Series 5**
**Aruba 3810 Switch Series 5**
**Aruba virtual switching framework (VSF)**
Aruba 2930F Series switches
commander 89
configuration 91–92
implementation 88–89
links 90–91
member 90
standby member 90
topologies 89–90
backplane stacking
*vs.* flooded traffic 93
*vs.* unicasts 92–93
fabric viewing 88
FSU 99
LLDP MAD
behavior 96–97
setup 95–96
manual configuration 86–88
OOBM MAD 94–95
physical and logical view 81–82
plug-and-play configuration 82–84
split-brain situation 94
use cases 84–86
VLAN MAD 97–99
**AS external (ASE) route 136**
ASBRs
advertisements 140–141
AOS-Switches 139–140
example route 141
routing table 139, 142
Type 4 LSA 142
Type 5 LSA 138–139, 143
excessive route elimination 143–144, 146
inter-area route elimination 146
need for redistributing 137–138
NSSA 148–149
scenario 149–150
stub areas 144–148
**ASICs 551**
**Assured Forwarding (AF) 517**
**Attribute Value Pair (AVP) 456**
**authen.html 414**
**Authentication, Authorization, and Accounting (AAA) 331–332, 430**
**Authorized servers 570–571**
**Autonomous system (AS) 106, 253–255**
**Autonomous System Border Router (ASBR)**
advertisements 140–141
AOS-Switches 139–140
example route 141
routing table 139, 142
Type 4 LSA 142
Type 5 LSA 138–139, 143

## B

**Backplane stacking**
- benefits 72
- chain topology 73
- deterministic configuration 76–77
- election process 78
- factors 73
- mesh topology 74
- plug-and-go installation method 77–78
- ring topology 73–74
- roles 74–76
- stack fragments 80–81
- stack operations 79–80
- standby member 78
- supporting on 72

**Backup Designated Router (BDR) 110–111**

**Bidirectional forwarding detection (BFD)**
- echo mode 171–172
- failed neighbor detection, speed 168–169
- messages and asynchronous mode 170–171

**Block action 595–596**

**Bootstrap Routers (BSR) 239**

**Border Gateway Protocol (BGP)**
- advertising routes 265–266
- AS 253–255
- connection states 258–260
- external routes, OSPF 267
- injecting routes 266–267
- MD5 authentication 257–258
- multihomed ISP connections
  - benefit 252
  - ISPs 253
  - primary use case 252–253
- neighbor addresses
  - AOS-Switches 255–256
  - eBGP 256–257
  - iBGP 257
  - receiving routes 260–261
- *vs.* OSPF 269
- route selection
  - attributes 263–265
  - ECMP 264
  - first criteria in 261–263
  - MED 264
- TCP session 255
- transit AS 268–269

**Bridge Protocol Data Units (BPDUs) 15–18, 520**
- filtering 23–24
- protection 21–23
- throttling 25–26

**Bring Your Own Device (BYOD) 2, 341, 404–405**

**Broadcast traffic 547**

## C

**Campus architectures 7–8**

**Campus network 8–9**

**Candidate BSRs (C-BSRs) 239**

**Candidate RPs (C-RPs) 238–241**

**Captive portal authentication**
- authentication enforced on 398–399
- authentication setup 408–409
- CA-signed certificate 406–407
- Ethernet jack 397–398
- full guest/BYOD access solution 397
- high-level overview 399
- login process 402–405
- redirection process 400–402
- self-signed certificate 407
- switch configuration 408
- unregistered devices, optional VLAN for 405–406

web-based 396
Windows Active Directory 398
**Certificate Authority (CA) 340**
**Certificate Revocation List (CRL) 407**
**Certificate signing request (CSR) 407**
**Challenge Handshake Authentication Protocol (CHAP) 342, 375–376**
**Change of authorization (CoA) 348, 349, 399**
**Class-based rate limiting 549–552**
**Classifier-based QoS policy 533–534**
AOS-Switch 542–544
configuring and applying 537–538
priority 540–541
review 541–542
Secure Shell packet 539
verification 538–539
**Classless Inter-Domain Routing (CIDR) 301**
**Class of Service (CoS) 288, 515**
**Class Selector (CS) 517**
**ClearPass 6–7, 348–349, 358–359, 366, 377**
**ClearPass Policy Manager 399**
**Command line interface (CLI) 407, 519**
**Congestion Experienced (CE) bits 518**
**Connection rate filtering 594**
ACL 599–600
action 595–596
IDSs and IPSs 594
implementation 598–599
operation 594–595
sensitivity 597–598
unblocking 596–597
Virtual Machine 599
**Continuous mode 582**
**Controlled port 333**
**Cyclic Redundancy Check (CRC) errors 484**


## D


**Data-driven mode 209–211**
**Data link layer redundancy technologies**
loop protection
edge loops 28–29
feature 30
port mode 31–32
spanning tree protocols 29–30
VLAN mode 32–33
RPVST+ 16–18
BPDU filtering 23–24
BPDU protection 21–23
BPDU throttling 25–26
*vs.* MSTP 15–16, 19–20
port cost differences 18
PVST protection 23
root guard 24–25
*vs.* RSTP 15–16
setting up 19
STP loop guard 26–28
vulnerability 20–21
UDLD
cross-connected fibers 33, 34
fiber optic link 33, 34
frames 35–36
guidelines 36
STP network 34
tagged/untagged 37
UDLD-enabled ports 38
**Dead time 347**
**Deep packet inspection (DPI) 424**
**Denial of Service (DoS) 424, 575**
**Designated Router (DR) 110–111, 232–235**
**DHCPv4 snooping 567**
**DHCPv6 snooping 567**

**Differentiated Services code points (DSCPs) 284**
AF and EF 517
definition 518
honoring 522–525
interaction with 531
with IP precedence 518
RFC 517
traffic classification 528–529
**Digital workplace 1–3**
**Dijkstra algorithm 114**
**Directed graph 113–114**
**Disconnect messages (DMs) 348, 349, 403**
**Discovery View 467**
**display command 50**
**Domain Name System (DNS) 333, 401, 600**
**drop option 573**
**Dynamic Host Configuration Protocol (DHCP) 333, 400**
address exhaustion 566, 567
address spoofing 566, 567
and ARP protection 577–578
authorized servers 570–571
configuration 569–570
option 82 insertion
Discover and Request packets 572
filtering 573–574
IP addresses 571–572
limitation 572
remote ID types 573
snooping 567–568
**Dynamic settings 353**

## E

**EAP-Transport Layer Security (EAP-TLS) 339**
advantages 340
disadvantages 340–341
EAP Request/TLS and EAP Response/TLS packets 340
**Eavesdropping access 580–581**
**Eavesdropping protection 590–591**
**802.1p value 520–522**
**802.1Q VLAN tag 516**
**802.1X authentication**
authenticator 334
EAP 333
framework 336
methods 338–339, 343–344
PEAP 341–343
RADIUS server 337–338
TLS 339–341
TTLS 341–343
logical ports 332–333
port-based authentication 331–332
port-based mode 361–362
RADIUS server 335
AOS-Switches 349–350
ClearPass 348–349, 358–359
customized settings 352
dynamic port ACLs 357–358
dynamic settings 353–356, 359–360
enabling 350–352
groups 345–348
key option 345
specification 344
requirements 335–336
roles 333–334
supplicant 334
user-based mode 362–365
user role-based authorization 367–368
**802.1X port-based authentication 588–589**

**802.1X Unauthorized-client VLAN**
- device's traffic 415
- guidelines 416–417
- multiple employees and guests 417–418

**Emergency Call Services (ECS) 554**
**Emergency Line Identification Number (ELIN) 558**
**encrypt-credentials 408**
**encrypted option 408**
**Enhanced Web-Auth (EWA) 396**
- authen.html 414
- guidelines 414–415
- index.html 414
- process for 413

**Equal-Cost Multi-Path (ECMP) 132, 264**
**Ethernet History group 485**
**ethernetHistoryTable 485**
**Ethernet protocol 532**
**Ethernet statistics group 485**
**ethernetStatsTable 485**
**Expedited Forwarding (EF) 517**
**Extensible Authentication Protocol (EAP) 333, 405**
- framework 336
- methods 338–339, 343–344
- PEAP 341–343
- RADIUS server 337–338
- TLS 339
  - advantages 340
  - disadvantages 340–341
  - EAP Request/TLS and EAP Response/TLS packets 340
- TTLS 341–343

**Exterior BGP (eBGP) 254, 256–257**
**External gateway protocol (EGP) 253**
**External routes 136**
- ASBRs
  - advertisements 140–141
  - AOS-Switches 139–140
  - example route 141
  - routing table 139, 142
  - Type 4 LSA 142
  - Type 5 LSA 138–139, 143
- excessive route elimination 143–144, 146
- inter-area route elimination 146
- need for redistributing 137–138
- NSSA 148–149
- scenario 149–150
- stub areas 144–148

## F

**Fabric 4**
**Failover and convergence**
- area borders 166
- BFD
  - echo mode 171–172
  - failed neighbor detection, speed 168–169
  - messages and asynchronous mode 170–171
- factors 165
- failed neighbor relationships, detecting 166–168
- graceful restart
  - commander 173
  - configuration process 176–177
  - default router 172
  - process 174–175
  - VRRP 177–178
- routers 166

**Fast Software Updates (FSU) 99**
**First In First Out (FIFO) 509**
**Fully adjacent 107**

## G

**Generic Routing Encapsulation (GRE) 424**
**Group address 196**

**Guaranteed minimum bandwidth (GMB) 509, 511**
percentages 511–512
port behavior 513
port's bandwidth 510–511
settings 512
SP traffic 513
unallocated and unused bandwidth 511

## H

**High availability solution 435**
backup controller 438–440
clustering 437–438
failure behavior, controlling 440–441
VRRP 436–437
**host option 287**

## I

**igmp filter-unknown-mcast command 210**
**ignore statement 535, 536**
**index.html 414**
**Interior BGP (iBGP) 254, 257**
**Interior Gateway Protocol (IGP) 106, 255**
**Internal routers 128**
**International Telecommunications Union (ITU) 507**
**Internet Assigned Numbers Authority (IANA) 196**
**Internet Control Message Protocol (ICMP) 546–547**
**Internet Engineering Task Force (IETF) 517**
**Internet Group Management Protocol (IGMP) 218**
membership tables 205–207
multicast
flooding within VLANs 198–200
overview 196–197
uses 198
queriers
behavior without PIM enabled 204
behavior with PIM enabled 204
enabling 202–203
multiple queriers and elections 203–204
snooping 207–209
unknown multicasts, AOS-Switches
data-driven mode 209–211
fast leave 209–211
nondata-driven mode 211
use cases 200–201
**Internet of Things (IoT) 2, 3, 374, 424**
**Internet Service Providers (ISPs)**
multihomed connections
benefit 252
ISPs 253
primary use case 252–253
OSPF 137, 146
**Internetwork Packet Exchange (IPX) traffic 532**
**intrusion detection systems (IDSs) 594**
**intrusion prevention systems (IPSs) 594**
**ip access-list command 280**
**IP precedence bits 516–518**

## K

**keep option 574**

## L

**Latency 505–506**
**Limited-continuous mode 582**
**Link Aggregation Control Protocol (LACP) 538**
**Link-keepalive interval 35**
**Link-keepalive retries 35**
**Link Layer Discovery Protocol-Media Endpoint Devices (LLDP-MED)**
enabling 555–556
review interoperation with authentication 554–555
SNMP servers 554
VLAN ID 554
VoIP phone 554

**Links 106**
**Link-state advertisements (LSAs) 106, 111–113**
**Link-state databases (LSDBs) 110, 127**
**Link State Updates (LSUs) 110, 114–115**
**Local MAC Authentication (LMA) 374, 592**
groups 380–381
lists 379
profiles 382–384
rudimentary access security 379
unauthorized-client 384–385
**Local Web-Auth 396**
**Loop protection**
edge loops 28–29
feature 30
port mode 31–32
spanning tree protocols 29–30
VLAN mode 32–33

## M

**MAC address 575**
extended 288–289
specifying ranges 306
standard 287–288
**MAC Authentication (MAC-Auth) 592**
local MAC-Auth
groups 380–381
lists 379
profiles 382–384
rudimentary access security 379
unauthorized-client 384–385
multiple clients
address limit 385
Authorized-client VLANs 389
combining 802.1X 386–388
IP phones 385
untagged VLANs 385
RADIUS-based
address format 376–377
Aruba ClearPass 377
configuration process 378
credentials 376
process 374–375
protocol 375–376
use cases 373–374
**MAC-based VLANs (MBVs) 418**
**MAC classes 536, 537**
**mac-count-notify 477**
**MAC forwarding table 592**
**MAC lockdown**
configuration 592
MAC-Auth 592
*vs.* port security 593–594
redundant links 593
switch blocks 591
VLAN 592
**mac-notify 477**
**Management user authentication options**
access levels 452–453
access types 452
AOS-Switches 451
default authentication methods 453
local authentication 453
RADIUS servers 451
operator/manager access 455–457
port-based authentication 454
RADIUS-based command authorization 457–458
secondary authentication method 455, 460–461
SSH login 455
TACACS+ server 452
VSAs, command authorization 458–460

**ManagerPriv group 466**
**managerRadius 460**
**ManagerReadView 467**
**ManagerWriteView 467**
**Master and backup responsibilities, VRRP 52**
**match statement 535, 536**
**Maximum transmission unit (MTU) 444**
**Message information base (MIB) 463**
**Microsoft Active Directory servers 598**
**Mobility Controller (MC) 295**
high availability 435
backup controller 438–440
clustering 437–438
failure behavior, controlling 440–441
VRRP 436–437
licensing and capacity 445–446
tunneled-node traffic
feature 425
guidelines 444
implementation restrictions 441–443
PAPI enhanced security 426–427
port-based node 427–431
role-based node 427–428, 432–435
server profile 425–426
use cases 423–425
**Mobility Master (MM) 428**
**Mobility Solution**
high availability 435
backup controller 438–440
clustering 437–438
failure behavior, controlling 440–441
VRRP 436–437
licensing and capacity 445–446
tunneled-node traffic
feature 425
guidelines 444
implementation restrictions 441–443
PAPI enhanced security 426–427
port-based node 427–431
role-based node 427–428, 432–435
server profile 425–426
use cases 423–425
**MS-CHAP v2 method 341, 342**
**Multi-Active Detection (MAD) 94**
**Multi-area OSPF systems**
ABRs 126
multiple areas 128
Type 3 LSAs 127, 129
aggregating summaries 131–133
inter-area routes, filtering 133–134
intra-areas routes *vs.* inter-area routes 126
LSDB size 127
need for route aggregation 130
Segment 1 and 2 127
**Multicast routes**
discovering 217–218
*vs.* unicast routes 216–217
use cases 216
**Multicast traffic 547**
flooding within VLANs 198–200
overview 196–197
uses 198
**Multi-Exit Discriminator (MED) 264**
**Multiple clients**
address limit 385
Authorized-client VLANs 389
combining 802.1X 386–388
IP phones 385
untagged VLANs 385
**Multiple Spanning Tree Protocol (MSTP) 233, 593**
instances 62
RPVST+ 15–16, 19–20
*vs.* VRRP 46, 59–61
**Must be zero (MBZ) bit 516**

## N


**Named Access Control List (NACL) context 308**

**NAS-Filter-Rules 357**

**Neighbor addresses**

- AOS-Switches 255–256
- eBGP 256–257
- iBGP 257
- receiving routes 260–261

**Netbeui 532**

**Network Access Server (NAS) 338**

**Network Time Protocol (NTP) 349**

**Non-broadcast multi-access (NBMA) network 110**

**Nondata-driven mode 211**

**Nonpreemptive mode 57**

**no-summary option 152**

**Notify-only action 595–596**

**Not so stubby area (NSSA) 148–149**


## O


**Object identifier (OID) 463**

**Open Shortest Path First (OSPF) 196, 252, 267, 520**

**OperatorReadView 467**

**Organizationally Unique Identifier (OUI) 381**

**OSPF link 110–111**

**Out of band management (OOBM) network 452**


## P


**Params 479–480**

**Password Authentication Protocol (PAP) 342**

**Per-user tunnel mode (PUTM) 428**

**plaintext option 408**

**Policy-based access management 6–7**

**Port-access learn mode 589**

**Port-based ACLs (PACLs) 293, 318–319**

**Port-based mode 361–362**

**Port-based rate limiting 545–546**

**Port security**

- actions
  - feature 583
  - limit devices 585
  - preventing changes 586
- address limit
  - limit devices 584–585
  - parameter 583
  - preventing changes 586
- controlling devices 587–588
- eavesdropping protection 590–591
- 802.1X port-based authentication 588–589
- learn modes 582
  - factors 582
  - limit devices 584–585
  - preventing changes 586
- MAC addresses 581
- vs. MAC lockdown 593–594
- unauthorized switch 583–584

**Power over Ethernet (PoE), 554**

**Power sourcing equipment (PSE) 556**

**Preemptive mode 56–57**

**Protected EAP (PEAP)**

- advantages 342
- developement 341
- disadvantages 343
- inner method 342
- outer method 342

**Protocol independent multicast (PIM)**

- AOS-Switch 219
- IGMP 218
- PIM-DM
  - configuration 220–221
  - elected forwarder 231–232

(*, G) entries 223–224
(S, G) entries 224–227
flooding and pruning 221–222
grafts 222–223
high bandwidth and high tolerance 219
pruned interface 219
state refreshes 227–229
tree and unicast routing table 229–231
PIM-SM
behavior as source 234–235
configuration 232
designated router (DR) 232–233
lower-bandwidth environment 219
RP 233–235, 237–243
switching to SPT 235–237

**Protocol Independent Multicast Dense Mode (PIM-DM)**
configuration 220–221
elected forwarder 231–232
(*, G) entries 223–224
(S, G) entries 224–227
flooding and pruning 221–222
grafts 222–223
high bandwidth and high tolerance 219
pruned interface 219
state refreshes 227–229
tree and unicast routing table 229–231

**Protocol Independent Multicast Sparse Mode (PIM-SM)**
behavior as source 234–235
configuration 232
designated router (DR) 232–233
lower-bandwidth environment 219
RP 233–235, 237–243
switching to SPT 235–237

**Provisioning API (PAPI) 426–427**
**Public Key Infrastructure (PKI) 340**
**PVST protection 23**

## Q

**Quality of Service (QoS)**
Aruba APs 526
challenges 507–508
classifier-based QoS policies
configuring and applying 537–538
verification 538–539
CoS 515, 516
default setting 526, 527
delay 507
device type setting 527–528
DSCP 517–518
802.1p 516
features 504
honoring DSCP 522–525
honoring 802.1p value 520–521
interaction with incoming DSCP 531
LLDP-MED
enabling 555–556
review interoperation with authentication 554–555
SNMP servers 554
VLAN ID 554
VoIP phone 554
none setting 527
physical interface 530
queuing and scheduling 509
controlling 514–515
egress queues 513–514
FIFO 509
GMB 509–513
SP 509–510

rate limition 545
broadcast and multicast traffic 547
class-based 549–552
egress per-queue 548–549
ICMP traffic 546–547
port-based 545–546
user-based 553
real-time traffic 505–506
service setting 525
strategies 519
TCP and UDP 505
ToS and IP precedence bits 516–517
traffic class creation 535–536
traffic classification 518–519
802.1p priority and DSCP 528–529
policy 531–534, 539–540
traffic template 521
use case 508
VLAN interface 530–531
**Queuing and scheduling 509**
controlling 514–515
egress queues 513–514
FIFO 509
GMB 509, 511
percentages 511–512
port behavior 513
port's bandwidth 510–511
settings 512
SP traffic 513
unallocated and unused bandwidth 511
SP 509–510

## R

**RADIUS attributes 354–356**
**RADIUS authentication 589**
**RADIUS-based MAC-Auth 400**
address format 376–377
Aruba ClearPass 377
configuration process 378
credentials 376
process 374–375
protocol 375–376
**RADIUS server 451, 553**
AOS-Switches 349–350
ClearPass 348–349, 358–359
customized settings 352
dynamic port ACLs 357–358
dynamic settings 353–356, 359–360
EAP 337–338
enabling 350–352
groups 345–348
key option 345
operator/manager access 455–457
port-based authentication 454
RADIUS-based command authorization 457–458
secondary authentication method 455, 460–461
specification 344
SSH login 455
**radius-server host command 345**
**RADIUS settings 353**
**Rapid Per-VLAN Spanning Tree Plus (RPVST+)**
BPDUs 16–18
filtering 23–24
protection 21–23
throttling 25–26
vs. MSTP 15–16, 19–20
port cost differences 18
PVST protection 23
root guard 24–25
vs. RSTP 15–16
setting up 19

STP loop guard 26–28
vulnerability 20–21
**Rapid Spanning Tree Protocol (RSTP) 15–16, 593**
**Rate limition, QoS 545**
broadcast and multicast traffic 547
class-based 549–552
egress per-queue 548–549
ICMP traffic 546–547
port-based 545–546
user-based 553
**Redundant networks**
ABRs 152–153
external route metrics 156
inter-area routes 154–155
interface cost setting 151–152
route selection 163–164
type 1 metric 160–161
type 2 metric 156–158
**Remote monitoring (RMON)**
alarm generation 486–488
AOS-Switches 485
conjunction with SNMP 484
information collection 485–486
local device monitoring 485
thresholds 476
**Rendezvous point (RP)**
RPT 233–235
selection from RP set
group prefixes 242
load balancing 243
priority 243
process 241
specifying
bootstrap mechanism 238–240
Core-1/Core-2 237
manual RP address 238
**replace option 574**
**Request for Comments (RFC) 517**
**Root guard 24–25**
**Routed Access Control List (RACL) 358**
**Routed ACL (RACL) 292**
inbound 310–311
outbound 311–312
**Route selection**
attributes 263–265
ECMP 264
first criteria in 261–263
MED 264
**Routing Information Protocol (RIP) 106, 252**
**rp-candidate command 240, 242**
**RP tree (RPT) 233–234**

## S

**samplingProbe MIB 467**
**Secondary authentication method 455, 460–461**
**Secure device management**
configuration auditing
Aruba AirWave 482–483
monitoring network traffic and events 483–484
network maintenance and monitoring tasks 482
network mapping and monitoring features 482
RMON 476, 484–488
destination switch 493–494
enabling jumbo frames 494–495
local traffic mirroring 491–492
management user authentication options
access levels 452–453
access types 452
AOS-Switches 451
default authentication methods 453

local authentication 453
RADIUS servers 451, 454–461
TACACS+ server 452
VSAs, command authorization 458–460
remote traffic mirroring 493
sFlow
agents 488, 489
on AOS-Switches 490
collector/receiver 488–490
SNMP 461–482
source switch 494
**Secure Shell (SSH) 9, 279, 452, 539**
**Security**
connection rate filtering 594
ACL 599–600
action 595–596
IDSs and IPSs 594
implementation 598–599
operation 594–595
sensitivity 597–598
unblocking 596–597
Virtual Machine 599
DHCP
address exhaustion 566, 567
address spoofing 566, 567
and ARP protection 577–578
authorized servers 570–571
configuration 569–570
Discover and Request packets 572
filtering 573–574
IP addresses 571–572
limitation 572
remote ID types 573
snooping 567–568
eavesdropping and unauthorized access 580–581
port security
actions 583, 585, 586
address limit 583–586
controlling devices 587–588
eavesdropping protection 590–591
802.1X port-based authentication 588–589
learn modes 582, 584–586
MAC addresses 581
*vs.* MAC lockdown 593–594
unauthorized switch 583–584
**send-alarm action 585**
**send-disable action 585**
**Sensitivity 597–598**
**Sequence number (SEQ) 298–299**
**Session Announcement Protocol (SAP) 196**
**sFlow**
agents 488, 489
on AOS-Switches 490
collector/receiver 488–490
**shared option 320**
**Shortest path first (SPF) algorithm 113–114**
**show dhcp-snooping command 569**
**show ip igmp command 203**
**show ip route ospf command 147**
**show port-access local-mac association command 384**
**show port-access local-mac mac-group default 381**
**show rmon statistics command 486**
**show snmp-server trap command 481**
**show vlan ports command 360**
**show vrrp command 50, 51**
**Simple Network Management Protocol (SNMP) 36, 583**
communities 463
concepts 462
consistent security and management policies 461
network devices configuration 461

objects, OIDs, and MIBs 463
operations 462
security weaknesses 463
servers 554
SNMPv2 462
control access 466
messages 468
trap hosts 480–482
SNMPv3
benefits 463–464
defining traps 476–478
notifications 475
notification targets 479–480
predefined groups and associated rights 466–467
settings in Aruba AirWave 471–475
settings on AOS-Switches 469–470
*vs.* SNMPv1/2c operation 467–469
users 464–465
**Single area OSPF system**
dedicated VLAN per link 124–125
enabling OSPF 117–120
example 116
LSUs 120–124
Router-1 configuration 117
VLAN 10, 22, and 32 120–124
**Site 2 switches 471**
**snmp-server enable trap commands 480**
**SNMPv2, 462**
control access 466
messages 468
trap hosts 480–482
**SNMPv3**
benefits 463–464
defining traps
enabling and disabling traps 478
event IDs 478
event traps 477–478
mac-notify and mac-count-notify options 477
types 476
notification
setting up 475
targets 479–480
predefined groups and associated rights 466–467
settings in Aruba AirWave 471–475
settings on AOS-Switches 469–470
*vs.* SNMPv1/2c operation 467–469
users 464–465
**Standby UAC (S-UAC) 438**
**Static MAC addressing 592**
**Static mode 582**
**Strict priority (SP) scheduling 509–510**
**stub no-summary option 151**
**Systems Network Architecture (SNA) 532**

## T

**Taglist 480**
**Target IP address 479**
**TCP applications 505**
**TCP session 255**
**TCP/UDP ports 532**
**Telnet 279, 452**
**Ternary content-addressable memory (TCAM) 319**
**Throttle action 595–596**
**Time to Live (TTL) 256**
**TLVs 557, 558**
**Traffic class 535–536**
**Trusted Anchor (TA) profile 407**
**Trusted ports 568**
**tunneled-node-server fallback-local-switching command 441**

**Tunneled-node traffic**
feature 425
guidelines 444
implementation restrictions 441–443
PAPI enhanced security 426–427
port-based node
configuration 427–428
MC handling 430–431
node enabling 429–430
role-based node
configuration 427–428
MC handling 435
roles for 432–434
user-role 432
server profile 425–426
**Tunneled Transport Layer Security (TTLS)**
advantages 342
developement 341
disadvantages 343
inner method 342
outer method 342
**Type of Service (ToS) 516–517**

U

**UDP 287, 505**
**Unauthorized access 580–581**
**Uncontrolled port 333**
**Unidirectional Link Detection (UDLD)**
cross-connected fibers 33, 34
fiber optic link 33, 34
frames 35–36
guidelines 36
STP network 34
tagged/untagged 37
UDLD-enabled ports 38
**Unified Communications (UC) 2**
**Unified wired and wireless management 5–6**
**Untrusted ports 568**
**User-based mode 362–365**
**User-based rate limits 553**

V

**Vendor-specific attribute (VSA) 432**
default commands 459
"HPE-Command-Exception," 458–460
"HPE-Command-String," 458–460
RADIUS 458
**Video-conferencing applications 200**
**Video traffic 506**
**Virtual LAN (VLAN) 231–232**
and ARP protection 577–578
dedicated per link 124–125
802.1X Unauthorized-client
device's traffic 415
guidelines 416–417
multiple employees and guests 417–418
**DHCP snooping 568, 569**
**interface 530–531, 536**
**multicast 198–200**
**VLAN 10, 22, and 32 120–124**
**Virtual links**
ABR 10.255.0.3 and ABR 10.255.0.2 180
configuration process 180–181
example situations 179
non-backbone and transit area 179–180
**Virtual router identifier (VRID), 47, 437**
**Virtual Router Redundancy Protocol (VRRP) 177–178, 204, 231**
configuration 49–51, 61
controlling 48–49
failover 52–54
high availability 436–437

IPv4 48
load sharing routing 58–59
MSTP 46, 59–61
operation 51–52
ping response behavior 55
preemptive and nonpreemptive modes 56–57
setting up 57
VRID 47
VSF 46–47
**Virtual Switching Framework (VSF) 4, 46, 253, 568**
Aruba 2930F Series switches
commander 89
configuration 91–92
implementation 88–89
links 90–91
member 90
standby member 90
topologies 89–90
**backplane stacking**
*vs.* flooded traffic 93
*vs.* unicasts 92–93
**fabric 88, 231**
**FSU 99**
**LLDP MAD**
behavior 96–97
setup 95–96
**manual configuration 86–88**
**OOBM MAD 94–95**
**physical and logical view 81–82**
**plug-and-play configuration 82–84**
**split-brain situation 94**
**use cases 84–86**
**VLAN MAD 97–99**
**Virus throttling 594**
**VLAN ACL (VACL) 292, 358**
at the edge 315–317
inbound 312–313
outbound 314–315
**vlan ID ip igmp command 209**
**Voice traffic 505–506**
**VoIP phone 554**

## W

**Web-based authentication**
advantages 394
AOS-switch support for 396–397
Aruba ClearPass 395–396
basic login pages 409
certificate 412
disadvantages 395
multiple clients 412–413
RADIUS server 410–411
redirect URL 411
switch enabling 413
types 395
unauthenticated clients 412
**Web browser 279**
**Wildcard bits**
adding rule 305–306
definition 302
examples 303–305
reverse logic from subnet masks 303
source and destination IP addresses 300, 303
**Wired and wireless network management 5–6**